CMC Supporting Papers

The Committee for Economic Development is publishing for the Commission on Money and Credit

THE FEDERAL RESERVE AND THE TREASURY: ANSWERS TO QUESTIONS FROM THE COMMISSION ON MONEY AND CREDIT

and fifty-eight individual essays organized into nine separate volumes, each centered around a particular aspect of monetary and fiscal policy. Their titles and the contributing authors are as follows:

IMPACTS OF MONETARY POLICY

Daniel B. Suits; Robert Eisner and Robert H. Strotz, with a bibliography by G. R. Post; Edwin Kuh and John R. Meyer; Leo Grebler and Sherman J. Maisel; Charlotte DeMonte Phelps; Irwin Friend

STABILIZATION POLICIES

E. Cary Brown, Robert M. Solow, Albert Ando, and John Kareken; Milton Friedman and David Meiselman; Lawrence E. Thompson; Arthur M. Okun; Merton H. Miller; Allan H. Meltzer; Oswald Brownlee and Alfred Conrad

MONETARY MANAGEMENT

Frank M. Tamagna; Warren L. Smith; Clark Warburton; Michael D. Reagan; C. P. Kindleberger; Robert Z. Aliber

FISCAL AND DEBT MANAGEMENT POLICIES

William Fellner; Richard A. Musgrave; James Tobin; James R. Schlesinger; Paul H. Cootner; Irving Auerbach; Ralph K. Huitt; John Lindeman

FEDERAL CREDIT AGENCIES

George F. Break; Jack Guttentag; Ernest Bloch; D. Gale Johnson; Dale E. Hathaway; George S. Tolley; Jack McCroskey

FEDERAL CREDIT PROGRAMS

Stewart Johnson; Warren A. Law; James W. McKie; D. Gale Johnson; James Gillies; Robert C. Turner and Ross Robertson; J. Fred Weston

PRIVATE CAPITAL MARKETS

Irwin Friend; Hyman P. Minsky; Victor L. Andrews

PRIVATE FINANCIAL INSTITUTIONS

Paul M. Horvitz; Deane Carson and Paul Cootner; Thomas G. Gies, Thomas Mayer, and Edward C. Ettin; Lawrence L. Werboff and Marvin E. Rozen; Fred H. Klopstock; E. Gordon Keith

INFLATION, GROWTH, AND EMPLOYMENT

Joseph W. Conard; Jesse W. Markham; Franklyn D. Holzman; John W. Kendrick; Daniel Creamer; Stanley Lebergott; Lawrence R. Klein and Ronald G. Bodkin; Tibor and Anne Scitovsky

TRADE ASSOCIATIONS MONOGRAPHS

THE COMMERCIAL BANKING INDUSTRY
The American Bankers Association

THE CONSUMER FINANCE INDUSTRY
National Consumer Finance Association

LIFE INSURANCE COMPANIES AS
FINANCIAL INSTITUTIONS
Life Insurance Association of America

MANAGEMENT INVESTMENT COMPANIES
Investment Company Institute

MORTGAGE COMPANIES: THEIR PLACE
IN THE FINANCIAL STRUCTURE
Miles L. Colean, for the
Mortgage Bankers Association of America

MUTUAL SAVINGS BANKING: BASIC CHARACTERISTICS
AND ROLE IN THE NATIONAL ECONOMY
National Association of Mutual Savings Banks

PROPERTY AND CASUALTY INSURANCE COMPANIES:
THEIR ROLE AS FINANCIAL INTERMEDIARIES
American Mutual Insurance Alliance
Association of Casualty and Surety Companies
National Board of Fire Underwriters

THE SAVINGS AND LOAN BUSINESS: ITS PURPOSES,
FUNCTIONS, AND ECONOMIC JUSTIFICATION
Leon T. Kendall, for the
United States Savings and Loan League

FEDERAL CREDIT PROGRAMS

PRENTICE-HALL INTERNATIONAL, INC., London
PRENTICE-HALL OF AUSTRALIA, PTY., LTD., Sydney
PRENTICE-HALL OF CANADA, LTD., Toronto
PRENTICE-HALL FRANCE, S.A.R.L., Paris
PRENTICE-HALL OF INDIA PRIVATE LIMITED, New Delhi
PRENTICE-HALL OF JAPAN, INC., Tokyo
PRENTICE-HALL DE MEXICO, S.A., Mexico City

Stewart Johnson
Warren A. Law
James W. McKie
D. Gale Johnson
James Gillies
Robert C. Turner and Ross M. Robertson
J. Fred Weston

FEDERAL CREDIT PROGRAMS

A SERIES OF RESEARCH STUDIES
PREPARED FOR THE

Commission on Money and Credit

Prentice-Hall, Inc.
Englewood Cliffs, N.J.

Library of Congress Catalog No.: 63-14709

Printed in the United States of America

C

The Commission on Money and Credit was established in 1957 as an independent organization by the unanimous vote of the Board of Trustees of the Committee for Economic Development. The bylaws governing the Commission on Money and Credit state that "It shall be the responsibility of the Commission to initiate studies into the United States monetary and financial system."

This volume was especially prepared for the Commission on Money and Credit as part of its research program leading to the publication in June 1961 of its final report: Money and Credit: Their Influence on Jobs, Prices, and Growth. It is published by direction of the Commission according to its bylaws, as a contribution to the understanding of the monetary and financial system of the United States. It is one of more than 100 research studies prepared for the Commission by trade organizations, individual scholars, the Federal Reserve System, and the Treasury of the United States.

A selected group of these papers including those of this volume, is being published for the Commission by the Information Division of the Committee for Economic Development in accordance with commitments to The Ford Foundation and the Merrill Foundation, which provided main financial support for the Commission.

Publication of this volume does not necessarily constitute endorsement of such study by the Commission, its Advisory Board, its Research Staff, or any member of any board or committee, or any officer of the Committee for Economic Development, The Ford Foundation, the Merrill Foundation, or any other organization participating in the work of the Commission.

COMMISSION ON MONEY AND CREDIT

Members

Frazar B. Wilde, CHAIRMAN
Chairman, Connecticut General Life Insurance Company

H. Christian Sonne, VICE CHAIRMAN
New York, New York

Adolf A. Berle, Jr.
New York, New York
(Withdrew to serve as Chairman of the U.S. State Department Latin American Task Force.)

James B. Black
Chairman of the Board, Pacific Gas & Electric Company

Joseph M. Dodge
Chairman of the Board, The Detroit Bank and Trust Company
(Resigned October 7, 1960.)

Marriner S. Eccles
Chairman of the Board, First Security Corporation

Lamar Fleming, Jr.
Chairman of the Board, Anderson, Clayton & Co.

Henry H. Fowler
Fowler, Leva, Hawes & Symington
(Resigned February 3, 1961, on his appointment as Under Secretary of the Treasury.)

Gaylord A. Freeman, Jr.
Vice Chairman, The First National Bank of Chicago
(Appointed April 29, 1960.)

Fred T. Greene
President, Federal Home Loan Bank of Indianapolis
(Died March 17, 1961.)

Philip M. Klutznick
Park Forest, Illinois
(Resigned February 8, 1961, on his appointment as United States Representative to the Economic and Social Council of the United Nations.)

Fred Lazarus, Jr.
Chairman of the Board, Federated Department Stores, Inc.

Isador Lubin
Arthur T. Vanderbilt Professor of Public Affairs, Rutgers University

J. Irwin Miller
Chairman of the Board, Cummins Engine Company

Robert R. Nathan
President, Robert R. Nathan Associates, Inc.

Emil Rieve
President Emeritus, Textile Workers of America, AFL-CIO
(Appointed May 19, 1960.)

David Rockefeller
President, The Chase Manhattan Bank

Beardsley Ruml
New York, New York
(Died April 18, 1960.)

Stanley H. Ruttenberg
Director, Department of Research, AFL-CIO

Charles Sawyer
Taft, Stettinius & Hollister

William F. Schnitzler
Secretary-Treasurer, AFL-CIO
(Resigned April 28, 1960.)

COMMISSION ON MONEY AND CREDIT

Earl B. Schwulst
President and Chairman of the Board, The Bowery Savings Bank

Charles B. Shuman
President, American Farm Bureau Federation

Jesse W. Tapp
Chairman of the Board, Bank of America, N.T. & S.A.

J. Cameron Thomson
Retired Chairman of the Board, Northwest Bancorporation

Willard L. Thorp
Director, Merrill Center for Economics, Amherst College

Theodore O. Yntema
Chairman, Finance Committee, Ford Motor Company

Advisory Board

Lester V. Chandler
Professor of Economics, Princeton University

Gerhard Colm
Chief Economist, National Planning Association

Gaylord A. Freeman, Jr.
Vice Chairman, The First National Bank of Chicago
(Resigned April 29, 1960, on his appointment to the Commission.)

Leo Grebler
Professor of Business Administration, University of California (Los Angeles)

Raymond W. Goldsmith
Professor of Economics, Yale University

Neil H. Jacoby
Dean, School of Business Administration, University of California (Los Angeles)

Richard A. Musgrave
Woodrow Wilson School of Public and International Affairs, Princeton University

Richard E. Neustadt
Professor of Public Law and Government, Columbia University

Paul A. Samuelson
Professor of Economics, Massachusetts Institute of Technology

Sumner H. Slichter
Lamont University Professor, Harvard University
(Died September 27, 1959.)

Edward S. Shaw
Professor of Economics, Stanford University

Alan H. Temple
New York, New York

Jacob Viner
Professor of Economics, Emeritus, Princeton University

Staff

Bertrand Fox
Research Director

Eli Shapiro
Deputy Research Director

FOREWORD

The Commission on Money and Credit came into being in May 1958 to appraise our monetary and financial system, both public and private, and the governmental regulations and controls that affect it. Based on such an examination, the Commission was to make recommendations on what changes, if any, should be made to improve the structure, operations, regulation and control of our monetary and credit system.

In its early meetings, the Commission blocked out the scope and major subdivisions of its inquiry. It then subdivided itself into topical subcommittees or "task forces," each of which was to identify and spell out the key policy issues related to each task force mission, to develop plans for analyzing these central problems, and to prepare recommendations in relation to each for presentation to the full Commission. When the Commission had reached agreement on the key policy issues to be investigated, the staff then prepared a program of proposed research projects around the issues to be considered by each task force.

The proposed research projects were then discussed at task force meetings, and each project to be undertaken was approved by the Commission. Each research project was to provide for the Commission's deliberations, information that would identify clearly the critical elements which underlay the policy questions under consideration. The projects were to mobilize the relevant facts, analytical findings, and the arguments for and against alternative positions.

Two sets of studies related to the work of the task force deal with federal credit programs. The first set, presented in the volume entitled, Federal Credit Agencies, deals with individual federal credit programs. The second set of seven studies is presented in this volume and deals with studies which cut across individual credit programs and with broader aspects of the federal credit problems. Because so little work had been done on many aspects of federal credit programs, many of these papers had to be prepared by scholars new to the field. Each paper, however, was prepared either by a scholar who had done significant work in the field or had done work in related fields which could be adapted to the problems assigned.

Stewart Johnson of the University of Connecticut was asked to assemble detailed statistics on all federal lending and loan insurance programs in the United States for the period 1929 to 1958. His instructions included, "This project will assemble data relating to the magnitudes of the various kinds of credit activities in such a manner that aggregate totals can be obtained. Data will be assembled by appropriate types of credit assistance on the volume of credit activity per year and outstanding credit at year end."

Warren A. Law of the Harvard Business School was asked to make a study of the aggregate impact of federal credit programs on the economy. His instructions included, "This study will deal with the aggregate impact of federal credit programs on the entire economy. It will involve an analysis of the aggregate effect of all programs combined on the federal budget, the government debt, the private financial system, and on total economic activity; it will also develop measures of cost of the programs in total. An important aspect of the study relates to the extent and degree to which these programs have counteracted or supplemented fiscal, debt management, and monetary policies in the past, and how they might contribute more effectively in the future to the goals of such policies, if such a course seems appropriate. Another important aspect of the effects to be considered relates to resource allocation and the possible contributions therefrom to economic growth."

James W. McKie of Vanderbilt University was asked to prepare a paper on criteria for federal credit assistance. His instructions included, "Among the criteria used for the establishment and continuation of some federal credit or loan guarantee programs are: 1) the alleged inadequacy of competition in the private financial system such that credit is not available for a particular purpose on reasonably adequate terms; 2) the alleged existence of credit gaps such that adequate credit is not available for a particular purpose on any terms. This study will examine the appropriateness of these two criteria for federal credit assistance on a theoretical basis, and it will attempt to develop operational tests for the identification of inadequate competition and credit gaps, which might justify federal credit programs. It will take into account also the empirical evidence involved in analyses of the situations that gave rise to and led to the abandonment of federal credit programs in the past."

D. Gale Johnson of the University of Chicago was asked to analyze the role of federal credit agencies in the agricultural sector as a whole. His instructions included, "The paper will set forth the place of federal agencies as compared to private financial institutions in providing various kinds of credit to agriculture, the relationships among the functions performed by the several federal agencies, and the nature of the competitive or complementary relationships with private institutions. It will discuss whether agricultural credit agencies facilitate or thwart the transmission of general monetary policies and whether specific agricultural credit policies can be developed to assist monetary, debt management, and fiscal policies in attaining high and stable levels of employment, reasonable stable prices and adequate economic growth."

James Gillies of U.C.L.A. was asked to make an aggregative analysis of federal credit programs in the housing sector of the economy. His instructions included, "This paper will set forth the place of federal credit agencies as compared to private financial institutions in providing various kinds of credit to housing, the relationships among the functions performed by the several federal agencies, and the nature of the competitive or complementary relationships with private institutions. It will discuss whether housing credit agencies facilitate or thwart the transmission of general monetary policies and whether specific housing credit policies can be developed to assist monetary, debt management, and fiscal policies in attaining our national economic objectives."

Robert C. Turner and Ross M. Robertson of the University of Indiana were asked to make a study of the sources of funds available to federal lending agencies. Their instructions included, "This study will consist of an analysis and appraisal of the methods of financing employed to support the various federal credit programs. The methods of financing used and the sources of funds tapped to support federal credit programs have differing impacts in the short and longer run on the economy. This study, which will cut across all credit programs—agricultural, housing, business, and international—will involve a comparative analysis of the effects of the different methods of financing used and an appraisal of the efficiency of one as compared to another method of financing in enabling the various credit programs to accomplish their objectives. A basic purpose of the study is to develop guides or criteria for recommendations relating to the possible redesign of the financing methods used for specific programs to enable them to accomplish their objectives more effectively."

J. Fred Weston of U.C.L.A. was asked to prepare an analysis of technical components of federal credit programs. His instructions included, "This study will cover an analysis of the costs, credit standards, and credit terms employed in federal credit programs. The purpose of this study is to show how variations in credit standards, credit costs, and other credit terms influence the behavior of federal credit activities and the ability of federal credit programs to achieve effectively their stated purposes. The study will cut across all credit programs, and by comparative analyses of relevant provisions among programs, the study will contribute findings suitable for appraising the technical efficiency of particular provisions found in individual programs, and for guiding recommendations for the possible redesign of specific programs to enable them to accomplish their objective more effectively."

These studies were submitted to and used by the Commission and its staff in preliminary form. The authors were then given an opportunity to revise them in the light of comments received from outside readers, the Commission's staff, and readers chosen from the Commission's Advisory Board. The final manuscripts are presented in this volume as they were received from their authors; there has been no final editing by the staff of the Commission.

The Commission is happy to present these research studies among the supporting papers behind its Report. The members of the Commission and its staff are grateful to the authors of the papers for their contributions to the deliberations of the Commission.

Bertrand Fox
Director of Research

Eli Shapiro
Deputy Director of Research

August 1962

CONTENTS

CONTENTS

FEDERAL CREDIT PROGRAMS

Research Study One

STATISTICS ON FEDERAL LENDING AND LOAN INSURANCE PROGRAMS IN THE UNITED STATES, 1929-1958

Stewart Johnson*
University of Connecticut

I. INTRODUCTION

Federal lending, loan insurance, and loan guarantee programs have expanded rapidly in recent years. And the variety of the programs is as striking as their size. To be able to examine the ways federal credit programs have affected the economy generally and in particular the operations of monetary, budget, and fiscal policies,

---

*This statistical report would have been impossible were it not for the many persons in the federal lending agencies who made available the published and unpublished data on which so many of the figures in the tables are based, particularly those of recent years. There are too many of them to thank individually for their cooperation and for the considerable amount of extra work our inquiries involved. We also appreciate their generous willingness to do this extra work promptly and to supply detailed data in the prescribed form.

Our second greatest debt is to the authors, the National Bureau of Economic Research, and Princeton University Press for giving us permission to use the statistics in Federal Lending and Loan Insurance, by Raymond J. Saulnier, Harold G. Halcrow, and Neil H. Jacoby, published in 1958. Many of the tables in the present report cite this publication as the source of some or all of the data.

Mrs. Vivian C. Howard and Ralph R. Nichols of the Commission staff helped in obtaining the data and in preparing and checking the tables.

the allocation of resources, and other financial institutions, both public and private, the Commission on Money and Credit required detailed, current information on their lending activities.

The present report provides basic data on the lending activities of all the domestic federal lending programs for the 30-year period of 1929 through 1958. The tables were prepared according to a standard procedure so that the data would be consistent and comparable from one program to another. This proved to be a difficult and time-consuming task, for the agencies operating such programs are many, their methods of lending and of keeping records are diverse, groups of loans frequently are transferred to a successor or sister agency handling similar loans, and some agencies are reluctant to divulge data on their lending activities. Insofar as possible the coverage of each program is complete.

These data were made available to economists preparing monographs on different parts or aspects of the federal credit programs for the Commission in the interests of consistency about the underlying facts. They are now being made available to the public in the hope that they may prove useful to others interested in studying the full range of this highly important activity of the federal government.

Coverage of the Report

This report covers only the domestic federal lending programs in the United States. The 51 federal lending programs are grouped in four categories: agricultural loans, (Tables I-1 to I-70), business loans (Tables 1-71 to I-133), housing loans (Tables I-134 to I-225), and miscellaneous loans (Tables I-226 to I-243). The total of all such loans outstanding at the end of 1929, 1939, 1949, and 1958 are shown in the Summary Table on page 3. In addition to loans made, insured, or guaranteed by government agencies, the statistics cover loans made by mutualized or federally sponsored agencies having a special financial or administrative connection with the federal government even though advances of capital funds by the government may have been discontinued or repaid. The Federal Land Banks are an example of such an agency.

Lending activities are included even when the lending is only incidental to the main purpose of an agency. Loans of the Commodity Credit Corporation are included, for example, as well as loans made in connection with the disposal of government property.

We attempted to include all domestic federal lending activity. We believe that omissions are small—probably not more than 1 percent of the total, but undoubtedly some federal lending activity has been missed. As the authors of a previous compilation noted, "it may be hard to believe that there should be no means of determining, even after persistent inquiry, how much was disbursed under federal programs that involved millions of dollars, but this in the case."[1]

SUMMARY TABLE I-A

Summary of Loans Outstanding, All Fifty-One Programs
Year End, 1929, 1939, 1949, and 1958

Type of Program	1929	1939	1949	1958
	(thousands of dollars)			
Agricultural loans	1,947,745	4,779,776	6,080,540	12,244,210
Business loans	129,073	957,451	1,483,643	1,469,321
Housing loans	---	5,177,521	20,509,087	67,059,777
Miscellaneous loans	52,130	347,745	179,982	431,546
Total	2,128,948	11,262,493	28,253,252	81,204,854
Subtractions to eliminate double counting:				
Agricultural loans	---	388,254	619,420	1,196,861
Housing loans	---	192,662	926,476	3,900,953
Total subtractions	---	580,916	1,545,896	5,097,814
Net total	2,128,948	10,681,577	26,707,356	76,107,040

Source: Summary Tables for agricultural loans (p. 7), business loans (p. 80), housing loans (p. 143), and miscellaneous loans (p. 225).

[1] R. J. Saulnier, Harold G. Halcrow, and Neil H. Jacoby, Federal Lending and Loan Insurance, for the National Bureau of Economic Research (Princeton: Princeton University Press, 1958), p. 6. Hereafter this book is referred to as Saulnier, et al.

Relationship to Other Compilations

As noted in the acknowledgments, many of the tables in this report used Federal Lending and Loan Insurance by Saulnier, Halcrow, and Jacoby as a source of data. This report adds five years to their series, which ended with 1953. We have also used calendar-year data, and have covered advances rather than commitments. This report differs from theirs, however, in having somewhat broader coverage. For example, it includes new lending programs, Commodity Credit Corporation loans, loans on government life insurance, loans in connection with disposal of government property, and Bureau of Indian Affairs cattle loans. We also separated out the non-insured or nonguaranteed part of insured and guaranteed loans. Some of their data have been corrected; most often the changes were made in data for the final years of their tabulations, 1952 and 1953, where agency revisions had been made after their report.

Beginning with the fiscal 1952 U.S. budget, special budget analyses of federal credit programs have been published each year. In fiscal 1961, the analysis gave descriptions of direct federal loans and mortgage purchases and of federal loan insurance and guarantee programs. It summarized new commitments, disbursements, repayments, loans outstanding, guarantees in force, new commitment authority, and status of credit authority for 22 major federal credit programs. The years covered by the fiscal 1961 analysis, available in January 1960, were fiscal 1959, fiscal 1960, and fiscal 1961, with actual figures for the first of these three years, and estimates for the latter two. Although quite helpful in the preparation of this report, the analyses do not contain long-time series.

In early 1960 a study of the federal insurance and guarantee programs by George F. Break, University of California, was published by the National Planning Association. An examination of the descriptions and statistical series proved helpful, but none of the series were used as direct sources for the present study.

Description of the Series

When possible the data were obtained on a calendar-year basis, but sometimes it was necessary to interpolate fiscal-year data to obtain estimates for calendar years. The period covered is the 30 years from 1929 through 1958. Occasionally data are given for 1959. But because some interpolation was necessary and the required data for the fiscal year, 1960, were not yet available, the collection of complete data for 1959 was impossible at the time the report was prepared; consequently no special effort was made to obtain 1959 data. Similarly, occasionally data are given for years before 1929, but federal lending activity was not very important in the 1920's and earlier, so again no effort was made to obtain them. For programs originating before 1929, only data on outstandings and loans made are shown for that year because the 1928 data required for derivation of loans repaid and changes in outstandings were not always available.

For most programs yearly series on loans outstanding, loans made, loans repaid or charged off, and net change in outstandings are shown. The loans outstanding at the end of each year are the net amount yet to be paid. Reductions in face value of original loans, through repayment, are taken into account. There is one exception to this general practice. The Veterans' Administration does not have records of partial repayment of their guaranteed and insured business loans and carry the full amount as outstanding until the loan is entirely repaid. An attempt was made to obtain estimates, but without success.

The data on loans made are for actual advances or disbursements, rather than for authorizations, commitments, or obligations. This distinction is significant. Often a commitment by a federal agency to a given borrower greatly exceeded the amount of its disbursement, and was later cancelled or withdrawn in whole or in part. The commitment performed an economic function enabling the potential borrower to conduct his operations differently, by virtue of his ability to "call" on federal credit. Although economically important, data on commitments are fragmentary and never appear in the published figures on federal credit outstanding. Consequently, the tables in this report contain data on disbursements, with one or two exceptions where the only data available were for commitments, and these data were used and so designated in the tables. In many of the tables the figures would have been materially different if the series had included money committed but not yet actually advanced.

The loans repaid or charged off are derived figures: the amount needed to balance out changes in outstandings and loans made. Occasionally they include sales of loans of the government agency to private concerns. The net changes in outstandings are also derived figures, calculated from the difference in outstandings between one year and the next.

There are a few other series shown, or variations in these series. For example, for the Federal National Mortgage Association, instead of the usual "loans repaid or charged off," sales and repayments of mortgages appear separately. For the Urban Renewal Administration, contract authorizations, capital grant reservations, and capital grant payments are shown as well as the standard series on lending activity. And for insured, guaranteed, or participation loans, in addition to the total series are tables giving the breakdown between the insured and non-insured parts, the guaranteed and non-guaranteed parts, or the government and private shares. Some of these breakdowns were readily available from the lending agency; others are estimates.

There are tables summarizing the data for the various parts of the lending program of each agency. In addition, to give a broad general picture of federal lending and insurance activity, year-end outstandings were summarized for each of the years 1929, 1939, 1949, and 1958. The last is the most recent year for which complete data were available. Total loans of the different programs were calculated for agricultural loans, business loans, housing loans, and miscellaneous loans.

In a few of the tables on housing loans there will be occasional internal or aggregative inconsistencies of $1,000 or $2,000, because of the rounding to thousands and because the totals were calculated from the nonrounded data.

II. AGRICULTURAL LENDING AND LOAN INSURANCE PROGRAMS

The oldest federal lending programs have been the agricultural ones. The largest program in terms of outstandings in 1929 and 1939 were that of the Federal Land Banks. In 1949 and 1958, this program was third in size, with the Commodity Credit Corporation first and the Rural Electrification program second.

Farm Credit Administration Programs and Related Credit Programs

The Farm Credit Administration, established as an independent government agency in 1933, supervises and coordinates a cooperative credit system for agriculture (in 1939 it was made a part of the Department of Agriculture but was made an independent agency again in 1953). The system provides mortgage credit through Federal Land Banks (FLB's) and Federal Land Bank Associations (FLBA's), production credit through Federal Intermediate Credit Banks (FICB's) and Production Credit Associations (PCA's), and marketing and purchasing credit through Banks for Cooperatives (BC's) and agricultural marketing, purchasing, and business service cooperatives. Financed originally with government funds, the system will ultimately be wholly privately owned and financed, and is mainly so already. The system is self-supporting, including the government's administrative and supervisory costs. Total loans under these programs are now about $3 billion and represent about 20 percent of all credit extended to farmers.

Mortgage Credit

FCA Program:
Federal Land Banks and Federal Land Bank Associations (Table I-1)

SUMMARY TABLE I-B

Summary of Agricultural Loans Outstanding, Eighteen Programs
Year End, 1929, 1939, 1949, and 1958

Table No.	Program of Agricultural Loans	1929	1939	1949	1958
			(thousands of dollars)		
I-62	Commodity Credit Corporation	--	575,267	1,728,530	3,298,382
I-55	Rural Electrification Administration	--	183,243	1,301,734	2,874,423
I-1	Federal Land Bank	1,213,953	2,002,061	916,862	2,088,791
I-12	Federal Intermediate Credit Banks	73,356	198,035	471,849	1,141,784
I-6	Production Credit Associations	--	153,425	387,454	1,114,694
I-50	Farmers Home Administration	7,976	449,943	568,312	1,007,269
I-19	Banks for Cooperatives	--	76,252	301,887	509,829
I-23	Agricultural Marketing Act Revolving Fund	14,510	236,207	179,865	134,799
I-65	Veterans' Administration	--	--	141,500	70,000
I-13	Production Credit Corporations	--	75,370	22,296	4,000
I-14	Regional Agricultural Credit Corporations	--	8,005	1,273	239
I-4	Federal Farm Mortgage Corporation	--	713,290	58,650	--
I-24	Joint Stock Land Banks	637,789	91,726	270	--
I-70	Reconstruction Finance Corporation Agricultural Loans	--	856	44	--
I-67	Tennessee Valley Authority	--	4,578	14	--
I-69	Electric Home and Farm Authority	--	11,228	--	--
I-68	Tennessee Valley Associated Cooperatives	--	290	--	--
I-66	War Finance Corporation	161	--	--	--
	Total	1,947,745	4,779,776	6,080,540	12,244,210
	Subtractions to eliminate double counting:				
I-7	FICB's loans to PCA's	--	146,323	372,662	1,058,062
I-22	AMARF loans to BC's	--	149,000	178,500	134,799
I-13	PCC stock purchases in PCA's	--	75,370	22,296	4,000
I-8	FICB's loans to BC's	--	17,561	45,962	--
I-10	FICB's loans to RACC's	--	--	--	--
I-18	BC's loans secured by CCC documents	--	--	--	--
	Total subtractions	--	388,254	619,420	1,196,861
	Net total	1,947,745	4,391,522	5,461,120	11,047,349

Related Programs:

Joint Stock Land Banks (Table I-24)

Federal Farm Mortgage Association including FLB Commissioner Loans (Tables I-2 to I-5).

Production Credit

FCA Programs:

Federal Intermediate Credit Banks (Tables I-7 to I-12)

Production Credit Associations (Table I-6)

Related Programs:

Regional Agricultural Credit Corporations (Table I-14)

Production Credit Corporations (Table I-13)

Marketing Credit

FCA Program:
Banks for Cooperative and Marketing, Purchasing, and Business Service Cooperatives (Tables I-15 to I-19)

Related Programs:
War Finance Corporation (Table I-66)
Agricultural Marketing Act Revolving Fund (Tables I-20 to I-23)
Tennessee Valley Associated Cooperatives (Table I-68)

Federal Land Banks (Table I-1)

The Federal Land Bank System is cooperative and is completely farmer owned. All of the stock of the approximately 900 Federal Land Bank Associations is owned by their member borrowers; all of the stock of the 12 district FLB's, by the local FLBA's. Farmers may obtain FLB loans (Table I-1) only through FLBA's, which endorse, but do not make, the loans. Funds for making loans are obtained from the sale of bonds to the investing public. These bonds are not guaranteed by the government as to principal or interest. The loans are extended on farm real estate, usually for 20 to 23 years.

Federal Farm Mortgage Corporation (Tables I-2 to I-5)

The Federal Farm Mortgage Corporation was established in 1934 as a direct agency of the federal government to extend emergency credit. Authority to make new Land Bank Commissioner loans expired on July 1, 1947 (except for the purpose of refinancing loans previously made), and on June 30, 1955, the remaining FFMC loans were sold to the 12 FLB's and the FFMC became inactive.

The FFMC direct Commissioner loans to farmers were made through the Federal Land Bank System. The bulk of these loans were made for refinancing and scaling down of debts of individual farmers. During the peak of operations in 1934 about 88 percent of the total credit extended was for refinancing. About 150,000 of the more than 620,000 refinancing loans closed by the Federal Land Banks or the Land Bank Commissioner from May 1, 1933 through December 31, 1940 involved scale-downs of other indebtedness. These debt reductions totaled about one-third of the original indebtedness. In 1934-36, the Commissioner also purchased consolidated farm loans of the Federal Land Banks.

During 1937 and 1938, and again in 1945 and 1947, the FFMC made direct loans to Federal Land Banks. In each case the loans were repaid within two years (Table I-3). During 1934-36 when the private market for Federal Land Bank bonds was poor, the FFMC also purchased about $800 million of FLB bonds, directly from the Land Banks (Table I-5).

Agricultural Loans

TABLE I-1

Federal Land Bank Direct Loans, 1917-1955[a]

Year ended December 31	Outstanding	Loans made	Loans repaid or charged off	Net change in outstandings
	(thousands of dollars)			
1917	38,800	39,112	312	38,800
1918	156,214	118,130	716	117,414
1919	293,595	144,987	7,606	137,381
1920	349,843	66,985	10,737	56,248
1921	432,870	91,030	8,003	83,027
1922	639,863	224,301	17,308	206,993
1923	799,869	192,083	32,077	160,006
1924	928,831	165,510	36,548	128,962
1925	1,008,359	127,355	47,827	79,528
1926	1,081,986	131,318	57,691	73,627
1927	1,161,838	140,384	60,532	79,852
1928	1,203,911	102,236	60,163	42,073
1929	1,213,953	64,253	54,211	10,042
1930	1,209,431	47,971	52,493	-4,522
1931	1,192,918	42,015	58,528	-16,513
1932	1,158,274	27,570	62,214	-34,644
1933	1,268,441	151,634	41,467	110,167
1934	1,959,106	730,367	39,702	690,665
1935	2,126,117	248,671	81,660	167,011
1936	2,133,192	109,170	102,095	7,075
1937	2,119,018	63,092	77,266	-14,174
1938	2,072,262	51,418	98,174	-46,756
1939	2,002,061	51,582	121,783	-70,201
1940	1,955,616	64,275	110,720	-46,445
1941	1,879,901	65,068	140,783	-75,715
1942	1,717,697	53,974	216,178	-162,204
1943	1,456,334	61,900	323,263	-261,363
1944	1,214,801	70,275	311,808	-241,533
1945	1,086,488	92,986	221,299	-128,313
1946	985,477	130,162	231,173	-101,011
1947	898,417	138,764	225,824	-87,060
1948	878,586	150,514	170,345	-19,831
1949	916,862	182,357	144,081	38,276
1950	959,789	205,933	163,006	42,927
1951	1,007,695	214,220	166,314	47,906
1952	1,086,289	254,581	175,987	78,594
1953	1,185,781	289,772	190,280	99,492
1954	1,285,365	306,276	206,692	99,584
1955	1,500,685	487,489	272,169	215,320
1956	1,744,052	522,357	278,990	243,367
1957	1,919,281	398,993	223,764	175,229
1958	2,088,791	429,424	259,914	169,510

[a]Series cover regular mortgage loans made in the United States and Puerto Rico. Outstandings also include purchase money mortgages and real estate sales contracts, which are excluded from the volume series because annual data are lacking.

Source: Data for 1917 to 1953 from Federal Lending and Loan Insurance by R. J. Saulnier, et al., p. 407. Data for 1954-58 from Farm Credit Administration.

Agricultural Loans

TABLE I-2

Federal Farm Mortgage Corporation
Land Bank Commissioner Loans, 1933-1955[a]

Year ended December 31	Outstanding[b]	Loans made	Loans repaid or charged off	Net change in outstandings
		(thousands of dollars)		
1933	70,738	70,812	74	70,738
1934	616,737	553,048	7,049	545,999
1935	794,147	195,869	18,459	177,410
1936	841,251	76,887	29,783	47,104
1937	824,151	39,707	56,807	-17,100
1938	774,377	29,152	78,926	-49,774
1939	713,290	27,230	88,317	-61,087
1940	685,149	36,391	64,532	-28,141
1941	634,885	37,308	87,572	-50,264
1942	543,895	28,242	119,232	-90,990
1943	429,751	30,077	144,221	-114,144
1944	347,307	34,469	116,913	-82,444
1945	239,365	28,692	136,634	-107,942
1946	146,621	14,611	107,355	-92,744
1947	107,066	10,345	49,900	-39,555
1948	77,920	17	29,163	-29,146
1949	58,650	19	19,289	-19,270
1950	44,008	25	14,667	-14,642
1951	32,778	57	11,287	-11,230
1952	23,899	41	8,920	-8,879
1953	17,628	40	6,311	-6,271
1954	12,834	31	4,825	-4,794
1955	---	-6	12,840	-12,834

[a]Authority to make Land Bank Commissioner loans expired July 1, 1947 except for the purpose of refinancing loans previously made.
[b]Mortgages in process of foreclosure were estimated for 1951 and 1952.

Note: Table I-4 is the total of Tables I-2 and I-3.

Source: Data are from Agricultural Statistics for 1952 and 1958. Excludes territories and possessions.

Agricultural Loans

TABLE I-3

Federal Farm Mortgage Corporation Loans to Federal Land Banks, 1937-1948[a]

Year ended December 31	Outstanding	Loans made	Loans repaid or charged off	Net change in outstandings
		(thousands of dollars)		
1937	41,000	44,000	3,000	41,000
1938	26,200	3,700	18,500	-14,800
1939	---	---	26,200	-26,200
1940	---	---	---	---
1941	---	---	---	---
1942	---	---	---	---
1943	---	---	---	---
1944	---	---	---	---
1945	---	172,300	172,300	---
1946	---	---	---	---
1947	21,000	21,000	---	21,000
1948	---	---	21,000	-21,000

[a]Excludes purchases of Land Bank bonds by the FFMC, covered in Table I-5.

Note: Table I-4 is the total of Tables I-2 and I-3.

Source: Data supplied by Farm Credit Administration.

Agricultural Loans

TABLE I-4

Total Loans of Federal Farm Mortgage Corporation, 1933-1955[a]

Year ended December 31	Outstanding	Loans made	Loans repaid or charged off	Net change in outstandings
		(thousands of dollars)		
1933	70,738	70,812	74	70,738
1934	616,737	553,048	7,049	545,999
1935	794,147	195,869	18,459	177,410
1936	841,251	76,887	29,783	47,104
1937	865,151	83,707	59,807	23,900
1938	800,577	32,852	97,426	-64,574
1939	713,290	27,230	114,517	-87,287
1940	685,149	36,391	64,532	-28,141
1941	634,885	37,308	87,572	-50,264
1942	543,895	28,242	119,232	-90,990
1943	429,751	30,077	144,221	-114,144
1944	347,307	34,469	116,913	-82,444
1945	239,365	200,992	308,934	-107,942
1946	146,621	14,611	107,355	-92,744
1947	128,066	31,345	49,900	-18,555
1948	77,920	17	50,163	-50,146
1949	58,650	19	19,289	-19,270
1950	44,008	25	14,667	-14,642
1951	32,778	57	11,287	-11,230
1952	23,899	41	8,920	-8,879
1953	17,628	40	6,311	-6,271
1954	12,834	31	4,825	-4,794
1955	--	6	12,840	-12,834

[a]Excludes purchases of Land Bank bonds by the FFMC, covered in Table I-5.

Note: Table I-4 is the total of Tables I-2 and I-3.

Source: Data supplied by Farm Credit Administration.

TABLE I-5

Federal Farm Mortgage Corporation Acquisitions and Dispositions of Federal Land Bank Bonds, 1934-1945

'ear ended December 31	Owned by FFMC, end of year	Acquired by purchase and exchange during year	Repurchased by FLBs and retired during year
		(thousands of dollars)	
1934	579,454	623,324	43,870
1935	754,630	175,176	---
1936	761,130	6,500	---
1937	761,130	---	---
1938	761,130	---	---
1939	761,130	---	---
1940	761,130	---	---
1941	761,130	---	---
1942	591,298	---	169,832
1943	438,135	---	153,163
1944	116,842	---	321,293
1945	---	---	116,842

Source: Data supplied by Farm Credit Administration.

Production Credit Associations (Table I-6)

The 494 Production Credit Associations make short- and intermediate-term loans to finance farm operations. Loans are made for repayment over a period of up to five years. PCA's obtain loan funds primarily by discounting borrower's notes with the 12 district Federal Intermediate Credit Banks. As of January 1, 1959, the PCA's as a whole were using only $4 million of government capital, whereas during the 1930's the government investment had amounted to as much as $90 million.

Unlike the Federal Land Bank Associations, which function merely as intermediaries between farmer-member borrowers and the Federal Land Banks, the PCA's actually extend credit to farmers. Originally, supervision of PCA's took place through 12 Production Credit Corporations, one in each farm credit district. When the Production Credit Corporation in each of the 12 districts was merged with the Federal Intermediate Credit Bank of the district on January 1, 1957, the FICB's assumed the responsibility for the supervision of the PCA's.

The first loans of the Production Credit Associations were made in 1933. The volume of loans made has grown steadily over the years, from $300 million in 1938 to $900 million in 1948 and to $2,500 million in 1958.

Year-end outstandings also have followed a steady sharply-upward course, increasing from $100 million in 1938 to $400 million in 1948 and to $1,400 million in 1958. The fact that year-end outstandings consistently have been below the volume of loans during the year is due to the heavy proportion of loans with maturities of less than one year.

Federal Intermediate Credit Banks (Tables I-7 to I-12)

The 12 district Federal Intermediate Credit Banks are primarily "wholesalers" of short- and intermediate-term farm credit, providing funds for organizations extending credit to farmers. Their own funds are obtained by the sale of debentures to the investing public. These are used to purchase loans made by Production Credit Associations, credit corporations, commercial banks, and other credit institutions. The FICB's also supervise and assist the 494 Production Credit Associations scattered throughout the United States, as a part of the Farm Credit Administration system.

The Federal Intermediate Credit Banks were established in the short- and intermediate-term farm credit markets in 1923 for much the same general reasons that the Federal Land Banks were established, namely, to provide farmers with more adequate credit at a

Agricultural Loans

TABLE I-6

Production Credit Association Loans, 1933-1959[a]

Year ended December 31	Outstanding	Loans made	Loans repaid or charged off	Net changes in outstandings
	(thousands of dollars)			
1933	27	27	---	27
1934	60,459	106,812	46,380	60,432
1935	93,400	194,959	162,018	32,941
1936	104,481	226,915	215,834	11,081
1937	136,918	284,886	252,449	32,437
1938	146,825	301,022	291,115	9,907
1939	153,425	319,401	312,801	6,600
1940	170,686	347,145	329,884	17,261
1941	185,611	414,815	399,890	14,925
1942	182,658	474,049	477,002	- 2,953
1943	196,637	497,178	483,199	13,979
1944	188,306	485,750	494,081	- 8,331
1945	194,788	509,579	503,097	6,482
1946	230,025	607,482	572,245	35,237
1947	289,077	747,967	688,915	59,052
1948	366,822	915,812	838,067	77,745
1949	387,454	946,440	925,808	20,632
1950	450,673	1,065,745	1,002,526	63,219
1951	561,371	1,310,034	1,199,336	110,698
1952	599,295	1,330,320	1,292,396	37,924
1953	541,786	1,213,786	1,271,295	- 57,509
1954	576,997	1,259,176	1,223,965	35,211
1955	644,449	1,373,081	1,305,629	67,452
1956	699,283	1,476,342	1,421,508	54,834
1957	885,918	1,718,436	1,531,801	186,635
1958	1,114,694	2,190,669	1,961,893	228,776
1959	1,361,198	2,501,721	2,255,217	246,504

[a]Series are for continental United States. They exclude loans guaranteed by CC and, beginning 1947, also exclude loans held by associations in liquidation. "Loans made" include renewals.

Source: Data from 1933 to 1953 from Saulnier et al., Table 32. Data from 1954 to 1957 from Agricultural Statistics for 1958, Table 700.

Agricultural Loans

TABLE I-7

Federal Intermediate Credit Banks Loans to Production Credit Associations, 1933-1959[a]

Year ended December 31	Outstanding	Loans made	Loans repaid or charged off a/	Net change in outstandings
	(thousands of dollars)			
1933	27	27	---	27
1934	60,595	109,680	49,112	60,568
1935	95,957	209,282	173,920	35,362
1936	106,845	240,274	229,386	10,888
1937	134,809	304,169	276,205	27,964
1938	141,964	329,961	322,806	7,155
1939	146,323	350,101	345,742	4,359
1940	169,565	384,017	360,775	23,242
1941	191,718	465,347	443,194	22,153
1942	194,564	532,338	529,492	2,846
1943	202,848	599,807	591,523	8,284
1944	198,754	644,022	648,116	-4,094
1945	197,333	656,560	657,981	-1,421
1946	231,285	796,614	762,662	33,952
1947	285,349	981,939	927,875	54,064
1948	354,708	1,188,446	1,119,087	69,359
1949	372,662	1,204,099	1,186,145	17,954
1950	435,717	1,325,072	1,262,017	63,055
1951	539,677	1,707,787	1,603,827	103,960
1952	573,434	1,666,140	1,632,383	33,757
1953	512,247	1,522,702	1,583,889	-61,187
1954	565,258	1,579,008	1,525,997	53,011
1955	610,378	1,725,208	1,680,088	45,120
1956	663,016	1,920,545	1,867,907	52,638
1957	849,808	2,199,750	2,012,958	186,792
1958	1,058,062	2,749,758	2,541,504	208,254
1959	1,285,109	3,077,513	2,850,466	227,047

[a]Data are for continental United States.

Note: Table I-12 is the total of Tables I-7 to I-11.

Source: Data from Agricultural Statistics for 1957, 1958, and 1959, and from Farm Credit Administration.

Agricultural Loans

TABLE I-8

Federal Intermediate Credit Banks Loans to Banks for Cooperatives, 1935-1959[a]

Year ended December 31	Outstanding	Loans made	Loans repaid or charged off	Net change in outstandings
	(thousands of dollars)			
1935	8,016	9,502	1,486	8,016
1936	22,247	29,631	15,400	14,231
1937	29,075	36,807	29,979	6,828
1938	25,045	38,430	42,460	-4,030
1939	17,561	28,879	36,363	-7,484
1940	15,554	31,061	33,068	-2,007
1941	31,582	68,608	52,580	16,028
1942	76,160	159,055	114,477	44,578
1943	103,685	222,782	195,257	27,525
1944	65,003	142,628	181,310	-38,682
1945	40,518	93,481	117,966	-24,485
1946	41,538	118,946	117,926	1,020
1947	44,534	134,555	131,559	2,996
1948	66,131	165,475	143,878	21,597
1949	45,962	201,421	221,590	-20,169
1950	45,125	108,418	109,255	- 837
1951	65,906	126,078	105,297	20,781
1952	47,071	110,568	129,403	-18,835
1953	24,659	55,702	78,114	-22,412
1954	27,200	73,350	70,809	2,541
1955	3,200	51,903	75,903	-24,000
1956	13,950	33,000	22,250	10,750
1957	3,000	5,200	16,150	-10,950
1958	---	---	3,000	-3,000
1959	---	400	400	---

[a]Data are for continental United States.

Note: Table I-12 is the total of Tables I-7 to I-11.

Source: Data from Agricultural Statistics for 1957, 1958, and 1959, and from Farm Credit Administration.

Agricultural Loans

TABLE I-9

Federal Intermediate Credit Banks Direct Loans to Cooperative Associations, 1923-1956[a]

Year ended December 31	Outstanding	Loans made	Loans repaid or charged off	Net change in outstandings
		(thousands of dollars)		
1923	33,627	60,000[b]	26,373[b]	33,627
1924	43,507	83,223	73,343	9,880
1925	53,686	100,148	89,969	10,179
1926	52,700	103,529	104,515	-986
1927	31,990	50,799	71,509	-20,710
1928	36,174	53,571	49,387	4,184
1929	26,073	43,588	53,689	-10,101
1930	64,377	109,927	71,623	38,304
1931	45,177	145,127	164,327	-19,200
1932	9,618	88,997	124,556	-35,559
1933	15,005	27,787	22,400	5,387
1934	33,969	57,357	38,393	18,964
1935	2,731	44,511	75,749	-31,238
1936	1,640	3,755	4,846	-1,091
1937	1,814	5,129	4,955	174
1938	920	2,668	3,562	-894
1939	1,835	4,155	3,240	915
1940	1,490	4,593	4,938	-345
1941	2,152	5,651	4,989	662
1942	2,000	9,397	9,549	-152
1943	2,000	5,000	5,000	---
1944	700	3,402	4,702	-1,300
1945	2,042	4,032	2,690	1,342
1946	4,151	11,579	9,470	2,109
1947	4,000	14,128	14,279	-151
1948	4,709	13,639	12,930	709
1949	2,400	9,900	12,209	-2,309
1950	3,233	9,044	8,211	833
1951	4,000	15,176	14,409	767
1952	2,000	8,000	10,000	-2,000
1953	500	4,000	5,500	-1,500
1954	2,200	4,200	2,500	1,700
1955	3,000	11,096	10,296	800
1956	---	12,167	15,167	-3,000

[a]Data are for continental United States.
[b]Estimates.

Note: Table I-12 is the total of Tables I-7 to I-11.

Source: Data from Agricultural Statistics of 1952 and 1958.

Agricultural Loans

TABLE I-10

Federal Intermediate Credit Banks Loans to Regional Agricultural Credit Corporations, 1933-1935

Year ended December 31	Outstanding	Loans made	Loans repaid or charged off	Net change in outstandings
		(thousands of dollars)		
1933	73,236	109,718	36,482	73,236
1934	38,651	113,435	148,020	-34,585
1935	---	32,533	71,184	-38,651

Note: Tables I-12 is the total of Tables I-7 to I-11.

Source: Worksheet material of the National Bureau of Economic Research.

Agricultural Loans

TABLE I-11

Federal Intermediate Credit Banks Loans to Others, 1923-1959[a]

Year ended December 31	Outstanding	Loans made	Loans repaid or charged off	Net change in outstandings
		(thousands of dollars)		
1923	9,105	13,000[b]	3,895[b]	9,105
1924	18,760	34,004	24,349	9,655
1925	25,974	53,191	45,977	7,214
1926	38,977	72,589	59,586	13,003
1927	42,334	85,456	82,099	3,357
1928	43,884	82,136	80,586	1,550
1929	47,283	90,591	87,192	3,399
1930	62,462	103,906	88,727	15,179
1931	71,960	118,380	108,882	9,498
1932	79,658	148,624	140,926	7,698
1933	60,382	140,527	159,803	-19,276
1934	55,083	124,429	129,728	- 5,299
1935	46,518	116,138	124,703	- 8,565
1936	40,508	105,587	111,597	- 6,010
1937	39,974	100,983	101,517	- 534
1938	32,612	88,698	96,060	- 7,362
1939	32,316	85,383	85,679	- 296
1940	33,116	87,315	86,515	800
1941	37,939	100,697	95,874	4,823
1942	38,182	106,881	106,638	243
1943	34,137	91,790	95,835	-4,045
1944	29,966	79,266	83,437	-4,171
1945	26,487	73,039	76,518	-3,479
1946	31,701	84,892	79,678	5,214
1947	37,915	107,545	101,331	6,214
1948	55,750	158,778	140,943	17,835
1949	50,825	154,636	159,561	- 4,925
1950	62,073	169,455	158,207	11,248
1951	77,842	216,394	200,625	15,769
1952	82,931	212,147	207,058	5,089
1953	63,558	175,504	194,877	-19,373
1954	58,276	153,253	158,535	- 5,282
1955	61,907	153,820	150,189	3,631
1956	60,007	150,276	152,176	- 1,900
1957	67,192	169,198	162,013	7,185
1958	83,722	215,262	198,732	16,530
1959	89,576	219,824	213,970	5,854

[a]Consists of loans to private financing institutions in continental United States.
[b]Estimates.

Note: Table I-12 is the total of Tables I-7 to I-11.

Source: Agricultural Statistics for 1952 and 1958. The years 1933 to 1935 were adjusted to remove loans to Regional Agricultural Credit Corporations. These loans are shown separately in Table I-10.

Agricultural Loans

TABLE I-12

Federal Intermediate Credit Banks Total Loans, 1923-1959[a]

Year ended December 31	Outstanding	Loans made	Loans repaid or charged off	Net change in outstandings
(thousands of dollars)				
1923	42,732	73,000[b]	30,268[b]	42,732
1924	62,267	117,227	97,692	19,535
1925	79,660	153,339	135,946	17,393
1926	91,677	176,118	164,101	12,017
1927	74,324	136,255	153,608	-17,353
1928	80,058	135,707	129,973	5,734
1929	73,356	134,179	140,881	- 6,702
1930	126,839	213,833	160,350	53,483
1931	117,137	263,507	273,209	- 9,702
1932	89,276	237,621	265,482	-27,861
1933	148,650	278,059	218,685	59,374
1934	188,298	404,901	365,253	39,648
1935	153,222	411,966	447,042	-35,076
1936	171,240	379,247	361,229	18,018
1937	205,672	447,088	412,656	34,432
1938	200,541	459,757	464,888	- 5,131
1939	198,035	468,518	471,024	- 2,506
1940	219,725	506,986	485,296	21,690
1941	263,391	640,303	596,637	43,666
1942	310,906	807,671	760,156	47,515
1943	342,670	919,379	887,615	31,764
1944	294,423	869,318	917,565	-48,247
1945	266,380	827,112	855,155	-28,043
1946	308,675	1,012,031	969,736	42,295
1947	371,798	1,238,167	1,175,044	63,123
1948	481,298	1,526,338	1,416,838	109,500
1949	471,849	1,570,056	1,579,505	-9,449
1950	546,148	1,611,989	1,537,690	74,299
1951	687,425	2,065,435	1,924,158	141,277
1952	705,436	1,996,855	1,978,844	18,011
1953	600,964	1,757,908	1,862,380	-104,472
1954	652,934	1,809,811	1,757,841	51,970
1955	678,485	1,942,027	1,916,476	25,551
1956	736,973	2,115,988	2,057,500	58,488
1957	920,000	2,374,148	2,191,121	183,027
1958	1,141,784	2,965,020	2,743,236	221,784
1959	1,374,685	3,297,737	3,064,836	232,901

[a]Includes loans to Production Credit Association, Banks for Cooperatives, Regional Agricultural Credit Corporations, direct loans to cooperative associations and loans to private financing institutions. Series are for continental United States.
[b]Estimates.

Note: Table I-12 is the total of Tables I-7 and I-11.

Source: Agricultural Statistics for 1952 and 1958.

lower cost. The FICB's originally were important in making direct loans to agricultural cooperatives, a function now largely served by the Banks for Cooperatives, as well as in discounting agricultural paper for private lenders. The volume of such discounting was small. Consequently, the PCA's were established in 1933 to do what it was hoped in 1923 the private lenders would do if they could discount paper with the FICB's.

Total loans of FICB's were $3.3 billion in 1959, more than double those of 10 years earlier, and a record high (Table I-12). Year-end outstandings grew from $73 million in 1929 to $198 million in 1939, $472 million in 1949, and $1,375 million in 1959.

Production Credit Corporations (Table I-13)

The Farm Credit Act of 1933 authorized the establishment of 12 Production Credit Corporations, one in each farm credit district. The PCC's were provided with government capital of $120 million and empowered to make subscriptions to non-voting stock of the local PCA's. They were also empowered to charter local PCA's and to supervise their activities. Thus, the PCA's extended short- and intermediate-term credit to farmers, drawing part of their equity funds from the PCC's, and part of their loanable funds by rediscounting short-term paper with the FICB's. The PCC's were a part of the Farm Credit Administration until January 1, 1957, when they were merged with the FICB's of each district. The FICB's were the remaining agency, but separate accounting continued of the government capital in the PCC's.

As of the end of 1958, only $4 million of PCC government capital remained invested in non-voting stock of the PCA's (Table I-13). This compared with a high of $90 million at the end of 1934. Most of the stock in the PCA's now is voting stock held by member borrowers.

Regional Agricultural Credit Corporations (Table I-14)

Regional Agricultural Credit Corporations were established as direct federal agencies in each of the 12 farm credit districts in 1932. Their purposes was to make short- and intermediate-term loans to farmers, filling in the gap resulting from the lack of such loans by private lending agencies. The RACC's were initially established and financed by the Reconstruction Finance Corporation. They were empowered to obtain additional funds by borrowing from the RFC, FICB's, and Federal Reserve Banks.

The RACC's were transferred to the Farm Credit Administration in 1933. With the growth within that system of PCA's supplying the same type of credit, the need for their existence diminished

Agricultural Loans

TABLE I-13

Purchases of Stock in Production Credit Associations by Production Credit Corporations, 1933-1958[a]

Year ended December 31	Outstanding	Loans made	Loans repaid or charged off	Net change in outstandings
		(thousands of dollars)		
1933	2,430	2,430	---	2,430
1934	90,086	89,405	1,749	87,656
1935	77,017	11,999	25,068	-13,069
1936	75,038	3,895	5,874	-1,979
1937	76,146	4,824	3,716	1,108
1938	75,788	2,419	2,777	-358
1939	75,370	2,558	2,976	-418
1940	61,445	1,301	15,226	-13,925
1941	81,498	21,464	1,411	20,053
1942	81,621	1,920	1,797	123
1943	76,090	621	6,152	-5,531
1944	63,587	538	13,041	-12,503
1945	55,491	596	8,692	-8,096
1946	46,034	292	9,749	-9,457
1947	34,918	225	11,341	-11,116
1948	29,139	30	5,809	-5,779
1949	22,296	115	6,958	-6,843
1950	15,728	965	7,533	-6,568
1951	11,371	1,015	5,372	-4,357
1952	7,596	100	3,875	-3,775
1953	4,946	640	3,290	-2,650
1954	3,165	160	1,941	-1,781
1955	2,160	---	1,005	-1,005
1956	1,830	250	580	-330
1957	1,700	50	180	-130
1958	4,000	2,860	560	2,300

[a]Effective January 1, 1957, under provision of the Farm Credit Act of 1956, the $1,830,010 of investment of the PCC in capital stock of the PCA's was transferred to the Governor of the Farm Credit Administration. Under the act, the PCC in each Farm Credit district was terminated and its activities were merged with the Federal Intermediate Credit Bank.

Source: Data for 1933 to 1953 from Saulnier, et al., page 407. Data for 1954-58 supplied by Farm Credit Administration.

Agricultural Loans

TABLE I-14

Regional Agricultural Credit Corporation Loans, 1932-58[a]

Year ended December 31	Outstanding	Loans made	Loans repaid or charged off	Net change in outstandings
		(thousands of dollars)		
1932	24,373	24,597	224	24,373
1933	144,636	223,116	102,853	120,263
1934	87,102	140,589	198,123	-57,534
1935	43,400	90,655	134,357	-43,702
1936	25,288	34,667	52,779	-18,112
1937	15,592	18,603	28,299	-9,696
1938	11,080	5,718	10,230	-4,512
1939	8,005	4,664	7,739	-3,075
1940	5,855	4,805	6,955	-2,150
1941	5,531	6,759	7,083	-324
1942	3,991	7,759	9,299	-1,540
1943	32,047	73,255	45,199	28,056
1944	12,195	15,665	35,517	-19,852
1945	6,151	9,646	15,690	-6,044
1946	2,560	1,470	5,061	-3,591
1947	1,862	77	775	-698
1948	1,522	77	417	-340
1949	1,273	130	379	-249
1950	1,236	8	45	-37
1951	868	--	368	-368
1952	656	5	217	-212
1953	501	--	155	-155
1954	442	1	60	-59
1955	386	--	56	-56
1956	336	--	50	-50
1957	283	--	53	-53
1958	239	--	44	-44

[a]This program is now being liquidated by the Farmers Home Administration.

Source: Data are from Saulnier, et al., page 403, and from Farmers Home Administration.

to the point that Congress in 1937 provided for their consolidation or merger. The last remaining RACC was dissolved in 1949, and the program turned over to the Farmers Home Administration for liquidation.

Banks for Cooperatives (Tables I-15 to I-19)

The Banks for Cooperatives make loans to farmers' cooperatives engaged in marketing farm products, purchasing farm supplies, and providing farm business services. Loans are made to finance the construction and improvement of physical facilities, and for operating capital purposes, including the financing of inventories. The Banks for Cooperatives provide agricultural cooperatives with a full line of credit, with a national source of funds, and supply certain management services not normally provided by private lenders. Loan funds are obtained from sale of debentures to private investors, borrowings from other Farm Credit banks and from commercial banks, and from use of the BC's capital, originally supplied by the government and now owned in part by borrowing cooperatives. In addition to the 12 district Banks for Cooperatives, there is a 13th Central Bank for Cooperatives in Washington, D.C. that may make loans directly itself or jointly with one or more district banks.

The Banks for Cooperatives made loans totaling \$559 million in 1958, and had \$510 million outstandings at the end of 1958 (Table I-19). Their volume of business has undergone steady growth since their first loans were made in 1934.

Operating capital loans, offered on a seasonal or term basis, amounted to \$378 million in 1958 (Table I-15). They represented about two-thirds of the total loans of the Banks for Cooperatives.

Commodity loans, to assist cooperatives in the effective merchandising of agricultural products and supplies, amounted to \$105 million in 1958 (Table I-16). This type of loan was of lesser importance in 1958 than in any of the preceding 8 years.

Facility loans, to construct or acquire physical facilities needed for operations or growth, amounted to \$76 million in 1958 (Table I-17).

A discontinued category of loans, those secured by CCC documents, were made in 1943-48 (Table I-18). All were repaid by the end of 1949.

Agricultural Loans

TABLE I-15

Banks for Cooperatives Operating Capital Loans, 1934-1958

Year ended December 31	Outstanding	Loans made	Loans repaid or charged off	Net change in outstandings
	(thousands of dollars)			
1934	21,991	61,254	39,263	21,991
1935	27,718	45,064	39,337	5,727
1936	28,868	43,166	42,016	1,150
1937	35,372	53,979	47,475	6,504
1938	36,176	52,595	51,791	804
1939	32,326	49,729	53,579	- 3,850
1940	35,354	61,849	58,821	3,028
1941	52,004	100,642	83,992	16,650
1942	54,485	128,099	125,618	2,481
1943	70,157	167,430	151,758	15,672
1944	64,746	160,413	165,824	- 5,411
1945	67,970	186,809	183,585	3,224
1946	101,696	262,942	229,216	33,726
1947	151,689	346,336	296,343	49,993
1948	173,720	321,666	299,635	22,031
1949	165,040	253,751	262,431	- 8,680
1950	177,426	250,471	238,085	12,386
1951	220,702	370,399	327,123	43,276
1952	216,929	345,007	348,780	- 3,773
1953	182,657	307,304	341,576	-34,272
1954	168,592	292,236	306,301	-14,065
1955	181,980	333,055	319,667	13,388
1956	242,752	420,498	359,726	60,772
1957	240,745	370,398	372,405	- 2,007
1958	258,678	377,990	360,057	17,933

Note: Table I-19 is the total of Tables I-15 to I-18.

Source: Data supplied by Farm Credit Administration.

Agricultural Loans

TABLE I-16

Banks for Cooperatives Commodity Loans, 1935-1958

Year ended December 31	Outstanding	Loans made	Loans repaid or charged off	Net change in outstandings
		(thousands of dollars)		
1935	8,702	11,756	3,054	8,702
1936	22,653	31,010	17,059	13,951
1937	30,052	36,484	29,085	7,399
1938	27,109	36,886	39,829	- 2,943
1939	20,950	30,143	36,302	- 6,159
1940	17,980	35,229	38,199	- 2,970
1949	37,735	73,536	53,781	19,755
1942	67,246	118,580	89,069	29,511
1943	55,500	124,443	136,189	-11,746
1944	35,646	107,835	127,689	-19,854
1945	37,112	82,271	80,805	1,466
1946	39,690	104,670	102,092	2,578
1947	48,158	123,897	115,429	8,468
1948	43,342	132,996	137,812	- 4,816
1949	37,777	100,871	106,436	- 5,565
1950	60,042	120,207	97,942	22,265
1951	79,357	155,015	135,700	19,315
1952	77,288	150,300	152,369	- 2,069
1953	52,189	143,309	168,408	-25,099
1954	39,199	127,042	140,032	-12,990
1955	44,838	156,564	150,925	5,639
1956	59,591	137,608	122,855	14,753
1957	38,276	109,264	130,579	-21,315
1958	42,059	104,982	101,199	3,783

Note: Table I-19 is the total of Tables I-15 to I-18.

Source: Data supplied by Farm Credit Administration.

Agricultural Loans

TABLE I-17

Banks for Cooperatives Facility Loans, 1934-1958

Year ended December 31	Outstanding	Loans made	Loans repaid or charged off	Net change in outstandings
		(thousands of dollars)		
1934	5,860	6,261	401	5,860
1935	13,593	9,528	1,795	7,733
1936	18,126	7,118	2,585	4,533
1937	22,209	7,121	3,038	4,083
1938	24,211	5,464	3,462	2,002
1939	22,976	3,488	4,723	- 1,235
1940	21,407	4,153	5,722	- 1,569
1941	23,705	7,391	5,093	2,298
1942	22,913	5,701	6,493	- 792
1943	20,880	7,534	9,567	- 2,033
1944	21,403	8,874	8,351	523
1945	23,963	11,024	8,464	2,560
1946	34,775	19,880	9,068	10,812
1947	66,983	43,972	11,764	32,208
1948	87,458	35,844	15,369	20,475
1949	99,070	27,995	16,383	11,612
1950	107,510	31,498	23,058	8,440
1951	123,893	43,547	27,164	16,383
1952	124,287	32,811	32,417	394
1953	137,264	46,403	33,426	12,977
1954	153,824	63,444	46,884	16,560
1955	143,865	38,017	47,976	- 9,959
1956	154,765	50,540	39,640	10,900
1957	175,431	61,670	41,004	20,666
1958	209,092	75,708	42,047	33,661

Note: Table I-19 is the total of Tables I-15 to I-18.

Source: Data supplied by Farm Credit Administration.

Agricultural Loans

TABLE I-18

Banks for Cooperatives Loans Secured by CCC Documents, 1943-1949

Year ended December 31	Outstanding	Loans made	Loans repaid or charged off	Net change in outstandings
	(thousands of dollars)			
1943	88,637	99,174	10,537	88,637
1944	91,040	86,515	84,112	2,403
1945	28,500	53,598	116,138	-62,540
1946	5,389	12,277	35,388	-23,111
1947	7,947	16,043	13,485	2,558
1948	164	4,172	11,955	- 7,783
1949	--	--	164	- 164

Note: Table I-19 is the total of Tables I-15 to I-18.

Source: Data supplied by Farm Credit Administration.

Agricultural Loans

TABLE I-19

Total Loans of Banks for Cooperatives, 1934-1958

Year ended December 31	Outstanding	Loans made	Loans repaid or charged off	Net change in outstandings
	(thousands of dollars)			
1934	27,851	67,515	39,664	27,851
1935	50,013	66,348	44,186	22,162
1936	69,647	81,294	61,660	19,634
1937	87,633	97,584	79,598	17,986
1938	87,496	94,945	95,082	-137
1939	76,252	83,360	94,604	-11,244
1940	74,741	101,231	102,742	-1,511
1941	113,444	181,569	142,866	38,703
1942	144,644	252,380	221,180	31,200
1943	235,174	398,581	308,051	90,530
1944	212,835	363,637	385,976	-22,339
1945	157,545	333,702	388,992	-55,290
1946	181,550	399,769	375,764	24,005
1947	274,777	530,248	437,021	93,227
1948	304,684	494,678	464,771	29,907
1949	301,887	382,617	385,414	-2,797
1950	344,978	402,176	359,085	43,091
1951	423,952	568,961	489,987	78,974
1952	418,504	528,118	533,566	-5,448
1953	372,110	497,016	543,410	-46,394
1954	361,615	482,722	493,217	-10,495
1955	370,683	527,636	518,568	9,068
1956	457,108	608,646	522,221	86,425
1957	454,452	541,332	543,988	-2,656
1958	509,829	558,680	503,303	55,377

Note: Table I-19 is the total of Tables I-15 to I-18.

Source: Data supplied by Farm Credit Administration.

Agricultural Marketing Act Revolving Fund (Tables I-20 to I-23)

Loans from the Agricultural Marketing Act Revolving Fund were of considerable significance in 1930-33, primarily for the purpose of supporting prices of farm products (mainly wheat and cotton), and secondarily for the purpose of making loans to farm cooperatives engaged in marketing. The Revolving Fund was placed in liquidation in 1933, because its functions were being taken over and expanded by the Commodity Credit Corporation (price support loans) and the Banks for Cooperatives (loans to agricultural cooperatives). However, a few loans to farmers' cooperatives to facilitate the collection of outstanding items continued in each year through 1952, and, of more importance, the Revolving Fund became and continues to be a major source of capital for the Banks for Cooperatives. The initial source of funds for the Revolving Fund was a $500 million appropriation from the U.S. Treasury. Currently, and since 1933, the Agricultural Marketing Act Revolving Fund has been administered by the Farm Credit Administration. In 1930-33, it was used and administered by the Federal Farm Board.

The Federal Farm Board used its full lending authority, with total loans of $517 million in 1931 (exceeding the total lending authority because some funds came from repayment of loans, and earnings), and with outstandings at the end of 1932 of $467 million (Table I-23). When resources of the Federal Farm Board were exhausted, prices of the products being supported dropped sharply. Losses on price-support loans amounted to about $330 million by 1935, including $197 million on donations of wheat and cotton to the American Red Cross, and $46 million on wheat sold to the Secretary of Agriculture under the provisions of the Agricultural Adjustment Act.

Joint Stock Land Banks (Table I-24)

The Joint Stock Land Banks were established as a result of the 1916 Federal Farm Loan Act for the purpose of making long-term mortgage loans on farm real estate. They made no loans after 1933, and their liquidation was complete by 1951.

The JSLB's were established under the same Act that initiated Federal Land Banks, as a compromise that set up a cooperative system with government sponsorship and financial aid, the Federal Land Banks, alongside a system of privately organized and financed land banks, the JSLB's. The bonds sold by the JSLB's to obtain loanable funds were tax exempt, but other than this they operated without special government assistance.

Eighty-eight JSLB's were chartered during the period from 1917 through 1931. Their loans exceeded $100 million in only four years: 1922, 1923, 1925, and 1926 (Table I-24). During 1929, their loans

Agricultural Loans

TABLE I-20

Agricultural Marketing Act Revolving Fund Loans to Farmers' Cooperatives, 1929-1953

Year ended December 31	Outstanding	Loans made	Loans repaid or charged off	Net change in outstandings
	(thousands of dollars)			
1929	14,510	14,823	313	14,510
1930	136,698	193,395	71,207	122,188
1931	156,280	126,773	107,191	19,582
1932	158,885	34,489	31,884	2,605
1933	157,752	40,687	41,820	-1,133
1934	54,863	9,555	112,444	-102,889
1935	44,433	7,402	17,832	-10,430
1936	53,754	20,450	11,129	9,321
1937	30,982	5,935	28,707	-22,772
1938	23,723	7,910	15,169	-7,259
1939	20,547	1,214	4,390	-3,176
1940	16,461	3,094	7,180	-4,086
1941	16,914	3,990	3,537	453
1942	12,551	5,017	9,380	-4,363
1943	7,351	1,417	6,617	-5,200
1944	3,067	809	5,093	-4,284
1945	2,693	660	1,034	-374
1946	2,232	975	1,436	-461
1947	2,602	1,400	1,030	370
1948	1,315	1,000	2,287	-1,287
1949	1,365	700	650	50
1950	1,309	700	756	-56
1951	1,451	700	558	142
1952	905	375	921	-546
1953	--	--	905	-905

Note: Table I-23 is the total of Tables I-20 to I-22.

Source: Data from Agricultural Statistics for 1952 and 1958.

TABLE I-21

Agricultural Marketing Act Revolving Fund Loans to Stabilization Corporations to Support Farm Commodity Prices, 1930-1940

Year ended December 31	Outstanding	Loans made	Loans repaid or charged off	Net change in outstandings
	(thousands of dollars)			
1930	97,058	155,157	58,099	97,058
1931	279,974	390,048	207,132	182,916
1932	307,616	194,538	166,896	27,642
1933	176,340	6,024	137,300	-131,276
1934	92,048	--	84,292	-84,292
1935	71,426	--	20,622	-20,622
1936	68,008	--	3,418	-3,418
1937	67,989	--	19	-19
1938	67,460	--	529	-529
1939	66,660	--	800	-800
1940	--	--	66,660	-66,660

Note: Table I-23 is the total of Tables I-20 to I-22.

Source: Worksheet material of the National Bureau of Economic Research.

Agricultural Loans

TABLE I-22

Agricultural Marketing Act Revolving Fund
Loans to Banks for Cooperatives, 1933-1958[a]

Year ended December 31	Outstanding	Loans made	Loans repaid or charged off	Net change in outstandings
		(thousands of dollars)		
1933	95,000	95,000	--	95,000
1934	110,000	15,000	--	15,000
1935	134,000	24,000	--	24,000
1936	137,500	3,500	--	3,500
1937	144,500	7,000	--	7,000
1938	149,000	4,500	--	4,500
1939	149,000	--	--	--
1940	109,000	--	40,000	-40,000
1941	140,000	51,000	20,000	31,000
1942	171,500	31,500	--	31,500
1943	174,000	3,000	500	2,500
1944	177,000	3,000	--	3,000
1945	178,500	3,500	2,000	1,500
1946	178,500	--	--	--
1947	178,500	--	--	--
1948	178,500	--	--	--
1949	178,500	--	--	--
1950	178,500	--	--	--
1951	178,500	--	--	--
1952	178,500	--	--	--
1953	178,500	--	--	--
1954	150,000	--	28,500	-28,500
1955	150,000	--	--	--
1956	147,314	--	2,686	-2,686
1957	141,588	--	5,726	-5,726
1958	134,799	--	6,789	-6,789

[a]Represents investments in capital stock of Banks for Cooperatives.

Note: Table I-23 is the total of Tables I-20 to I-22.

Source: Data supplied by Farm Credit Administration.

Agricultural Loans

TABLE I-23

Total Loans from Agricultural Marketing Act Revolving Fund, 1929-1958

Year ended December 31	Outstanding	Loans made	Loans repaid or charged off	Net change in outstandings
		(thousands of dollars)		
1929	14,510	14,823	313	14,510
1930	233,756	348,552	129,306	219,246
1931	436,254	516,821	314,323	202,498
1932	466,501	229,027	198,780	30,247
1933	429,092	141,711	179,120	-37,409
1934	256,911	24,555	196,736	-172,181
1935	249,859	31,402	38,454	-7,052
1936	259,262	23,950	14,547	9,403
1937	243,471	12,935	28,726	-15,791
1938	240,183	12,410	15,698	-3,288
1939	236,207	1,214	5,190	-3,976
1940	125,461	3,094	113,840	-110,746
1941	156,914	54,990	23,537	31,453
1942	184,051	36,517	9,380	27,137
1943	181,351	4,417	7,117	-2,700
1944	180,067	3,809	5,093	-1,284
1945	181,193	4,160	3,034	1,126
1946	180,732	975	1,436	-461
1947	181,102	1,400	1,030	370
1948	179,815	1,000	2,287	-1,287
1949	179,865	700	650	50
1950	179,809	700	756	-56
1951	179,951	700	558	142
1952	179,405	375	921	-546
1953	178,500	--	905	-905
1954	150,000	--	28,500	-28,500
1955	150,000	--	--	--
1956	147,314	--	2,686	-2,686
1957	141,588	--	5,726	-5,726
1958	134,799	--	6,789	-6,789

Note: Table I-23 is the total of Tables I-20 to I-22.

Source: Data supplied by Farm Credit Administration.

Agricultural Loans

TABLE I-24

Joint Stock Land Bank Loans, 1917-1950

Year ended December 31	Outstanding	Loans made	Loans repaid or charged off	Net change in outstandings
		(thousands of dollars)		
1917	1,888	1,890	2	1,888
1918	8,384	6,600	104	6,496
1919	60,038	53,030	1,376	51,654
1920	77,959	19,324	1,403	17,921
1921	85,017	9,335	2,277	7,058
1922	218,775	138,685	4,927	133,758
1923	392,639	189,748	15,884	173,864
1924	446,429	74,587	20,797	53,790
1925	545,559	131,431	32,301	99,130
1926	632,476	123,026	36,109	86,917
1927	669,798	83,719	46,397	37,322
1928	656,516	40,572	53,854	-13,282
1929	637,789	18,186	36,913	-18,727
1930	605,858	5,236	37,167	-31,931
1931	552,180	5,407	59,085	-53,678
1932	474,954	2,181	79,407	-77,226
1933	412,346	739	63,347	-62,608
1934	277,020	a/	135,326	-135,326
1935	200,617	--	76,403	-76,403
1936	162,786	--	37,831	-37,831
1937	133,554	--	29,232	-29,232
1938	114,992	--	18,562	-18,562
1939	91,726	--	23,266	-23,266
1940	73,455	--	18,271	-18,271
1941	55,919	--	17,536	-17,536
1942	37,015	--	18,904	-18,904
1943	10,097	--	26,918	-26,918
1944	5,455	--	4,642	- 4,642
1945	3,208	--	2,247	- 2,247
1946	1,641	--	1,567	- 1,567
1947	645	--	996	- 996
1948	462	--	183	- 183
1949	270	--	192	- 192
1950	---	--	270	- 270

[a]After JSLB's were put into liquidation (1933), loans made a e assumed to be zero.

Source: Saulnier, et al., p. 160.

were only \$18 million, and in 1930 and 1931, only \$5 million in each year. During the early 1930's their policy of foreclosing on mortgages, selling acquired properties at market-breaking prices, and buying their own outstanding bonds at high discounts brought them into disrepute. The Farm Mortgage Act of 1933 prohibited them from issuing additional tax exempt bonds or from making additional loans except to refinance outstanding accounts or in connection with the sale of acquired real estate.

Farmers Home Administration (Tables I-25 to I-50)

The Farmers Home Administration, established in 1946 as a division of the U.S. Department of Agriculture, operates a program aimed at developing efficient individual farms, by loans to farmers unable to obtain credit elsewhere, of four types:

1. Operating loans,
2. Farm ownership loans,
3. Farm housing loans,
4. Soil and water conservation, and water facilities, loans.

In addition the Farmers Home Administration makes loans designed to dampen the effects on farmers of natural and economic disasters. All loans are supervised closely, and most are to low-income low-equity farm families. A large share of the loans have been made in the South. Funds for making loans have come mainly from money appropriated by Congress, although in recent years insured loans from private credit sources have been growing in importance.

The FHA program represented reorganization, continuation, and expansion of the programs of the following defunct agencies: Farm Security Administration (1937-46), Resettlement Administration (1935-37), and the Rural Rehabilitation Division of the Federal Emergency Relief Administration (1933-35). On establishment in 1946 it also took over the functions previously performed by the Emergency Crop and Feed Division of the Farm Credit Administration. In 1949, the assets of the Regional Agricultural Credit Corporations were transferred to the FHA for liquidation.

The early emphasis of the FHA program was in aiding borrowers to become self-sufficient on subsistence farms. A grant program was important in conjunction with loans. During 1934-41, nearly one-half of the borrowers also received grants. At the present time, emphasis is in the direction of serving a group of farmers who were or could be expected to become commercial farmers. The program has become more nearly that of serving commercial farmers who for various reasons cannot obtain credit elsewhere.

Total loans of the Farmers Home Administration were larger in 1958 than in any preceding year, $358 million (Table I-50). In 1958, total loans were more than triple those of 10 and 20 years earlier, $113 million and $111 million, respectively. Outstandings at the end of 1958 exceeded $1.0 billion for the first time in the agency's history.

Eleven parts of loans of the Farmers Home Administration, adding to the totals in Table I-50, are as follows:

1. Table I-25 — direct farm ownership loans. These loans are made to improve and buy family-type farms, enlarge undersized farms to family-type size, and refinance debts. With veterans' preference applicable to such loans, most of such loans since World War II have been to veterans. Their volume in 1958 was only $27 million, about one-half their 1941 amount, and less than 10 percent of total FHA activity. Division of such loans between those from appropriated funds and those from Corporation Trust Funds of the states is shown in Tables I-26 and I-27. Most loans were from appropriated funds. The FHA made a small amount of loans from State Corporation Trust Funds, with the income therefrom reverted to the states supplying them. Sometimes the FHA in compiling their statistics omits these loans from State Corporation Trust Funds, as being made by them as an agent for the states, even though such business is intermingled with their other loaning activity.

2. Table I-28 — insured farm ownership loans. These loans are of a similar type as the direct farm ownership loans, except that the source of funds is different. Fewer of them are made to veterans. They were first made in 1948, in a volume of $3 million, but have expanded rapidly so that in 1958 the volume of $35 million exceeded that of direct farm ownership loans.

3. Table I-29 — direct farm housing loans. These are loans to construct and repair farm houses and other essential farm buildings. This type of loan was authorized in 1949, and first made in 1950. The volume of such loans was $49 million in 1958. The welfare aspect of this program is shown by the authorization of loans if the borrower agreed to follow farm improvement plans that in five years would provide the necessary earnings to meet repayments. For such cases, the FHA was authorized, if the borrower could not meet full payments during the first five years, to contribute up to half the principal and all of the interest installments due.

4. Table I-30 — direct operating loans from appropriated funds. These are loans primarily to obtain chattel resources needed to become successfully established in farming. About 75 percent of such loans are invested in equipment and livestock.

Agricultural Loans

TABLE I-25

Farmers Home Administration Direct Farm Ownership Loans, 1938-1958

Year ended December 31	Outstanding	Loans made	Loans repaid or charged off	Net change in outstandings
	(thousands of dollars)			
1938	10,275	10,275	--	10,275
1939	32,301	22,287	261	22,026
1940	66,286	36,406	2,421	33,985
1941	116,610	51,558	1,234	50,324
1942	160,258	48,131[a]	4,483	43,648
1943	174,946	28,998	14,310	14,688
1944	193,810	39,497	20,633	18,864
1945	185,060	14,256	23,006	- 8,750
1946	192,306	37,984	30,738	7,246
1947	199,193	36,229	29,342	6,887
1948	192,440	19,623	26,376	- 6,753
1949	192,434	17,487	17,493	- 6
1950	191,433	18,564	19,565	- 1,001
1951	190,220	22,908	24,121	- 1,213
1952	192,842	23,482	20,860	2,622
1953	193,749	17,872	16,965	907
1954	198,781	19,828	14,796	5,032
1955	198,657	16,688	16,812	- 124
1956	208,560	26,390	16,487	9,903
1957	238,774	45,029	14,815	30,214
1958	248,873	27,406	17,307	10,099

[a]See footnote a/ to Table I-27.

Note: Table I-25 is the total of Tables I-26 and I-27.

Source: Data supplied by the Farmers Home Administration.

Agricultural Loans

TABLE I-26

Farmers Home Administration Direct Farm
Ownership Loans from Appropriated Funds, 1938-1958

Year ended December 31	Outstanding	Loans made	Loans repaid or charged off	Net change in outstandings
		(thousands of dollars)		
1938	10,275	10,275	--	10,275
1939	32,301	22,287	261	22,026
1940	66,286	36,406	2,421	33,985
1941	116,610	51,558	1,234	50,324
1942	159,626	47,298	4,282	43,016
1943	174,215	28,750	14,161	14,589
1944	192,757	39,326	20,784	18,542
1945	180,972	10,585	22,370	-11,785
1946	188,535	37,844	30,281	7,563
1947	195,808	36,107	28,834	7,273
1948	188,753	18,424	25,479	- 7,055
1949	188,919	17,094	16,928	166
1950	188,447	18,559	19,031	- 472
1951	187,307	21,901	23,041	- 1,140
1952	190,331	23,342	20,318	3,024
1953	191,551	17,862	16,642	1,220
1954	196,869	19,827	14,509	5,318
1955	197,125	16,687	16,431	256
1956	207,263	26,366	16,228	10,138
1957	237,597	45,028	14,694	30,334
1958	247,905	27,406	17,098	10,308

Note: Table I-25 is the total of Tables I-26 and I-27.

Source: Data supplied by the Farmers Home Administration.

Agricultural Loans

TABLE I-27

Farmers Home Administration Direct Farm Ownership Loans from Corporation Trust Funds, 1942-1958

Year ended December 31	Outstanding	Loans made	Loans repaid or charged off	Net change in Outstanding
	(thousands of dollars)			
1942	632	833[a]	201	632
1943	731	248	149	99
1944	1,053	171	151	322
1945	4,088	3,671	636	3,035
1946	3,771	140	457	- 317
1947	3,385	122	508	- 386
1948	3,687	1,199	897	302
1949	3,515	393	565	- 172
1950	2,986	5	534	- 529
1951	2,913	1,007	1,080	- 73
1952	2,511	140	542	- 402
1953	2,198	10	323	- 313
1954	1,912	1	287	- 286
1955	1,532	1	381	- 380
1956	1,297	24	259	- 235
1957	1,177	1	121	- 120
1958	968	--	209	- 209

[a]Cumulative from 1938 through December 31, 1942. The amount for each year during this period and the amount outstanding at the end of each year through 1941 are not available.

Note: Table I-25 is the total of Tables I-26 and I-27.

Source: Data supplied by the Farmers Home Administration.

Agricultural Loans

TABLE I-28

Farmers Home Administration Insured Farm Ownership Loans, 1948-1958

Year ended December 31	Outstanding	Loans made	Loans repaid or charged off	Net change in outstandings
	(thousands of dollars)			
1948	2,908	2,972	64	2,908
1949	12,396	9,728	240	9,488
1950	29,359	17,632	669	16,963
1951	43,084	15,899	2,174	13,725
1952	51,599	11,156	2,641	8,515
1953	58,535	10,473	3,537	6,936
1954	66,330	11,430	3,635	7,795
1955	97,226	36,396	5,500	30,896
1956	128,117	38,533	7,642	30,891
1957	146,402	26,732	8,447	18,285
1958	170,144	34,504	10,762	23,742

Source: Data supplied by the Farmers Home Administration.

TABLE I-29

Farmers Home Administration Direct Farm Housing Loans, 1950-1958

Year ended December 31	Outstanding	Loans made	Loans repaid or charged off	Net change in Outstanding
		(thousands of dollars)		
1950	26,782	27,634	852	26,782
1951	47,631	23,809	2,960	20,849
1952	69,680	26,432	4,383	22,049
1953	78,913	14,737	5,504	9,233
1954	77,177	4,646	6,382	-1,736
1955	70,640	67	6,604	-6,537
1956	72,979	9,539	7,200	2,339
1957	91,442	25,814	7,351	18,463
1958	131,195	49,369	9,616	39,753

Source: Data supplied by the Farmers Home Administration.

Their volume in 1958 was $179 million, exactly one-half of total FHA loans. Such loans represent the most important lending activity of the FHA. Taken by themselves, the data in Table I-30 seem to indicate a rapid expansion in such loans beginning in 1946. However, the rural rehabilitation loans shown in Table I-42 were of a similar type, and their peak volume in 1941, $114 million, was over one-half of the 1958 volume of direct operating loans. Of a similar type and grouped together are the direct operating and rural rehabilitation loans from Corporation Trust Funds (Table I-45).

5. Table I-31 — water facilities and soil and water conservation direct loans. This program was initiated in several steps. Water facilities loans were first made in 1939. These were loans to individual farmers and to groups of farmers in the 17 arid and semiarid states. The initial goal was the financing of water facilities to enable low-income farmers to improve their farm productivity and level of living. In 1954 Congress extended the program to include the entire United States and broadened it to include loans for soil and water conservation purposes — the latter including drainage, improved permanent pasture, and forestation. Both direct and insured loans are included in this program.

6. Table I-38 — soil and water conservation insured loans. These loans are for the same purposes as the direct loans described above. They were first made in 1954. Despite their shorter history, outstandings at the end of 1958 were larger than for direct loans of this type, $19 million compared with $14 million.

7. Table I-41 — emergency loans. These loans were for the purpose of aiding farmers who were in trouble because of drought, flood, or other disaster. On some occasions, recessions were also contributory to the magnitude of the aid provided. In the bookkeeping of the FHA, such loans are divided into production emergency, economic emergency, special emergency, and special livestock loans. Their volume is an important part of total FHA lending activity, amounting to one-sixth of the total in 1958 and one-third in 1954. Emergency crop and feed loans, shown in Table I-48, were of a similar nature in the 1929-46 period.

8. Table I-42 — rural rehabilitation loans from appropriated funds. These loans were for operating purposes. Their division as between loans to individuals and loans to associations is shown in Tables I-43 and I-44. Loans to associations were made for a variety of reasons, including cooperative marketing.

Agricultural Loans

TABLE I-30

Farmers Home Administration Direct Operating Loans from Appropriated Funds, 1946-1958[a]

Year ended December 31	Outstanding	Loans made	Loans repaid or charged off	Net change in outstandings
	(thousands of dollars)			
1946	5,310	5,313	3	5,310
1947	51,037	78,571	32,844	45,727
1948	86,177	80,576	45,436	35,140
1949	119,992	79,660	45,845	33,815
1950	144,339	85,332	60,985	24,347
1951	165,734	107,225	85,830	21,395
1952	210,874	122,758	77,618	45,140
1953	245,203	118,427	84,098	34,329
1954	278,454	136,236	102,985	33,251
1955	272,174	112,151	118,431	-6,280
1956	297,807	156,838	131,205	25,633
1957	318,612	172,214	151,409	20,805
1958	319,721	179,444	178,335	1,109

[a]Operating loans from Corporation Trust Funds are included in Table I-45.

Source: Data supplied by the Farmers Home Administration.

TABLE I-31

Farmers Home Administration Water Facilities and Soil and Water Conservation Direct Loans, 1939-1958

Year ended December 31	Outstanding	Loans made	Loans repaid or charged off	Net change in outstandings
	(thousands of dollars)			
1939	251	251	--	251
1940	650	528	129	399
1941	1,096	589	143	446
1942	2,023	1,176	249	927
1943	2,577	1,053	499	554
1944	2,880	925	622	303
1945	3,014	801	667	134
1946	3,489	1,269	794	475
1947	3,752	1,014	751	263
1948	4,442	1,601	911	690
1949	5,868	2,261	835	1,426
1950	7,923	3,169	1,114	2,055
1951	9,927	3,624	1,620	2,004
1952	13,733	5,629	1,823	3,806
1953	18,642	7,088	2,179	4,909
1954	21,729	5,812	2,725	3,087
1955	20,543	1,982	3,168	-1,186
1956	20,436	2,755	2,862	-107
1957	23,814	6,236	2,858	3,378
1958	23,252	2,827	3,389	-562

Note: Table I-31 is the total of Tables I-32 and I-33.

Source: Data supplied by the Farmers Home Administration. In 1939-54, the loans are all for water facilities.

Agricultural Loans

TABLE I-32

Farmers Home Administration Water Facilities and Soil and Water Conservation Direct Loans to Individuals, 1939-1958

Year ended December 31	Outstanding	Loans made	Loans repaid or charged off	Net change in outstandings
	(thousands of dollars)			
1939	251	251	--	251
1940	650	528	129	399
1941	1,096	589	143	446
1942	1,590	728	234	494
1943	1,932	824	482	342
1944	2,142	794	584	210
1945	2,230	695	607	88
1946	2,654	1,108	684	424
1947	2,858	913	709	204
1948	3,435	1,390	813	577
1949	4,446	1,773	762	1,011
1950	6,057	2,632	1,021	1,611
1951	7,435	2,873	1,495	1,378
1952	10,321	4,576	1,690	2,886
1953	14,038	5,664	1,947	3,717
1954	15,940	4,389	2,487	1,902
1955	13,768	615	2,787	-2,172
1956	13,267	2,025	2,526	- 501
1957	15,378	4,644	2,533	2,111
1958	14,206	1,825	2,997	-1,172

Note: Table I-31 is the total of Tables I-32 to I-33. In 1955-58, Table I-32 is the total of Tables I-34 and I-35.

Source: Data supplied by the Farmers Home Administration. In 1939-54, the loans are all for water facilities.

Agricultural Loans

TABLE I-33

Farmers Home Administration Water Facilities and Soil and Water Conservation Direct Loans to Associations, 1942-1958

Year ended December 31	Outstanding	Loans made	Loans repaid or charged off	Net change in outstandings
		(thousands of dollars)		
1942	433	448	15	433
1943	645	229	17	212
1944	738	131	38	93
1945	784	106	60	46
1946	835	161	110	51
1947	894	101	42	59
1948	1,007	211	98	113
1949	1,422	488	73	415
1950	1,866	537	93	444
1951	2,492	751	125	626
1952	3,412	1,053	133	920
1953	4,604	1,424	232	1,192
1954	5,789	1,423	238	1,185
1955	6,775	1,367	381	986
1956	7,169	730	336	394
1957	8,436	1,592	325	1,267
1958	9,046	1,002	392	610

Note: Table I-31 is the total of Tables I-32 and I-33. In 1955-58, Table I-33 is the total of Tables I-36 and I-37.

Source: Data supplied by the Farmers Home Administration. In 1942-54, the loans are all for water facilities.

TABLE I-34

Farmers Home Administration Water Facilities Direct Loans to Individuals, 1955-1958

Year ended December 31	Outstanding	Loans made	Loans repaid or charged off	Net change in outstandings
		(thousands of dollars)		
1955	13,233	20	2,727	- 2,707
1956	10,925	10	2,318	- 2,308
1957	9,031	4	1,898	- 1,894
1958	7,019	3	2,015	- 2,012

Note: In 1955-58, Table I-32 is the Total of Tables I-34 and I-35.

Source: Data supplied by the Farmers Home Administration.

Agricultural Loans

TABLE I-41

Farmers Home Administration Emergency Loans, 1949-1958[a]

Year ended December 31	Outstanding	Loans made	Loans repaid or charged off	Net change in outstandings
	(thousands of dollars)			
1949	7,143	7,311	168	7,143
1950	15,861	26,378	17,660	8,718
1951	15,184	19,774	20,451	-677
1952	24,853	37,114	27,445	9,669
1953	47,818	60,595	37,630	22,965
1954	68,333	88,289	67,774	20,515
1955	71,029	83,090	80,394	2,696
1956	80,922	88,271	78,378	9,893
1957	78,738	63,672	65,856	-2,184
1958	59,681	60,494	79,551	-19,057

[a]Includes production emergency, economic emergency, special emergency, and special livestock loans.

Source: Data supplied by the Farmers Home Administration.

Agricultural Loans

TABLE I-42

Farmers Home Administration Rural Rehabilitation Loans from Appropriated Funds, 1935-1958[a]

Year ended December 31	Outstanding	Loans made	Loans repaid or charged off	Net change in outstandings
		(thousands of dollars)		
1935	36,096	42,600	6,504	36,096
1936	76,328	53,537	13,305	40,232
1937	121,685	65,690	20,333	45,357
1938	173,173	80,694	29,206	51,488
1939	249,017	111,588	35,744	75,844
1940	296,418	95,157	47,756	47,401
1941	336,965	113,972	73,425	40,547
1942	366,886	113,119	83,198	29,921
1943	345,756	107,553	128,683	-21,130
1944	304,323	63,273	104,706	-41,433
1945	274,303	67,753	97,773	-30,020
1946	260,563	87,086	100,826	-13,740
1947	194,885	2,655	68,333	-65,678
1948	150,802	---	44,083	-44,083
1949	122,492	93	28,403	-28,310
1950	92,255	15	30,252	-30,237
1951	69,003	50	23,302	-23,252
1952	53,658	60	15,405	-15,345
1953	41,344	1	12,315	-12,314
1954	34,982	---	6,362	-6,362
1955	29,419	---	5,563	-5,563
1956	22,144	---	7,275	-7,275
1957	16,916	---	5,228	-5,228
1958	12,682	---	4,234	-4,234

[a]Rural rehabilitation loans from Corporation Trust Funds are included in Table I-45.

Note: Table I-42 is the total of Tables I-43 and I-44.

Source: Data supplied by the Farmers Home Administration.

Agricultural Loans

TABLE I-43

Farmers Home Administration Rural Rehabilitation Loans to Individuals from Appropriated Funds, 1935-1958[a]

Year ended December 31	Outstanding	Loans made	Loans repaid or charged off	Net change in outstandings
	(thousands of dollars)			
1935	35,200	41,700	6,500	35,200
1936	73,852	51,952	13,300	38,652
1937	118,017	64,490	20,325	44,165
1938	169,150	80,292	29,159	51,133
1939	242,296	108,785	35,639	73,146
1940	286,440	91,747	47,603	44,144
1941	316,851	103,561	73,150	30,411
1942	339,079	104,913	82,685	22,228
1943	318,135	105,534	126,478	-20,944
1944	280,512	63,168	100,791	-37,623
1945	258,525	67,739	89,726	-21,987
1946	249,733	87,086	95,878	-8,792
1947	186,005	2,655	66,383	-63,728
1948	143,234	---	42,771	-42,771
1949	115,587	93	27,740	-27,647
1950	86,026	13	29,574	-29,561
1951	63,561	33	22,498	-22,465
1952	49,229	60	14,392	-14,332
1953	37,454	---	11,775	-11,775
1954	31,147	---	6,307	-6,307
1955	25,615	---	5,532	-5,532
1956	20,565	---	5,050	-5,050
1957	15,411	---	5,154	-5,154
1958	11,800	---	3,611	-3,611

[a]Rural rehabilitation loans from Corporation Trust Funds are included in Table I-45.

Note: Table I-42 is the total of Tables I-43 and I-44.

Source: Data supplied by the Farmers Home Administration.

Agricultrual Loans

TABLE I-44

Farmers Home Administration Rural Rehabilitation Loans to Associations from Appropriated Funds, 1935-1958[a]

Year ended December 31	Outstanding	Loans made	Loans repaid or charged off	Net change in outstandings
		(thousands of dollars)		
1935	896	900	4	896
1936	2,476	1,585	5	1,580
1937	3,668	1,200	8	1,192
1938	4,023	402	47	355
1939	6,721	2,803	105	2,698
1940	9,978	3,410	153	3,257
1941	20,114	10,411	275	10,136
1942	27,807	8,206	513	7,693
1943	27,621	2,019	2,205	- 186
1944	23,811	105	3,915	- 3,810
1945	15,778	14	8,047	- 8,033
1946	10,830	--	4,948	- 4,948
1947	8,880	--	1,950	- 1,950
1948	7,568	--	1,312	- 1,312
1949	6,905	--	663	- 663
1950	6,229	2	678	- 676
1951	5,442	17	804	- 787
1952	4,429	--	1,013	- 1,013
1953	3,890	1	540	- 539
1954	3,835	--	55	- 55
1955	3,804	--	31	- 31
1956	1,579	--	2,225	- 2,225
1957	1,505	--	74	- 74
1958	882	--	623	- 623

[a]Rural rehabilitation loans from Corporation Trust Funds are included in Table I-45.

Note: Table I-42 is the total of Tables I-43 and I-44.

Source: Data supplied by the Farmers Home Administration.

9. Table I-45 — direct operating and rural rehabilitation loans from Corporation Trust Funds. This type of loan was described previously along with direct operating loans. Their division as between loans to individuals and loans to associations is shown in Tables I-46 and I-47.

10. Table I-48 — emergency crop and feed loans. These loans were made primarily for the purpose of aiding farmers who were in trouble because of drought, flood, or economic disaster. Thus they were the 1929-46 counterpart to the 1949-58 emergency loans shown in Table I-41. Also, some of these loans were similar to the direct operating loans shown in Table I-30. This particular category of loans ceased in 1946.

11. Table I-49 — miscellaneous loans. This is the catch-all category of what remains of the large basket of different lending activity of the FHA. It includes Wartime Civil Control Administration loans; flood and wind-storm restoration, flood damage, and fur and orchard loans; seed loans; water conservation and utilization project loans; credit sales of real property; and Puerto Rican hurricane relief loans.

Rural Electrification Administration (Tables I-51 to I-55)

The Rural Electrification Administration operates a rural development program by credit extensions to cooperatives engaged in supplying electric and telephone service to rural areas. Since 1935 the REA has been making loans with maturities of up to 35 years, chiefly to cooperatives, to provide electric service to farmers and other rural people; these loans are mainly for generation, transmission, and distribution. Since 1950 similar loans have been made to finance the construction and improvement of rural telephone systems. Originally, the REA was part of a general program for relief of unemployment. The flow of funds to REA cooperatives under this program originally was from the RFC, and since 1947 has been directly from the U.S. Treasury in amounts determined by Congress. The REA originally was established as an independent agency. Under the 1939 Reorganization Act, it was placed in the U.S. Department of Agriculture, where it has remained to date.

The amount of a construction loan, the most important type, may be up to 100 percent of the total costs. Applications are approved after legal, engineering, economic, and financial studies. Funds are obligated by a loan contract and the borrower gives a note, mortgage, or other security. Funds are advanced as needed for carrying out the construction.

Agricultural Loans

TABLE I-45

Farmers Home Administration Operating and Rural Rehabilitation Loans from Corporation Trust Funds, 1938-1958

Year ended December 31	Outstanding	Loans made	Loans repaid or charged off	Net change in outstandings
	(thousands of dollars)			
1938	29	29	--	29
1939	44	18	3	15
1940	60	20	4	16
1941	56	6	10	- 4
1942	25,935[a]	55,111	29,232	25,879
1943	24,346	18,909	20,498	- 1,589
1944	22,443	466	2,369	- 1,903
1945	20,931	5,356	6,868	- 1,512
1946	27,481	16,059	9,509	6,550
1947	28,304	13,314	12,491	823
1948	22,775	4,970	10,499	- 5,529
1949	30,281	18,847	11,341	7,506
1950	26,211	9,740	13,810	- 4,070
1951	19,487	5,222	11,946	- 6,724
1952	23,881	13,832	9,438	4,394
1953	25,142	10,139	8,878	1,261
1954	24,260	7,188	8,070	- 882
1955	25,500	10,587	9,347	1,240
1956	23,244	9,171	11,427	- 2,256
1957	18,466	3,474	8,252	- 4,778
1958	12,352	1,786	7,900	- 6,114

[a]Includes some loans made to individuals in 1936-41 and not previously included in the data because a break-down by years is not available.

Note: Table I-45 is the total of Tables I-46 and I-47.

Source: Data supplied by the Farmers Home Administration.

Agricultural Loans

TABLE I-46

Farmers Home Administration Operating and Rural Rehabilitation Loans to Individuals from Corporation Trust Funds, 1942-1958

Year ended December 31	Outstanding	Loans made	Loans repaid or charged off	Net change in outstandings
		(thousands of dollars)		
1942	25,685[a]	54,811	29,126	25,685
1943	23,699	18,482	20,468	-1,986
1944	21,841	458	2,316	-1,858
1945	20,245	5,260	6,856	-1,596
1946	26,946	16,059	9,358	6,701
1947	27,868	13,314	12,392	922
1948	22,502	4,970	10,336	-5,366
1949	30,034	18,847	11,315	7,532
1950	25,970	9,740	13,804	-4,064
1951	19,260	5,222	11,932	-6,710
1952	23,663	13,832	9,429	4,403
1953	25,056	10,139	8,746	1,393
1954	24,180	7,188	8,064	-876
1955	25,422	10,587	9,345	1,242
1956	23,174	9,171	11,419	-2,248
1957	18,397	3,474	8,251	-4,777
1958	12,284	1,786	7,899	-6,113

[a]Includes some loans made in 1936-41 and not previously included in the data because a breakdown by years is not available.

Note: Table I-45 is the total of Tables I-46 and I-47.

Source: Data supplied by the Farmers Home Administration.

Agricultural Loans

TABLE I-47

Farmers Home Administration Operating and Rural Rehabilitation Loan to Associations from Corporation Trust Funds, 1938-1958

Year ended December 31	Outstanding	Loans made	Loans repaid or charged off	Net change in outstandings
		(thousands of dollars)		
1938	29	29	--	29
1939	44	18	3	15
1940	60	20	4	16
1941	56	6	10	-4
1942	250	300	106	194
1943	647	427	30	397
1944	602	8	53	-45
1945	686	96	12	84
1946	535	--	151	-151
1947	436	--	99	-99
1948	273	--	163	-163
1949	247	--	26	-26
1950	241	--	6	-6
1951	227	--	14	-14
1952	218	--	9	-9
1953	86	--	132	-132
1954	80	--	6	-6
1955	78	--	2	-2
1956	70	--	8	-8
1957	69	--	1	-1
1958	68	--	1	-1

Note: Table I-45 is the total of Tables I-46 and I-47.

Source: Data supplied by the Farmers Home Administration.

Agricultural Loans

TABLE I-48

Farmers Home Administration Emergency Crop and Feed Loans, 1929-1958

Year ended December 31	Outstanding	Loans made	Loans repaid or charged off	Net change in Outstanding
	(thousands of dollars)			
1929	7,976	5,760	-2,216	7,976
1930	8,946	5,340	4,370	970
1931	49,769	55,788	14,965	40,823
1932	90,353	64,205	23,621	40,584
1933	90,863	57,376	56,866	510
1934	111,238	70,471	50,096	20,375
1935	172,470	96,382	35,150	61,232
1936	164,762	16,135	23,843	-7,708
1937	172,701	31,815	23,876	7,939
1938	171,489	19,648	20,860	-1,212
1939	168,330	15,079	18,238	-3,159
1940	168,438	19,517	19,409	108
1941	164,974	18,346	21,810	-3,464
1942	156,676	19,687	27,985	-8,298
1943	147,650	18,697	27,723	-9,026
1944	139,541	18,439	26,548	-8,109
1945	130,505	16,465	25,501	-9,036
1946	118,120	16,972	29,357	-12,385
1947	106,189	--	11,931	-11,931
1948	90,240	--	15,949	-15,949
1949	71,341	--	18,899	-18,899
1950	53,347	--	17,994	-17,994
1951	38,212	--	15,135	-15,135
1952	27,955	--	10,257	-10,257
1953	19,976	--	7,979	-7,979
1954	16,359	--	3,617	-3,617
1955	13,527	--	2,832	-2,832
1956	11,105	--	2,422	-2,422
1957	8,331	--	2,774	-2,774
1958	5,874	--	2,457	-2,457

Source: Data supplied by the Farmers Home Administration.

Agricultural Loans

TABLE I-49

Farmers Home Administration
Miscellaneous Loans,
1942-1958[a]

Year ended December 31	Outstanding	Loans made	Loans repaid or charged off	Net change in outstandings
	(thousands of dollars)			
1942	2,748	3,590	842	2,748
1943	1,646	706	1,808	- 1,102
1944	2,149	1,373	870	503
1945	1,828	267	588	- 321
1946	3,683	8,972[b]	7,117	1,855
1947	3,207	1,408	1,884	- 476
1948	3,682	3,235	2,760	475
1949	6,365	3,970	1,287	2,683
1950	7,261	4,125	3,229	896
1951	5,924	1,725	3,062	- 1,337
1952	5,236	1,727	2,415	- 688
1953	4,493	1,332	2,075	- 743
1954	6,130	3,509	1,872	1,637
1955	5,828	1,027	1,329	- 302
1956	5,619	1,076	1,285	- 209
1957	5,385	921	1,155	- 234
1958	4,869	911	1,427	- 516

[a]Includes the following loan program:
Wartime Civil Control Administration Loans, 1942-58; Flood and Windstorm Restoration, Flood Damage, Fur and Orchard Loans, 1943-58; Credit Sales of Real Property, 1946-58; Agriculture Credit Corporation Loans, 1948-58 (Saulnier, et al., included these loans under the heading "Farmers Seed Loan Office" in a table on p. 403); Water Conservation and Utilization Project Loans, 1954-58; Puerto Rican Hurricane Relief Loans, 1956-58.

[b]This figure is unusually high because it is cumulative through December 31, 1946 for credit sales of real property.

Source: Data supplied by the Farmers Home Administration.

Agricultural Loans

TABLE I-50

Total Loans of Farmers Home Administration, 1929-1958

Year ended December 31	Outstanding	Loans made	Loans repaid or charged off	Net change in outstandings
	(thousands of dollars)			
1929	7,976	5,760	-2,216	7,976
1930	8,946	5,340	4,370	970
1931	49,769	55,788	14,965	40,823
1932	90,353	64,205	23,621	40,584
1933	90,863	57,376	56,866	510
1934	111,238	70,471	50,096	20,375
1935	208,566	138,982	41,654	97,328
1936	241,090	69,672	37,148	32,524
1937	294,386	97,505	44,209	53,296
1938	354,966	110,646	50,066	60,580
1939	449,943	149,223	54,246	94,977
1940	531,852	151,628	69,719	81,909
1941	619,701	184,471	96,622	87,849
1942	714,526	240,814	145,989	94,825
1943	696,921	175,916	193,521	-17,605
1944	665,146	123,973	155,748	-31,775
1945	615,641	104,898	154,403	-49,505
1946	610,952	173,655	178,344	-4,689
1947	586,567	133,191	157,576	-24,385
1948	553,466	112,977	146,078	-33,101
1949	568,312	139,357	124,511	14,846
1950	594,771	192,589	166,130	26,459
1951	604,406	200,236	190,601	9,635
1952	674,311	242,190	172,285	69,905
1953	733,815	240,664	181,160	59,504
1954	792,684	277,087	218,218	58,869
1955	821,342	280,301	251,643	28,658
1956	892,754	341,102	269,690	71,412
1957	967,935	346,801	271,620	75,181
1958	1,007,269	358,386	319,052	39,334

Note: Table I-50 is the total of Tables I-25, I-28, I-29, I-30, I-31, I-38, I-41, I-42, I-45, I-48, and I-49.

Source: Data supplied by the Farmers Home Administration.

Agricultural Loans

TABLE I-51

Rural Electrification Administration Loans for Distribution, Generation, and Transmission, 1935-1959

Year ended December 31	Outstanding	Loans made: Distribution	Loans made: Generation and transmission	Loans repaid or charged off	Net change in outstandings
		(thousands of dollars)			
1935	10	9	1	--	10
1936	3,329	3,108	211	--	3,319
1937	34,219	28,922	1,968	--	30,890
1938	87,881	50,234	3,428	--	53,662
1939	182,728	88,769	6,078	--	94,847
1940	248,529	63,740	4,395	2,334	65,801
1941	321,840	72,450	4,996	4,135	73,311
1942	344,759	29,728	2,050	8,859	22,919
1943	346,218	13,047	900	12,488	1,459
1944	360,337	23,624	3,933	13,438	14,119
1945	406,677	54,971	1,456	10,087	46,340
1946	526,802	122,526	9,369	11,770	120,125
1947	733,049	208,880	16,212	18,845	206,247
1948	998,020	261,287	23,153	19,469	264,971
1949	1,300,068	281,026	45,964	24,942	302,048
1950	1,540,905	219,464	52,018	30,645	240,837
1951	1,737,484	181,915	55,448	40,784	196,579
1952	1,899,662	156,205	54,810	48,837	162,178
1953	2,048,211	145,836	53,413	50,700	148,549
1954	2,143,229	129,413	31,975	66,370	95,018
1955	2,219,070	122,733	26,643	73,535	75,841
1956	2,297,410	126,001	31,595	79,256	78,340
1957	2,420,372	134,687	73,823	85,548	122,962
1958	2,522,780	132,100	67,975	97,667	102,408
1959	2,639,535	138,290	73,715	95,250	116,755

Note: Table I-53 is the total of Tables I-51 and I-52.

Source: Data supplied by Rural Electrification Administration. In 1935-43, the estimated distribution of loans made was obtained by applying to total electric loans in the given year and the ratio of 1935-43 loans of the given category to total 1935-43 electric loans. The percentages were 92.062 percent for distribution loans, 6.348 percent for generation and transmission loans, and 1.590 percent for consumer facilities loans. Further adjustment was necessary so that "loans repaid or charged off" would not be a negative figure by adding to distribution loans the amounts of $43,000 in 1936, $384,000 in 1937, $515,000 in 1938, and $616,000 in 1939. Outstandings in 1935-42 were estimated by applying to total outstandings the ratio of distribution, generation, and transmission outstandings to total outstandings in 1943 (99.719 percent).

Agricultural Loans

TABLE I-52

Rural Electrification Administration Loans for Consumer Facilities, 1936-1959

Year ended December 31	Outstanding	Loans made	Loans repaid or charged off	Net change in outstandings
	(thousands of dollars)			
1936	9	10	1	9
1937	96	109	22	87
1938	248	344	192	152
1939	515	907	640	267
1940	700	1,101	916	185
1941	907	1,251	1,044	207
1942	972	513	448	65
1943	975	225	222	3
1944	703	317	589	-272
1945	1,053	544	194	350
1946	1,199	294	148	146
1947	1,399	321	121	200
1948	1,529	286	156	130
1949	1,666	342	205	137
1950	2,798	1,725	593	1,132
1951	2,907	1,289	1,180	109
1952	3,556	2,071	1,422	649
1953	4,260	2,770	2,066	704
1954	4,601	2,752	2,411	341
1955	5,767	3,917	2,751	1,166
1956	6,172	3,814	3,409	405
1957	6,855	4,235	3,552	683
1958	6,545	3,147	3,457	-310
1959	6,832	2,868	2,581	287

Note: Table I-53 is the total of Tables I-51 and I-52.

Source: Data supplied by Rural Electrification Administration. In 1936-43, estimated outstandings and loans in Table I-34 subtracted from total electric loans as reported by REA to obtain estimated outstandings and loans for consumer facilities.

Agricultural Loans

TABLE I-53

Rural Electrification Administration Total Electric Loans, 1935-1959

Year ended December 31	Outstanding	Loans made	Loans repaid or charged off	Net change in outstandings
		(thousands of dollars)		
1935	10	10	--	10
1936	3,338	3,329	1	3,328
1937	34,315	30,999	22	30,977
1938	88,129	54,006	192	53,814
1939	183,243	95,754	640	95,114
1940	249,229	69,236	3,250	65,986
1941	322,747	78,697	5,179	73,518
1942	345,731	32,291	9,307	22,984
1943	347,193	14,172	12,710	1,462
1944	361,040	27,874	14,027	13,847
1945	407,730	56,971	10,281	46,690
1946	528,001	132,189	11,918	120,271
1947	734,448	225,413	18,966	206,447
1948	999,549	284,726	19,625	265,101
1949	1,301,734	327,332	25,147	302,185
1950	1,543,703	273,207	31,238	241,969
1951	1,740,391	238,652	41,964	196,688
1952	1,903,218	213,086	50,259	162,827
1953	2,052,471	202,019	52,766	149,253
1954	2,147,830	164,140	68,781	95,359
1955	2,224,837	153,293	76,286	77,007
1956	2,303,582	161,410	82,665	78,745
1957	2,427,227	212,745	89,100	123,645
1958	2,529,325	203,222	101,124	102,098
1959	2,646,367	214,873	97,831	117,042

Note: Table I-53 is the total of Tables I-51 and I-52.
Table I-55 is the total of Tables I-53 and I-54.

Source: Obtained by adding Tables I-51 and I-52.

Agricultural Loans

TABLE I-54

Rural Electrification Administration Loans
for Telephones, 1950-1959

Year ended December 31	Outstanding	Loans made	Loans repaid or charged off	Net change in outstandings
	(thousands of dollars)			
1950	45	45	--	45
1951	2,602	2,572	15	2,557
1952	17,733	15,134	3	15,131
1953	43,603	26,001	131	25,870
1954	77,949	35,402	1,056	34,346
1955	123,145	46,026	830	45,196
1956	184,633	62,988	1,500	61,488
1957	260,358	78,367	2,642	75,725
1958	345,098	88,886	4,146	84,740
1959	436,382	97,737	6,453	91,284

Note: Table I-55 is the total of Tables I-53 and I-54.

Source: Data supplied by Rural Electrification Administration.

Agricultural Loans

TABLE I-55

Total Loans of the Rural Electrification Administration, 1935-1959

Year ended December 31	Outstanding	Loans made	Loans repaid or charged off [a]	Net change in outstandings
	(thousands of dollars)			
1935	10	10	--	10
1936	3,338	3,329	1	3,328
1937	34,315	30,999	22	30,977
1938	88,129	54,006	192	53,814
1939	183,243	95,754	640	95,114
1940	249,229	69,236	3,250	65,986
1941	322,747	78,697	5,179	73,518
1942	345,731	32,291	9,307	22,984
1943	347,193	14,172	12,710	1,462
1944	361,040	27,874	14,027	13,847
1945	407,730	56,971	10,281	46,690
1946	528,001	132,189	11,918	120,271
1947	734,448	225,413	18,966	206,447
1948	999,549	284,726	19,625	265,101
1949	1,301,734	327,332	25,147	302,185
1950	1,543,748	273,252	31,238	242,014
1951	1,742,993	241,224	41,979	199,245
1952	1,920,951	228,220	50,262	177,958
1953	2,096,074	228,020	52,897	175,123
1954	2,225,779	199,542	69,837	129,705
1955	2,347,982	199,319	77,116	122,203
1956	2,488,215	224,398	84,165	140,233
1957	2,687,585	291,112	91,742	199,370
1958	2,874,423	292,108	105,270	186,838
1959	3,082,749	312,610	104,284	208,326

[a]Only $44,000 has been charged off to date in the history of the agency.

Note: Table I-55 is the total of Tables I-53 and I-54.

Source: Obtained by adding Tables I-53 and I-54.

The most rapid development of the REA program has occurred since 1945. At the end of 1945 only $0.4 billion in loans was outstanding, whereas at the end of 1955 the total was over $2.3 billion, and at the end of 1959 had risen to $3.1 billion (Table I-55). As a result of this expansion, REA borrowers in recent years have served about one-half of the farms in the United States. At present, about 96 percent of U.S. farms are electrified, compared with 11 percent when the program began in 1935.

The magnitude of the REA program has been relatively large compared with the other farm credit programs. Total outstandings at the beginning of 1960 were about 50 percent more than those of the Federal Land Banks, three times those of the Production Credit Associations, and about equal to the maximum amount the Commodity Credit Corporation has had outstanding at any one time.

Electrification loans made were of the largest annual amount in 1949, $327 million (Table I-53). They decreased by more than one-half to only $153 million in 1955, and were two-thirds of the 1949 volume in 1959, $215 million. Outstandings at the end of 1959 were $2.6 billion.

The electrification loans for generation, transmission, and distribution are shown in Table I-51. These are the bulk of the electrification loans. Data on the other and much smaller part, loans for consumer facilities, appear in Table I-52. The consumer facilities loans are for the wiring of farmsteads, and the purchase and installation of electrical appliances and plumbing. The loans generally are required to be repaid in five years. No loans are made direct to consumers. The funds are loaned to REA borrowers operating electric systems for relending to their members.

The outstandings on loans to independent telephone companies and cooperatives for extending or improving rural service were $436 million at the end of 1959 (Table I-54). This was a sharp increase from the similar total five years earlier of $78 million, and from nothing ten years earlier.

Commodity Credit Corporation (Tables I-56 to I-62)

The Commodity Credit Corporation guarantees loans made by private lending agencies and makes direct loans to farmers and cooperative marketing associations for the purpose of supporting prices of agricultural commodities. It also uses price-support techniques not involving the use of credit, such as direct purchase of commodities and purchase agreements. The CCC also makes loans for the construction or repair of farm storage facilities. From October 17, 1933 through June 30, 1939, the CCC was an independent agency managed and operated in close affiliation with the RFC. Since July 1, 1939, it has been in the U.S. Department of Agriculture.

Commodity price support loans at 100 percent of the price support level are nonrecourse loans. They are secured by pledged agricultural commodities, and the borrowers may discharge their obligations without further liability by turning over these commodities to the CCC. In such event, there is no interest on direct loans, and the CCC pays the private lender the interest on guaranteed loans. The borrower pays the interest only when the loan is paid in cash.

Direct loans obtained from county committees of the Commodity Stabilization Service represent a direct extension of credit by the CCC. The committees are acting as agents of the CCC, and the CCC borrows from the U.S. Treasury to obtain the necessary funds. If the farmer gets his loan from a local bank, he gets his money from the bank and would, therefore, appear to owe the bank money. However, the local bank retains a "certificate of interest" equal to the amount loaned. This certificate is a highly liquid interest-bearing security. The banker can either retain it to maturity, present it for payment to the designated Federal Reserve Bank any time prior to maturity, or transfer it to another bank, the other bank having the same three alternatives as did the bank making the actual loan to the farmer.

Total loans of the CCC were at their highest annual volume in 1958, $3.6 billion (Table I-62). This was only slightly larger than the 1949 volume of $3.4 billion. Prior to 1948, the annual volume never reached $1.0 billion, and since 1948, have been in excess of $1.0 billion in all years except 1951.

The two parts of the CCC lending activities, commodity loans and storage facilities loans, are shown in Tables I-58 and I-61. The program of loans for storage facilities has been relatively small.

The division of commodity loans into their direct and guaranteed parts is shown in Tables I-56 and I-57. Direct loans were larger than guaranteed loans in each year from 1933 through 1940. Since then, guaranteed loans were larger in each year. In 1957-59, guaranteed loans were 4.4 times as great as direct loans, compared with 1.9 times as great 10 years earlier, in 1947-49, indicating a continuing trend toward more guaranteed loans. Year-end outstandings of guaranteed loans have fluctuated widely, depending in large part on the relative yields on certificates of interest and comparable paper.

The division of storage facilities loans into their direct and guaranteed parts is shown in Tables I-59 and I-60. These are recourse loans, and their guaranteed volume never has been large relative to their direct volume.

Agricultural Loans

TABLE I-56

Commodity Credit Corporation Direct Commodity Loans, 1933-1959

Year ended December 31	Outstanding	Loans made[a]	Loans repaid or charged off[b]	Net change in outstandings
	(thousands of dollars)			
1933	102,694	113,549	10,855	102,694
1934	178,561	197,436	121,569	75,867
1935	197,719	218,617	199,459	19,158
1936	183,593	202,998	217,124	-14,126
1937	182,309	201,579	202,863	-1,284
1938	300,900	332,704	214,113	118,591
1939	264,878	292,875	328,897	-36,022
1940	206,707	228,556	286,727	-58,171
1941	205,422	227,135	228,420	-1,285
1942	107,884	119,287	216,825	-97,538
1943	47,909	52,973	112,948	-59,975
1944	46,701	52,638	53,846	-1,208
1945	39,975	45,200	51,926	-6,726
1946	57,961	64,087	46,101	17,986
1947	104,946	116,038	69,053	46,985
1948	436,199	487,064	155,811	331,253
1949	957,084	1,058,248	537,363	520,885
1950	595,286	198,045	559,843	-361,798
1951	511,933	245,088	328,441	-83,353
1952	773,283	286,767	25,417	261,350
1953	793,461	1,109,571	1,089,393	20,178
1954	601,773	304,430	496,118	-191,688
1955	1,542,764	463,637	-477,354	940,991
1956	1,835,681	739,100	446,183	292,917
1957	1,445,806	252,153	642,028	-389,875
1958	2,466,301	511,788	-508,707	1,020,495
1959	1,549,798	492,082	1,408,585	-916,503

[a]In 1934-47, figures for fiscal years were estimates based on the ratio of loans made to outstandings in 1948, when loans made were 110.5 percent of outstandings. This ratio also was applied to calendar year outstandings for 1949 to obtain estimate of 1949 loans made.

[b]This column is derived as a balancing item and thus reflects loans purchased by CCC from private lending agencies. These purchases are not included in loans made because the information is unavailable.

Note: Table I-58 is the total of Tables I-56 and I-57.

Source: Data supplied by the Commodity Stabilization Service. For 1933-48, data for calendar years are interpolations of fiscal year data.

Agricultural Loans

TABLE I-57

Commodity Credit Corporation Guaranteed Commodity Loans, 1933-1959

Year ended December 31	Outstanding a/	Loans made b/	Loans repaid or charged off c/	Net change in outstandings
	(thousands of dollars)			
1933	97,262	111,875	14,613	97,262
1934	194,525	183,488	86,225	97,263
1935	215,394	121,708	100,839	20,869
1936	200,006	50,094	65,482	-15,388
1937	198,607	64,085	65,484	-1,399
1938	327,807	129,200	---	129,200
1939	310,389	125,833	143,251	-17,418
1940	171,446	151,994	290,937	-138,943
1941	142,311	304,015	333,150	-29,135
1942	299,720	605,663	448,254	157,409
1943	409,688	632,377	522,409	109,968
1944	325,663	477,012	561,037	-84,025
1945	137,970	308,800	496,493	-187,693
1946	26,395	198,043	309,618	-111,575
1947	27,892	200,887	199,390	+1,497
1948	270,798	741,888	498,982	242,906
1949	764,054	2,287,960	1,794,704	493,256
1950	284,711	1,187,967	1,667,310	-479,343
1951	244,751	683,735	723,695	-39,960
1952	625,490	1,091,763	711,024	380,739
1953	2,253,171	2,077,387	449,706	1,627,681
1954	2,338,489	2,323,014	2,237,696	85,318
1955	1,041,365	2,334,266	3,631,390	-1,297,124
1956	786,514	2,456,400	2,711,251	-254,851
1957	307,070	1,008,613	1,488,057	-479,444
1958	801,379	3,083,992	2,589,683	494,309
1959	151,697	1,391,208	2,040,890	-649,682

[a] For 1934-38 fiscal years, outstandings are based on the ratio of guaranteed to direct loan outstandings in 1939, which was 108.94 percent.

[b] In 1934-46, figures for fiscal years were estimates based on subtracting estimated direct loans made, as given in Table I-56, from total loans made, as given in Table I-58, except that occasional additions to the resulting figure were required to reconcile with increases in outstandings. Additions were necessary in 1934, 1936, 1938, and 1939. In calendar 1949, loans made were estimated by applying fiscal 1947-49 ratio of loans made to outstandings, which was 299.45 percent.

[c] Includes loans sold to the CCC.

Note: Table I-58 is the total of Tables I-56 and I-57.

Source: Data supplied by the Commodity Stabilization Service. For 1933-48, data for calendar years are interpolations of fiscal year data.

Agricultural Loans

TABLE I-58

Total Commodity Loans of Commodity Credit Corporation, 1933-1959

Year ended December 31	Outstanding	Loans made	Loans repaid or charged off	Net change in outstandings
		(thousands of dollars)		
1933	199,956	225,424	25,468	+199,956
1934	373,086	380,924	207,794	+173,130
1935	413,113	340,325	300,298	+40,027
1936	383,599	253,092	282,606	-29,514
1937	380,916	265,664	268,347	-2,683
1938	628,707	461,904	214,113	+247,791
1939	575,267	418,708	472,148	-53,440
1940	378,153	380,550	577,664	-197,114
1941	347,733	227,135	257,555	-30,420
1942	407,604	724,950	665,079	+59,871
1943	457,597	685,350	635,357	+49,993
1944	372,364	529,650	614,883	-85,233
1945	177,945	354,000	548,419	-194,419
1946	84,356	262,130	355,719	-93,589
1947	132,838	316,925	268,443	+48,482
1948	706,997	1,228,952	654,793	+574,159
1949	1,721,138	3,346,208	2,332,067	+1,014,141
1950	879,997	1,386,012	2,227,153	-841,141
1951	756,684	928,823	1,052,136	-123,313
1952	1,398,773	1,378,530	736,441	+642,089
1953	3,046,632	3,186,958	1,539,099	+1,647,859
1954	2,940,262	2,627,444	2,733,814	-106,370
1955	2,584,129	2,797,903	3,154,036	-356,133
1956	2,622,195	3,195,500	3,157,434	+38,066
1957	1,752,876	1,260,766	2,130,085	-869,319
1958	3,267,680	3,595,780	2,080,976	+1,514,804
1959	1,701,495	1,883,290	3,449,475	-1,566,185

Note: Table I-58 is the total of Tables I-56 and I-57.
Table I-62 is the total of Tables I-58 and I-61.

Source: Data supplied by the Commodity Stabilization Service. Computed by adding Tables I-56 and I-57.

Agricultural Loans

TABLE I-59

Commodity Credit Corporation Direct Storage Facility Loans, 1949-1959

Year ended December 31	Outstanding	Loans made	Loans repaid or charged off a/	Net change in outstandings
	(thousands of dollars)			
1949	4,691	4,691	---	4,691
1950	11,954	6,720	-543	7,263
1951	19,400	9,189	1,743	7,446
1952	21,872	7,231	4,759	2,472
1953	24,226	8,406	6,052	2,354
1954	33,530	17,812	8,508	9,304
1955	30,316	7,839	11,053	-3,214
1956	24,703	5,544	11,157	-5,613
1957	21,751	7,122	10,074	-2,952
1958	29,455	16,734	9,030	7,704
1959	42,995	23,910	10,370	13,540

[a]This column is derived as a balancing item, and thus reflects loans purchased by the CCC from private lending agencies. These purchases are not included in loans made because the information is unavailable.

Note: Table I-61 is the total of Tables I-59 and I-60.

Source: Data supplied by the Commodity Stabilization Service.

TABLE I-60

Commodity Credit Corporation Guaranteed Storage Facilities Loans, 1949-1959

Year ended December 31	Outstanding	Loans made	Loans repaid or charged off	Net change in outstandings
	(thousands of dollars)			
1949	2,701	2,701	---	2,701
1950	5,866	4,650	1,485	3,165
1951	6,263	2,928	2,531	397
1952	5,783	1,810	2,290	-480
1953	5,014	1,400	2,169	-769
1954	7,113	3,250	1,151	2,099
1955	6,360	2,210	2,963	-753
1956	4,757	1,640	3,243	-1,603
1957	3,474	1,200	2,483	-1,283
1958	1,247	910	3,137	-2,227
1959	507	---	740	-740

Note: Table I-61 is the total of Tables I-59 and I-60.

Source: Data supplied by the Commodity Stabilization Service.

Agricultural Loans

TABLE I-61

Total Storage Facilities Loans of Commodity Credit Corporation, 1949-1959

Year ended December 31	Outstanding	Loans made	Loans repaid or charged off	Net change in outstandings
	(thousands of dollars)			
1949	7,392	7,392	---	7,392
1950	17,820	11,370	942	10,428
1951	25,663	12,117	4,274	7,843
1952	27,655	9,041	7,049	1,992
1953	29,240	9,806	8,221	1,585
1954	40,643	21,062	9,659	11,403
1955	36,676	10,049	14,016	-3,967
1956	29,460	7,184	14,400	-7,216
1957	25,225	8,322	12,557	-4,235
1958	30,702	17,644	12,167	5,477
1959	43,502	23,910	11,110	12,800

Note: Table I-61 is the total of Tables I-59 and I-60.
Table I-62 is the total of Tables I-58 and I-61.

Source: Data supplied by the Commodity Stabilization Service.

Agricultural Loans

TABLE I-62

Total Loans of the Commodity Credit Corporation, 1933-1959

Year ended December 31	Outstanding	Loans made	Loans repaid or charged off	Net change in outstandings
	(thousands of dollars)			
1933	199,956	225,424	25,468	+199,956
1934	373,086	380,924	207,794	+173,130
1935	413,113	340,325	300,298	+40,027
1936	383,599	253,092	282,606	-29,514
1937	380,916	265,664	268,347	-2,683
1938	628,707	461,904	214,113	+247,791
1939	575,267	418,708	472,148	-53,440
1940	378,153	380,550	577,664	-197,114
1941	347,733	227,135	257,555	-30,420
1942	407,604	724,950	665,079	+59,871
1943	457,597	685,350	635,357	+49,993
1944	372,364	529,650	614,883	-85,233
1945	177,945	354,000	548,419	-194,419
1946	84,356	262,130	355,719	-93,589
1947	132,838	316,925	268,443	+48,482
1948	706,997	1,228,952	654,793	+574,159
1949	1,728,530	3,353,600	2,332,067	+1,021,533
1950	897,817	1,397,382	2,228,095	-830,713
1951	782,347	940,940	1,056,410	-115,470
1952	1,426,428	1,387,571	743,490	+644,081
1953	3,075,872	3,196,764	1,547,320	+1,649,444
1954	2,980,905	2,648,506	2,743,473	-94,967
1955	2,620,805	2,807,952	3,168,052	-360,100
1956	2,651,655	3,202,684	3,171,834	+30,850
1957	1,778,101	1,269,088	2,142,642	-873,554
1958	3,298,382	3,613,424	2,093,143	+1,520,281
1959	1,744,997	1,907,200	3,460,585	-1,553,385

Note: Table I-62 is the total of Tables I-58 and I-61.

Source: Data supplied by the Commodity Stabilization Service. Computed by adding Tables I-58 and I-61.

Veterans' Administration (Tables I-63 to I-65)

The Administrator of Veterans' Affairs guarantees or insures loans to small-scale, low-income farmer-veterans for the purchase, construction, or improvement of farm properties. The first loans were made in 1945. There were 19,862 farm loans closed in 1947, but the number had dwindled to only 254 in the entire country in 1958. The farm, business, and housing loans are administered by the Veterans' Administration, an independent agency, as one of a large number of programs.

The authority to guarantee or insure such loans for veterans of World War II is scheduled to expire on July 25, 1962. The original expiration date was 1957, but this was first extended to 1958, then to 1960, and then to 1962. For veterans of the Korean conflict, the expiration date for such loans is January 31, 1965.

The bulk of the loans are guaranteed by the VA rather than insured. Funds are obtained from private lenders.

The annual volume of loans under the program was greatest in 1947, $78 million (Table I-65). In 1959, they were only $1 million.

The division of total VA farm loans into their guaranteed or insured, and nonguaranteed and non-insured, parts is given in Tables I-63 and I-64. At the end of 1949, the guaranteed or insured part of outstandings was 40 percent of the total, and at the end of 1959, 45 percent.

War Finance Corporation (Table I-66)

In 1921-22, the War Finance Corporation made significant volumes of agricultural loans to financial institutions and cooperatives for the marketing of farm products and livestock. The volume was $83 million in 1921 and $149 million in 1922. No new loans for any purpose were made after 1928, and the agency was placed in liquidation in 1929. Loan funds were obtained from the U.S. Treasury. In the 1929-58 period covered by this study, this series is important only for repayments and dwindling outstandings.

Tennessee Valley Authority (Table I-67)

A rural development program of minor importance was that conducted by the TVA itself in making loans to municipalities and cooperative wholesale power distribution companies in the TVA area, for the purpose of acquiring and operating power plants and distribution facilities. Loans made during the entire 1934-43 period totaled only $5.3 million.

Agricultural Loans

TABLE I-63

Veterans' Administration Guaranteed and Insured Farm Loans, Part Guaranteed or Insured, 1945-1959

Year ended December 31	Outstanding	Loans made	Loans repaid or charged off	Net change in outstandings
	(thousands of dollars)			
1945	400	500	100	+ 400
1946	29,000	29,600	1,000	+28,600
1947	50,000	36,600	15,600	+21,000
1948	55,000	18,560	13,560	+ 5,000
1949	56,000	7,560	6,560	+ 1,000
1950	57,000	7,970	6,970	+ 1,000
1951	50,000	5,930	12,930	- 7,000
1952	45,000	2,600	7,600	- 5,000
1953	42,000	1,640	4,640	- 3,000
1954	40,000	1,830	3,830	- 2,000
1955	35,000	2,950	7,950	- 5,000
1956	34,000	1,690	2,690	- 1,000
1957	30,000	740	4,740	- 4,000
1958	28,000	350	2,350	- 2,000
1959	25,000	360	3,360	- 3,000

Note: Table I-65 is the total of Tables I-63 and I-64.

Source: Estimates made by Veterans' Administration.

TABLE I-64

Veterans' Administration Guaranteed and Insured Farm Loans, Part Nonguaranteed and Non-Insured, 1945-1959

Year ended December 31	Outstanding	Loans made	Loans repaid or charged off	Net change in outstandings
	(thousands of dollars)			
1945	2,500	2,500	--	+ 2,500
1946	31,000	34,240	5,740	+28,500
1947	70,000	41,149	2,149	+39,000
1948	85,000	23,829	8,829	+15,000
1949	85,500	9,973	9,473	+ 500
1950	85,000	11,431	11,931	- 500
1951	90,000	21,521	16,521	+ 5,000
1952	90,000	5,372	5,372	--
1953	87,000	4,603	7,603	- 3,000
1954	80,000	4,673	11,673	- 7,000
1955	75,000	6,970	11,970	- 5,000
1956	66,000	4,959	13,959	- 9,000
1957	55,000	3,014	14,014	-11,000
1958	42,000	1,256	14,256	-13,000
1959	30,000	858	12,858	-12,000

Note: Table I-65 is the total of Tables I-63 and I-64.

Source: Data obtained by subtracting Table I-63 from Table I-65.

Agricultural Loans

TABLE I-65

Veterans' Administration Guaranteed and Insured Farm Loans in Total, 1945-1959

Year ended December 31	Outstanding	Loans made	Loans repaid or charged off	Net change in outstandings
	(thousands of dollars)			
1945	2,900	3,000	100	+ 2,900
1946	60,000	63,840	6,740	+57,100
1947	120,000	77,749	17,749	+60,000
1948	140,000	42,389	22,389	+20,000
1949	141,500	17,533	16,033	+ 1,500
1950	142,000	19,401	18,901	+ 500
1951	140,000	16,020	18,020	- 2,000
1952	135,000	7,972	12,972	- 5,000
1953	129,000	6,243	12,243	- 6,000
1954	120,000	6,503	15,503	- 9,000
1955	110,000	9,920	19,920	-10,000
1956	100,000	6,646	16,646	-10,000
1957	85,000	3,754	18,754	-15,000
1958	70,000	1,606	16,606	-15,000
1959	55,000	1,218	16,218	-15,000

Note: Table I-65 is the total of Tables I-63 and I-64.

Source: Exact data or estimates supplied by Veterans' Administration.

Agricultural Loans

TABLE I-66

War Finance Corporation Agricultural Loans, 1918-1939

Year ended December 31	Outstanding	Loans made	Loans repaid or charged off	Net change in outstandings
	(thousands of dollars)			
1918	3,079	6,403	3,324	3,079
1919	1,459	1,424	3,044	- 1,620
1920	793	1	667	- 666
1921	82,997	82,967	763	82,204
1922	148,692	186,143	120,448	65,695
1923	70,201	18,135	96,626	-78,491
1924	40,269	9,872	39,804	-29,932
1925	15,589	937	25,617	-24,680
1926	7,670	355	8,274	- 7,919
1927	1,362	178	6,486	- 6,308
1928	454	126	1,034	- 908
1929	161	--	293	- 293
1930	59	--	102	- 102
1931	45	--	14	- 14
1932	14	--	31	- 31
1933	13	--	1	- 1
1934	9	--	4	- 4
1935	8	--	1	- 1
1936	7	--	1	- 1
1937	4	--	3	- 3
1938	3	--	1	- 1
1939	--	--	3	- 3

Source: Saulnier, et al., p. 388.

Agricultural Loans

TABLE I-67

Tennessee Valley Authority Loans to Municipalities and Cooperative Wholesale Power Distribution Companies, 1934-1952

Year ended December 31	Outstanding	Loans made	Loans repaid or charged off	Net change in outstandings
	(thousands of dollars)			
1934	96	214	118	96
1935	524	491	63	428
1936	1,226	725	23	702
1937	1,633	823	416	407
1938	2,543	873	-37	910
1939	4,578	1,134	-901	2,035
1940	4,172	853	1,259	- 406
1941	4,018	135	289	- 154
1942	3,611	28	435	- 407
1943	3,295	3	319	- 316
1944	2,938	--	357	- 357
1945	2,428	--	510	- 510
1946	724	--	1,704	- 1,704
1947	98	--	626	- 626
1948	69	--	29	- 29
1949	14	--	55	- 55
1950	9	--	5	- 5
1951	3	--	6	- 6
1952	--	--	3	- 3

Source: Saulnier, et al., p. 412.

Agricultural Loans

TABLE I-68

Tennessee Valley Associated Cooperatives Loans to Cooperatives, 1934-1948[a]

Year ended December 31	Outstanding	Loans made	Loans repaid or charged off	Net change in outstandings
	(thousands of dollars)			
1934	73	52	-21	73
1935	167	78	-16	94
1936	131	79	115	- 36
1937	179	97	49	48
1938	291	140	28	112
1939	290	54	55	- 1
1940	292	7	5	2
1941	287	1	6	- 5
1942	286	1	2	- 1
1943	276	--	10	- 10
1944	270	--	6	- 6
1945	287	17[b/]	--	17
1946	165	13	135	- 122
1947	75	--	90	- 90
1948	--	--	75	- 75

[a]Direct loans and stock purchases.
[b]Adjusted to $17,000 from the $14,000 reported so as to cross-check with changes in outstandings.

Source: Saulnier, et al., p. 403.

TABLE I-69

Electric Home and Farm Authority Loans, 1934-1942

Year ended December 31	Outstanding	Loans made	Loans repaid or charged off	Net change in outstandings
	(thousands of dollars)			
1934	116	386	270	116
1935	986	1,009	139	870
1936	1,913	2,426	1,499	927
1937	5,092	4,804	1,625	3,179
1938	7,892	7,211	4,411	2,800
1939	11,228	10,106	6,770	3,336
1940	14,305	13,013	9,936	3,077
1941	15,934	10,306	8,677	1,629
1942[a/]	---	---	15,934	-15,934

[a]Outstanding accounts were transferred to the Reconstruction Finance Corporation in 1942 for liquidation.

Source: Saulnier, et al., p. 403.

Agricultural Loans

TABLE I-70

Reconstruction Finance Corporation Direct Agricultural Loans, 1932-1951

Year ended December 31	Outstanding	Loans made	Loans repaid or charged off	Net change in outstandings
	(thousands of dollars)			
1932	1,325	1,440	115	1,325
1933	10,389	11,475	2,411	9,064
1934	19,434	18,448	9,403	9,045
1935	22,246	5,277	2,465	2,812
1936	1,369	2,508	23,385	-20,877
1937	991	560	938	-378
1938	20,743	20,073	321	19,752
1939	856	7,161	27,048	-19,887
1940	490	--	366	-366
1941	434	2	58	-56
1942	339	--	95	-95
1943	57	--	282	-282
1944	55	--	2	-2
1945	55	--	--	--
1946	55	--	--	--
1947	55	--	--	--
1948	47	--	8	-8
1949	44	--	3	-3
1950	44	--	--	--
1951	--	--	44	-44

Source: Saulnier, et al., pp. 381-382.

Tennessee Valley Associated Cooperatives (Table I-68)

The Tennessee Valley Associated Cooperatives, Inc., a government corporation, made direct loans to and purchased stock in farmers' cooperatives and canning associations in the Tennessee Valley, in the years between 1934 and 1946. Funds were supplied by the U.S. Treasury. This lending program was of minor significance.

Electric Home and Farm Authority (Table I-69)

The Electric Home and Farm Authority was a government lending agency that discounted installment contracts arising out of the sale by accredited dealers of electrical home appliances and equipment. Originally, in 1933, it operated only in the TVA region. In 1935, its operations were extended to the entire country, and it became affiliated with the RFC. Funds for making loans came partly from the government ($850,000), and partly from the sale to commercial banks of the Authorities' notes, issued under an RFC commitment to purchase them if not paid at maturity. In 1942, the Electric Home and Farm Authority was placed in liquidation.

Reconstruction Finance Corporation Agricultural Loans (Table I-70)

A minor part of the lending activity of the Reconstruction Finance Corporation was in making direct agricultural loans. These were for the purpose of financing (1) livestock marketing, (2) exports of agricultural surpluses, and (3) storage and marketing of agricultural commodities. The last RFC agricultural loans were made in 1941. Outstandings were liquidated by the end of 1951.

III. BUSINESS LENDING AND LOAN INSURANCE PROGRAMS

The largest programs of business federal lending in 1929 were those for railroad loans and loans by the Maritime Administration. In 1939 and 1949, year-end outstandings of the Reconstruction Finance Corporation constituted more than one-half of total outstandings on all federal loans to business. In 1958, year-end outoutstandings on defense loans were largest, followed by those for loans of the Maritime Administration and Small Business Administration. Use of year-end outstandings rather than volume of loans made as an indication of the size of a program under-emphasizes the importance of the programs with loans of short maturities. Many defense loans had short maturities, and so their importance is under-emphasized in the tabulation.

SUMMARY TABLE I-C

Summary of Business Loans Outstanding, Twelve Programs, Year End 1929, 1939, 1949, and 1958

Table No.	Program of Business Loans	1929	1939	1949	1958
		(thousands of dollars)			
I-125	Defense Loans	--	--	8,893	529,110
I-105	Maritime Administration	69,500	57,179	443,900	377,933
I-90	Small Business Administration	--	--	--	370,390
I-93	Veterans' Administration	--	--	244,843	121,728
I-73	Reconstruction Finance Corporation Loans to Business Firms	--	642,528	764,362	41,884
I-106	Civil Aeronautics Board	--	--	--	14,788
I-109	Inland Waterways Corporation	828	456	271	6,967
I-92	U.S. Department of the Interior Direct Loans to Fisheries	--	--	--	4,248
I-130	Federal Reserve Banks Industrial Loans	--	33,884	7,413	2,116
I-131	Virgin Island Corporation	--	--	4	157
I-99	Railroad Loans	58,745	52,197	13,928	--
I-132	Reconstruction Finance Corporation Loans to Financial Institutions	--	171,207	29	--
	Total	129,073	957,451	1,483,643	1,469,321

Subtractions to eliminate double counting -- none

Reconstruction Finance Corporation Loans to Business Firms (Tables I-71 to I-75)

The most complicated, and most varied in operating methods and types of loans, of all federal lending agencies was the Reconstruction Finance Corporation, active in loaning from 1932 through 1953, and since then in clean-up and liquidating operations. From time of establishment until dissolution in 1953, the RFC operated as a direct agency of the federal government. It operated under a Board of Directors, with Jesse H. Jones as Chairman of the Board until 1945 and a succession of chairmen thereafter until 1951 when the Board of Directors was replaced by an Administrator and a Loan Policy Board.

The RFC made direct loans and participated with private lending institutions in making loans to business, including railroads, and to states and other public bodies (some of which were corporations established by the RFC), when credit was not otherwise available on reasonable terms. The RFC also made disaster and civil defense loans, and a great many other loans of a bewildering variety. No loan of any type seemed to be outside its authority. This description covers only the business loans of the RFC, with agricultural loans, loans to minor governmental units, and loans to financial institutions covered elsewhere in this study by other tables than I-71 to I-75. Also, loans to certain public bodies, such as the Commodity Credit Corporation, are not covered in this section, being considered sources of government funds for other federal lending activity rather than federal lending itself.

In 1932 and 1933, most of the business loans of the RFC were made to railroads. Beginning in 1934, many were to industrial firms. The aim was to prevent bankruptcies and the spread of unemployment. During World War II and the Korean conflict, many of the business loans were for the purpose of stimulating output of war and defense materials. Nearly three-fourths of total RFC loans during its life-time were to manufacturing and mining firms.

The annual volume of business loans was greatest in 1942, 1943, and 1946, being $0.5 billion in each of these years (Table I-73). Loans in the last full year before dissolution, 1952, were $109 million. Outstandings were at their peak at the end of 1943, $922 million, and dwindled to $21 million by the end of 1959.

The division of the RFC business loans into their direct and guaranteed parts is shown in Tables I-71 and I-72. Except in 1946 and 1947, the volume of direct loans was larger than the volume of guaranteed loans in each of the active years of the RFC.

The division of guaranteed RFC business loans into their guaranteed and nonguaranteed parts is shown in Tables I-74 and I-75. The guaranteed part usually was from three to four times as large as the nonguaranteed part, indicating a guarantee of about 75 to 80 percent of the total loan.

Small Business Administration (Tables I-76 to I-91)

The Small Business Administration makes loans to (1) small businesses, (2) victims of disaster, (3) small business investment companies, and (4) state and local development companies. Its first loans were made in 1954, and loans of the third and fourth types listed above were first made in 1959. Funds for SBA loans and the SBA share of participation loans come from a revolving fund established with government capital. The SBA is an independent agency of the federal government. Loans are made through 15 regional offices and numerous branch offices.

Business Loans

TABLE I-71

Reconstruction Finance Corporation Direct Business Loans,
1932-1959

Note: Table I-73 is the total of Tables I-71 and I-72.

Year ended December 31	Outstanding	Loans made	Loans repaid or charged off	Net change in outstandings
	(thousands of dollars)			
1932	272,472	284,312	11,840	272,472
1933	337,087	109,789	45,174	64,615
1934	388,340	60,684	9,431	51,253
1935	442,568	77,412	23,184	54,228
1936	414,261	63,153	91,460	-28,307
1937	434,735	44,571	24,097	20,474
1938	547,161	140,567	28,141	112,426
1939	581,296	93,916	59,781	34,135
1940	596,570	149,788	134,514	15,274
1941	616,087	117,798	98,281	19,517
1942	794,838	385,706	206,955	178,751
1943	775,876	287,849	306,811	-18,962
1944	718,136	198,883	256,623	-57,740
1945	486,924	227,895	459,107	-231,212
1946	393,689	53,871	147,106	-93,235
1947	444,404	200,038	149,323	50,715
1948	442,945	102,996	104,455	-1,459
1949	568,499	239,554	114,000	125,554
1950	524,098	246,583	290,984	-44,401
1951	502,444	149,521	171,175	-21,654
1952	451,749	103,238	153,933	-50,695
1953	383,485	78,028	146,292	-68,264
1954	170,940	20,708	233,253	-212,545
1955	118,524	942	53,358	-52,416
1956	79,023	199	39,700	-39,501
1957	42,508	---	36,515	-36,515
1958	38,243	---	4,265	-4,265
1959	18,951	409	19,701	-19,292

Note: The break-down of loans outstanding among loans of different types were as follows, in thousands of dollars:

	Railroad loans	Foreign mining loans	Other business loans	Total
December 31, 1953	76,908	4,300	302,277	383,485
" ", 1954	9,495	--	161,445	170,940
" ", 1955	9,150	--	109,374	118,524
" ", 1956	8,762	--	70,261	79,023
" ", 1957	6,613	--	35,895	42,508
" ", 1958	6,284	--	31,959	38,243
" ", 1959	5,994	--	12,957	18,951

These loans included direct loans, government share of immediate participations, and deferred participations purchased. On July 1, 1957, loans with balances of less than $250,000 were transferred to the SBA. Disbursements in 1954-59 were for authorizations prior to September 28, 1953, or, in 1959, for purchase of deferred participation.

Source: Computed from Saulnier, et al., Table A-9, pp. 381-382, to 1952 for outstanding and to 1953 for loans made; Treasury Dept., 1953-59. From Saulnier data, subtractions were made in 1947-53 of the data for the Smaller War Plants Corporation, appearing in Table I-121; in 1953, of the Section 409 Civil Defense loans, appearing in Table I-229; and in 1951-53, of the Section 302 Defense Loans, appearing in Tables I-113 and I-115.

Business Loans

TABLE I-72

Reconstruction Finance Corporation Business Loan Guarantees, 1934-1959

Year ended December 31	Outstanding	Loans made	Loans repaid or charged off	Net change in outstandings
	(thousands of dollars)			
1934	1,416	1,498	82	1,416
1935	3,506	3,746	1,656	2,090
1936	5,091	3,668	2,083	1,585
1937	4,996	1,161	1,256	-95
1938	45,579	47,332	6,749	40,583
1939	61,232	38,934	23,281	15,653
1940	44,830	10,551	26,953	-16,402
1941	40,785	17,117	21,162	-4,045
1942	118,261	145,454	67,978	77,476
1943	145,761	176,279	148,779	27,500
1944	107,337	127,150	165,574	-38,424
1945	136,058	169,989	141,268	28,721
1946	434,774	469,152	170,436	298,716
1947	363,786	221,485	292,473	-70,988
1948	245,481	89,604	207,909	-118,305
1949	195,863	92,649	142,267	-49,618
1950	126,734	49,958	119,087	-69,129
1951	78,419	12,449	60,764	-48,315
1952	48,148	5,960	36,231	-30,271
1953	31,172	5,897	22,873	-16,976
1954	27,672	19,495	22,995	-3,500
1955	18,843	9,765	18,594	-8,829
1956	11,210	8,332	15,965	-7,633
1957	4,492	5,555	12,273	-6,718
1958	3,641	--	851	-851
1959	2,496	--	1,145	-1,145

Note: Table I-73 is the total of Tables I-71 and I-72.
Table I-72 is the total of Tables I-74 and I-75.

Source: Based on estimates of Treasury Department of division between government and private parts, and data in Table I-74. Outstandings and loans made as given in Table I-74 divided by .75 in 1934-46, .80 in 1947-49, .85 in 1950-52, and .90 in 1953-59.

Business Loans

TABLE I-73

Total Business Loans of the Reconstruction Finance Corporation, 1932-1959

Year ended December 31	Outstanding	Loans made	Loans repaid or charged off	Net change in outstandings
	(thousands of dollars)			
1932	272,472	284,312	11,840	272,472
1933	337,087	109,789	45,174	64,615
1934	389,756	62,182	9,513	52,669
1935	446,074	81,158	24,840	56,318
1936	419,352	66,821	93,543	-26,722
1937	439,731	45,732	25,353	20,379
1938	592,740	187,899	34,890	153,009
1939	642,528	132,850	83,062	49,788
1940	641,400	160,339	161,467	-1,128
1941	656,872	134,915	119,443	15,472
1942	913,099	531,160	274,933	256,227
1943	921,637	464,128	455,590	8,538
1944	825,473	326,033	422,197	-96,164
1945	622,982	397,884	600,375	-202,491
1946	828,463	523,023	317,542	205,481
1947	808,190	421,523	441,796	-20,273
1948	688,426	192,600	312,364	-119,764
1949	764,362	332,203	256,267	75,936
1950	650,832	296,541	410,071	-113,530
1951	580,863	161,970	231,939	-69,969
1952	499,897	109,198	190,164	-80,966
1953	414,657	83,925	169,165	-85,240
1954	198,612	40,203	256,248	-216,045
1955	137,367	10,707	71,952	-61,245
1956	90,233	8,531	55,665	-47,134
1957	47,000	5,555	48,788	-43,233
1958	41,884	--	5,116	-5,116
1959	21,447	409	20,846	-20,437

Note: Table I-73 is the total of Tables I-71 and I-72.

Source: Obtained by adding Tables I-71 and I-72.

Business Loans

TABLE I-74

Guaranteed Part of Reconstruction Finance Corporation
Guaranteed Business Loans, 1934-1959

Year ended December 31	Outstanding	Loans made	Loans repaid or charged off	Net change in outstandings
	(thousands of dollars)			
1934	1,062	1,124	62	1,062
1935	2,630	2,810	1,242	1,568
1936	3,819	2,752	1,563	1,189
1937	3,748	871	942	-71
1938	34,193	35,508	5,063	30,445
1939	45,935	29,208	17,466	11,742
1940	33,631	7,915	20,219	-12,304
1941	30,596	12,841	15,876	-3,035
1942	88,718	109,118	50,996	58,122
1943	109,348	132,242	111,612	20,630
1944	80,523	95,386	124,211	-28,825
1945	102,069	127,524	105,978	21,546
1946	326,162	351,952	127,859	224,093
1947	291,029	177,188	212,321	-35,133
1948	196,385	71,683	166,327	-94,644
1949	156,690	74,119	113,814	-39,695
1950	107,767	42,481	91,404	-48,923
1951	66,683	10,586	51,670	-41,084
1952	40,942	5,068	30,809	-25,741
1953	28,058	5,308	18,192	-12,884
1954	24,907	17,547	20,698	-3,151
1955	16,961	8,790	16,736	-7,946
1956	10,090	7,500	14,371	-6,871
1957	4,043	5,000	11,047	-6,047
1958	3,277	--	766	-766
1959	2,247	--	1,030	-1,030

Note: Table I-72 is the total of Tables I-74 and I-75.

Source: Saulnier, et al., pp. 381-382, for 1934-53 data; Treasury Department for 1954-59 data. Includes regular deferred participation commitments and loans sold subject to deferred participation. On July 1, 1957, all deferred participation commitments with balances of less than $250,000 were transferred to the SBA. No new regular deferred participation commitments were authorized subsequent to September 28, 1953.

Business Loans

TABLE I-75

Non-Guaranteed Part of Reconstruction Finance Corporation Guaranteed Business Loans, 1934-1959

Year ended December 31	Outstanding	Loans made	Loans repaid or charged off	Net change in outstandings
	(thousands of dollars)			
1934	354	374	20	354
1935	876	936	414	522
1936	1,272	916	520	396
1937	1,248	290	314	-24
1938	11,386	11,824	1,686	10,138
1939	15,297	9,726	5,815	3,911
1940	11,199	2,636	6,734	-4,098
1941	10,189	4,276	5,286	-1,010
1942	29,543	36,336	16,982	19,354
1943	36,413	44,037	37,167	6,870
1944	26,814	31,764	41,363	-9,599
1945	33,989	42,465	35,290	7,175
1946	108,612	117,200	42,577	74,623
1947	72,757	44,297	80,152	-35,855
1948	49,096	17,921	41,582	-23,661
1949	39,173	18,530	28,453	-9,923
1950	18,967	7,477	27,683	-20,206
1951	11,736	1,863	9,094	-7,231
1952	7,206	892	5,422	-4,530
1953	3,114	589	4,681	-4,092
1954	2,765	1,948	2,297	-349
1955	1,882	975	1,858	-883
1956	1,120	832	1,594	-762
1957	449	555	1,226	-671
1958	364	--	85	-85
1959	249	--	115	-115

Note: Table I-72 is the total of Tables I-74 and I-75.

Source: Obtained by subtracting Table I-74 and I-75.

Business Loans

TABLE I-76

Small Business Administration Direct Loans to Small Businesses, 1954-1958

Year ended December 31	Outstanding	Loans made a/	Loans repaid or charged off	Net change in outstandings
	(thousands of dollars)			
1954	7,203	7,902 b/	699 b/	7,203
1955	14,154	10,390	3,439	6,951
1956	30,634	22,504	6,024	16,480
1957	57,332	37,025	10,327	26,698
1958	98,249	37,567	-3,350	40,917

[a]Includes loans later converted entirely to a private non-SBA status.
[b]From September 29, 1953 (beginning of program) through December 31, 1954.

Note: Through 1958, Tables I-76, I-77, I-80, and I-81 add to total SBA loans in Table I-90; beginning in 1959, these four plus Tables I-84, I-85, and I-86 add to total SBA loans in Table I-90.

Source: Data was supplied by the SBA.

Business Loans

TABLE I-77

Small Business Administration Participation Loans to Small Businesses, Total Amounts, 1954-1958

Year ended December 31	Outstanding	Loans made a/	Loans repaid or charged off	Net change in outstandings
		(thousands of dollars)		
1954	17,921	19,351 b/	1,430 b/	17,921
1955	40,151	29,586	7,356	22,230
1956	86,927	62,383	15,607	46,776
1957	148,625	92,864	31,166	61,698
1958	219,371	113,073	42,327	70,746

[a]Includes loans later converted entirely to a private non-SBA status.
[b]From September 29, 1953 (beginning of program) through December 31, 1954.

Note: Through 1958, Tables I-76, I-77, I-80, and I-81 add to total SBA loans in Table I-90; beginning in 1959, these four plus Tables I-84, I-85, and I-86 add to total SBA loans on Table I-90. Table I-77 is the total of Tables I-78 and I-79.

Source: Data were supplied by the SBA.

Business Loans

TABLE I-78

Small Business Administration Participation Loans to Small Businesses, SBA Share, 1954-1958

Year ended December 31	Outstanding	Loans made a/	Loans repaid or charged off	Net change in outstandings
		(thousands of dollars)		
1954	13,691	14,802 b/	1,111 b/	13,691
1955	30,290	22,545	5,946	16,599
1956	66,179	47,492	11,603	35,889
1957	114,304	74,887	26,762	48,125
1958	169,092	84,122	29,334	54,788

[a] Includes loans later converted entirely to a private non-SBA status.
[b] From September 29, 1953 (beginning of program) through December 31, 1954.

Note: Table I-77 is the total of Tables I-78 and I-79.

Source: Data were supplied by the SBA.

Business Loans

TABLE I-79

Small Business Administration Participation Loans to Small Businesses, Private Participation, 1954-1958

Year ended December 31	Outstanding	Loans made a/	Loans repaid or charged off	Net change in outstandings
		(thousands of dollars)		
1954	4,230	4,549 b/	319 b/	4,230
1955	9,861	7,041	1,410	5,631
1956	20,748	14,891	4,004	10,887
1957	34,321	17,977	4,404	13,573
1958	50,279	28,951	14,993	15,958

[a] Includes loans later converted entirely to a private non-SBA status.
[b] From September 29, 1953 (beginning of program) through December 31, 1954.

Note: Table I-77 is the total of Tables I-78 and I-79.

Source: Data were supplied by the SBA.

Business Loans

TABLE I-80

Small Business Administration Direct Disaster Loans, 1954-1958

Year ended December 31	Outstanding	Loans made a/	Loans repaid or charged off	Net change in outstandings
		(thousands of dollars)		
1954	1,969	2,018 b/	49 b/	1,969
1955	17,391	16,343	921	15,422
1956	33,183	19,181	3,389	15,792
1957	36,883	8,954	5,254	3,700
1958	42,479	11,745	6,149	5,596

[a]Includes loans later converted entirely to a private non-SBA status.
[b]From September 29, 1953 (beginning of program) through December 31, 1954.

Note: Through 1958, Tables I-76, I-77, I-80, and I-81 add to total SBA loans in Table I-90; beginning in 1959, these four plus Tables I-84, I-85, and I-86 add to total SBA loans in Table I-90.

Source: Data were supplied by the SBA.

Business Loans

TABLE I-81

Small Business Administration Participation Disaster Loans, Total Amounts, 1955-1958

Year ended December 31	Outstanding	Loans made [a]	Loans repaid or charged off	Net change in outstandings
		(thousands of dollars)		
1955	736	739	3	736
1956	6,299 [b]	6,076 [b]	513	5,563
1957	9,842	4,899	1,356	3,543
1958	10,291	1,818	1,369	449

[a]Includes loans later converted entirely to a private non-SBA status.
[b]Adjustment made to correct overstatement of book figure in 1956, which adjustment is reflected in 1958 on SBA's reports.

Note: Through 1958, Tables I-76, I-77, I-80, and I-81 add to total SBA loans in Table I-90; beginning in 1959, these four plus Tables I-84, I-85, and I-86 add to total SBA loans in Table I-90.

Source: Data were supplied by the SBA.

Business Loans

TABLE I-82

Small Business Administration Participation Disaster Loans, SBA Share, 1955-1958

Year ended December 31	Outstanding	Loans made [a]	Loans repaid or charged off	Net change in outstandings
		(thousands of dollars)		
1955	583	585	2	583
1956	5,340	5,222	465	4,757
1957	8,359	4,338	1,319	3,019
1958	8,377	1,407	1,389	18

[a] Includes loans later converted entirely to a private non-SBA status.

Note: Table I-81 is the total of Tables I-82 and I-83.

Source: Data were supplied by the SBA.

Business Loans

TABLE I-83

Small Business Administration Participation Disaster Loans, Private Participation, 1955-1958

Year ended December 31	Outstanding	Loans made a/	Loans repaid or charged off	Net change in outstandings
	(thousands of dollars)			
1955	153	154	1	153
1956	959	854	48	806
1957	1,483	561	37	524
1958	1,914	411	- 20 b/	431

[a]Includes loans later converted entirely to a private non-SBA status.

[b]Results from incorrect reporting of deferred participations purchased and converted to direct loans. Correction subsequent to 12/31/58.

Note: Table I-81 is the total of Tables I-82 and I-83.

Source: Data were supplied by the SBA.

Business Loans

TABLE I-84

Small Business Administration Purchases of Debentures in Small Business Investment Companies, 1959

Year ended December 31	Outstanding	Loans made	Loans repaid or charged off	Net change in outstandings
		(thousands of dollars)		
1959	1,147	1,147	---	1,147

Note: Through 1958, Tables I-76, I-77, I-80, and I-81 add to total SBA loans in Table I-90; beginning in 1959, these four plus Tables I-84, I-85, and I-86 add to total SBA loans in Table I-90.

Source: Data supplied by Small Business Administration.

TABLE I-85

Small Business Administration Direct Loans to State and Local Development Companies, 1959

Year ended December 31	Outstanding	Loans made	Loans repaid or charged off	Net change in outstandings
		(thousands of dollars)		
1959	455	466	11	455

Note: Through 1958, Tables I-76, I-77, I-80, and I-81 add to total SBA loans in Table I-90: beginning in 1959, these four plus Tables I-84, I-85, and I-86 add to total SBA loans in Table I-90.

Source: Data supplied by Small Business Administration.

Business Loans

TABLE I-86

Small Business Administration Participation Loans to State and Local Development Companies, 1959

Year ended December 31	Outstanding	Loans made	Loans repaid or charged off	Net change in outstandings
		(thousands of dollars)		
1959	939	942	3	939

Note: Through 1958, Tables I-76, I-77, I-80, and I-81 add to total SBA loans in Table I-90; beginning in 1959, these four plus Tables I-84, I-85, and I-86 add to total SBA loans in Table I-90. Table I-86 is the total of Tables I-87 and I-88.

Source: Data supplied by Small Business Administration.

TABLE I-87

Small Business Administration Participation Loans to State and Local Development Companies, SBA Share, 1959

Year ended December 31	Outstanding	Loans made	Loans repaid or charged off	Net change in outstandings
		(thousands of dollars)		
1959	845	848	3	845

Note: Table I-86 is the total of Tables I-87 and I-88.

Source: Data supplied by Small Business Administration.

Business Loans

TABLE I-88

Small Business Administration Participation Loans to State and Local Development Companies, Private Participation, 1959

Year ended December 31	Outstanding	Loans made	Loans repaid or charged off	Net change in outstandings
		(thousands of dollars)		
1959	94	94	---	94

Note: Table I-86 is the total of Tables I-87 and I-88.

Source: Data supplied by Small Business Administration.

TABLE I-89

Small Business Administration Loans to Hospitals and Nursing Homes Operated for Profit, 1957-1958

Year ended December 31	Outstanding	Loans approved	Loans repaid or charged off	Net change in outstandings
		(thousands of dollars)		
1957		3,454		
1958		6,180		

[a]Other statistics, and data for years prior to 1957, are not readily available.

Note: These data are included in Tables I-76 and I-77, and were not added in obtaining SBA total loans in Table I-90.

Source: Data were supplied by the SBA.

Business Loans

TABLE I-90

Total Loans of the Small Business Administration, 1954-1958

Year ended December 31	Outstanding	Loans made a/	Loans repaid or charged off	Net change in outstandings
	(thousands of dollars)			
1954	27,093	29,271	2,178	27,093
1955	72,432	57,058	11,719	45,339
1956	157,043	110,144	25,533	84,611
1957	252,682	143,742	48,103	95,639
1958	370,390	164,203	46,495	117,708

[a]Includes loans later converted entirely to a private non-SBA status.

Note: Through 1958, Tables I-76, I-77, I-80, and I-81 add to total SBA loans in Table I-90; beginning in 1959, these four plus Tables I-84, I-85, and I-86 add to total SBA loans in Table I-90.

Source: Data were supplied by the SBA. Liquidating business of SBA for RFC appears in RFC tables, and is not included here.

TABLE I-91

Sales to Private Investors of Notes, Mortgages, and other Paper Received from SBA Direct Loans, 1955-1958

Year ended December 31	Unpaid balance at date of sale	Cumulative
	(thousands of dollars)	
1955	295	295
1956	359	654
1957	61	715
1958	---	715

Source: Data were supplied by the SBA.

There are two types of business and disaster loans—direct loans and participation loans. In a participation loan, the SBA joins with a private lending institution in a loan to a small business concern. In a direct loan, funds come entirely from the SBA and go directly to the borrower. By law, the SBA may not make a direct loan if a private lending institution will join with it in the loan.

The business loans are limited in size to a maximum of $350,000. In practice, the average size is about $50,000. Disaster loans are made to persons whose homes or businesses have been damaged by storm, flood, or other disaster, and to small business firms that have suffered economic injury because of excessive rainfall or drought in their areas.

Beginning in 1959, the SBA has provided financial assistance to privately owned investment companies that make equity-type and long-term financing available to small business concerns. This is done through the purchase of debentures from the investment company up to a maximum of $150,000, and through loans of up to 50 percent of the investment company's paid-in capital and surplus. The SBA also makes loans to state and local development companies to help them assist small businesses in their areas.

At the end of 1958, the SBA had loans outstanding of $370 million (Table I-90). Loans expanded each year, from $29 million in 1954 to $164 million in 1958.

Purchases of debentures in Small Business Investment Companies amounted to $1,147,000 in 1959 (Table I-84). No other direct loans were made to Small Business Investment Companies. Loans to state and local development companies amounted to $1,408,000.

The policy of the SBA is to sell to private investors as much as possible of the notes, mortgages, and other paper received from direct loans. A total of $715,000 of such paper was sold in 1955-58, with the greatest sales in 1956 (Table I-91).

U.S. Department of the Interior Direct Loans to Fisheries (Table I-92)

Loans are made to owners of fishing vessels and fishing gear, and to persons doing research into basic problems of fisheries in the capture or landing of fish, for the purpose of stengthening the domestic fishing industry. Approval for loans is made by the Department of the Interior. Subsequent to this approval, administrative work is handled by the Small Business Administration.

Loans are made only in the absence of credit from other sources on reasonable terms. Excluded from eligibility are loans to finance shore operations, to replace vessels or gear where the applicant's

Business Loans

TABLE I-92

U.S. Department of the Interior Direct Loans to Fisheries, 1957-1959

Year ended December 31	Outstanding	Loans made	Loans repaid or charged off	Net change in outstandings
		(thousands of dollars)		
1957	3,140	3,280	140	3,140
1958	4,248	1,601	493	1,108
1959	4,127	1,186	1,307	-121

Source: Data were supplied by the SBA, but the SBA does the book-keeping only. The SBA does not furnish the money. It services these loans for the Fish and Wildlife Service of the U.S. Department of the Interior.

ownership is less than 20 percent, or to finance new business ventures involving fishing operations. Funds for loans come out of a Fisheries Loan Fund, a revolving fund established with government capital.

The first loans under this program were made in 1957. Total loans in the 1957-59 period were $6 million.

Veterans' Administration (Tables I-93 to I-95)

The purpose of business loans of the Veterans' Administration is to aid the civil re-establishment of returning veterans who wish to begin businesses of their own, by making credit available under more liberal terms than would otherwise exist. The authority to guarantee or insure such loans is scheduled to expire in 1962 for veterans of World War II, and in 1965 for veterans of the Korean conflict. Funds for such loans come from private sources. The loan program is administered by the Loan Guaranty Service of the Department of Veterans' Benefits of the VA. Field offices have authority to approve or disapprove applications for loan guarantee or insurance without reference to Washington.

Loans may be guaranteed in an amount not exceeding 50 percent of the loan, provided that the guaranteed part does not exceed $4,000 for real-estate loans or $2,000 for other loans. By agreement between a lender and the VA, the lender may substitute insurance against loss up to 15 percent of the aggregate amount of his eligible loans, in place of individual guaranteed loans. In case of default on any loan, he may then recover the full amount so long as total losses are not more than 15 percent of all his VA loans. The loan insurance option was applied much more extensively to VA business loans than to VA farm or home loans. Through May 25, 1951, only 0.4 percent of VA home loans were insured, 6.5 percent of VA farm loans, and 39.4 percent of VA business loans. Apparently the insurance option was more popular with VA business loans because of their smaller size and more risky nature.

Guaranteed and insured business loans of the VA were greatest in the first two years they were made, 1946 and 1947, when the volume was $136 million and $126 million, respectively (Table I-93). Year-end outstandings decreased from a peak of $320 million in 1952 to $122 million in 1958; these figures do not reflect partial amortization, however.

The break-down of total VA business loans into their guaranteed and insured, and nonguaranteed and non-insured parts, is shown in Tables I-94 and I-95. At the peak of year-end outstandings in 1952, the guaranteed and insured part was 26 percent of the total.

Business Loans

TABLE I-93

Veterans' Administration Guaranteed and Insured Business Loans, 1946-1958

Year ended December 31	Outstanding c/	Loans made	Loans repaid or charged off b/	Net change in outstandings c/
	(thousands of dollars)			
1946 a/	131,072	136,047	4,975	131,072
1947	234,105	126,047	23,014	103,033
1948	253,523	58,450	39,032	19,418
1949	244,843	32,290	40,970	-8,680
1950	242,437	32,351	34,757	-2,406
1951	292,041	82,729	33,125	49,604
1952	320,487	64,855	36,409	28,446
1953	257,883	33,646	96,250	-62,604
1954	216,314	21,317	62,886	-41,569
1955	180,471	21,669	57,512	-35,843
1956	154,834	15,787	41,424	-25,637
1957	134,400	13,123	33,557	-20,434
1958	121,728	8,609	21,281	-12,672

[a]Includes a small volume of loans made in 1945.
[b]Amounts repaid in full or charged off as claims paid.
[c]Does not reflect reductions from partial amortization.

Note: Table I-93 is the total of Tables I-94 and I-95.

Source: Data from special tabulations supplied by Veterans' Administration.

Business Loans

TABLE I-94

Guaranteed and Insured Part of Veterans' Administration Guaranteed and Insured Business Loans, 1946-1958

Year ended December 31	Outstanding c/	Loans made	Loans repaid or charged off b/	Net change in outstandings c/
	(thousands of dollars)			
1946 a/	51,024	53,297	2,273	51,024
1947	88,098	47,344	10,270	37,074
1948	92,876	21,347	16,569	4,778
1949	85,657	9,468	16,687	-7,219
1950	80,636	8,572	13,593	-5,021
1951	83,067	14,969	12,538	2,431
1952	82,098	11,198	12,167	-969
1953	67,665	5,883	20,316	-14,433
1954	57,853	3,869	13,681	-9,812
1955	49,516	4,214	12,551	-8,337
1956	43,255	2,908	9,169	-6,261
1957	38,575	2,234	6,914	-4,680
1958	35,395	1,413	4,593	-3,180

[a]Includes a small volume of loans made in 1945.
[b]Amounts repaid in full or charged off as claims paid.
[c]Does not reflect reductions from partial amortization.

Note: Table I-93 is the total of Tables I-94 and I-95.

Source: Data from special tabulations supplied by Veterans' Administration.

Business Loans

TABLE I-95

Non-Guaranteed and Non-Insured Part of Veterans' Administration Guaranteed and Insured Business Loans, 1946-1958

Year ended December 31	Outstanding c/	Loans made	Loans repaid or charged off b/	Net change in outstandings c/
		(thousands of dollars)		
1946 a/	80,048	82,750	2,702	80,048
1947	146,007	78,703	12,744	65,959
1948	160,647	37,103	22,463	14,640
1949	159,186	22,822	24,283	-1,461
1950	161,801	23,779	21,164	2,615
1951	208,974	67,760	20,587	47,173
1952	238,389	53,657	24,242	29,415
1953	190,218	27,763	75,934	-48,171
1954	158,461	17,448	49,205	-31,757
1955	130,955	17,455	44,961	-27,506
1956	111,579	12,879	32,255	-19,376
1957	95,825	10,889	26,643	-15,754
1958	86,333	7,196	16,688	-9,492

[a] Includes a small volume of loans made in 1945.
[b] Amounts repaid in full or charged off as claims paid.
[c] Does not reflect reductions from partial amortization.

Note: Table I-93 is the total of Tables I-94 and I-95.

Source: Data from special tabulations supplied by Veterans' Administration.

Railroad Loans (Tables I-96 to I-99)

The Interstate Commerce Commission guarantees against loss of principal or interest loans to railroads to finance the acquisition, construction, or maintenance of road, property, or equipment, and administers the program as an independent government agency. As predecessor programs, the Director General of Railroads, in 1919, and the ICC, in 1920, were empowered to lend to railroads. From 1918 through February 1920, railroads were under federal operation. The Director General made operating loans out of a $500 million revolving fund. The ICC in a previous program made loans from a $300 million revolving fund set up under the Transportation Act of 1920. No new loans were made under these programs after 1924. Another predecessor agency was the Public Works Administration, which made loans to railroads totaling $201 million in the period from 1933 through 1937. The RFC also made loans to railroads; these are included with its business loans described and tabulated elsewhere in this study.

The ICC program is one of guaranteeing loans to railroads in financial need. A guarantee may be granted only if necessary funds on reasonable terms are not otherwise available. Guarantees can take either of 2 forms, (1) a commitment to purchase the loan under specified conditions, or (2) an agreement to share losses. A guarantee fee is provided at rates intended to cover administrative expenses of the program. Administrative expenses and any payments to lenders under the guarantee agreements are to be financed by congressional appropriations. The aggregate principal amount of guaranteed loans is limited to $500 million.

The three parts of railroad loans are shown in Tables I-96, I-97, and I-98. Interstate Commerce Commission loans under the present program were $61 million in 1959 (Table I-96). The 1933-37 railroad loans of the Public Works Administration had been liquidated by the end of 1951 (Table I-97). Outstandings from earlier railroad loans, in 1919-24, were down to $59 million by the end of 1929, but were not finally extinguished until 1958 (Table I-98).

Maritime Administration (Tables I-100 to I-105)

The Maritime Administration's present lending activity consists of guaranteeing or insuring loans from private sources of funds for the financing of the construction, conversion, or reconditioning of ships. The present program covers construction loans, mortgages on completed ships, and mortgage bonds of shipping companies. The purpose of such loans is to encourage the building of U.S. cargo and passenger-carrying vessels, considered necessary for national strength and prestige as well as for regular trade.

Business Loans

TABLE I-96

Interstate Commerce Commission Guaranteed Loans to Railroads, 1959

Year ended December 31	Outstanding	Loans made	Loans repaid or charged off	Net change in outstandings
		(thousands of dollars)		
1959	60,817	60,817		60,817

Note: Table I-99 is the total of Tables I-96 to I-98.

Source: Data furnished by Interstate Commerce Commission.

TABLE I-97

Public Works Administration Direct Loans to Railroads, 1933-1951

Year ended December 31	Outstanding	Loans made	Loans repaid or charged off	Net change in outstandings
		(thousands of dollars)		
1933	39,864	39,864	-	39,864
1934	133,478	93,615	1	93,614
1935	148,780	55,113	39,811	15,302
1936	57,107	12,233	103,906	-91,673
1937	50,731	150	6,526	- 6,376
1938	46,506	-	4,225	- 4,225
1939	22,011	-	24,495	-24,495
1940	13,548	-	8,463	- 8,463
1941	11,696	-	1,852	- 1,852
1942	10,877	-	819	- 819
1943	10,188	-	689	- 689
1944	9,457	-	731	- 731
1945	7,839	-	1,618	- 1,618
1946	5,990	-	1,849	- 1,849
1947	3,035	-	2,955	- 2,955
1948	3,035	-	-	-
1949	2,123	-	912	- 912
1950	2,123	-	-	-
1951	-	-	2,123	- 2,123

Note: Table I-99 is the total of Tables I-96 to I-98.

Source: Saulnier, *et al.*, p. 389, with estimates added for 1933 and 1951 on outstandings.

Business Loans

TABLE I-98

Director General of Railroads and Interstate Commerce Commission Direct Loans to Railroads, 1929-1958

Year ended December 31	Outstanding	Loans made	Loans repaid or charged off	Net change in outstandings
	(thousands of dollars)			
1929	58,745	-		
1930	47,367	-	11,378	-11,378
1931	39,434	-	7,933	- 7,933
1932	38,704	-	730	- 730
1933	38,097	-	607	- 607
1934	34,452	-	3,645	- 3,645
1935	30,915	-	3,537	- 3,537
1936	30,238	-	677	- 677
1937	30,230	-	8	- 8
1938	30,230	-	-	-
1939	30,186	-	44	- 44
1940	30,080	-	106	- 106
1941	25,213	-	4,867	- 4,867
1942	25,213	-	-	-
1943	25,121	-	92	- 92
1944	21,598	-	3,523	- 3,523
1945	21,598	-	-	-
1946	21,598	-	-	-
1947	11,964	-	9,634	- 9,634
1948	11,929	-	35	- 35
1949	11,805	-	124	- 124
1950	11,805	-	-	-
1951	11,805	-	-	-
1952	6,019	-	5,786	- 5,786
1953	5,759	-	260	- 260
1954	4,000	-	1,759	- 1,759
1955	3,000	-	1,000	- 1,000
1956	2,000	-	1,000	- 1,000
1957	1,000	-	1,000	- 1,000
1958	-	-	1,000	- 1,000

Note: Table I-99 is the total of Tables I-96 to I-98.

Source: Saulnier, et al., pp. 409-410, with estimates on liquidation for 1954-58.

Business Loans

TABLE I-99

Total Direct and Guaranteed Loans to Railroads, 1929-1959

Year ended December 31	Outstanding	Loans made	Loans repaid or charged off	Net change in outstandings
	(thousands of dollars)			
1929	58,745			
1930	47,367	-	11,378	-11,378
1931	39,434	-	7,933	- 7,933
1932	38,704	-	730	- 730
1933	77,961	39,864	607	39,257
1934	167,930	93,615	3,646	89,969
1935	179,695	55,113	43,348	11,765
1936	87,345	12,233	104,583	- 92,350
1937	80,961	150	6,534	-6,384
1938	76,736	-	4,225	-4,225
1939	52,197	-	24,539	-24,539
1940	43,628	-	8,569	-8,569
1941	36,909	-	6,719	-6,719
1942	36,090	-	819	- 819
1943	35,309	-	781	- 781
1944	31,055	-	4,254	-4,254
1945	29,437	-	1,618	-1,618
1946	27,588	-	1,849	-1,849
1947	14,999	-	12,589	-12,589
1948	14,964	-	35	- 35
1949	13,928	-	1,036	-1,036
1950	13,928	-	-	-
1951	11,805	-	2,123	-2,123
1952	6,019	-	5,786	-5,786
1953	5,759	-	260	-260
1954	4,000	-	1,759	-1,759
1955	3,000	-	1,000	-1,000
1956	2,000	-	1,000	-1,000
1957	1,000	-	1,000	-1,000
1958	-	-	1,000	-1,000
1959	60,817	60,817	-	60,817

Note: Table I-99 is the total of Tables I-96 to I-98. Does not include RFC loans to railroads which are included along with loans to other businesses by the RFC.

Business Loans

TABLE I-100

Maritime Administration Direct Construction Loans to American Shipowners, 1929-1949

Year ended December 31	Outstanding	Loans made	Loans repaid or charged off	Net change in outstandings
	(thousands of dollars)			
1929	29,000	13,600		
1930	51,700	24,600	1,900	22,700
1931	88,000	39,800	3,500	36,300
1932	120,800	37,700	4,900	32,800
1933	120,900	12,600	12,500	100
1934	108,000	400	13,300	-12,900
1935	96,500	150	11,650	-11,500
1936	82,400	--	14,100	-14,100
1937	64,800	--	17,600	-17,600
1938	50,300	--	14,500	-14,500
1939	45,800	--	4,500	- 4,500
1940	37,800	--	8,000	- 8,000
1941	27,400	--	10,400	-10,400
1942	20,600	--	6,800	- 6,800
1943	15,500	--	5,100	- 5,100
1944	12,600	--	2,900	- 2,900
1945	11,500	--	1,100	- 1,100
1946	10,200	--	1,300	- 1,300
1947	4,700	--	5,500	- 5,500
1948	50	--	4,650	- 4,650
1949	--	--	50	- 50

Note: Table I-105 is the total of Tables I-100, I-101, and I-104.

Source: Merrill J. Roberts, "Government Credit Aids to Transportation," (unpublished CMC Research Study), Table 1 fiscal-year data placed on calendar-year basis by interpolation.

Business Loans

TABLE I-101

Maritime Administration Direct Loans in Connection with Sale of Government-Owned Ships, 1929-1959

Year ended December 31	Outstanding	Loans made	Loans repaid or charged off	Net change in outstandings
		(thousands of dollars)		
1929	40,500	--		
1930	37,300	--	3,200	- 3,200
1931	31,500	--	5,800	- 5,800
1932	27,200	--	4,300	- 4,300
1933	28,100	1,000	100	900
1934	25,093	--	3,007	- 3,007
1935	15,188	--	9,905	- 9,905
1936	14,892	--	296	- 296
1937	20,281	10,000	4,611	5,389
1938	9,693	--	10,588	-10,588
1939	10,316	1,000	377	623
1940	33,405	30,000	6,911	23,089
1941	35,552	10,000	7,853	2,147
1942	48,272	20,000	7,280	12,720
1943	108,280	70,000	9,992	60,008
1944	88,162	--	20,118	-20,118
1945	99,935	20,000	8,227	11,773
1946	116,156	20,000	3,779	16,221
1947	312,300	200,000	3,856	196,144
1948	486,450	180,000	5,850	174,150
1949	441,500	--	44,950	-44,950
1950	430,500	--	11,000	-11,000
1951	427,500	--	3,000	- 3,000
1952	381,000	--	46,500	-46,500
1953	335,000	--	46,000	-46,000
1954	292,623	--	42,377	-42,377
1955	260,659	38,792	70,756	-31,964
1956	276,450	68,813	53,022	15,791
1957	261,492	24,348	39,306	-14,958
1958	226,309	--	35,183	-35,183
1959	199,000	--	27,309	-27,309

Note: Table I-105 is the total of Tables I-100, I-101, and I-104.

Source: For 1929-53, Saulnier, et al., p. 393, with direct loans outstanding shown in Table I-100 subtracted from the totals appearing in Saulnier, after interpolation, when necessary, to put on calendar-year basis. For "loans made," rough estimates were made.
For 1954-58, data were supplied by Maritime Administration, and for 1959, estimates were made from U.S. 1961 Budget. Includes sales to both American and foreign firms.

Business Loans

TABLE I-102

Maritime Administration Insured Construction Loans to American Shipowners, 1954-1959

Year ended December 31	Outstanding	Loans made	Loans repaid or charged off	Net change in outstandings
	(thousands of dollars)			
1954	900	900	--	900
1955	2,025	1,125	--	1,125
1956	3,479	3,704	2,250	1,454
1957	11,627	11,627	3,479	8,148
1958	27,563	53,799	37,863	15,936
1959	42,954	61,328	45,937	15,391

Note: Table I-104 is the total of Tables I-102 and I-103.

Source: Data supplied by Maritime Administration. Assumes that insurance covers 100% of construction loans, as understood from Maritime Administration personnel. The figures given are the M.A. insurance liabilities.

Business Loans

TABLE I-103

Maritime Administration Insured Mortgages on Completed Ships, 1938-1959

Year ended December 31	Outstanding	Loans made	Loans repaid or charged off	Net change in outstandings
	(thousands of dollars)			
1938	162	162	--	162
1939	1,063	901	--	901
1940	2,900	1,837	--	1,837
1941	7,875	4,975	--	4,975
1942	5,036	282	3,121	-2,839
1943	3,036	33	2,033	-2,000
1944	815	--	2,221	-2,221
1945	--	--	815	- 815
1946	--	--	--	--
1947	--	--	--	--
1948	1,200	1,200	--	1,200
1949	2,400	1,200	--	1,200
1950	2,313	--	87	- 87
1951	553	--	1,760	-1,760
1952	446	--	107	- 107
1953	371	--	75	- 75
1954	300	--	71	- 71
1955	176	176	300	- 124
1956	14,514	14,356	18	14,338
1957	36,170	26,153	4,497	21,656
1958	124,061	94,185	6,294	87,891
1959	212,136	97,974	9,899	88,075

Note: Table I-104 is the total of Tables I-102 and I-103.

Source: For 1939-53, Saulnier, et al., p. 393, with interpolations to put on calendar-year basis. For 1954-59, data supplied by Maritime Administration. Assumes that insurance covers 100 percent of each mortgage, as understood from Maritime Administration personnel. The figures given are the M.A. insurance liabilities.

Business Loans

TABLE I-104

Total Insured Loans of the Maritime Administration, 1938-1959

Year ended December 31	Outstanding	Loans made	Loans repaid or charged off	Net change in outstandings
		(thousands of dollars)		
1938	162	162	--	162
1939	1,063	901	--	901
1940	2,900	1,837	--	1,837
1941	7,875	4,975	--	4,975
1942	5,036	282	3,121	- 2,839
1943	3,036	33	2,033	- 2,000
1944	815	--	2,221	- 2,221
1945	--	--	815	- 815
1946	--	--	--	--
1947	--	--	--	--
1948	1,200	1,200	--	1,200
1949	2,400	1,200	--	1,200
1950	2,313	--	87	- 87
1951	553	--	1,760	- 1,760
1952	446	--	107	- 107
1953	371	--	75	- 75
1954	1,200	900	71	829
1955	2,201	1,301	300	1,001
1956	17,993	18,060	2,268	15,792
1957	47,797	37,780	7,976	29,804
1958	151,624	147,984	44,157	103,827
1959	255,090	159,302	55,836	103,466

Note: Table I-104 is the total of Tables I-102 and I-103.

Table I-105 is the total of Tables I-100, I-101, and I-104.

Source: Data supplied by Maritime Administration.

Business Loans

TABLE I-105

Total Insured and Direct Loans of the Maritime Administration, 1929-1959

Year ended December 31	Outstanding	Loans made	Loans repaid or charged off	Net change in outstandings
	(thousands of dollars)			
1929	69,500	13,600		
1930	89,000	24,600	5,100	+19,500
1931	119,500	39,800	9,300	+30,500
1932	148,000	37,700	9,200	+28,500
1933	149,000	13,600	12,600	+ 1,000
1934	133,093	400	16,307	-15,907
1935	111,688	150	21,555	-21,405
1936	97,292	--	14,396	-14,396
1937	85,081	10,000	22,211	-12,211
1938	60,155	162	25,088	-24,926
1939	57,179	1,901	4,877	-2,976
1940	74,105	31,837	14,911	+16,926
1941	70,827	14,975	18,253	- 3,278
1942	73,908	20,282	17,201	+ 3,081
1943	126,816	70,033	17,125	+52,908
1944	101,577	--	25,239	-25,239
1945	111,435	20,000	10,142	+ 9,858
1946	126,356	20,000	5,079	+14,921
1947	317,000	200,000	9,356	+190,644
1948	487,700	181,200	10,500	+170,700
1949	443,900	1,200	45,000	-43,800
1950	432,813	--	11,087	-11,087
1951	428,053	--	4,760	- 4,760
1952	381,446	--	46,607	-46,607
1953	335,371	--	46,075	-46,075
1954	293,823	900	42,448	-41,548
1955	262,860	40,093	71,056	-30,963
1956	294,443	86,873	55,290	+31,583
1957	309,289	62,128	47,282	+14,846
1958	377,933	147,984	79,340	+68,644
1959	454,090	159,302	83,145	+76,157

Note: Table I-105 is the total of Tables I-100, I-101, and I-104.

Source: Data supplied by Maritime Administration.

The Maritime Administration is a part of the U.S. Department of Commerce, and has had this status since 1950 when its predecessor the independent Maritime Commission was abolished. The Administration carries out its functions under a delegation of authority from the Secretary of Commerce. Many of its actions are based on determinations made by the Federal Maritime Board, composed of three members appointed by the President with the advice and consent of the U.S. Senate. The Maritime Administration is the successor to the U.S. Shipping Board, the U.S. Shipping Board Bureau, and the U.S. Maritime Commission.

In addition to insured construction loans on ships being built, the M. A. insures mortgage loans on completed ships. The insurance covers up to 100 percent of the mortgage, but the mortgage may not exceed 75 percent of the cost to the purchaser of vessels built with federal subsidies and 87 1/2 percent of the cost of nonsubsidized vessels. Beginning on October 15, 1958, the M. A. has insured publicly issued merchant marine bonds, and this has been a rapidly expanding part of the program. Prior to this, only privately placed mortgages were insured. The first insured publicly issued bonds were on completed ships, but following enabling legislation passed by Congress on July 31, 1959, they have also been on ships in the process of construction. In case of default, such bonds in some cases are backed by the entire assets of the shipping company, but in the case of certain passenger vessels are backed only by the vessel covered by the mortgage.

The insured loans program was preceded by direct construction loans to American shipowners in the period from 1920 to 1935. Advances and mortgage loans in connection with the sale of government-owned ships also were made by the Maritime Administration and its predecessors, beginning in 1920 and continuing to date.

Direct loans in connection with sales of government-owned ships amounted to $200 million in 1947, $180 million in 1948, $70 million in 1943, and $69 million in 1956 (Table I-101). Year-end outstandings decreased from $486 million at the end of 1948 to $199 million at the end of 1959.

Insured loans have expanded rapidly in recent years. Their annual volume never exceeded $5 million prior to 1956, but was $148 million in 1958 and $159 million in 1959. The division of total insured loans between those for construction and those on completed ships is shown in Tables I-102 and I-103. In 1959, year-end outstandings were about five times as large for insured loans on completed ships as for construction loans. Under present law, the ceiling on the unpaid balance of insured loans outstanding is $1 billion.

Civil Aeronautics Board (Tables I-106 to I-108)

The Civil Aeronautics Board guarantees loans by private lending institutions to local service and other small airlines for the purchase of aircraft. The CAB loans are administered by the Bureau of Air Operations of the CAB. The purpose of such loans is to promote the development of local, feeder, and shorthaul air transportation in the United States. Loans are insured against loss of interest and 90 percent of principal, up to a total of $5 million per airline. Loans must be repaid within ten years. A guarantee fee of three-eights of 1 percent of the guaranteed unpaid principal has been charged borrowers since December 16, 1958; prior to that date, a variable fee was charged.

Total loans in 1958 were $15 million (Table I-106). A smaller amount, $10 million, was loaned in 1959. The division of total loans into their guaranteed and non-guaranteed shares is shown in Tables I-107 and I-108. The outstandings of the guaranteed share at the end of 1959 were $22 million.

Inland Waterways Corporation (Table I-109)

The Inland Waterways Corporation made loans to states, municipalities, and transportation companies for the construction of terminal facilities. The first and largest loans were made in 1921, and the last loan in 1935. The purpose of the IWC loans was to improve the transportation facilities of the United States. Funds for loans were obtained from the U.S. Treasury, and repayments and liquid assets turned over to the Treasury when operations ceased.

Except for a mortgage received in connection with the sale of its property and operating equipment, the unpaid balance of which was $9 million in 1953, total loans in the 1929-58 period were less than $500,000 (Table I-109). Outstandings were $7 million at the end of 1958.

Defense Loans (Tables I-110 to I-125)

Federal loan guarantees and direct lending to firms producing war or defense materials are for the purpose of obtaining military supplies sooner and in larger quantity than would otherwise occur. Loans are primarily for working capital of defense contractors whose output is sold to the federal government. Secondarily, they are for expansion of defense facilities. Under the Defense Production Act of 1950, guarantees of loans by public or private financing institutions to defense contractors or subcontractors are authorized by one of several designated departments of the U.S. Government. More than 90 percent of the authorizations have been by the Air Force, the Army, and the Navy. The Federal Reserve banks act as fiscal agents. Procedures are governed by Regulation V of the

Business Loans

TABLE I-106

Civil Aeronautics Board Guaranteed Loans to Airlines, 1958-1959

Year ended December 31	Outstanding	Loans made	Loans repaid or charged off	Net change in outstandings
	(thousands of dollars)			
1958	14,788	14,806	18	14,788
1959	23,947	10,304	1,145	9,159

Note: Table I-106 is the total of Tables I-107 and I-108.

Source: Data were obtained from Civil Aeronautics Board.

TABLE I-107

Civil Aeronautics Board Guaranteed Loans to Airlines, Guaranteed Share, 1958-1959

Year ended December 31	Outstanding	Loans made	Loans repaid or charged off	Net change in outstandings
	(thousands of dollars)			
1958	13,309	13,325	16	13,309
1959	21,552	9,274	1,031	8,243

Note: Table I-106 is the total of Tables I-107 and I-108.

Source: Data were obtained from Civil Aeronautics Board.

Business Loans

TABLE I-108

Civil Aeronautics Board Guaranteed Loans to Airlines, Non-Guaranteed Share, 1958-1959

Year ended December 31	Outstanding	Loans made	Loans repaid or charged off	Net change in outstandings
		(thousands of dollars)		
1958	1,479	1,481	2	1,479
1959	2,395	1,030	114	916

Note: Table I-106 is the total of Tables I-107 and I-108.

Source: Data were obtained from Civil Aeornautics Board.

TABLE I-109

Direct Loans of the Inland Waterways Corporation, 1929-1958

Year ended December 31	Outstanding	Loans made	Loans repaid or charged off	Net change in outstandings
		(thousands of dollars)		
1929	828	65		
1930	793	14	49	-35
1931	731	---	62	-62
1932	643	---	88	-88
1933	618	---	25	-25
1934	594	---	24	-24
1935	604	38	28	10
1936	576	---	28	-28
1937	547	---	29	-29
1938	514	---	33	-33
1939	456	---	58	-58
1940	435	---	21	-21
1941	409	---	26	-26
1942	390	---	19	-19
1943	363	---	27	-27
1944	343	---	20	-20
1945	312	---	31	-31
1946	264	---	48	-48
1947	224	---	40	-40
1948	189	---	35	-35
1949	271	226	144	82
1950	219	27	79	-52
1951	185	29	63	-34
1952	109	---	76	-76
1953	9,073	9,000	36	8,964
1954	8,608	---	465	-465
1955	8,196	---	412	-412
1956	7,779	---	417	-417
1957	7,369	---	410	-410
1958	6,967	---	402	-402

Source: Data supplied by Treasury Department. In 1931-34, data were not available on loans made, and it was estimated that the volume was zero.

Business Loans

TABLE I-110

Guaranteed Loans under Section 301 of the Defense Production Act of 1950 and Regulation V of the Federal Reserve Board, Total Amounts, 1950-1959

Year ended December 31	Outstanding	Loans made	Loans repaid or charged off	Net change in outstandings
		(thousands of dollars)		
1950	8,000	8,000	--	8,000
1951	675,000	1,463,000	796,000	667,000
1952	979,000	2,882,000	2,578,000	304,000
1953	805,000	2,413,000	2,587,000	- 174,000
1954	472,000	1,562,000	1,895,000	- 333,000
1955	294,000	932,000	1,110,000	- 178,000
1956	389,000	1,122,000	1,027,000	95,000
1957	395,000	1,085,000	1,079,000	6,000
1958	310,000	728,000	813,000	- 85,000
1959	340,000	1,147,000	1,117,000	30,000

Note: Table I-110 is the total of Tables I-111 and I-112.
Table I-123 is the total of Tables I-110 and I-118.

Source: Data supplied by Federal Reserve Bank. The figures shown cover loans made by private financing institutions and guaranteed by one of the departments and agencies authorized to guarantee defense production loans. These are the Departments of the Army, Navy, and Air Force; the Atomic Energy Commission; the Departments of Commerce, Interior, and Agriculture; and General Services Administration. (Note: The National Aeronautics and Space Administration was authorized as a guaranteeing agency in 1959). The Departments of the Interior and Agriculture have not been active in the program, however, and have not guaranteed any loans.

Business Loans

TABLE I-111

Guaranteed Loans under Section 301 of the Defense Production Act of 1950 and Regulation V of the Federal Reserve Board, Guaranteed Part, 1950-1959

Year ended December 31	Outstanding	Loans made a/	Loans repaid or charged off b/	Net change in outstandings
		(thousands of dollars)		
1950	6,000	6,000	--	6,000
1951	547,000	1,186,000	645,000	541,000
1952	803,000	2,364,000	2,108,000	256,000
1953	666,000	1,996,000	2,133,000	- 137,000
1954	368,000	1,218,000	1,516,000	- 298,000
1955	226,000	716,000	858,000	- 142,000
1956	289,000	834,000	771,000	63,000
1957	300,000	824,000	813,000	11,000
1958	236,000	554,000	618,000	- 64,000
1959	256,000	864,000	844,000	20,000

[a]Data were derived from applying ratio of guaranteed outstandings to total outstandings to the total loans made, using data in Table I-110.

[b]Data were derived as a balancing item.

Note: Table I-110 is the total of Tables I-111 and I-112.

Source: Data supplied by Federal Reserve Bank.

Business Loans

TABLE I-112

Guaranteed Loans under Section 301 of the Defense Production Act of 1950 and Regulation V of the Federal Reserve Board, Non-Guaranteed Part, 1950-1959

Year ended December 31	Outstanding	Loans made	Loans repaid or charged off	Net change in outstandings
	(thousands of dollars)			
1950	2,000	2,000	--	2,000
1951	128,000	277,000	151,000	126,000
1952	176,000	518,000	470,000	48,000
1953	139,000	417,000	454,000	- 37,000
1954	104,000	344,000	379,000	- 35,000
1955	68,000	216,000	252,000	- 36,000
1956	100,000	288,000	256,000	32,000
1957	95,000	261,000	266,000	- 5,000
1958	74,000	174,000	195,000	- 21,000
1959	84,000	283,000	273,000	10,000

Note: Table I-110 is the total of Tables I-111 and I-112.

Source: This table was derived by subtracting Table I-111 from table I-110.

TABLE I-113

Direct Loans under Section 302 of the Defense Production Act of 1950, 1951-1959

Year ended December 31	Outstanding	Loans made	Loans repaid or charged off	Net change in outstandings
	(thousands of dollars)			
1951	27,667	31,441	3,774	27,667
1952	88,842	68,076	6,901	61,175
1953	146,828	74,974	16,988	57,986
1954	162,624	50,040	34,244	15,796
1955	185,784	41,688	18,528	23,160
1956	178,562	4,415	11,637	-7,222
1957	177,511	3,556	4,607	-1,051
1958	176,277	6,000	7,234	-1,234
1959	169,948	---	6,329	-6,329

Note: Table I-124 is the total of Tables I-113, I-114, I-117, I-121, and I-122.

Source: Data furnished by Treasury Department.

Business Loans

TABLE I-114

Participation Loans under Section 302 of the Defense Production Act of 1950, 1951-1959

Year ended December 31	Outstanding	Loans made	Loans repaid or charged off	Net change in outstandings
	(thousands of dollars)			
1951	160	160	---	160
1952	566	430	24	406
1953	2,056	1,800	310	1,490
1954	17,430	21,888	6,514	15,374
1955	22,489	11,633	6,574	5,059
1956	21,673	6,462	7,278	- 816
1957	20,081	---	1,592	-1,592
1958	18,929	850	2,002	-1,152
1959	16,698	---	2,231	-2,231

Note: Table I-114 is the total of Tables I-115 and I-116.
Table I-124 is the total of Tables I-113, I-114, I-117, I-121, and I-122.

Source: Data supplied by Treasury Department.

TABLE I-115

Government Part of Participation Loans under Section 302 of the Defense Production Act of 1950, 1951-1959

Year ended December 31	Outstanding	Loans made	Loans repaid or charged off	Net change in outstandings
	(thousands of dollars)			
1951	112	112	---	112
1952	351	263	24	239
1953	1,625	1,470	196	1,274
1954	15,688	19,588	5,525	14,063
1955	19,778	9,865	5,775	4,090
1956	19,542	5,816	6,052	- 236
1957	18,118	---	1,424	-1,424
1958	17,078	765	1,805	-1,040
1959	15,067	---	2,011	-2,011

Note: Table I-114 is the total of Tables I-115 and I-116.

Source: Data supplied by Treasury Department.

Business Loans

TABLE I-116

Private Part of Participation Loans under Section 302 of the Defense Production Act of 1950, 1951-1959

Year ended December 31	Outstanding	Loans made	Loans repaid or charged off	Net change in outstandings
	(thousands of dollars)			
1951	48	48	--	48
1952	215	167	--	167
1953	431	330	114	216
1954	1,742	2,300	989	1,311
1955	2,711	1,768	799	969
1956	2,131	646	1,226	- 580
1957	1,963	--	168	- 168
1958	1,851	85	197	- 112
1959	1,631	--	220	- 220

Note: Table I-114 is the total of Tables I-115 and I-116.

Source: Data supplied by Treasury Department.

TABLE I-117

Direct Advances of the General Services Administration under Section 303 of the Defense Production Act of 1950, 1951-1959

Year ended December 31	Outstanding	Loans made	Loans repaid or charged off	Net change in outstandings
	(thousands of dollars)			
1951	28,660	28,660	--	28,660
1952	54,797	55,143	29,006	26,137
1953	72,483	44,850	27,164	17,686
1954	90,165	31,699	14,017	17,682
1955	76,952	16,789	30,002	-13,213
1956	63,196	11,491	25,247	-13,756
1957	53,710	14,693	24,179	-9,486
1958	15,114	18,092	56,688	-38,596
1959	8,684	12,900	19,330	-6,430

Note: Table I-124 is the total of Tables I-113, I-114, I-117, I-121, and I-122.

Source: Data furnished by General Services Administration.

Business Loans

TABLE I-118

World War II Guaranteed Loans under Regulation V, Total Amounts, 1942-1949

Year ended December 31	Outstanding	Loans made	Loans repaid or charged off	Net Change in outstandings
		(thousands of dollars)		
1942	804,000	1,134,000	330,000	804,000
1943	1,914,000	4,940,000	3,830,000	1,110,000
1944	1,736,000	4,044,000	4,222,000	- 178,000
1945	511,000	2,103,000	3,328,000	-1,225,000
1946	19,000	99,000	591,000	- 492,000
1947	2,000	6,000	23,000	- 17,000
1948	1,000	--	1,000	- 1,000
1949	--	--	1,000	- 1,000

Note: Table I-118 is the total of Tables I-119 and I-120.
Table I-123 is the total of Tables I-110 and I-118.

Source: Data supplied by Federal Reserve Bank. No loans under the World War II guaranteed loan program were authorized after May 1946. Advances subsequent thereto were on loans previously authorized, and balances outstanding were gradually reduced. Data (in thousands of dollars) were published in the Federal Reserve Bulletin table entitled "War Production Loans Guaranteed by War Department, Navy Department, and Maritime Commission Through Federal Reserve Banks under Regulation V." The last figures published were for March 31, 1949 (May 1949 Federal Reserve Bulletin) when loans outstanding were $873 thousand and the guaranteed portion $801 thousand.

Business Loans

TABLE I-119

World War II Guaranteed Loans under Regulation V, Guaranteed Part, 1942-1949

Year ended December 31	Outstanding	Loans made [a]	Loans repaid or charged off [b]	Net change in outstandings
		(thousands of dollars)		
1942	632,000	891,000	259,000	632,000
1943	1,602,000	4,135,000	3,165,000	970,000
1944	1,482,000	3,452,000	3,572,000	- 120,000
1945	436,000	1,794,000	2,840,000	- 1,046,000
1946	17,000	89,000	508,000	- 419,000
1947	2,000	--	15,000	- 15,000
1948	1,000	--	1,000	- 1,000
1949	--	--	1,000	- 1,000

[a]Data were derived from applying ratio of guaranteed outstandings to total outstandings to the total loans made, using data in Table I-118.
[b]Data were derived as a balancing item.

Note: Table I-118 is the total of Tables I-119 and I-120.

Source: Data supplied by Federal Reserve Bank.

Business Loans

TABLE I-120

World War II Guaranteed Loans under Regulation V, Non-Guaranteed Part, 1942-1949

Year ended December 31	Outstanding	Loans made	Loans repaid or charged off	Net change in outstandings
		(thousands of dollars)		
1942	172,000	243,000	71,000	172,000
1943	312,000	805,000	665,000	140,000
1944	254,000	592,000	650,000	- 58,000
1945	75,000	309,000	488,000	- 179,000
1946	2,000	10,000	83,000	- 73,000
1947	--	6,000	8,000	- 2,000
1948	--	--	--	--
1949	--	--	--	--

Note: Table I-118 is the total of Tables I-119 and I-120.

Source: This table was derived by subtracting Table I-119 from Table I-118.

Business Loans

TABLE I-121

Direct Loans of the Smaller War Plants Corporation, 1942-1958

Year ended December 31	Outstanding	Loans made	Loans repaid or charged off	Net change in outstandings
	(thousands of dollars)			
1942	774	3,090	2,316	774
1943	14,519	46,686	32,941	13,745
1944	35,756	167,767	146,530	21,237
1945	28,500	120,794	128,050	-7,256
1946	21,336	12,183	19,347	-7,164
1947	13,756	--	7,580	-7,580
1948	7,550	--	6,206	-6,206
1949	4,442	172	3,280	-3,108
1950	2,920	97	1,619	-1,522
1951	2,203	--	717	- 717
1952	1,801	--	402	- 402
1953	1,340	--	461	- 461
1954	1,068	--	272	- 272
1955	1,014	--	54	- 54
1956	918	--	96	- 96
1957	800	--	118	- 118
1958	700	--	100	- 100

Note: Table I-124 is the total of Tables I-113, I-114, I-117, I-121, and I-122.

Source: Saulnier, et al., p. 414, for 1942-45 data on outstandings, and 1942-46 data on loans made. Treasury Department, for remaining data, with estimates for 1957 and 1958 following transfer of accounts to GSA on July 1, 1957. Fiscal year data have been interpolated to obtain calendar year data. Includes government share of immediate participations, and deferred participations purchased.

Business Loans

TABLE I-122

Direct Loans to War Contractors by the War Department in 1943-1945, and Purchases by the Department of Defense of Principal Balances of Loans Guaranteed by the Army and Navy, 1942-1958

Year ended December 31	Outstanding	Loans made[a]	Loans repaid or charged off	Net change in outstandings
	(thousands of dollars)			
1942	118	124	6	118
1943	9,769	10,603	952	9,651
1944	39,582	42,618	12,805	29,813
1945	14,526	5,390	30,446	-25,056
1946	6,219	4,409	12,716	- 8,307
1947	5,417	2,292	3,094	- 802
1948	4,867	6	556	- 550
1949	4,451	-	416	- 416
1950	4,335	-	116	- 116
1951	11,988	8,050	397	7,653
1952	12,599	7,342	6,731	611
1953	11,214	3,134	4,519	- 1,385
1954	2,879	1,573	9,908	- 8,335
1955	5,238	4,439	2,080	2,359
1956	6,367	3,777	2,648	1,129
1957	14,490	9,415	1,292	8,123
1958	8,090	12,252	18,652	- 6,400

[a]Includes purchases of V loans of World War II, and Section 301 loans of Defense Production Act of 1950.

Note: Table I-124 is the total of Tables I-113, I-114, I-117, I-121, and I-122.

Source: 1942-53, Saulnier, et al., p. 417, Columns 1 and 3.
1954-58, Department of Defense.

Business Loans

TABLE I-123

Total Guaranteed Loans for the Expansion of Defense Production, 1942-1959

Year ended December 31	Outstanding	Loans made	Loans repaid or charged off	Net change in outstandings
		(thousands of dollars)		
1942	804,000	1,134,000	330,000	804,000
1943	1,914,000	4,940,000	3,830,000	1,110,000
1944	1,736,000	4,044,000	4,222,000	- 178,000
1945	511,000	2,103,000	3,328,000	-1,225,000
1946	19,000	99,000	591,000	- 492,000
1947	2,000	6,000	23,000	- 17,000
1948	1,000	--	1,000	- 1,000
1949	--	--	1,000	- 1,000
1950	8,000	8,000	--	8,000
1951	675,000	1,463,000	796,000	667,000
1952	979,000	2,882,000	2,578,000	304,000
1953	805,000	2,413,000	2,587,000	- 174,000
1954	472,000	1,562,000	1,895,000	- 333,000
1955	294,000	932,000	1,110,000	- 178,000
1956	389,000	1,122,000	1,027,000	95,000
1957	395,000	1,085,000	1,079,000	6,000
1958	310,000	728,000	813,000	- 85,000
1959	340,000	1,147,000	1,117,000	30,000

Note: Table I-123 is the total of Tables I-110 and I-118.
Table I-125 is the total of Tables I-123 and I-124.

Source: See Tables I-110 and I-118.

Business Loans

TABLE I-124

Total Direct and Participation Loans for the Expansion of Defense Production, 1942-1958

Year ended December 31	Outstanding	Loans made	Loans repaid or charged off	Net change in outstandings
		(thousands of dollars)		
1942	892	3,214	2,322	892
1943	24,288	57,289	33,893	23,396
1944	75,338	210,385	159,335	51,050
1945	43,026	126,184	158,496	-32,312
1946	27,555	16,592	32,063	-15,471
1947	19,173	2,292	10,674	- 8,382
1948	12,417	6	6,762	- 6,756
1949	8,893	172	3,696	- 3,524
1950	7,255	97	1,735	- 1,638
1951	70,678	68,311	4,888	63,423
1952	158,605	130,991	43,064	87,927
1953	233,921	124,758	49,442	75,316
1954	274,166	105,200	64,955	40,245
1955	291,477	74,549	57,238	17,311
1956	270,716	26,145	46,906	-20,761
1957	266,592	27,664	31,788	- 4,124
1958	219,110	37,194	84,676	-47,482

Note: Table I-124 is the total of Tables I-113, I-114, I-117, I-121, and I-122.
Table I-125 is the total of Tables I-123 and I-124.

Source: See Tables I-113, I-114, I-117, I-121, and I-122.

Business Loans

TABLE I-125

Total Loans under Federal Lending Programs for the Expansion of Defense Production, 1942-1958

Year ended December 31	Outstanding	Loans made	Loans repaid or charged off	Net change in outstandings
	(thousands of dollars)			
1942	804,892	1,137,214	332,322	804,892
1943	1,938,288	4,997,289	3,863,893	1,133,396
1944	1,811,338	4,254,385	4,381,335	- 126,950
1945	554,026	2,229,184	3,486,496	-1,257,312
1946	46,555	115,592	623,063	- 507,471
1947	21,173	8,292	33,674	- 25,382
1948	13,417	6	7,762	- 7,756
1949	8,893	172	4,696	- 4,524
1950	15,255	8,097	1,735	6,362
1951	745,678	1,531,311	800,888	730,423
1952	1,137,605	3,012,991	2,621,064	391,927
1953	1,038,921	2,537,758	2,636,442	- 98,684
1954	746,166	1,667,170	1,959,925	- 292,755
1955	585,477	1,006,549	1,167,238	- 160,689
1956	659,716	1,148,145	1,073,906	74,239
1957	661,592	1,112,664	1,110,788	1,876
1958	529,110	765,194	897,676	- 132,482

Note: Table I-125 is the total of Tables I-123 and I-124.

Federal Reserve Board. Direct loans are made for the expansion of industrial capacity, development of technological processes, or the production of essential materials by the U.S. Treasury under authorization by one of four departments of U.S. Government. The General Services Administration also makes direct loans on purchase commitments for strategic minerals, metals, and industrial equipment. Funds for direct loans come from the department or agency making them.

Most of the loans under the Defense Production Act of 1950 have been guaranteed loans to defense contractors who are relatively small and cannot obtain credit from regular channels at reasonable cost, or who are growing rapidly and have large credit needs relative to assets, and who sell their output to the federal government for military purposes. Under the loan guarantee program, charges are made for guarantees to cover administrative expenses and possible losses. The rate of charge depends on the percentage of the loan guaranteed, which has averaged about 75 percent in the past few years. Upon the request of the lender, the guaranteed part of the loan must be purchased by the procurement agency.

Most important of the predecessors in defense loans was the V-loan program of World War II, with loans made over a six-year period, 1942-47. The administrative set-up was similar to that for V-loans under the Defense Production Act of 1950, except that only the armed forces and the U.S. Maritime Commission could authorize guarantee of loans. Another predecessor was the Smaller War Plants Corporation of World War II, making direct loans to small business concerns engaged in the production of war and essential civilian goods. The War Department also made direct loans to war contractors in 1943-45.

Total loans under federal lending programs for the expansion of defense production were as large as $5.0 billion in 1943, $4.3 billion in 1944, and $3.0 billion in 1952 (Table I-125). In 1958, they were $0.8 billion. Year-end outstandings have been small relative to loans made, reflecting the short life-time of many such loans, and were only $0.5 billion in 1958.

The two parts of defense loans, guaranteed loans and direct or participation loans, are shown in Tables I-123 and I-124. Guaranteed loans exceeded direct loans by about 20 times.

The World War II guaranteed loans are shown in Table I-118, and those since 1950 in Table I-110. The World War II volume of loans exceeded $12 billion, and had all been repaid or charged off by the end of 1949. The 1950-59 volume exceeded $13 billion, and outstandings at the end of 1959 were $0.3 billion. These loans are divided into their guaranteed and non-guaranteed shares in Tables

I-119 and I-120, for World War II loans, and in Tables I-111 and I-112, for 1950-59 loans. The guaranteed share was by far the largest part under both programs.

The details of the direct and participation loans for the expansion of defense production appear in the data on their six parts in Tables I-113, I-114, I-117, I-121, and I-122.

Federal Reserve Banks Industrial Loans (Tables I-126 to I-130)

The Federal Reserve banks made loans, and participations in loans, to industrial and commercial businesses for working capital during the period from 1934 through 1958. Most loans were to small business firms. The intent was to meet the intermediate credit needs of small businesses in financial difficulty and, originally, to alleviate the effects of the depression. At the hearings preceding authorization of such loans, it was indicated that the RFC, with parallel puproses in many respects, had not succeeded in helping small businesses. The program was terminated by the Small Business Investment Act signed by the President on August 24, 1958. SBA loans of types authorized by this and prior legislation were intended to take the place of FRB industrial loans.

From 1934 to its termination in 1958, the FRB industrial loans numbered 3,787. About one-half were made as direct loans, and one-half in cooperation with banks and other financial institutions as guarantees of participation loans. In participation loans, the guarantee averaged about 50 percent of the amount of the loan. Fees on participation loans ranged from 1/2 percent to 2 percent. Maturities of direct and participation loans were not in excess of five years. Their average size was $175,000. Funds for direct loans came partly from advances from the U.S. Treasury, and partly from the FRB's themselves. Funds for participation loans came from private lending agencies.

Industrial loans and participations of Federal Reserve banks were largest in 1942 and 1943, with total loans for the two years of $217 million (Table I-130). In their year of greatest volume, 1942, the $126 million of loans was made up of $68 million direct loans and $58 million participation loans (Tables I-126 and I-129).

Virgin Islands Corporation (Table I-131)

Loans to aid agricultural and business enterprises in the Virgin Islands were made between 1949 and 1958 by the Virgin Islands Corporation. The program was administered within the Division of Insular Affairs of the U.S. Department of Interior. The program has been of minor significance. Over one-half of total loans were made in the one year of 1956, $208,000. Outstandings at the end of 1958 were $157,000.

Business Loans

TABLE I-126

Industrial Loans of Federal Reserve Banks, 1934-1959[a]

Year ended December 31	Outstanding	Loans made	Loans repaid or charged off	Net change in outstanding
	(thousands of dollars)			
1934	13,589	14,884	1,295	13,589
1935	32,493	28,479	9,575	18,904
1936	25,526	8,519	15,486	-6,967
1937	20,216	4,932	10,242	-5,310
1938	17,345	6,500	9,371	-2,871
1939	13,683	3,805	7,467	-3,662
1940	9,152	2,860	7,391	-4,531
1941	10,337	15,695	14,510	1,185
1942	14,126	68,032	64,243	3,789
1943	10,532	60,265	63,859	-3,594
1944	3,894	20,381	27,019	-6,638
1945	1,995	14,043	15,942	-1,899
1946	554	3,445	4,886	-1,441
1947	1,387	9,296	8,463	833
1948	995	15,994	16,386	-392
1949	2,178	4,005	2,822	1,183
1950	2,632	6,530	6,076	454
1951	4,687	27,656	25,601	2,055
1952	3,921	31,193	31,959	-766
1953	1,900	22,009	24,030	-2,021
1954	719	7,477	8,658	-1,181
1955	702	2,901	2,918	-17
1956	794	2,846	2,754	92
1957	524	3,333	3,603	-270
1958	335	948	1,137	-189
1959	--	--	335	-335

[a]Includes (1) loans made "directly" to borrowers, i.e., those in which no commercial bank or other financing institution took part, and (2) loans in which commercial banks or other financing institutions participated, either originally or on a deferred participation basis. The figures shown are for Federal Reserve Bank disbursements and loans outstanding, and do not include FRB commitments or private financing institutions' participations.

Note: Table I-130 is the total of Tables I-126 and I-129.

Source: Data supplied by Federal Reserve Bank.

Business Loans

TABLE I-127

Commitments to Make Industrial Loans by Federal Reserve Banks, 1934-1959[a]

Year ended December 31	Outstanding	Commitments made	Commitments cancelled used, or expired	Net change in outstandings
		(thousands of dollars)		
1934	8,225	11,443	3,218	8,225
1935	27,649	29,223	9,799	19,424
1936	20,959	12,283	18,973	-6,690
1937	12,780	6,978	15,157	-8,179
1938	14,161	11,217	9,836	1,381
1939	9,220	4,621	9,562	-4,941
1940	5,226	4,374	8,368	-3,994
1941	14,597	19,530	10,159	9,371
1942	10,661	22,207	26,143	-3,936
1943	9,270	10,221	11,612	-1,391
1944	4,165	4,769	9,874	-5,105
1945	1,644	2,350	4,871	-2,521
1946	8,309	8,845	2,180	6,665
1947	7,434	6,069	6,944	-875
1948	1,643	2,187	7,978	-5,791
1949	2,288	4,130	3,485	645
1950	3,754	4,019	2,553	1,466
1951	6,036	9,078	6,796	2,282
1952	3,210	3,468	6,294	-2,826
1953	3,569	980	621	359
1954	1,148	510	2,931	-2,421
1955	2,293	2,412	1,267	1,145
1956	2,365	630	558	72
1957	1,109	1,035	2,291	-1,256
1958	975	--	134	-134
1959	--	--	975	-975

[a]These commitments were almost all "deferred participations," with the private financing institution advancing the money but the FRB being responsible for the part given above. Data on the private financing institution's part of such loans appear in Table I-128.

Note: Table I-129 is the total of Tables I-127 and I-128.

Source: Data supplied by Federal Reserve Bank. Prior to 1940 the year-end figure was for the last Wednesday, which may not have been the last day of the year. The dates were: 1934-December 26; 1935-December 31; 1936-December 30; 1937-December 29; 1938-December 28; and 1939-December 27.

Business Loans

TABLE I-128

Participations of Private Financing Institutions in Industrial Loans of Federal Reserve Banks, 1934-1959

Year ended December 31	Outstanding	Loans made [a]	Loans repaid or charged off [b]	Net change in outstandings
		(thousands of dollars)		
1934	1,296	1,803	507	1,296
1935	8,775	9,277	1,798	7,479
1936	7,208	4,225	5,792	-1,567
1937	7,238	3,952	3,922	30
1938	12,722	10,077	4,593	5,484
1939	10,981	5,503	7,244	-1,741
1940	6,386	5,344	9,939	-4,595
1941	19,600	26,224	13,010	13,214
1942	17,305	36,046	38,341	-2,295
1943	17,930	19,770	19,145	625
1944	2,705	3,097	18,322	-15,225
1945	1,086	1,552	3,171	-1,619
1946	2,670	2,842	1,258	1,584
1947	4,869	3,975	1,776	2,199
1948	1,990	2,650	5,529	-2,879
1949	2,947	5,319	4,362	957
1950	3,745	4,009	3,211	798
1951	11,985	18,025	9,785	8,240
1952	3,289	3,554	12,250	-8,696
1953	3,469	952	772	180
1954	1,027	459	2,901	-2,442
1955	1,103	1,160	1,084	76
1956	1,129	300	274	26
1957	1,122	1,048	1,055	-7
1958	806	826	1,142	-316
1959	--	--	806	-806

[a] Obtained by applying to outstandings in this table the ratio of commitments made to outstandings in Table I-127.
[b] Obtained by the difference required as a balancing item.

Note: Table I-129 is the total of Tables I-127 and I-128.

Source: Data supplied by Federal Reserve Bank. Prior to 1940 the year-end figure was for the last Wednesday, which may not have been the last day of the year. The dates were: 1934-December 26; 1935-December 31; 1936-December 30; 1937-December 29; 1938-December 28; and 1939-December 27.

Business Loans

TABLE I-129

Total Participation Loans under Industrial Loan Program of Federal Reserve Banks, 1934-1959

Year ended December 31	Outstanding	Loans made	Loans repaid or charged off	Net change in outstandings
	(thousands of dollars)			
1934	9,521	13,246	3,725	9,521
1935	36,424	38,500	11,597	26,903
1936	28,167	16,508	24,765	- 8,257
1937	20,018	10,930	19,079	- 8,149
1938	26,883	21,294	14,429	6,865
1939	20,201	10,124	16,806	- 6,682
1940	11,612	9,718	18,307	- 8,589
1941	34,197	45,754	23,169	22,585
1942	27,966	58,253	64,484	- 6,231
1943	27,200	29,991	30,757	- 766
1944	6,870	7,866	28,196	-20,330
1945	2,730	3,902	8,042	- 4,140
1946	10,979	11,687	3,438	8,249
1947	12,303	10,044	8,720	1,324
1948	3,633	4,837	13,507	- 8,670
1949	5,235	9,449	7,847	1,602
1950	7,499	8,028	5,764	2,264
1951	18,021	27,103	16,581	10,522
1952	6,499	7,022	18,544	-11,522
1953	7,038	1,932	1,393	539
1954	2,175	969	5,832	- 4,863
1955	3,396	3,572	2,351	1,221
1956	3,494	930	832	98
1957	2,231	2,083	3,346	- 1,263
1958	1,781	826	1,276	- 450
1959	-	-	1,781	- 1,781

Note: Table I-129 is the total of Tables I-127 and I-128.
Table I-130 is the total of Tables I-26 and I-129.

Source: Data supplied by Federal Reserve Banks.

Business Loans

TABLE I-130

Total Loans under Industrial Loan Program of Federal Reserve Banks, 1934-1959

Year ended December 31	Outstanding	Loans made	Loans repaid or charged off	Net change in outstandings
	(thousands of dollars)			
1934	23,110	28,130	5,020	23,110
1935	68,917	66,979	21,172	45,807
1936	53,693	25,027	40,251	-15,224
1937	40,234	15,862	29,321	-13,459
1938	44,228	27,794	23,800	3,994
1939	33,884	13,929	24,273	-10,344
1940	20,764	12,578	25,698	-13,120
1941	44,534	61,449	37,679	23,770
1942	42,092	126,285	128,727	- 2,442
1943	37,732	90,256	94,616	- 4,360
1944	10,764	28,247	55,215	-26,968
1945	4,725	17,945	23,984	- 6,039
1946	11,533	15,132	8,324	6,808
1947	13,690	19,340	17,183	2,157
1948	4,628	20,831	29,893	- 9,062
1949	7,413	13,454	10,669	2,785
1950	10,131	14,558	11,840	2,718
1951	22,708	54,759	42,182	12,577
1952	10,420	38,215	50,503	-12,288
1953	8,938	23,941	25,423	- 1,482
1954	2,894	8,446	14,490	- 6,044
1955	4,093	6,473	5,269	1,204
1956	4,288	3,776	3,586	190
1957	2,755	5,416	6,949	- 1,533
1958	2,116	1,774	2,413	- 639
1959	-	-	2,116	- 2,116

Note: Table I-130 is the total of Tables I-126 and I-129.

Source: Data supplied by the Federal Reserve Banks.

Business Loans

TABLE I-131

Direct Business and Agricultural Loans by the Virgin Islands Corporation, 1949-1958

Year ended December 31	Outstanding	Loans made	Loans repaid or charged off	Net change in outstandings
	(thousands of dollars)			
1949	4	4	---	4
1950	14	14	4	10
1951	78	89	25	64
1952	21	27	84	-57
1953	33	29	17	12
1954	21	10	22	-12
1955	21	20	20	---
1956	199	208	30	178
1957	171	4	32	-28
1958	157	7	21	-14

Source: Tabulations supplied by Division of Insular Affairs, U.S. Department of Interior.

Reconstruction Finance Corporation Loans to Financial Institutions (Tables I-132 and I-133)

The Reconstruction Finance Corporation made substantial loans to financial institutions in distress during the 1932-35 period. Smaller and decreasing volumes of such loans were made from 1936 through 1945. These loans were made to a variety of financial institutions in varying degrees of financial liquidity. According to Saulnier, et al, they included banks and trust companies, trustees of closed banks and trust companies, insurance companies, building and loan associations, mortgage loan companies, agricultural and livestock credit corporations, credit unions, and joint stock land banks.

Some loans were made directly to financial institutions of the types listed above, usually secured by notes or mortgages. Others were made in the form of purchases of preferred stock of financial institutions, and of their capital notes and debentures; this type of loan was made to insurance companies, banks, and trust companies.

The direct RFC loans to financial institutions amounted in their peak year, 1932, to $1.1 billion (Table I-132). They were $0.8 billion in 1933, and $0.5 billion in 1934. Stock purchases amounted to $687 million in 1934, and were under $50 million annually in each year after 1935 (Table I-133).

Business Loans

TABLE I-132

Reconstruction Finance Corporation Direct Loans to Financial Institutions, 1932-1955

Year ended December 31	Outstanding	Loans made	Loans repaid or charged off	Net change in outstandings
	(thousands of dollars)			
1932	831,432	1,119,419	287,987	831,432
1933	1,035,208	758,614	554,838	203,776
1934	841,676	460,961	654,493	-193,532
1935	519,518	138,203	460,361	-322,158
1936	322,836	68,207	264,889	-196,682
1937	249,959	41,865	114,742	- 72,877
1938	208,541	30,442	71,860	- 41,418
1939	171,207	15,764	53,098	- 37,334
1940	172,353	45,063	43,917	1,146
1941	117,537	4,640	59,456	- 54,816
1942	111,076	20,097	26,558	- 6,461
1943	80,103	8,409	39,382	- 30,973
1944	29,921	260	50,442	- 50,182
1945	25,418	3,274	7,777	- 4,503
1946	21,841	--	3,577	- 3,577
1947	887	--	20,954	- 20,954
1948	344	--	543	- 543
1949	29	--	315	- 315
1950	27	--	2	- 2
1951	26	--	1	- 1
1952	24	--	2	- 2
1953	24	--	--	--
1954	24	--	--	--
1955	--	--	24	-24

Source: Saulnier, et al., pp. 381-382, for data to 1953; Treasury Dept. supplied data for 1953-55.

Business Loans

TABLE I-133

Reconstruction Finance Corporation Stock Purchases in Financial Institutions, 1933-1958

Year ended December 31	Outstanding	Purchases of preferred stock	Redemption of stock	Net change in outstandings
		(thousands of dollars)		
1933	268,564	268,722	158	268,564
1934	882,717	687,009	72,856	614,153
1935	917,168	103,118	68,667	34,451
1936	693,651	26,294	249,811	-223,517
1937	593,622	17,379	117,408	-100,029
1938	571,070	30,868	53,420	- 22,552
1939	521,657	23,516	72,929	- 49,413
1940	505,326	44,257	60,588	- 16,331
1941	448,661	1,786	58,451	- 56,665
1942	422,109	13,921	40,473	- 26,552
1943	389,539	563	33,133	- 32,570
1944	336,192	16	53,363	- 53,347
1945	284,422	269	52,039	- 51,770
1946	190,189	--	94,233	- 94,233
1947	151,817	5,000	43,372	- 38,372
1948	128,566	--	23,251	- 23,251
1949	114,362	3,000	17,204	- 14,204
1950	102,557	--	11,805	- 11,805
1951	84,344	--	18,213	- 18,213
1952	46,776	--	37,568	- 37,568
1953	41,539	--	5,237	- 5,237
1954	20,497	--	21,042	- 21,042
1955	4,927	--	15,570	- 15,570
1956	4,779	--	148	- 148
1957	4,779	--	--	--
1958	--	--	4,779	- 4,779

Source: Saulnier, et al., pp. 381-382, to 1953; Treasury Dept., 1953-58. Covers loans on, and subscriptions for, preferred stock of insurance companies and of banks and trust companies; and purchases of capital notes and debentures of banks.

IV. HOUSING LENDING AND LOAN INSURANCE PROGRAMS

Nonexistent in 1929, federal lending for the housing area is now larger than for the other three groups combined. In 1939, the emergency Home Owners' Loan Corporation outstandings were largest, with Federal Housing Administration outstandings a close second. In 1958, outstandings on Veterans' Administration guaranteed and insured housing loans were the greatest, with those for the Federal Housing Administration not far behind.

SUMMARY TABLE I-D

Summary of Housing Loans Outstanding, Eleven Programs, Year End 1929, 1939, 1949, and 1958

Table No.	Program of Housing Loans	1929	1939	1949	1958
			(thousands of dollars)		
I-213	Veterans' Administration	--	--	8,104,173	31,331,569
I-141	Federal Housing Administration	--	2,137,655	9,979,940	26,192,778
I-173	Federal National Mortgage Association	--	146,760	828,354	3,900,953
I-169	Public Housing Administration	--	367,568	756,777	3,520,038
I-219	Federal Home Loan Banks	--	181,313	433,429	1,298,320
I-200	Community Facilities Administration	--	--	51,186	521,131
I-204	Urban Renewal Administration	--	--	--	294,988
I-223	Home Owners' Loan Corporation	--	2,247,169	232,575	--
I-225	RFC Mortgage Company	--	57,377	122,653	--
I-224	Treasury Department	--	39,679	--	--
I-170	Defense Homes Corporation	--	--	--	--
	Total	--	5,177,521	20,509,087	67,059,777
	Subtractions to eliminate double counting:				
I-173	Federal National Mortgage Association	--	146,760	828,354	3,900,953
I-225	RFC Mortgage Company (80% of total)	--	45,902	98,122	--
	Total subtractions	--	192,662	926,476	3,900,953
	Net total	--	4,984,859	19,582,611	63,158,824

Federal Housing Administration (Tables I-134 to I-161)

The Federal Housing Administration, one of the five constituent agencies of the Housing and Home Finance Agency, insures against default (a) the full principal amount of a wide variety of mortgage loans on new and existing housing, and (b) up to 90 percent of the principal amount of unsecured home-improvement loans. Housing mortgage insurance is primarily on one- to four-family houses, but also is provided for rental housing, housing under cooperative ownership, housing for armed services personnel, housing in urban renewal areas, and housing for the relocation of displaced families. The FHA also engages in direct lending to finance sales of acquired property resulting from defaults on insured loans.

The FHA program was a depression measure adopted in 1934. It was intended to bring new methods into home financing that would prevent a repetition of the mortgage collapse of the 1930's. Today, about 17 percent of all outstanding home mortgages are insured by the FHA. Of total new construction, FHA insurance helps finance about one-third. Of new loans for home modernization and repairs, the FHA insures about 40 percent.

The FHA's program is self-supporting. Funds for loans come from private lending agencies. The FHA's income comes primarily from insurance premiums and fees. The FHA issues 20-year debentures in payments of claims when mortgages go into default. These bear a government guarantee as to principal and interest.

The law under which the FHA insures home mortgages provides maximum mortgage amounts for different types of dwellings, maximum interest rates, maximum maturities, and maximum percentages of appraised values that can be covered by the insured mortgage. Advance payment of mortgages without penalty is permitted. Certain physical specifications of the properties carrying insured mortgages must be met. On property improvement loans, a maximum amount, currently $10,000, and a maximum maturity, currently three years, is provided by law.

Some of the early FHA activities have since been discontinued. Direct loans to financial institutions were made only in 1935 and 1936; authority to make such loans was repealed by an amendment to the National Housing Act in April 1936. Short-term insured loans to finance production of prefabricated houses, begun in 1948, were ended in 1955.

Some present FHA activities were added after World War II. The FHA did not insure loans on cooperative housing projects until 1950. It began its program of insurance of mortgages for housing for the elderly in 1957.

Housing Loans

TABLE I-134

Federal Housing Administration Insured Loans under Home Mortgage Programs, 1935-1958

Year ended December 31	Outstanding	Loans made	Loans repaid or charged off	Net change in outstandings
	(thousands of dollars)			
1935[a]	107,300	201,414	94,114	107,300
1936[a]	398,407	366,659	75,552	291,107
1937[a]	781,364	455,093	72,136	382,957
1938[a]	1,362,061	590,288	9,591	580,697
1939	1,755,113	694,764	301,712	393,052
1940	2,349,475	762,084	167,722	594,362
1941	3,030,059	910,770	230,186	680,584
1942	3,742,483	973,271	260,847	712,424
1943	4,060,027	763,097	445,553	317,544
1944	4,189,903	707,363	577,487	129,876
1945	4,077,619	474,245	586,529	-112,284
1946	3,692,323	421,949	807,245	-385,296
1947	3,781,347	894,675	805,651	89,024
1948	5,269,251	2,116,043	628,139	1,487,904
1949	6,905,692	2,209,842	573,401	1,636,441
1950	8,563,312	2,492,367	834,747	1,657,620
1951	9,676,916	1,928,433	814,829	1,113,604
1952	10,770,134	1,942,307	849,089	1,093,218
1953	11,989,743	2,288,626	1,069,017	1,219,609
1954	12,778,803	1,942,266	1,153,206	789,060
1955	14,337,601	3,084,767	1,525,969	1,558,798
1956	15,505,545	2,638,230	1,470,286	1,167,944
1957	16,501,426	2,251,064	1,255,183	995,881
1958	19,725,565	4,551,483	1,327,344	3,224,139

[a]Figures for 1935-38 are interpolations of the following figures for years ended June 30:

	Outstanding	Loans made
1935	11,505	93,882
1936	203,094	308,945
1937	593,720	424,373
1938	969,009	485,813

Note: Table I-138 is the total of Tables I-134 to I-137.

Source: Data supplied by Federal Housing Administration.

Housing Loans

TABLE I-135

Federal Housing Administration Insured Loans under Multiple-Family Project Mortgage Programs, 1935-1958

Year ended December 31	Outstanding	Loans made	Loans repaid or charged off	Net change in outstandings
	(thousands of dollars)			
1935[a]	1,615	2,355	740	1,615
1936[a]	4,375	2,101	-659	2,760
1937[a]	21,419	10,483	-6,561	17,044
1938[a]	66,569	47,638	2,488	45,150
1939	104,935	51,851	13,485	38,366
1940	104,381	12,949	13,503	-554
1941	107,268	13,565	10,678	2,887
1942	124,221	21,215	4,262	16.953
1943	201,751	84,622	7,092	77,530
1944	240,519	56,096	17,328	38,768
1945	237,092	19,817	23,244	-3,427
1946	213,430	13,175	36,837	-23,662
1947	549,218	359,944	24,156	335,788
1948	1,142,331	608,711	15,598	593,113
1949	2,134,251	1,021,230	29,310	991,920
1950	3,218,674	1,156,681	72,258	1,084,423
1951	3,705,610	583,773	96,837	486,936
1952	3,920,034	321,911	107,487	214,424
1953	4,028,294	259,194	150,934	108,260
1954	4,110,528	234,022	151,788	82,234
1955	3,993,738	76,489	193,279	-116,790
1956	3,937,808	130,247	186,177	-55,930
1957	4,365,838	597,348	169,318	428,030
1958	5,031,628	908,671	242,881	665,790

[a]Figures for 1935-38 are interpolations of the following figures for years ended June 30:

	Outstanding
1935	875
1936	2,355
1937	6,395
1938	36,443

Note: Table I-138 is the total of Tables I-134 to I-137.

Source: Data supplied by Federal Housing Administration.

Housing Loans

TABLE I-136

Federal Housing Administration Insured Property Improvement Loans, 1934-1958

ar ended cember 31	Outstanding	Loans made [a/]	Loans repaid or charged off	Net change in outstandings
	(thousands of dollars)			
1934	20,000[b/]	30,451	10,451[b/]	20,000[b/]
1935	150,000[b/]	223,620	93,620[b/]	130,000[b/]
1936	175,000[b/]	246,150	221,150[b/]	25,000[b/]
1937	100,000[b/]	60,382	135,382[b/]	-75,000[b/]
1938	175,000[b/]	160,181	85,181[b/]	75,000[b/]
1939	275,800	207,719	106,919	100,800
1940	342,100	250,949	184,649	66,300
1941	365,600	262,084	238,584	23,500
1942	229,300	140,742	277,042	-136,300
1943	132,600	95,448	192,148	-96,700
1944	111,900	125,223	145,923	-20,700
1945	186,200	189,023	114,723	74,300
1946	332,600	362,743	216,343	146,400
1947	636,900	606,386	302,086	304,300
1948	862,900	698,029	472,029	226,000
1949	918,200	675,350	620,050	55,300
1950	1,003,400	789,639	704,439	85,200
1951	1,085,700	707,070	624,770	82,300
1952	1,228,000	848,327	706,027	142,300
1953	1,506,200	1,334,287[c/]	1,056,087	278,200
1954	1,376,600	890,606	1,020,206	-129,600
1955	1,060,200	645,645	962,045	-316,400
1956	1,070,200	691,992	681,992	10,000
1957	1,131,500	868,568	807,268	61,300
1958	1,299,000	868,443	700,943	167,500

Loans made for 1951-58 reflect net proceeds rather than face amounts. This is in keeping with change in reporting procedures made several years ago by the FHA.

Data were not available and rough estimates were made. For a more detailed estimating procedure see Saulnier, et al., p. 395.

The increase in 1953 loans over 1952 loans insured is due in part to authorization controls which resulted in a tabulation backlog of approximately $200 million as of December 31, 1952.

ote: Table I-138 is the total of Tables I-134 to I-137.
Table I-136 is the total of Tables I-142 and I-143.

urce: The series for loans made was supplied by the Federal Housing Administration. The series for outstandings is from Housing Statistics for 1958, p. 191.

Housing Loans

TABLE I-137

Federal Housing Administration Insured Loans to Finance Production of Prefabricated Houses, 1948-1955

Year ended December 31	Out-standing a/	Loans made	Loans repaid or charged off	Net change in outstandings
	(thousands of dollars)			
1948	1,900	1,900	---	1,900
1949	1,700	1,466	1,666	-200
1950	700	568	1,568	-1,000
1951	300	560	960	-400
1952	200	288	388	-100
1953	200	221	221	---
1954	200	356	356	---
1955	---	36	236	-200

[a]Outstandings rounded to nearest $100 thousand.

Note: Table I-138 is the total of Tables I-134 to I-137.

Source: The series for loans made was supplied by the Federal Housing Administration. Outstandings are from Housing Statistics for 1958, p. 192.

Housing Loans

TABLE I-138

Total Mortgages and Loans Insured by the Federal Housing Administration, 1934-1958

Year ended December 31	Outstanding	Loans made	Loans repaid or charged off	Net change in outstandings
		(thousands of dollars)		
1934	20,000	30,451	10,451	20,000
1935	258,915	427,389	188,474	238,915
1936	577,782	614,910	296,043	318,867
1937	902,783	525,958	200,957	325,001
1938	1,603,630	798,107	97,260	700,847
1939	2,135,848	954,334	422,116	532,218
1940	2,795,956	1,025,982	365,874	660,108
1941	3,502,927	1,186,419	479,448	706,971
1942	4,096,004	1,135,228	542,151	593,077
1943	4,394,378	943,167	644,793	298,374
1944	4,542,322	888,682	740,738	147,944
1945	4,500,911	683,085	724,496	-41,411
1946	4,238,353	797,867	1,060,425	-262,558
1947	4,967,465	1,861,005	1,131,893	729,112
1948	7,276,382	3,424,655	1,115,738	2,308,917
1949	9,959,843	3,907,888	1,224,427	2,683,461
1950	12,786,086	4,439,255	1,613,012	2,826,243
1951	14,468,526	3,219,836	1,537,396	1,682,440
1952	15,918,368	3,112,833	1,662,991	1,449,842
1953	17,524,437	3,882,328	2,276,259	1,606,069
1954	18,266,131	3,067,250	2,325,556	741,694
1955	19,391,539	3,806,937	2,681,529	1,125,408
1956	20,513,553	3,460,469	2,338,455	1,122,014
1957	21,998,764	3,716,980	2,231,769	1,485,211
1958	26,056,193	6,328,597	2,271,168	4,057,429

Note: Table I-138 is the total of Tables I-134 to I-137.
Table I-141 is the total of Tables I-138 to I-140.

Source: Data supplied by Federal Housing Administration.

Housing Loans

TABLE I-139

Federal Housing Administration Direct Loans to Financial Institutions, 1935-1938

Year ended December 31	Out-standings	Loans made	Loans repaid or charged off	Net change in outstandings
		(thousands of dollars)		
1935	110	125	15	110
1936	18	16	108	-92
1937	2	---	16	-16
1938	---	---	2	-2

Note: Table I-141 is the total of Tables I-138 to I-140.

Source: Data supplied by Federal Housing Administration.

Housing Loans

TABLE I-140

Federal Housing Administration Direct Housing Loans in Connection with Property Acquired by Default and Foreclosure of Insured Loans, 1937-1958[a]

Year ended December 31	Outstanding	Loans made	Loans repaid or charged off	Net change in outstandings
	(thousands of dollars)			
1937	46	47	1	46
1938	657	625	14	611
1939	1,807	1,278	128	1,150
1940	4,693	3,589	703	2,886
1941	11,481	7,203	415	6,788
1942	17,457	8,523	2,547	5,976
1943	19,463	3,600	1,594	2,006
1944	17,172	1,534	3,825	-2,291
1945	19,108	6,338	4,402	1,936
1946	25,756	11,163	4,515	6,648
1947	24,801	3,025	3,980	-955
1948	21,670	953	4,084	-3,131
1949	20,097	768	2,341	-1,573
1950	20,211	4,404	4,290	114
1951	29,498	10,779	1,492	9,287
1952	34,986	7,391	1,903	5,488
1953	40,503	7,758	2,241	5,517
1954	48,323	11,881	4,061	7,820
1955	67,417	21,620	2,526	19,094
1956	93,841	29,238	2,814	26,424
1957	122,457	32,714	4,098	28,616
1958	136,585	19,746	5,618	14,128

[a]Covers loans made in connection with disposition of properties acquired through foreclosure on mortgages originally insured by the FHA under Titles I, II, VI, VIII, and IX of the National Housing Act.

Note: Table I-141 is the total of Tables I-138 to I-140.

Source: Data supplied by Federal Housing Administration.

Housing Loans

TABLE I-141

Total Loans, Direct and Insured, of the Federal Housing Administration, 1934-1958

Year ended December 31	Outstanding	Loans made	Loans repaid or charged off	Net change in outstandings
	(thousands of dollars)			
1934	20,000	30,451	10,451	20,000
1935	259,025	427,514	188,489	239,025
1936	577,800	614,926	296,151	318,775
1937	902,831	526,005	200,974	325,031
1938	1,604,287	798,732	97,276	701,456
1939	2,137,655	955,612	422,244	533,368
1940	2,800,649	1,029,571	366,577	662,994
1941	3,514,408	1,193,622	479,863	713,759
1942	4,113,461	1,143,751	544,698	599,053
1943	4,413,841	946,767	646,387	300,380
1944	4,559,494	890,216	744,563	145,653
1945	4,520,019	689,423	728,898	-39,475
1946	4,264,109	809,030	1,064,940	-255,910
1947	4,992,266	1,864,030	1,135,873	728,157
1948	7,298,052	3,425,608	1,119,822	2,305,786
1949	9,979,940	3,908,656	1,226,768	2,681,888
1950	12,806,297	4,443,659	1,617,302	2,826,357
1951	14,498,024	3,230,615	1,538,888	1,691,727
1952	15,953,354	3,120,224	1,664,894	1,455,330
1953	17,564,940	3,890,086	2,278,500	1,611,586
1954	18,314,454	3,079,131	2,329,617	749,514
1955	19,458,956	3,828,557	2,684,055	1,144,502
1956	20,607,394	3,489,707	2,341,269	1,148,438
1957	22,121,221	3,749,694	2,235,867	1,513,827
1958	26,192,778	6,348,343	2,276,786	4,071,557

Note: Table I-141 is the total of Tables I-138 to I-140.

Source: Data supplied by Federal Housing Administration.

Housing Loans

TABLE I-142

Insured Part of Property Improvement Insured Loans of the Federal Housing Administration, 1934-1958

Year ended December 31	Outstanding contingent liability a/	Liability for new loans made b/	Reduction in liability for loans repaid	Net change in outstandings
	(thousands of dollars)			
1934	7,408	6,090	-1,318	7,408
1935	54,403	44,724	-2,271	46,995
1936	59,884	24,615	19,134	5,481
1937	14,689	6,038	51,233	-45,195
1938	38,969	16,018	-8,262	24,280
1939	50,535	20,772	9,206	11,566
1940	55,851	25,095	19,779	5,316
1941	70,193	26,208	11,866	14,342
1942	74,753	14,074	9,514	4,560
1943	77,452	9,545	6,846	2,699
1944	74,661	12,522	15,313	-2,791
1945	87,835	18,902	5,728	13,174
1946	77,911	36,274	46,198	-9,924
1947	115,456	60,639	23,094	37,545
1948	158,327	69,803	26,932	42,871
1949	178,821	67,535	47,041	20,494
1950	192,552	78,964	65,233	13,731
1951	253,226	70,707	10,033	60,674
1952	233,252	84,833	104,807	-19,974
1953	261,311	133,429	105,370	28,059
1954	237,148	89,061	113,224	-24,163
1955	236,586	64,565	65,127	-562
1956	296,064	69,199	9,721	59,478
1957	285,016	86,857	97,905	-11,048
1958	320,011	86,844	51,849	34,995

[a]Data for 1939-58 supplied by the Federal Housing Administration. Figures for 1934-38 were estimated on the basis of the 1939 ratio between liability for new loans made and outstanding contingent liability.

[b]Equal to 10 percent of net proceeds of new property improvement loans made; see Tables I-136. The percentage was 20 instead of 10 in 1934 and 1935.

Note: Table I-136 is the total of Tables I-142 and I-143.

Source: Data supplied by Federal Housing Administration. Under FHA regulations each financial institution's portfolio of loans is insured up to 10 percent of the total aggregate amount of net proceeds outstanding with individual claims payments being limited since the Housing Act of 1954, to 90 percent of the calculated principal loss sustained by the lender on each defaulted note. The figures in Column 1 represent the FHA's estimate of its maximum liability in case of defaults.

Housing Loans

TABLE I-143

Noninsured Part of Property Improvement Insured Loans of the Federal Housing Administration, 1934-1958

Year ended December 31	Outstanding	Loans made	Loans repaid or charged off	Net change in outstandings
		(thousands of dollars)		
1934	12,592	24,361	11,769	+ 12,592
1935	95,597	178,896	95,891	+ 83,005
1936	115,116	221,535	202,016	+ 19,519
1937	85,311	54,344	84,149	- 29,805
1938	136,031	144,163	93,443	+ 50,720
1939	225,265	186,947	97,713	+ 89,234
1940	286,249	225,854	164,870	+ 60,984
1941	295,407	235,876	226,718	+ 9,158
1942	154,547	126,668	267,528	-140,860
1943	55,148	85,903	185,302	- 99,399
1944	37,239	112,701	130,610	- 17,909
1945	98,365	170,121	108,995	+ 61,126
1946	254,689	326,469	170,145	+156,324
1947	521,444	545,747	278,992	+266,755
1948	704,573	628,226	445,097	+183,129
1949	739,379	607,815	573,009	+ 34,806
1950	810,848	710,675	639,206	+ 71,469
1951	832,474	636,363	614,737	+ 21,626
1952	994,748	763,494	601,220	+162,274
1953	1,244,889	1,200,858	950,717	+250,141
1954	1,139,452	801,545	906,982	-105,437
1955	823,614	581,081	896,919	-315,838
1956	774,136	622,793	672,271	- 49,478
1957	846,484	781,711	709,363	+ 72,348
1958	978,989	781,599	649,094	+132,505

Note: Table I-136 is the total of Tables I-142 and I-143.

Source: Derived by subtracting data in Table I-142 from data in Table I-136.

Housing Loans

TABLE I-144

Federal Housing Administration Insured Home Mortgages for New and Existing Housing in Urban Renewal Areas, 1956-1958

Year ended December 31	Outstanding	Loans made	Loans repaid or charged off	Net change in outstandings
	(thousands of dollars)			
1956	596	597	1	596
1957	5,419	4,887	64	4,823
1958	11,541	6,261	139	6,122

Note: Table I-146 is the total of Tables I-144 and I-145.

Source: Data supplied by Federal Houing Administration. Covers mortgages insured under Title II, Section 220 of the National Housing Act.

TABLE I-145

Federal Housing Administration Insured Home Mortgages for Displaced Families Formerly Living in Urban Renewal Areas, 1956-1958

Year ended December 31	Outstanding	Loans made	Loans repaid or charged off	Net change in outstandings
	(thousands of dollars)			
1956	123	124	1	123
1957	4,595	4,512	40	4,472
1958	44,006	39,719	308	39,411

Note: Table I-146 is the total of Tables I-144 and I-145.

Source: Data supplied by Federal Housing Administration. Covers mortgages insured under Title II, Section 221 of the National Housing Act.

Housing Loans

TABLE I-146

Federal Housing Administration Total Insured Mortgages under Urban Renewal, 1956-1958

Year ended December 31	Outstanding	Loans made	Loans repaid or charged off	Net change in outstandings
		(thousands of dollars)		
1956	719	721	2	719
1957	10,014	9,399	104	9,295
1958	55,547	45,980	447	45,533

Note: Table I-146 is the total of Tables I-144 and I-145.

Source: Data supplied by Federal Housing Administration.

TABLE I-147

Federal Housing Administration Insured Mortgages for Family Housing under Cooperative Ownership, 1951-1958

Year ended December 31	Outstanding	Loans made	Loans repaid or charged off	Net change in outstandings
		(thousands of dollars)		
1951	2,451	2,464	13	2,451
1952	32,371	30,355	435	29,920
1953	58,175	27,062	1,258	25,804
1954	98,401	42,095	1,869	40,226
1955	104,443	9,026	2,984	6,042
1956	107,698	7,220	3,965	3,255
1957	157,528	54,169	4,339	49,830
1958	230,669	78,279	5,138	73,141

Note: Table I-149 is the total of Tables I-147 and I-148.

Source: Data supplied by Federal Housing Administration. Covers mortgages insured under Title II, Section 213 of the National Housing Act.

Housing Loans

TABLE I-148

Federal Housing Administration Insured Mortgages for Projects under Cooperative Ownership, 1950-1958

Year ended December 31	Outstanding	Loans made	Loans repaid or charged off	Net change in outstandings
	(thousands of dollars)			
1950	2,691	2,691	---	2,691
1951	73,437	72,921	2,175	70,746
1952	148,450	91,701	16,688	75,013
1953	182,565	74,880	40,765	34,115
1954	211,214	56,417	27,768	28,649
1955	195,658	13,854	29,410	15,556
1956	224,967	36,366	7,057	29,309
1957	293,045	110,306	42,228	68,078
1958	314,278	97,800	76,567	21,233

Note: Table I-149 is the total of Tables I-147 and I-148.

Source: Data supplied by Federal Housing Administration. Covers mortgages insured under Title II, Section 213 of the National Housing Act.

TABLE I-149

Federal Housing Administration Total Insured Mortgages for Family Housing and Projects under Cooperative Ownership, 1950-1958

Year ended December 31	Outstanding	Loans made	Loans repaid or charged off	Net change in outstandings
	(thousands of dollars)			
1950	2,691	2,691	---	2,691
1951	75,888	75,385	2,188	73,197
1952	180,821	122,056	17,123	104,933
1953	240,740	101,942	42,023	59,919
1954	309,615	98,512	29,637	68,875
1955	300,101	22,880	32,394	-9,514
1956	332,665	43,586	11,022	32,564
1957	450,573	164,475	46,567	117,908
1958	544,947	176,079	81,705	94,374

Note: Table I-149 is the total of Tables I-147 and I-148.

Source: Data supplied by Federal Housing Administration.

Housing Loans

TABLE I-150

Federal Housing Administration Insured Mortgages for Homes for Servicemen, 1954-1958

Year ended December 31	Outstanding	Loans made	Loans repaid or charged off	Net change in outstandings
	(thousands of dollars)			
1954	141	141	---	141
1955	85,676	86,545	1,010	85,535
1956	231,839	151,556	5,393	146,163
1957	369,084	147,434	10,189	137,245
1958	570,208	218,333	17,209	201,124

Note: Table I-153 is the total of Tables I-150 and I-152.

Source: Data supplied by Federal Housing Administration. Covers mortgages insured under Title II, Section 222 at the National Housing Act.

TABLE I-151

Federal Housing Administration Insured Mortgages for Homes for Civilians Employed by the Military, 1956-1958

Year ended December 31	Outstanding	Loans made	Loans repaid or charged off	Net change in outstandings
	(thousands of dollars)			
1956	152	152	---	152
1957	8,747	8,679	84	8,595
1958	25,365	16,963	345	16,618

Note: Table I-153 is the total of Tables I-50 to I-152.

Source: Data supplied by the Federal Housing Administration. Covers mortgages insured under Title VIII, Section 809 of the National Housing Act.

Housing Loans

TABLE I-152

Federal Housing Administration Insured Mortgages for Military and Armed Services Project Housing, 1949-1958

Year ended December 31	Outstanding	Loans made	Loans repaid or charged off	Net change in outstandings
	(thousands of dollars)			
1949	12,071	12,071	---	12,071
1950	135,123	123,052	---	123,052
1951	340,458	205,653	318	205,335
1952	473,800	135,842	2,500	133,342
1953	568,898	100,558	5,460	95,098
1954	635,797	74,763	7,864	66,899
1955	639,760	22,406	18,443	3,963
1956	703,408	79,065	15,417	63,648
1957	1,070,314	385,748	18,842	366,906
1958	1,674,910	626,392	21,796	604,596

Note: Table I-153 is the total of Tables I-150 to I-152.

Source: Data supplied by Federal Housing Administration. Covers mortgages insured under Title VIII, Section 803 of the National Housing Act.

TABLE I-153

Federal Housing Administration Total Insured Mortgages for Armed Services Housing, 1949-1958

Year ended December 31	Outstanding	Loans made	Loans repaid or charged off	Net change in outstandings
	(thousands of dollars)			
1949	12,071	12,071	--	12,071
1950	135,123	123,052	--	123,052
1951	340,458	205,653	318	205,335
1952	473,800	135,842	2,500	133,342
1953	568,898	100,558	5,460	95,098
1954	635,938	74,904	7,864	67,040
1955	725,436	108,951	19,453	89,498
1956	935,399	230,773	20,810	209,963
1957	1,448,145	541,861	29,115	512,746
1958	2,270,483	861,688	39,350	822,338

Note: Table I-153 is the total of Tables I-150 to I-152.

Source: Data supplied by Federal Housing Administration.

Housing Loans

TABLE I-154

Federal Housing Administration Insured Mortgages for Housing for the Elderly, 1957-1959

Year ended December 31	Mortgages insured	Cumulative mortgages insured
	(thousands of dollars)	
1957	5,853	5,853
1958	10,808	16,661
1959 (Sept. 30)	12,097	28,758

Source: Data supplied by Federal Housing Administration.

TABLE I-155

Federal Housing Administration Insured Home Mortgages for Publicly Constructed Housing Sold after World War II, 1948-1958

Year ended December 31	Outstanding	Loans made	Loans repaid or charged off	Net change in outstandings
		(thousands of dollars)		
1948	3,379	3,390	11	3,379
1949	8,885	5,677	171	5,506
1950	11,352	2,880	413	2,467
1951	14,580	3,909	681	3,228
1952	13,931	182	831	- 649
1953	13,017	44	958	- 914
1954	11,463	6	1,560	- 1,554
1955	10,428	--	1,035	- 1,035
1956	9,417	--	1,011	- 1,011
1957	8,639	--	778	- 778
1958	7,875	--	764	- 764

Note: Table I-157 is the total of Tables I-155 and I-156.

Source: Data supplied by Federal Housing Administration. Covers mortgages insured under Title VI, Section 603-610 of the National Housing Act.

Housing Loans

TABLE I-156

Federal Housing Administration Insured Project Mortgages for Publicly Constructed Housing Sold after World War II, 1948-1958

Year ended December 31	Outstanding	Loans made	Loans repaid or charged off	Net change in outstandings
	(thousands of dollars)			
1948	2,829	2,848	19	2,829
1949	6,341	3,608	96	3,512
1950	6,385	1,868	1,824	44
1951	6,225	35	195	- 160
1952	6,007	--	218	- 218
1953	5,796	--	211	- 211
1954	5,547	--	249	- 249
1955	5,103	--	444	- 444
1956	4,820	--	283	- 283
1957	4,587	--	233	- 233
1958	4,311	--	276	- 276

Note: Table I-157 is the total of Tables I-155 and I-156.

Source: Data supplied by Federal Housing Administration. Covers mortgages insured under Title VI, Section 608-610 of the National Housing Act.

TABLE I-157

Federal Housing Administration Insured Home and Project Mortgages for Publicly Constructed Housing Sold after World War II, 1948-1958

Year ended December 31	Outstanding	Loans made	Loans repaid or charged off	Net change in outstandings
	(thousands of dollars)			
1948	6,208	6,239	31	6,208
1949	15,226	9,285	267	9,018
1950	17,737	4,748	2,237	2,511
1951	20,805	3,944	876	3,068
1952	19,938	182	1,049	- 867
1953	18,813	44	1,169	- 1,125
1954	17,010	6	1,809	- 1,803
1955	15,531	---	1,479	- 1,479
1956	14,237	---	1,294	- 1,294
1957	13,226	---	1,011	- 1,011
1958	12,186	---	1,040	- 1,040

Note: Table I-157 is the total of Tables I-155 and I-156.

Source: Data supplied by Federal Housing Administration.

Housing Loans

TABLE I-158

Federal Housing Administration Insured Home Mortgages in Critical Defense Areas, 1952-1958

Year ended December 31	Outstanding	Loans made	Loans repaid or charged off	Net change in outstandings
	(thousands of dollars)			
1952	108,039	108,535	496	108,039
1953	304,752	202,086	5,373	196,713
1954	460,334	170,290	14,708	155,582
1955	451,457	27,915	36,792	- 8,877
1956	421,221	8,150	38,386	- 30,236
1957	399,042	294	22,473	- 22,179
1958	382,259	---	16,783	- 16,783

Note: Table I-160 is the total of Tables I-158 and I-159.

Source: Data supplied by Federal Housing Administration. Covers mortgages insured under Title IX, Section 903 of the National Housing Act.

TABLE I-159

Federal Housing Administration Insured Project Mortgages in Critical Defense Areas, 1952-1958

Year ended December 31	Outstanding	Loans made	Loans repaid or charged off	Net change in outstandings
	(thousands of dollars)			
1952	22,179	22,186	7	22,179
1953	52,536	30,497	140	30,357
1954	59,869	9,820	2,487	7,333
1955	55,267	923	5,525	-4,602
1956	47,744	---	7,523	-7,523
1957	44,821	---	2,923	-2,923
1958	42,512	---	2,309	-2,309

Note: Table I-160 is the total of Tables I-158 and I-159.

Source: Data supplied by Federal Housing Administration. Covers mortgages insured under Title IX, Section 908 of the National Housing Act.

Housing Loans

TABLE I-160

Federal Housing Administration Insured Home and Project Mortgages in Critical Defense Areas, 1952-1958

Year ended December 31	Outstanding	Loans made	Loans repaid or charged off	Net change in outstandings
		(thousands of dollars)		
1952	130,218	130,721	503	130,218
1953	357,288	232,583	5,513	227,070
1954	520,203	180,110	17,195	162,915
1955	506,724	28,838	42,317	-13,479
1956	468,965	8,150	45,909	-37,759
1957	443,863	294	25,396	-25,102
1958	424,771	---	19,092	-19,092

Note: Table I-160 is the total of Tables I-158 and I-159.

Source: Data supplied by Federal Housing Administration.

Housing Loans

TABLE I-161

Housing Group

Federal Housing Administration Insured Mortgage Loans Made as Divided between New and Existing Strucutres, 1935-1958

Year ended December 31	Home mortgage loans made: On new houses	Home mortgage loans made: On existing houses	Multi-family project mortgages loans made: On new structures	Multi-family project mortgages loans made: On existing structures
	(thousands of dollars)			
1935	22,400	71,600	2,400	---
1936	95,000	213,900	2,100	---
1937	168,800	255,500	10,500	---
1938	239,900	245,800	47,600	---
1939	486,300	208,400	51,900	---
1940	587,100	175,000	12,900	---
1941	727,700	183,000	12,000	1,600
1942	765,800	207,600	19,500	1,700
1943	553,100	210,000	84,000	600
1944	483,800	223,700	46,100	9,900
1945	257,200	217,100	16,000	4,000
1946	119,900	301,900	11,700	1,400
1947	476,800	417,800	358,500	1,300
1948	1,432,000	684,100	605,800	3,000
1949	1,317,300	892,500	1,017,300	4,000
1950	1,636,700	855,500	1,154,700	2,000
1951	1,215,500	712,700	577,600	6,200
1952	968,500	973,600	321,900	---
1953	1,258,600	1,030,100	259,200	---
1954	1,035,400	906,700	234,000	---
1955	1,269,100	1,815,500	73,400	3,200
1956	1,133,100	1,505,200	129,500	700
1957	880,000	1,371,000	596,500	800
1958	1,665,900	2,885,600	908,200	500

Source: Housing and Home Finance Agency, Twelfth Annual Report, 1958, p. 319.

In total, lending activity of the FHA reached a peak of $6.3 billion in 1958, well above the previous peak in 1950 of $4.4 billion (Table I-141). Between 1950 and 1958, the annual volume varied between $3.1 and $3.9 billion. In the 1930's, annual volume was below $1.0 billion in each year. Year-end outstandings have risen steadily from year to year since 1946, from $4.3 billion in that year to $26.2 billion in 1958.

The three parts of total FHA lending activity are shown in Tables I-138, I-139, and I-140. By far the largest part has been the insuring of mortgages and loans (Table I-138), with total direct loans to financial institutions only $131,000 (Table I-139), and direct loans in connection with property acquired by default and foreclosure of insured loans having an annual volume no larger at its annual high than $33 million (Table I-140).

The breakdown of the insured FHA loans into their four parts is shown in Tables I-134, I-135, I-136, and I-137. Insured loans under the home mortgage programs have been most important, with outstandings at the end of 1958 of $19.7 billion (Table I-134). Insured loans under multiple-family project mortgage programs amounted to $1.2 billion in 1950 and $1.0 billion in 1949, and year-end outstandings in 1958 were $5.0 billion (Table I-135). Property improvement insured loans were $0.9 billion in 1958, and year-end outstandings in that year were $1.3 billion (Table I-136). Total insured loans to finance the production of prefabricated houses were only $5 million and were liquidated by 1955 (Table I-137).

The breakdown of the insured property loans into their insured and noninsured parts is given in Tables I-142 and I-143. Each financial institution's portfolio of loans is insured up to 10 percent of the total aggregate amount of net proceeds outstanding, with payments on individual claims limited, since the Housing Act of 1954, to 90 percent of the calculated principal loss sustained by the lender on each defaulted note. On new loans made in each year, the FHA maximum liability in case of defaults, 10 percent is shown as the insured part in Table I-142. The remainder, 90 percent, appears as the noninsured part in Table I-143.

The remainder of the FHA tables, I-144 to I-161, give partial breakdowns into meaningful parts of loans already tabulated in Table I-138, the total insured lending activity of the FHA.

Data on insured Urban Renewal Area mortgage loans appear in Tables I-144, I-145, and I-146. Most of these were on new houses bought by displaced persons formerly living in Urban Renewal areas, $40 million in 1958 being of this type (Table I-145). Only $6 million of FHA insured home mortgages in 1958 were on new and existing housing in Urban Renewal areas (Table I-144).

FHA insurance on mortgages for family housing and projects under cooperative ownership reached a peak of $176 million in 1958 (Table I-149). Year-end outstandings in 1958 were $545 million. Of these, $314 million were on projects (Table I-148), and $231 million were on family housing.

Special classification of FHA insured mortgages on housing for the armed services began in 1949, and has continued to date. The total of such loans expanded from a low of $75 million in 1954 to $862 million in 1958 (Table I-153). Most of these were on multi-family project housing for the military and armed services (Table I-152). A substantial additional amount were on homes for service-men (Table I-150), and only a minor part were on homes for civilians employed by military establishments (Table I-151).

Beginning in 1957, special provisions have applied for FHA insurance on housing for the elderly. Through September 1959, $29 million of such mortgages had been insured by the FHA (Table I-154).

A minor FHA program concerned the insurance of mortgages issued upon the sale of publicly constructed housing. This was done between 1948 and 1954, with total lending activity at a high of $9 million in 1949 (Table I-157). Insured home mortgages of this type were slightly greater than insured multi-family project mortgages (Tables I-155 and I-156).

Insured home and project mortgage loans in critical defense areas were made between 1952 and 1957. The greatest volume, $233 million, was in 1953 (Table I-160). Most of these were on homes, and only a small part were on projects (Tables I-158 and I-159).

In the four most recent years, new FHA insured mortgage loans have been greater in volume on existing houses than on new houses (Table I-161). In 1947-54 the reverse was true in all except one year. Multi-family project mortgages insured by the FHA have been almost entirely on new structures.

Public Housing Administration (Tables I-162 to I-169)

The Public Housing Administration guarantees (in fact, or in effect) short-term notes and long-term obligations sold to private investors by local housing authorities to finance construction and capital costs of PHA-approved low-rent housing projects. To a lesser extent, the PHA makes direct loans to local housing authorities. The purpose of the program is to provide decent housing for low-income families. Since 1947 the PHA has been administered as one of five constitutents of the Housing and Home Finance Agency. Its immediate predecessors were the Federal Public Housing Authority, established in 1942, and the United States Housing

Housing Loans

TABLE I-162

Public Housing Administration Total Loans Except Those Made as a Liquidating Agency and in Sale of Acquired Property, 1938-1959

Year ended December 31	Outstanding	Loans made	Loans repaid or charged off[b]	Net change in outstandings
	(thousands of dollars)			
1938	16,285	16,285	--	16,285
1939	160,916	172,736	28,105	144,631
1940	435,974	976,551	701,493	275,058
1941	597,760	952,124	790,338	161,786
1942	709,136	740,680	629,304	111,376
1943	679,622	380,519	410,033	- 29,514
1944	661,249	274,149	292,522	- 18,373
1945	657,484	230,580	234,345	- 3,765
1946	655,130	268,630	270,984	- 2,354
1947	642,517	250,867	263,480	- 12,613
1948	641,165	375,616	376,968	- 1,352
1949	640,905	381,992	382,252	- 260
1950	765,435	649,559	525,029	124,530
1951	1,399,728	1,608,748	974,455	634,293
1952	1,966,759	1,917,668	1,350,637	567,031
1953	2,443,244	2,965,600	2,489,115	476,485
1954	2,753,090	3,062,152	2,752,306	309,846
1955	2,864,248	2,055,301	1,944,143	111,158
1956	2,963,561	1,755,678	1,656,365	99,313
1957	3,080,876	1,708,298	1,590,983	117,315
1958	3,331,391	2,058,391	1,807,876	250,515
1959	3,529,717	2,085,549a/	1,887,223	198,326

[a] Includes $99,142 collection loss recoveries.
[b] Includes repossessions and charge-offs.

Note: Table I-165 is the total of Tables I-162 to I-164. Table I-169 is the total of Tables I-165 to I-168.

Housing Loans

TABLE I-163

Public Housing Administration Guaranteed Temporary Financing Loans to Local Housing Authorities, 1939-1959

Year ended December 31	Outstanding	Loans made	Loans repaid or charged off	Net change in outstandings
		(thousands of dollars)		
1939	50,671	50,671	---	50,671
1940	240,651	495,858	305,878	189,980
1941	201,830	392,135	430,956	-38,821
1942	245,152	424,882	381,560	43,322
1943	222,975	245,763	267,940	-22,177
1944	226,024	261,298	258,249	3,049
1945	229,218	228,314	225,120	3,194
1946	231,571	260,185	257,832	2,353
1947	222,976	249,999	258,594	-8,595
1948	216,851	303,201	309,326	-6,125
1949	220,627	378,499	374,723	3,776
1950	282,509	553,954	492,072	61,882
1951	351,407	742,515	673,617	68,898
1952	313,374	861,480	899,513	-38,033
1953	813,626	1,759,536	1,259,284	500,252
1954	1,065,866	1,902,093	1,649,853	252,240
1955	753,301	1,365,690	1,678,255	-312,565
1956	672,460	1,266,922	1,347,763	-80,841
1957	769,468	1,469,030	1,372,022	97,008
1958	890,524	1,649,663	1,528,607	121,056
1959	836,360	1,622,830	1,676,994	-54,164

Note: Table I-165 is the total of Tables I-162 to I-164.

Source: Data supplied by the Public Housing Administration.

Housing Loans

TABLE I-164

Public Housing Administration Guaranteed Long-Term Financing Loans to Local Housing Authorities, 1940-1959

Year ended December 31	Outstanding	Loans made	Loans repaid or charged off	Net change in outstandings
	(thousands of dollars)			
1940	19,120	19,806	686	19,120
1941	38,315	22,701	3,506	19,195
1942	99,845	65,153	3,623	61,530
1943	139,881	44,333	4,297	40,036
1944	146,210	10,052	3,723	6,329
1945	143,884	1,215	3,541	-2,326
1946	146,671	6,576	3,789	2,787
1947	142,863	---	3,808	-3,808
1948	139,835	904	3,932	-3,028
1949	135,683	---	4,152	-4,152
1950	131,495	---	4,188	-4,188
1951	454,517	328,019	4,997	323,022
1952	753,890	307,509	8,136	299,373
1953	1,119,327	384,363	18,926	365,437
1954	1,575,739	497,238	40,826	456,412
1955	2,020,660	473,810	28,889	444,921
1956	2,184,971	198,671	34,360	164,311
1957	2,205,867	65,156	44,260	20,896
1958	2,344,862	186,894	47,899	138,995
1959	2,605,733	312,446	51,575	260,871

Note: Table I-165 is the total of Tables I-162 to I-164.

Source: Data supplied by the Public Housing Administration.

Housing Loans

TABLE I-165

Public Housing Administration Direct Loans to Local Housing Authorities, 1938-1959

Year ended December 31	Outstanding	Loans made	Loans repaid or charged off[b]	Net change in outstandings
		(thousands of dollars)		
1938	16,285	16,285	---	16,285
1939	110,245	122,065	28,105	93,960
1940	176,203	460,887	394,929	65,958
1941	357,615	537,288	355,876	181,412
1942	364,139	250,645	244,121	6,524
1943	316,766	90,423	137,796	-47,373
1944	289,015	2,799	30,550	-27,751
1945	284,382	1,051	5,684	-4,633
1946	276,888	1,869	9,363	-7,494
1947	276,678	868	1,078	-210
1948	284,479	71,511	63,710	7,801
1949	284,595	3,493	3,377	116
1950	351,431	95,605	28,769	66,836
1951	593,804	538,214	295,841	242,373
1952	899,495	748,679	442,988	305,691
1953	510,291	821,701	1,210,905	-389,204
1954	111,485	662,821	1,061,627	-398,806
1955	90,287	215,801	236,999	-21,198
1956	106,130	290,085	274,242	15,843
1957	105,541	174,112	174,701	-589
1958	96,005	221,834	231,370	-9,536
1959	87,624	150,273 a/	158,654	-8,381

[a]Includes $99,142 collection loss recoveries.
[b]Includes repossessions and charge-offs.

Note: Table I-165 is the total of Tables I-162 to I-164.

Source: Data supplied by the Public Housing Administration.

Housing Loans

TABLE I-166

Public Works Administration Limited Dividend Housing Corporation Loans, 1934-1957

Year ended December 31	Outstanding	Loans made	Loans repaid or charged off	Net change in outstandings
	(thousands of dollars)			
1934	3,000	3,000	--	3,000
1935	7,000	4,000	--	4,000
1936	9,000	2,000	--	2,000
1937	10,142	1,397	255	1,142
1938	9,533	--	609	- 609
1939	9,272	81	342	- 261
1940	6,479	--	2,793	-2,793
1941	1,884	--	4,595	-4,595
1942	1,640	--	244	- 244
1943	1,594	--	46	- 46
1944	1,558	--	36	- 36
1945	1,540	--	18	- 18
1946	1,412	--	128	- 128
1947	954	--	458	- 458
1948	927	--	27	- 27
1949	894	--	33	- 33
1950	888	--	6	- 6
1951	861	--	27	- 27
1952	822	--	39	- 39
1953	800	--	22	- 22
1954	743	--	57	- 57
1955	698	--	45	- 45
1956	645	--	53	- 53
1957	--	--	645	- 645

Note: Table I-169 is the total of Tables I-165 to I-168.

Source: Data supplied by the Public Housing Administration.

Housing Loans

TABLE I-167

Public Housing Administration Loans Made in Sale of Acquired Property, 1942-1959

Year ended December 31	Outstanding	Loans made [a]	Loans repaid or charged off [b]	Net change in outstandings
		(thousands of dollars)		
1942	2,310	2,310	--	2,310
1943	7,433	5,244	121	5,123
1944	7,025	--	408	-408
1945	6,498	575	1,102	-527
1946	5,162	261	1,597	-1,336
1947	6,742	3,992	2,412	1,580
1948	10,636	5,275	1,381	3,894
1949	12,079	3,031	1,588	1,443
1950	16,953	6,455	1,581	4,874
1951	14,589	1,370	3,734	-2,364
1952	22,111	8,623	1,101	7,522
1953	33,409	12,749	1,451	11,298
1954	63,453	34,743	4,699	30,044
1955	120,127	61,851	5,177	56,674
1956	144,596	36,744	12,275	24,469
1957	181,190	48,850	12,256	36,594
1958	178,647	11,012	13,555	-2,543
1959	148,010	30	30,667	-30,637

[a] Amounts reported for 1942, 1943, and 1944 were estimated by the PHA.
[b] Includes repossessions, charge-offs, and transfers.

Note: Table I-169 is the total of Tables I-165 to I-168.

Source: Data supplied by the Public Housing Administration.

Housing Loans

TABLE I-168

Public Works Administration Direct Loans to Agencies Constructing Low-Cost Housing Projects, 1933-1959

Year ended December 31	Outstanding	Loans made	Loans repaid or charged off	Net change in outstanding
		(thousands of dollars)		
1933	45,000	50,021	5,021	45,000
1934	132,655	110,929	23,274	87,655
1935	181,290	147,728	99,093	48,635
1936	198,115	102,900	86,075	16,825
1937	186,230	34,854	46,739	-11,885
1938	175,574	40,921	51,577	-10,656
1939	197,380	66,679	44,873	21,806
1940	215,531	33,471	15,320	18,151
1941	218,857	14,947	11,621	3,326
1942	204,869	6,973	20,961	-13,988
1943	160,635	270	44,504	-44,234
1944	152,030	--	8,605	- 8,605
1945	147,986	--	4,044	- 4,044
1946	134,738	--	13,248	-13,248
1947	133,383	--	1,355	- 1,355
1948	147,001[a]	--	-13,618[a]	13,618
1949	102,899	--	44,102	-44,102
1950	100,457	--	2,442	- 2,442
1951	92,108	--	8,349	- 8,349
1952	89,825	--	2,283	- 2,283
1953	88,366	--	1,459	- 1,459
1954	60,000[b]	--	28,366	-28,366
1955	40,000[b]	--	20,000	-20,000
1956	30,000[b]	--	10,000	-10,000
1957	20,000[b]	--	10,000	-10,000
1958	10,000[b]	--	10,000	-10,000
1959	--[b]	--	10,000	-10,000

[a]Includes $13,900,000 in revenue bonds transferred from the Department of the Interior.
[b]These data are rough estimates based on information received from the Treasury, HHFA, and GSA. By successive steps PWA assets were transferred between the RFC, Treasury, and HHFA. With each step the successor agency merged such outstandings with similar loans which it had originated, i.e., the RFC merged its own receivables with those transferred from PWA and in turn the Treasury and HHFA did the same. For example, $6,294,000 of the $88,366,000 outstandings at the end of 1953 were transferred to the RFC in September 1953, and the balance of this transferral was $2,880,000 at the end of 1953, when the remaining loans were taken over and merged with similar RFC loans in the Treasury. The $2,880,000 also is covered in Table I-240. The comptroller of GSA stated that it is probable that most PWA loans are now liquidated–through repayment, sale to private investors, or donation to local governments.

Note: Table I-169 is the total of Tables I-165 to I-168.

Source: Saulnier, et al. Table A-14. From 1934 to 1937 loans to limited dividend housing corporations (shown in Table I-166) were deducted from Saulnier's figures.

Housing Loans

TABLE I-169

Total Public Housing Administration Loans and Public Works Administration Loans of Similar Nature, 1933-1959

Year ended December 31	Outstanding	Loans made	Loans repaid or charged off	Net change in outstandings
	(thousands of dollars)			
1933	45,000	50,021	5,021	45,000
1934	135,655	113,929	23,274	90,655
1935	188,290	151,728	99,093	52,635
1936	207,115	104,900	86,075	18,825
1937	196,372	36,251	46,994	-10,743
1938	201,392	57,206	52,186	5,020
1939	367,568	239,496	73,320	166,176
1940	657,984	1,010,022	719,606	290,416
1941	818,501	967,071	806,554	160,517
1942	917,955	749,963	650,509	99,454
1943	849,284	386,033	454,704	-68,671
1944	821,862	274,149	301,571	-27,422
1945	813,508	231,155	239,509	-8,354
1946	796,442	268,891	285,957	-17,066
1947	783,596	254,859	267,705	-12,846
1948	799,729	394,791	378,658	16,133
1949	756,777	385,023	427,975	-42,952
1950	883,733	656,014	529,058	126,956
1951	1,507,286	1,610,118	986,565	623,553
1952	2,079,517	1,926,291	1,354,060	572,231
1953	2,565,819	2,978,349	2,492,047	486,302
1954	2,877,286	3,096,895	2,785,428	311,467
1955	3,025,073	2,117,152	1,969,365	147,787
1956	3,138,802	1,792,422	1,678,693	113,729
1957	3,282,066	1,757,148	1,613,884	143,264
1958	3,520,038	2,069,403	1,831,431	237,972
1959	3,677,727	2,085,579	1,927,890	157,689

Note: Table I-169 is the total of Tables I-165 to I-168.

Source: Data supplied by the Public Housing Administration.

Authority, established in 1937. The loan programs for low-cost housing projects of the Public Works Administration, established in 1933, are also covered in this section.

Local housing authorities are agencies created under state laws to plan, develop, own, and operate public housing. Loans to local authorities are made by the PHA under Annual Contribution Contracts. For project development, PHA loan commitments may be made up to 90 percent of the cost. For permanent financing, the Contracts provide for payment of contributions over a 40-year period to cover the debt service (interest plus capital) on bonds sold privately by the local authority. Funds for Annual Contribution Contracts come from the U.S. Treasury. The PHA also is authorized to borrow from the Treasury.

Low-rent public housing units approved under federal projects reached a prewar peak of 65,057 in 1938 but declined sharply during World War II. No new authorizations were possible from 1946 through 1949. Various legislative acts over the years have given the PHA authority to enter into new commitments for specified numbers of units of low-rent public housing. For example, the Housing Act of 1956 authorized the PHA to enter into new commitments for 70,000 units—35,000 by August 1958 and another 35,000 by June 1959.

Total PHA loans, plus PWA loans of a similar nature, reached a peak volume in 1954, $3.1 billion (Table I-169). The volume in 1959 was $2.1 billion. The highest volume in the prewar years was in 1940, $1.0 billion. Year-end outstandings have risen steadily since 1949, from $0.8 billion in that year to $3.7 billion in 1959.

The PHA-PWA loans are divided in four parts. Most important are the short-term and long-term loans to local housing authorities of the three types described above: direct loans, guaranteed temporary loans, and guaranteed long-term loans. These in total amounted to $2.1 billion in 1959, and outstandings at the end of 1959 were $3.5 billion (Table I-165). Second, the PHA made loans in connection with the sale of acquired property that reached a top volume of $62 million in 1955, and with year-end outstandings in 1959 of $148 million (Table I-167). Third, the Public Works Administration made direct loans to agencies constructing low-cost housing projects from 1933 through 1943. The highest annual volume of these loans was in 1935, $148 million (Table I-168). Fourth, and of minor importance, were loans to limited dividend housing corporations during 1933-39 by the Public Works Administration (Table I-166).

In PHA loans to local housing authorities there has been a marked shift from direct to guaranteed loans during the past decade. Year-end outstandings of direct loans decreased from a high of $899 million in 1952 to $87 million in 1959 (Table I-162). During this same period, outstandings of guaranteed temporary financing loans increased from $313 million to $836 million (Table I-163), and of guaranteed long-term financing loans from $754 million to $2606 million (Table I-164).

Defense Homes Corporation (Table I-170)

The Defense Homes Corporation made $1 million of mortgage loans in 1941-44 for the construction of housing in defense production areas (Table I-170). In 1947, the program was transferred to the Reconstruction Finance Corporation for liquidation. Its loans were made as a part of the program of the Federal Public Housing Authority of the National Housing Agency.

Federal National Mortgage Association (Tables I-171 to I-187)

The Federal National Mortgage Association purchases and sells mortgages guaranteed by the Veterans' Administration or insured by the Federal Housing Administration. Its purpose is to assure an adequate secondary market for such mortgages, increasing their liquidity and encouraging greater private investment in housing. When first established in 1938 (by the RFC under the name of National Mortgage Association of Washington), it was intended to be a lender of last resort for mortgage investors, combating the depression by increasing the solvency of mortgage lenders and by encouraging greater employment in the home construction industry. Originally, it bought and sold only FHA-insured mortgages. In 1948, it was granted authority to buy and sell VA-guaranteed home mortgages. Its operations are administered through five field offices, a fiscal agency and mortgage sales office in New York, and an administrative office in Washington, D.C.

Regulations on eligibility for purchase have varied from time to time. For example, in the early 1950's there was a regulation in force that mortgages must have been held by the original lender for at least two months before being eligible for FNMA purchase. In 1957, as another example, eligible mortgages were required to have a maturity of at least ten years and an unpaid principal balance of at least $4,000. Originally, mortgages were purchased at their principal amounts. Since 1954 they have been purchased at market prices, varying from time to time depending in large part on prevailing interest rates. Prices paid also vary by area and by the amount of the mortgagor's equity. Through the years to date, FNMA has been more active on the buying than on the selling side of the market.

In the reorganization of activities when it became a constituent of the HHFA in 1954, the activities of FNMA were divided three ways, each with its own assets, liabilities, and borrowing authority,

Housing Loans

TABLE I-170

Direct Housing Loans of the Defense Homes Corporation, 1941-1947[a]

Year ended December 31	Outstanding	Loans made	Loans repaid or charged off	Net change in outstandings
		(thousands of dollars)		
1941	130	130 b/	---	130
1942	557	428	1	427
1943	905	395	47	348
1944	936	31c/	---	31
1945	901	---	35	-35
1946	787	---	114	-114
1947	---	---	787	-787

[a]Represents mortgage loans for construction of housing in defense production areas. The program was transferred to the Reconstruction Finance Corporation for liquidation in March 1947.

[b]Was reported in Saulnier, et al. as $90,000, but corrected to $130,000 so as to cross-check with data on outstandings at year-end.

[c]Was reported in Saulnier, et al., as $27,000, but corrected to $31,000 so as to cross-check with data on outstandings at year-end.

Source Saulnier, et al., p. 414.

Housing Loans

TABLE I-171

Federal National Mortgage Association Purchase and Sale of FHA-Insured Mortgages, 1938-1958

Year ended December 31	Outstanding	Purchases	Sales	Repayments[a]	Net change in outstandings
	(thousands of dollars)				
1938	80,266	82,166	--	1,900	80,266
1939	146,760	74,081	351	7,236	66,494
1940	181,100	48,041	6	13,695	34,340
1941	206,840	42,321	3	16,578	25,740
1942	210,929	23,179	--	19,090	4,089
1943	64,487	1,502	126,646	21,298	-146,442
1944	52,423	200	11	12,253	- 12,064
1945	7,442	58	38,623	6,418	- 44,981
1946	5,591	32	2	1,881	- 1,851
1947	4,420	60	--	1,231	- 1,171
1948	188,184	186,811	--	3,047	183,764
1949	403,258	252,673	19,366	18,233	215,074
1950	169,199	49,255	261,392	21,922	-234,059
1951	203,689	74,452	28,144	11,818	34,490
1952	319,769	167,706	35,733	15,893	116,080
1953	621,035	355,093	32,309	21,517	301,266
1954	802,171	353,576	134,318	38,123	181,136
1955	901,049	184,465	13,839	71,748	98,878
1956	978,402	153,229	1,250	74,626	77,353
1957	1,237,221	313,372	2,049	52,504	258,819
1958	1,483,472	469,431	155,419	67,761	246,251

[a]Includes repayments, sales discounts, and other credits.

Note: Table I-173 is the total of Tables I-171 and I-172. In 1955-58, Table I-171 is the total of Tables I-175, I-178, and I-181.

Source: Semiannual reports of Federal National Mortgage Association.

Housing Loans

TABLE I-172

Federal National Mortgage Association Purchase and Sale of VA-Guaranteed Mortgages, 1948-1958

Year ended December 31	Outstanding	Purchases	Sales	Repayments[a]	Net change in outstandings
		(thousands of dollars)			
1948	11,110	11,134	--	24	11,110
1949	425,096	419,540	387	5,167	413,986
1950	1,177,465	995,039	207,990	34,680	752,369
1951	1,645,845	602,857	82,971	51,506	468,380
1952	1,921,898	370,166	20,188	73,925	276,053
1953	1,840,602	187,364	181,377	87,283	- 81,296
1954	1,631,574	260,846	381,070	88,804	-209,028
1955	1,714,109	226,969	46,916	97,518	82,535
1956	2,068,821	455,489	3,764	97,013	354,712
1957	2,737,008	782,645	838	113,620	668,187
1958	2,417,481	153,364	326,845	146,046	-319,527

[a]Includes repayments, sales discounts, and other credits.

Note: Table I-173 is the total of Tables I-171 and I-172. In 1955-58, Table I-172 is the total of Tables I-176, I-179, and I-182.

Source: Semiannual reports of Federal National Mortgage Association.

Housing Loans

TABLE I-173

Federal National Mortgage Association Purchase and Sale of FHA-Insured and VA-Guaranteed Mortgages, 1938-1958

Year ended December 31	Outstanding	Purchases	Sales	Repayments[a]	Net change in outstandings
		(thousands of dollars)			
1938	80,266	82,166	--	1,900	80,266
1939	146,760	74,081	351	7,236	66,494
1940	181,100	48,041	6	13,695	34,340
1941	206,840	42,321	3	16,578	25,740
1942	210,929	23,179	--	19,090	4,089
1943	64,487	1,502	126,646	21,298	-146,442
1944	52,423	200	11	12,253	-12,064
1945	7,442	58	38,623	6,418	-44,981
1946	5,591	32	2	1,881	-1,851
1947	4,420	60	--	1,231	-1,171
1948	199,294	197,945	--	3,071	194,874
1949	828,354	672,213	19,753	23,400	629,060
1950	1,346,664	1,044,294	469,382	56,602	518,310
1951	1,849,534	677,309	111,115	63,324	502,870
1952	2,241,667	537,872	55,921	89,818	392,133
1953	2,461,637	542,457	213,686	108,800	219,970
1954	2,433,745	614,422	515,388	126,927	-27,892
1955	2,615,158	411,434	60,755	169,266	181,413
1956	3,047,223	608,718	5,014	171,639	432,065
1957	3,974,229	1,096,017	2,887	166,124	927,006
1958	3,900,953	622,795	482,264	213,807	-73,276

[a] Includes repayments, sales discounts, and other credits.

Note: Table I-173 is the total of Tables I-171 and I-172. In 1955-58, Table I-173 is the total of Tables I-174, I-177, and I-180.

Source: Semiannual reports of Federal National Mortgage Association.

Housing Loans

TABLE I-174

Federal National Mortgage Association Secondary Market Operations, Purchase and Sale of FHA-Insured and VA-Guaranteed Mortgages, 1955-1958

Year ended December 31	Outstanding	Purchases	Sales	Repayments a/	Net change in outstandings
		(thousands of dollars)			
1955	85,681	86,049	---	392	85,657 b/
1956	648,715	574,539	5,014	6,491	563,034
1957	1,635,841	1,021,043	2,886	31,031	987,126
1958	1,380,690	259,536	465,571	49,116	-255,151

[a]Includes repayments, sales discounts, and other credits.
[b]The total increase in FNMA outstandings between 1954 and 1955 was $181,413,000. Of this increase $85,657,000 occurred in the "secondary market operations" account, and $95,756,000 in the "management and liquidating" account.

Note: Table I-174 is the total of Tables I-175 and I-176. In 1955-58, Table I-173 is the total of Tables I-174, I-177, and I-180.

Source: Semiannual reports of Federal National Mortgage Association.

TABLE I-175

Federal National Mortgage Association Secondary Market Operations, Purchase and Sale of FHA-Insured Mortgages, 1955-1958

Year ended December 31	Outstanding	Purchases	Sales	Repayments a/	Net change in outstandings
		(thousands of dollars)			
1955	19,833	19,933	--	111	19,822
1956	138,590	121,620	1,250	1,613	118,757
1957	367,504	238,799	2,049	7,836	228,914
1958	398,738	184,551	138,844	14,473	31,234

[a]Includes repayments, sales discounts, and other credits.

Note: Table I-174 is the total of Tables I-175 and I-176. In 1955-58, Table I-171 is the total of Tables I-175, I-178, and I-181.

Source: Semiannual reports of Federal National Mortgage Association.

Housing Loans

TABLE I-176

Federal National Mortgage Association Secondary Market Operations, Purchase and Sale of VA-Guaranteed Mortgages, 1955-1958

Year ended December 31	Outstanding	Purchases	Sales	Repayments[a/]	Net change i outstanding
		(thousands of dollars)			
1955	65,848	66,116	--	281	65,835
1956	510,125	452,919	3,764	4,878	444,277
1957	1,268,337	782,244	837	23,195	758,212
1958	981,952	74,985	326,727	34,643	-286,385

[a]Includes repayments, sales discounts, and other credits.

Note: Table I-174 is the total of Tables I-175 and I-176. In 1955-58, Table I-172 is the total of Tables I-176, I-179, and I-182.

Source: Semiannual report of Federal National Mortgage Association.

TABLE I-177

FNMA Special Assistance Functions, Purchase and Sale of FHA-Insured and VA-Guaranteed Mortgages, 1956-1958

Year ended December 31	Outstanding	Purchases	Sales	Repayments[a]	Net change in outstandings
		(thousands of dollars)			
1956	5,559	5,582	--	23	5,559
1957	72,174	67,063	--	448	66,615
1958	418,553	363,259	13,341	3,539	346,379

[a]Includes repayments, sales discounts, and other credits.

Note: Table I-177 is the total of Tables I-178 to I-179. In 1955-58, Table I-173 is the total of Tables I-174, I-177, and I-180.

Source: Semiannual reports of Federal National Mortgage Association.

Housing Loans

TABLE I-178

FNMA Special Assistance Functions, Purchase and Sale of FHA-Insured Mortgages, 1956-1958

Year ended December 31	Outstanding	Purchases	Sales	Repayments[a]	Net change in outstandings
	(thousands of dollars)				
1956	5,552	5,574	--	22	5,552
1957	71,979	66,874	--	447	66,427
1958	340,198	284,880	13,341	3,320	268,219

[a]Includes repayments, sales discounts, and other credits.

Note: Table I-177 is the total of Tables I-178 and I-179. In 1955-58, Table I-171 is the total of Tables I-175, I-178, and I-181. Table I-178 is the total of Tables I-183 to I-187.

Source: Semiannual reports of Federal National Mortgage Association.

TABLE I-179

FNMA Special Assistance Functions, Purchase and Sale of VA-Guaranteed Mortgages, 1956-1958

Year ended December 31	Outstanding	Purchases	Sales	Repayments a/	Net change in outstanding
	(thousands of dollars)				
1956	7	8	---	1	7
1957	195	189	---	1	188
1958	78,355	78,379	---	219	78,160

[a]Includes repayments, sales discounts, and other credits.

Note: Table I-177 is the total of Tables I-178 and I-179. In 1955-58, Table I-172 is the total of Tables I-176, I-179, and I-182.

Source: Semiannual reports of Federal National Mortgage Association.

Housing Loans

TABLE I-180

Federal National Mortgage Association Management and Liquidating Functions, Purchase and Sale of FHA-Insured and VA-Guaranteed Mortgages, 1955-1958

Year ended December 31	Outstanding	Purchases	Sales	Repayments a/	Net change in outstandings
		(thousands of dollars)			
1955	2,529,477	325,385	60,755	168,874	95,756 b/
1956	2,392,949	28,597	---	165,125	-136,528
1957	2,266,215	7,911	1	134,645	-126,734
1958	2,101,710	---	3,352	161,152	-164,505

[a]Includes repayments, sales discounts, and other credits.

[b]The total increase in FNMA outstandings between 1954 and 1955 was $181,413,000. Of this increase $85,657,000 occurred in the "secondary market operations" account, and $95,756,000 in the "management and liquidation" account.

Note: Table I-180 is the total of Tables I-181 and I-182. In 1955-58, Table I-173 is the total of Tables I-174, I-177, and I-180.

Source: Amounts outstanding are from semiannual reports of the Federal National Mortgage Association; other figures were derived by subtraction from combined operations.

TABLE I-181

Federal National Mortgage Association Management and Liquidating Functions, Purchase and Sale of FHA-Insured Mortgages, 1955-1958

Year ended December 31	Outstandings	Purchases	Sales	Repayments a/	Net change i outstandings
		(thousands of dollars)			
1955	881,215	164,532	13,839	71,637	79,056
1956	834,260	26,035	---	72,991	-46,955
1957	797,738	7,699	---	44,221	-36,522
1958	744,536	---	3,234	49,968	-53,202

[a]Includes repayments, sales discounts, and other credits.

Note: Table I-180 is the total of Tables I-181 and I-182. In 1955-58, Table I-171 is the total of Tables I-175, I-178, and I-181.

Source: Amounts outstanding are from semiannual reports of Federal National Mortgage Association. Other series obtained by subtraction from combined operations.

Housing Loans

TABLE I-182

Federal National Mortgage Association Management and Liquidating Functions, Purchase and Sale of VA-Guaranteed Mortgages, 1955-1958

Year ended December 31	Outstanding	Purchases	Sales	Repayments a/	Net change in outstandings
		(thousands of dollars)			
1955	1,648,261	160,853	46,916	97,237	16,700
1956	1,558,689	2,562	---	92,134	-89,572
1957	1,468,476	212	1	90,424	-90,213
1958	1,357,174	---	118	111,184	-111,302

[a]Includes repayments, sales discounts, and other credits.

Note: Table I-180 is the total of Tables I-181 and I-182. In 1955-58, Table I-172 is the total of Tables I-176, I-179, and I-182.

Source: Outstandings are from semiannual reports of Federal National Mortgage Association. Other series obtained by subtraction from combined operations.

TABLE I-183

FNMA Special Assistance Functions, Purchase and Sale of FHA-Insured Urban Renewal Mortgages, 1956-1958

Year ended December 31	Outstanding	purchases	Sales	Repayments	Net change in outstandings
		(thousands of dollars)			
1956	298	300	---	2	298
1957	7,643	7,437	---	92	7,345
1958	45,583	38,363	---	423	37,940

Note: Table I-178 is the total of Tables I-183 to I-187.

Source: Semiannual reports of Federal National Mortgage Association.

Housing Loans

TABLE I-184

FNMA Special Assistance Functions, Purchase and Sale of FHA-Insured Low-Cost Housing Mortgages, 1956-1958

Year ended December 31	Outstanding	Purchases	Sales	Repayments	Net change in outstandings
	(thousands of dollars)				
1956	455	460	---	5	455
1957	5,257	4,899	---	97	4,802
1958	41,084	36,543	---	716	35,827

Note: Table I-178 is the total of Tables I-183 to I-187.

Source: Semiannual reports of Federal National Mortgage Association.

TABLE I-185

FNMA Special Assistance Functions, Purchase and Sale of FHA-Insured Cooperative Housing Mortgages, 1956-1958

Year ended December 31	Outstanding	Purchase	Sales	Repayments	Net change in outstandings
	(thousands of dollars)				
1956	1,360	1,360	---	---	1,360
1957	35,987	34,784	---	157	34,627
1958	89,207	58,542	4,434	888	53,220

Note: Table I-178 is the total of Tables I-183 to I-187.

Source: Semiannual reports of Federal National Mortgage Association.

Housing Loans

TABLE I-186

FNMA Special Assistance Functions, Purchase and Sale of FHA-Insured Armed Services Family Housing Mortgages, 1956-1958

Year ended December 31	Outstanding	Purchases	Sales	Repayments	Net change in outstandings
	(thousands of dollars)				
1956	1,695	1,697	---	2	1,695
1957	21,376	19,755	---	74	19,681
1958	162,639	151,432	8,907	1,262	141,263

Note: Table I-178 is the total of Tables I-183 to I-187.

Source: Semiannual reports of Federal National Mortgage Association.

TABLE I-187

FNMA Special Assistance Functions, Purchase and Sale of FHA-Insured Critical Defense Areas Mortgages, 1956-1958

Year ended December 31	Outstanding	Purchases	Sales	Repayments	Net change in outstandings
	(thousands of dollars)				
1956	1,744	1,757	---	13	1,744
1957	1,716	---	---	27	-28
1958	1,685	---	---	31	-31

Note: Table I-178 is the total of Tables I-183 to I-187.

Source: Semiannual reports of Federal National Mortgage Association.

and conducted in much the same way as though it constituted a separate corporation, as follows:

1. Management and liquidation functions—to liquidate mortgages of the predecessor FNMA, with no new mortgage purchase authority except from other constituents of the HHFA in order to permit efficient liquidation of their mortgage portfolios.

2. Secondary market operations—the long-established program of purchase and sale of FHA-insured and VA-guaranteed home mortgages, with funds for operations coming principally from the sale of debentures to private investors, and with provision for this part of the program ultimately to become privately owned by the mortgage lending institutions using its facilities.

3. Special assistance functions—the financing and purchase of mortgages, upon specific authorization by the President or Congress, of selected types of home mortgages originating under special housing programs, such as urban renewal or housing for the elderly, with funds obtained by borrowing from the U.S. Treasury.

Data on the total activity of FNMA from 1938 through 1958 are shown in Table I-173. Annual purchases did not exceed $100 million until 1948, and have exceeded $1 billion in only two years, 1950 and 1957. Sales as great as $0.5 billion occurred in each of three years: 1950, 1954, and 1958. Repayments amounted to $0.2 billion in 1958. Year-end outstandings increased from $0.2 billion in 1948 to $3.9 billion in 1958.

The division of total FNMA activity as between FHA-insured and VA-guaranteed mortgages is shown in Tables I-171 and I-172. Of outstandings at the end of 1958, $2.4 billion were of VA-guaranteed mortgages and $1.5 billion were of FHA-insured mortgages. The relation between purchases of the two types has varied erratically from year to year in the period since VA-guaranteed mortgages were first purchased in 1948.

In the 1955-58 period, when activities were clearly divided as between secondary market operations, special assistance functions, and management and liquidating functions, purchases and sales of FHA-insured mortgages are shown separately for these divisions in Tables I-175, I-178, and I-181. Similar breakdowns of data for VA-guaranteed mortgages are shown in Tables I-176, I-179, and I-182.

The totals for the three separate divisions of FNMA activity, with FHA and VA mortgages combined, appear in Tables I-174, I-177, and I-180. Year-end outstandings in 1958 were $2.1 billion for management and liquidation, $1.4 billion for secondary market operations, and $0.4 billion for special assistance functions.

Through 1958, the most important type of purchases and sales of FHA-insured mortgages under the special assistance program was for armed services family housing (Table I-186). Next most important was cooperative housing (Table I-185), followed by urban renewal (Table I-183), low-cost housing (Table I-184), and housing in critical defense areas (Table I-187).

Community Facilities Administration (Tables I-188 to I-200)

The Community Facilities Administration makes loans for college housing; loans to states, municipalities, and other public agencies for the planning of public works; and loans to communities for public facilities (mainly for water supply and sewage disposal in small communities). Lending under these current programs began in 1951, 1955, 1956, respectively. Loanable funds for the programs come from borrowings from the U.S. Treasury.

College housing loans are made to educational institutions of higher learning and nonprofit corporations established by them to construct student and faculty housing and related services. The primary purpose is to alleviate an acute shortage in student housing facilities. Public or nonprofit hospitals that operate training programs for student nurses or interns also are eligible for loans under this part of the program. The maximum amortization period for repayment, originally 40 years, is now 50 years.

Planning loans are made to public agencies to help finance the planning of various public works. Their purpose is to encourage public agencies to maintain a reserve of plans for needed public works and to promote efficiency in planning and construction. Loans become payable to a revolving fund, without interest, when the public works contemplated by the approved plans is placed under construction.

Public facility loans are made to any nonfederal public body which has authority to finance, construct, and operate the proposed public work. Loan applications by smaller communities, with populations under 10,000, are given priority. Interest rates on these loans are required to be set at rates that will cover all expenses of the program.

In addition to the three current programs described above, the CFA is responsible for management and liquidation of certain related programs whose legislative authority has terminated. These include programs of loans for prefabricated housing, Alaskan housing, two previous advance planning programs, war public works under the Lanham Act, and defense community facilities provided under Public Law 139, 82nd Congress.

Housing Loans

TABLE I-188

Community Facilities Administration Loans for College Housing, 1951-1959

Year ended December 31	Outstanding	Loans made	Loans repaid or charged off	Net change in outstandings
	(thousands of dollars)			
1951	85	85	--	85
1952	5,414	5,339	10	5,329
1953	28,887	23,498	25	23,473
1954	64,882	36,605	610	35,995
1955	90,939	26,547	490	26,057
1956	146,755	58,397	2,580	55,816
1957	273,848	128,804	1,711	127,093
1958	449,984	179,063	2,928	176,136
1959	682,526	238,986	6,444	232,542

Note: Table I-200 is the total of Tables I-188, I-193, I-197, I-198, and I-199.

Source: Data supplied by the Community Facilities Administration.

TABLE I-189

Community Facilities Administration Public Facilities Loans Program, Current Activity, 1956-1959

Year ended December 31	Outstanding	Loans made	Loans repaid or charged off	Net change in outstandings
	(thousands of dollars)			
1956	49	49	--	49
1957	4,713	4,664	--	4,664
1958	16,371	11,662	4	11,658
1959	40,677	24,366	60	24,306

Note: Table I-193 is the total of Tables I-189 to I-192.

Source: Data supplied by the Community Facilities Administration.

Housing Loans

TABLE I-190

Community Facilities Administration Public Facilities Loans Program, Liquidation of RFC Loans, 1957-1959[a]

Year ended December 31	Outstanding	Loans made	Loans repaid or charged off	Net change in outstandings
		(thousands of dollars)		
1957	4,497	4,527[b]	30	4,497
1958	4,265	-	232	-232
1959	4,155	-	110	-110

[a]This table records the CFA liquidation of the Public Facilities Loan Program of the Reconstruction Finance Corporation. The CFA Public Facilities Loan Program which superseded this is shown in Table I-189. The volume of loans acquired from the RFC on July 1, 1957 was $4,527,000.

[b]Loans acquired from the RFC on July 1, 1957.

Note: Table I-193 is the total of Tables I-189 to I-192.

Source: Data supplied by the Community Facilities Administration.

TABLE I-191

Community Facilities Administration Lanham Act Bonds Loan Activity, 1942-1959

Year ended December 31	Outstanding	Loans made[a]	Loans repaid or charged off	Net change in outstandings
		(thousands of dollars)		
1942	324	500	176	324
1943	3,711	4,000	613	3,387
1944	4,663	1,500	548	952
1945	6,477	2,115	301	1,814
1946	4,996	-	1,481	- 1,481
1947	4,294	-	702	- 702
1948	2,784	-	1,510	- 1,510
1949	1,940	-	844	- 844
1950	1,680	-	260	- 260
1951	1,319	-	361	- 361
1952	1,267	-	52	- 52
1953	1,022	-	245	- 245
1954	959	-	63	- 63
1955	903	-	56	- 56
1956	703	-	200	- 200
1957	625	-	78	- 78
1958	587	-	38	- 38
1959	555	-	32	- 32

[a]Total loans were $8,115,000, and the distribution among years was estimated. When acquired by CFA from the GSA on May 24, 1950, the outstandings were $1,704,000.

Note: Table I-193 is the total of Tables I-189 to I-192.

Source: Data supplied by the Community Facilities Administration for 1950-59. For 1942-50, from p. 412 of Saulnier, et al.

Housing Loans

TABLE I-192

Community Facilities Administration Defense Community Facilities Program, 1952-1959

Year ended December 31	Outstandings	Loans made	Loans repaid or charged off	Net change in outstandings
		(thousands of dollars)		
1952	663	663	--	663
1953	2,718	2,055	--	2,055
1954	3,515	813	16	797
1955	3,569	74	20	54
1956	3,581	49	36	12
1957	3,538	--	43	-43
1958	3,490	--	48	-48
1959	3,362	--	128	-128

Note: Table I-193 is the total of Tables I-189 to I-192.

Source: Data supplied by the Community Facilities Administration.

TABLE I-193

Community Facilities Administration Loans for Construction of Public Facilities, 1942-1959

Year ended December 31	Outstandings	Loans made	Loans repaid or charged off	Net change in outstandings
		(thousands of dollars)		
1942	324	500	176	324
1943	3,711	4,000	613	3,387
1944	4,663	1,500	548	952
1945	6,477	2,115	301	1,814
1946	4,996	--	1,481	-1,481
1947	4,294	--	702	- 702
1948	2,784	--	1,510	-1,510
1949	1,940	--	844	- 844
1950	1,680	--	260	- 260
1951	1,319	--	361	- 361
1952	1,930	663	52	611
1953	3,740	2,055	245	1,810
1954	4,474	813	79	734
1955	4,472	74	76	- 2
1956	4,333	98	237	- 139
1957	13,373	9,191	151	9,040
1958	24,713	11,662	322	11,340
1959	48,749	24,366	330	24,036

Note: Table I-193 is the total of Tables I-189 to I-192.
Table I-200 is the total of Tables I-188, I-193, I-197, I-198, and I-199.

Source: Data supplied by the Community Facilities Administration.

Housing Loans

TABLE I-194

Community Facilities Administration Loans for Advance Planning of Public Works, Current Programs, 1955-1959

Year ended December 31	Outstanding	Loans made	Loans repaid or charged off	Net change in outstandings
	(thousands of dollars)			
1955	6	6	-	6
1956	391	394	9	385
1957	1,991	2,200	600	1,600
1958	5,576	4,995	1,410	3,586
1959	9,851	7,065	2,790	4,275

Note: Table I-197 is the total of Tables I-194 to I-196.

Source: Data supplied by the Community Facilities Administration.

TABLE I-195

Community Facilities Administration First Advance Planning Program, 1945-1959[a]

Year ended December 31	Outstanding	Loans made	Loans repaid or charged off	Net change in outstandings
	(thousands of dollars)			
1945	6,624	6,624	---	6,624
1946	24,625	18,271	270	18,001
1947	35,425	12,282	1,482	10,800
1948	33,884	6,812	8,353	-1,541
1949	33,246	6,403	7,041	-638
1950	33,641	2,488	2,093	395
1951	30,759	240	3,123	-2,882
1952	29,093	80	1,746	-1,666
1953	27,437	95	1,751	-1,656
1954	25,879	---	1,558	-1,558
1955	23,961	---	1,918	-1,918
1956	23,321	---	640	-640
1957	22,883	---	438	-438
1958	22,463	---	420	-420
1959	22,014	---	450	-450

[a]This table records the CFA liquidation of the First Advance Planning Program of the War Mobilization and Reconversion Act of 1944. The CFA advance planning program is shown in Table I-194. When acquired from the GSA on May 24, 1950, outstandings were $35,630,000: the cumulative total of loans made was $45,983,000: and the cumulative total of loans repaid was $10,353,000.

Note: Table I-197 is the total of Tables I-194 to I-196.

Source: Data supplied by the Community Facilities Administration for 1950-59. The earlier data appear on p. 391 of Saulnier, *et al.*

Housing Loans

TABLE I-196

Community Facilities Administration Second Advance Planning Program, 1950-1959[a]

Year ended December 31	Outstanding	Loans made	Loans repaid or charged off	Net change in outstandings
		(thousands of dollars)		
1950	4,270	4,349	79	4,270
1951	9,226	6,302	1,346	4,956
1952	10,598	3,688	2,316	1,372
1953	10,165	1,391	1,824	-433
1954	8,913	436	1,687	-1,252
1955	7,806	8	1,115	-1,107
1956	7,031	---	775	-775
1957	6,296	---	735	-735
1958	5,349	---	948	-948
1959	4,916	---	433	-433

[a]This table records the CFA liquidation of the Second Advance Planning Program originally authorized by Congress in 1949. The CFA advance planning program is shown in Table I-194. When acquired from the GSA on May 24, 1950, $446,000 of loans had been made and all were outstanding.

Note: Table I-197 is the total of Tables I-194 to I-196.

Source: Data supplied by the Community Facilities Administration.

Housing Loans

TABLE I-197

Community Facilities Administration Total Loans for Advance Planning of Public Works, 1945-1959

Year ended December 31	Outstanding	Loans made	Loans repaid or charged off	Net change in outstandings
	(thousands of dollars)			
1945	6,624	6,624	---	6,624
1946	24,625	18,271	270	18,001
1947	35,425	12,282	1,482	10,800
1948	33,884	6,812	8,353	-1,541
1949	33,246	6,403	7,041	-638
1950	37,911	6,837	2,172	4,665
1951	39,985	6,542	4,468	2,074
1952	39,691	3,768	4,062	-294
1953	37,602	1,486	3,575	-2,089
1954	34,792	436	3,246	-2,810
1955	31,773	14	3,033	-3,019
1956	30,743	394	1,424	-1,030
1957	31,170	2,200	1,773	427
1958	33,388	4,995	2,777	2,218
1959	36,781	7,065	3,672	3,393

Note: Table I-197 is the total of Tables I-194 to I-196. Table I-200 is the total of Tables I-188, I-193, I-197, I-198, and I-199.

Source: Data supplied by the Community Facilities Administration.

TABLE I-198

Community Facilities Administration Loans for Prefabricated Housing, 1949-1959

Year ended December 31	Outstanding	Loans made	Loans repaid or charged off	Net change in outstandings
	(thousands of dollars)			
1949 [a]	16,000	16,428	428	16,000
1950 [a]	21,917	10,000	4,083	5,917
1951	30,425	11,390	2,881	8,508
1952	9,344	4,983	26,063	-21,081
1953	8,138	8,837	10,043	-1,206
1954	5,835	1,283	3,586	-2,303
1955	5,496	71	410	- 339
1956	5,107	--	390	- 390
1957	4,798	--	308	- 308
1958	4,629	--	170	- 170
1959	4,278	--	351	- 351

[a]Distribution of loans between 1949 and 1950 were estimated. The total of loans made in these two years were $26,428,000, $23,231,000 before September 7, 1950, when the program was transferred from the RFC to CFA, and $3,197,000 between September 7 and December 31, 1950. Loans repaid were $3,141,000 before September 7, 1950 and $1,369,000 in the remainder of 1950.

Note: Table I-200 is the total of Tables I-188, I-193, I-197, I-198, and I-199.

Source: Data supplied by the Community Facilities Administration.

Housing Loans

TABLE I-199

Community Facilities Administration Loans for Alaskan Housing, 1950-1959

Year Ended December 31	Outstanding	Loans made	Loans repaid or charged off	Net change in outstandings
	(thousands of dollars)			
1950	1,574	1,593	20	1,574
1951	5,224	3,718	68	3,650
1952	10,748	6,601	1,077	5,524
1953	11,863	5,839	4,724	1,115
1954	9,127	-	2,736	-2,736
1955	9,027	-	99	-99
1956	8,925	-	102	-102
1957	8,816	-	109	-109
1958	8,417	-	399	-399
1959	8,051	-	366	-366

Note: Table I-200 is the total of Tables I-188, I-193, I-197, I-198, and I-199.

Source: Data supplied by the Community Facilities Administration.

TABLE I-200

Total Loans of the Community Facilities Administration, 1942-1959

Year ended December 31	Outstanding	Loans made	Loans repaid or charged off	Net change in outstandings
	(thousands of dollars)			
1942	324	500	176	324
1943	3,711	4,000	613	3,387
1944	4,663	1,500	548	952
1945	13,101	8,739	301	8,438
1946	29,621	18,271	1,751	16,520
1947	39,719	12,282	2,184	10,098
1948	36,668	6,812	9,863	-3,051
1949	51,186	22,831	8,313	14,518
1950	63,082	18,430	6,534	11,896
1951	77,038	21,735	7,779	13,956
1952	67,127	21,354	31,265	-9,911
1953	90,230	41,715	18,612	23,103
1954	119,110	39,137	10,257	28,880
1955	141,707	26,706	4,109	22,597
1956	195,863	58,889	4,733	54,156
1957	332,005	140,195	4,053	136,142
1958	521,131	195,720	6,594	189,126
1959	780,385	270,417	11,163	259,254

Note: Table I-200 is the total of Tables I-188, I-193, I-197, I-198, and I-199.

Source: Data supplied by the Community Facilities Administration.

Total loans of the Community Facilities Administration were $270 million in 1959, and outstandings at the end of 1959 were $780 million (Table I-200). In the 1942-59 lifetime of the CFA and its predecessors, the record was one of slow expansion until 1955, and rapid expansion thereafter.

The five parts of CFA lending activity have been tabulated as follows:

1. College housing loans. This has been by far the most important lending activity of the CFA. In 1959, such loans made up 88 percent of total loans made, and 87 percent of year-end outstandings (Table I-188).

2. Loans for advance planning. These loans exceeded $10 million in only two years of the 1945-59 period—1946 and 1947, when they were $18 million and $12 million, respectively (Table I-197). Division of these loans into their three parts are shown in Table I-195, the first advance planning program, with loans made from 1945 through 1953; in Table I-196, the second advance planning program, with loans made from 1950 through 1955; and in Table I-194, the current program, with loans made from 1955 through 1959.

3. Loans for construction of public facilities. The total of such loans in the 1942-59 period was under $60 million, and over one-half were made in the two years of 1958 and 1959 (Table I-193). Most of these were under the current program, under which loans have been made since 1956 (Table I-189). The volumes of outstandings in 1959 and earlier years were relatively small for liquidation of the Public Facilities Loan Program of the RFC (Table I-190), loans in connection with the sale of war public works constructed in World War II under the Lanham Act (Table I-191), and loans for defense community facilities in 1952-56 (Table I-192).

4. Loans for prefabricated housing. The peak volume of such loans was in 1949, $16 million (Table I-198). Loans of this type were not made after 1955, and year-end outstandings, at a high of $30 million in 1951, were down to $4 million in 1959.

5. Loans for Alaskan housing. These loans, made in 1950-53, totaled $18 million (Table I-199).

<u>Urban Renewal Administration (Tables I-201 to I-209)</u>

The Urban Renewal Administration makes loans and grants to local public agencies for the planning and execution of slum clearance and urban renewal projects. Loans are either of short-term or

Housing Loans

TABLE I-201

Urban Renewal Administration Planning Advances, 1950-1959

Year ended December 31	Outstanding	Loans made	Loans repaid or charged off	Net change in outstandings
	(thousands of dollars)			
1950	889	889	---	889
1951	3,470	2,581	---	2,581
1952	5,908	3,041	604	2,438
1953	6,373	1,954	1,488	465
1954	6,688	1,562	1,247	315
1955	7,930	2,406	1,163	1,242
1956	9,571	3,920	2,279	1,641
1957	12,000	5,171	2,741	2,429
1958	14,175	7,935	5,760	2,175
1959 (Oct.)	16,285	7,378	5,268	2,110

Note: Table I-204 is the total of Tables I-201 to I-203.

Source: Data supplied by Urban Renewal Administration.

TABLE I-202

Urban Renewal Administration Temporary Loans, 1952-1959

Year ended December 31	Outstanding	Loans made	Loans repaid or charged off	Net change in outstandings
	(thousands of dollars)			
1952	9,574	9,714	140	9,574
1953	32,836	31,976	8,716	23,262
1954	53,665	36,649	15,819	20,829
1955	63,411	52,244	42,498	9,746
1956	100,998	64,368	26,780	37,587
1957	170,252	105,529	36,275	69,254
1958	278,069	160,602	52,785	107,817
1959 (Oct.)	397,213	210,824	91,680	119,144

Note: Table I-204 is the total of Tables I-201 to I-203. Table I-202 is the total of Tables I-205 and I-206.

Source: Data supplied by Urban Renewal Administration.

Housing Loans

TABLE I-203

Urban Renewal Administration Long-Term Guaranteed Loans, 1958-1959[a]

Year ended December 31	Outstanding	Loans made	Loans repaid or charged off	Net change in outstandings
	(thousands of dollars)			
1958	2,744	2,744	---	2,744
1959 (Oct.)	2,744	---	---	---

[a]There have been no direct long-term loans under this program to date.

Note: Table I-204 is the total of Tables I-201 to I-203.

Source: Data supplied by Urban Renewal Administration.

TABLE I-204

Total Loans of Urban Renewal Administration, 1950-1959

Year ended December 31	Outstanding	Loans made	Loans repaid or charged off	Net change in outstandings
	(thousands of dollars)			
1950	889	889	---	889
1951	3,470	2,581	---	2,581
1952	15,482	12,755	744	12,012
1953	39,209	33,930	10,204	23,727
1954	60,353	38,211	17,066	21,144
1955	71,341	54,650	43,661	10,988
1956	110,569	68,288	29,059	39,228
1957	182,252	110,700	39,016	71,683
1958	294,988	171,281	58,545	112,736
1959 (Oct.)	416,242	218,202	96,948	121,254

Note: Table I-204 is the total of Tables I-201 to I-203.

Source: Data supplied by Urban Renewal Administration.

Housing Loans

TABLE I-205

Direct Part of Urban Renewal Administration Temporary Loans, 1952-1958

Year ended December 31	Outstanding	Loans made	Loans repaid or charged off a/	Net change in outstandings
		(thousands of dollars)		
1952	9,574	9,714	140	9,574
1953	21,903	21,043	8,716	12,329
1954	37,835	24,832	8,899	15,932
1955	27,359	18,203	28,679	-10,476
1956	33,570	21,294	15,082	6,211
1957	43,232	31,397	21,735	9,662
1958	67,577	51,540	27,195	24,345
1959 (Oct.)	66,288	54,634	55,923	-1,289

[a]Includes direct loans refunded by "guaranteed" loans during the year.

Note: Table I-202 is the total of Tables I-205 and I-206.

Source: Data supplied by Urban Renewal Administration.

TABLE I-206

Guaranteed Part of Urban Renewal Administration Temporary Loans, 1953-1959

Year ended December 31	Outstanding	Loans made	Loans repaid or charged off[a]	Net change in outstandings
		(thousands of dollars)		
1953	10,933	10,933	---	10,933
1954	15,830	11,817	6,920	4,897
1955	36,052	34,041	13,819	20,222
1956	67,428	43,074	11,698	31,376
1957	127,020	74,132	14,540	59,592
1958	210,492	109,062	25,590	83,472
1959 (Oct.)	330,925	156,190	35,757	120,433

[a]Includes loans refunded by direct loans during the year.

Note: Table I-202 is the total of Tables I-205 and I-206.

Source: Data supplied by Urban Renewal Administration.

Housing Loans

TABLE I-207

Urban Renewal Administration Capital Grant Payments, 1953-1959

Year ended December 31	Capital grant payments
	(thousands of dollars)
1953	8,673
1954	12,597
1955	37,580
1956	16,291
1957	30,618
1958	50,080
1959 (Oct.)	74,425

Source: Data supplied by Urban Renewal Administration.

TABLE I-208

Urban Renewal Administration Capital Grant Reservations Approved, 1950-1958[a]

Year ended December 31	Outstanding	Net change in outstandings
	(thousands of dollars)	
1950	198,774	198,774
1951	282,725	83,951
1952	329,229	46,504
1953	348,540	19,312
1954	377,171	28,631
1955	553,793	176,622
1956	827,738	273,944
1957	1,021,056	193,318
1958	1,326,239	305,183

[a]Includes reservations for urban renewal projects, general neighborhood renewal planning, and demonstration projects.

Source: Calaculated from Table VII-1, p. 270, Twelfth Annual Report of Housing and Home Finance Agency, 1958.

Housing Loans

TABLE I-209

Urban Renewal Administration Contract Authorizations, 1950-1958

Year ended December 31	For planning advances	For temporary loans	For capital grants	Total
	(thousands of dollars)			
1950	3,066	--	--	3,066
1951	2,758	282	402	3,442
1952	3,584	33,608	53,696	90,888
1953	2,076	70,178	51,108	123,362
1954	2,951	28,007	41,392	72,350
1955	6,272	52,982	38,438	97,692
1956	10,441	52,156	35,739	98,336
1957	7,050	219,411	168,365	394,826
1958	11,992	350,576	226,717	589,285

Source: Calculated from Table VII-2, p. 270, Twelfth Annual Report of Housing and Home Finance Agency, 1958.

long-term duration, and directly from appropriated government funds or from private lending institutions under URA guarantee. The purpose of the URA program is to assist municipalities in redeveloping land so that it can be used most advantageously, and to eliminate slums and potential slums. Prior to 1954, the Division of Slum Clearance and Urban Development administered he program.

To be eligible for URA projects a local public agency must be authorized by state or local law to carry out the various activities nvolved. It may be a specially created redevelopment agency, a ocal housing authority, or a city or county itself. Loans to these ocal public agencies are of two types. Short-term loans — either planning advances or temporary loans — are made for project planning and carrying out the plans. Long-term loans, with maturiies of up to 40 years, are made to finance any part of a project area that is leased for redevelopment rather than sold, after the project is completed.

Loans by private lenders are guaranteed in the sense that loan commitments of the URA are pledged as security by the local agency. The intent of the statute is that guaranteed private financing be used to the maximum extent practicable. Since 1953, when first used, guaranteed loans have been about three times as great as direct loans of the URA.

When the project is completed and the area is sold or leased, he local public agency is eligible to receive a capital grant from he URA which covers two-thirds of its net cost (three-fourths if he local agency pays separately all costs of planning, surveys, egal fees, and administrative work). The remaining one-third is covered by the local public agency. These two sources plus proceeds rom the sale of the area furnish the necessary funds for the repayment of the temporary loan. As a simplified example, assume hat the cost of a project is $4 million. This would be covered by a emporary URA loan. The cleared land is sold for $1 million. The URA capital grant would be $2 million and the local public agency would supply $1 million. These three items total $4 million, and would be used to repay the temporary URA loan. If the land were eased instead of sold, however, the URA would make a long-term oan of $1 million, the proceeds from which would be added to the $2 million capital grant and the $1 million local agency contribution o enable repayment of the $4 million temporary loan.

Total loans of the URA expanded from $1 million in 1950 to $38 million in 1954 and $171 million in 1958 (Table I-204). Outtandings were $295 million at the end of 1958, and $416 million at the end of October 1959.

More than 90 percent of the loans made since the inception of the program have been temporary loans (Table I-202). The annual volume of planning advances has never exceeded $8 million (Table I-201). No long-term loans were made until 1958, and the volume in that year was $3 million, all of the guaranteed rather than the direct type (Table I-203).

The distribution of temporary loans into their direct and guaranteed parts is shown in Tables I-205 and I-206. Outstandings at the end of October 1959 were $66 million for direct loans and $331 million for guaranteed loans.

Between 1949 and 1958, about 700 separate URA projects had been approved, 300 had moved from the planning to the development stage, and ten had been completed. Because of the considerable period of time taken for completion of a project, capital grant reservations approved have greatly exceeded capital grant payments. At the end of 1958, there were $1.3 billion approved capital grant reservations outstanding, but only $50 million capital grant payments had been made during the year (Tables I-207 and I-208). Similarly, contract authorizations for temporary loans in 1958 were $351 million (Table I-209), compared with temporary loans made of $161 million (Table I-202).

Veterans' Administration (Tables I-210 to I-218)

The Veterans' Administration guarantees loans made by private lenders for buying or improving homes to veterans of World War II and the Korean conflict. It makes direct housing loans in rural areas and small towns if it is found that private capital is not available for financing loans under the guarantee program. The VA also makes vendee loans covering purchase-money mortgages and real estate sales contracts in connection with the term sales of homes acquired through foreclosure of VA-guaranteed loans. The program has been the largest of all federal loan programs, with outstandings of $31 billion at the end of 1958, $5 billion in excess of the $26 billion for the second largest, the Federal Housing Administration program. Expenses of the guarantee program are paid from appropriations by Congress. Direct loans of the VA are made from funds from the U.S. Treasury.

The purpose of the program is partly to facilitate home ownership by veterans of World War II and the Korean conflict, partly to benefit veterans for their contribution to national welfare by serving in the armed forces, and partly to encourage home construction and ownership.

The first guaranteed VA loans were made in 1944, the first vendee loans in 1947, and the first direct loans in 1950. The

Housing Loans

TABLE I-210

Veterans' Administration Guaranteed Home Loans, 1944-1959

Year ended December 31	Outstanding	Loans made	Loans repaid or charged off	Net change in outstandings
		(thousands of dollars)		
1944	18,000	18,629	629	18,000
1945	100,000	88,997	6,997	82,000
1946	2,400,000	2,442,434	142,434	2,300,000
1947	5,500,000	3,271,618	171,618	3,100,000
1948	7,200,000	1,870,287	170,287	1,700,000
1949	8,100,000	1,417,886	517,886	900,000
1950	10,300,000	3,058,916	858,916	2,200,000
1951	13,200,000	3,574,724	674,724	2,900,000
1952	14,600,000	2,684,425	1,284,425	1,400,000
1953	16,100,000	3,045,928	1,545,928	1,500,000
1954	19,300,000	4,234,975	1,034,975	3,200,000
1955	24,600,000	7,270,548	1,970,548	5,300,000
1956	28,400,000	5,868,383	2,068,383	3,800,000
1957	30,700,000	3,760,715	1,460,715	2,300,000
1958	30,400,000	1,864,884	2,164,884	- 300,000
1959	30,000,000	2,786,671	3,186,671	- 400,000

Note: Table I-210 is the total of Tables I-214 and I-215. Table I-213 is the total of Tables I-210 to I-212.

Source: Data supplied by the Veterans' Administration. Includes primary and secondary loans for home purchase, and home improvement loans. Also includes insured home loans, a minor part of the program, the initial insurance credits for which amounted to only $8,488,000 between their authorization in 1945 and May 25, 1951.

Housing Loans

TABLE I-211

Veterans' Administration Direct Home Loans, 1950-1958

Year ended Dec. 31	Outstanding	Loans made	Loans repaid or charged off	Net change in outstandings
		(thousands of dollars)		
1950	6,342	6,342	--	6,342
1951	108,000	103,095	1,437	101,658
1952	167,000	67,522	8,522	59,000
1953	274,684	113,899	6,215	107,684
1954	328,569	109,353	55,468	53,885
1955	412,801	119,939	35,707	84,232
1956	462,777	80,924	30,948	49,976
1957	638,922	207,679	31,534	176,145
1958	743,098	148,512	44,336	104,176

Note: Table I-213 is the total of Tables I-210 to I-212.

Source: 1950-53 data from Saulnier, et al., pp. 384 and 385. 1954-58 data supplied by the Veterans' Administration.

TABLE I-212

Veterans' Administration Vendee Home Loans, 1947-1958

Year ended Dec. 31	Outstanding	Loans made	Loans repaid or charged off	Net change in outstandings
		(thousands of dollars)		
1947	130	130	--	130
1948	1,239	1,133	24	1,109
1949	4,173	3,111	177	2,934
1950	10,453	6,716	436	6,280
1951	21,633	12,191	1,011	11,180
1952	31,891	12,082	1,824	10,258
1953	41,111	11,877	2,657	9,220
1954	51,527	61,548	51,132	10,416
1955	64,160	79,154	66,521	12,633
1956	87,228	107,464	84,396	23,068
1957	126,898	154,849	115,179	39,670
1958	188,471	225,661	164,088	61,573

Note: Table I-213 is the total of Tables I-210 to I-212.

Source: 1947-53, Saulnier, et al., pp. 384-5. 1954-58, data supplied by Veterans' Administration.

Housing Loans

TABLE I-213

Total Home Loans of the Veterans' Administration, 1944-1958

Year ended December 31	Outstanding	Loans made	Loans repaid or charged off	Net change in outstandings
	(thousands of dollars)			
1944	18,000	18,629	629	+ 18,000
1945	100,000	88,997	6,997	+ 82,000
1946	2,400,000	2,442,434	142,434	+2,300,000
1947	5,500,130	3,271,748	171,618	+3,100,130
1948	7,201,239	1,871,420	170,311	+1,701,109
1949	8,104,173	1,420,997	518,063	+ 902,934
1950	10,316,795	3,071,974	859,352	+2,212,622
1951	13,329,633	3,690,010	677,172	+3,012,838
1952	14,798,891	2,764,029	1,294,771	+1,469,258
1953	16,415,795	3,171,704	1,554,800	1,616,904
1954	19,680,096	4,405,876	1,141,575	3,264,301
1955	25,076,961	7,469,641	2,099,776	5,396,865
1956	28,950,005	6,056,771	2,183,727	3,873,044
1957	31,465,820	4,123,243	1,607,428	2,515,815
1958	31,331,569	2,239,057	2,373,308	- 134,251

Note: Table I-213 is the total of Tables I-210 to I-212.

Source: Calculated by adding Tables I-210 to I-212.

Housing Loans

TABLE I-214

Part of Veterans' Administration Guaranteed Home Loans that Was Guaranteed, 1944-1959

Year ended December 31	Outstanding	Loans made	Loans repaid or charged off	Net change in outstandings
	(thousands of dollars)			
1944	8,000	8,390	390	+ 8,000
1945	42,285	37,075	2,790	+ 34,285
1946	1,150,000	1,177,510	69,795	+1,107,715
1947	2,600,000	1,553,555	103,555	+1,450,000
1948	3,300,000	921,510	221,510	700,000
1949	3,700,000	722,280	322,280	+ 400,000
1950	5,100,000	1,655,420	255,420	+1,400,000
1951	6,750,000	2,097,760	447,760	1,650,000
1952	7,700,000	1,568,100	618,100	950,000
1953	8,900,000	1,771,830	571,830	+1,200,000
1954	10,600,000	2,430,630	730,630	+1,700,000
1955	13,700,000	4,095,315	995,315	+3,100,000
1956	15,900,000	3,244,180	1,044,180	+2,200,000
1957	17,000,000	2,027,855	927,855	+1,100,000
1958	16,800,000	978,010	1,178,010	- 200,000
1959	16,000,000	1,454,080	2,254,080	- 800,000

Note: Table I-210 is the total of Tables I-214 and I-215.

Source: Data supplied by Veterans' Administration. Includes only primary and secondary loans. Home improvement VA loans were 0.0 percent of total VA guaranteed home loans in 1944, 0.32 percent in 1949, 0.11 percent in 1954, and 0.18 percent in 1959. Since the guaranteed part of these home improvement loans is not included above, the data slightly understate the total volume, and correspondingly slightly overstate the total nonguaranteed volume in Table I-215. Also includes insured home loans, a minor part of the program, the initial insurance credits for which amounted to only $8,488,000 between their authorization in 1945 and May 25, 1951.

Housing Loans

TABLE I-215

Part of Veterans' Administration Guaranteed Home Loans That Was Not Guaranteed, 1944-1959

Year ended December 31	Outstanding	Loans made	Loans repaid or charged off	Net change in outstandings
	(thousands of dollars)			
1944	10,000	10,239	239	+10,000
1945	57,715	51,922	-4,793	+ 56,715
1946	1,250,000	1,264,924	72,639	+1,192,285
1947	2,900,000	1,718,063	68,063	+1,650,000
1948	3,900,000	948,777	-51,223	+1,000,000
1949	4,400,000	965,606	465,606	+ 500,000
1950	5,200,000	1,403,496	603,496	+ 800,000
1951	6,450,000	1,476,964	226,964	+1,250,000
1952	6,900,000	1,116,325	666,325	+ 450,000
1953	7,200,000	1,274,098	974,098	+ 300,000
1954	8,700,000	1,804,345	304,345	+1,500,000
1955	10,900,000	3,175,233	975,233	+2,200,000
1956	12,500,000	2,624,203	1,024,203	+1,600,000
1957	13,700,000	1,732,860	532,860	+1,200,000
1958	13,600,000	886,874	986,874	- 100,000
1959	14,000,000	1,332,591	932,591	+ 400,000

Note: Table I-210 is the total of Tables I-214 and I-215.

Source: Calculated by subtracting Table I-214 from Table I-210.

Housing Loans

TABLE I-216

Division of Veterans' Administration Guaranteed Primary Home Loans as Between New and Existing Houses, 1944-1959

Year ended December 31	New houses: Number	New houses: Thous. of dollars original principal amounts	Existing houses: Number	Existing houses: Thous. of dollars original principal amounts
1944			1,999	18,629
1945	1,353	7,662	18,510	79,054
1946	66,816	433,427	347,194	1,993,562
1947	198,446	1,463,538	289,221	1,741,778
1948	107,573	836,602	140,967	890,871
1949	83,777	669,340	89,642	597,260
1950	208,420	1,713,765	160,784	1,171,898
1951	272,364	2,585,414	122,851	937,082
1952	188,765	1,788,560	109,576	888,655
1953	201,965	2,032,982	114,800	1,006,772
1954	242,114	2,673,793	163,612	1,556,315
1955	397,643	4,690,703	256,348	2,569,544
1956	313,332	3,908,838	188,713	1,949,692
1957	218,800	2,889,946	83,247	862,705
1958	94,049	1,310,987	49,470	548,839
1959	145,414	2,051,281	65,097	730,414

Source: Data supplied by Veterans' Administration. Cannot be reconciled with Table I-210 because Table I-210 contains secondary and home improvement loans not tabulated in this table. This table summarizes only primary loans for home purchases.

Housing Loans

TABLE I-217

Division of Veterans' Administration Guaranteed Home Loans as Between (a) Primary Loans for Purchase of New and Existing Homes and Home Improvement Loans, and (b) Second Mortgage Loans for Purchase of New and Existing Houses, 1944-1959

Year ended December 31	Primary loans for purchase of new and existing homes and home improvement loans	Second mortgage loans for purchase of new and existing homes	Total
	(thousands of dollars)		
1944	18,629	--	18,629
1945	86,809	2,188	88,997
1946	2,429,631	12,803	2,442,434
1947	3,212,275	59,343	3,271,618
1948	1,734,109	136,178	1,870,287
1949	1,271,192	146,694	1,417,886
1950	2,891,005	167,911	3,058,916
1951	3,528,845	45,879	3,574,724
1952	2,683,361	1,064	2,684,425
1953	3,045,850	78	3,045,928
1954	4,234,905	70	4,234,975
1955	7,270,514	34	7,270,548
1956	5,868,378	5	5,868,383
1957	3,760,705	10	3,760,715
1958	1,864,884	--	1,864,884
1959	2,786,671	--	2,786,671

Source: Data supplied by Veterans' Administration. Totals in this table are the same as those for total loans made that appear in Table I-210.

Housing Loans

TABLE I-218

Veterans' Administration Sales of Direct and Vendee Home Mortgages to Private Investors, 1952-1958

Year ended December 31	Direct loans		Vendee accounts	
	Sales	Cumulative total	Sales	Cumulative total
		(thousands of dollars)		
1952	7,515	7,515	---	---
1953	3,079	10,594	---	---
1954	20,779	31,373	---	---
1955	13,924	45,297	---	---
1956	3,233	48,530	---	---
1957	238	48,768	319 a/	319
1958	3,881	52,649	303	622

[a]Cumulative amount.

Source: Data supplied by Veterans' Administration.

World War II authority for loan guarantees is due to expire on July 25, 1962, and that for the Korean conflict in 1965. Direct housing loans to veterans of both wars are scheduled to expire on July 25, 1962.

Loan guarantees protect the private lender against losses of up to 60 percent of the loan or $7,500, whichever is less. To qualify for VA guarantee, terms specified as to interest rate charged, type of construction, ratio of loan to value of property, and maximum maturity must be complied with by the private lender. Terms generally have been more favorable than on FHA-insured loans. As with VA business and farm loans, provision is also made for insured home loans, but they have never been an important part of the program, accounting for less than 1 percent of total VA home loans. VA guarantees on home improvement loans have been well below 1 percent of the guarantees on ownership loans.

Total home loans by the Veterans' Administration had their greatest annual volume in 1955 and 1956, $7.5 billion and $6.1 billion, respectively (Table I-213). Year-end outstandings increased from $5.5 billion in 1947 to a high of $31.5 billion in 1957, and declined slightly to $31.3 billion in 1958.

Guaranteed home loans made up the bulk of the VA home loan program. Loans made in 1959 were $2.8 billion, well below the peak volume of $7.3 billion in 1955, while year-end outstandings in 1959 were $30.0 billion, only slightly below the 1957 peak of $30.7 billion (Table I-210).

Direct home loans, begun in 1950 in specified rural areas for veterans certifying that they were unable to obtain regular VA-guaranteed loans, were largest in 1957, $208 million (Table I-211). In 1958, the volume was $149 million.

Vendee home loans reached their peak in 1958, $226 million (Table I-212). Year-end outstandings have been small relative to loans made, indicating a short life for loans of this type, and were $188 million in 1958.

The division of VA-guaranteed home loans into their guaranteed and nonguaranteed parts is shown in Tables I-214 and I-215. In the year of greatest loans, 1955, 56 percent of the loans made was guaranteed, and 44 percent not guaranteed. The corresponding percentages in 1959 were 52 and 48 percent, respectively. Of the total year-end outstandings in 1959 of $30.0 billion, $16.0 billion was the guaranteed part and $14.0 billion the nonguaranteed part.

In the early years of the program, 1944-49, more VA-guaranteed home loans were on existing houses than on new houses (Table

I-216). Since then, about twice as much money has been loaned on new structures as on existing ones. In 1955, the amount loaned on new houses was 1.8 times the amount loaned on existing houses, and in 1959, 2.8 times.

Unlike the FHA, the VA guarantees second mortgages as well as first mortgages on residential loans. These have been of relatively minor importance, however. No second mortgages were guaranteed in 1958 and 1959, and in their year of greatest volume, 1950, the amount was $168 million (Table I-217).

Whenever possible, the VA sells its direct and vendee home mortgages to private investors. A total of $53 million home mortgages were sold during the 1952-58 period, with peak sales of $21 million in 1954 (Table I-218).

Federal Home Loan Banks (Tables I-219 and I-220)

The 11 district Federal Home Loan Banks make both short-term and long-term loans to their members (mostly savings and loan associations) on the security of home mortgages. They also make unsecured short-term loans to members.

The FHLB's were established in 1932 as permanent central credit banks for member institutions. Their principal function is to provide additional liquidity for their members by making advances to them when required for unusual or heavy withdrawals, and to meet the recurring needs of member institutions for funds for seasonal mortgage lending. Another important function is the transfer of funds from areas in which there is a surplus to areas with a shortage (such as the West Coast in recent years), thereby facilitating the flow of credit.

Initial capital of $100 million was provided by the government. This was later increased to $125 million, all of which was retired in full by 1951, so that the 11 FHLB's are now privately owned by members.

Loanable funds come in large part from sale of short-term consolidated FHLB notes or bonds, not guaranteed or insured by the government. The Treasury is authorized to buy and hold up to $1 billion of such notes and bonds, but no such purchase has ever been made. The authorization is important only in providing liquidity for savings and loan associations in the event of a severe emergency.

There were 4,570 members of the Federal Home Loan Bank System on December 31, 1958. These were 1,804 federal savings and loan associations chartered and supervised by the Federal Home

Housing Loans

TABLE I-219

Loans of Federal Home Loan Banks to Member Institutions, 1932-1959

Year ended December 31	Outstanding	Loans made	Loans repaid or charged off	Net change in outstandings
		(thousands of dollars)		
1932	838	838	---	838
1933	85,442	90,032	5,427	84,604
1934	86,603	38,676	37,515	1,161
1935	102,686	59,130	43,047	16,083
1936	145,227	93,257	50,716	42,541
1937	200,038	123,251	68,440	54,811
1938	198,842	81,958	83,154	-1,196
1939	181,313	94,781	112,310	-17,529
1940	201,492	134,212	114,033	20,179
1941	219,446	157,600	139,646	17,954
1942	129,213	99,462	189,695	-90,233
1943	110,068	156,926	176,070	-19,145
1944	130,563	239,254	218,759	20,495
1945	194,872	277,748	213,439	64,309
1946	293,455	329,232	230,649	98,583
1947	435,572	351,079	208,962	142,117
1948	515,016	359,613	280,169	79,444
1949	433,429	255,663	337,250	-81,587
1950	815,957	674,757	292,229	382,528
1951	805,937	422,977	432,997	-10,020
1952	864,189	585,813	527,562	58,252
1953	951,555	727,517	640,150	87,366
1954	867,478	734,249	818,326	-84,077
1955	1,416,759	1,251,680	702,400	549,281
1956	1,228,156	744,936	933,539	-188,603
1957	1,265,195	1,116,148	1,079,109	37,039
1958	1,298,320	1,363,699	1,330,574	33,125
1959	2,134,322	2,066,819	1,230,817	836,002

Source: Federal Home Loan Bank Board, Annual Report, 1958, p. 49. Data for 1959 supplied by Federal Home Loan Bank Board.

Housing Loans

TABLE I-220

Inter-District Loans Among Federal Home Loan Banks, 1933-1958

Year ended December 31	Outstanding	Loans made	Loans repaid or charged off	Net change in outstandings
		(thousands of dollars)		
1933	3,000	3,000	---	3,000
1934	1,550	4,250	5,700	- 1,450
1935	2,500	5,500	4,550	950
1936	12,700	22,500	12,300	10,200
1937	4,450	15,300	23,550	-8,250
1938	1,000	12,900	16,350	-3,450
1939	8,150	12,900	5,750	7,150
1940	2,000	17,700	23,850	-6,150
1941	11,000	14,000	5,000	9,000
1942	---	6,500	17,500	-11,000
1943	500	14,500	14,000	500
1944	3,000	13,500	11,000	2,500
1945	7,800	24,300	19,500	4,800
1946	6,500	36,000	37,300	-1,300
1947	11,500	66,000	61,000	5,000
1948	6,250	62,250	67,500	-5,250
1949	28,700	47,700	25,250	22,450
1950	1,000	121,500	149,200	-27,700
1951	1,500	9,500	9,000	500
1952	---	30,000	31,500	-1,500
1953	9,000	90,400	81,400	9,000
1954	13,500	87,500	83,000	4,500
1955	---	149,500	163,000	-13,500
1956	---	58,412	58,412	---
1957	43,000	120,000	77,000	43,000
1958	7,000	98,894	134,894	-36,000

Source: Supplied by Federal Home Loan Bank Board.

Loan Bank Board; 2,739 state chartered savings and loan associations; 25 savings banks; and two insurance companies. These institutions make more than one-third of the home mortgage loans in the United States, primarily conventional mortgages not federally guaranteed or insured.

The FHLB's provide a way by which relatively small mortgage lending institutions have access at lower cost to large-scale capital markets for loanable funds. Since April 15, 1958, each member's limit on allowable loans has been 20 percent of its withdrawable accounts, except that additional loans have been allowed to meet withdrawals. Loans not exceeding one year in maturity may be made on a secured or unsecured basis. Loans with longer maturities must be secured by home mortgages or U.S. obligations, and must be amortized on a monthly or quarterly basis. Members may also make deposits in the FHLB's, on which interest is earned.

Loans by FHLB's to member institutions have always provided a relatively small part of their total loanable funds. Loans at no time have exceeded 5 percent of the combined assets of member institutions, and were about 2 1/2 percent at the end of 1958.

In 1959, loans of FHLB's to member institutions were $2.1 billion (Table I-219). This was considerably more than the previous peak in annual volume, $1.4 billion in 1958. Year-end outstandings in 1959 were $2.1 billion.

Interdistrict loans among FHLB's have occurred in each year since 1933, and have exceeded $100 million in each of three years: 1950, 1955, and 1957 (Table I-220). In 1958, interdistrict loans totaling $99 million were made; $92 million of these plus all outstandings as of January 1, 1958 were repaid, leaving $7 million outstanding at the year-end.

Home Owners' Loan Corporation (Tables I-221 to I-223)

The Home Owners' Loan Corporation made emergency loans, mostly in the 1930's, primarily to refinance defaulted home mortgages. In addition to direct loans, it purchased shares in insured savings and loan associations. The purpose of HOLC loans was to alleviate the distress situation in the home mortgage area in the depression years of the early 1930's. The HOLC operated in the home mortgage area as a temporary agency performing an emergency function in much the same manner as the Federal Farm Mortgage Corporation operated in the farm mortgage area. The HOLC was supplied with government capital of $200 million and was authorized to issue bonds bearing a government guarantee.

Housing Loans

TABLE I-221

Home Owners' Loan Corporation Direct Loans, 1933-1952[a]

Year ended December 31	Outstanding	Loans made	Loans repaid or charged off	Net change in outstandings
		(thousands of dollars)		
1933	141,520	141,604	84	141,520
1934	2,366,463	2,240,162	15,219	2,224,943
1935	2,897,162	596,631	65,932	530,699
1936	2,765,098	128,533	260,597	-132,064
1937	2,397,646	33,703	401,155	-367,452
1938	2,168,100	109,135	338,681	-229,546
1939	2,035,716	203,196	335,580	-132,384
1940	1,955,572	166,448	246,592	-80,144
1941	1,776,918	84,323	262,977	-178,654
1942	1,566,971	53,838	263,785	-209,947
1943	1,338,102	73,534	302,403	-228,869
1944	1,091,363	41,816	288,555	-246,739
1945	852,319	5,314	244,358	-239,044
1946	636,463	1,896	217,752	-215,856
1947	485,909	2,065	152,619	-150,554
1948	368,908	2,050	119,051	-117,001
1949	230,623	2,097	140,382	-138,285
1950	9,592	868	221,899	-221,031
1951	9,588	--	4	- 4
1952	--		9,588	- 9,588

[a]Includes refinancing loans and vendee instruments.

Note: Table I-223 is the total of Tables I-221 and I-222.

Source: Saulnier, et al., p. 387, and HOLC annual reports.

Housing Loans

TABLE I-222

Home Owners' Loan Corporation Purchases of Shares in Insured Savings and Loan Associations, 1935-1951

Year ended December 31	Outstanding	Loans made	Loans repaid or charged off	Net change in outstandings
	(thousands of dollars)			
1935	19,846	19,846	--	19,846
1936	125,621	105,775	--	105,775
1937	206,475	80,999	145	80,854
1938	214,801	8,921	595	8,326
1939	211,453	4,385	7,733	-3,348
1940	194,264	1,720	18,909	-17,189
1941	175,167	1,613	20,710	-19,097
1942	152,311	598	23,454	-22,856
1943	63,286	--	89,025	-89,025
1944	34,551	--	28,735	-28,735
1945	21,421	--	13,130	-13,130
1946	15,192	--	6,229	-6,229
1947	8,063	--	7,129	-7,129
1948	5,883	--	2,180	-2,180
1949	1,952	--	3,931	-3,931
1950	414	--	1,538	-1,538
1951	--	--	414	- 414

Note: Table I-223 is the total of Tables I-221 and I-222.

Source: Saulnier, et al., p. 387, and annual reports of HOLC.

Housing Loans

TABLE I-223

Home Owners' Loan Corporation Total Loans, 1933-1952

Year ended December 31	Outstanding	Loans made	Loans repaid	Net change in outstandings
	(thousands of dollars)			
1933	141,520	141,604	84	141,520
1934	2,366,463	2,240,162	15,219	2,224,943
1935	2,917,008	616,477	65,932	550,545
1936	2,890,719	234,308	260,597	-26,289
1937	2,604,121	114,702	401,300	-286,598
1938	2,382,901	118,056	339,276	-221,220
1939	2,247,169	207,581	343,313	-135,732
1940	2,149,836	168,168	265,501	-97,333
1941	1,952,085	85,936	283,687	-197,751
1942	1,719,282	54,436	287,239	-232,803
1943	1,401,388	73,534	391,428	-317,894
1944	1,125,914	41,816	317,290	-275,474
1945	873,740	5,314	257,488	-252,174
1946	651,655	1,896	223,981	-222,085
1947	493,972	2,065	159,748	-157,683
1948	374,791	2,050	121,231	-119,181
1949	232,575	2,097	144,313	-142,216
1950	10,006	868	223,437	-222,569
1951	9,588	--	418	-418
1952	--	--	9,588	- 9,588

Note: Table I-223 is the total of Tables I-221 and I-222.

Source: Two types of loans may have been omitted from the HOLC statistics, due to unavailability of data. These are: (1) wholesale purchases of home mortgages from banks in receivership, and (2) direct cash loans for maintenance or reconditioning of home properties.

Most of the home mortgage loans were made by substitution of HOLC bonds for defaulted or distressed mortgages of home owners. Eligible applicants were owner-occupants of one- to four-family nonfarm properties valued at not more than $20,000. The average amount of loan was $3,000. About a million refinancing loans were made, totaling $3 billion. In 1935, the HOLC held about 13 percent of total home mortgage debt.

The HOLC also made so-called vendee loans, on the sale of property acquired in foreclosures, totaling about $600 million. Other home loans included direct cash loans for payment of taxes where a tax sale was imminent, for refinancing defaulted home mortgages where the mortgagor refused to take HOLC bonds, and for the purchase of groups of home mortgages held by banks in receivership.

Purchases of shares in insured savings and loan associations, together with those of the Treasury described in the following section, amounted to about $275 million in the 1933-42 period, and in the mid-1930's supplied about one-seventh of the total capital of such associations. Of total purchases, the HOLC made $224 million and the Treasury $49 million.

Over one-half of the total loans of the HOLC were made in the single year of 1934, $2.2 billion (Table I-223). Loans exceeded $100 million in each year of the 1933-40 period, but were under $100 million in each year of the 1941-50 period. Year-end outstandings reached $2.9 billion in 1935, were down to $0.9 billion by 1945, and were extinguished in 1952. The two parts of total HOLC loans, the direct part and the purchases of shares in insured savings and loan associations, are shown in Tables I-221 and I-222. The former were more than ten times the volume of the latter.

Treasury Department (Table I-224)

In 1933-35 the U.S. Treasury Department purchased shares in insured savings and loan associations amounting to $49 million. Along with $224 million of similar purchases by the Home Owners' Loan Corporation, these purchases helped keep savings and loan associations solvent during the depression, supplemented their investment resources, and increased the supply of home mortgage credit.

Repayments on these loans were at a slow rate until 1939, but with rapid repayments in 1939-44 the outstandings at the end of 1944 were only $3 million. The last of such loans was repaid in 1949.

Housing Loans

TABLE I-224

Treasury Department Purchases of Shares in Insured Savings and Loan Associations, 1933-1949

Year ended December 31	Outstanding	Loans made	Loans repaid or charged off	Net change in outstandings
		(thousands of dollars)		
1933	18	18	---	18
1934	10,725	10,707	---	10,707
1935	49,273	38,575	27	38,548
1936	48,991	---	282	- 282
1937	48,051	---	940	- 940
1938	47,053	---	998	- 998
1939	39,679	---	7,374	- 7,374
1940	26,748	---	12,931	- 12,931
1941	21,284	---	5,464	- 5,464
1942	17,548	---	3,736	- 3,736
1943	6,884	---	10,664	- 10,664
1944	3,489	---	3,395	- 3,395
1945	1,982	---	1,507	- 1,507
1946	1,150	---	832	- 832
1947	555	---	595	- 595
1948	247	---	308	- 308
1949	---	---	247	- 247

Source: Saulnier, et al., p. 398.

RFC Mortgage Company (Table I-225)

The Reconstruction Finance Corporation Mortgage Company's primary lending activity was the purchase and sale of federally insured home and project mortgages during 1935-48. Secondarily, it made direct loans on new or existing income-producing residential properties. Its programs were among those of the 1930's designed to bring the country out of the depression through stimulating construction and stabilizing the financial markets. Loanable funds came primarily from the Reconstruction Finance Corporation, through subscriptions to capital stock and borrowings. The program of the RFC Mortgage Company was administered by the RFC in accordance with RFC amendment legislation in 1935. In 1954, its portfolio of outstanding loans was transferred to the Federal National Mortgage Association.

Operations of the RFC Mortgage Company in the secondary market area were nearly four times as great in volume as its direct lending. Of $383 million purchases of federally insured home and project mortgages, $252 million were FHA-insured and $141 million were VA-guaranteed. A successor already in existence, the Federal National Mortgage Association, was duplicating its chief activity, secondary market operations, at the time the RFC Mortgage Company stopped making purchases and sales in 1948.

The standard direct loans on income-producing residential property were supplemented during World War II by special loans to the Defense Homes Corporation and special loans to defray taxes and fixed charges on income properties in distress because of wartime restrictions and regulations.

Loans and mortgage purchases of the RFC Mortgage Company varied between $26 million and $46 million in each of the years from 1936 through 1944 (Table I-225). The peak volume, $124 million, was in 1947. Year-end outstandings decreased from a high of $131 million in 1948 to $65 million in 1953. In 1954, when $62 million of VA-guaranteed and FHA-insured mortgages, and $2 million of direct loans, were transferred to FNMA, they were considered liquidated insofar as the RFC Mortgage Company was concerned.

Housing Loans

TABLE I-225

Housing Group

RFC Mortgage Company Direct Housing Loans and Purchases of Mortgages, 1935-1954

Year ended December 31	Outstanding	Loans made and mortgages purchased	Loans repaid, mortgages sold, and charge-offs	Net change in outstandings
		(thousands of dollars)		
1935	5,705	5,744	39	5,705
1936	36,126	33,880	3,459	30,421
1937	67,534	45,395	13,987	31,408
1938	54,227	35,316	48,623	-13,307
1939	57,377	27,824	24,674	3,150
1940	67,300	26,148	16,225	9,923
1941	73,036	29,034	23,298	5,736
1942	97,578	45,646	21,104	24,542
1943	104,634	41,625	34,569	7,056
1944	102,211	45,048	47,471	- 2,423
1945	39,240	17,436	80,407	-62,971
1946	13,610	2,715	28,345	-25,630
1947	122,715	123,744	14,639	109,105
1948	131,296	16,060	7,479	8,581
1949	122,653	-	8,643	- 8,643
1950	91,909	-	30,744	-30,744
1951	78,477	-	13,432	-13,432
1952	71,920	-	6,557	- 6,557
1953	65,529	-	6,391	- 6,391
1954	-	-	65,529[a]	-65,529

[a]The outstanding balance of the FHA, VA, and direct mortgages in the portfolio of the RFC Mortgage Company was transferred to the FNMA from the RFC on July 1, 1954. Since the FNMA portfolio contained FHA and VA mortgages of the same type, the transferred FHA and VA mortgages, aggregating $61,998,000, were intermingled, and statistics of FNMA from then on contained the combined data only. The direct mortgages transferred were kept separate in statistical compilations, but since they amounted to only $2,153,000 on July 1, 1954, they are included with other loans in the FNMA statistics, and are not tabulated separately in a special table.

Source: Saulnier, et al., p. 411, and information supplied by FNMA.

V. MISCELLANEOUS LOAN PROGRAMS

Total lending under the miscellaneous programs has been insignificant in comparison with other federal lending. The largest of these programs in terms of outstandings was that of loans on Veterans' Administration life insurance.

SUMMARY TABLE I-E

Summary of Miscellaneous Loans Outstanding, Ten Programs, Year-End 1929, 1939, 1949, and 1958

Table No.	Program of Miscellaneous Loans	1929	1939	1949	1958
		(thousands of dollars)			
I-242	Veterans' Administration Life Insurance Loans	52,130	149,663	139,697	356,778
I-236	Lease-Purchase Program Loans	---	---	---	42,305
I-227 & I-228	Treasury Department Loans to District of Columbia	---	---	---	10,973
I-238	Bureau of Indian Affairs	---	2,624	7,537	9,157
I-231	Treasury Department Civil Defense Loans	---	---	---	5,042
I-237 & I-241	Disaster Loans	---	20,970	4,745	4,362
I-243	Bureau of Reclamation	---	---	---	2,558
I-226	Loans to College Students	---	---	1,329	371
I-240	Reconstruction Finance Corporation Loans to Minor Governmental Units	---	170,346	18,766	---
I-239	Puerto Rico Reconstruction Administration	---	4,142	7,908	---
	Total	52,130	347,745	179,982	431,546

Subtractions to eliminate double counting -- none

Loans to College Students (Table I-226)

The Federal Security Agency made loans to students enrolled in accelerated courses during World War II. This was the only college student loan program under which money was disbursed through December 31, 1958. In 1953, the Federal Security Agency was dissolved, and its activities transferred to the Department of Health, Education, and Welfare. In 1959, student loans not included in these tabulations were made under Title II of the National Defense Education Act of 1958, under a new program that is described at the end of this section.

Loans were made to college students in the technical and professional fields of medicine, engineering, dentistry, chemistry, pharmacy, veterinary, and physics. War-created shortages of personnel in these fields appeared to be serious, and the loans were made to enable students to accelerate their courses so as to be available earlier for service in the war effort. Over two-thirds of the loans were made to students of medicine and engineering.

In the 1943 fiscal year, loans were made to 11,081 students in 286 colleges and universities. In the 1944 fiscal year, loans were made only to students who had received loans the previous year, and the number of loans was 1,572. These loans in fiscal 1944 were made to enable students to finish the accelerated program for which earlier loans had been made. Funds for loans came from a congressional appropriation of $5 million.

The terms of repayment called for four equal annual installments covering principal and interest, beginning one year after graduation or separation for other purposes. Provision was made for cancellation of the unpaid balance of the loan when the borrower was inducted into the military services, before graduation, under the Selective Training and Service Act. Repayments were deferred during the military service of the borrower.

The new program of the Office of Education of the U.S. Department of Health, Education, and Welfare, with initial loans made in 1959, provides for the following types of loans:

1. Loans to college students, with federal capital contributions covering up to 90 percent of the loan fund at each college or university, and the remainder provided by the institution of higher education.

2. Loans to institutions of higher education to cover their 10 percent of the college or university loan fund, in instances where the institution is unable to secure funds from other sources on reasonable terms.

Miscellaneous Loans

TABLE I-226

Federal Security Agency World War II Loans to College Students in Accelerated Courses, 1942-1958

Year ended December 31	Outstanding	Loans made	Loans repaid or charged off	Net change in outstandings
	(thousands of dollars)			
1942	935	935	0	935
1943	3,089	2,216	62	2,154
1944	3,044	173	218	- 45
1945	2,698	4	350	- 346
1946	2,273	---	425	- 425
1947	1,871	8	410	- 402
1948	1,577	---	294	- 294
1949	1,329	---	248	- 248
1950	1,154	---	175	- 175
1951	1,018	---	136	- 136
1952	924	---	94	- 94
1953	837	---	87	- 87
1954	756	---	81	- 81
1955	709	---	47	- 47
1956	551	---	158	- 158
1957	503	---	48	- 48
1958	371	---	132	- 132

Source: Data supplied by U.S. Department of Health, Education, and Welfare.
No loans under new program—to college students, to colleges for loan programs, and to nonprofit private elementary and secondary schools for equipment—were made prior to January 1, 1959.

3. Loans to nonprofit private elementary and secondary schools for the acquisition of equipment for science, mathematics, and foreign language instruction.

The loans to college students, most important of the above three types, are to be in amounts not exceeding $1,000 per student per year, and $5,000 in total per student. They are repayable over a ten-year period beginning one year after the borrower ceases to be a full-time student. Up to 50 percent of the loan, plus interest, will be canceled if the student becomes a teacher in a public elementary or secondary school. The interest rate, beginning one year after the borrower ceases to be a full-time student, is 3 percent.

Treasury Department Loans to District Of Columbia (Tables I-227 and I-228)

The U.S. Treasury Department made loans of $1.9 million to the District of Columbia in 1942-44, primarily for purposes of civilian defense (Table I-227). None of these loans was outstanding at the end of 1944.

In 1953, and again in 1956-58, the Treasury Department made loans totaling $11,250,000 for the construction of public works (Table I-228). Year-end outstandings in 1958 were $10,973,000. These loans were made under legislation enacted on June 2, 1950, authorizing loans to the District of Columbia for financing the construction of water, sewage, and highway construction projects. Loans must be specifically requested of Congress in connection with the budget submitted for the District each fiscal year. Maturities of loans may be up to 30 years. Interest charged the District reflects the cost of money to the Treasury for borrowings of a maturity approximately equal to one-half of the period of time the loan is to be outstanding.

Treasury Department Civil Defense Loans (Tables I-229 to I-233)

The Treasury Department is authorized to make loans to finance projects for civil defense purposes up to $250 million outstanding at any one time, upon certification of the Director of Civil and Defense Mobilization. Loans are to be made only if financial assistance is not otherwise available on reasonable terms. These may be either direct loans, none of which has been made since 1955, or deferred participation loans, some of which were made through 1958. Most of the loans made were to hospitals, and most of these were for hospitals located in the New York–New Jersey area. The lending program is financed by borrowings from the U.S. Treasury.

Miscellaneous Loans

TABLE I-227

Treasury Department Loans to the District of Columbia for Civilian Defense and other Purposes, 1942-1944

Year ended December 31	Outstanding	Loans made	Loans repaid or charged off	Net change in outstandings
		(thousands of dollars)		
1942	800	800	---	800
1943	701	900	999	-99
1944	---	200	901	-701

Source: Saulnier, et al., p. 398.

TABLE I-228

Treasury Department Loans to the District of Columbia for the Construction of Public Works, 1953-1958

Year ended December 31	Outstanding	Loans made	Loans repaid or charged off	Net change in outstandings
		(thousands of dollars)		
1953	1,900	1,900	---	1,900
1954	1,900	---	---	---
1955	1,865	---	35	-35
1956	5,523	3,700	42	3,658
1957	8,846	3,400	77	3,323
1958	10,973	2,250	123	2,127

Source: Data supplied by Treasury Department.

Miscellaneous Loans

TABLE I-229

Treasury Department Civil Defense Direct Loans Made under Section 409 of the Federal Civil Defense Act of 1950, 1953-1958

Year ended December 31	Outstanding	Loans made	Loans repaid or charged off	Net change in outstandings
	(thousands of dollars)			
1953	1,866	1,876	10	1,866
1954	2,338	618	146	472
1955	2,051	99	386	-287
1956	1,302	--	749	-749
1957	1,199	--	103	-103
1958	1,098	--	101	-101

Note: Table I-231 is the total of Tables I-229 and I-230.

Source: Data supplied by Treasury Department. The only loans made were to hospitals, mostly in the New York-New Jersey area. The program was transferred to the Treasury from the RFC on September 28, 1953.

TABLE I-230

Treasury Department Civil Defense Deferred Participation Loans Made under Section 409 of the Federal Civil Defense Act of 1950, 1954-1958

Year ended December 31	Outstanding	Loans made	Loans repaid or charged off	Net change in outstandings
	(thousands of dollars)			
1954	1,675	1,675	--	1,675
1955	3,150	1,525	50	1,475
1956	4,233	1,150	67	1,083
1957	4,060	--	173	-173
1958	3,944	75	191	-116

Note: Table I-231 is the total of Tables I-229 and I-230. Table I-230 is the total of Table I-232 and I-233.

Source: Data supplied by Treasury Department, usually for fiscal years, with interpolation necessary to put data on calendar-year basis.

Miscellaneous Loans

TABLE I-231

Treasury Department Total Civil Defense Loans, 1953-1958

Year ended December 31	Outstanding	Loans made	Loans repaid	Net change in outstandings
		(thousands of dollars)		
1953	1,866	1,876	10	1,866
1954	4,013	2,293	146	2,147
1955	5,201	1,624	436	1,188
1956	5,535	1,150	816	334
1957	5,259	--	276	- 276
1958	5,042	75	292	- 217

Note: Table I-231 is the total of Tables I-229 and I-230.

Source: Obtained by adding Tables I-229 and I-230.

TABLE I-232

Treasury Department Civil Defense Deferred Participation Loans, Government Part, 1954-1958

Year ended December 31	Outstanding	Loans made	Loans repaid or charged off	Net change in outstandings
		(thousands of dollars)		
1954	1,508	1,508	--	1,508
1955	2,310	802	--	802
1956	2,774	510	46	464
1957	2,663	--	111	-111
1958	2,399	62	326	-264

Note: Table I-230 is the total of Tables I-232 and I-233.

Source: Data supplied by Treasury Department for fiscal years, with interpolation necessary to put data on calendar-year basis.

Miscellaneous Loans

TABLE I-233

Treasury Department Civil Defense Deferred Participation Loans
Private Part, 1954-1958

Year ended December 31	Out-standing	Loans made	Loans repaid or charged off	Net change in outstandings
		(thousands of dollars)		
1954	167	167	---	167
1955	840	723	50	673
1956	1,459	640	21	619
1957	1,397	---	62	-62
1958	1,545	13	-135	148

Note: Table I-230 is the total of Tables I-232 and I-233.

Source: Obtained by subtracting Table I-232 from Table I-230.

The loan program was authorized by the Federal Civil Defense Act of 1950. Originally it was administered by the Reconstruction Finance Corporation. On September 28, 1953, in accordance with the Reconstruction Finance Corporation Liquidation Act approved July 30, 1953, it was transferred to the U.S. Treasury.

Lease-Purchase Program Loans (Tables I-234 to I-236)

Between 1954 and 1957, lease-purchase contracts covering the construction of buildings for the General Services Administration and Post Office Department were authorized, with the commitment to purchase in one sense a guarantee of loans of private capital used in their construction. Inclusion within the definition of federal lending activity is debatable. In the CMC Research Study by Warren Law,[1] these commitments were excluded, while in the National Planning Association report on federal loans and guarantees by George Break, they were included. In this report, these commitments are included as a part of federal lending activity. Although Congress in 1957 provided for termination of the program, commitments under previous authorizations continued in 1958 and 1959.

No public funds are involved initially. The mechanics of the program are such that the cost of construction is paid by private investors who take and hold title to the buildings until the payments under the leases to the government are equal to total costs plus interest. This occurs in from ten to 25 years.

Total commitments under the lease-purchase program for public buildings were $43 million in the period ended December 31, 1958 (Table I-236). Year-end outstandings in 1958 were $42 million.

Most of the commitments were for buildings of the General Services Administration (Table I-234). Commitments for buildings of the Post Office Department were less (Table I-235).

With the termination of authority for new lease-purchase authorizations in 1957, and a cancellation of all projects except those under construction, a new "commercial leasing program" was begun in 1958, under which the private investor retains title to the building after the long-term lease to the government runs out. This new program resulted in private investment in post offices of $0.3 billion by early 1960, and was expected to result in private investment of $1.5 billion in 12,000 new post offices by 1966. In the tabulations in this study, commitments under commercial leasing programs were excluded from the definition of federal loan and insurance activity.

---

[1]See Research Study Two of this volume.

Miscellaneous Loans

TABLE I-234

Commitments of U.S. Post Office Department under Lease-Purchase Program for Public Buildings, 1958

Year ended December 31	Outstanding	Loans made	Loans repaid or charged off	Net change in outstandings
		(thousands of dollars)		
1958[a]	487	495	8	487

[a]No commitments under this program until 1958. Program extinguished in 1959.

Note: Table I-236 is the total of Tables I-234 and I-235.

Source: Special tabulations supplied by Post Office Department.

TABLE I-235

Commitments of General Services Administration under Lease-Purchase Program for Public Buildings, 1956-1959

Year ended December 31	Outstanding	Loans made	Loans repaid or charged off	Net change in outstandings
		(thousands of dollars)		
1956	1,675	1,675	--	1,675
1957	1,570	--	105	-105
1958	41,818	40,353	105	40,248
1959	47,832	6,382	368	6,014

Note: Table I-236 is the total of Tables I-234 and I-235.

Source: Data supplied by General Services Administration.

Miscellaneous Loans

TABLE I-236

Total Commitments under Lease-Purchase Program for Public Buildings, 1956-1958

Year ended December 31	Out-standing	Loans made	Loans repaid or charged off	Net change in outstandings
		(thousands of dollars)		
1956	1,675	1,675	---	1,675
1957	1,570	---	105	-105
1958	42,305	40,848	113	40,735

Note: Table I-236 is the total of Tables I-234 and I-235.

Source: Data supplied by Post Office Department and General Services Administration.

Disaster Loans (Tables I-237 and I-241)

The Reconstruction Finance Corporation—directly and through funds supplied to a corporation chartered by it, the Disaster Loan Corporation—made disaster loans to victims of floods and other catastrophes in each of the years from 1933 through 1955.

The Disaster Loan Corporation made loans between 1937 and 1945. The RFC made direct loans between 1933 and 1938, and again between 1945 and 1955; in the middle years when the DLC was active, the RFC made either no or few direct loans. Outstanding balances of the DLC were transferred to the RFC for liquidation on June 30, 1945, when the DLC was dissolved. Outstanding balances of the RFC were transferred to the Small Business Administration on July 1, 1954, as part of the liquidation process of the RFC.

Bureau of Indian Affairs (Table I-238)

The Bureau of Indian Affairs, of the U.S. Department of the Interior makes loans to Indians and Indian organizations for educational purposes, to promote industry, and to provide emergency relief. Loans to encourage industry and self-support among Indians have been made since 1911. Loans for educational purposes, and to Indian tribes, credit associations, and cooperative associations, have been made since 1934. A unique type of loan, cattle instead of money, with repayment in kind, has been made to Indians for several years from a "revolving cattle pool."

From incomplete data covering most but not all of the lending activity of the Bureau of Indian Affairs, Table I-238 was prepared, covering the period from 1934 through 1958. In 1951-58, the following programs were included: (1) the revolving credit program of loans to tribes, credit associations, and cooperatives; (2) reimbursable loans exclusive of tribal funds for education and other purposes; (3) loans from the revolving cattle pool, with each head valued at $100.

Puerto Rico Reconstruction Administration (Table I-239)

A program of minor significance has been that of loans to farmers, farm tenants, laborers, stockmen, farm partnerships, and cooperative associations in Puerto Rico, for the purpose of rural rehabilitation. The program was administered by the Puerto Rico Reconstruction Administration, an independent government agency. It was liquidated in 1955, and assets transferred to other agencies of the U.S. Government for liquidation.

Reconstruction Finance Corporation Loans to Minor Governmental Units (Table I-240)

Among the wide variety of loans of the Reconstruction Finance Corporation were those to minor governmental units for miscellaneous purposes. Their emergency characteristics in the depression, and their use for defense purposes in 1941, are indicated by the description of their coverage by Saulnier, et al., as follows: "Construction loans to public agencies for defense and nondefense projects; loans to drainage, levee, and similar districts; loans to establish state funds for securing repayment of deposits of public moneys in banks and other depositories; loans to refinance obligations of public school districts; and loans for payment of teachers' salaries, for self-liquidating public works, and for relief and work relief under the Emergency Relief and Construction Act of 1932 as amended."[2] This type of RFC loan exceeded $100 million in only two years, 1933 and 1941, when the volume was $273 million and $151 million, respectively (Table I-240). Year-end outstandings were considered extinguished in 1957 when the small amount of loans then outstanding were transferred to Housing and Home Finance Agency.

[2] Saulnier, et al., p. 383

Miscellaneous Loans

TABLE I-237

Direct Loans of the Disaster Loan Corporation, 1937-1945

Year ended December 31	Outstanding	Loans made	Loans repaid or charged off	Net change in outstandin
		(thousands of dollars)		
1937	5,907	7,571	1,664	5,907
1938	6,932	2,982	1,957	1,025
1939	19,302	14,976	2,606	12,370
1940	20,905	5,444	3,841	1,603
1941	16,290	2,595	7,210	-4,615
1942	6,876	1,108	10,522	-9,414
1943	2,677	603	4,802	-4,199
1944	1,735	848	1,790	-942
1945	---	188	1,923	-1,735

Source: Saulnier, et al., pp. 415-416. Represents withdrawals from funds held by the RFC loans to victims of floods and other catastrophes. The Corporation was dissolved June 30, 1945, and outstanding balances transferred to the RFC for liquidiation.

Miscellaneous Loans

TABLE I-238

Direct Loans of the Bureau of Indian Affairs, 1934-1958

Year ended December 31	Outstanding	Loans made	Loans repaid or charged off	Net change in outstandings
	(thousands of dollars)			
1934	80	139	59	80
1935	110	205	175	30
1936	179	344	275	69
1937	849	1,076	406	670
1938	2,091	1,461	219	1,242
1939	2,624	1,073	540	533
1940	2,648	665	641	24
1941	2,788	619	479	140
1942	2,700	775	863	- 88
1943	2,569	875	1,006	- 131
1944	5,879	1,011	- 2,299 a/	3,310
1945	5,576	1,019	1,322	- 303
1946	5,808	1,381	1,149	232
1947	6,132	2,214	1,890	324
1948	6,952	1,907	1,087	820
1949	7,537	2,239	1,654	585
1950	9,984	2,973	526	2,447
1951	15,407	2,604	- 2,819 b/	5,423
1952	15,044	1,773	2,136	- 363
1953	13,500	764	2,308	- 1,544
1954	11,653	330	2,177	- 1,847
1955	9,865	1,022	2,810	- 1,788
1956	8,860	2,020	3,025	- 1,005
1957	8,585	2,324	2,599	- 275
1958	9,157	2,486	1,914	572

[a] This is a negative figure apparently because of the addition of a program hitherto excluded.

[b] This is a negative figure because of the addition of the "revolving cattle pool" data to the series for the first time in 1951.

Source: 1934-50—pp. 415-416 of Saulnier, et al., with estimates of outstandings added for 1934 and 1935. The volume of loans made was estimated by linear interpolation of fiscal year data. Year-end outstandings were from the Daily Statements of, and material supplied by, the Treasury Department. Includes loans for educational purposes only since 1939. Emergency relief loans during 1935-37 are excluded from loans made. Includes loans to promote industry, and revolving fund loans to Indians and Indian organizations. Loans for the former totaled $5,441,000 in 1911-33.
1951-59—Data from Bureau of Indian Affairs. Calendar year estimates were based on linear interpolation of fiscal year data. Includes (1) the revolving credit program, (2) reimbursable loans exclusive of tribal funds, and (3) the revolving cattle pool, with each head valued at $100.

Miscellaneous Loans

TABLE I-239

Direct Loans of the Puerto Rico Reconstruction Administration, 1936-1958

Year ended December 31	Outstanding	Loans made [a]	Loans repaid or charged off	Net change in outstandings
		(thousands of dollars)		
1936	1,955	2,000	45	1,955
1937	3,990	2,100	65	2,035
1938	4,598	1,000	392	608
1939	4,142	--	456	-456
1940	4,216	100	26	74
1941	4,281	100	35	65
1942	4,165	--	116	-116
1943	5,977	2,000	188	1,812
1944	6,708	1,000	269	731
1945	6,037	--	671	-671
1946	5,588	--	449	-449
1947	5,418	--	170	-170
1948	6,959	2,000	459	1,541
1949	7,908	1,000	51	949
1950	9,130	2,000	778	1,222
1951	8,878	--	252	-252
1952	8,758	--	120	-120
1953	8,098	--	660	-660
1954	3,287	--	4,811	-4,811
1955	--	--	3,287	-3,287

[a] Loans made were estimated.

Source: Saulnier, et al., p. 415 and data supplied by Treasury Department. All functions of the Puerto Rico Reconstruction Administration ceased as of the close of business on February 15, 1955, in accordance with the Act approved August 15, 1953 (67 Stat. 584). Outstanding loans and other assets as of that date were transferred to other agencies of the U.S. Government for liquidation.

Miscellaneous Loans

TABLE I-240

Reconstruction Finance Corporation Direct Loans to Minor Governmental Units for Miscellaneous Purposes, 1932-1957

Year ended December 31	Outstanding	Loans made	Loans repaid or charged off	Net change in outstandings
	(thousands of dollars)			
1932	95,704	95,704	--	95,704
1933	368,002	273,425	1,127	272,298
1934	425,083	96,937	39,856	57,081
1935	485,837	99,908	39,154	60,754
1936	546,319	75,217	14,735	60,482
1937	591,807	60,023	14,535	45,488
1938	268,089	61,447	385,165	-323,718
1939	170,346	70,028	167,771	- 97,743
1940	126,878	56,222	99,690	- 43,468
1941	132,433	150,813	145,258	5,555
1942	136,044	12,275	8,664	3,611
1943	97,670	3,773	42,147	- 38,374
1944	79,167	1,896	20,399	- 18,503
1945	62,982	1,123	17,308	- 16,185
1946	55,955	12,796	19,823	- 7,027
1947	68,990	18,419	5,384	13,035
1948	77,836	13,806	4,960	8,846
1949	18,766	7,060	66,130	- 59,070
1950	13,623	1,624	6,767	- 5,143
1951	12,780	1,909	2,752	- 843
1952	18,442	8.167	2,505	5,662
1953	29,836a/	13,959	2,565	11,394
1954	24,795	31,565	36,606	- 5,041
1955	23,063	173	1,905	- 1,732
1956	4,698	--	18,365	- 18,365
1957b/	--	--	4,698	- 4,698

[a]The 1953 outstandings include $2,880,000 of housing PWA loans, a small part of total PWA outstandings on that date, and in the remaining recent years the liquidation of this small part of total PWA loans are also included in the outstandings.

[b]A small amount of loans were transferred to the HHFA on June 30, 1957, but the program was so close to final liquidation that in this table it was considered to be closed out at the end of 1957.

Source: Saulnier, et al., pp. 381-383 for data through 1952; Treasury Dept., for 1953-57 data.

Miscellaneous Loans

TABLE I-241

Reconstruction Finance Corporation Loans to Repair Damage Caused by Floods and other Catastrophes, 1933-1959

Year ended December 31	Outstanding	Loans made	Loans repaid or charged off	Net change in outstandings
	(thousands of dollars)			
1933	2,692	2,761	69	2,692
1934	8,272	5,859	279	5,580
1935	9,157	1,169	284	885
1936	8,722	1,624	2,059	- 435
1937	6,401	570	2,891	-2,321
1938	2,481	19	3,939	-3,920
1939	1,668	--	813	- 813
1940	1,234	--	434	- 434
1941	1,027	--	207	- 207
1942	936	--	91	- 91
1943	656	--	280	- 280
1944	509	--	147	- 147
1945	1,464	1,497	542	955
1946	940	61	585	- 524
1947	1,178	518	280	238
1948	3,034	2,259	403	1,856
1949	4,745	2,509	798	1,711
1950	4,090	655	1,310	- 655
1951	13,112	10,342	1,320	9,022
1952	17,130	7,579	3,561	4,018
1953	16,022	2,195	3,303	-1,108
1954	12,983	869	3,908	-3,039
1955	10,424	148	2,707	-2,559
1956	7,815	--	2,609	-2,609
1957	5,983	--	1,832	-1,832
1958	4,362	--	1,621	-1,621
1959	2,998	--	1,364	-1,364

Source: Saulnier, et al., pp. 381-382, to 1953; Small Business Administration, 1954-59. Program transferred to SBA on July 1, 1954.

Veterans' Administration Life Insurance Loans (Table I-242)

The Veterans' Administration makes loans to holders of VA life insurance policies of veterans and servicemen, in much the same manner as private insurance companies make loans to their policy holders. The program of loans is administered by the Department of Insurance of the Veterans' Administration.

Loans on GI insurance policies are made up to a maximum of 94 percent of their cash value. The rate of interest payable on loans in September 1960 was 4 percent. Loans may be repaid at any time in full or in installments of at least $5 per month.

Outstandings on loans to holders of U.S. Government life insurance policies reached a peak of $400 million in 1959 (Table I-242). This resulted from a steady year-to-year increase from the corresponding figure of $115 million in 1946. The prewar peak of year-end outstandings was $151 million in 1941.

Bureau of Reclamation (Table I-243)

The Bureau of Reclamation makes loans (1) to irrigation districts and other local water user organizations for the development of irrigation facilities, the so-called distribution system loans, and (2) to irrigation districts, conservancy districts, other public agencies, and states for the construction of small projects generally similar to those of the regular Reclamation program, the so-called small project loans. Funds for both types of loans come from the U.S. Treasury, with each small project loan requiring specific congressional approval, and the distribution system loans requiring approval by the Secretary of the Interior.

The local organization seeking a loan for the development of irrigation facilities is required itself to finance a part of construction costs, up to 10 percent for distribution systems, and up to 25 percent for small projects. The maturity of loans must not exceed 50 years. No interest is charged on those portions of the loan used to irrigate lands not in excess of 160 acres in a single ownership. The total cost of a small project receiving a small project loan must not exceed $10 million. No such limit applies to distribution system loans.

Miscellaneous Loans

TABLE I-242

Veterans' Administration Loans to Holders of U.S. Government Life Insurance Policies, 1929-1959

Year ended December 31	Outstanding	Loans made	Loans repaid or charged off	Net change in outstandings
	(thousands of dollars)			
1929	52,130	43,190		
1930	70,830	64,839	46,139	18,700
1931	89,660	84,185	65,355	18,830
1932	110,642	113,128	92,146	20,982
1933	121,764	112,050	100,928	11,122
1934	121,681	116,456	116,539	- 83
1935	127,580	117,338	111,439	5,899
1936	128,560	114,446	113,466	980
1937	138,468	126,179	116,271	9,908
1938	147,426	118,791	109,833	8,958
1939	149,663	140,783	138,546	2,237
1940	150,645	149,547	148,565	982
1941	151,206	112,976	112,415	561
1942	144,762	109,316	115,760	- 6,444
1943	133,414	130,457	141,805	-11,348
1944	123,125	9,295	19,584	-10,289
1945	116,379	9,469	16,215	- 6,746
1946	114,507	13,832	15,704	- 1,872
1947	115,555	17,128	16,080	1,048
1948	125,569	22,167	12,153	10,014
1949	139,697	27,757	13,629	14,128
1950	157,311	33,834	16,220	17,614
1951	175,309	37,409	19,411	17,998
1952	188,744	34,933	21,498	13,435
1953	208,150	42,695	23,289	19,406
1954	231,933	48,878	25,095	23,783
1955	256,668	80,993	56,258	24,735
1956	284,051	93,570	66,187	27,383
1957	319,778	111,813	76,086	35,727
1958	356,778	121,505	84,505	37,000
1959	399,899	133,156	90,035	43,121

Source: Special tabulations supplied by Veterans' Administration. In 1929-43 and 1955-59, the figures for "Loans made" include the full amount of outstanding loans on policies in cases where existing loans were increased. The existing loans in such cases were included in the repayment figures. Therefore, the figures in the "Loans made" and "Loans repaid or charged off" columns for these years are inflated. During the years 1944-54, only the increases in the loans in such cases were included in the "Loans made" column.

Miscellaneous Loans

TABLE I-243

Bureau of Reclamation Direct Loans for Construction of Irrigation Distribution Systems and Small Reclamation Projects, 1957-1958

Year ended December 31	Outstanding	Loans made	Loans repaid or charged off	Net change in outstandings
		(thousands of dollars)		
1957	110	110	-	110
1958	2,558	2,448	-	2,448

Source: Data furnished by Bureau of Reclamation, Department of the Interior.

Research Study Two

THE AGGREGATE IMPACT OF FEDERAL CREDIT PROGRAMS ON THE ECONOMY

Warren A. Law
Harvard University

INTRODUCTION

An important phenomenon of the United States economy since World War II has been the growth of programs involving either the extension of credit by the federal government or government insurance or guarantee of loans made by private institutions. The first such program was established in 1917 with the organization of the Federal Land banks. By 1940 loans made or guaranteed by the federal government totaled almost $4 billion, and in 1958, the last year covered in this essay, the total exceeded $20 billion.

The primary purpose of the present study is to assess the aggregate impact of all these programs on the level of economic activity in the United States. In addition, the study briefly considers the extent to which these programs have supplemented or counteracted deliberate fiscal or monetary policy directed toward stabilizing the economy. Some attention is devoted to costs of the programs, their effect upon resource allocation, and their relation to national goals.

Scope of the Study. A difficult initial task is to define the limits to the study. The basic work on this subject, by Saulnier, Halcrow, and Jacoby,[1] includes 58 direct federal agencies and 6 federally

---

[1] R.J. Saulnier, H.G. Halcrow, N.H. Jacoby, Federal Lending and Loan Insurance (Princeton, 1958).

sponsored agencies with credit programs in existence at some time. Of these, 27 were still active in 1953. The list runs the gamut from the Virgin Islands Corporation, which makes direct loans to aid that area, to Prencinradio Incorporated, which made loans during World War II to radio stations in Uruguay. In all, 146 separate credit programs are included, and 10 others excluded only because annual data were unavailable.

In general, the present study embraces the same programs, and the reader is referred to Saulnier, et al. for a list. However, certain important inclusions or exclusions require comment here. First, loans to foreign governments are excluded where possible, partly on the grounds that inclusion would make the study unmanageable and partly because many of these "loans" are, in fact, direct grants. Second, loans of the Commodity Credit Corporation are included. Although it may be argued that their primary purpose is not credit assistance but support of agricultural prices, they are included because of their size and because the true timing of their impact on GNP is misstated under present budgetary treatment. Finally, in addition to revising some of Saulnier's data and bringing them up to date, this study includes loans made in connection with disposition of government property, whereas the former does not.

CREATION OF GROSS NATIONAL PRODUCT

Any attempt to determine the contribution of federal lending or loan insurance programs to real output is beset with statistical, theoretical and conceptual difficulties. A major hurdle is the simple accumulation of data, much of which is unavailable in published sources.[1] Then some answer must be given to such questions as: To what extent did public credit substitute for private credit or for federal spending? Was federal credit financed by taxes, sales of government securities to the public, creation of new money, or by still other methods? But we may start with even simpler difficulties.

Problems of Definition:

Net or Gross Flow? There are at least three possible series of value in our analysis—total loans authorized, total loan funds disbursed, and net change in loans outstanding. The first, total amount

---

[1]The herculean task of gathering data for this and other studies was under the direction of Professor Stewart Johnson. As an extreme example of his problems, the Bureau of Indian Affairs has one program in which credit is extended in the form of cattle instead of money, and repayments made in kind. Fortunately for the accuracy of our data, the more difficult problems relate to programs of insignificant size.

of new loan commitments each year, is important because it is often the commitment which sets the economic wheels in motion. A private firm, for example, may begin production on the basis of a government commitment to lend at a later date.[2] Moreover, the loan commitment is the only point at which a lending program may be controlled (just as the provision of "new commitment authority" is the point at which Congress has control). Total commitments, however, have an upward bias because loans may be included which are subsequently cancelled and because two or more types of federal assistance are sometimes provided for the same transaction at different stages in the financing process. More important, data are often unavailable for commitments of minor credit programs, and have been readily available for major programs only since 1952.[3]

Of the two remaining series, the second—annual volume of loan funds disbursed—is clearly more important when we are concerned with the impact of federal credit on a particular industry or area of economic activity. Although the borrower must repay the loan, any reduction in his propensity to spend which results from those repayments will be felt in areas other than that in which the loan was originally made. Thus, extension of a mortgage loan will probably result in increased housing expenditures, but it is unlikely that repayments on that mortgage will induce the homeowner to curtail his expenditures on housing.

On the other hand, repayment does reduce the borrower's ability to spend somewhere, otherwise there would be no difference in the effect of a federal loan versus a federal grant. It is possible, of course, that new loans will increase borrowers' expenditures more than repayments will reduce them, i.e., that the expansionary effect of a given loan exceeds the contractionary effect of an equal amount of repayments. It is also probable that the timing of repayments will not coincide with the timing of the expenditure reductions resulting therefrom. But unfortunately we know very little about borrower behavior and assume below that the effects of a loan and repayment are roughly symmetrical.[4]

---

[2]See M. L. Weidenbaum, "The Federal Government Spending Process," in Joint Economic Committee, Federal Expenditure Policy for Economic Growth and Stability, 1957. A "commitment" is an approval by a federal agency of a direct loan or of insurance or guarantee of a private loan.

[3]In Bureau of the Budget, Special Analysis of Federal Credit Programs, published annually.

[4]We also assume that repayments do not increase the government's propensity to spend. The relatively small share of total loans which are direct government loans (rather than insured private loans) strengthens this assumption. When repayments go to private lenders they tend to be reloaned, of course, but this is reflected in the "gross flow" series.

If new loans increase and repayments decrease aggregate spending, then the difference between the two—the change in loans outstanding—provides the best measure of the stimulating or depressing force of credit on total spending in a given period.[5] We so assume hereafter. In view, however, of the many weaknesses of this assumption, we shall also include data on the gross flow of credit, and point out where the latter is a more significant measure for a particular purpose.

Inclusion of Loan Insurance. It is obvious on the surface that federal insurance or guarantee of private loans has some expenditure-generating effect. By reducing default and liquidity risks, such insurance persuades lenders to extend loans to otherwise unacceptable credit risks and to liberalize terms to all borrowers, while easier terms may induce borrowers to increase their demands for funds. In all of these events private lending is increased. Hence we cannot ignore loan insurance in estimating the effects of federal credit activities on total spending. In fact, for this purpose the only reasons for differentiating between direct federal lending and loan insurance are the possibility that direct loans are made with new money or that a larger share of the insured lending would have taken place even in the absence of any federal action. The question of the extent to which federal credit (including insured loans) has increased total credit or merely substituted for other forms of credit is discussed later as is the question of the source of loan funds. At this point, however, we simply add federally insured loans to direct federal loans and participations to derive a picture of total federal credit activities. Moreover, no distinction is made between an insured and a guaranteed loan, with both being lumped hereafter under one heading—insured loans.

Noninsured Parts. In computing a figure to be called "total federal credit," including both direct loans of federal or federally sponsored agencies and loans of private agencies insured or guaranteed by the federal government, should we also include the

---

[5] Cf. G. Haberler, Consumer Instalment Credit and Economic Fluctuations, (New York, 1942), Ch. 3. We refer here, of course, only to the primary effect of credit and disregard any "multiplier" or "accelerator" effects. These are discussed later. Also, the statement is valid only when applied to total credit in the economy. That is, an increase in net federal credit outstanding would have little or no effect on total spending if it merely substituted for an increase in some other type of credit. Whether or not the extension of a given type of credit diminishes significantly the availability of credit elsewhere depends on liquidity conditions in the economy. This problem is recognized later.

noninsured or nonguaranteed parts of the latter loans? (Similarly, should we include the private portion of those loans in which the federal government participates jointly with private lenders, as in loans extended under Section 302 of the Defense Production Act?) Clearly the Treasury assumes no risk of loss and has none of the usual characteristics of a creditor with respect to this part of the loan. On the other hand, if our purpose is to estimate the total impact of federal credit programs we must admit that the private portion of many of these loans would not have been made at all without federal participation, or would have been made only under terms so onerous as to be unacceptable to the borrower. Thus to exclude this portion entirely would understate the effect of federal credit. However, we have not included hereafter the uninsured parts of insured loans in total federal credit. The understatement resulting therefrom will partially offset the overstatement resulting from inclusion of the insured parts, since many of the latter would have been granted without federal aid. Since 1950 the uninsured parts of these loans have been about one-fourth of the total, so the offset is considerable. Data are included in Table II-1.

"Federal Credit" Defined. The term "federal credit" as used hereafter includes, the total of: (a) direct federal loans; (b) the federally insured or guaranteed parts of private loans (but not the uninsured parts); and (c) federal participations in private loans. Where the terms "gross" or "net" are not used, we are referring to net flows—i.e., we have deducted from total federal credit all repayments or expirations of insurance (the latter being small). In all cases we are referring to loans actually disbursed, rather than merely authorized.

A First Look at the Picture

Gross federal credit extended annually has risen from less than \$0.3 billion in 1929 to more than \$20 billion in 1958, but the rise has not been a steady one. Instead there have been several noticeable jumps, first with the advent of New Deal legislation in the early 1930's, another during World War II, and still another with the postwar boom. Before 1932 the only significant federal credit programs were in the agricultural area, primarily those of the Federal Land banks and Federal Intermediate Credit banks, although the Agricultural Marketing Act had adumbrated later legislation by extending \$740 million of loans in 1930-32 to support commodity prices. Total loans doubled in 1932, to \$2.2 billion, with the advent of the Reconstruction Finance Corporation. As that agency's loans to financial institutions declined steadily in subsequent years, the drop was more than offset by new programs. The prewar peak was reached in 1934, with \$6.2 billion loaned or insured, more than \$2.2 billion of which was accounted for by the Home Owners Loan Corporation alone. From that year until the

TABLE II-1

Federal Lending and Loan Insurance, 1929-1958
(Millions of dollars)

	(1) Direct loans (a)	(2) Insured loans (b)	(3) Total federal credit	(4) Noninsured Parts (c)	(5) Grand Total Cols. 3 and 4
1929	0.3	-	0.3	-	0.3
1930	0.7	-	0.7	-	0.7
1931	1.0	-	1.0	-	1.0
1932	2.2	-	2.2	-	2.2
1933	2.8	0.1	2.9	-	2.9
1934	6.0	0.2	6.2	(d)	6.2
1935	2.8	0.4	3.2	0.2	3.4
1936	1.8	0.5	2.2	0.2	2.4
1937	1.6	0.5	2.2	0.1	2.3
1938	1.9	0.8	2.7	0.2	2.9
1939	2.1	1.0	3.1	0.2	3.3
1940	2.5	1.4	4.0	0.2	4.2
1941	2.7	1.7	4.4	0.2	4.6
1942	2.5	3.1	5.6	0.4	6.0
1943	2.4	6.0	8.5	0.9	9.4
1944	2.0	5.1	7.1	0.7	7.8
1945	2.2	3.0	5.2	0.6	5.8
1946	2.1	2.6	4.8	1.8	6.6
1947	3.0	3.6	6.6	2.4	9.0
1948	3.6	4.9	8.5	1.7	10.2
1949	4.4	6.8	11.2	1.6	12.8
1950	4.7	7.2	11.9	2.2	14.1
1951	5.0	7.7	12.8	2.5	15.3
1952	5.5	8.6	14.1	2.5	16.6
1953	6.4	10.7	17.1	2.9	20.0
1954	5.5	10.7	16.2	3.0	19.2
1955	5.9	12.3	18.2	4.0	22.2
1956	6.2	11.0	17.3	3.6	20.9
1957	6.9	8.5	15.5	2.8	18.3
1958	7.6	12.3	20.0	1.9	21.9

[a] Includes participations (which average less than $10 million annually).
[b] Insured and guaranteed parts only.
[c] Noninsured or nonguaranteed parts of loans in column 2. Also includes private parts of participation loans. Latter average less than $10 million annually.
[d] Less than $50 million.

Totals may not add, due to rounding.

Source: Tables II-9 to II-12.

beginning of the war, annual lending and insurance averaged about \$3 billion, of which about 40 percent went into the agricultural sector—primarily via loans of the Federal Land Bank—and about 45 percent into housing, with FHA insured loans gradually replacing HOLC direct loans as the most important program in the latter area. Loans to business averaged a relatively modest \$243 million during the 1935-40 period.

Gross federal credit jumped in World War II, reaching a peak of \$8.5 billion in 1943. Most of the increase was due to war production loans guaranteed through Federal Reserve banks under Regulation V. From the high of 1943, federal credit declined almost to the prewar level in 1946, only to begin the rapid postwar rise due largely to FHA and VA mortgage insurance. Housing credit alone cannot explain the sizable postwar increases, however. Credit extended to the agricultural sector has been several times the prewar level, with most of the increase accounted for by price-support loans. Finally, loans to business jumped again during the Korean conflict and have remained substantially above their previous level ever since.

These totals, of course, obscure much of interest. Lending programs blossom overnight and disappear as rapidly. The Disaster Loan Corporation, for example, managed to lend only \$36 million during its eight-year life. Some programs are subject to recurrent spurts of activity. The Inland Waterways Corporation, which had loaned only \$400,000 in the preceding 24 years, loaned \$9 million in 1953 and has not made another loan since. Some relatively moribund programs have shown new vigor in the last few years—insured loans of the Maritime Administration, for example. Finally, some programs, such as the Civil Aeronautics Board guarantee of loans to airlines, are so new as to preclude any real estimate of their lending potential.

Of more interest to us than total lending and insurance is the net yearly change in outstandings—total credit extended less repayments. Here the over-all picture is even more likely to hide significant detail. The net flow of federal credit was insignificant until 1931 and only in the 1932-35 period did it exceed \$1 billion annually before World War II. In fact, the \$4.1 billion level of 1934 was not reached again until 1949. Repayment of the vast 1932-35 outpouring of federal credit held the net flow down during the rest of the 1930's, with the net for 1936-37 actually being negative. Most of this consisted of repayments of RFC loans (both by business and by state and local governments) and repayments of HOLC loans by homeowners. Net credit flows of both agencies were negative throughout the 1935-40 period. In addition, several agricultural programs had negative net flows over the same time.

After a brief spurt in 1942 net flows again declined and were negative in both 1944 and 1945, reaching a total of -$2.0 billion in the latter year, attributable to repayment of the V-loans extended to businessmen early in the war and to continued repayment of depression-incurred HOLC loans and farm loans. In fact, every sector of federal credit had negative net flows in 1944 and 1945. Since World War II net federal credit flows have been heavily positive, with housing credit playing an overwhelming role. Of the $54 billion net federal credit injected into the economy in 1946-58, $46 billion was housing credit. The business sector had a negative net flow for the period, while agriculture had a positive flow of $8 billion. Both housing flows and agricultural flows have been erratic, at times reinforcing and at times offsetting one another. The lowest postwar year (1954) was one in which both sectors had small credit flows, while the highest year (1958) saw large net flows in both sectors.

Some Analytical Problems

Before attempting to generalize about past relationships between federal credit and gross national product, we should recognize the many qualifications to which our discussion is subject. We cannot state that federal credit made a real "net" addition to GNP without assuming that: (1) the credit extended was truly income-generating and did not merely result in a transfer payment; (2) federal credit did not simply replace private credit; and (3) it is possible to determine the source of the loaned funds and to estimate the effects thereof on the money market. Each of these assumptions requires discussion.

Lending and Income Creation. Any use of the ratio of federal credit to gross national product implies, of course, that expenditures resulting from the credit are true income-generating and output-generating expenditures. This assumption may not be valid. Loans obtained to refinance old loans or pay for acquisition of existing assets, including land, do not have the same initial effect on output and income as loans to acquire newly produced goods and services. Loans of Federal Land banks, for example, may be used largely for refinancing mortgages or repayment of current liabilities; FHA-guaranteed loans may be used to purchase existing housing; and all housing loans involve some payment for land.[6] Data to make the necessary adjustments are unfortunately unavailable, although using a series of ingenious assumptions, Freedman has estimated that 87 percent of the loans of eight major federal agencies were

---

[6]A loan to purchase existing housing may generate some income in the form of capital gains by bidding up prices. This effect has certainly been important since World War II.

income-creating in 1948.[7] Since one of the largest agencies, the Commodity Credit Corporation, was virtually dormant in 1948, and since all of its loans are income-creating, Freedman's work suggests that we may not be wildly misled in assuming that all federal credit in recent years has been income-generating. Also, of course, the multiplier effects of a loan may be the same whether it originally generates output or not. Finally, there is the fact that only in the housing area are non-income-generating loans likely to be large, and there is enough margin of error in estimating the true timing of effects of housing credit on GNP to suggest spurious accuracy if refinements of the Freedman type were instituted.[8] For all these reasons, no such refinement is attempted here. Needless to say, the same argument applies in reverse, i.e., if borrowers repay loans by liquidating assets, the primary deflationary effect of repayment would not be as great as if repayment were made by curtailing consumption.

Competition with Private Credit and Direct Federal Spending. The crucial problem in estimating the "net" addition to GNP resulting from federal credit is whether it is complementary to or competitive with private credit.

Fortunately, in many cases the answer is relatively clear. Some programs are aimed deliberately at marginal and submarginal borrowers.[9] The Farmers Home Administration, for example, has directed its aid toward farmers who are expected eventually to improve their credit rating and "graduate" to private financing. The Public Housing Administration has deliberately subsidized low-income tenants. The Reconstruction Finance Corporation, the Small Business Administration, and the Civil Aeronautics Board have extended or guaranteed loans which were unavailable at "reasonable" rates, and so on. Clearly it would be rash to assert that none of the credit extended under programs of this type would have been extended in their absence, but there is a strong presumption that little of it would have been.

---

[7]Robert Freedman, Jr., "The Inflationary Impact of Eight Federal Aid Agencies," unpublished Ph.D. dissertation, Yale, 1953.

[8]For example, suppose a large speculative builder sells a new house from his "inventory." The proceeds of an insured loan in this case initially adds to the builder's working capital but will generate new output only when paid to factors of production for replacement of the depleted inventory. This time lag may be considerable. Other lags are noted later.

[9]The various insurance programs are categorized along these lines by George F. Break, The Economic Impact of Federal Loan Insurance (Washington, D.C.: National Planning Association, 1962), Ch. 2.

Other federal credit programs merely postpone federal budget expenditures. Price-support loans guaranteed by the Commodity Credit Corporation, for example, have in recent years usually resulted in "repayment" by the CCC at a later date, at which time these repayments are included in the federal budget as expenditures. Since repayments are deducted from gross flows of credit in computing net flow there would be no net federal credit extended in the long run if all these loans were eventually transformed into federal expenditures.[10] The same argument applies to defense production loans (V-loans) and local authority obligations guaranteed by the Public Housing Administration and Urban Renewal Administration. The point to be made here, however, is simply that these loans are not substitutes for private credit.[11]

But there still remains a broad spectrum of programs where there is clearly some overlapping of federal and private credit. Most of the Farm Credit Agency lenders are competitive to some extent with private institutions, as are the Rural Electrification Administration, the Federal Home Loan banks, etc. However, it is simply impossible to make any meaningful estimate of the degree of overlapping. A few generalizations may be made. First, the stage of the business cycle is important. Undoubtedly many of the loans made under various farm credit programs in the 1930's would not have been made by private lenders, while there might be considerable competition for the same loan today. Second, most of the programs in this category involve some sort of farm credit, and a small rural lender might be competitive for any given federal loan but still be quite unable or unwilling to compete for all the loans of that type in his area. Third, there is a strong element of subsidy in almost all these programs (via low rates, unusually long maturities, government absorption of administrative expenses, etc.) which suggests that private lenders would be unwilling to lend on the same terms. Fourth, competition from federal credit has probably liberalized private lending policies and resulted in more private lending. Finally, and fortunately, the net credit flows of most of these programs are relatively unimportant so that any error resulting from treating the entire net flow as a net addition to GNP will not be large.

---

[10]On the other hand, there would be a positive net flow in any year in which gross loans exceeded the federal "repayment." Thus the budget expenditure and net credit flow would not jibe in any given year, and the latter would be a better measure of the primary economic effect of the program in that year.

[11]This raises the interesting question of whether we can speak of any program as representing a "net" addition to GNP unless we are certain that federal grants, subsidies, or expenditures would be unchanged in the program's absence. This question is discussed later.

The important exceptions to this last statement are the mortgage insurance programs of VA and FHA.

By far the most important problem in measuring the impact of federal credit programs is that of determining the effect of mortgage insurance programs on the volume of residential construction. VA and FHA mortgages are designed neither for marginal credit risks nor as substitutes for federal spending. In short, they fall in our third category—programs competing with private lenders—and unfortunately in recent years they have overshadowed all other forms of federal credit. In 1955, of a $5.5 billion net flow of federal credit, VA and FHA mortgage insurance accounted for $4.5 billion. Thus most of our other questions are insignificant beside this one.

Much has been written on the effects of VA and FHA insurance programs on economic stability, the composition and location of residential construction, and related subjects, but only two studies have gone beyond the level of generalization in estimating the effect of these programs on the level of home building in the postwar period. Unfortunately, the two reach widely disparate conclusions. One study, by Saulnier, Halcrow, and Jacoby, rather startlingly concludes that government housing programs "failed to produce a level of housing output even in the peak year 1950 which, considering the population factors at work, was as high as that achieved in the twenties without benefit of federal financing aids."[12] This statement is based on a comparison of the 1948-50 period with 1923-25. In the earlier period the ratios of nonfarm housing starts to housing stock, to increase in nonfarm population, and to increase in nonfarm families were all higher than in the post-World War II period. Moreover, construction costs and housing prices rose less in the earlier period. Thus, although careful to qualify their statements, the authors conclude that the evidence "suggests that the primary manifestation of credit liberalization program must be found in construction costs and housing prices. . . "

These conclusions have been attacked on several grounds, in addition to a general complaint of inaccurate data.[13] First, liberalized housing credit after World War II has been due to much more pervasive forces than federal credit programs alone—among them

[12]R.J. Saulnier, H.G. Halcrow, N.H. Jacoby, Federal Lending and Loan Insurance for the National Bureau of Economic Research Princeton: Princeton University Press, 1958), pp. 341-47.

[13]Leo Grebler and Sherman J. Maisel, "Determinants of Residential Construction: A Review of Present Knowledge," Research Study Four in Impacts of Monetary Policy, prepared for the Commission on Money and Credit (Englewood Cliffs, N.J.; Prentice-Hall, Inc., 1963), Ch. 6, "Federal Credit Programs as Determinants."

the general monetary and fiscal policies affecting the supply of and demand for loanable funds. Second, Saulnier's finding ignores a secular trend toward a weaker response of housing output to differences in credit terms pointed out earlier by Grebler, et al.[14] Third, there was a marked shift between 1923-25 and 1948-50 from unamortized to amortized mortgages, which tended to offset much of the advantages to borrowers of lower interest rates. Fourth, the supply-demand relationship for housing was in much greater disequilibrium in the later period than in the earlier. And finally, costs have also risen in nonresidential construction since World War II, although there has been no federal aid in this area, suggesting that the explanation is more complex than implied by Saulnier.

A more sophisticated analysis by George Break has reached conclusions quite different from those of Saulnier.[15] Break's minimum estimate of the postwar impact of federal mortgage insurance is that these programs have increased housing expenditures in the short run by $2 billion to $3 billion a year (in 1957-58 dollars), while his middle-range estimate raises this figure to almost $4 billion, or about 30 percent of current housing expenditures.[16]

Break reaches these conclusions in several steps. He constructs a "composite terms of credit" variable, including interest rate, average term to maturity, and average loan-to-value ratio. He measures the impact of federal loan insurance on mortgage credit terms by comparing the value of this variable for conventional home loans with its value for FHA, VA and conventional loans combined. He then estimates the sensitivity of housing demand to a difference in this variable. (This involves a complex econometric model, derived both from successive-approximation graphic methods and least-square analysis, and including five independent variables.)

Break's model has been criticized on a number of statistical grounds. It assumes, for example, that disturbances are small, have a normal distribution with mean equal to zero, and are not

---

[14]Leo Grebler, David Blank, and Louis Winnick, Capital Formation in Residential Real Estate, (Princeton, 1956).

[15]George F. Break, "Federal Loan Insurance for Housing," Research Study One in Federal Credit Agencies, prepared for the Commission on Money and Credit (Englewood Cliffs, N.J.: Prentice-Hall, Inc., 1963). See also Break's "Hidden Effects of Federal Credit Programs," in Joint Economic Committee, Federal Expenditure Policy for Economic Growth and Stability, 1957.

[16]Break's model deals with short-run effects. Long-run effects should be smaller, since credit conditions are less likely to affect home purchases as the time period being considered is lengthened.

serially correlated. The time series used are also assumed to act in a linear manner. Grebler and Maisel have shown the assumption of lack of serial correlation to be false and have pointed out that there is no logical reason for assuming that a single linear relationship in the time series of credit terms will be satisfactory.[17]

A choice between Saulnier's and Break's conclusions could be made with complete confidence only by repeating the postwar experience without the presence of federal mortgage insurance. However, despite its statistical weaknesses, Break's approach seems superior. He has not merely compared two brief periods 25 years apart, ignoring secular change, but has instead constructed models for 1925-41 and 1948-56. He has tested his equations carefully, using them to predict changes in housing starts for several periods. In every case the direction of change was correctly predicted, although the magnitude was usually understated. Moreover, Saulnier's implication that federal housing programs have merely increased prices rather than expanded housing construction does not jibe with other studies of borrower behavior. There is ample evidence that housing credit has been available on more liberal terms under these programs than elsewhere, and many studies have shown that credit terms have significant effect on the demand for other types of nonbusiness credit.[18] Other studies have found veterans buying more expensive homes than nonveterans and a decline in typical mortgagor's income following liberalized mortgage terms, suggesting both a widening and deepening effect of these programs.[19]

It is probable that the effect of federal credit on housing starts has increased in the last decade. The unprecedented personal liquidity at the end of World War II, coupled with the great supply-demand disequilibrium in housing at that time and the relatively inelastic nature of supply in the industry, suggests that a large proportion of those who took advantage of insured or guaranteed financing in the immediate postwar period would have turned to conventional financing had these programs been unavailable. In more recent years, as liquidity has decreased and the housing shortage abated, home building has probably become more sensitive

---

[17]Grebler and Maisel, op. cit., Ch. 3, "Statistical-Econometric Models," and Ch. 4, "Critique of Statistical-Econometric Models."

[18]See A. Kisselgoff, Factors Affecting the Demand for Consumer Installment Credit, Technical Paper No. 7 (New York; National Bureau of Economic Research, 1952). Board of Governors of the Federal Reserve System, Consumer Installment Credit, Pt. I, Vol. I.

[19]Federal Reserve Bulletin (July 1951), pp. 787-89; Herbert Shapiro, "Characteristic of One-Family Houses with FHA Mortgages, 1949-54," Construction Review (November 1955).

to credit terms, and thus to the existence of governmental intervention. This may explain some of the disparity between Saulnier's conclusion, which was based only on 1948-50 experience, and that of Break, which includes data for 1950-56.

Finally, we should note that Break's estimates do not include repair or modernization loans, which are presumably more responsive than construction loans to terms and availability of credit since their purpose is more easily postponable. These loans have averaged over $1 billion annually since 1950. This omission helps to offset any overstatement in his estimates of the effect of federal housing credit.

Source of Federal Credit Funds. Still another complication in estimating gross national product attributable to federal credit arises because the credit utilizes funds which might have been spent by others. Similarly, repayment of federal credit has a reverse effect.

Net funds loaned under federal credit programs (i.e., after repayments) come from many sources: borrowings from the Treasury, bond sales on the open market, direct Treasury appropriations, insurance premiums, fees, etc. Basically, of course, they come either from the Treasury or the public. If they are borrowed from the public, other potential users will be deprived of funds unless there are excess reserves in the banking system. If they are received from the public as profits (due to excess of interest payments, insurance premiums, and fees over operating expenses) we may treat them the same as repayments, i.e., as reductions in the net flow of credit. If funds are obtained from the Treasury, again the reserve position of the banking system is critical. If the Treasury is running a cash deficit, clearly other potential borrowers are deprived of funds unless there are excess reserves in the system. But this is also true even if the Treasury has a cash surplus, as long as that surplus is being used to retire publicly-held debt.[20]

The presence of excess reserves is doubly important in estimating GNP attributable to federal credit. Not only do they assure that funds involved have not been taken over from other borrowers, but their presence also suggests that federal credit is less likely

---

[20]We are treating the tax system here as exogenous, i.e., determined without reference to federal revenue programs, just as we are ignoring for the time being any change in other federal spending programs which might exist in the absence of federal credit. We are also obviously assuming complete mobility of funds throughout the capital market.

at that time to be a simple substitute for private credit.[21] When money is easy, private lenders compete more vigorously with those federal programs in which government and private credit overlap, and the gap between low-interest federal loans and private interest rates is narrower. Thus federal credit extended under these conditions is more likely to represent lending unavailable elsewhere. The 1930's provide an example.

The only study of the sources of loan funds in federal credit programs has been made by Ross Robertson.[22] The tentative results for 1950-58 are shown in Table II-2. These are difficult to reconcile with our data on net loans extended because: (a) Robertson's data include earnings used for administrative expenses rather than loans, and an unknown amount of principal repayments (less than $1 billion for the period), (b) his treatment of CCC funds differs considerably from ours, and (c) his study includes only programs actively lending in 1950-58, while our data include over $1 billion received during the period from repayments on loans made under earlier programs.

After elimination of CCC programs from his totals and ours, we have the following comparisons between funds obtained by federal lending agencies and net direct government loans (including the government's share of participation loans). All data in billions of dollars:

TABLE II-3

	Obtained by Federal Lenders			
	Privately	From Treasury	Total	Net Loans
1950	0.4	2.4	2.6	1.1
1951	0.3	1.3	1.7	1.4
1952	0.1	1.1	1.2	1.1
1953	0.1	0.6	0.7	0.3
1954	0.1	0.4	0.5	(0.4)
1955	1.5	0.0	1.5	1.2
1956	0.6	0.8	1.4	1.0
1957	2.3	0.0	2.3	2.1
1958	(0.4)	1.7	1.4	1.1

[21]Of course data may show zero excess reserves when, in fact, excess reserves would exit were it not for the income effects generated by federal credits. In this case funds would not have been taken from other users. Or the Federal Reserve could create reserves as fast as they were borrowed, and the data might still show no excess reserves.

[22]Unpublished study for the Commission on Money and Credit.

TABLE II-2

Sources of Loanable Funds, Selected Government Lending Agencies, 1950-58 (a)

(Millions of dollars)

	Obtained from Private Sector			Obtained from Government				
Year (c)	Sale of Debt	Sale of Stock	Total	Borrowed	Stock Purchased	Appropriation(b)	Total	Grand Total
1950	391	56	447	1790	(50)	629	2369	2816
1951	243	106	349	207	(61)	467	613	962
1952	22	56	78	930	(3)	312	1239	1317
1953	(1)	60	59	2230	(7)	244	2467	2526
1954	(20)	77	57	1473	37	537	2047	2104
1955	1445	95	1540	3885	-	427	4312	5852
1956	515	122	637	2065	(7)	522	2580	3217
1957	2203	130	2333	345	38	761	1144	3477
1958	(499)	132	(367)	505	7	578	1090	723

[a] In addition to above, most loan programs are revolving, i.e., repayments on old loans may be reloaned.

[b] "Government appropriation" includes earnings. Total also includes funds used for administrative expenses if paid from earnings rather than special appropriations.

[c] Totals include programs using both calendar and fiscal years, with former representing by far the larger share.

Source: Unpublished study by Ross Robertson for Commission on Money and Credit.

In every year Robertson's totals exceed ours. The discrepancy is assumed to be due to the factors mentioned above, although the difference in 1950 is too large to be so easily explained.

The major point to note, however, is the relatively small role played by Treasury funds in the total picture of federal credit. From 1950 through 1958 total loans extended (direct and insured) averaged about $16 billion annually. Of this total, about $11 billion was provided from repayments and about $3.5 billion from "new" private sources. However, repayments include Treasury repayment of CCC loans, so the average annual Treasury contribution was about $2.5 billion, while private sources provided about $13.5 billion annually.

The importance of this is that it minimizes the error resulting from our treating Treasury funds as a total, ignoring whether they represent taxes or borrowings. Admittedly it makes a difference whether taxes would be cut or the public debt reduced in the absence of federal credit programs, but we cannot judge which would happen. Thus we merely assume that a dollar injected into a federal credit program by the Treasury represents diversion of funds from a potential borrower, unless there are excess reserves in the banking system.

Secondary Effects. Thus far we have referred only to the primary economic effects of federal credit, i.e., to the original income- and output-generating expenditures resulting from these programs. In addition there exist countless other secondary influences. Only the most important can be mentioned here.[23]

First is the familiar "multiplier effect," the endless flow of respending resulting from the primary increase in incomes, a flow probably exceeding the primary increase alone.

Second are the expenditures induced by the acquisition of goods obtained by federal credit. This includes not only the conventional "accelerator" effects (investment induced by the rate of change in income and in different life spans of consumer and capital goods) but also "completive investment."[24] Thus construction of new houses results in expenditures for furniture and equipment, additional public utilities to serve the house, and "household-oriented" construction (new stores, schools, hospitals, parks, etc.).

---

[23]See Break, The Growth and Significance of Federal Loan Insurance, op. cit., Ch. 1.

[24]See J.M. Mattila and W.R. Thompson, "Residential-Service Construction: A Study of Induced Investment," Review of Economics and Statistics (November 1956).

Third, there are all the effects derived from federal credit-induced changes in money markets, general credit terms, financial institutions, etc. Some of these changes will be discussed later.[25] As examples, we may note here that: (a) federal credit may expand aggregate demand by inducing a competitive liberalization of credit terms offered by private lenders; (b) by stabilizing the mortgage market (and thus reducing precautionary demand for cash) federal credit may result in more lending; and (c) creation of a secondary mortgage market in the United States and development of the amortized mortgage as a standardized credit instrument, both due to federal mortgage insurance, have probably increased the supply of funds available for investment in home building.[26]

Fourth, federal credit may produce variations in private demand through substitution effects induced by changes in relative prices or in expectations, and these may contract or expand private demand still further. (This introduces all those unknown influences on expectations. Some businessmen may be discouraged from investing by fear of governmentally financed competition, while others may be encouraged to do so by expectation of continuous and dependable credit flows. This effect is, if possible, even more nebulous than the preceding ones.)

Finally, there is always the possibility that federal credit may cause direct federal spending to be lower. In such a case the federal credit program may not truly increase GNP above the level which would exist without it. The existence of such cases cannot be proved, anymore than we can prove whether a borrower seeking an income-generating federal loan would not, if the loan were refused, still make the expenditure for which the loan was sought but cut his purchases of land or another existing asset.

In view of all these difficulties, we have attempted only to estimate the primary effects of federal credit on national income and output.

Real or Money Income? Finally there remains the question of whether an increase in GNP attributable to federal credit results in a real increase in goods and services or simply in higher prices. Traditionally we have argued that when unemployed resources exist on a large scale increased spending is reflected in increased output

---

[25]Cf. also Robert Freedman, Jr., "Federal Credit Agencies and the Structure of Money Markets, Interest Rates and the Availability of Capital," Quarterly Journal of Economics (August 1955).

[26]Earl S. Garver, Mortgage Insurance, unpublished Ph.D. thesis (Yale, 1943), pp. 664-73.

and employment and that, as full employment is approached, further increases in spending tend increasingly to be channeled into rising prices.

Over most of the history of federal credit we may apply the traditional wisdom with safety. Certainly most of any income increase derived from this source in the 1930's was real, just as federal credit in the immediate postwar reconversion period served only to feed the fires of inflation.

The answer is less obvious when we consider the relatively mild inflation of recent years. Federal credit may have affected the general level of prices during this period in several ways. Most important is the upward bias imparted to the entire price structure by farm price supports. On the other hand, if there is validity to the familiar "cost-push" explanation of recent inflation, federal credit may have dampened inflation by increasing competition through easier credit for small firms and the channeling of funds into more competitive sectors of the economy.[27] Finally, the newer argument that recent inflation has been caused by rapid shifts in the composition of demand has implications for federal credit, since the latter could be one cause of excess demand in particular sectors of the economy. However, the major study propounding this explanation traced the 1955-57 inflation to sectors where federal credit had little efffect, and found housing playing an offsetting role.[28]

Even though federal credit may have contributed to higher price levels in postwar periods of less than full employment, it does not follow that any increase in GNP attributable to the credit program is illusory rather than real. If the loan is output-generating and the loaned funds are not diverted from other users, then the output induced by federal credit does not replace other goods and services, and is a true net addition.

A Second Look at the Picture

Remembering all the above qualifications, we may not take another look at the relationship of federal credit and gross national product. The reader will be struck by the imprecision of the statements. The evidence is incomplete and the methodology imperfect. Accurate isolation of the net effects of federal credit

---

[27] See J.K. Galbraith, "Market Structure and Stabilization Policy," Review of Economics and Statistics (May 1957), p. 131.

[28] C.L. Schultze, Recent Inflation in the United States, Study Paper No. 1, prepared for the Joint Economic Committee of Congress, September 1959).

programs from the multitude of other forces simultaneously at work is clearly impossible. Nevertheless, some facts stand out with relative clarity.

Before 1932 net federal credit flows were insignificant. In 1932, however, net flows exceeded 2 percent of GNP (Table II-4). But member bank free reserves were heavily negative in that year, and it may be argued that federal credit merely diverted funds from other users. In this case, however, the cause of negative reserves was not heavy loan demand (loans and investments of commercial banks declined almost 20 percent during the year) but continued deposit declines, and it is unlikely that federal credit deprived potential borrowers of funds. On the other hand, more than two-thirds of the net flow in this year represented RFC loans to financial institutions, which in most cases were not output-generating loans. On balance, the significant effects of federal credit in 1932 were due not to the primary impact of income-generating loans but to the secondary effects derived from bolstered confidence in financial institutions.

The same thing is true of the next two years, when net federal credit flows reached their all-time peak in relation to GNP. Net flows totaled \$5.7 billion in 1933-34, but more than \$4.2 billion of this was credit without direct primary income-generating and output-generating effects—RFC stock purchases in financial institutions, HOLC loans to homeowners, Federal Land Bank advances, etc. In short, federal credit programs in 1932-34, like many of the early New Deal actions, were essentially defensive emergency devices devoted to averting the threatened collapse of the financial system and real-estate market.[29] To the extent that federal credit did so, its contribution to the economy, though immeasurable, was great. But it is impossible to give a meaningful answer to the question, "How much would GNP have been in 1932-34 without federal credit?"

The reverse is true in the last half of the 1930's. Federal credit played a minor role, with net flows declining drastically after 1934, actually becoming negative in 1936, and averaging less than one-half of 1 percent of GNP over 1937-41. But the picture is slightly misleading, for in this period the gross flow of credit increasingly consisted of direct output-generating programs, while much of the repayments had relatively little depressing effect on

---

[29] The owners of one-fifth of the nation's nonfarm dwellings sought HOLC loans. By the end, HOLC held about one-sixth of the total urban home mortgage debt. See A.M. Schlesinger, Jr., The Coming of the New Deal (Boston, 1958), pp. 297-98 for an assessment of the effect of this program on public morale.

TABLE II-4

Federal Credit in Relation to Gross National Product, 1929-58

(Dollar figures in billions)

	Gross Credit Extended		Net Change in Outstandings		Repayments
	Amount	As % of GNP	Amount	As % of GNP	During Year (a)
1929	0.30	0.3	N.A.	N.A.	N.A.
1930	0.71	0.8	0.28	0.3	0.43
1931	1.01	1.3	0.20	0.3	0.80
1932	2.24	3.8	1.20	2.1	1.03
1933	2.91	5.2	1.53	2.7	1.38
1934	6.23	9.6	4.14	6.4	2.09
1935	3.24	4.5	1.06	1.5	2.19
1936	2.24	2.7	-0.07	-0.1	2.31
1937	2.18	2.4	0.05	0.1	2.13
1938	2.72	3.2	0.48	0.6	2.23
1939	3.07	3.4	0.29	0.3	2.78
1940	3.95	3.9	0.56	0.6	3.40
1941	4.37	3.5	0.70	0.6	3.67
1942	5.62	3.5	1.33	0.8	4.30
1943	8.47	4.4	0.54	0.3	7.93
1944	7.12	3.4	-0.94	-0.4	8.06
1945	5.17	2.4	-2.00	-0.9	7.16
1946	4.75	2.3	0.12	0.1	4.64
1947	6.58	2.8	2.46	1.1	4.12
1948	8.50	3.3	3.93	1.5	4.57
1949	11.24	4.4	4.76	2.5	6.48
1950	11.88	4.2	4.44	2.6	7.44
1951	12.77	3.9	5.44	1.7	7.34
1952	14.08	4.0	4.50	1.3	9.57
1953	17.06	4.7	5.18	1.4	11.87
1954	16.21	4.5	2.46	0.7	13.75
1955	18.23	4.6	5.45	1.4	12.78
1956	17.27	4.1	4.64	1.1	12.62
1957	15.48	3.5	3.91	0.9	11.56
1958	20.04	4.5	6.71	1.5	13.33

Totals may not add, due to rounding.

[a] Includes expirations of insurance.

Source: Stewart Johnson, "Statistics on Federal Lending and Loan Insurance Programs in the United States, 1929-1958," see Research Study One of this Volume. GNP from Economic Report of the President.

spending. About $500 million of repayments were made by financial institutions, probably with minimal effects either on their willingness to lend or on spending. About $2.5 billion of repayments were in the form of Treasury assumption of CCC price-support loans. We cannot, of course, tell whether these Treasury repayments came from taxes or borrowing, but to the extent that it was the latter there was little effect on spending, in view of the large free reserves in the banking system. Thus it is likely that real GNP attributable to federal credit was at least twice that indicated by net flows alone. Even so, the amount is small. Moreover, if we compare credit flows with "full employment" GNP, which was about 25 percent above "actual" GNP in 1935-39, the relative weakness of federal credit is even more marked.[30]

During World War II federal credit made no real contribution to GNP, but played a useful role in dampening inflationary pressures and in channelling resources into war production. With the single exception of housing in 1942, the three non-business sectors had negative net flows throughout the war. The savings thus generated were more than offset in 1942-43 by V-loans to business, but repayments of these loans caused negative net flows in all sectors in the last two years of the war, and an over-all negative net flow of more than $1 billion for 1942-45.

In the immediate postwar period, however, federal credit generated significant inflationary pressures. In 1946 continued repayment of V-loans almost offset the jump in housing credit and the net effect of federal credit was very small; but in 1947-48 almost $6.4 billion was pumped via these programs into an economy already suffering from excessive liquidity, too-easy money, and spiraling prices. It seems probable that federal credit had little effect on real GNP in this period, serving only to offset about half the surplus collected in the federal cash budget in 1946-48.

In 1949, however, federal credit provided an important stimulus to a sagging economy. Net flow in this year was more than 2.5 percent of GNP. Since prices were stable at this time, free reserves plentiful, and unemployment high, much of this represented a real increase in output. Here for the first time our conclusions are importantly affected by the Break-Saulnier dispute over the significance of mortgage insurance. More than two-thirds of the net flow of federal credit in 1949 consisted of VA and FHA loans. In addition, FNMA provided over $600 million of funds for the mortgage market. There is no doubt that housing provided powerful support to the

---

[30]Full employment GNP for the period is estimated by E.C. Brown, "Fiscal Policy in the Thirties: A Reappraisal," American Economic Review, (December 1956).

initial recovery. During the first half of 1950, prior to the impact of the Korean War, residential construction contributed $2.9 billion of the $17 billion increase in GNP (annual rates)—much more than the normal share of housing in total output.[31]

If we accept Break's middle estimates, and if we apply an instantaneous multiplier of two or more, we conclude that federal credit added more than 3 percent to real GNP in 1949 and early 1950—certainly the greatest impact of these programs on real output and income since 1934, and possibly the greatest in their history.[32]

For a number of reasons, federal credit had little effect on real output from mid-1950 through 1953. To begin with, the relative importance of net federal credit flows fell steadily, averaging less than 1.5 percent of GNP during 1951-53. In addition, resources became fully employed as the Korean conflict progressed, and federal credit was dissipated in rising prices. Finally, a new consideration arose—tight money. With negative free reserves in 1952 and 1953 and unemployment less than 3 percent, we may assume that credit flows and resource allocations resulting from federal credit programs were largely diverted from other borrowers and other users, and that federal credit had relatively little effect on real GNP.

In 1954 none of these factors were present. Money was easy, unemployment high, and prices stable. Under these circumstances net flows of federal credit are likely to add to real GNP as they did in 1949, but unfortunately net flows in 1954 reached the lowest point since 1946, less than 0.7 percent of GNP. This is odd, since the gross flow was only slightly less than the preceding year. The explanation, of course, is the level of repayments—$13.8 billion, an all-time record. In this case, net flow presents a misleading picture, since $2.2 billion of the repayments were on privately

---

[31]Leo Grebler, Housing Issues in Economic Stabilization Policy, National Bureau of Economic Research, Occasional Paper 72, 1960, p. 101.

[32]In view of the many potential errors in our estimate of the primary impact of federal lending, an attempt to apply an accurate multiplier would be ludicrous. It is interesting, however, to note the number of studies which have derived a multiplier of 2.0 to 2.5. Cf., e.g., Arthur Smithies, "Keynesian Economics: The Propensity to Consume and the Multiplier," American Economic Review (May 1948), and Oswald Brownlee and Alfred Conrad, "Effects upon the Distribution of Income of a Tight Money Policy," Research Study Seven in Stabilization Policies, prepared for the Commission on Money and Credit (Englewood Cliffs, N.J.: Prentice-Hall, Inc., 1963).

held price-support loans guaranteed by CCC. Most of these "repayments" consisted in fact of direct purchases by CCC of paper held by private lenders, and were reflected in the federal budget, which had a $1.1 billion cash deficit in 1954. In view of the large free reserves, we may infer that the federal deficit did not entirely represent a diversion of funds from private borrowers and thus that CCC repayments did not depress private spending by their full amounts. Hence the net flow understates the influence of federal credit on real GNP.[33] But even if we add total CCC repayments to net flows, thus erring in the opposite direction, we still find the ratio of federal credit to GNP lower than in most postwar years. Thus it fell far short of providing a stimulus to revival equal to its 1949 performance.

In 1955, however, net federal credit more than doubled over 1954, reaching the record level of almost $5.5 billion. The increase was almost entirely due to housing credit, since all other sectors combined had negative flows. Net flow in this year was 4.6 percent of GNP, a ratio unequalled before or since.

Here we confront a basic difficulty in estimating the effect of federal credit on economic activity in a given year, that of timing the true primary impact of housing credit. As we have seen, housing accounted for most of the fluctuations in federal credit in 1954-55. Here are the changes in net flow for these years (in billions):

TABLE II-5

	All Sectors	Housing
1954	-$2.7	-$0.7
1955	+ 3.0	+ 2.8

Yet this picture does not jibe with the fact that private housing starts under FHA and VA programs increased more than 40 percent in 1954 and only 15 percent in 1955. One explanation, of course, is that starts are not affected by repayments of past loans, while net credit flows are. But even when we compare FHA and VA home loans made (including noninsured parts) with starts under government programs, the pieces still do not fit:[34]

33On the other hand, by this line of reasoning the 1954 federal cash budget becomes less inflationary.

34Data from Grebler, Housing Issues in Economic Stabilization Policy, op. cit., Tables 1, 2. Note that loan volume may not agree exactly with data used elsewhere in our study, since definitions differ slightly.

TABLE II-6

	Government Underwritten Loans (billions)		Starts (thousands)	
	FHA	VA	FHA	VA
1953	$2.2	$3.1	252	157
1954	1.9	4.3	276	307
1955	3.1	7.2	277	393

The basic cause for this discrepancy is that starts may coincide with a commitment to lend upon completion, but may precede by a significant period the actual granting of the loan. There was a sharp increase in commitments during 1954, some of which was not reflected in loan acquisitions until 1955.[35]

There is no easy way with existing data to remove this source of error. A rough solution is to combine the years 1954-55. If so, we find net federal credit was approximately 1 percent of GNP for the two years. Since (a) the 1948-58 average for this ratio is slightly above 1.5 percent; (b) 1954-55 includes the trough and initial revival from recession; and (c) net credit flows for all sectors other than housing are negative for the period (and the housing sector is the one most likely to represent a mere transfer from private credit)—we may still conclude that federal credit programs as a whole not only did not provide a stimulus to revival equal to their impact in 1949, but even that their contribution fell short of what might have been regarded as "normal." In absolute terms, the net flow of federal credit in 1954-55 fell below any other two-year period since 1947.

The 1956-57 period repeated the experience of 1951-53—increasingly tight money, rising prices, relatively full employment, and a declining ratio of federal credit to GNP. Again housing accounted for almost all the net flow of federal credit during the period. With a federal cash budgetary surplus far in excess of net direct federal loans, and the tightest money market (largest negative reserves) in recent history, we may assume that much of the flow of federal credit represented funds which would have been loaned or spent in

---

[35]Toward the end of 1954 new commitments for residential mortgage loans by life insurance companies were more than two and a half times the level of August 1953. Grebler, ibid., p. 25. For a discussion of the time lapse between commitment and final loan, see M. Wilkerson and D.K. Newman, "FHA and VA Housing Statistics and the Housing Market," Construction Review (June 1957).

the absence of these programs. In view of this, and since the net flow of federal credit averaged less than 1 percent of GNP, it is doubtful that real GNP was influenced significantly by their presence.

Net federal credit jumped 70 percent in 1958, the last year of our study, due primarily to a large increase in CCC price-support loans. If these programs are omitted, both net and gross flows show about the same relation to GNP as in 1956-57.

Conclusion

In conclusion, we may make a few generalizations about the relationship of federal credit to income and output since 1929:

(1) In the early years of the Great Depression, federal credit programs played an important role in preventing massive foreclosures of real estate loans, supporting financial institutions, and generally restoring public confidence. They did not, however, generate significant increases in output or employment. In the later years of the depression these programs, although helpful, had a relatively small effect on GNP.

During World War II their impact was deflationary, as repayments were made on depression loans. Since World War II their effect has been consistently expansionary, the net flow of federal credit averaging about 1.5 percent of GNP. In most years the programs have added more to rising prices than real output; although in the three brief postwar recessions, and particularly in 1954, they have mitigated the downturn and stimulated revival by making a real contribution to output.

(2) Since World War II the story of federal credit has been basically the story of credit in the housing sector. In 1950-58 the net flow of federal credit was $42.7 billion, of which $37.1 billion went into housing. (Agriculture accounted for the rest, with business and miscellaneous sectors together having a zero net flow.) Thus fluctuations in federal credit have been largely attributable to fluctuations in housing. There is little doubt that the volume of construction in the short run has been heavily influenced by federal credit programs and, therefore, that federal credit has influenced the level of GNP in any given year. Whether or not home building in the long run has been influenced by these programs (and thus whether or not real GNP has been significantly affected over the last decade by federal credit) is still a moot point, although George Break's model suggests that it has.

(3) The only other major source of instability in the net flow of federal credit in recent years has been CCC commodity loans. The

extent to which these loans account for fluctuations in the net flow of credit is emphasized by the last three years of our study:

TABLE II-7

	Net flow to agriculture	Net flow to agriculture other than commodity loans
1956	+$38 million	+$658 million
1957	−869 million	+ 625 million
1958	+1,514 million	+ 696 million

This again raises the question of whether these programs should properly be included in our study, since their principal function has been to postpone the making of federal expenditures (admittedly an important function to a Treasury operating close to a debt ceiling).[36] If they are omitted, our argument that housing dominates the picture of federal credit is strengthened.

STABILITY, RESOURCE ALLOCATION AND OTHER PROBLEMS

Contribution to Stability.

We may now consider whether federal credit programs have contributed to or detracted from economic stability. This can be done in several ways. Saulnier, et al. have simply considered whether the flow of credit increased in years when GNP declined, and vice versa, and concluded that in such years federal credit had a countercyclical influence.[1] By also counting as countercyclical an increased flow of credit in an initial year of business revival, they find that gross credit volume moved in a countercyclical direction 15 years out of 24 studied, and net credit flow in 17 of the years.

But this approach is questionable. It suggests, for example, that since GNP increased in each year during 1933-37 then federal credit should have decreased in each year but the first, in order to be regarded as countercyclical, even though unemployment in each of those years exceeded 14 percent of the civilian labor force.

Another approach would be to ask whether federal credit flows have contributed to stability at levels of relatively full employment with relatively stable prices. Thus we may ask whether the major economic problem in a given year was inflation or deflation. If the former, federal credit flows should be negative, and vice versa.

---

[36]Of course, only the guaranteed loans do not enter the budget when made.

[1]R.J. Saulnier, H.G. Halcrow, N.H. Jacoby, Federal Lending and Loan Insurance (Princeton, 1958), pp. 111-15.

As a rough approximation we may consider the important problem to be deflation in those years in which unemployment exceeded 5 percent of the labor force, and inflation in those years in which it fell below that figure and the Consumer Price Index rose one percent or more.[2] Only two years since 1929 fall in neither category—1953 and 1955. Admitting room for debate, let us consider the major problem in those years as inflation.

Thus we have a simple picture of the economy since 1929 and one which would probably be endorsed by most observers. From 1930 through 1941 our major problem was unemployment. From 1942 through 1958 it was inflation, with the exception of three brief periods of recession (1949-50, 1954, and 1958, using annual data).

Viewed in this light, the countercyclical record of federal credit looks less impressive. True, the net flow of credit had the hoped-for sign in 16 of the 29 years, but this is simply the result of consistent positive flows over a period when a majority of the years have been deflationary ones. During the depression of 1931-41, federal credit played a proper inflationary role in every year but one—1936. (Possibly 1937 should also be included, since transformation of fiscal year data to calendar years by interpolation has a possible range of error larger than the small positive flow estimated for that year.) But since 1941 federal credit has continued its positive flow when our criteria would usually require negative flows. In 1944-45 (and possibly 1946) flows were negative, but since then federal credit has consistently given the economy an inflationary thrust.

When we examine the movements of federal credit in different sectors of the economy the record is unimproved. The business sector, for example, has a somewhat better anti-inflationary record, with negative flows in six inflationary years, but a worse record against recessions, with positive flows in only 8 of the 15 years of deflation. Credit aid to agriculture has the best record, with flows having the proper sign in 19 of 29 years, although absolute amounts have been highly erratic.

In general, then, the past contribution of federal credit to stability at full employment has been a standoff. This is to be expected, considering the origin and nature of the programs. Each credit program has been designed to meet a specific need at a given time, with little relation to general economic stability. Thus V-loans have been related to need for war production, agricultural price-

---

[2]We are forced to use annual data, and thus to increase the imprecision of our approach, because quarterly data on federal credit are unavailable.

support credit to crop surpluses, urban renewal credit to congressional pressures, etc. Admittedly credit needs tend to increase in periods of serious recession, and congressional willingness to lend increases at the same time. But long-term repayment of these loans exerts deflationary pressure in the unforeseeable future. When loans in a program decline from a peak, repayments eventually produce a negative flow. Federal credit to the business sector in 1932-37 provides a classic example. Thus injections of credit at the onset of a recession must, unless the recession is halted thereby, be continued or the program will soon be contributing to deflationary pressures.

In one significant area of federal credit–VA and FHA mortgage insurance–there is evidence of some countercyclical effects in recent years. This is discussed later, in connection with the relation of federal credit to monetary policy.

Relation to Other Government Policies

Fiscal Policy. Most of the loans included in our definition of "federal credit" do not influence the federal budget. We may ask, therefore, whether federal credit has reinforced or offset the other federal expenditure programs in their effects on the level of economic activity.

One way to approach this question is to compare net credit flow with the size of the surplus or deficit in the consolidated cash budget. We may compare: (a) Whether the net flow is positive when the cash budget balance is negative, and vice versa, thus indicating whether the two influence economic activity in the same direction; and (b) the relative magnitudes of the two. These comparisons are made in Table II-8.

Again the story may be divided into two parts. During the prewar depression the cash budget was uniformly unbalanced and federal credit flows almost as consistently positive. Since 1940, however, the two measures have exerted opposite pressures in 9 of 18 years.

In the early stages of the depression both federal credit and the cash deficit were important in mitigating the downturn. In the five-year period 1930-34 the cash budget was unbalanced by a total of $8.7 billion, while net credit flows were $8.4 billion.[3] However, more than $5 billion of the credit flow came from RFC, HOLC, and the Federal Land Bank, which derived some of their loan funds from

[3]The two figures are not strictly comparable, since calendar-year data for the cash budget are unavailable until 1943.

TABLE II-8

Federal Credit Flow Compared to Member Bank Reserves
and Federal Cash Budget, 1930-58

Calendar Year	Net Credit Flow (billions)	Average Free Reserve (millions)	Balance of Cash Budget (a) (billions)
1930	$0.3	-$216	+$0.9
1931	0.2	- 234	- 1.0
1932	1.2	- 262	- 2.7
1933	1.5	294	- 2.6
1934	4.1	1,535	- 3.3
1935	1.1	2,462	- 2.4
1936	-0.1	2,506	- 3.5
1937	0.1	1,206	- 2.8
1938	0.5	2,513	- 0.1
1939	0.3	4,388	- 2.9
1940	0.6	6,323	- 2.7
1941	0.7	5,319	- 4.8
1942	1.3	2,663	-19.4
1943	0.5	1,486	-51.1
1944	-0.9	911	-46.7
1945	-2.0	755	-36.7
1946	0.1	761	+ 0.04
1947	2.5	697	+ 5.7
1948	3.9	697	+ 8.0
1949	4.8	707	- 1.3
1950	4.4	677	+ 0.5
1951	5.4	468	+ 1.2
1952	4.5	- 66	- 1.6
1953	5.2	- 91	- 6.1
1954	2.5	628	- 1.1
1955	5.5	- 21	- 0.7
1956	4.6	- 269	+ 5.5
1957	3.9	- 320	+ 1.2
1958	6.7	298	- 7.3

[a] Fiscal year through 1942, calendar year thereafter.

Sources: Table II-4 and Economic Report of the President, 1959.

the Treasury and were included in the cash budget. If these were deducted from the budget, the deficit in this period would be less than net flows of federal credit. However, federal expenditures were more directly income-creating than the credit flows, and more important as an economic stimulant. In the remaining years of the depression, as repayments from the initial spurt of credit exerted their influence, net federal credit flows were small relative to budgetary deficits, equalling about 10 percent of the latter during 1935-41.

As we have seen, net credit flows were negative in 1942-45, withdrawing slightly more than $1 billion from the income stream in this period, in sharp contrast to the budgetary cash deficit of $154 billion. Since then the record has been reversed. During 1946-57, the cash budget achieved a total surplus of $11.4 billion, exerting a significant deflationary pressure, which was much more than offset by the $47.3 billion net flow of federal credit in the period. Moreover, in contrast to the early 1930's, very little of federal credit is now reflected in the budget, so that the two may properly be regarded as separate influences on the economy.

However, we have noted above that a deliberate change in federal credit <u>policy</u> will be better reflected in gross credit flow in the short run, since repayments are determined by past loan extensions. Also, although the cash budget is a better measure of the economic impact of federal spending and taxation, most fiscal policy debates center on the conventional budget, particularly on the expenditure side, with revenues usually being determined by a tax structure subject to infrequent major changes. Thus if we are interested in whether federal credit policy has been harmonious with fiscal policy we might compare gross credit flow with federal expenditures in the conventional budget.[4]

The important question, however, is not whether federal credit has complemented or counteracted fiscal policy in the past, but whether it will do so in the future. And the important reality is that, under our present budgetary system, there is no way of assuring that the two will not conflict. Federal credit programs have important effects on the economic system, but increasingly they are excluded from either the conventional or cash budget. Thus, by a simple change in accounting policy, the government may change its budgetary balance, without in any way changing the effects of its activities on incomes, outputs, or prices.

---

[4]This implies that federal expenditure policies have always been deliberately based on their countercyclical effect. This is untrue, but to the extent that there has been such a fiscal policy, conventional budget expenditures provide a better measure of the policy.

One illustration should suffice. In 1954 Congress directed the Federal National Mortgage Association to reorganize as a corporation. Previously, FNMA had operated with funds borrowed from the Treasury, and its activities were reflected in the budget. In January 1955, FNMA sold $570 million of nonguaranteed notes to private investors to reimburse the Treasury for some of the previous loans. This transaction, although it withdrew money from the income stream and had a deflationary effect, did not affect budget totals because the management and liquidation functions of FNMA are classified as "wholly owned government enterprise" for budgetary accounting policy, and the issuing of obligations by such enterprises is classified as a debt operation, not as an ordinary receipt.[5] In contrast, in fiscal 1960 FNMA exchanged $388 million of the government-backed mortgages in its portfolio for nonmarketable 2 3/4 percent Treasury bonds held by private investors, then turned the bonds over to the Treasury for retirement. These transactions, which had no effect on the money supply or income stream, were reflected in the budget as a receipt item.[6] Thus these two transactions had budgetary effects directly opposed to their true effects on the economy.

At least three different measures of federal receipts and expenditures are in common use:[7] The conventional or administrative budget, the cash budget, and Department of Commerce estimates of federal receipts and expenditures on income and product account. Federally insured or guaranteed loans are, of course, reflected in none of them. Direct government loans and repayments are excluded from the Department of Commerce statement on grounds that government lending, like consumer lending, is a part of savings rather than an expenditure.[8] We have just seen that direct federal loans and receipts may not be included in the conventional budget,

---

[5]See Sidney G. Tickton, The Budget in Transition, Planning Pamphlet No. 89, National Planning Association, 1955, p. 20.

[6]See Senate Banking and Currency Committee Hearing, "Exchanging FNMA Mortgages for Treasury Bonds," 86th Cong. 1st Sess., June 1959. Of course, the transactions did affect the money market, by decreasing the supply of Governments and increasing the supply of mortgages. It also had certain tax consequences.

[7]The three are reconciled for fiscal 1953 by Marilyn J. Young, "Three Statements of Federal Receipts and Expenditures: A Reconciliation," in Comparability of National Accounts, Studies in Income and Wealth, Vol. 20, National Bureau of Economic Research.

[8]There is one exception. CCC price-support loans are counted as purchases for inventory. See Gerhard Colm, The Federal Budget and The National Economy, Planning Pamphlet No. 90, National Planning Association, 1955, p. 80.

or may be included in a misleading way. Thus there is a serious need for budgetary changes which will make possible quantitative estimates of the economic impact of federal credit programs.

Budgetary reform has attracted a great deal of attention in recent years, and the U. S. Chamber of Commerce has argued that "there is probably no part of government more in need of reform . . ."[9] Detailed suggestions for improvement are outside the scope of this study, but certainly the administrative budget should include (preferably on a quarterly basis, and in an appendix if necessary) data on each credit program, showing: (1) volume of loans authorized and expected to be extended or insured; (2) commitments to make or insure loans; (3) volume of loans actually made or insured, including the noninsured part of any partially insured loan; (4) volume of credit outstanding; and (5) sources of funds used.[10] Correspondingly, the total budget, including federal credit programs, should be considered by a joint congressional committee concerned only with growth and stability, which would recommend appropriate levels of taxation and borrowing.[11]

Monetary Policy. Saulnier, Halcrow, and Jacoby have stated that: "On the whole. . . federal loan and loan insurance policy shows less correlation with monetary policy than fiscal policy" and that the countercyclical record of federal credit is "appreciably" better than that of Federal Reserve monetary policy although "the record reflects defects in federal monetary policies as well as inadequacies in the management of the credit programs of federal agencies."[12]

This conclusion is debatable. To begin with, it uses the definition of "countercyclical" noted above, which would recognize the propriety of a tight money policy in any year (except the first) in which GNP increases, no matter how far it still falls below the level of full employment. In addition, Saulnier, et al. have used as their measure of Federal Reserve policy the annual net change in Federal Reserve Bank credit outstanding, arguing that proper central banking policy would require progressive reduction in this measure

---

[9]See the report of the Chamber's Committee on Government Expenditures, The Federal Budget System, 1954.

[10]The Special Analysis of Federal Credit Programs, appended to the budget since 1952, includes some of this but covers only major programs, has much overlapping, contains little on sources of funds, etc.

[11]Similar suggestions have been made many times. Cf. Committee for Economic Development, Control of Federal Government Expenditures, 1955; and National Planning Association, The Need for Further Budget Reform, 1955.

[12]Saulnier, et al., op. cit., p. 138.

"during advanced stages of economic upswing" (i.e., in any year after the first upward change in GNP) and vice versa. Using these two criteria, one may be surprised to learn that money was tight in 1936 (when member bank free reserves averaged more than $2.5 billion) and that this was the proper monetary policy "if economic stabilization were a major objective" (even though unemployment averaged 16.9 percent of the civilian labor force).

The picture changes, however, if we use different criteria—if, for example, we use the rough definition of "good" stabilization policy outlined above, based on unemployment and price levels, and a commonly accepted criterion of monetary ease, the presence of substantial free reserves in the banking system. With these measures we find that federal credit and monetary policy were correlated (positive net flows of federal credit accompanying easy money, and vice versa) in 18 of the 29 years during 1930-58 (see Table II-8). Of the 11 remaining years in which the two conflicted, the Federal Reserve was "right" in six.[13] Thus, of Saulnier's conclusions, we can agree only that the record reflects inadequacies on both sides.

Such comparisons, though interesting, prove very little, for there is no deliberate "federal credit policy" as such, only a myriad of unrelated programs. Still the comparisons do demonstrate that the effects of federal credit programs as a whole may diverge from those desired by monetary authorities.

The activities of federal credit agencies reflect mandates and powers given by Congress, but the agencies often have considerable latitude in their operations. FNMA may, for example, issue or retire debt obligations and purchase or sell mortgages at its own discretion, subject only to limits imposed by Congress. In other programs, basic legislation restricts the possibility of control. There is little Congress can do, short of changing the basic law, to limit the number of persons applying for FHA-insured loans. In all programs the federal agencies have no responsibility for the general credit and monetary situation; and the impact of these agencies in the money market may at times interfere with or make difficult the implementation of Federal Reserve policies.

Conflict may arise in many ways. Federal credit agencies, for example, may prevent monetary restraint from falling with equal weight on all sectors of the economy. As an illustration, the Rural Electrification Administration has made 35-year loans since 1935 at 2 percent, no matter what the cost of long-term money to the

[13]The five other years are 1944-45, when we had easy money for obvious reasons, and 1930-32, when we had tight money for well-known but less accepted reasons.

Treasury. On the other hand, much of the impact of tight money in recent years has been concentrated on residential construction, due partly to interest ceilings in the VA and FHA programs.

A second possible difficulty pertains to the velocity of money. During the boom of 1955-57 the money supply was held down by Federal Reserve policy, but the economy seemed to escape through an increase in velocity. One cause of velocity changes may be federal credit agencies. Assume, for example, an increased demand for mortgage money and a constant supply of money. As the public exchanges cash for mortgages, inflationary pressures result, but continued exchanges are dampened as the public finds its supply of liquid assets declining relative to its total assets and income, which creates resistance to continued inflation. If, however, FNMA issues its securities and buys mortgages with the proceeds, then the public's total liquid assets would increase and restraints to inflation would be weakened.[14] In short, the public has supplied mortgage credit with less reduction in liquidity than would have occurred without intervention of a federal agency, and the credit demand has generated a greater increase in velocity.[15]

Conflicts may also arise because obligations of federal credit agencies are directly competitive with Government securities when sold publicly. If the amount of such offerings exceeds the demand for low-interest assets, the Treasury may find it more difficult to sell its own long-term bonds. Constructive coordination of debt management with monetary policy has thus been complicated by the existence of federal credit agencies authorized to issue such obligations.

Conflict between federal credit programs and monetary policy are most likely to be important when Federal Reserve policy is one of restraint. In fact, the well-known weakness of monetary policy in stimulating the economy may be partly mitigated by federal credit programs which utilize, or encourage private utilization of, reserves being created by the Federal Reserve. However, the potential conflicts suggest a need for greater coordination. No

---

[14]This example is based on a similar one by Herbert Stein, "The Financial Structure," American Economic Review (May 1958), p. 70.

[15]In general, this seems to be the major way in which nonbank financial intermediaries weaken aggregate Federal Reserve control. However, it has been argued that they, in fact, may create money. See G.W. McKinley, "The Federal Home Loan Bank System and the Control of Credit," Journal of Finance (December 1957). The argument requires a definition of money which includes savings deposits in the total. See comment by C.F. Haywood, Journal of Finance (December 1958).

formal arrangements exist at present for cooperation between federal lending agencies as a group and the Federal Reserve, although provision for cooperation with agencies affecting real estate credit existed during the life of Regulation X.[16] Many suggestions have been made for the establishment of some sort of national monetary council.[17] At different times the idea has been endorsed by the Federal Reserve and the Treasury, although never simultaneously. The danger exists that, even if such a body were only consultative, Federal Reserve independence would be weakened, but this fear is most often voiced by those who believe that the central bank would be pushed in the direction of easier money during inflationary periods, and we have seen that Federal Reserve restraints tend to be weakened by federal credit programs in the absence of coordination between the two. Since this is so, and since these programs are increasingly outside the normal budgetary controls of Congress, the opinion here is that a formal coordinating body between major federal lending agencies, the central bank and the Treasury is long overdue.

It was mentioned above that VA-guaranteed and FHA-insured mortgage loans have behaved countercyclically in recent years. Here is a situation in which monetary policy and federal credit flows have clearly been positively correlated, for the major reason for fluctuations in VA and FHA housing starts has been that tight money causes a diversion of investment funds into other areas, due largely to the interest rate ceilings imposed under those programs. The data are persuasive. For example, as interest rates rose from December 1954 to February 1958, FHA-financed starts declined 45 percent and VA-financed starts dropped 92 percent, while conventionally financed starts rose 8 percent. Due to these ceilings general monetary controls have had more impact in recent years on residential construction than any other sector.[18] The desirability of this is discussed later.

---

[16]See Joint Committee on the Economic Report, Monetary Policy and the Management of the Public Debt, 1952, Part 1, pp. 269-71.

[17]See, e.g., G. L. Bach, "Monetary Policy Formulation," American Economic Review (December 1949). President Eisenhower has recommended "exchanges of views." Economic Report of the President, 1958, p. 59. Cf. also Roy Blough, "Political and Administrative Requisites for Achieving Economic Stability," American Economic Review (May 1950).

[18]See W. L. Smith, "The Impact of Monetary Policy on Residential Construction," in Senate Banking Committee, Study of Mortgage Credit, Washington, D.C., 1958. The use of discounts does not fully offset the ceilings. The impact is magnified by the fact that insurance companies and banks, the institutions most active in FHA (Continued on the following page.)

Resource Allocation

Federal credit programs have affected not only the level of economic activity, but also its pattern. However, appraisal of the resource allocational effects of these programs is even more difficult than measurement of their impact on GNP. Individual studies of the major programs are being prepared by the Commission on Money and Credit. We can only outline a few obvious results here.

Business. Flows of federal credit into the business sector have been very much smaller than into agriculture or housing, and minute in relation to other sources of credit utilized by business. From 1947 through 1958, for example, the net flow of federal credit into this sector was only $60 million.[19] Thus the really significant effects on investment, incomes, and employment in this sector have been those induced by federal credit aid to agriculture and housing.

However, within the sector there have been noticeable selective effects. Investment has been stimulated, for example, in the merchant marine, railroads and related transportation enterprises, and fisheries, while industries engaged in foreign trade have been helped by activities of the Export-Import Bank, etc.[20]

Many of the credit programs in the business sector have been directed to the small and new enterprise, on grounds that private facilities for financing such firms are inadequate. Data to support this hypothesis are sketchy, although clearly these firms are the weakest borrowers and poorest credit risks, and there are

---

(Footnote 18, continued from the previous page.)
and VA lending, are more sensitive to yield differentials and have a wider choice of investment outlets than savings and loan associations, which are most active in conventional lending. Leo Grebler, Housing Issues in Economic Stabilization Policy, National Bureau of Economic Research, 1960, p. 92.

[19]All figures are subject to qualification, since allocation of some loans to a given sector is arbitrary.

[20]Cf. Merrill J. Roberts, "Government Credit Aids to Transportation," unpublished study prepared for the Commission on Money and Credit.

indications of limited access to the capital market.[21] True or not, there may be other grounds for encouraging easier credit for small firms, as a part of antitrust policy. Carl Kaysen takes this position, but contends that to date the credit aids of the Small Business Administration have been of such limited scale and scope that they have had little bearing on competition.[22] He finds a need for some sort of guarantee program, along the lines of FHA, which would make possible readier access to institutional capital for the growing but still relatively new and small firm. To a limited extent the Small Business Investment Act may meet this need.[23]

Another familiar argument is over the extent to which small firms are unduly affected by general credit restrictions implemented through general monetary controls. Again evidence is sketchy, but fairly persuasive, that general credit controls do discriminate against small firms.[24] If so, federal lending programs may moderate the "inequity," but at the cost of weakening general monetary controls.

Housing. The debate over the extent to which federal housing credit has increased the use of resources in residential construction has already been discussed in detail. In addition, however, there have been some secondary effects of these programs on resource allocation.

While categorical statistical evidence is lacking, there is little doubt that mortgage insurance has had much to do with the national movement toward individual homeownership. The percentage of nonfarm owner-occupied housing has increased from 53 percent in

---

[21]See V.L. Andrews, et al., "Who Finances Small Business?" in Board of Governors of Federal Reserve System, Financing Small Business, Washington, D.C., 1958. For evidence that the inadequacy of small business financing has been exaggerated, see Irving Schweiger, "Adequacy of Financing Small Business since World War II," Journal of Finance (September 1958). See also Jack McCroskey, "Federal Credit Programs for Small Business," Research Study Seven in Federal Credit Agencies, prepared for the CMC (Englewood Cliffs, N.J.: Prentice-Hall, Inc., 1963).

[22]C. Kaysen, Antitrust Policy (Cambridge, 1959), p. 230. RFC, the most important federal lending program in the business sector to date, provided relatively little credit for small firms. Saulnier, et al., op. cit., p. 437.

[23]But cf. Paul Donham and C.L. Fitzgerald, Jr., "More Reason in Small Business Financing," Harvard Business Review (July-August 1959).

[24]See Joint Economic Committee, Staff Report on Employment Growth and Price Levels, Washington, D.C., 1959, pp. 378-81; and J.K. Galbraith, op. cit.

1947 to 61 percent in 1959. There has also been a substantial increase in the percentage of single-family houses (from 62 percent of all dwelling units started in the 1920's to 87 percent in 1949-58).[25] These developments in turn have stimulated the dispersion of cities into the suburbs (a flight admittedly aided by the rise of the automobile). In addition to the familiar transportation, fiscal, and political problems arising from this migration, the effect on national capital requirements is important. The household-oriented investment in schools, highways, and community facilities induced by urban decentralization has led to a more capital-intensive way of life than would be required by greater concentration.

On the other hand, there is some modest support for arguing that federal credit programs have increased productivity in home building, since it has encouraged the growth of speculative large-scale developers and mass merchandisers.[26] This, coupled with the decrease in average size of homes (which has probably been influenced by federal credit programs), has led to some capital saving.

Agriculture. Discussion of the effect of federal credit on agriculture is always overshadowed by the vast impact of the price-support program in general. The diversion of resources into agriculture resulting therefrom is one of the major problems of the day, but one much too complex to be discussed in detail here.[27]

The technological revolution in agriculture during the last two decades is familiar. Capital investment requirements per farm have increased sharply. As farmers have obtained more efficient equipment they have also obtained the potential to handle larger acreages with the same family labor supply. Thus farms have been consolidated and large amounts of labor released from agriculture to industry. Acquisition of the equipment and the acreage have required large supplies of credit. Federal credit programs have both lowered the cost and increased the supply of credit to farmers, and have thus been partly responsible for the agricultural revolution. Whether or not the revolution should be carried further depends on whether

---

[25]George F. Break, "Federal Loan Insurance for Housing," Research Study One in Federal Credit Agencies, prepared for the Commission on Money and Credit (Englewood Cliffs, N.J.: Prentice-Hall, Inc., 1963), Table I-19.

[26]But it is claimed that government support of British home building has retarded technological change. Anglo-American Council on Productivity, Productivity Team Report: Building (New York, 1950), p. 4.

[27]For an estimate of changes resulting from gradual abandonment of price supports, see Farm Price and Income Projections 1960-65, Senate Doc. No. 77, 86th Congress, 2d Sess., 1960.

our country faces a greater shortage of capital or of manpower in the future.[28]

Much of the technological change has been due to provision of electrical power. About half the farmers using central-station power in the United States obtain it from facilities constructed with REA loans. The direct capital investment in wiring and appliances by farmer-customers of REA borrowers was estimated at more than $5 billion in 1953.

Regional Resource Allocation

Federal credit programs have influenced the regional allocation of resources in two ways. First, they have channeled funds into areas where are located certain industries or groups which specific credit programs were designed to aid. Second, they have transmitted loan funds from capital surplus areas into areas of shortage.

The first effect is obvious. Although data are unavailable, it is clear that resources have been diverted into large cities (via urban rehabilitation and other programs), areas of commercial fishing, Indian reservations, and into all the other areas where are concentrated recipients of the dozens of special loan programs. In agriculture, the regions producing the five basic price-supported crops have similarly been affected.

The second effect is more important. Again empirical evidence is sketchy, but several studies have shown that federal credit programs have transmitted funds into areas where loan funds are in relatively short supply. Roosa, for example, has found that interregional distribution of RFC funds in the 1930's supplemented bank credit in areas where needed, and Saulnier found that relatively large numbers of RFC loans were made in capital-deficit areas.[29] In some cases the regional allocation has been deliberate, as with REA loan funds, which are allocated among states largely according to the number of unelectrified farms.

---

28 For development of the ideas in this paragraph, see C.P. Heisig, "Long-Term Adjustments in Composition of Farm Production and in Production Inputs," and E.T. Baughman, "The Contribution of Credit Policy to Financing Needed Farms," both in Joint Economic Committee, Policy for Commercial Agriculture, Washington, D.C., 1957. (Also unpublished studies for the Commission on Money and Credit by Karl Fox, etc.)

29 Robert Roosa, The Monetary Powers of Some Federal Agencies Outside the Federal Reserve System, Ph.D. thesis (Michigan, 1941), p. 296. Saulnier, et al., op. cit., pp. 443-44.

As might be expected, the most noticeable regional effects have been felt in housing. The new FHA mortgage, with its extended maturity period and liberalized loan-to-value ratio, created a standardized credit instrument in the 1930's; and the development of a secondary mortgage market, aided first by the RFC Mortgage Company and later by FNMA, has given the residential mortgage greater liquidity and made it a more fungible investment medium. As a result, the boundaries within which lenders have been willing to make mortgage loans have been enlarged from the city or state to the entire nation.

The spread in interest rates narrowed almost immediately following FHA. In 1931 effective savings and loan rates varied from 6.2 percent in Connecticut to 15.3 percent in Tennessee. By 1936 the range was only 5.0 percent to 7.3 percent.[30] Today, as the individual lender has declined and the large institutional investor increased in importance, the spread is still narrower.[31] As a by-product, this increased institutionalization of the mortgage market has made the interregional flow of mortgage money more sensitive to monetary policy than total mortgage loans would suggest. Thus the 1955 restraints on mortgage warehousing loans and on borrowings from Home Loan Banks had a pronounced impact on home building in such capital-deficit areas as the West and Southwest.[32]

The general attitude toward FHA and VA lending varies by type of lender. Life insurance companies have been the strongest supporters of government programs, judged by the percentage of such loans in their mortgage portfolios, while commercial banks have engaged less in this type of lending, and savings and loans associations least of all.[33] Thus differences in the structure of the mortgage market have made a difference in the flow of funds into federally insured mortgage loans. One study of 25 major metropolitan areas with 54 percent of all mortgage lending in the United States found the percentage of FHA and VA loans to all mortgage loans in the area ranging from 19 percent in Cincinnati to 57 percent in Atlanta.[34] In those markets where life insurance companies were

---

[30]Garver, op. cit., p. 669.

[31]Cf. Saulnier, et al., op. cit., pp. 357-59. A recent policy change has allowed individual lenders to buy FHA mortgages. Wall Street Journal (July 14, 1960).

[32]For evidence on the volatility of the supply of funds to these areas, see Grebler, Housing Issues in Economic Stabilization Policy, op. cit., pp. 92-95.

[33]For evidence of the strong early opposition to FHA by savings and loan associations, see Garver, op. cit., p. 427.

[34]James Gillies and Clayton Curtis, "The Structure of Local Mortgage Markets and Government Housing Finance Programs," Journal of Finance (September 1955).

the dominant lenders the median percentage was 52 percent, while in areas dominated by savings and loan associations the median was 28.5 percent. Two other studies found that the proportion of FHA and VA mortgages varied inversely with the size of the lending institution and that small cities, usually having small lenders, made relatively less use of government programs than the large ones.[35]

This suggests that all citizens may not have an equal chance to share in any benefits of federal mortgage insurance. It may also account for some intercity variations in interest rates.

The Distribution of Income

Federal credit aid to small business, to the extent that it reduces "monopoly," may be considered by economists to promote an optimal resource allocation. But economic discussions of "optimal" take the currently existing distribution of wealth as given. Yet most people, including a majority of economists, feel that wealth distribution is a matter of public concern, and there is a strong belief that government should promote a greater degree of equality than would exist in its absence.

Nothing quantitative can be said about the effect of federal credit on the distribution of incomes, but it may be doubted that, despite a large number of programs aimed at lower income groups, there has been any significant redistribution downward. Aid to the business sector has largely benefited stockholders. Programs in the housing and agricultural sectors have increased the incomes of all who own resources either specialized to, or with a comparative advantage in, these sectors, but these gains cannot easily be allocated to different income groups.

The direct benefits of federal mortgage insurance—the really important part of the housing sector—have accrued largely to middle-income groups. In 1956, for example, approximately 35 percent of the spending units in the nation had money incomes after taxes of less than $3,600; and in the same year only 10 percent of those with VA mortgages and 11 percent with FHA loans had incomes below $4,000, while nearly 25 percent of those with conventional home mortgages had incomes below that figure.[36]

Similarly, price-support loans, which constitute a major share of federal agricultural credit, have gone primarily to large

---

[35]Gillies and Curtis, "A Note on the Small Mortgage Market," Journal of Finance (September 1959); J.E. Morton, Urban Mortgage Lending (Princeton, 1956), p. 53.

[36]Break, Federal Loan Insurance for Housing, op. cit., Table I-13.

farmers.[37] And most of the Farm Credit Administration programs for extending production, intermediate- and long-term credit are out of reach of low-income farmers. The only exception is the loan program of the Farmers Home Administration.[38] Finally, it is a recognized economic principle that increased agricultural incomes tend to be absorbed eventually by the landowner either in rise of rents or value of property. Needless to say, the poorer farmers are least likely to be landowners.

The Cost of Federal Credit

Default and Loss Experience. Saulnier, et al. have described the lending experience of federal credit agencies in some detail.[39] It should be sufficient here to summarize their findings:

(1) The record is very good for those programs aimed at refinancing debt during the depression of the 1930's (HOLC, farm mortgage financing, etc.). In general, the experience of federal programs in this area approximated those of private lenders.

(2) The experience of the cooperative financial institutions sponsored by the federal government (Federal Land banks, Production Credit Associations, etc.) has also been favorable and broadly comparable to private institutions, which they have come to resemble and with which they compete. This is particularly true of those programs designed to help borrowers who could meet private credit standards but were unable to borrow because of inadequate credit facilities.

(3) Substantial losses have been incurred in those programs designed to help low-income farmers or business firms unable to find private financing on reasonable terms. As might be expected, losses in these programs were greater than could be sustained by a private agency needing to earn a reasonable return on invested capital.

(4) In general, most programs have been self-supporting in the long run, but none (possibly excepting the Export-Import Bank) has realized "satisfactory" profits by conventional private standards.

Of course, many programs were deliberately intended to include

---

[37]See W.W. Wilcox and W.C. Hendrix, Under-Employment of Rural Families, Report prepared for Joint Economic Committee, 1951, p. 45.

[38]F.J. Welch, "The Evolving Low-Income Problems in Agriculture," American Economic Review (May 1960), pp. 236-37.

[39]Saulnier, et al., op. cit., ch. 4.

some element of subsidy, and the presence of profits at a satisfactory private level would suggest failure in that respect. In contrast, a loss experience comparable to that of private institutions tells us nothing about the presence or absence of subsidy. The use of subsidies in federal credit is being covered in another Commission on Money and Credit study, but some observations seem pertinent here.

Subsidy in Direct Loans. Almost all federal credit programs involve some degree of subsidy but, as is so often the case in this essay, the degree is immeasurable. This stems from the fundamental difficulty in defining "subsidy." When applied to an enterprise, the term has been defined as "an increase in the demand for its output, or a decrease in the costs which it must bear to produce its output, which are not the result of market forces or 'natural' changes in consumer tastes, techniques of production, or availabilities of natural resources, but rather result from the deliberate action of the subsidy giver (government)."[40] But even the author of this definition admits that it is "of little practical value in analyzing actual government subsidy policies."

Clearly the support of farm prices above the "natural" market price fits this definition. But is the support of butter prices, which has greatly increased consumption of margarine, also to be considered a subsidy to the latter? Similarly, it will be recognized that taxes are higher as a result of federal credit programs (although which taxes is moot) and that these taxes, by influencing demand, will generate some subsidy effects of the kind defined above, but no one would be willing to attempt a description of them.

Even when we confine the definition to deliberate effects, foreseen and desired by the Congress, we still have trouble. To begin with, it is difficult to determine from legislative history the intentions of Congress in a specific program, and in many cases the intent is multiple.[41] Public housing loans, for example, are designed not only to subsidize low-income groups but also to provide a sort of "collective good," free to all residents of the city, namely, decreased crime, less disease, etc. Such collective consumption expenditures are usually distinguished from subsidies. In some cases (e.g., urban redevelopment loans) the major purpose of a federal credit program is to provide such a collective benefit.

Remembering these problems, we can still note examples of

---

[40]Carl Kaysen, "On Defining A Subsidy," in C.J. Friedrich and J.K. Galbraith, eds., Public Policy (Cambridge, 1953).

[41]For a summary of some congressional debates concerning major programs, see Appendix B of Robert Freedman, Jr., "The Inflationary Impact of Eight Federal Aid Agencies," unpublished Ph.D. dissertation, Yale, 1953.

two broad categories of subsidy involved in federal credit programs: (a) purchases by government for more than market price, and (b) sales by government for less than market price.

The outstanding example of the first type of subsidy is, of course, the farm price support program. But even in this case quantitative measurement is impossible. The amount of subsidy is usually said to be the realized losses of CCC, but the government accounts showing losses do not relate to the year in which payments were made, so the farmer is receiving an added subsidy in the form of an interest-free loan in the interim. In addition, certain specialized operations of CCC are paid by Treasury appropriations which are not considered reimbursements for losses; and other parts of the subsidy are "hidden" in foreign aid appropriations, since CCC stocks are often transferred to them at the support price rather than the market price.[42] Finally, since there is substantial and constant deterioration of stocks in storage, operating figures alone do not disclose the total amount of the subsidy.[43] Even ignoring these problems, losses on resale have exceeded $1 billion in some years.

The second type of subsidy, sales by government at less than market price, is found in almost every federal credit program, if the failure of government to collect a "market" rate of interest on its loans is included in this category. Again, defining the market rate is difficult, but several lending agencies charge the borrower (or pay to the Treasury) a lower rate than the Treasury must pay for long-term money. In some cases the equivalent of an interest-free loan is made, in the form of purchase of capital stock.

The Hoover Commission has recommended that the Treasury impose interest rates on lending agencies for federal advances or contributions equal to the going rate of interest paid by the Treasury on its own obligations of comparable maturity.[44] But even in those cases where the Treasury already does this, it does not eliminate the subsidy. Assuming the agency relends at this rate, this still ignores the premium which the market would demand for risk and loss of liquidity on a similar private loan to the same borrower.

---

[42]R.L. Hubbell, "Concealed Subsidies in the Federal Budget," National Tax Journal (September 1947), p. 224.

[43]One study has assumed an eventual total loss of 30 percent of gross acquisitions in 1955 and 1956. R. Hubbell and Wilfred Lewis, Jr., "Capital Consumption by the Federal Government," National Tax Journal (March 1959), p. 34.

[44]Lending Agencies, Report of Commission on Organization of the Executive Branch of the Government, House Doc. No. 107, 84th Cong., 1st Sess., 1955, Recommendation No. 43.

The "proper" interest rate on a federal loan is discussed below.

Another hidden subsidy causing government to lend at less than the market rate is the absorption by the Treasury of administrative expenses of the lending agency, rather than charging the borrower for these costs. Again the Hoover Commission has recommended that these costs be charged to the beneficiaries of lending programs, but again the costs are difficult to obtain. The Commission, for example, cited administrative expenses of $26 million for the Farmer's Home Administration in 1954, but this includes costs of technical assistance programs, which presumably should not be borne by borrowers. Several other lending agencies also have multiple roles, and it is difficult to allocate joint costs. Finally, all federal agencies have some overhead expenses (personnel recruitment, buildings, etc.) paid from general Treasury funds. Thus even those lending agencies which attempt to cover administrative expenses from earned income do not cover all cost.[45]

The Hoover Commission has pointed out still another aspect of the second type of subsidy, the income received by lending agencies on funds invested in United States securities. Where this situation exists, according to the Commission, "the government is in the position of paying the interest on the money borrowed to make the investment in the agency and at the same time paying to the agency interest on that part of the government's investment which the agency has used to buy United States securities." The Commission recommends that such securities be returned to the Treasury in exchange for a non-interest-bearing account and that "the agencies display to the public the amount of these hidden subsidies."[46]

It is difficult to accept this reasoning, unless the lending agency's interest receipts from Treasury securities are deducted from administrative costs in calculating the interest rate to be charged on loans. If, in fact, an agency is charging rates sufficiently high to cover all costs as described above, then interest received on Treasury securities does not constitute a subsidy. If the government has purchased stock in the lending agency, it might be argued that surplus funds should be used to retire this stock rather than to invest in Treasury securities, but in this case the subsidy consists of the original stock purchases, not the investment, and the

---

[45]Senate Bill 2427, 85th Cong., required agencies to charge not less than the Treasury rate plus administrative expenses "to the extent consistent with the purposes of the loan program," certainly a question-begging solution. Cf. Hubbell, op. cit., p. 222.

[46]Lending Agencies, op. cit., pp. 105-7.

use of surplus funds to retire stock indicates either that the Treasury originally invested more than was necessary to operate the program or that the program is making a "profit."

It is not the purpose to discuss here whether federal lending should be subsidized. The important point to be derived from the above generalizations is that all these programs involve subsidies and subsidy effects, sometimes of significant size, and that much of the subsidy is concealed. The moral is that Congress should make a greater effort to distinguish these effects, should mark intended subsidies as such, and make other programs self-sustaining. This would, of course, require budgetary changes, both on the part of the lending agencies and the Treasury.

Subsidy in Loan Insurance. Everything said above about administrative costs of federal lending agencies applies also to agencies insuring private loans. In addition there is the question of whether the fees charged by the latter are adequate to cover the true cost of the insurance, i.e., whether the insurance program is "actuarially sound."

In the case of VA-guaranteed or insured loans the answer is clear, since no fees or premiums are charged, and all losses are borne by the taxpayer. FHA, however, charges both fees and premiums for the various types of insurance it writes, building up reserves for losses with the income therefrom. The Hoover Commission noted that "serious doubts have been raised concerning the adequacy" of these reserves,[47] and the report of the President's Advisory Committee on Government Housing Policies and Programs admitted in 1953 that "there has, as yet, been no test of the adequacy of the loss reserves of the Federal Housing Administration during any prolonged period of declining property values."

One early study, using "semiactuarial" tests, concluded that "on the basis of reasonable expectations" the system was sound. This lukewarm endorsement was further tempered by the admission that there was at that time (1943) no intention to repay the RFC for funds previously advanced.[48] A more recent (1956) and more rigorous study concluded that in early years the actuarial formula was unsound but that the situation is now sound.[49] Again, however, the judgment was tentative and surrounded by ceteris paribus assumptions.

---

[47] Lending Agencies, op. cit., p. 27.

[48] E.S. Garver, Mortgage Insurance, unpublished Ph.D. thesis (Yale, 1943), p. 760.

[49] Cf. Charles M. Haar, Federal Credit and Private Housing (New York: McGraw-Hill, 1960), p. 177.

In essence, these discussions of actuarial soundness are meaningless. In anything short of a serious depression the FHA program is probably "sound," but in a really serious, prolonged depression its reserves might be inadequate. But this is precisely the situation in which many other "reserves" would be exhausted (unemployment compensation, for example) and in which the government would, and should, intervene on a massive scale. It is unreasonable to expect private individuals, via an insurance premium, to obtain complete protection against this sort of a catastrophe.

At any rate, the system has been self-supporting to date, collecting premiums sufficient to cover all losses and operating expenses, repay the original RFC investment (plus interest), and accumulate reserves of over $200 million. Loss experience of both FHA and VA has been minimal. Of 4,764,000 VA home loans guaranteed before 1957 only 29,400 claims had been paid, while 974,800 loans had already been repaid. Of 3,395,900 FHA mortgages insured under Section 203, only 12,400 had been foreclosed and 1,520,000 repaid.[50]

The Cost of Federal Loan Funds. If Congress is to make a greater effort to distinguish the subsidy involved in federal credit programs, a measure is needed of the cost of the funds involved. Presumably a program should not be undertaken unless the anticipated benefits outweigh these costs. Admittedly the measurement of benefits is difficult. In addition to those benefits for which monetary values can be assigned, many federal credit programs have intangible ones—preservation of the family-sized farm, improved public health, etc. Equally difficult is the determination of the true cost of loan funds, particularly where they come from the federal Treasury.

The Hoover Commission's insistence that a federal lending program cover its "costs," including interest equal to that on long-term federal securities, implies that this is an acceptable criterion for justifying such a program. The same approach is taken by non-lending government agencies in assessing the benefits and costs of a proposed project. The Bureau of the Budget specifically recommends, for example, "A rate based upon the average rate of interest bearing marketable securities of the United States. . . which, upon original issue, had terms to maturity not more than twelve months [different from] the economically useful life of the project."[51]

Does the interest rate on Treasury securities measure the true

---

[50] Housing Amendments of 1957, Senate Banking Committee Hearings, 85th Cong., 1st Sess., p. 437.
[51] Circular A-47, December 1952, Section 15, p. 14.

social cost of the funds employed in a federal lending program? To argue so overlooks two important factors: the social cost of risk bearing and the compulsory nature of federal tax collections.[52]

First, the Treasury bond rate understates the full social cost of capital used in a lending program, since it makes no allowance for the risks of the particular loan. The holder of a federal security is unworried about the safety of, for example, a loan to an Indian family for cattle purchase. If the loan is not repaid, the taxpayer makes up the loss, not the bondholder. Yet, unless the interest rate reflects the risk of a loan, there will be misallocation of loanable funds.

Second, some of the funds loaned directly by a federal agency come from taxes. Since the individual has no choice about payment, the social cost of taxes depends upon the circumstances and desires of the taxpayer. That is, marginal taxes may be collected from individuals whose "rate of time preference" is far different from that of the purchaser of Treasury bonds.[53]

This merely reminds us that the real economic cost of a good is its "opportunity cost," i.e., the alternative output which society must forego in order to obtain it. According to the theory of welfare economics, a purely private competitive economy will allocate resources, production and consumption in an optimal way.[54] The interest rate produces an intertemporal distribution of resources which is also optimal by reflecting both the time preference of consumers and the returns which can be earned on investments. In the real economy, there is no single "market rate of interest," and the question here is which rate best measures the social cost of federal loan funds, i.e., the opportunity cost of federal capital. Formulation of sound public policy requires such a measure, since use of a rate too low could waste the nation's capital in loan programs yielding less satisfaction to borrowers than if left in alternative uses, and vice versa.

---

[52]Cf. Otto Eckstein, Water Resource Development (Cambridge, 1958), p. 95. Much of the following is based on arguments developed in this book and in John Krutilla and O. Eckstein, Multiple Purpose River Development (Baltimore, 1958).

[53]Of course, many loan programs use funds borrowed from savers, but even here it may be argued that taxes could be lowered in the absence of the program, since the borrowed funds could be used elsewhere by the government.

[54]I.e., so that no change is possible which would make anyone better off and still leave all other individuals as well off as before. See T. Scitovsky, Welfare and Competition (Chicago, 1951), for a description of the mechanism and for qualifications to the statement, some of which are discussed below.

Opportunity costs may differ according to the level of economic activity. It is a commonplace that in a deep depression government spending does not force any sacrifice on private groups and thus the social cost of government capital may be zero.[55] But this assumes that unemployment can be reduced only by increased government expenditure. If, for example, government could increase private demand by a tax reduction, alternative use of resources again becomes relevant, since private ends are being sacrificed for public objectives. The important comparison is not between the situations existing before and after a government expenditure but between what is and what might be.[56] As long as employment could be increased by fiscal or monetary measures, government's use of resources has a social cost. However, that cost will differ with the level of activity, since the alternatives available to private groups vary therewith.

We have seen that the rate on Treasury bonds is an inadequate guide for the investment (lending) of federal funds. Another solution might be the rate earned on private investments, since the funds could theoretically be used for this purpose instead. We noted above that, with one possible exception, no federal credit program has earned rates (of profit) comparable to those of private lenders. But this approach assumes that a decrease in federal loans would result in an equal increase in private investment, and that the return on the increase would equal that on existing (and presumably better) investments. Neither of these assumptions is tenable, so we must also reject this suggestion.

However, an estimate of the social cost of federal capital can be obtained in theory by tracing the tax money that provides the capital to its source and estimating the value attached to these funds in their alternative uses. The problems associated with this approach are obvious. It requires an estimate of the incidence of marginal tax dollars and assumptions as to which taxes would be

---

[55]Krutilla and Eckstein argue that, expressed as an interest rate, it is not inconceivable that the social cost would be negative in such circumstances. Op. cit., p. 119.

[56]See Earl Rolph, The Theory of Fiscal Economics (Berkeley, 1954), pp. 49-50. For an argument that social costs are not contemporaneous, i.e., that the costs of achieving government ends (including war expenditures) may be postposed to future generations, see James Buchanan, Public Principles of Public Debt (Homewood, 1958).

increased or cut if the government raised or reduced its spending.[57] Estimates must be made of the rate of return foregone on private investments when taxes are levied on different kinds of business, and rates of return must be inputed to money raised from taxes on households at different income levels.

Krutilla and Eckstein have made an extensive empirical investigation using this method, in assessing the economic efficiency of particular river basin development programs.[58] Using data for 1955, a year "considered typical of long-term conditions," they have constructed two models using different sets of assumptions about the potential tax cuts forestalled by public spending. In one model, consisting of tax cuts particularly favorable to low-income groups (and thus designed to stimulate consumption) they estimate the social cost of federal capital at 5.79 percent. In the other, with tax cuts designed to stimulate investment, the cost is estimated at 5.44 percent. They contend that the actual level lies within a range of 1 percent of these estimates and that the probable value "for the economic conditions postulated," i.e., those of 1955, lies between 5 and 6 percent.[59]

Of course the potential sources of error in the study are numerous. The true incidence of most taxes, particularly the corporate income tax, is debatable, to engage in understatement. In much of the analysis, average rates were used as an approximation to marginal rates of return. The approach itself begs all the familiar questions of welfare theory (mobility of resources, rationality of consumer and producer behavior, etc.), and the model implicitly assumes

---

[57] The approach assumes that a loan program is not at the expense of other federal expenditures and that a fiscal policy is pursued sufficient to produce stability at full employment. It does not necessarily assume tax changes equal to the change in spending, since multiplier effects of one may exceed the other. In effect, the approach measures Richard Musgrave's "differential incidence" of government expenditures. "General Equilibrium Aspects of Incidence Theory," American Economic Review (May 1953).

[58] Krutilla and Eckstein, op. cit., Ch. 5. The results are summarized in, "The Cost of Federal Money, Hells Canyon, and Economic Efficiency," National Tax Journal (March 1958), Part 1.

[59] As we have seen the cost would be lower in severe depression. In an inflationary period, it would probably be higher, since monetary policy would drive interest rates up and, among other things, more personal savings would probably find their way into business uses in which high rates of return prevail. Thus the alternative return foregone by the individual saver through his marginal tax dollar would be higher.

that the allocation of resources and structure of prices are approximately those which would result in a perfectly competitive economy. Finally, it abstracts from changes in income distribution, assuming that it does not matter to whom the benefits of a government expenditure accrue.[60]

Despite these qualifications, the substantial gap between the social cost of federal money as estimated by Krutilla and Eckstein and the rate on long-term Treasury securities should give us pause. (The average yield on long-term Governments in 1955 was 2.84 percent.) Assuming for the moment that the Krutilla-Eckstein estimate is correct, this would imply that those loan programs using Treasury funds are reducing rather than increasing "welfare" when the benefits derived from those programs during the life of the loan do not equal the amount of the loan plus 5 to 6 percent of the outstanding balance.[61] In those cases where no subsidy is intended, and where there are no intangible social benefits other than to the borrower, it would also imply that the lending agency should charge this interest rate (plus administrative costs).

This implication does not hold for those programs which obtain loan funds through sale of their own obligations to the public, since they, in fact, act as private lenders do. They should, however, "earn" a rate of return on any capital stock purchased by the Treasury equal to the 5 to 6 percent rate (again including an imputed value to intangible social benefits).

On the other hand, one might argue on several grounds that the Krutilla-Eckstein criterion should not be applied in the case of federal credit, and possibly not at all. First, we have seen that the assumptions of conventional welfare economics are not very well fulfilled in our economy. Second, there is a vast difficulty of measuring the intangible benefits, the so-called external economies of consumption. The very existence of these economies is a matter of social judgment and for political decision. Similarly, we have noted possible external diseconomies in some lending programs—

---

[60]For more technical qualifications and criticisms, see the study itself and review thereof by Julius Margolis, American Economic Review (March 1959).

[61]This clearly applies when tax funds are used, but it may not be so obvious if the Treasury is borrowing. However, we cannot (and should not for the purposes of this analysis) allocate specific revenues to the funds involved in a loan program. It is only important that taxes could be cut if federal loans were reduced. Note also that the analysis applies only to marginal changes in loan programs and taxes. (Otherwise the government could increase welfare by removing all taxes and shifting to borrowed funds exclusively.)

increased traffic problems, for example. The point is that the community, acting collectively through the political process, must judge the extent of these economies and diseconomies and often can only do it to the extent of agreeing that a certain government program is vaguely "desirable."

Third, the Krutilla-Eckstein analysis yields a rate which reflects only the preferences of the present generation of decision makers. Future generations have no role in the market place and thus in the allocation of resources over time. It may be argued that the government is more likely to be, and should be, more concerned with long-run national welfare than the individual. Using a lower rate of return as a criterion for adopting governmental programs would favor projects which are particularly long-lived. This point may have more relevance to water resource development than to the typical federal lending program, but is pertinent to some of the latter, e.g., REA loans.

More important, economic efficiency is not the only, or even necessarily the dominant, value in our scheme of values. We often politically invalidate market criteria. A lending program may be undertaken for social or other objectives which may be incompatible with maximum economic efficiency.

Nevertheless, the Krutilla study reminds us that efficiency criteria are relevant in considering the economic costs incurred by society in undertaking a government program. These costs are rarely recognized explicitly, and they are not found by a simple calculation of the interest rate on long-term Treasury securities.

THE ROLE OF FEDERAL CREDIT

Appropriate Use of Federal Credit

Three main types of situations have been described where the extension of federal credit may be socially beneficial: (1) competition may be inadequate in certain cases, i.e., credit may be available but not on terms in line with comparable competitive situations; (2) "credit gaps" may exist, i.e., credit may not be available for a particular purpose on any terms. These gaps may be chronic or depression-induced; and (3) there may be a divergence between the private and social valuation of the returns from a potential investment. Since private returns guide resource allocations in a pure market economy, we may improve economic efficiency through an extra-market device, e.g., federal lending. These three situations, and criteria for their identification, are being discussed in other Commission on Money and Credit studies. However, there are two other ways, not directly subsumable under any of the above situations, in which federal credit may be usefully employed—first, as an incentive and, second, as a substitute for direct government spending.

Federal Credit as an Incentive to Investment. The use of federal credit programs as deliberate incentives to encourage businessmen to invest either in specific industries or in specific geographic areas has been largely unexplored, but offers interesting possibilities. Of course, many business loan programs have incentive aspects, but they are designed primarily for the firm which is willing to invest but unable to raise the necessary funds on acceptable terms. We are referring here to cases where the firm is unwilling to take the risk involved in a capital expenditure, even though it may have adequate funds. An obvious example is the reluctance of businessmen to expand facilities in the Korean emergency for fear they would become redundant at a peacetime level of demand.

Government loans were utilized at that time as aids to business expansion, but, as an incentive, principal reliance was placed on the issuance of Certificates of Necessity permitting accelerated tax amortization. In the words of an RFC official, both were "government aids to business expansion, with the Necessity Certificate being more of a stimulation and the loans being more of an enabling device."[1]

However, accelerated amortization has been widely criticized on the ground that it offers more lavish inducements than are strictly necessary to achieve the desired objectives.[2] Since firms will demand protection against the worst foreseeable eventuality, but since it is unlikely that all these dangers will actually materialize, the average value of the grant of tax relief will be greater than the loss actually incurred. Moreover, accelerated amortization may decrease tax revenues when they should be high, and vice versa.

A better alternative would be a government-guaranteed, nonrecourse loan. This would make it possible to wait until loss actually resulted from the investment before determining the amount of compensation, which could be limited to the exact loss. For example, the government might guarantee the loan for a specified period,

---

[1]Edward C. Welch, "Government Aids to Business Expansion," American Economic Review (May 1952), p. 423.

[2]Kermit Gordon, "Government Policy on Business Practices: Comments," American Economic Review (May 1952), pp. 432-37; E.C. Brown, "Weakness of Accelerated Depreciation as an Investment Stimulus," Joint Economic Committee, Federal Tax Policy for Economic Growth and Stability, 1955.

giving the businessman the option at the end of the period either of turning the facility over to the government at depreciated value or of retaining it and relieving the government of further responsibility.[3] This is obviously very similar to the technique used in agricultural price supports.

Credit as a Substitute for Federal Spending. Federal loan guarantees may substitute not only for direct federal loans but also for federal spending. This is the effect of CCC guarantees of price-support loans, and the technique could be widely extended. For example, the government could extend grants to students for higher education, make direct loans, or guarantee private loans for the same purpose. As we have seen, the effects on resource allocation would differ according to whether the funds involved came from voluntary savings or taxation.

There is still another difference. Guaranteed loans have a considerably smaller effect than direct loans on the federal budget. This may be a strength or a weakness. It may be argued that budget discipline is necessary to prevent indiscriminate dishing-out of benefits, that budgetary limitations alone can temper the demand for additional government services. Whatever the validity of this argument, it is weakened when we recognize the ease with which a separate government "corporation" can be established to make loans, using funds obtained by sale of its own securities, and escape inclusion either in the federal budget or in the public debt. On the other hand, exclusion from the debt may be a godsend to a harassed administration working near an arbitrary debt ceiling, just as it has been claimed that too much "tax consciousness" may prevent public or congressional approval of needed public programs. This begs the definition of "needed," but the theme of "public poverty amid private plenty" is now a familiar one, and there seems to be a tendency for the public to increase its valuation of most governmental services after some experience with them.

Obviously, federal credit programs have many weaknesses. The Hoover Commission has compiled the following list:[4]

1. The tendency of such agencies to expand their functions beyond their original purposes.

---

[3]Cf. R. Schlaifer, et al., "Accelerated Amortization," Harvard Business Review (May 1951).

[4]Lending Agencies, op. cit., p. 14. For other criticisms see Library of Congress, Legislative Reference Service, "An Examination of the Growth of Federal Credit Agencies and Certain Detrimental Effects on the Private Economy," part of a study of Adverse Effects of the Expanding Activities of the National Government of the Private Economy and Federal System, Washington, D.C., 1957.

2. When the function for which such agencies were established has been completed, there is an inner impulse to continue when they should be liquidated.

3. There is a tendency to create activities which could be undertaken by private agencies.

4. In some of these agencies there are concealed subsidies.

5. Congressional policies which permit the making of loans or guarantees by such agencies to individuals or concerns without adequate equities.

6. The making of loans or guarantees without adequate premiums or fees or interest rates from beneficiaries out of which administrative expenses can be paid and reserves against losses built up.

7. Departmental lending or guaranteeing programs have a fatal attraction politically. Pressure groups, whether business, farmers, or veterans, often force the abandonment of the normal standards of prudence in the organization of these agencies which alone can assure the repayments of credits granted. Thus some of these operations practically become subsidies to a small fraction of the people from the taxpayer at large.

8. Where easy money is obtainable from the government, financial integrity tends to deteriorate and windfalls and corruption frequently flourish.

With the exception of numbers 5 and 6, this reads like a list of the deadly sins of government activities in general, and a complete cure would require, among other things, a reform of human nature.

However, two steps could accomplish a great deal. First is the implementation of budgetary reforms along lines described above. Until it is considerably easier to find out exactly what is happening in federal credit programs it will be difficult to remedy any weaknesses. Second is the often-mentioned need for coordination of the policies of federal credit programs with the general economic and credit policies of the government.

This second step would be simplified by consolidation of the numerous federal credit programs into three or four centralized lenders. At present the heads of many smaller lending agencies, who operate under congressional mandates to action and are subject to organized private pressures, may have less interest in the effect of their programs on economic stability than in self-survival. A smaller number of agency heads should be better able to resist pressure and more responsive to the needs of general stabilization policy, while, at the legislative level, piecemeal consideration by small congressional subcommittees would be reduced.

Relation to National Objectives

Discussion of the proper role of government in economic life is far beyond the scope of this essay. However, there is some consensus about three basic commitments. Government is generally agreed to have responsibility for maintaining economic stability at relatively full employment. There is an increasing sense of its responsibility for more conscious pursuit of economic growth. And, although there may be semantic objections to the term "income redistribution," there is emphasis on the ideal of equal opportunity for all and general concern over the living standards of low-income groups. Federal credit programs have some relation to all three commitments.

Economic Stability. The case for federal credit programs as a stabilizing device is the same as the case for selective controls in general. The debate over the desirability and usefulness of selective controls is familiar and need not be repeated here.[5] As we have seen, the countercyclical record of federal credit is unimpressive so far. Can it be improved?

Prospects are not sanguine for much improvement in stabilizing short-run fluctuations. Our ability to forecast these fluctuations is still only fair. Changes in credit flows are relatively slow to accomplish (in contrast, e.g., with tax changes), and the time lag between a change in policy and the effect of the change is great. The possible advantages of expanding and contracting these programs in the short run are offset by lowered organizational inefficiency and increased business uncertainty. (This is especially true in housing, where the customary annual omnibus "housing bill" has compounded the usual market uncertainties.)

However, there is one way in which the contribution of federal credit to short-run stability could be improved—through countercyclical changes in the source of funds. Most direct lending

---

[5]For favorable arguments, see Arthur Smithies, "Uses of Selective Credit Controls," in United States Monetary Policy, Papers prepared for the American Assembly (December 1958); H.P. Minsky, "Central Banking and Money Market Changes," Quarterly Journal of Economics (May 1957); Erwin Miller, "Monetary Policy in a Changing World," Quarterly Journal of Economics (February 1956); and Smithies, "The Control of Inflation," Review of Economics and Statistics (August 1957).

programs can (or could be designed to) obtain loan funds from more than one source. By shifting from funds currently made available out of income to those newly created by the banking system, the impact of a given amount of lending could be varied considerably. (In essence, this is the same as orthodox financial policy, which would call for the Treasury to shift from taxes to borrowed funds in a recession.) Similarly, a program financed entirely by debt sales to private investors could shift from long-term to short-term issues during recession and back to long maturities during inflationary periods. This would require, of course, conscious direction by the programs' administrators and is another argument for greater coordination between the operation of these programs and monetary and fiscal policy in general. Actual countercyclical changes in volume of lending would be politically difficult, and would require at best a long-run educational campaign, but shifts in sources of funds require only an administrative reform—the coordination of policy.

For longer-run changes, federal credit programs have more possibilities for offsetting inflationary pressures than for counteracting recession. The deflationary potential of a reduction in lending is enormous today, when repayments on previous loans are running in excess of $12 billion annually. The experience of 1944-45 demonstrated how repayments following a peak in total federal credit could produce a negative net flow in a very short time. In contrast, we may expect less help from federal credit in a long contraction. This is partly due to the well-known weakness of monetary policy in general when private demand has dropped precipitously. However, there are several ways in which federal credit programs may be useful in depression.

First, in a really serious emergency, federal credit may be invaluable. When a vicious circle of contraction and liquidation sets in, as in the 1930's, private lenders, governed by fear of loss, are increasingly forced to withhold credit and to foreclose. Private demand for funds may be substantial at the very time lenders are least willing to lend. Only the government, acting without fear of loss, can supply funds necessary to prevent further deterioration. By extending the loan term, i.e., refinancing, federal credit may carry borrowers, most of them ordinarily credit-worthy, through their temporary difficulty. The experience of HOLC is the classic example.[6]

---

[6]Actually, more has been done in agricultural lending to fit the amortization period to the income pattern of the borrower. See Robert Rosa, The Monetary Powers of Some Federal Agencies Outside the Federal Reserve System, Ph.D. thesis (Michigan, 1941), p. 344. We should note also that the amortized mortgage (popularized by FHA) and government loan insurance programs both reduce the threat of future liquidity crises.

Second, some of the cyclical perversity of state and local spending may be reduced by the granting of federal credit to these levels of government in a depression, as RFC did in the 1930's.[7] It has been argued that a better solution is to make outright unconditional grants in depression on the basis of need, since this would obviate the later repayment of these loans by state tax systems, which are generally inferior to the federal system.[8] However, this abstracts from sectional opposition to the potential strings attached to federal grants. In fact, "States' rights" feeling today may be strong enough to make even federal lending politically difficult. An inferior possibility is a federal guarantee of state and local obligations issued for specified purposes in depression to increase their marketability.

Finally, there is some hope that housing would respond to easier federal credit in recession. The reaction in 1953-54 lends credence to this possibility, and expansion of residential building after 1934 and 1937-38 also supports it.[9] But in fact we have no experience about how the demand for new residential construction would respond to still further easing of credit terms during any significant decline in economic activity. It may be doubted that there would be much effect. If terms were changed from 10 percent minimum down payment with 25-year maximum maturity and 4 percent interest, to zero down payment, 35-year maturity and 3 1/2 percent, this would reduce monthly mortgage carrying charge by 13 percent (from $4.75 per $1,000 of purchase price to $4.13). But real estate taxes and home operating expenses would not change, substantial outlays for closing costs would remain, and uncertainty would still discourage the undertaking of fixed commitments.[10] Moreover, the large supply of existing housing which would be offered at declining prices or rents would discourage both the demand for new con-

---

[7]Cf. Ansel M. Sharp, "A Study of the Countercyclical Aspects of Total Government Fiscal Policy, 1929-40," Ph.D. thesis, Louisiana State University, 1956.

[8]Paul Strayer, Fiscal Policy and Politics, (New York, 1958), pp. 199-200.

[9]M.L. Colean and R. Newcomb, Stabilizing Construction: The Record and Potential (New York, 1952), p. 145.

[10]See Leo Grebler, David Blank, and Louis Winnick, Capital Formation and Financing in Residential Real Estate, (National Bureau of Economic Research, 1955), Chs. 18 and 19 for a pessimistic view of the effect of further easing of FHA and VA terms. It is summarized in Leo Grebler, The Role of Federal Credit Aids in Residential Construction, (National Bureau of Economic Research Occasional Paper, 1953), pp. 59-62.

struction and the willingness of lenders to finance it.[11]

In recessions of smaller magnitude, however, housing may be an important stimulant. A quarterly comparison of GNP (annual rates) and residential construction expenditures for the postwar period indicates that, on the whole, housing "conformed positively to business fluctuations with a lead, cushioned recession, gave strong support to initial recovery from business contraction, and tapered off in advanced phases of general business expansion."[12] The governmentally assisted programs have been more volatile, and more countercyclical, than the nongovernmental. All of the expansion of 1953-54 and most of the contraction of 1955-57 was in the government-assisted sector. One reason is that much of the demand for government-assisted credit comes from consumers who are only in the market when the most liberal programs permitted under the programs are available.[13] More important has been the interest rate ceiling on VA loans, which has driven lenders out of this market when yields rise on alternative investments.[14]

The postwar behavior of housing has not been systematically countercyclical, but much of the difference is due to time lags between changes in credit terms and the supply of mortgage funds and the initiating, financing, and actual construction of houses. Little can be done to improve the timing of response as long as the forward-commitment process is regarded as essential for the efficient operation of the construction industry.[15] However, because of the substantial time lags in residential construction, there is even greater need than usual for better data on early decisions (commitments and builders' programs), the inventory of unsold new homes, vacancies in rental property and old homes, etc., if selective credit measures in this sector are to be employed for economic stabilization purposes.

---

[11]The declining value of existing houses would be aggravated by easier terms on new construction. It should not be forgotten that the government has, through its contingent liability, a substantial stake in debt on existing property and thus an interest in maintaining values.

[12]Grebler, Housing Issues in Economic Stabilization Policy, National Bureau of Economic Research, 1960, p. 104.

[13]Ibid., p. 92.

[14]It has also led indirectly to inflexibility in FHA maximum rates. For a discussion of mortgage discounts, showing that they are inadequate substitutes for flexible rates, see Grebler, ibid., Appendix A.

[15]James J. O'Leary, "Monetary Policies and the Mortgage Market," Journal of Finance (May 1958).

We have already noted the overwhelming role played by housing in the total picture of postwar federal credit. This means that, unless new programs are added, any substantial countercyclical effect of federal credit must come from housing programs. Fortunately, we have also noted that housing seems more susceptible to changes in credit terms than most other types of lending and that it has, in general, behaved in a countercyclical fashion.[16] This raises the question of whether economic stability conflicts with the social objective, as stated in the 1949 Housing Act, of providing "a decent home and suitable environment for every American family." Should residential building be the balance wheel of the economy, to use Grebler's phrase, or is the attainment of the housing objective, like national defense, of such importance that it should not be deterred even though there is full employment and general pressure on resources? The question, since it involves a value judgment about social priorities, cannot be answered categorically.[17] The case for maximum stability in housing is based not only on social welfare but also on the contention that general credit restraint acts with "unfair" harshness on housing, and that optimum efficiency cannot be obtained with variable output. It is even argued that some liberalization of government housing credit may help maintain an otherwise restrictive monetary and fiscal policy by forestalling congressional attempts to legislate more aid to housing and relieving public pressure for a change in over-all policy.

On the other side, it is claimed that housing objectives can be attained at best only in the very long run, while economic stability has a shorter time horizon and must therefore be attained in the short run or fail; that housing demand is not eliminated but merely postponed by decreased federal credit; and that varying a subsidy can hardly be considered unfair discrimination against housing. Finally, housing uses much the same resources as other forms of construction, and, in a boom, when demand for nonresidential building is high, the resulting rise in construction costs if housing demand also continues at a maximum level may be more harmful to potential

---

16Changes in housing expenditures also seem to have a greater effect on employment than many other kinds of spending. The man-years of primary employment resulting from $1,000 spent on residential construction has been estimated at 0.231 (based on 1947 interindustry relationships), compared, e.g., to 0.207 for highway construction and 0.194 for defense procurement. Alan M. Strout, "Primary Employment Effect of Alternative Spending Programs," Review of Economics and Statistics (November 1958).

17For both sides, see Charles M. Haar, Federal Credit and Private Housing (New York: McGraw-Hill, 1960), Ch. 5 and Grebler, Housing Issues in Economic Stabilization Policy, op. cit., Ch. 5.

homeowners than postponing their ownership via credit restrictions.

Whatever the merits of these arguments, the question points up again the need for coordination of federal credit programs generally with monetary stabilization policy. If all those sectors which, like housing, are commonly believed to be more responsive to general credit controls are sheltered by federal credit from the effects of those restraints, then general monetary restriction either will be useless or must be executed with such severity as to obviate its use.

Economic Growth. Maintenance of relatively full employment without inflation is, of course, directly related to economic growth and to the extent that federal credit programs contribute to one they also promote the other. In addition, federal credit affects growth in other ways.

It is doubtful that the rate of saving may be affected significantly by these programs, but resources may be directed into capital saving uses or, conversely, into areas requiring a scrapping of existing capital or involving a high rate of obsolescence. We have noted that federal housing programs may have promoted a way of life which is capital-intensive, and the emphasis of our agricultural credit programs on preserving the family farm may have had similar results. In contrast, urban renewal programs may save a great deal more capital through rehabilitation of marginal areas than would be required to finance them. (In fact, any really significant effects of federal credit on capital formation will be felt in the housing area, since more than a quarter of gross private domestic investment goes into residential construction and peripheral facilities.)

Abramovitz has shown that the increase in per capita output since 1870 is due not to increased capital inputs per head but to "the complex of little understood forces which caused productivity, that is, output per unit of utilized resources, to rise."[18] True, we know little about the causes of productivity increase, but an important one is undoubtedly investment of resources in education. In fact, we could argue that educational expenditures should be classified as investment rather than consumption, on the ground that they increase the demand for current resources but add to future output. Moreover, higher education, like capital formation, is often financed out of accumulated savings.

---

[18]Moses Abramovitz, "Resources and Output Trends in the United States Since 1870," American Economic Review (May 1956). See also, B.F. Massell, "Capital Formation and Technological Change in United States Manufacturing," Review of Economics and Statistics (May 1960).

Here an obvious contribution to growth can be made by federal credit. The Commission on Human Resources and Advanced Training has concluded that college graduating classes could currently be twice as large as they are, without loss of quality.[19] A large program of federal scholarships could improve this situation, but might not be an efficient use of public funds, since many recipients would go to college in any case. A loan program is preferable, and Title II of the National Defense Education Act of 1958, providing for government aid to universities in establishing student loan funds, is a small step in the right direction. Numerous studies have shown that investment in professional training yields a high return to the trainee and thus should make repayment possible. In addition, there are some true external economies involved, since the amount of such training consumed by one person enters into the utility functions of others, and thus gives grounds for subsidizing the loans. (The interest rate on loans made from funds established under the above act is set at 3 percent.)

Federal credit programs to aid small business have some effect on economic growth, since (a) increased competition should increase efficiency, and (b) small firms are the source of many innovations. On the other hand much small business is inefficient, constituting "disguised unemployment" for the entrepreneur and wasting resources for the economy. There is always danger that support of marginal firms (or depressed areas) will prevent needed adjustments to shifts in supply and demand or technology. On balance, the impact of federal credit on growth is probably negligible in this area.

Finally, Fellner has pointed out that technological improvements may yield changes in the marginal productivity of labor, capital or resources which may not correspond with the relative scarcities of these factors, and the growth process will be hindered thereby.[20] In theory, federal credit could help in such cases since, as we have seen, it can be used as an incentive to make certain investments, search for resources, etc. Actual identification of cases meeting Fellner's description and application of a credit program to its cure would, however, present obvious difficulties.

Income Redistribution. Our society has a general bias toward egalitarianism, and particularly toward equality of opportunity. This explains much of the support for federal credit programs for public housing, small business, and low income farmers. Probably

---

[19]Dael Wolfle, America's Resources of Specialized Talent (New York, 1954), p. 269.

[20]William Fellner, Trends and Cycles in Economic Activity (New York, 1956), Ch. 8.

a loan program for higher education would receive support partly for the same reason. As we have seen, however, it is doubtful that federal credit in the past has made much of a change in income distribution and, by its nature, a credit program is inferior to tax changes or grants of free services or goods if "fair shares for all" becomes a basic issue in the United States.

CONCLUSION

Federal lending or loan insurance is a powerful technique for directing funds into a particular activity or sector. By (a) lending without regard to loss, either of capital or of liquidity; (b) guaranteeing private lenders against these losses; (c) pooling risks; (d) stabilizing money markets; (e) subsidizing lending operations through payment of administrative costs, provision of free federal capital, or tax advantages, the federal government can channel resources into a specific industry, region, city, crop, or firm.

There are dozens of these programs, with new ones being added much faster than older ones are abandoned. Since 1957 new programs have been introduced to aid feeder airlines, guarantee loans to railroads for equipment purchase, establish student loan funds, help schools purchase classroom equipment, make loans in foreign currencies to private firms for trade expansion, develop small reclamation projects, lend to state and local development companies, purchase debentures in small business investment companies, lend to fisheries, insure export credit against "political risks," and for several other purposes. Total new commitments for the major federal credit programs alone have been estimated at $25 billion for fiscal 1960.

The desirability of any specific program rests, of course, on the case that can be made for selective aid to the economic sector toward which the program is directed. There is danger, however, that in debating this case for each program we may overlook the total impact of all lending programs on the economy. Their combined influence is great. They may ease the problems of the Treasury and Federal Reserve or magnify them, contribute to economic fluctuations or increase the system's stability. Since World War II they have created inflationary pressures in every year, but their deflationary potential is enormous. They may modify the character of growth and reduce departures from it.

Like an iceberg, the major part of these programs is not visible. Many do not affect the budget or the public debt. This relative invisibility may lead Congress to devote less attention to these programs than their importance deserves, or to assume that their cost is less than it is. A recurrent theme of this essay has been the need for the regular publication of more information about these programs, their sources of funds, lending commitments, contingent liabilities, etc.

But information should be combined with action. Federal credit programs may be viewed as selective economic controls of great promise, and their use should be coordinated with other instruments of stabilization policy, general or selective. This would be facilitated by combining many diverse programs into a few lending agencies, as the Housing and Home Finance Agency combined several programs in that area. The heads of these agencies should then coordinate their operations and policies with the Treasury, Federal Reserve and Budget Bureau, preferably as members of an economic council with an authority and status in economic policy similar to that of the National Security Council in defense policy.

TABLE II-9

Federal Credit Extended to Housing, 1932-58[a]
(Millions of dollars)

	Direct Loans	Insured Loans	Total	Repayments (b)	Net change
1932	1	-	1	-	1
1933	282	-	282	10	272
1934	2,404	6	2,410	75	2,335
1935	872	248	1,120	301	821
1936	466	394	860	448	412
1937	319	471	790	704	85
1938	375	654	1,029	531	499
1939	595	819	1,414	891	519
1940	874	1,316	2,190	1,346	845
1941	874	1,366	2,240	1,530	711
1942	492	1,498	1,990	1,450	542
1943	378	1,148	1,526	1,678	(151)
1944	333	1,055	1,388	1,514	(127)
1945	316	779	1,095	1,242	(141)
1946	366	1,916	2,282	1,881	544
1947	497	3,120	3,617	1,616	2,000
1948	662	4,023	4,685	1,682	2,998
1949	963	4,401	5,364	1,944	3,417
1950	1,858	5,938	7,796	2,841	4,955
1951	1,789	5,752	7,541	2,989	4,555
1952	2,003	5,086	7,089	3,769	3,318
1953	2,304	6,608	8,912	5,397	3,512
1954	2,295	7,107	9,402	6,598	2,802
1955	2,209	9,195	11,404	5,834	5,568
1956	1,982	7,590	9,572	5,651	3,919
1957	3,007	6,571	9,578	5,506	4,068
1958	2,871	8,471	11,342	6,938	4,403

Columns may not add due to rounding.

[a]None prior to 1932.
[b]Including expirations of insurance.

Source: Stewart Johnson, "Statistics on Federal Lending and Loan Insurance Programs in the United States, 1929-1958," Research Study One of this Volume, Tables I-134 to I-225.

TABLE II-10

Federal Credit Extended to Agriculture, 1929-58
(Millions of dollars)

Calendar Year	Direct Loans	Insured Loans	Total Loans	Repayments	Net Change
1929	238	-	238	230	7
1930	621	-	621	383	236
1931	883	-	883	720	162
1932	590	-	590	630	(44)
1933	941	112	1,053	653	397
1934	2,091	183	2,274	1,098	1,176
1935	1,352	122	1,474	1,099	373
1936	945	50	995	976	19
1937	1,006	64	1,070	977	89
1938	1,117	129	1,246	994	249
1939	1,133	126	1,259	1,332	(68)
1940	1,113	152	1,265	1,500	(237)
1941	1,368	304	1,672	1,593	81
1942	1,362	606	1,968	2,005	(41)
1943	1,406	632	2,038	2,280	(242)
1944	1,259	477	1,736	2,231	(487)
1945	1,435	310	1,745	2,235	(491)
1946	1,620	228	1,848	1,933	(83)
1947	2,045	238	2,283	1,981	304
1948	2,619	764	3,383	2,513	866
1949	3,196	2,309	5,505	4,134	1,370
1950	2,506	1,219	3,725	4,139	(415)
1951	3,005	709	3,714	3,384	330
1952	3,186	1,108	4,294	3,301	993
1953	3,757	2,090	5,847	3,999	1,845
1954	2,993	2,339	5,332	5,157	179
1955	3,450	2,393	5,843	5,775	69
1956	4,032	2,508	6,540	5,919	620
1957	3,694	1,041	4,735	4,977	(244)
1958	4,536	3,122	7,658	5,450	2,210

Source: Stewart Johnson, "Statistics on Federal Lending and Loan Insurance Programs in the United States, 1929-1958," Research Study One of this Volume, Tables I-1 to I-70.

TABLE II-11

Federal Credit Extended to Business, 1929-58
(Millions of dollars)

Calendar Year	Direct Loans	Insured Loans	Participations	Total Loans	Repayments	Net Change
1929	14	-	-	14	-	14
1930	25	-	-	25	5	20
1931	40	-	-	40	18	22
1932	1,441	-	-	1,441	310	1,131
1933	1,191	-	-	1,191	614	577
1934	1,318	1	11	1,330	760	568
1935	401	3	29	433	625	(205)
1936	178	3	12	193	760	(568)
1937	119	1	7	127	312	(185)
1938	208	36	11	255	207	46
1939	139	30	5	174	249	(76)
1940	272	10	4	286	298	(13)
1941	151	18	20	189	281	(95)
1942	520	1,000	22	1,542	703	839
1943	485	4,267	10	4,762	3,784	979
1944	430	3,547	5	3,982	4,279	(297)
1945	391	1,922	2	2,315	3,656	(1,341)
1946	93	494	9	596	929	(331)
1947	416	224	6	646	482	147
1948	299	94	2	395	354	41
1949	247	84	4	335	318	16
1950	254	57	4	315	430	(117)
1951	246	1,212	9	1,467	945	521
1952	264	2,380	3	2,647	2,471	171
1953	232	2,007	3	2,242	2,442	(200)
1954	114	1,241	36	1,391	1,924	(528)
1955	132	730	36	898	1,100	(203)
1956	134	863	59	1,056	960	93
1957	104	869	80	1,053	995	58
1958	109	716	86	911	851	61

Source: Stewart Johnson, "Statistics on Federal Lending and Loan Insurance Programs in the United States, 1929-1958," Research Study One of this Volume, Tables I-71 to I-133.

TABLE II-12

Federal Credit Extended for Miscellaneous Puposes, 1929-58
(Millions of dollars)

	Direct Loans	Repayments	Net Change
1929	43	28	16
1930	65	46	19
1931	84	65	19
1932	209	92	117
1933	388	102	286
1934	219	157	63
1935	218	150	68
1936	193	130	63
1937	198	134	62
1938	185	501	(316)
1939	227	312	(84)
1940	212	253	(40)
1941	268	264	2
1942	125	137	(10)
1943	141	191	(49)
1944	14	41	(27)
1945	12	38	(25)
1946	28	38	(10)
1947	38	23	14
1948	42	18	24
1949	40	83	(41)
1950	42	26	15
1951	52	20	31
1952	53	30	23
1953	61	32	28
1954	85	73	11
1955	83 (a)	67	16
1956	101 (a)	91	9
1957	118	87	32
1958	129	89	40

Source: Stewart Johnson, "Statistics on Federal Lending and Loan Insurance Programs in the United States, 1929-1958," Research Study One of this Volume, Tables I-226 to I-243.

TABLE II-13

Noninsured Parts of Federally Insured Loans and Private Parts of Federal Participation Loans, 1934-1958
(Millions of dollars)

Calendar Year	Loans Extended	Repayments	Net Change
1934	24	12	13
1935	180	96	84
1936	223	203	20
1937	54	84	(30)
1938	156	95	61
1939	197	104	93
1940	229	172	57
1941	240	232	8
1942	406	356	50
1943	935	887	48
1944	747	831	(85)
1945	576	627	(49)
1946	1,833	378	1,459
1947	2,434	450	1,984
1948	1,656	467	1,189
1949	1,626	1,100	525
1950	2,158	1,303	855
1951	2,482	1,040	1,443
1952	2,457	1,771	683
1953	2,926	2,468	458
1954	2,974	1,653	1,321
1955	3,995	2,183	1,814
1956	3,552	2,000	1,554
1957	2,790	1,550	1,239
1958	1,852	1,862	(9)

Columns may not add due to rounding.

Note: Loans in this table are included in "federal credit" as defined in this study. Above totals are not included in any other table herein, except Column 4 of Table II-1.

Source: Stewart Johnson, "Statistics on Federal Lending and Loan Insurance Programs in the United States, 1929-1958," Research Study One of this Volume.

Research Study Three

CREDIT GAPS AND FEDERAL CREDIT PROGRAMS

James W. McKie
Vanderbilt University

INTRODUCTION

The federal government has undertaken a wide variety of programs to make credit available to business firms and individuals. It has guaranteed the credit of private institutions. It has taken steps to increase the flow of credit or alter its direction to promote public ends. These programs are often instituted in response to a "credit gap." The term has been used loosely. The main purpose of this paper is to investigate the meaning, and to devise rough tests for the recognition of credit gaps.

Credit gaps can exist only in imperfect markets. They can result from inadequate market organization or imperfect knowledge; on the other hand they may be a sign of ineffective competition. We are concerned with both symptoms and fundamental causes of credit gaps and inadequate competition in credit markets.

THE OPTIMUM ALLOCATION OF CAPITAL RESOURCES AND CREDIT

Capital is a scarce resource. A "credit gap" is not simply a scarcity of capital, but a particular kind of scarcity. This fact is often lost to sight in discussions of credit "needs." The mere existence of an "opportunity" to invest does not of itself create a valid claim on capital resources. The opportunities for investment are practically boundless. Capital must be rationed, and our problem is to decide by what means and according to what criteria it should be rationed.

Perhaps our best criteria are based on the behavior of an economic system assumed to be perfectly competitive, without institutional frictions and without uncertainty. In such a system, interest rates would be the sole and sufficient mechanism for rationing capital and credit among competing uses. Potential borrowers and users of equity capital would register their wants in an interrelated system of demand schedules for capital funds. Their demand prices in the form of interest rates would depend on the ultimate profitability of capital in productive uses or on the urgency of their wants for consumer credit. The market would strike a simultaneous balance between the supply and demand for credit in each market and the supply of capital to various markets, e.g., the relationship of the short-term market to the long-term market and the relationship of debt to equity capital. In equilibrium, differences in interest rates would persist only because of (1) differences in risk among various classes of borrowers and capital-users; (2) differences in the cost of serving various classes of borrowers; (3) differences in the liquidity of loans. There would be no "credit gaps."

Does this mean that the rationing of credit by some means other than the interest rate is evidence of an inadequate economic performance? Clearly, some credit rationing is inevitable because of uncertainty in the actual world and because of institutional lags and frictions. General credit rationing by financial intermediaries is not necessarily indicative of credit gaps. If interest rates should respond sluggishly to changes in the level of economic activity, a general shortage of credit might result, but the lenders might well ration it in precisely the same way that interest rates would ration it if the market were in equilibrium.

Frictions and lags can become great enough to interfere seriously with optimum allocation of capital funds. Monopoly in credit markets may have similar effects. General monopoly could produce a general level of interest rates that is too high when measured against the basic supply-price of capital and which unnecessarily excludes many borrowers from the market. Local monopoly would show up as rate discrimination against certain classes of borrowers or rate differentials among localities. In either case the "gap" might be invisible, in that no borrower willing to borrow at the monopolistic interest rate need go unsatisfied.

It appears, then, that inadequate competition can affect the level and structure of interest rates without creating visible credit gaps; conversely, credit rationing, both general and specific, can occur in markets that are not monopolistic. But in some instances a visible credit gap may accompany structural monopoly.

THE MEANING OF "CREDIT GAP"

The term "credit gap" is used in several different senses. It may mean that investment opportunities exist whose prospective benefits would exceed the cost but which do not attract investable funds because of some barrier to the flow of private capital. Apart from monopolistic exclusion, barriers may result from legal restrictions, prejudice, habit, and routine. If lending institutions are prohibited by law from undertaking sound investments and investment demands are therefore unsatisfied, or if banks refuse to lend to certain classes of persons or firms not because of any objective element of risk but simply because of inertia, prejudice, or habit, a gap is indicated. This kind of credit gap might be easy to bridge, as with the removal of legal restrictions; on the other hand, gaps resulting from prejudice can be very difficult to overcome.

Often a "credit gap" is alleged when private capital is not pursuing some socially desirable end. The possibilities are vast. "Social benefits" is largely a subjective notion. Assertions that the social benefits of some enterprise exceed the private benefits usually mean that certain activities or ends ought to be subsidized even though they do not directly repay the costs. In the ensuing discussion we shall exclude consideration of social benefits when we identify credit gaps. If the public authority contributes funds to realize social benefits (private parties being uninterested because the private costs exceed the private benefits), it is not remedying a credit gap but subsidizing, or spending public funds for a public purpose. To exclude the object of subsidies and collective expenditure from the category of credit gaps is not to imply that they are unworthy objectives of public finance; it is simply to give the category a more definite meaning. When we encounter a gap between social benefit and private benefit it is not a credit gap so much as an eligible opportunity for subsidy, which might well take the form of a credit subsidy.

Exclusion of subsidies still leaves the possibility that the public authority can supply credit for certain purposes at lower economic cost than private lending institutions can supply it. We must consider the possible sources of economies in the public supply of funds or in public guarantees of private investment in such cases, and also whether the relative economies that may be realized by governmental actions are likely to be transitory or permanent. If the public authority can indeed make funds available at a genuinely lower cost for particular purposes, and if the calculable economic benefits exceed such cost, it can bridge a credit gap. This second class of credit gaps involves a cost difference rather than an artificial barrier to the flow of funds. To evaluate the possible sources of public economies we must take a closer look at the "cost" of capital.

RISK AND THE COST OF CREDIT

Ordinary commodities may have one price in one market, but credit does not. Credit is made available at a variety of prices which depend on the risks of the investments as lenders view them. The interest rate in the market finds a level appropriate to the risk. But "risk" is a multidimensional concept, hard to measure or even to define. In one sense the riskiness of an investment refers to the parameters of its mathematical probability of return. Investors must choose among investment opportunities that present different combinations of risk characteristics. One investing institution may give heavy weight to investment opportunities having a small dispersion of expected return and accept lower returns in preference to greater dispersion of expectations and a higher mean return. Others will prefer a different assortment of investments. The market rates of interest in a pure-risk economy would reflect the weighted balance of preferences of persons and institutions having funds to invest among different classes of risk. This weighted balance of risk preferences would simply be a datum of the market. Borrowers who were disadvantaged by it could not claim a credit gap existed merely because they offered a return with a higher actuarial mean value than some more favored borrower.

In the business world, not many risks approach pure mathematical insurability. The insurance business itself is evidence that some do, but most of the ventures and decisions of business enterprises are not insurable in the same sense, and no definite mathematical probability can be assigned to them. The lender or investor may be able to classify investment opportunities into categories within which the individual items are more or less interchangeable and homogeneous, like residential mortgages; even so, he cannot exactly calculate the mathematical risk because no case nor group of cases is exactly like another. And there are large categories of investments in which the decision is unique or nonrepetitive, for which there is no similar precedent, and for which the chances of success or failure have to be inferred from the circumstances of the individual trial. This lack of information is what we mean by uncertainty.[1] Most estimates of risk by lenders involve a component of uncertainty, and if it is large the opinions of different parties concerning the "riskiness" of the investment may well differ.

---

[1]A unique trial drawn from a universe of possibilities about which nothing is known represents "...not actuarial risk which is a form of knowledge, but uncertainty which is another name for ignorance." Shackle, Expectation in Economics (Cambridge, 1949), pp. 115-16. This is of course the well-known distinction pointed out long ago by Frank Knight.

Another element of investment risk is its degree of generality. Some risks are specific to the investment, or to the class to which they belong. These are the credit risks, involving the expected profit of the investment and its dispersion compared to other investments, the specific risk of catastrophe, and the probable variation in return over time. Other risks are general, involving inflation or depression. These market risks are common to all investments, though they may have different effects on the various investment classes.

Where and how will these risks differ for private enterprise and for the public authority? And to what extent will other costs be different? These questions contain the key to identification of our second class of credit gaps. It is clear that the public authority has no over-all advantage over private lenders in the form of lower credit risks or lower investment costs for all classes of lending. It is even more certain that the rate at which the federal government borrows does not represent the "social cost" of capital. If the whole economy were suddenly converted to a regime of state socialism, it could not invest capital in all investment opportunities at this rate. The government cannot render the economy riskless, though it might well transform the interest cost of risk into some other form of cost such as the costs of inflation. In the present economy, an investment in a government security is "riskless" only because of the certainty of repayment of principal at maturity (and of interest) in dollars then current, assuming the continuity of the government. But if the government should attempt to invest in all outlets that cannot borrow from private sources at this rate, an inflationary effect would be inevitable. Other distortions would also be likely as the government attempted to compensate for the shortage of capital relative to investment demand at the government rate.

The government as lender (or as guarantor of loans) thus stands in a quite different position from the government as borrower. When it lends, the government must set rates that are appropriate to all the risks and other costs of the investments, and (since we are not including subsidies in our definitions) it must have a normal expectation of return of the principal advanced. The only question is whether its risk costs or other costs are lower than those of private institutions in any particular case.

SOURCES OF PUBLIC ECONOMIES IN GOVERNMENT CREDIT PROGRAMS

It seems very likely that most costs of investment are independent of government action. Governmentally guaranteed investment is subject to both market risks and specific credit risks. But the government may realize risk advantages or lower costs in some circumstances.

1. The risk element most subject to government control is the risk associated with depression. (This is to be distinguished from other risks of catastrophe or bankruptcy that are specific to certain investments.) We do not know how much private lenders are influenced by the possibility of catastrophic deflation, but the public authority can do what no private institution can do in reducing the probability of such an event. Ideally, it should try to ensure that investments which are sound credit risks will not produce principal losses merely because they cannot survive a deflationary crisis, without guaranteeing the survival of investments that are unsound due to high specific credit risks. This may be quite difficult in practice. The public authority can give a general promise of fiscal and monetary action to forestall or remedy a deflationary crisis. It might also find a few opportunities to eliminate the risk of a "crisis of confidence" by offering a contingent guarantee or insurance of a type of credit whose specific risks are small and diffuse and whose uncertainties are slight. Deposit insurance is the best example, since it eliminates an unnecessary uncertainty and reduces risk cost to a true minimum. But these opportunities are strictly limited, and the government cannot offer specific survival guarantees of most types of credit without actual or potential cost to itself. To absorb or conceal these costs amounts to subsidization.

2. In classes of investments where aggregation of similar cases is possible, considerable economies of scale may exist. Average risk costs would continue to decline as similar cases are added to provide more risk offsets, though the additional cost reductions might become negligible at some point on the expansion path, while other unit costs of doing business might rise as scale increases. The facts will vary from one credit market to another. For the most part these economies are available to private institutions, but occasionally the government may be in a better position to seize them. At any given stage of historical development, the scope of the economies of scale for particular types of investment may transcend the scale on which private credit institutions operate. (Legal barriers and other limits on the discretion of private institutions may reinforce this cost effect.) It takes time and experience to develop a large-scale credit pool, and there may be threshold barriers or developmental difficulties that would endanger the survival of a private pool before it could break through to the realization of full-scale economies. If the government can accurately perceive such opportunities, it can push the development through the formative stage with loan guarantees, or with direct lending programs by governmentally-created institutions if no private lenders exist within the designated credit field. Then, once the program has reached maturity, the government can turn over the institutions to private enterprise and reduce its own commitment to a guarantee of support that is likely to be invoked only during a deflationary crisis.

It should be emphasized that these large-scale economies are not necessarily beyond the reach of private institutions in all instances. Where the government has any advantage over private institutions in realizing them it is most likely to have only a temporary or threshold advantage. For some types of investment economies of scale are not especially significant. Large uncertainties tend to nullify the advantages of risk aggregation. The credit market is heterogeneous and differentiated. Local specialization is a distinct advantage in some of its segments, notably in commercial bank loans, because of local advantages in appraising risks, in personal acquaintance with the borrower, in maintenance of a close check on the use of the loan, and the continued solvency of the borrower. Economies of scale in this class of lending would thus partly depend on the scale of the local community, and might turn into diseconomies as the lender extended his activities over greater distances or into more diverse areas and as his information began to thin out. (A government program to surmount barriers to the flow of credit in this field would have to take this element into account.) The effect of scale-economies, on the other hand, is more likely to be seen in investments like residential mortgages, where the advantages of large-scale processing and risk pooling are considerable.

3. A more lasting cost advantage may be available to the government when a credit program is complementary to the government's pre-existing organization and wide geographical coverage. Because of its nonfinancial activities in practically every community, the government already has crossed an organizational threshold. It may be able to gather information, make evaluations and decisions, and administer programs related to those activities at a lower additional cost than a new private organization could achieve. This is particularly important in "thin" or scattered credit markets that are uneconomical for an institution specializing in particular forms of credit. However, the advantages of complementarity and geographical coverage are limited, and they can disappear with growing credit volume and community development which make private specialist institutions economical.

To summarize the discussion to this point, a credit gap may arise when there is some artificial barrier to the flow of private credit in response to investment opportunities, or when the government can supply a credit demand which private sources at that time and place do not supply because of higher costs. We do not include unrealized "social benefits" in the category of credit gaps, but only the direct returns and the calculable costs of investment or credit. The public authority has no general economic cost advantage over private credit intermediaries, and in particular the low rate at which it borrows does not confer any such cost advantage on it. But it may realize cost advantages where it can achieve economies of scale that are currently beyond the reach of private lenders, or where it already engages in complementary activities. It may also be able to reduce one element of risk cost by supporting credit during a deflationary crisis.

In addition to gaps in the availability of credit, imperfect competition may produce other forms of distortion in credit markets.

To assert that the public may benefit when the government bridges a credit gap or remedies competitive imperfections is not to say that these actions have entirely neutral effects. Even when the public authority merely guarantees private investment rather than advancing public funds, it makes private debt partly interchangeable with public debt or otherwise alters the supply-demand balances in the various hetergeneous sectors of the capital market. This is bound to change interest rates and affect the allocation of resources. If credit gaps are distortions, however, correction of the distortions improves the allocation of resources.

SIGNS AND SYMPTOMS OF CREDIT GAPS

The foregoing general discussion should help us to recognize actual credit gaps and noncompetitive situations eligible for federal credit programs. But it is much easier to make retrospective judgments of existing programs than of the need for new or different ones, since a program may well produce its own evidence of the need for it. We shall consider several possible signs and symptoms of credit gaps and inadequate competition that may be useful guides under various conditions.

Credit Rationing: Chronic

It is tempting to identify a credit gap wherever there is an unsatisfied demand for credit at the market price, but assessments of risk and allowance for the varying terms of price are prerequisites for such a judgment. That credit rationing occurs is undeniable. We are looking for classes of borrowers (using that word in the broadest sense) who are excluded from the market but who are willing to pay a return on capital commensurate with the risks of the investment. Such cases are not easy to find. To assert that the failure of the market to supply them must necessarily be due to risk preference is to turn that concept into an empty tautology; yet the risk preferences of lenders as well as uncertainty do undoubtedly disfavor some classes of borrowers. It is easy to find unsatisfied borrowers. It is not too difficult to find examples of both large- and small-scale credit rationing, but they may be related to causes other than a credit gap.

Short-run credit rationing may often be due simply to stickiness of interest rates when the supply of credit varies. If the stickiness is caused primarily by institutional frictions and not by oligopolistic tacit collusion or something similar, one can expect that the situation will correct itself after a lag. Similar phenomena can be observed in a great many markets; hardly any prices are perfectly flexible. At all events they suggest a distinction between cyclical rationing and structural or semipermanent rationing.

Credit rationing unrelated to risk or return might be chronic. If certain groups claim prejudice, it should be possible to examine their credit-worthiness to see whether the claim is well-founded. Claims of this sort have been made, e.g., on behalf of Negroes in both the South and North, and on behalf of American Indians. The difficulty that immediately suggests itself is that lack of credit is, or discriminatory terms against certain groups are, merely one facet of a generally underprivileged economic status, and it is pointless to single out that one. The argument here merges with a welfare problem. If members of a particular minority group cannot borrow on equitable terms for business purposes, and if only short-run difficulties need to be overcome to establish such enterprises on a self-sustaining basis, then a kind of infant-industry aid might well form part of any general welfare program for such groups. A credit-aid plan should soon produce evidence on whether or not a credit gap exists—whether self-sustaining enterprises managed by or employing members of the underprivileged group can establish themselves without requiring net government expenditure in the long run.

Other groups may not be able to claim that they suffer prejudicial credit discrimination, but they may be "rationed out" of the credit market by over-rigid rules, habit, or inertia on the part of lending institutions. Bankers' codes of proper behavior tend to be strict, and at times may be shortsighted. A conservative policy is best for a fiduciary institution, of course, but all the same one may wonder why it took so long for bankers to find out that personal consumer loans, for example, were safe, sound, and profitable. No doubt a questionnaire circulated 50 years ago would have revealed that bankers thought that consumer loans were too risky, as well as a general feeling that bank loans should be for "productive" purposes. Perhaps the evolution of financial responsibility, increased stability of individual employment, the growth of discretionary income, and sustained prosperity <u>have</u> made consumer loans less risky. But probably the gap was there.

Banks and other credit institutions may also suffer from legal restrictions of various kinds. These tend to hem in the lending institutions and interfere with the free flow of capital resources into certain uses or certain areas. Everyone recognizes the need for restrictions on types of investments by fiduciary institutions, assuming that self-regulation does not work, but the rationale for prohibitions on branch banking, for instance, or out-of-state investments by insurance companies, is questionable. When these restrictions result in the growth of makeshift institutions to fill the gap, such as money-changers operating out of drugstores, the existence of the gap is obvious. This is true also, when there is a large discrepancy in interest rates from one locality to another which banks or other lenders cannot rectify because of legal barriers. Detection of such cases should not be difficult.

Credit Rationing: Cyclical

A cyclical credit gap arises when some investment needs or some borrowers are periodically discriminated against, so that they are repeatedly excluded from the market whenever credit gets tight for reasons unrelated to risk or cost. (This means systematic discrimination, not merely haphazard effects of sticky interest rates in a period of tightening credit.) Cyclical credit gaps might result from inertia, habit, or personal discrimination.

Evidence of cyclical discriminatory rationing is very thin, as usual, because of the difficulty of getting an objective measure of risk. Commercial banks use several methods of rationing credit in periods of tight money, but one which is common to almost all is the practice of favoring their own depositors, roughly in proportion to the size of the deposit, other things being equal. Since certain classes of borrowers typically keep deposit balances that are low relative to their average needs for bank credit, these classes are cut off the eligible list first when credit tightens, even though they may be willing to pay the same interest rate as before in proportion to the rates paid by more favored borrowers. Is this arbitrary and discriminatory rationing? While bankers may tend to think in terms of availability of funds or of expanding and contracting quantitative limits, it seems likely that the implicit rate of earnings on demand deposits is what actually governs their actions. Prevented by law from paying interest on demand deposits, they allocate credit to those who provide them with the reserves that support their loans. This allocation is the equivalent of a higher interest rate. It may also happen during a credit stringency that a bank will accommodate a borrower who has not in the past kept adequate balances on deposit, provided the borrower will agree to maintain compensating balances from then on, and is also willing to pay a higher interest rate. These policies are not necessarily discriminatory, but they may be. The criterion of optimum allocation of capital resources might be better satisfied if banks merely accepted proportionally higher rates of interest from borrowers with low deposit ratios, rather than excluded them altogether while keeping the same relative structure of interest rates in effect.

Among the cyclically disfavored credit classes are construction company (since contractors usually do not maintain large balances), finance company, and mortgage company loans. The last-mentioned usually suffer a shortening of the term of the loan rather than complete exclusion; it is only those which must have longer terms that are excluded. This effect is general. In times of tight money, besides raising interest rates and favoring deposit customers, banks may choose to eliminate riskier loans, to draw in the geographic boundaries of their lending, to reduce the length of loans, and to require larger down payments on installment loans.[1] These are not arbitrary rationing devices, either; the interest rate is only one dimension of the "price" of credit. If bankers tend to think of construction loans as particularly risky loans, they may think that a general rise in interest rates will make it difficult for such borrowers to repay the rate which would be appropriate to that risk, and may therefore withhold credit entirely.[2]

Another kind of cyclical credit gap may occur in the opposite phase of the business cycle: the credit stringency which may result from autodeflation and deep depression. Here the problem is not credit rationing but a general reluctance to make loans because of uncertainty that borrowers will survive the crisis, coupled with the disappearance of bank reserves and loanable funds in general collapse of credit and a general freezing of assets. It is clearly the mission of monetary and fiscal authorities to extend emergency credit to arrest an autodeflation and stabilize the situation enough to permit the survival of borrowers whose assets are perfectly good in the long run but temporarily illiquid. This is a general rather than a particular credit problem.

---

[1]See the Ph.D. thesis of Weston Edwards, "Study of the Management of Investment and Loan Portfolios of Selected Commercial Banks," Harvard Graduate School of Business Administration, 1961.

I am also indebted to several other members of the Cambridge capital markets study group for illuminating discussion of credit rationing.

[2]As Donald R. Hodgman says in a recent article ". . . the higher interest rates go, the more numerous are the borrowers who become marginal in terms of credit rationing (risk consideration), regardless of their willingness to commit themselves to higher interest charges. Ultimately every borrower is limited by his capacity rather than his willingness. Accordingly the higher interest rates go, the more pervasive will become the influence of credit rationing. More and more borrowers will find that 'availability' rather than interest determines their access to credit." "Credit Risk and Credit Rationing," Quarterly Journal of Economics (May 1960), p. 277. See also Jack Guttentag, "Credit Availability, Interest Rates, and Monetary Policy," Southern Economic Journal (January 1960), pp. 219 ff.

Direct Calculation of Returns

In some fields of economic activity, information on costs, markets, and technology is complete enough to support a fairly reliable calculation of prospective returns to investment. Students of such fields may detect (or verify) the presence of a credit gap by direct comparison of expected net cash flow with the investment costs. Agriculture is the field that most readily comes to mind. It may be possible to show, for example, that a reorganization of family farms in a certain area into commercial farms that are larger and more heavily capitalized will produce added returns considerably in excess of the added capital cost. If it can further be shown that the unavailability of capital at a cost commensurate with the risk is the reason that such reorganizations have not been carried out, a credit gap is indicated.

Obviously such a conclusion should be reached only after the most searching and cautious appraisal of the facts. The principal stumbling block, as always, is the evaluation of risk. If commercial sources of capital refuse to make it available to this activity, is it because of shortsightedness and inertia or because of risk appraisal? If the latter, is there some rate at which lenders would lend to the entrepreneurs? Would this rate reflect monopoly? If not, are existing lending agencies mistaken in their evaluation of the riskiness of the investment opportunity? What objective evidence exists concerning the frequency of success of the proposed types of investment, and concerning the reliability of predictions of net return? Is this evidence accessible to private lenders? Are there economies of scale or of complementarity available to the government in this case but not available to private lenders? Only when studies of costs and returns have provided answers to these questions can we attach much significance to their conclusions on credit gaps. They should be based on concrete calculation of risks and costs; purely intuitive statements that this or that program would be profitable are no better than present lenders' intuitive judgments that they would not.

Discontinuities in Credit Terms

The various forms of credit and capital funds, and their terms of availability, form a kind of spectrum in several dimensions. But it is not necessarily an unbroken continuum. Because of institutional specialization, or barriers created by law or custom, or lags in economic development, discontinuities in the credit spectrum may exist. While even a perfectly functioning credit system would not make equity capital, for example, available on the same terms as debt capital, because of differences in risk and in risk preferences, it would nevertheless provide a continuum of terms for different prospective risks and a means of arbitrage if the supply of debt capital should become too large or too small in relation to the supply of equity capital. Malfunctions would result in blocks to the transfer of capital between the markets, or to the movement of borrowers from the debt market to the equity market and vice versa, or to changes in relative interest rates.

In a frictionless economic system, new lending institutions would spring up to fill the gaps, or other institutions would expand their programs to bridge the intervals. To a large extent emerging gaps have been filled by the rise of new forms of financial intermediaries, but the process may work sluggishly and imperfectly. Thin spots may occur when a particular credit demand will not fit into the organization and outlook of existing intermediaries while the uncertainties are still so great as to restrain the growth of new types of lenders, and when the potential borrowers are small-scale.

It has been suggested, for instance, that the supplies of revolving credit and of permanent credit may get out of balance with their respective demands. Bank credit is predominantly of the former type, while equity capital and capital available through national investing agencies is predominantly of the latter type. Institutions providing long-term capital, whether debt or equity, tend to specialize in certain kinds of lending and virtually all of them favor large-sized borrowers operating on a national scale themselves. As a result local borrowers constantly importune banks to lend on a quasi-permanent basis, such as working capital term loans indefinitely renewed. Commercial banks themselves have differing policies regarding the use of that portion of their resources represented by time deposits, and some even limit their term loans to some percentage of time deposits. The nature of commercial banking imposes such restrictions.

Thin spots in the spectrum of availability can also be caused by overly rigid rules such as arbitrary limits to debt-equity ratios. These ratios may or may not be consistent with the objective risks of the borrowing companies, and lending agencies may be disinclined to experiment with alternative criteria even though the existing ones may have demonstrably failed to produce the desired risk avoidance.

Many of these discontinuity problems affect small business. It has often been pointed out that small businesses have to pass through a kind of pessimum point if they are to grow into large ones. As long as they can operate on the personal resources of the entrepreneurs, the equity available on local markets, and the relatively high-cost revolving capital supplied by banks, they do not feel the pinch; but they find it very difficult to get access to any source of risk capital other than retained earnings until they have grown up to the point where the national financial institutions can or will serve them on a large scale.[3] It is partly a problem of the fixed costs of capital flotation, which work against the small borrower, and partly a problem of information (hence of "risk"). Private intermediaries have not contrived an institution that will fully bridge this interval, though small business financing agencies have sprung up in some areas. The emergence of agencies primarily interested in underwriting risky innovation by small business is noteworthy.

There may be gaps at the end of the credit spectrum as well as within it. Among the many dimensions of the price of credit is the term of the loan. For any class of loan the maximum term available to the bulk of the borrowers marks the end of the credit spectrum. This boundary must depend, in part, on the probability of repayment of the loan plus interest, which probability may diminish as maturities lengthen. Imperfect knowledge of the actual probabilities, so far as they can be calculated, and adherence to fixed forms of lending may unduly constrict the range of credit terms.

The best example of this possibility is residential mortgages. As late as the 1920's savings institutions typically offered residential mortgages with a maximum 15-year maturity, and usually without an amortization feature. It was the Home Owners Loan Corporation's emergency mortgage program that made amortization practically universal in residential mortgages; and the FHA liberalization of terms that followed brought lengthened maturities to the mortgage market, as well as increased loan-to-value ratios. A diminishing average loan ratio as a loan is amortized makes longer maturities and higher initial ratios more attractive. The average term of private mortgages increased from 7 to 9 years in the 1920's to 15 to 20 years in the 1950's.[4] It was not that lending

---

[3]The separation of investment banking functions from commercial banking functions by the Banking Act of 1933 may have widened this gap. Banks had often made and renewed term loans to a small business until the firm had developed to the point where it could sell an equity issue to the public, with the commercial bank acting as underwriter and arranging brokerage in the local financial community. Underwriting services are still available for growing firms, but they must now go through a transplanting process when they cease to rely solely on term bank credit. But even under the former regime most developing small businesses experienced difficulty in getting access to equity markets.

[4]George F. Break, "Federal Loan Insurance for Housing," Research Study One in Federal Credit Agencies, prepared for the Commission on Money and Credit (Englewood Cliffs, N.J.: Prentice-Hall, Inc., 1963). Professor Break ascribes this to the "competitive

(Footnote continued on following page)

institutions were reluctant to undertake any long-term lending, since long maturities were common for bonds. The explanation seems to be an overly conservative evaluation of risk, coupled with an unwillingness to experiment.

We do not now know whether the term of loans as well as other dimensions of price could at present be extended on a sound basis, for any class of investment, into ranges not now supplied from any source of capital. Only detailed study and experiment could answer the question. We do know that credit terms cover a much wider and more varied range than they formerly did.

Differences in Interest Rates

Among the signs and symptoms of inadequate competition or credit gaps must be listed variation in interest rates among localities and discrimination in rates among classes of borrowers at any given time. Discrimination among borrowers has already been touched on under a different aspect: discrimination in credit availability against certain groups. The usual problem of evaluating risk differences is encountered here, since rate discrimination must mean that rates are not in proportion to cost and to risk. Discrimination can result from ignorance, obsolescent rules, or irrational prejudice. Or it may result from local monopoly, which would permit lenders to charge what the traffic will bear and maximize net revenues in each segment of the loan market. The practice should be evaluated in the context of market structure.

Variations in interest rates among localities may also draw attention to situations of local monopoly. But they are not invariably a sign of monopoly. We expect that interest rates will be higher in a capital-importing region than in a capital-exporting region because lenders usually feel that more distant loans are riskier. Local investment situations which are superficially similar may also show considerable variation in true risk. Furthermore, local lenders may have differing risk preferences. For some classes of investment this will make little difference because the capital funds come partly from nonlocal sources which tend to iron out the local variations. But for commercial bank loans the natural barriers of local differentiation may produce significant differences.

(Footnote 4 continued from previous page)
pressure" of FHA and VA loans. This does not necessarily mean that they broke down a private monopoly of mortgage credit. In the context of the present study one can perhaps say that the FHA and VA loans demonstrated the soundness of longer-term mortgages to private lenders, and that they probably would not revert to the old shorter-term limits if the federal programs were terminated.

Though their market areas overlap somewhat, commercial banks are generally dependent on local sources of funds and make loans (though not all investments) on a local basis, primarily. The spatial differentiation which enables them to do this is a barrier to the full operation of competitive forces in the credit market, but the spatial barrier may permit only small local differences in interest rates.

The dependence of local banks on local depositors for their resources has another implication for our problem of credit gaps. Some communities or regions suffer from instability in income because of their dependence on a single major industry, especially an extractive industry like agriculture. Other economic activities which are not as unstable may also suffer from the resulting instability in the supply of bank credit. The major industry itself may be made even more unstable because cycles in bank credit exacerbate its problems. A situation like this indicates a possibility of economic benefit in a program of pooling risks in different localities, breaking down the local barriers to movements of bank credit in order to make the whole system more stable. This might reduce variations in interest rates among localities.[5]

MARKET ORGANIZATION AND MONOPOLY

Some varieties of credit gaps may reveal themselves by symptoms that are fairly easy to observe. Monopoly (or "inadequate competition"), however, whether or not accompanied by a credit gap, is not so easy to diagnose symptomatically. There is often no substitute for a thorough examination of market structure and the complete pattern of behavior that it exhibits. In any case, the configuration of structural elements in a market helps us to understand its symptoms. By "structure" is meant such features as the number and size distribution of lenders and borrowers, differentiation of institutional position, freedom of entry to the several segments of the market, the variability of demand, and so on. Close examination of credit-market structures would probably turn up many instances of non-optimal structure and imperfectly competitive behavior. Without such detailed studies we cannot generalize on the facts. But some possibilities may be pointed out.

---

[5]Professor D. Gale Johnson makes this point for farm credit agencies. See D. Gale Johnson, "The Credit Programs Supervised by the Farm Credit Administration," Research Study Four in Federal Credit Agencies, prepared for the Commission on Money and Credit (Englewood Cliffs, N.J.: Prentice-Hall, Inc., 1963).

Entry and Numbers

The conditions of entry are the most important determinants of competition in the long run. They will vary from one kind of credit market to another. It seems hardly likely that entry restrictions have any significance for national credit institutions—insurance companies, acceptance and finance companies, underwriters and brokerage houses. Are they important in commercial banking markets? The number of banks in the aggregate has not increased since the great shake-out of the early 1930's, but it is not easy to draw any inference from this fact because commercial banks obviously have been realizing increased economies of scale. Many students think that the number of banks was formerly excessive, and may still be. A few local markets that have expanded rapidly in the postwar period have attracted new commercial banks to some degree. The older banking markets have mostly had a static structure, and while we do not have much information on the threshold conditions that would induce entry, we certainly do not have any evidence that existing banks have combined to restrict entry nor that they would have the power to do so.

The extreme case, natural monopoly, is found where a single bank can economically serve its entire market. There are many one-bank towns in the United States that do not really fall into the category of monopoly because banks in nearby communities can compete for loan opportunities and borrowers can reach other sources of supply. There are others, however, in which the single bank undoubtedly has appreciable market power. Having little fear of entry, it need only concern itself with the competition of imperfect substitutes for bank credit, like finance company loans, factoring, open lines of credit from suppliers, etc. If the lending unit is too small to realize the full economies of scale associated with its type of lending and if it must charge higher rates because it cannot achieve adequate risk balance in its portfolio, the borrowing public must pay an additional cost of inefficiency. Such banks are also more likely to restrict the total volume of commercial loans for the sake of risk avoidance.

In medium-sized commercial bank markets, economies of scale may still create barriers to entry. Four large commercial banks, for example, could easily serve a good-sized city and handle the correspondent business of smaller banks in a considerable region. With only four in the market, a new entrant would face a substantial threshold, affording some opportunity to the established banks to maintain credit terms above "cost" (if they can avoid price competition among themselves) without inducing the entry of a fifth. Again this margin may be partially limited by the capital that can flow in from other markets and by substitutes for bank credit.

Bank mergers should be considered in this light. There are different kinds of mergers. Combination of large banks in the major money markets certainly reduce the alternatives available to borrowers in those markets, though recent combinations may still leave those situations more competitive than small markets. (In any event it seems that this kind of structural change is the concern of antitrust policy rather than of federal credit policy.) Acquisitions by banking chains of individual banks in separated markets do not change the concentration in those markets, and by giving the bank access to a larger pool of capital (and possibly of executive talent) it may improve competition, on balance.

The most thorough study of the structure of a banking market now available is the study of California banks by David Alhadeff. In summarizing his judgments on the effect of the growth of banking chains like the Bank of America, Alhadeff says, "As a result of their superior lending power in local markets, branch banks have produced a larger volume of loans per dollar of assets than unit banks as a group. As a function of their structure, branch banks have also been able to make banking facilities available in areas where unit banks could not survive. Finally, branch banks have demonstrable economies of scale and of structure which are not available to unit banks . . . The price society must pay for the various efficiencies and other advantages of branch banking is an unavoidable concentration of financial power."[1]

Oligopoly in Banking

In almost any market, competition among the few will differ markedly from competition among the many, and banking is probably no exception. In most banking markets, numbers are few enough to indicate a possibility of "oligopolistic rationality"—that is, tacit and mutual avoidance of price competition accompanied sometimes by a deflection of the competitive impulse into other channels, such as services or salesmanship. The scope for maintenance of noncompetitive prices or terms of lending is limited by the threat of entry, as already mentioned, and by substitute forms of credit. In view of the peculiarly sensitive position of commercial banks, or other fiduciary lending institutions, unrestrained price competition would be dangerous if the market structure were oligopolistic. Price competition in oligopoly means price warfare, i.e., chaos and not competitive equilibrium. Nor would free entry conditions necessarily lead to a

---

[1]David A. Alhadeff, Monopoly and Competition in Banking (Berkeley, 1954), p. 232. Alhadeff also says that " ... the concentration of California banking in which branches of one of the four large branch systems replace formerly independent unit banks in small towns would not significantly alter the existing market structure of those towns," (p. 219).

stable market in oligopoly. Unfortunately we have very little evidence on the actual flexibility of price in the banking field.

Other Credit Markets

Aside from commercial banking, is there evidence of monopoly or monopoloid structure in the markets for credit? The proliferation of finance companies and personal loan companies of every description in recent years, offering rates over a wide range (with a high minimum) is evidence that there are no substantial barriers to entry here. The market is differentiated, however, and rates may be somewhat sticky while much competitive effort goes into advertising. In other words, it is a case of monopolistic competition.[2] Government regulations add some obstacles to the free operation of competitive forces. While no federal credit program is likely to be considered in this field, the various regulatory authorities could make their regulations more simple and more uniform as a contribution to better economic performance.

The finance companies controlled by the major automobile and appliance firms have been forced to break the tie that used to exist between sales and financing. This removed a kind of monopoly leverage from this market, though it has had little discernible effect on the terms of credit.[3]

Another field that has been involved in antitrust action is investment banking. Allegations of monopoly and conspiratorial control in investment banking are an old story; the public imagination has often been exercised by tales of the "money trust." Proof of monopoly in investment banking would require detailed study of conditions of entry and of alternative market channels such as private placement, as well as of the competitive relationships among investment bankers. The opportunity to investigate at least some aspects of the matter came with the Investment Bankers Case of 1950-1953. Seventeen banking houses were accused of combining to monopolize flotation of the best security issues of large corporations and to exclude other investment houses from the market. The government alleged that the banking houses

---

[2]For an early appraisal of the characteristics of this market, see T.O. Yntema, "The Market for Consumer Credit: A Case in 'Imperfect Competition,'" Annals of the American Academy of Political and Social Science (March 1938), pp. 79-85. A thorough institutional description is given in Chapter 2 of The Consumer Finance Industry, a Monograph prepared for the Commission on Money and Credit by the National Consumer Finance Association (Englewood Cliffs, N.J.: Prentice-Hall, Inc., 1962).

[3]Exclusive captive financing was held to be illegal in General Motors Corp. v. U.S., 121 F. 2d 376 (1941), cert. den. 314 U.S. 618.

avoided competition among themselves by following a "triple concept": (1) the "traditional banker," meaning that the banker first managing a security issue for a particular firm is thereafter entitled to manage all issues for that firm; (2) "historical position," meaning that once a banker participates in a syndicate he is entitled to participate on equivalent terms in all future issues by that firm; (3) "reciprocity," meaning that the banking firms ". . . recognize a mutual obligation to exchange participations with one another in the buying groups which they respectively manage."[4]

Judge Medina said, "If the charge is true the restraints are ingeniously devised to create a controlled rather than a free market at every level. The operation of the 'triple concept' prevents competition as between defendants themselves; the domination and control over issues deprives issuers of a free market in which to raise the money they need; nondefendant firms are deprived of an opportunity to purchase securities in a free market."[5]

Though the antitrust proceedings did not thoroughly investigate all aspects of market structure in investment banking, such as conditions of entry, they did produce a wealth of evidence on competitive behavior among the defendant bankers. The judge found that the charge of conspiracy was wholly without merit. Competition may have been somewhat less than sanguinary. The formation and conduct of syndicates, however, and the stability of the banker-client relationship, merely reflected the particular characteristics of investment banking, such as the need for spreading risks, the expertise of certain houses in particular industrial fields, and the tendency for security issues to perpetuate a satisfactory relationship with banking houses familiar with their problems.[6] We need not raise the question again here. In any event, the rise of private placement and direct term lending in the 1930's created a new kind of competitive pressure that must have seriously reduced any monopoly power that the investment banking houses might have had

---

[4]U.S. v. Morgan et al., 118 F. Supp. 621 at p. 629 (quoting the Trial Brief for the United States).

[5]Ibid., p. 632.

[6]"I have come to the settled conviction and accordingly find that no such combination, conspiracy and agreement as is alleged in the complaint, nor any part thereof, was ever made, entered into, conceived, constructed, continued, or participated in by these defendants, or any of them." 118 F. Suppl. 621 at p. 829. The judge naturally looked to questions of "good faith" and "ordinary business purpose" rather than to indexes of the vigor of competition in deciding the issue of conspiracy. The TNEC hearings (Vol. 22-24) had developed much evidence and testimony purporting to show conspiracy among investment bankers but similar material was not accepted as evidence at the trial.

earlier. Presumably the many regulations that the Securities and Exchange Commission has imposed on the operations of investment bankers have as one of their purposes the maintenance of effective competition of a kind that is compatible with the characteristics of investment banking. These regulations therefore have an indirect relationship to the general subject of federal credit programs.

Even if "monopoly" in investment banking were not illusory, it would still be secondary to what appears to be the chief problem of security markets from our point of view: the difficulty that all but large businesses have in gaining access to them. We would not have supposed that the financing problems or credit gaps facing small businesses were due to an investment bankers' "monopoly" even without the evidence turned up in the Investment Bankers Case. Such a "monopoly" would instead have attempted to victimize those best able to protect their own interests: the large American corporations.

THE CHOICE OF POLICIES

When the public authority has detected a credit gap or a case of inadequate competition in a credit market important enough to warrant action, it can choose among several different forms of policy. The choice will usually lie among (1) direct government lending; (2) indirect lending through contributions to private credit institutions such as cooperatives, on a temporary or on a permanent basis; (3) loan guarantees to private lenders or insurance of loans without initial government financial contributions; (4) regulation, antitrust policy, or information programs. The government may decide to use a combination of these policies to meet the particular circumstances of the problem.

We shall give the matter of choice among different types of credit programs only brief attention here, since we are specifically concerned only with their relation to credit gaps and market imperfections, and not with a wide range of other institutional effects and criteria for choice.

Direct Lending

It has already been said that credit gaps should be distinguished from situations eligible for subsidy. When the government subsidizes, it may well spend appreciable sums to produce the desired social benefits; but when it merely closes a credit gap, it should anticipate no permanent or continuing net expenses. (Capital investments which are in theory subject to return through depreciation charges, and on which the appropriate rate of return is anticipated, are not "expenses" in this sense.) Most persons would doubtless agree that the government can best serve the interests of a private enterprise economy by stimulating private investors and intermediaries to close credit gaps whenever it can open the necessary channels without creating costs greater than those of direct government lending. It is possible, of course, that the government will add a measure of subsidy to the aid necessary to close a credit gap. In that case it might be difficult to rely on private sources of lending to the same extent in the absence of subsidy. But these can be analytically distinguished.

In line with this judgment, the government should rely on direct lending only if it cannot stimulate or persuade private sources to make the funds available at a sound and appropriate rate, or when its own direct costs of lending are demonstrably lower. The public authority is likely to have lower direct lending costs only when the granting of credit is complementary with some other established federal activity, and the program would be concerned with a credit gap in the administrative field of that agency. In most cases the "availability" of credit is the important question. Private lenders may not respond to guarantees or insurance where they have a local monopoly, or when they are too unenterprising, or when borrowers are spread too thinly in a locality to support an effective lending unit. These are fringe-end cases, though they might add up to a substantial total.

Direct lending has an administrative advantage in choice of terms and conditions. The federal government can determine the rate which will repay costs and compensate for risks and set that rate on the loans. (If borrowers will not borrow at this rate, the indicated conclusion is that no credit gap exists.) A loan guarantee, on the other hand, is complicated by the degree of interchangeability between the guaranteed securities and the government's own debt, and the cost of the guarantee is sometimes lost to sight.

Indirect Lending

A kind of intermediate step between direct lending and loan guarantees is indirect lending, in which the government makes funds available to privately owned or cooperative lending agencies, which in turn deal with the ultimate borrower. Typically the government supplies only part of the funds. This type of program is often appropriate when the gap is caused by a threshold barrier of some sort. When information is so poor that private sources will not invest unless a pool of capital has already been contributed by the government, which itself believes that lending experience will provide favorable information, it may help the lending institution to cross the threshold. A similar situation may arise when potential borrowers are so scattered that no private unit, unassisted, can encompass them; the government provides the starting capital for a cooperative having the necessary wide horizons. What the government does is to enter a new territory which private institutions have shunned because of institutional barriers or uncertainty due to lack of information; the government funds provide the impetus necessary to cross the unknown territory, to gather together and pool risks in large new units, etc.

The logic of this argument implies that after the feasibility of operation has been demonstrated, the threshold crossed, the necessary information provided, and the risks evaluated, the government should then begin to extricate its contribution and turn the entire operation over to private agencies. In practice many such programs also might contain an element of subsidy, which would inhibit termination of federal aid, but the principal difficulty would usually be the continued expansion of the program. Any growing lending institution must compete for additional funds against other intermediaries, and is likely to resist stubbornly the withdrawal of any part of its existing resources, however persuasive is the logic of doing so. But a continued expansion of the government contribution long after the infant has grown to maturity does not seem appropriate to bridging a credit gap.

Federal contributions or loans to private lending institutions to help them survive a general emergency do not require discussion here. Ordinarily one expects the aid to be short term, and in many cases to be replaced by an insurance program to deal with similar future contingencies.

Loan Guarantees and Insurance

Since an unconditional government guarantee of a private loan makes the loan instrument fully interchangeable with government debt, the government must decide whether to set a government-security rate on the loans it is guaranteeing. To do so would almost always involve a subsidy. It seems better policy, when the object of policy is simply to close a credit gap, to offer a limited or partial guarantee.[1]

Loan insurance is best suited to situations involving large numbers of similar events or risks. The government may perceive economies of scale in accumulating these risks so as to provide maximum risk offsets, transcending the local boundaries that most

[1]A ceiling on interest rates charged borrowers as a condition of a loan guarantee has no effect in closing a credit gap Ordinarily either the interest limitation will be ineffective, if private lenders decide that the guarantee has reduced risks enough to justify loans at or below the ceiling rate, or else lenders will begin to discount the loans to raise the effective rate above the ceiling.

investing institutions must inevitably observe, and pushing back the limits which private institutions must impose on investment commitments of any particular type. The availability of economies of scale would be the best reason for instituting such a program. Loan guarantees might be appropriate where local custom or other artificial barriers inhibit private sources from undertaking certain kinds of loans on a basis which can be proved sound by experience. In either case the need for the program might well be temporary. Loan guarantees would probably not work as well in meeting the credit needs of enterprises which are unique or for which uncertainty is very large. Direct or indirect lending if necessary, including limited participation, might be a more effective way to close credit gaps in such situations until some kind of risk experience can be accumulated.

Regulation, Antitrust Action, and Information Programs

These are too varied in detail for summary analysis. We can say merely that some kinds of regulation may promote a more competitive and better informed market, which should improve its economic performance. Ordinarily markets are expected to regulate themselves, using the force of competition. Credit markets and credit institutions are subjected to special rules and regulations because of their fiduciary nature and because they are peculiarly vulnerable to the effects of misinformation, panic, or manipulation. Remediable cases of monopoly should be dealt with by antitrust policy under the appropriate administrative agency. Only the cases which are not remediable, in which the forces of competition cannot be made to work, should be considered eligible for credit programs designed to compensate for monopoly. Credit gaps can often be reduced by more adequate information, so the value of programs that disseminate better information about market characteristics and risk experience is plain.

Quite often it appears that private institutions are prevented from realizing full economies of scale or specialization by restrictive state regulations of one kind or another, limiting their geographical territory, restricting the type of their investment, etc. These regulations, which differ markedly from one jurisdiction to another, should be closely examined to see whether they are individually justified by any public purpose. In many cases credit gaps could be reduced or eliminated if these regulations were made more realistic or more uniform.

THE PROGRAMS

The following section briefly examines some of the major credit programs of the federal government in the light of the criteria set forth in earlier sections of this paper. Our main concern is whether a given program was designed to close a credit gap and/or remedy inadequate competition in the market, and whether it has been mixed with a subsidy in actual application. (This inquiry is guided largely by the Research Studies on federal credit programs prepared for the Commission on Money and Credit.)

Housing Programs

The housing programs, as a group, are by all odds the most important of the federal credit programs. FHA and VA commitments alone constituted 58 percent of the total new commitments incurred under all federal credit programs between 1950 and 1959.[1] Other past and present programs include those of the Home Owners' Loan Corporation, the Federal Home Loan Bank System, and the Federal National Mortgage Association. (We do not consider farm housing programs here.)

HOLC. The Home Owners' Loan Corporation, as is well known, was an emergency program designed to prevent wholesale foreclosures of mortgages in the Great Depression, to restore liquidity to the mortgage market, to salvage the lending institutions and to provide a means for homeowners to disentangle themselves from the trap they found themselves in at that time. The emergency relief provisions of the HOLC were akin to other elements in fiscal and monetary policy of the federal government, and had nothing much to do with any normal, long-term credit gap—still less to do with any imperfections in competition. One could argue, of course, that the provisions of a secondary lender for institutions investing in mortgages itself filled a credit gap, in the same sense that the establishment of the Federal Reserve system earlier did for commercial banks. Other agencies have now largely absorbed this function.

The real contribution of the HOLC was its establishment, on a large scale, of the practice of periodic mortgage amortization. This contribution to home finance became standard practice very quickly, and brought other changes in its train such as the lengthening of mortgage maturities. It was an improvement which private lenders had somehow overlooked. In response to the mortgage crisis the HOLC uncovered and closed a credit gap.

Because of the emergency nature of HOLC, we cannot tell whether the federal contributions to it and its loss experience resulted in a subsidy to homeowners and financial institutions. It is

---

[1]George F. Break, "Federal Loan Insurance for Housing," Research Study One in Federal Credit Agencies, prepared for the Commission on Money and Credit (Englewood Cliffs, N J.: Prentice-Hall, Inc., 1963), Table I-2.

noteworthy, however, that the Treasury's initial $200 million contribution sustained its operation for many years.[2] It did sell several billion dollars worth of its bonds, mostly to the Treasury, at low rates; but since the mortgages it acquired were to a large extent in default, it is difficult to calculate the extent of the subsidy, if any.

FHA and VA. HOLC might have chosen to guarantee mortgages rather than to acquire them in exchange for its own bonds. While private refinancing of old mortgages might have presented some difficulties, private financing of new mortgages on an amortized basis rapidly became standard practice, and the federal government instituted a guarantee program for new private lending to homeowners. The VA program after 1945 was similar. Leaving details aside, the FHA program was (and is) a virtually complete guarantee of the mortgage amount. It does not, however, cover the lenders' administrative expenses, and FHA promises payment not in cash but in its own tax-exempt debentures. The VA program is a partial guarantee of cash payment. In addition, the VA makes some direct loans to homeowners. Both FHA and VA mortgages are subject to minimum down payment and maximum interest rate limitations, which have been changed from time to time.

If these programs were intended to close credit gaps, that objective was not the only one.

> Initiated primarily to expand output and employment in the construction industry during the Great Depression, the Federal Housing Administration now pursues the threefold purpose of promoting sound home financing on reasonable terms, stabilizing the mortgage market, and improving housing standards and conditions. GI home loans were originally thought of as a form of rehabilitation aid designed to enable returning veterans, over a two-year period, to acquire homes at prewar prices. By this means support was to be given to the construction industry during the difficult period, as it was then viewed, of reconversion to peacetime production. Needless to say, all of these goals were soon given up, and in their place we have the desire not only to protect the veteran against excessive prices and deficient housing quality but also to provide him with mortgage credit on more favorable terms that are available to nonveterans.[3]

---

[2]Robert C. Turner and Jospeh R. Ewers, "The Emergency Aid Program of the Home Owners' Loan Corporation," unpublished Research Study prepared for the Commission on Money and Credit.

[3]Break, op. cit., p. 2.

Protecting the veteran against excessive prices and deficient housing quality relates to the veteran's handicap of ignorance in the very complex housing market, not to the effects of any credit monopoly. "Promoting sound home financing on reasonable terms" might or might not turn out to be a euphemism for a housing subsidy. The facts show that the FHA and VA housing programs have not actually utilized Treasury funds to any great extent. The FHA has consistently collected (from insurance premiums and sale of assets seized in default) more than it has paid out. The VA, which charges no insurance premiums, has drawn small amounts to pay off lenders on defaulted mortgages, but has acquired almost that much in defaulted assets. This experience does not include any period of sharply falling real-estate values and large-scale unemployment—the possibility of which is a major factor in risk evaluation by private lenders. Nevertheless, the fact that FHA has been able to maintain a self-financing mortgage program for many years at rates usually less than the "conventional" rate, without specially selecting more favorable risks, indicates that it has been able to achieve economies of scale through self-insurance and pooling of risks that were beyond the reach of private lenders before the federal guarantee, and hence that it has bridged a credit gap. It has also continued the extension of maturities begun when HOLC instituted mortgage amortization, demonstrating the soundness of longer maturities than were formerly thought to be feasible.

Unfortunately the conclusions that might be drawn from the FHA and VA experience may have to be modified when we take account of the activities of the Federal National Mortgage Association. This agency has consistently pumped funds into the secondary market for insured mortgages. While the volume of its purchases has been far too small to keep FHA and VA mortgages at par in the primary market during periods of tight mortgage credit, it has produced some distortions and some windfall gains. We cannot be sure that its activities have not affected the price of insured mortgages, and hence the rate, in the primary market. It very likely has done so for VA-guaranteed mortgages.[4]

Leaving aside the possible effect of secondary-market purchases on the interest rate, the FHA itself has helped to create a wider and more effectively functioning market for mortgages. Insured mortgages have become more or less fungible instruments of investment, somewhat similar to commercial bonds. It is probable that a private agency could now attain practically all the economies

---

[4]See Jack Guttentag, "The Federal National Mortgage Association," Research Study Two in Federal Credit Agencies, prepared for the Commission on Money and Credit (Englewood Cliffs, N.J.: Prentice-Hall, Inc., 1963).

of scale that the FHA has established, if it could reasonably expect emergency government support in case of a severe deflationary crisis. While no comparable secondary market has developed for uninsured conventional mortgages, they have become enough like the FHA mortgages to bring the rates and terms very close together, in spite of the guarantee on the latter.

VA mortgages have more welfare-program aspects than FHA mortgages, and part of their costs are buried in other budgets rather than charged to the program. They have received more support from FNMA. They are intended for a special group, though a large one. The VA experience is therefore less illuminating than the FHA. The most interesting part of the VA program is the policy of direct lending to veterans who cannot secure credit from private sources. Apparently veterans living in rural areas have frequently found no credit available on the terms of a VA loan, though in metropolitan areas plenty was available, while no channel existed to transfer the funds into the deficit areas. We cannot tell whether this credit deficiency was due to local monopoly or to variations in local risk evaluation, and in truth it does not make much difference. The effect of the direct-loan program (assuming it contained no element of subsidy) would be to break down barriers to the flow of funds and make the market more homogeneous and competitive.

The same sort of effect could be expected from the Voluntary Home Mortgage Credit Program, which channels demand for VA and FHA credit from deficit areas to participating lenders having funds available.[5] The program was further extended with the Certified Agency Program, designed to overcome some of the barriers of location for FHA loans. The FHA offices were experiencing some difficulties in appraising properties and processing loans in areas remote from their offices, and the CAP permits approved lenders in such areas to act as FHA agents in processing loans. It promises to improve market homogeneity and to keep costs low by utilizing the facilities of established institutions. All of these programs seem well conceived to remedy credit gaps in certain areas and to reduce impediments to effective competition.

The Home Loan Banks. The Federal Home Loan Bank system was organized in the midst of the liquidity crisis that struck the savings and loan associations in the early 1930's. These associations invest most of their funds in conventional mortgages, for

---

[5] "With its impact concentrated on small towns, on families with annual incomes between $3,000 and $6,000 and on racial minorities everywhere who otherwise would have been unable to obtain mortgage credit, VHMCP had, by the end of 1959, arranged private loans amounting to $400 million." Break, op cit., p. 49.

which no secondary market has ever existed. As a result, the associations in the 1920's met their needs for liquid funds in the short run not by selling mortgages but by borrowing from commercial banks, and hence they shared in the banking crisis of 1932. The Home Loan Bank System was set up to provide a "lender of first resort" for holders of conventional mortgages. After a long period of Treasury participation, the FHLBS was converted to private ownership in 1950, retaining a Treasury guarantee of ultimate support.[6]

It is clear that the Banks were designed to perform a banking function, not to provide a continuing flow of long-term investible funds. Yet the Banks seem to be doing the latter too. The System makes advances everywhere at about the same rate, based on the rate at which it can sell its own securities plus administrative costs. As a result the System raises capital in surplus areas and makes the most of its advances in capital-short areas, where mortgage rates are high and the savings and loan associations find it profitable to borrow. In turn this has meant a rapidly rising volume of advances coupled with an increasing volume of sales of the Banks' own securities. The Home Loan Banks have thus apparently created a national market for mortgage funds and a kind of brokerage among the local mortgage markets.

A better organized national market in mortgage funds is certainly an objective worth promoting. But many observers have expressed an uneasy suspicion that the Banks are not exercising firm control over the volume of their advances. Even after the conversion of the System to private ownership it continued to finance long-term investments at a short-term rate that was still based on a Treasury guarantee. The System has not yet passed through any severe deflationary crisis, which could freeze and devalue its assets and require it to call on the Treasury for aid in behalf of the savings and loan associations. It is probably fair to say that the cost and incidence of this guarantee are unknown; yet the apparent liquidity that it lends to the obligations of the System supports the advances to the associations. The result has been a breakdown of the distinction between short-run revolving credit accommodation and the flow of long-term investment funds.[7]

---

[6]Ernest Bloch, "The Federal Home Loan Bank System," Research Study Three in <u>Federal Credit Agencies</u>, prepared for the Commission on Money and Credit, (Englewood Cliffs, N.J.: Prentice-Hall, Inc., 1963).

[7]An anonymous critic of this paper has suggested that if the savings and loan associations need a lender of first resort, a direct channel could be opened for them to the Federal Reserve banks, or possibly the Home Loan Banks could become a virtual intermediary in such a channel. This would keep the banking activities of the Home Loan Banks under the influence of the Reserve Banks and ensure that their operations conformed to over-all monetary policy. In this event the Treasury guarantee would become superfluous.

FNMA. The Federal National Mortgage Association exhibits a parallel, though perhaps more serious, problem: a swelling volume of advances to the secondary market for insured mortgages. It has expanded its holdings of insured mortgages, particularly the less attractive VA and no-down-payment FHA mortgages. Up to 1954 it largely used federal funds for this purpose and purchased mortgages at par even when they were selling at a discount in the primary market. The reorganization of 1954 was intended to produce a partial conversion to private ownership and to limit the extension of the associations' mortgage holdings. While FNMA has raised most of its funds since then by sale of its debentures to the public, it has not succeeded in retiring any substantial part of its debt to the Treasury, and the effort to control the volume of purchases has failed several tests.[8]

The objective of improving market organization in insured mortgages is again quite worthwhile, but here too we observe a continued flow of funds into the market. It is not clear why any government assistance or guarantee is necessary, once the organizational threshold has been crossed, to sustain the brokerage and warehousing functions in a national mortgage market. What we have instead is an ineffective market-support program, with sterilized inventories of surplus mortgages. It is hard to avoid the conclusion that FNMA may have produced a small subsidy for some classes of insured mortgages and concealed the true actuarial basis that would be appropriate for governmentally-insured mortgages, particularly the VA type, and that it certainly produced windfall gains for some investors. The reforms of 1954 went only part way toward solving the problem.

Small Business Programs

The federal government has shown solicitude for the problems of small business in many ways. We cannot survey them all. Our chief concern is with the programs that have been important since 1950: those of the Small Business Administration and the Small Investment Act of 1958. The others were either designed for emergency conditions or else were only incidentally small business programs.[9]

---

[8]Guttentag, op. cit.

[9]Details are given in Jack McCroskey, "Federal Credit Programs for Small Business," Research Study Seven in Federal Credit Agencies, prepared for the Commission on Money and Credit (Englewood Cliffs, N.J.: Prentice-Hall, Inc., 1963).

Those who think that small business faces a "credit gap" do not always agree on what it is. Some believe that all small businesses suffer from a credit gap (unless unusually lucky in their access to private capital sources), and that this handicap bears most heavily on the smallest businesses of all, which must pay the highest interest rates for funds and which have the highest mortality rates. This handicap would be reflected in the rate of entry and the conditions on which new firms may obtain financial backing. Others think that the gap relates to a point or range in the growth of successful small businesses considerably larger than the very smallest and newest firms in the respective industries. In this view it is the shallows between the local and private sources available to quite small businesses and the pools of capital available to large firms on organized regional and national markets that constitute the credit gap.

The following discussion inclines toward the second view. We do not rule out the possibility of a credit gap for all small business, particularly the smallest, but a mere difference in rates is not evidence of a gap so much as an inherently greater cost in serving the credit needs of small business and an inherently irreducible uncertainty for very small firms, particularly newly-entering ones. Many small new firms are simply not viable, and no credit bridge is going to help them to survive. Very small firms seem to have access to several sources of funds other than the personal resources of the proprietors—notably banks (the institution best fitted to gather the available information about small entrepreneurs and their ventures) and trade suppliers.

There is voluminous testimony that a gap in the continuity of credit availability handicaps the growth of small firms beyond a certain size, but very little concrete evidence. Some observers have expressed skepticism, believing that the barrier the closely held smaller firm encounters in entering the organized markets for equity funds is primarily due to the unwillingness of the owners to surrender or dilute control.[10] But even firms which are willing to

[10] "There is. . . a great reluctance on the part of many closely held small firms to share power and information with outsiders. . . . Although there are no reliable data on this point, it may be that the greatest difficulty in expanding equity is experienced by closely held firms which have exhausted their informal sources of funds and which do not represent an attractive 'growth' situation, or whose owners have curtailed reinvestment of earnings in the business." Irving Schweiger, "Adequacy of Small Business Financing: Another View," in Financing Small Business, Report by the Federal Reserve System to the Committees on Banking and Currency and the Select Committees on Small Business, 85th Congress, 2d Session (Washington, D.C., 1953), p. 149. But the credit gap facing small business includes not only equity capital but long-term debt financing.

share the control seem often to encounter difficulties. The large corporation gets the benefit of a scale-effect in accumulation of information and diffusion of risks in a large organized capital market which assembles buyers in large numbers, but the smaller and relatively unknown firm usually runs out of local funds, or can no longer sustain the high cost of more short-term debt, before it reaches the rim within which these economies become available. There are numerous exceptions, of course, and the handicap is a matter of degree. But few specialized financial intermediaries have grown up to deepen the flow of capital in this range, and one cannot tell what the relevant costs and returns might be until some risk experience is accumulated. This is the kind of situation that is often promising for an experimental federal credit program, particularly of the contributory type to launch private institutions across a threshold of uncertainty if the program is successful.

SBA. If the credit gap is a growth gap, the loan program of the Small Business Administration is not very well conceived to deal with it. The SBA has in effect acted as a bank with more liberal standards than ordinary banks, often with private participation in the loan. It has not done much to give growing businesses access to national capital markets, nor has it developed sources of equity capital (for which it has no statutory authorization). But the principal evidence that the SBA program is not primarily functioning to bridge a credit gap is its continued operating deficits. In most years its interest income has not even covered its administrative expenses, leaving nothing to repay the interest on funds advanced by the Treasury and nothing to provide for losses, which have been appreciable.[11] Since the program does not promise to become self-financing, we conclude that it is a subsidy for small business. The banks which provide the same kind of credit charge higher rates because the full costs of lending to small business are demonstrably higher, not because of any monopolistic element in the banking structure.

Yet we must insert one proviso. The SBA has ventured into one region which is only thinly supplied by commercial banks and other credit institutions: the longer-term small business loan of over three years maturity. We cannot easily evaluate its success because this part of the program is mixed with loans of other types and is affected by the general subsidy of SBA operations. Still, there may be a legitimate need for an experimental program in this area. If the SBA longer-term loan were dissociated from disaster relief

---

[11] Financing Small Business, op. cit., p. 276. McCroskey points out that some of this deficit is attributable to the disaster loans bearing a very low rate of interest, which are intermingled with the others.

and similar activities and if the rate were set at a level expected to make the program compensatory and self-supporting in the long run, it might fill a real need and also entice more private institutions into this area.

SBIC. Small business, from all reports, needs long-term debt and equity capital; the short-term loan market does not reveal any credit gaps. "The greatest need is for an institution to which small business can bring its case for capital."[12] The Act which authorized the formation of the Small Business Investment Corporations was an attempt to develop an institution that would supply long-term debt and equity capital to small business. The SBIC is not a true investment bank for small business, since it purchases securities to hold rather than to sell, and it makes intermediate- and long-term loans from its own resources. It is ingeniously designed to meet the special need of small business. Being privately and locally controlled, the SBIC's should be able to combine organizational flexibility and knowledge of local conditions with the advantage of partial risk absorption by the government.

It is too early to tell whether the SBIC program will be fully successful. The defects that have revealed themselves so far have been mainly technical. Some have been outstandingly successful, particularly those specializing in investments in certain booming electronics companies. But others have experienced difficulty in raising capital from the general public, and have themselves suffered from diseconomies of small size. In 1961 Congress raised the limit for SBA advances to any one SBIC from $150,000 to $400,000, and increased the over-all limit as well. This may help to encourage larger-sized lending units from which the government investment can be withdrawn after the experimental period is over, but it also increases the possibility of subsidy.[13]

Farm Programs

Federal aid to agriculture has taken so many forms under so many programs that a small catalog is necessary to list them all. They range from the operations of the Commodity Credit Corporation, which have nothing to do with credit gaps, to programs which in whole or in part are designed to bridge credit gaps. Often a welfare purpose is mixed with this design and may obscure the gap. It is interesting to note how many of the programs which began as emergency aid or aid to promote some nonfinancial objective, such

---

[12] A.D.H. Kaplan and Paul H. Banner, "Adequacy of Small-Business Financing: One View," in Financing Small Business, op. cit., p. 123.
[13] See Business Week, April 9, 1960 and May 20, 1961; U.S. News and World Report, October 2, 1961.

as preservation of the family farm, have moved toward a self-sustaining basis and have become more like the credit operations of private lenders.

Farm credit programs that are related to genuine credit gaps fall into two categories:

(1) Loans for individual farm development—to enlarge the scope of its operations; to modernize, equip, and mechanize it; to develop its soil and water resources; and to reorganize family subsistence farms into commercially viable units. One example of a self-supporting federal credit plan in this category is the water facilities loan program which has repaid private benefits well in excess of all costs, but which an individual private institution could not easily finance because of the uncertainties of the new program and because it could not secure the necessary risk offsets within the limited scope of its operations. Here the government was able to take advantage of economies of scale, and with the closure of the gap such economies have become more available to private lenders.[14]

(2) Provision of mortgage credit for farm land and farm housing. (This can merge into the other type, of course.) Here the trend toward a commercial, privately owned type of operation has been even more striking (leaving aside the obvious welfare programs designed to help the subsistence farmer, etc.). The outstanding example is the Federal Land Bank System, under the general supervision of the Farm Credit Administration. Instituted because of a widespread conviction that farm mortgage terms were too restrictive (for too short a term, too small in relation to appraised value, and too costly), the Banks at first used federal funds and acted in part as agents of relief in the farm depression of the 1920's and 30's. Through the National Farm Loan Associations they began to provide long-term, amortized farm mortgages. But the private institutions existing previously have continued to supply the bulk of farm mortgage credit, changing their terms and their practices in response to the impact of the Federal Land banks.

The Banks now raise their funds on the open market, without government guarantee of any kind. All the Banks in the System are responsible for the securities of each. They have created a national market for farm mortgage funds. Previously the money market for

---

[14]See Dale E. Hathaway, "The Federal Credit Programs for Individual Farm Development," Research Study Five in Federal Credit Agencies, prepared for the Commission on Money and Credit (Englewood Cliffs, N.J.: Prentice-Hall, Inc., 1963), esp. pp. 347-353.

farm mortgages had been highly segmented and local in character. In some areas it was economically organized and large in scope, but in others it was not—notably the South. The Land Banks demonstrated genuine economies of scale in transcending these local boundaries, and even the low-cost areas benefited. While the Banks have been in existence, interest rates have declined, regional differences in rates have tended to narrow, maturities have lengthened, and loan-to-value ratios have increased. Most of these trends were already under way earlier, and it is difficult to say how much the Banks may have contributed to them. (In at least one respect—the loan-to-value ratio—the Banks followed rather than led.) But the successful history of the Federal Land banks and their conversion to private ownership indicate that the federal program bridged a credit gap. It brought the benefits of scale economies to the market and then transferred the system it had constructed to private hands when its net contribution has been realized.[15] The remaining elements of government subsidy in the other programs supervised by the Farm Credit Administration may eventually disappear in the same way.

If agriculture still suffers from a credit gap, it is probably due to the increasing resemblance of agricultural enterprise to small and medium-sized business. The need of such enterprises for funds for equipment, modernization and expansion transcends the ordinary scope of a "mortgage," and a self-supporting insurance for intermediate-term loans for acquisition of capital assets may be feasible. While the risks of agricultural income instability are not like the specific risks of small business, the expansion problem for the enterprise has some points of resemblance. An experimental loan program might build up better information on the risk costs.

Other Programs

The other credit programs of the federal government require only brief discussion here. Few of the important ones seem to be designed principally to overcome a credit gap In the international field, one program that might qualify is that of the Export-Import Bank, in the sense that the government's contribution made the Bank better able to bear the political risks of international events than unsupported private institutions can. But this departs from the usual economic meaning of "risk." Another possible candidate is

---

[15]A complete and concise account of the history and functions of the Land Banks is given by D. Gale Johnson in "The Credit Programs Supervised by the Farm Credit Administration," Research Study Four in Federal Credit Agencies, prepared for the Commission on Money and Credit (Englewood Cliffs, N.J.: Prentice-Hall, Inc., 1963).

the International Finance Corporation. The experience of these agencies does not yet support an inference on the extent of subsidy nor on their viability. The other international programs are usually both heavily subsidized and interwoven with political objectives. On the whole the international programs are outside our field of inquiry.

Federal credit programs for community development are likewise not designed to bridge credit gaps, in the sense used here, almost by definition. The localities may need federal funds for community development because of a deficiency of local revenues, but this falls within the category of public finance. It is seldom true that private sources are not doing the particular job because of a credit gap.

Government credit aids to transportation are subsidies, not means of closing credit gaps. The credit sources available to transportation are well-organized; they do not suffer from diseconomies of small size nor from provincial shortsightedness; there is no evidence that they are monopolistic. When they have withheld capital it is because of well-founded estimates of the risk involved, and the inability of certain kinds of transportation companies to earn the market rate of interest is not evidence of a credit gap.

The Rural Electrification Administration might have had a stronger case if it had been able to demonstrate that a unit of economic size exceeded the limits of a typical electrical utility, or that electrical utilities had failed to seize economical opportunities for serving rural areas, or that an initial government contribution would help the cooperatives surmount a high-risk threshold and eventually reach an unsubsidized basis of operations. But the REA has in fact benefited from a continuing and substantial subsidy.[16] We do not have any basis for estimating how the private financial market would have reacted to a simple, limited government guarantee of REA bonds, or to any other alternative.

CONCLUDING REMARKS

Perhaps other credit gaps would be promising candidates for federal credit programs if they could be brought to light, but the

---

[16] G.S. Tolley, "The Rural Electrification Administration," Research Study Six in Federal Credit Agencies, prepared for the Commission on Money and Credit (Englewood Cliffs, N.J.: Prentice-Hall, Inc., 1963). Tolley asserts that the advantage conferred on the cooperatives by exemption from the federal income tax is several times as important as low interest rates on funds advanced them by the Treasury in lowering the coop "cost" of electricity.

proliferation of such programs in the last 20 or 30 years probably means that most of the outstanding possibilities have been explored.

The credit programs have not had uniform success. Some have undoubtedly closed credit gaps by providing better information and breaking down obsolete custom, by pooling risks, or by surmounting an uncertainty threshold—often merely by demonstrating that a credit program was feasible. Sometimes the program has hastened trends that were already in operation. The convergence between private and public credit programs is noteworthy. The private credit institutions very frequently have been able to sustain and continue what the federal programs began, and conversely the government programs have become enough like the private ones to encourage the belief that government participation will eventually be almost entirely eliminated from most of them.

Of the credit gap programs discussed here, the most successful by these criteria, and the most advanced, is the Federal Land Bank System. Probably the least success has been found in remedying the gap facing small growing businesses, if indeed such a gap exists. More experimentation in the small business field may support a more reliable judgment of this gap in the future. Of course there are many federal credit programs which are not designed to remedy credit gaps, and others which ostensibly are intended to do so but which in fact are subsidy programs.

This survey also leads us to the conclusion that except for isolated and "fringe-end" cases, few credit gaps appear to have been caused by monopoly in credit markets.

Research Study Four

AGRICULTURAL CREDIT, CAPITAL AND CREDIT POLICY IN THE UNITED STATES

D. Gale Johnson
University of Chicago

INTRODUCTION

Agriculture is one of the most capital intensive sectors of the American economy. This is true whether capital intensity is measured by capital-output or capital-labor ratio. In recent years the ratio of the value of farm productive assets to the gross national product produced in agriculture (both in current prices) has been at least 6:1. In the private part of the nonfarm economy the ratio has not exceeded 1.5:1 in the post-World War II period. Even if all farm real estate (land and buildings) is excluded, the capital-output ratio in agriculture is larger than for the private nonfarm economy, namely about 2.5:1 or about double the ratio in the private nonfarm economy. In 1957 the average value of productive assets per farm worker mainly engaged in agriculture was approximately $21,000, while the average for nonfarm private workers was $10,000.

The enterprise structure of agriculture, with its dependence upon the individual proprietorship, might be considered inappropriate for an industry so capital intensive. Debt and credit have only a modest role in the financial structure of agriculture. Self-financing is the primary means of acquisition of productive assets. The ratio of debt to total farm assets is now approximately 10 percent, which is significantly lower than exists in other private productive sectors. An important substitute for debt is the renting of assets, primarily land and buildings, which provides a partial explanation for the low debt-asset ratio in agriculture. Currently farm operators rent about a third of their agricultural land and buildings.

Part I of this study presents background information on the role of capital and credit in agriculture for the past half century, including certain comparisons to the private nonfarm economy. Because capital assets, including land, make up only a part of the total resources used in agriculture, the changes in all resources used in agriculture are considered.

In Part II, I discuss the competitive and complementary relations among the various private, public and semipublic agencies that provide credit to farmers and attempt an evaluation of the credit facilities available to farmers. The last part presents a series of suggestions on the role that credit can perform in the adjustment problems faced by agriculture and changes that might be made in credit institutions.

I. CAPITAL AND CREDIT IN AGRICULTURE

The purpose of this part of the monograph is to provide a background for the discussion of the role of credit in agriculture and for consideration of changes or modifications in credit policy as it relates to agriculture. Emphasis upon the structure of the agricultural production process and changes in it are emphasized. It is necessary to study not only the role of capital, which is usually assumed to include land, building, machinery and livestock, but to include labor and current production inputs in our analysis as well.

At the present time no modification of credit policy can be considered independently of decisions made with respect to other aspects of agricultural policy. Agricultural output is now 6 to 9 percent larger than the quantity demanded at current prices. Any change in farm credit policy that would increase the availability of credit would have the effect of increasing the excess of production over demand, unless the level of farm prices declined. It should not be concluded, however, that no change in credit policy that increased the availability of credit should be considered, but only that the impact of changes in credit policy should be recognized and that consideration should be given to changes in other policies that might have the effect of offsetting some of the output consequences of changes in credit availability.

A. Agriculture's Share of Tangible Assets, Output and Employment in the U.S.

A relatively large fraction of the total tangible assets used in production in the private sector of the economy is used in agriculture, and this has been true throughout the 20th century. Table IV-1 presents estimates of the total value of privately owned tangible assets used in production by the nonfarm and farm sectors. Tangible assets include land, buildings and machinery, but exclude all kinds

TABLE IV-1

Agriculture's Share in Total Privately Owned Tangible Assets Used in Production 1901 to 1957[a]

Year	Nonfarm Productive Assets[b] (billions)	Farm Productive Assets[b] (billions)	Percentage of Total in Agriculture	Assets Per Worker[c] Farm (dollars)	Assets Per Worker[c] Private Nonfarm (dollars)
	(1)	(2)	(3)	(4)	(5)
1901	31.7	21.8	40.7	2,000	1,780
1910	49.5	40.2	44.8	3,470	2,010
1913	55.6	44.8	44.6	3,900	2,140
1920	134.8	80.8	37.5	7.030	4,650
1923	120.7	59.1	32.9	5,320	3,770
1930	161.1	53.9	25.1	5,130	4,560
1940	132.0	38.1	22.4	3,990	4,120
1950	286.7	100.6	26.0	13,400	6,205
1956	455.1	115.1	20.2	17,480	9,030
1957	483.1	122.9	20.3	21,030	9,550
1959	559.6	145.3	20.6	25,510	10,580

[a]All values in current prices.

[b]Productive assets exclude residential property (buildings and land), consumer durables, all public and institutional property, monetary metals, and net foreign assets. Nonfarm residential land for 1950 and later estimated to be 54 percent of private nonfarm land: farm residences estimated at 55 percent of farm structures.

[c]Private nonfarm employment is total nonagricultural employment minus government employment.

Sources: Assets: Raymond W. Goldsmith, A Study of Saving in the United States, Vol. III, pp. 14 and 15; Statistical Abstract of the United States, 1959, pp. 324, and ibid., 1960, pp. 326 and 423, Economic Report of the President, January 1962, p. 294. Employment: Historical Statistics of the United States: Colonial Times to 1957, (1959), pp. 710-1, and Table IV-2 below. State and local government employment estimated for years before 1930.

of financial assets; the values expressed in Table IV-1 are in current prices for each year. At the turn of the century approximately 40 percent of all privately owned tangible assets in the United States economy were used in agriculture. According to the estimates the relative importance of agriculture increased during the first decade of the century. There was a substantial decline from 45 to 25 percent in the share of agriculture between 1913 and 1930. The decline in the relative importance of agriculture continued through the decade of the thirties, but during the forties agriculture's share increased somewhat. In the two most recent years for which data are available, 1957 and 1959, agriculture's share of the tangible assets was approximately one-fifth, which was almost as large as the share in 1940.

The decline in the share of the total private productive assets used in agriculture has been significantly less than the decline in agriculture's share of the labor force or the gross national product. Table IV-2 presents data on the absolute and relative levels of farm employment. Between 1910 and 1959 the percentage of the total labor force engaged in agriculture declined from 31 to less than 9 percent. Thus, agriculture's share in employment fell by more than two-thirds, while its share in total tangible assets declined by slightly more than one-half. The implications of these relative movements are shown in the last two columns of Table IV-1 where estimates of the value of tangible assets per worker are given for farm and private nonfarm. It may be noted that between 1910 and 1957 the money value of assets per worker in the private nonfarm sector increased by about 375 percent, while the increase for agriculture was 500 percent.[1]

The absolute value of assets per worker was higher in agriculture than in the private nonfarm sector for the years included in Table IV-1, excepting only 1940. In 1959 productive assets per worker in agriculture were more than double the assets in the private nonfarm sector. While it is true that the value of farm land is a very large fraction of the assets per farm worker, if the value of land is excluded for both nonfarm and farm, the average value of other tangible assets, including nonresidential buildings, was approximately $8,500 per worker in both sectors in 1959.

Table IV-3 presents estimates of agriculture's share of the gross national product. If the third column of that table, which indicates the percentage ratio of the farm gross national product to the total gross national product, is compared with column 4 of Table IV-1, two important differences are at once apparent. First, agriculture's share of tangible assets is substantially larger than agriculture's share of the gross national product. In 1910 agriculture produced about 16 percent of the gross national product and had almost 45

---

[1]Since the value of productive assets is expressed in current dollars in each year, the increases in real assets per worker were substantially smaller than indicated in the text.

TABLE IV-2

Agriculture's Share in Employment, 1910-1959

Year	Total Civilian (thousands)	Agricultural Employment (thousands)	Nonagricultural Employment (thousands)	Percentage of Total Employment in Agriculture (thousands)
	(1)	(2)	(3)	(4)
1910[a]	37,371	11,592	25,779	31.0
1920[a]	42,434	11,449	30,985	27.0
1930[a]	48,830	10,472	38,358	21.4
1940	47,520	9,540	37,980	20.1
1950	59,957	7,507	52,450	12.5
1955	63,193	6,730	56,464	10.6
1956	64,979	6,585	58,394	10.1
1957	65,011	6,222	58,789	9.6
1958	63,966	5,844	58,122	9.1
1959	65,581	5,836	59,745	8.9
1960	66,392	5,696	60,697	8.6

[a]1910-1930, gainful workers aged 10 or more; other years, average annual employment.

Sources: 1910-1930: 1940 to date: Statistical Abstract of the United States, 1959, Economic Report of the President, (January 1962), p. 230.

percent of the tangible assets used in private production.[2] Thus agriculture's share of tangible assets was almost three times as

---

[2]A more appropriate comparison of changes in the share of the gross national product produced by agriculture would be agriculture's share of the business gross product. Specific estimates of the business gross product are available only since 1929, but on the basis of an estimate which should be subject to only minor error, agriculture's share of the business gross product in 1910 was 17.6 percent; in 1929, 10.3 percent; in 1940, 7.7 percent; 1950, 8.1 percent; and 1957, 5.0 percent. A comparison of these figures with those in column three of Table IV-3 indicates that the relative decline of agriculture's share of the gross business product is only moderately less than the decline of agriculture's share of the gross national product.

TABLE IV-3

Agriculture's Share of Gross National Product and of Gross Private Productive Investment[a]

Year	Gross National product (billions) (1)	Farm Gross National product (billions) (2)	Percentage Farm of Total (3)	Gross Private Productive Investment[b] (billions) (4)	Gross Farm Productive Investment[b] (billions) (5)	Percentage Farm of Total (6)
1910	35.7	5.9	16.5		0.42	
1920	91.9	12.2	13.3		1.13	
1929	104.4	9.8	9.4	10.1	0.82	8.1
1930	91.1	7.7	8.5	8.5	0.61	7.2
1940	100.6	6.8	6.8	7.9	0.73	9.2
1950	284.6	20.5	7.2	29.1	3.85	13.2
1951	329.0	23.6	7.2	32.8	4.04	12.3
1952	347.0	22.8	6.6	33.1	3.81	11.5
1953	365.4	20.9	5.7	35.3	3.93	11.1
1954	363.1	20.3	5.6	35.1	3.44	9.8
1955	397.5	19.6	4.9	38.6	3.45	9.0
1956	419.2	19.3	4.6	44.3	3.12	7.0
1957	442.5	19.4	4.4	46.6	3.22	6.9
1958	441.7	22.0	5.0	40.6	3.75	9.2
1959	478.8	20.5	4.3	43.1	3.88	9.0
1960	504.4	20.8	4.1	46.4	3.38	7.3

[a]All values are in current prices.
[b]Excludes residential gross investment and changes in inventories.

Sources: Survey of Current Business, (October 1958), pp. 12-13, and (February 1960), p. 23; U.S. Income and Output (1958), pp. 118 and 139; The Farm Income Situation, (July 1961), p. 51; and Economic Report of the President, (January 1962), pp. 218 and 220.

great as its share of the gross national product. In general, throughout the period, agriculture's share of tangible assets has been substantially greater than its share of gross national product. Second, the decline in the farm share of gross national product has been greater than the decline in the share of tangible assets. Roughly speaking, agriculture's share of tangible assets declined slightly more than 50 percent between 1910 and 1957, while agriculture's share of the gross national product declined by about 70 percent.

The capital-output ratio in agriculture is much greater than in the rest of the economy. Capital-output ratios are shown in Table IV-4 for private nonfarm business and for agriculture, both including and excluding land. If land is included the capital-output ratio for private nonfarm in 1910 was almost exactly 1.6 while the capital-output ratio in agriculture was approximately 7. In the nonfarm part of the economy, the capital-output ratio in 1929 was significantly

TABLE IV-4

Capital-Output Ratios

	Including Land		Excluding Land	
Year	Private Nonfarm[a] (1)	Agriculture[b] (2)	Private Nonfarm (3)	Agriculture (4)
1910	1.5	6.8	1.2	2.1
1920	1.8	6.6	1.5	2.1
1929	1.9	5.5	1.5	2.9
1940	1.6	5.6	1.3	2.2
1950	1.2	4.9	1.1	2.3
1957	1.3	6.4	1.2	2.6
1959	1.2	7.2	1.1	2.8

[a]Capital includes only private business tangible productive capital; output equals gross nonfarm business product.

[b]Capital includes only tangible productive assets used in agriculture; output is farm GNP minus gross rental value of dwellings plus gross rents paid nonfarm landlords.

n.b. All monetary estimates underlying the capital-output ratios expressed in current dollars.

Sources: See Table IV-1 and Table IV-3.

higher in 1910, while there was a small decline in the capital-output ratio in agriculture. Following 1929 the capital-output ratio fell in the nonfarm part of the economy, and in 1959 was approximately 1.2. In agriculture, the capital-output ratio tended to be fairly stable between 5 and 6 until the mid-fifties and in the most recent year exceeded 7. Columns 3 and 4 of Table IV-4 indicate the magnitude of the capital-output ratios when land is excluded from both nonfarm and farm sectors. The exclusion of land has relatively little impact on the capital-output ratio in nonagriculture, but as would be expected, the capital-output ratio in agriculture excluding land is substantially reduced. Instead of being from 5 to 7, it tends to fall in the range of 2 to 3. But it should be noted that even excluding land the capital-output ratio in agriculture is substantially higher than it is in the nonfarm part of the economy.

The last three columns of Table IV-3 provide estimates of annual gross private productive investment and of gross farm productive investment. In 1929, gross farm productive investment was 8.1 percent of total private productive investment. Agriculture's share rose slightly to 1940 and by 1950 amounted to more than 13 percent of the national gross private investment. Since 1950 agriculture's share has declined and in recent years has been approximately at the 1929 level. In 1929 agriculture's share of gross private investment was slightly less than its share of gross private national output. In each year since 1955, agriculture's share of investment has remained substantially higher than its share of gross private national product. In recent years the farm share of investment has been almost twice as high as the farm share of the gross national product. Since the gross farm productive investment is a concept that excludes land, the data in columns 3 and 6 of Table IV-3 are consistent with the fact that the capital-output ratio (excluding land) in agriculture is approximately double the capital-output ratio in the rest of the nonfarm sector. These data also imply that unless gross farm investment declines significantly, the capital-output ratio in agriculture is likely to continue to be considerably higher than it is in the rest of the nonfarm economy.

B. Agricultural Output, Inputs, and Productivity.

During the past half century, farm output in the United States has doubled. During the same period of time the quantity of inputs or production factors used has increased by slightly less than a quarter. Thus output per unit of input has increased by about two-thirds. The data presented in Table IV-5 indicate that between 1910 and 1930 the increase in output was associated with an equal increase in the inputs, indicating that there was no increase in the quantity of output per unit of input. Since 1930 the total quantity of inputs used in agriculture has remained almost constant; but during the same period of time output increased by approximately 70 percent, and there has been a dramatic increase in the ratio of output per unit of input.

While it is true that there was only a modest increase in the total quantity of production inputs between 1910 and 1930, and virtually no increase since 1930, there have been large changes, both increases and decreases, in the quantities of certain broad categories of inputs. In Table IV-6 total production inputs are broken down into six categories which together compromise all production inputs. Farm real estate, which includes both land and buildings, is the only input for which there has been no significant increase or decrease. As indicated earlier, the reduction in the labor input has been very large. The earlier data were in terms of persons employed in agriculture, whereas the data in Table IV-6 reflect a measure of the number of hours worked. The small increase in

TABLE IV-5

Index Numbers of Output, Inputs and Productivity, United States Agriculture 1910-60 (1947-49 = 100)

Year	Farm Output (1)	Production Inputs (2)	Productivity (3)
1910	61	82	74
1920	70	93	75
1929	74	98	76
1930	72	97	74
1940	82	97	85
1950	101	101	100
1951	104	104	100
1952	108	104	104
1953	109	103	106
1954	109	102	107
1955	113	102	111
1956	114	102	112
1957	114	100	114
1958	124	101	123
959	125	102	123
960	128	102	125

ource: U.S.D.A., Agricultural Outlook Charts '60, p. 50, and Economic Report of the President (January 1962), pp. 291-93.

he total quantity of inputs required that the remaining categories of inputs increase severalfold. Comparing 1960 with 1910-19, nechanical power and machinery increased almost threefold, fer-ilizer and lime increased almost sevenfold, and the nonfarm com-onent of feed, seed and livestock purchases increased approximately ixfold. It is probable that much of the new technology that flowed

TABLE IV-6

Indexes of Agricultural Inputs
1947-49 = 100

Input	1910-19	1920-29	1930-39	1940-49	1950-59[a]	1960
A. Total	88	94	92	100	102	102
Farm real estate	95	96	94	97	105	106
Farm labor	140	139	129	113	77	62
Mech. power and mach.	35	47	50	78	133	140
Fertilizer and lime	22	29	31	77	151	189
Feed, seed, livestock services[b]	23	37	38	88	122	152
Misc.				97	119	135
B. Paid vs. unpaid						
Paid	58	70	70	93	112	
Unpaid[c]	134	133	126	108	90	
Labor	148	149	139	115	79	
Capital	96	90	91	88	120	
Output	64	70	73	95	112	128

[a] Data in Part B of table are for 1950-58.
[b] Nonfarm inputs associated with farmers purchases.
[c] Farm operator and unpaid labor plus inputs of real estate and other capital owned by farm operators.

Source: Economic Report of the President, (January 1960), pp. 101-04, and Economic Report of the President (January 1962), p. 292.

into agriculture came through these last three categories of inputs. The miscellaneous category was probably an important carrier of new and better production techniques, since it includes insecticides, herbicides and livestock medicines.

Part B of Table IV-6 reclassifies the inputs according to whether the current services of input are paid for by farm operators or are inputs owned by farm operators. It is quite obvious from the relative changes in input quantities indicated in Part A of Table IV-6 that the relative importance of paid inputs should have risen substantially over the half century; the quantity of paid inputs almost doubled between 1910-1919 and 1950-58. On the other hand, the quantity of unpaid inputs decreased by approximately 40 percent, and all of the decrease was due to the reduction in operator and unpaid family labor. The capital owned by the operator actually increased by approximately a third over the period of time.

C. Financial and Income Implications of the Changing Structure of Agriculture.

It is well known that the significance of monetary expenditures in agriculture have become much more important in recent years. A rough indication of the increasing importance may be obtained by comparison of the sum of production expenses and the net income of farm operators. From 1910 through 1919 the net income of farm operators was generally in excess of the total of production expenses; thus net returns to farm operators were somewhat more than half of gross farm income. During the 1920's production expenses were higher than net income by roughly a third. Except for the worst years in the Great Depression, the same pattern prevailed during the 30's. Some shift in this relationship occurred during World War II, and by the end of that war net farm operator income was approximately equal to production expenses. In 1948, production expenses totaled almost $19 billion and net farm income, including changes in inventories, was almost $18 billion. Since 1948 there has been a substantial growth in production expenses, not fully offset by an increase in gross farm income. By 1960, when net farm operator income had declined to $11.3 billion, total production expenses were $26.3 billion, or more than twice the level of net operator income.[3]

Table IV-7 presents, in some detail, estimates of the percentage of gross farm income that was required to cover certain cash expenditures and depreciation on productive capital for selected years since 1910. Current production expenditures include purchases from the nonfarm sector of the economy plus feed and livestock purchases. Wages paid to hired workers are excluded. The percentage of gross income required for current expenses has risen from about 21 percent in 1910 to approximately 42 percent in 1960. The increase in the percentage of gross income required for current expenditures is apparently not due to an unfavorable turn in the prices of the items included in current expenditures relative to the prices received by farmers. The index of prices received by farmers was

[3]See the U.S.D.A., The Farm Income Situation, (July 1961), p. 34.

TABLE IV-7

Current Farm Operating Expenditures, Fertilizer and Lime Expenditures, Repair and Operation of Capital Items, All Cash Expenditures, and Depreciation of Productive Capital as Percentage of Gross Farm Income, 1910-60[a]

Year	Current Production Expenditures[b] (1)	Fertilizer and lime (2)	Repair and Operation of Capital items (3)	All cash Expenditures[c] (4)	Depreciation, Productive Capital (5)
1910	21.4	2.0	3.3	44.8	4.2
1920	25.3	2.4	4.2	51.9	6.0
1929	26.8	2.2	6.4	53.7	5.5
1930	29.0	2.7	7.0	57.6	7.2
1940	33.0	2.7	8.9	58.8	6.0
1950	34.4	2.9	8.8	62.1	7.3
1951	35.0	2.8	8.3	60.5	7.5
1952	35.8	3.2	9.0	61.9	8.0
1953	35.9	3.6	9.9	63.9	9.1
1954	37.0	3.7	9.8	63.5	9.4
1955	38.0	3.7	10.2	65.3	9.9
1956	39.1	3.6	10.6	65.2	9.7
1957	39.6	3.6	10.7	65.4	9.9
1958	39.7	3.4	9.8	65.3	9.1
1959	43.0	3.9	10.6	70.1	9.8
1960	41.9	3.8	10.4	67.7	9.6

[a]Gross farm income includes cash income, value of inventory change, government payments, and nonmoney items.
[b]Includes feed, livestock and seed purchased, fertilizer and lime, repairs and operations of capital items and miscellaneous. Does not include wages for hired labor.
[c]Includes in addition to current production expenditures (column 1) the following items: cash wages, interest on farm mortgages, property taxes, gross investment expenditures and net rent to nonfarm landlords (share and cash).

Source: U.S.D.A., The Farm Income Situation, (July 1961).

238 in 1960 when calculated on a 1910-14 base. The index of prices paid by farmers for all production items was 264. However, the prices paid index includes the prices of motor vehicles and farm machinery, which are capital items and not current expenses. If these two categories are removed from the index of prices paid for production items, the 1960 index of prices paid for the types of expenditures included in current expenditures would be less than 240. It seems reasonable to assume that the physical quantity of the items included in the current expenditures increased very substantially between 1910 and 1960; in fact, almost twice as rapidly as the increase in total output of farm products.

Columns 2 and 3 of Table IV-7 show the percentage of gross farm income spent on fertilizer and lime and on repair and operation of capital items. In both cases there was a significant rise in the percentage of gross income spent. The increase was particularly large for repair and operation of capital items, which increased from 3.3 percent of gross farm income in 1910 to more than 10 percent in recent years. Such a large increase reflects the substitution of mechanical power for animal, which required relatively large expenditures for fuel, lubricants and repairs of tractors, trucks and automobiles.

Column 4 of Table IV-7 reflects the relationship between all cash expenditures and gross farm income. The total cash expenditures include farm capital expenditures, as well as all current expenses, the cash outlay for hired labor, property taxes, farm mortgage interest and net rent to nonfarm landlords. The behavior of the percentage of gross farm income required to cover cash expenditures is not unexpected in terms of the other data included in the table. Since 1910, when the percentage was approximately 45, there has been a persistent increase. In 1960, 68 percent of gross farm income was required for all cash expenditures.[4]

Table IV-7 also includes the percentage of gross farm income that was allocated to depreciation of productive capital. While the depreciation of productive capital does not require immediate cash outlay, the depreciation estimates presumably reflect the dollar

---

[4]It might seem more appropriate to relate cash expenditures to cash receipts. This was not done. Cash expenditures are required to produce nonmoney income such as food consumed in the farm household and the rental value of farm dwellings. However, it may be of interest to indicate the percentage of cash receipts required to pay for all cash expenditures for a selected number of years: 1910, 60 percent; 1929, 65 percent; 1950, 72 percent; and 1960, 75 percent. The increase in the percentage of cash expenditures to cash receipts is thus seen to be less than the changes indicated in column 4 of Table IV-7. The reason for this is that the relative importance of nonmoney income has declined over the past 50 years.

amout that must be put aside if the capital stock is to be maintained at a constant level. The percentage of gross farm income required for depreciation more than doubled between 1910 and 1960. The increase has been fairly gradual and it reflects primarily three forces. First, there has been a significant increase in the quantity of depreciable capital used on farms. This increase is, in part, indicated by the substantial rise in the input of power and farm machinery (see Table IV-6). Second, there has been a change in the composition of farm capital with a distinct shift in proportions toward capital with relatively short productive life. The relative importance of buildings as an item of farm capital has declined compared to tractors, trucks, automobiles and machinery. Third, the relative prices of farm capital items have apparently increased compared to prices received by farmers. Consequently even if the quantity of capital had increased at the same rate as farm output over the period, the percentage of gross farm income required for depreciation would have increased.

D. Have Capital Items Become More Important in Agriculture During the Past Half Century?

If capital is defined to include land, which it should if we are concerned with the credit aspects of capital utilization in agriculture, it does not seem possible to answer this question in an unequivocal fashion. If capital is measured as land and buildings and other tangible assets normally included in a balance sheet, the absolute amount of such inputs has unquestionably increased since 1910 and increased substantially, though not by the magnitudes implied by the changes in the value measured in current prices of these assets. According to the excellent study made by Tostlebe, the total value of physical assets used in agriculture, measured in 1910-14 prices, increased from $45.4 billion in 1910 to $53.7 billion in 1950. This amounted to an increase of about 19 percent and may appear to be somewhat surprising when compared to the increases in broad categories of inputs given in Table IV-6. However, it should be remembered that a large part of the increase in mechanical power was offset by a decline in the number of horses and mules. Similarly a significant part of the gross investment in machinery other than power that occurred after 1920 constituted a substitution of tractor drawn machinery for horse drawn machinery.[5]

If Tostlebe's estimates of the value of physical farm assets measured in constant prices are linked to the estimates contained

[5]Alvin S. Tostlebe, Capital in Agriculture, Its Formation and Financing Since 1870, National Bureau of Economic Research, (Princeton University Press, 1957), p. 66.

in the Balance Sheet of Agriculture at the year 1940, the increase in the estimated quantity of physical farm assets between 1910 and 1960 is approximately 30 percent.[6]

Since the absolute amount of capital, including land, has increased in physical terms and the labor input has declined substantially over the same period of time, it is obvious that the ratio of physical assets to labor has risen significantly. In fact, the increase in this ratio has been approximately 175 percent.

It should be noted that the real value of capital assets increased less than farm output over the period 1910 through 1959 (Table IV-8). During that period farm output more than doubled, while, as noted above, the real value of physical assets increased 30 percent. Consequently, when measured in real terms, the ratio of capital to farm output declined quite substantially over the period of time. However farm output is not the most appropriate measure of output change for the present purposes.[7] A more appropriate concept of output, especially if comparisons are to be made with the rest of the economy, is the real value added by agriculture. This measure of output is approximated by the Department of Commerce's estimates of gross national product of farms measured in constant prices. Between 1910 and 1958 the real value of the gross farm product increased by 53 percent, which was still a greater increase than occurred in the real value of physical assets used by farmers. Consequently the elimination of intermediate products purchased from the nonfarm sector of the economy from the measure output does not contradict the statement that the real capital-output ratio has declined.

While it is of interest to know that real capital has increased substantially compared to the labor input, but has at the same time declined relative to either gross or net farm output, these comparisons tell us nothing about the financial aspects of the changes in capital use in agriculture since 1910. From a financial standpoint, the implications of the increase in the physical use of capital are of two kinds: first, the effect the increased amount of capital has had on the amount of financial assets required in agriculture; and, second, how the share of income, either gross or net, required to maintain and/or to acquire the additional assets has changed over time. These two elements are certainly interrelated, but the factors affecting them are not identical. With respect to

---

[6]U.S.D.A., The Balance Sheet of Agriculture, 1961, Agriculture Information Bulletin No. 247, p. 3. The increase in productive physical assets in agriculture (1940 prices) between 1940 and 1960 was 22 percent.

[7]Farm output is a measure of the volume of farm production available for human use.

TABLE IV-8

Capital-Output Ratios in Real Terms, 1910-59

Year	Physical Capital[a] to Farm Output (1)	Physical Capital[b] to Farm GNP (2)
1910	6.1	7.4
1920	6.3	7.7
1929[c]	5.3	6.7
1930	5.5	7.2
1940	4.3	6.3
1950	4.2	6.4
1957	3.8	6.4
1958	3.7	6.1
1959	3.8	6.2

[a]All physical farm assets, except consumer durables included. 1910 to 1950 from Tostlebe; 1957-59 estimated from Balance Sheet of Agriculture estimates of physical assets of agriculture (1940 prices) linked to Tostlebe estimate for 1950. Farm income is total gross farm income, including changes in inventories.

[b]Physical assets as in Column 1. Farm gross national product includes gross rental value of homes and gross rents paid to nonfarm landlords. Estimate in Survey of Current Business in 1954 prices; adjusted to 1910-14 by multiplying by 0.402.

[c]Value of physical capital used in calculating 1929 ratio was for Jan. 1, 1930.

Sources: Alvin S. Tostlebe, Capital in Agriculture, Its Formation and Financing Since 1870, p. 101; U.S.D.A., Balance Sheet of Agriculture, 1958, p. 27; Survey of Current Business, (October 1958), p. 13 and (February 1960), p. 23; U.S.D.A., The Farm Income Situation, (July 1959), p. 34; and U.S.D.A., Agricultural Outlook Charts '60, p. 54.

the first, comparisons may be made between the value of farm assets measured in current prices and various concepts of farm income. The variations of these magnitudes, relative one to another over time, will depend upon changes in productivity, and relative prices of capital items and prices received by farmers for their products. The claim of capital upon farm income will be affected by additional factors, especially depreciation, repairs and maintenance, and the net return to farmer-owned resources.

Table IV-9 presents a series of ratios that are relevant to an understanding of changes in the ratio of the value of physical farm assets to various concepts of income. The value of physical farm assets included in Table IV-9 differs from that used in Table IV-8, since in Table IV-9 the value of farm dwellings is included and the rental value of farm residencies is included in all concepts of income. These changes in the concepts of value of assets and of income were made primarily for statistical reasons, since estimates of the net rental value of farm housing are not available, and because the value of dwellings is certainly a factor influencing the amount that can be borrowed by farmers.

TABLE IV-9

Ratio of Value of Physical Farm Assets to Gross Farm Income, Farm Gross National Product, Net Agricultural Income and Net Farm Operator Income in Current Dollars[a]

Year	Gross Farm Income[b]	Farm GNP	Net Agricultural Income[b]	Net Farm Operator Income[b]
	(1)	(2)	(3)	(4)
1910	5.6	6.8	7.9	10.2
1920	5.4	6.8	8.4	10.2
1929	4.5	5.5	7.1	9.9
1940	3.8	5.8	6.8	9.3
1950	3.5	5.2	6.3	8.2
1957	4.0	6.8	8.8	12.0
1958	3.8	6.4	8.1	10.7
1959	4.4	7.6	10.3	14.2

[a]Value of physical farm assets does not include consumer durables.
[b]Includes changes in value of inventories and government payments.

Sources: See Table IV-3.

The results indicated in Table IV-9 are not especially surprising. When a very gross concept of income is used, such as gross farm income, the ratio of the value of physical farm assets to income declines over time and declines rather significantly. When the purchases from the nonagricultural sector of the economy for current use are eliminated, as is done in the case of the gross national product, the ratio declines until 1950 and then increases again, and by 1959 is slightly higher than it was in 1910. The difference between net agricultural income and the farm gross national product is the capital consumption allowance or depreciation. As the data in Table IV-7 indicated, depreciation increased as a percentage of gross farm income over the period under consideration. And we see in column

3 of Table IV-9, the ratio of the value of physical farm assets to net agricultural income is now significantly higher than it was in 1910. It may be noted that this ratio remained fairly constant until 1929, and then declined during the thirties and even further during the forties. However, the rise in the value of farm real estate, particularly since 1950, has increased the ratio to a level above that prevailing at the beginning of the period.

The ratios in the last column of Table IV-9, which have net farm operator income in the denominator, reflect the fact that net farm operator income has generally been a declining fraction of each of the other concepts of agricultural income.[8]

From 1910 through 1940 the value of physical farm assets was approximately 10 times net operator income. The ratio declined to about 8 in 1950 (it was approximately 6 in the very prosperous year of 1948), but the ratio has tended to rise more or less continuously since 1950. In 1959 it was slightly in excess of 14.

The concept of net agricultural income includes the return to the owners of all of the assets included in physical farm assets and to all farm labor. It is of some interest to note that if all of net agricultural income were allocated as a return to farm assets (which implies that labor received nothing), the return on assets would have been slightly in excess of 12 percent during 1910 and about 11 percent for the averages of three years, 1957 through 1959. However, if 1959 represents the situation for the next few years with respect to the value of farm assets and net agricultural income, the rate of return would be somewhat less than 10 percent.

It has been indicated that the change in the capital structure of agriculture has resulted in increasing claims against farm income when those claims are measured as a percentage of gross farm income, value added by agriculture, or net agricultural income. The increase in the claims, however, grew primarily out of the cost of repairs and operation of capital items and of depreciation, and not out of claims arising out of increased aggregate expenditures for credit. Actually, the interest cost on borrowed funds has declined as a relative claim upon any one of the concepts of income or product of agriculture.

Data are presented in Table IV-10 that show the relationship between total interest charges, including mortgage and non-real estate debt, for selected years from 1910 through 1959. Interest

[8]Net agricultural income is equal to net farm operator income, plus wages paid to hired workers, interest on farm mortgage debt, and net rent to nonfarm landlords.

charges increased between 1910 and 1929, then declined and reached a low point in 1950. Since 1950 interest charges have increased as a percentage of the various measures of farm income, though in each instance interest charges in 1959 constituted a smaller percentage of income than in 1910.

TABLE IV-10

Interest Charges as Percent of Gross Farm Income, Farm Gross National Product and Net Agricultural Income, 1910-1959

(percent)

Year	Gross Farm Income	Farm GNP	Net Agricultural Income
1910	6	7	8
1920	7	9	10
1929	7	9	11
1940	4	6	8
1950	2	3	3
1955	2	4	5
1956	3	4	6
1957	3	4	6
1958	3	4	6
1959	3	5	7

Sources: See Table IV-3 and The Farm Income Situation (July 1961), p. 34.

E. Farm Assets and Farm Debts.

Total interest cost on borrowed funds and its relationship to agricultural income is only one facet of the impact of debt on the functioning of our agriculture. Another important aspect is the relationship between debt and the value of assets against which the debt represents a claim. If the ratio of debt to assets is high, either in the aggregate or for an important segment of farms, further capital investment, if it requires borrowed funds, may be inhibited. In addition, if the ratio is high and increasing, a significant decline in the level of farm income and of the market value of farm assets could result in economic distress and liquidation of farm firms. Since 1910 agriculture has passed through two periods when many farm operators were faced with foreclosure, or an equally unsatisfactory situation, because the value of their assets had fallen to or below the amount of their debts, and their level of net income was too low to permit servicing their financial obligations. Forced liquidation of farms was important during the 1920's because of borrowing during and immediately after World War I and the failure of land prices and farm income to continue to increase during the twenties. During the period of the Great Depression, forced liquidations became very high, indeed, and in some years involved from 3 to 5 percent of all farms.

The average relationship between debts and value of farm assets, whether for the nation or for regions, does not adequately indicate if a decline in land prices or farm incomes would result in significant financial distress, as evidenced by forced liquidations among an important number of farmers. Nevertheless, we may gain some insight by observing changes in the relationship since 1910. Table IV-11 presents estimates of the value of all farm assets and total farm debt and the ratio of debt to assets. While the absolute magnitude of farm debt on January 1, 1960 was the highest on record, the ratio of debt to assets was lower than it was in the early part of the present century, and only half of the magnitude of that ratio during the twenties and most of the thirties. Thus, on the average, it does not appear that the present ratio of debt to assets is at a level that would lead to significant financial distress. However, as implied above, the averages include the many farmers who have little or no debt, as well as an important proportion of all farm operators who have recently purchased real estate on the basis of minimal down payments. The latter group might find either that the market value of their real estate was less than their debt, or that their level of net income was insufficient to meet their debt commitments if farm incomes dropped over the next few years. The specific problems of the group of farmers who now have a relatively high ratio of debt to assets, and the implications of their problems to agricultural credit policy, will be considered in some detail in Part III.

F. Sources of Financing of New Farm Capital.

Net annual increases in the amount of total farm debt are primarily the result of two major uses of credit by farmers — credit

TABLE IV-11

Value of Farm Assets and Farm Debt, 1901-60

Year (Jan. 1)	Farm Assets[a] (billions) (1)	Farm Debt[b] (billions) (2)	Ratio of Farm Debt to Assets (per cent) (3)
1901	25.5	3.5	13.7
1913	52.2	7.7	14.8
1923	75.9	17.7	23.3
1930	71.2	15.5	21.8
1934	47.2	11.4	24.2
1940	54.4	10.6	19.5
1940	53.0	10.0	18.9
1946	102.0	8.0	7.8
1950	130.8	12.5	9.5
1955	164.7	17.8	10.8
1957	176.4	19.5	11.1
1958	186.7	20.2	10.8
1960	202.9	24.0	11.9

[a]Includes consumer durables and value of housing.
[b]Includes borrowings from the Commodity Credit Corporation.

Sources: 1901-1940; Raymond Goldsmith, A Study of Saving in the United States, Vol. III, p.75, 1940 to date: U.S.D.A., The Balance Sheet of Agriculture, 1958, Agriculture Information Bulletin No. 201, p. 26 and, The Balance Sheet of Agriculture, 1961 Agriculture Information Bulletin No. 247, p. 2.

to acquire real estate and credit to acquire new capital assets. A third major reason why an individual farmer borrows from a credit institution, namely to refinance existing obligations, does not, of course, result in a net increase in debt. Farmers also borrow for other reasons, such as for production needs and consumption purposes, but most of these debts are liquidated within a year.

It is almost impossible to allocate the increase in farm debt between the first two reasons noted above. A borrower who ostensibly obtains funds to purchase real estate may well use part of the proceeds of the mortgage to acquire additional capital assets. Similarly, a farmer who borrows for the purpose of purchasing equipment or machinery may use funds that he might otherwise have used for these purchases in order to buy farm land. The purpose of this discussion is to justify a simplifying assumption in the discussion immediately below. A consideration of agricultural credit policy must rest on, among other things, knowledge of the importance that farm credit has played in financing investment in agriculture. In the analysis that follows, the assumption has been made that all changes in farm debt are a consequence of or are related to capital investment which, in the present context, excludes the purchase and sale of real estate, but does include improvements that affect the value of real estate such as buildings and other measured investments.

The excellent study by Tostlebe of capital formation and financing provides estimates of the importance of credit in financing new capital in agriculture for the period from 1910 through 1949. In Table IV-12, I present a slightly modifed version of his results for that period and have brought his estimates up to date through 1958. Because certain data have been revised since Tostlebe completed his work and because some of my estimates are not quite as exhaustive or complete as his, Table IV-12 includes two sets of estimates for the period 1945 to 1949. All dollar values, it should be noted, are in terms of the dollars of the period involved.

The top part of Table IV-12 indicates the uses of new capital and farmer-owned financial reserves for each five-year period beginning with 1910. A negative figure implies that there was a reduction in that particular component during the five-year period. Lines 1 and 2 indicate the gross investment in land and buildings and machinery and motor vehicles. These were the major uses of new funds. Lines 9 through 12 indicate the sources of funds for capital investment or increasing cash working balances or other financial reserves. It may be noted that depreciation represents the major single source in every period excepting one, namely 1940 to 1944. In most periods, depreciation represents one-half to two-thirds of the total amount required for gross investment, increase in inventories, and increase in cash or financial reserves. Net income was the second most important source since 1935 except for the period 1954-58. It was only during 1915 to 1919 that increases in loans and credit provided more than half of the total funds that were used for all investment purposes.[9]

Line 14 shows the relationship between the increase in loans and credit and the gross physical capital investment for each period. These ratios undoubtedly overestimate the importance of loans and credit as a source for creation of new capital, since funds borrowed for purchase of real estate were undoubtedly important in most periods. Consequently, the ratios given in line 14 constitute the upper limit of the importance of credit as a source of financing investment. In the most recent period included in the table, namely 1954-58, loans and credit provided 29 percent of the gross investment in physical assets and 27 percent of all uses of funds.[10] Depreciation is almost three times as important as loans and credit.

The data in Table IV-12 indicate that even when it is assumed that all increases in loans and credit were used to increase agricultural assets, their contribution has generally been less important over the past two decades than either depreciation or net income as a source of financing. It is true that if a comparison were made with net investment, the role of borrowing would appear to be substantially larger. For example, during 1950 to 1954 net investment was approximately $10 billion and of this amount, increases in debt would have accounted for slightly less than 45 percent. During 1954-58, net investment was substantially smaller, slightly in excess of $5 billion, and during this four-year period the increase in total debts slightly exceeded net investment. However, since we were not able to isolate the net increase in debt used to purchase real estate, it hardly seems reasonable to assume that net income made no contribution to net investment during the period 1954-58.

---

[9]Refer to line 15, Table IV-12.

[10]The data in line 15 of Table IV-12 may be compared with reasonably comparable data for all nonfinancial corporations. External sources supplied 36 percent of the total uses of corporate funds for 1950-54 and 32 percent for 1954-58. (See Economic Report of the President (January 1962), p. 283.) In both periods agriculture relied less upon external sources.

TABLE IV-12

Uses and Sources of New Capital in Farming and in Farmer-Owned Reserves, United States, by Five-Year Periods, 1910-1958[a]

(billions of dollars)

	1910-1914	1915-1919	1920-1924	1925-1929	1930-1934	1935-1939	1940-1944	1945-1949[b]	1945-1949[c]	1950-1954	1955-1958
USES											
To maintain, increase or improve:											
(1) Land and buildings	3.8	4.3	2.1	4.4	2.2	2.1	4.0	7.9	5.8	8.7	6.3
(2) Machinery and motor vehicles	2.3	3.3	3.1	3.5	1.6	3.5	5.0	10.8	9.9	14.5	10.2
To increase inventories;											
(3) Livestock	0.5	0.2	-0.7	-0.4	-0.2	0.0	0.3	-1.9	-1.7	0.7	0.0
(4) Stored crops	0.3	0.1	-0.3	-0.1	-1.1	1.1	0.6	0.4	0.0	1.1	2.5
(5) Sum (1)+(2)+(3)+(4)	6.9	7.9	4.2	7.4	2.5	6.7	9.6	17.2	14.0	25.0	19.0
(6) To increase cash working balances	0.1	1.4	-0.3	-0.2	-0.1	0.7	2.9	2.4	1.7	0.3	0.6
(7) To increase financial reserves	0.3	3.5	0.0	0.3	0.0	1.2	7.9	3.3	2.8	1.1	0.9
(8) Total (5)+(6)+(7)	7.3	12.8	3.9	7.5	2.4	8.6	20.7	22.9	18.5	26.6	20.5

TABLE IV-12 — Continued

	1910-1914	1915-1919	1920-1924	1925-1929	1930-1934	1935-1939	1940-1944	1945-1949[b]	1945-1949[c]	1950-1954-	1954-1958
					(billions of dollars)						
SOURCES											
(9) Loans and credit	2.6	7.1	0.8	0.6	-2.6	0.6	-2.0	3.0	4.2	4.3	5.5
(10) Financial reserves	0.0	0.0	1.5	0.3	0.5	0.0	0.0	0.0	0.0	0.0	0.0
(11) Depreciation	3.7	5.3	7.0	6.2	4.8	4.9	7.3	13.3	8.7	16.5	15.3
(12) Net Income	1.0	0.4	-5.4	0.4	-0.3	3.1	15.4	6.6	5.8	5.8	-0.3
(13) Total	7.3	12.8	3.9	7.5	2.4	8.6	20.7	22.9	18.5	26.6	20.5
RATIOS						(per cent)					
(14) (9) / (5)	38	90	19	8	--	7	--	17	28	17	29
(15) (9) / (8) or 13	36	55	21	8	--	7	--	13	23	16	27

[a]Last period, 1955-58, is a four year period.

[b]Based on Tostlebe.

[c]Estimated from Balance Sheet of Agriculture, 1959 and The Farm Income Situation by this writer. Source of differences in lines (1) and (2) and (11) was revision by U.S.D.A. of concepts of gross investment and depreciation. Difference in line (7) due to greater inconclusiveness of concept of financial assets used by Tostlebe. Difference in line (9) due to exclusion of CCC loans from Tostlebe's estimates.

Sources: 1910-49: Alvin S. Tostlebe, Capital in Agriculture, Its Formation Since 1870, pp. 136-139 (Tables 35 and 36). 1945-58: U.S.D.A., The Balance Sheet of Agriculture, 1959 (Agriculture Information Bulletin No. 214), pp. 30-31 and 32, and The Farm Income Situation (July 1959), p. 51.

G. Ownership of Agricultural Resources.

Thus far our discussion of capital formation, value of farm assets and debts, and the financing of capital expansion has treated agriculture as a single entity. In other words, we have not been concerned about the ownership of agricultural resources. When a farmer does not have sufficient financial assets to purchase real estate or other capital, he can often acquire such control, either by borrowing or renting. Under some circumstances both alternatives are open to him, while under others perhaps only renting is available.

It is possible for the period since 1930 to indicate the financial interests of three groups in farm real estate. The three groups are owner-operators, landlords, and creditors.[11] If we assume that farm mortgages represent the only creditor claim against real estate, Table IV-13 provides such a breakdown. The first three lines of Table IV-13 provide the simplest set of categories, one in which all landlords are grouped together. The estimates indicate that there was very little change in the ownership of agricultural resources between 1930 and 1940. Between 1940 and 1950, with the increased money and real incomes of farm operators, the relative importance of creditors declined and owner-operators increased their share of the ownership of agricultural real estate from approximately 46 percent to 57 percent (line 1). Since 1950 there has been an increase in the absolute and relative magnitudes of farm mortgage credit and the share of owner-operators may have declined slightly, though the change indicated between 1950 and 1959 is well within the range of possible error in the data. It is perhaps surprising that the relative importance of landlords has remained so constant over the period of almost three decades.[12]

The other aspect of the landlord interest that is of significance in the present context is the much more important role of the landlord than of the creditor in supplying capital required for farm real estate. Not only has the percentage contribution of the landlord been greater than that of the creditor, but the landlord's contribution has remained stable in relative terms, while the creditor role has declined significantly. A set of calculations made on somewhat less

---

[11]The estimates exclude all public lands.

[12]In estimating the ownership interest of landlords and operators, the farm mortgage debt was allocated between these two groups of farm real estate owners. Manager-operated farms were counted as owner-operated. It was necessary to estimate the amount of mortgage debt on manager-operated farms. The total value of manager-operated farms may be estimated at $3 billion for 1950 out of a total farm real estate value of almost $75 billion.

complete data for 1910 indicates that the ownership of agricultural real estate was divided among the three groups in almost exactly the same proportions as in 1959.

TABLE IV-13

Ownership of Agricultural Real Estate[a]

(percent)

	1930	1940	1950	1956	1959
(1) Owner-Operators	46.7	46.4	57.1	55.8	56.4
(2) Landlords	34.1	33.9	35.3	35.6	34.6
(3) Creditors	20.1	19.6	7.5	8.5	9.0
(4) Nonfarm Landlords[b]	21.8	22.7	22.2	22.4	21.4
(5) Farm Landlords[b]	12.3	11.2	13.1	13.2	13.2
(6) Farmer Ownership	59.0	57.6	60.2	69.0	69.6

[a]The sum of lines (1), (2) and (3) equal 100, except for rounding error. The sum of lines (4) and (5) equal line (2).

[b]Estimated percentages of all rented land owned by nonfarm landlords: 1930-64%; 1940-67%; 1950 and 1956-63% and 1959-62%.

Sources: Statistical Abstract of the United States, 1959, p. 628; The Balance Sheet of Agriculture, 1959, p. 10; Agricultural Statistics, 1957, p. 587. Data for 1930 and 1959 partly estimated by writer.

Approximately a third of the value of all land owned by landlords is owned by landlords who live on the farms. A substantial proportion of the landlords living on farms are relatives of the tenants operating the farm. In lines 4 and 5 of Table IV-13, the landlord interest has been divided between those landlords living on farms and those not living on farms. The nonfarm landlord, it may be noted, has a larger financial interest in agricultural real estate than do creditors. The two interests were almost equal in 1930, but in 1959 the nonfarm landlords' interest was more than double that of creditors. Line 6 in the table, which is the sum of lines 1 and 5, indicates that farmer ownership of agricultural real estate has risen from 59 percent in 1930 to almost 70 percent in 1959.

Similar data on the ownership of all agricultural resources are not available. Real estate, however, constitutes almost three-quarters of the total value of physical assets used in farm production, and approximately 65 percent of all financial assets and physical assets, excluding consumer durables, owned by agriculture.

Aside from non-real estate debt, nonfarmers have limited financial resources in livestock, machinery and motor vehicles, and stored crops. A study made in the Great Plains area as of mid-1957 indicates that farm operators owned slightly less than 90 percent of the non-real estate physical capital used on their farms.[13]

If this relationship is assumed to hold for all of U.S. agriculture and if it is assumed that all non-real estate debt is a claim against the assets of farm operators, the following rough estimate of the distribution of ownership of all farm physical assets, except consumer durables, and financial assets, may be made for 1959: farm operators 63 percent, landlords and other owners of physical farm assets 25 percent, and creditors 12 percent. According to these estimates farm operators own a larger share of all agricultural resources than of agricultural real estate. It may also be noted that landlords and owners of non-real estate farm capital are more important suppliers of all agricultural resources than are creditors. In fact, their importance is approximately twice as great as that of creditors.

The estimated distribution of the ownership of all agricultural resources is admittedly somewhat rough. Yet, even if a considerable margin of error is allowed for, and whatever error there is would primarily affect the distribution between farm operators and landlords, it is quite clear that credit plays a relatively limited role in either the ownership of farm resources at any time or in the creation of new farm capital. A limited role should not be assumed to mean an unimportant role. The marginal effect of the use of credit can be substantially more important than indicated by its average importance.

II. COMPETITIVE AND COMPLEMENTARY RELATIONS AMONG AGRICULTURAL CREDIT INSTITUTIONS

In this part of the monograph, the interrelationships among the various credit agencies that are federally owned or supervised and other credit institutions serving agriculture will be presented. Little specific attention is given to the background and development of the federally owned or supervised credit agencies since these agencies have been described in some detail in a series of Research Studies prepared for the Commission on Money and Credit.[1] Our

---

[13] The Balance Sheet of Agriculture, 1959, Agriculture Information Bulletin No. 214, p. 12.

[1] In the volume, Federal Credit Agencies, see D. Gale Johnson, "The Credit Programs Supervised by the Farm Credit Administration," Research Study Four; Dale E. Hathaway, "The Federal Credit Programs for Individual Farm Development," Research Study Five; and George S. Tolley, "The Rural Electrification Administration," Research Study Six (Englewood Cliffs, N.J.: Prentice-Hall, Inc., 1963).

concern is almost wholly with those credit agencies that serve farmers directly and whose major purpose is the supply of agricultural credit. This means that the credit activities of the Commodity Credit Corporation, the Rural Electrification Administration, and the banks for cooperatives are not considered. Furthermore, since our concern is primarily with the longer-run and more permanent interrelationships, we will largely ignore the emergency credit activities of the 1930's. This is not to imply that these emergency programs were unnecessary, unimportant, or did not make substantial contributions to the welfare of farmers, other credit agencies and the economy as a whole. However, most of these programs, especially those started after 1933, were developed for a unique situation and were liquidated within a reasonable period of time. Certain emergency or distress types of credit are still available, but these are now largely administered by the Farmers Home Administration and are here considered as a part of that agency's activities.

A. Sources of Farm Credit.

While the studies referred to above have described the purposes, origins and development of the federally owned or supervised credit agencies, it was not the purpose of any one of the monographs to provide an over-all picture of the sources of farm credit or to describe the activities of the private institutions or individuals providing credit to farmers. In order that the total credit picture may be seen and the federal agencies put in their proper perspective, it is necessary to describe, at least briefly, the other sources of agricultural credit and to present some data and information on the changes in the sources of credit over the past half century.

If all farmers are considered as a group, they have available to them a large number of different credit sources. These include commercial banks, insurance companies, farm mortgage companies, merchants and dealers in farm supplies, installment loan companies, and individuals. Table IV-14 presents estimated distributions of total mortgages and loans outstanding for the beginning of six selected years. The table is divided into three parts: the top part provides the distribution for mortgages, the middle part for non-real estate loans, and the final part is a distribution for all outstanding farm credit.

When the distribution of mortgage credit outstanding is compared for the first and last period given in the table, it is seen that the relative importance of life insurance companies has almost doubled and the relative importance of commercial banks has remained rather stable. The introduction of the federally sponsored or owned credit agencies, in this instance the Federal Land banks and the Farmers Home Administration, has apparently primarily displaced

TABLE IV-14

Distribution of Agricultural Credit by Source for Real Estate Mortgages, Non-Real Estate Loans and All Credit, U. S., January 1, Selected Years

(Percent)

Type and Source	1913	1930	1940	1950	1955	1960
A. Real estate mortgages						
Banks	15.5	10.4	8.1	16.8	14.6	13.2
Insurance companies	12.6	22.0	14.9	21.0	24.7	22.9
Others	71.9	48.5	33.7	41.4	41.7	41.3
Federal Land banks		12.5	30.5	16.2	15.4	19.0
FFMC[b]			10.8	1.0		
Joint Stock Land banks		6.6	1.4			
FHA[c]			0.4	3.6	3.5	3.6
B. Non-real estate[a]						
Banks	50.0	50.0	30.0	39.1	40.2	45.6
PCA[d]			5.1	7.4	7.9	12.9
FICB[e]			1.0	1.0	0.8	0.9
FHA			13.9	6.6	5.7	3.7
Others	50.0	50.0	50.0	45.8	45.3	36.9
C. Total[a]						
Banks	29.7	23.9	15.0	27.6	26.6	28.2
Insurance companies	7.4	14.5	10.3	10.8	13.2	12.3
Others	62.9	49.1	38.8	43.6	43.4	39.3
FLB and FFMC		8.2	28.4	8.9	8.2	10.2
Joint Stock Land banks		4.4	1.0			
FHA			4.7	5.0	4.5	3.6
PCA and PICB			1.9	4.0	4.1	6.4

[a]Excludes all loans guaranteed by Commodity Credit Corporation as well as all loans held by CCC.
[b]Federal Farm Mortgage Corporation.
[c]Farmers Home Administration and predecessor organizations.
[d]Production Credit Associations.
[e]Federal Intermediate Credit banks loans, and discounts to livestock loan companies and agricultural credit corporations.

Sources: Raymond Goldsmith, A Study of Saving in the United States, Vol. III, p. 76; U.S.D.A., The Balance Sheet of Agriculture, 1959 (Agricultural Information Bulletin No. 214), pp. 25, 27, 30-31; U.S.D.A., Agricultural Statistics, 1952, p. 721; U.S.D.A., 27th Annual Report of the Farm Credit Administration, 1959-60, p. 6.

individuals and other sources of mortgage credit. The combined percentage of loans held by insurance companies and commercial banks increased from 28 percent to 36 percent between 1913 and 1960. By 1930 the Federal Land banks and the joint stock Land banks, which were privately owned but had the right to issue tax-exempt bonds, held about 19 percent of the outstanding farm mortgage debt.

As a result of the refinancing of a very large fraction of the farm mortgage debt during the 1930's, the various federally supervised or owned agencies held 43 percent of the mortgage debt on January 1, 1940. This proportion declined significantly during the prosperous war and immediate postwar period. Throughout the 1940's, 80 percent or more of the mortgages recorded each year were made by private agencies, and as farmers paid off existing mortgages held by the Federal Land banks and the Federal Farm Mortgage Corporation, the percentage of total mortgages held by the federally sponsored or owned agencies declined from 43 percent in 1940 to 21 percent in 1950. It was not until 1956 that the downward trend in the proportion of mortgages held by the Federal Land banks and the Farmers Home Administration was halted. It may be noted that the proportion of the outstanding mortgage debt held by individuals and others has remained remarkably constant since 1950.

The estimates of non-real estate loans are made on the basis of less complete data than are available for farm mortgages. The proportion held by the category designated by "others" is based on quite fragmentary data, and the estimates given for the two earlier periods are certainly very rough. According to these rough estimates commercial banks supplied about 50 percent of the non-real estate credit prior to 1930. The proportion dropped to 30 percent in 1940 and since that time has steadily increased and now stands at about 46 percent. In 1940, the federal agencies held about 20 percent of the non-real estate debt; the percentage declined to 14 percent by 1950 and has since increased slightly to 17 percent. Thus approximately five-sixths of the total non-real estate debt is currently supplied by private agencies. The single most important source of such credit in 1960 was commercial banks.

The bottom part of Table IV-14 shows the distribution of total farm mortgages and loans. According to these estimates banks now supply about the same proportion as in 1913. Insurance companies have increased their relative importance from approximately 7 percent to 12 percent. The federally supervised or owned agencies supplied about a fifth of the total credit on January 1, 1960. There was a slight increase in the relative importance of federal agencies in the 10 years preceding 1960, but the change was hardly large enough to indicate a significant trend.

The reasons for the origins of the various federal credit agencies as presented in the Research Studies referred to earlier, may be classified under five major criticisms of the private sources of credit that existed prior to these agencies: (1) there was not enough credit available to farmers; (2) change in the supply or availability of credit was unrelated to the needs of farmers; (3) credit was not available on terms suited to the particular needs of farmers; (4) farm credit provided by private sources was too costly; and (5) certain categories of farmers, especially low-income farmers and tenant farmers who desired to become farm owners, either could not obtain credit at all or could obtain it only in inadequate amounts. These five reasons might be interpreted as very serious indictments of the private credit system.[2] Does the fact that the public agencies now supply only a fifth of the total credit to farmers imply that most of these criticisms were unwarranted? Such a conclusion does not necessarily follow since it is possible that the federal agencies have acted primarily as pace setters and the private agencies have reacted to the competition provided by the federal agencies. While our discussion of the competitive and complementary relations among the private and public credit agencies is not specifically organized in terms of these criticisms of the private credit sources, it is hoped that the analysis and discussion will throw some light upon the possible validity or importance of each of the points.

B. The Element of Subsidy in the Federally Sponsored and Owned Credit Agencies.

Private credit agencies, especially commercial banks and insurance companies, have often criticised the federal agencies as unfair competitors. Each of the agencies has had or still has some element of subsidy from the federal government. The subsidy has taken various forms for the Federal Land banks, the Federal Intermediate Credit banks and the Production Credit Associations. Most of the subsidy has been due to the provision of interest-free capital by the federal government. In addition, until 1941 the bonds issued by the Federal Land banks were exempt from federal and state income taxation and are still exempt from state income taxation, and the Federal Land banks, the National Farm Loan Associations, and the Federal Intermediate Credit banks are given favored

[2]The first four of these criticisms are considered in some detail in Section II of my Research Study, "The Credit Programs Supervised by the Farm Credit Administration" [Research Study Four in Federal Credit Agencies, prepared for the Commission on Money and Credit (Englewood Cliffs, N.J.:Prentice-Hall, Inc., 1963)]. I feel that these reasons, if accepted literally, do not provide an accurate appraisal of the functioning of private credit agencies before the introduction of the public agencies.

treatment with respect to payment of federal income and state and local taxes.

Any estimate of the value of the subsidy growing out of the provision of government capital without the payment of interest must be based upon certain assumptions. The usual procedure is to estimate how much the interest-free provision of capital would have cost the government. However, it is probably just as meaningful to estimate what it would have cost the particular agency to have borrowed the same amount. Neither estimate, however, reflects the fact that the existence of the government free capital reduced the subjective risk as evaluated by the purchaser of the bonds or the debentures, as the case may be, and thus reduced the cost of funds actually borrowed.

In their excellent study, Federal Lending and Loan Insurance, Saulnier, Halcrow and Jacoby present estimates of the extent of subsidy for the period until June 30, 1954.[3] Their estimates were made by calculating the number of dollar-years of interest-free capital and multiplying by a simple rate of interest of 2 percent, which they believed to be roughly the cost of borrowing to the government during the period of time involved. Their estimates might be criticized on the grounds that compound rather than simple interest should have been used since the agency involved gained by not having to pay the interest and by being able to add the amount of interest they would otherwise have had to pay to their surplus accounts. These surplus accounts were either invested in farm loans or Government bonds from which the agency earned a return. However, for the time periods involved, and assuming that the appropriate rate of interest was 2 percent, the use of compound rather than simple interest has a relatively small effect.[4]

In 1947 the Federal Land banks repaid all of the government capital that had been invested in them. In the period from 1917 through 1947 the government provided approximately 3,400 million dollar-years of capital without interest cost to them. Almost all of the interest-free capital was provided after 1932.[5] At the time

---

[3] R. J. Saulnier, H. G. Halcrow, and N. H. Jacoby, Federal Lending and Loan Insurance, (New York: National Bureau of Economic Research, 1958), pp. 94-6, 174-5, 191-2, and 199.

[4] One dollar invested at 2 percent has the following values for two time periods:

15 years:		25 years:	
simple interest	$1.30	simple interest	$1.50
compound interest	1.35	compound interest	1.64

[5] From 1917 through 1932 the number of dollar-years of interest-free capital was 52 million.

the Land Banks were established the government invested less than $9 million in the capital stock of these institutions. Practically all of this was repaid by 1929 and it was not until 1932 that a substantial amount of interest-free government capital was made available as government stock and paid-in surplus. Had it not been for the severity of the depression it is reasonable to assume that the Federal Land banks could have been established and could have continued their operations with only a very minor element of interest subsidy. Taking the situation as it actually existed, however, the interest subsidy may be estimated as $67 to $75 million depending upon whether simple or compound interest is used and assuming an interest rate of 2 percent. The interest savings to the Land Banks, measured in terms of the rates paid on Federal Land Bank bonds, would have been substantially greater than the $67 to $75 million. The rate of interest paid on bonds during the period was 3.5 to 4.6 percent and the interest savings based on actual bond rates was $117 to $161 million.[6] As of June 30, 1947, at which time all governmental capital had been retired, the total reserve and surplus accounts of the Federal Land banks was $193 million while the combined reserves and surplus accounts of the Federal Land banks and the National Farm Loan associations was $215 million. Thus it would appear that even if the Federal Land banks and National Farm Loan Associations had paid to the government an amount equal to the cost of the funds borrowed on the basis of Land Bank bonds, the reserve and surplus accounts would have been positive as of June 30, 1947. In fact, the remainder of these accounts would have been at least equal to the value of capital stock subscribed by borrowers which, as of June 30, 1947, amounted to $65 million.[7]

Because of the close interrelationships between the Federal Intermediate Credit banks, the Production Credit Corporations and the Production Credit Associations, it is necessary to consider all three institutions as a unit in calculating the subsidy resulting from provision of interest-free capital. Furthermore, the Production Credit Corporations were dissolved as of December 31, 1956 and their assets and liabilities transferred to the Federal Intermediate Credit banks. Assuming a 2 percent (simple) rate of interest on the governmental capital supplied free for the period 1933-54 and a 25 percent rate for more recent years, the subsidy may be estimated

---

[6]Bond rates from Agricultural Statistics, 1952, p. 717. In making the calculations it was assumed all governmental capital and paid-in surplus was retired on December 31, 1946. The lower estimate was derived by using simple interest; the higher resulted from assuming compound interest.

[7]For data on financial accounts of the Land Bank System on June 30, 1947, see Fourteenth Annual Report of the Farm Credit Administration, 1946-47, pp. 28 and 108-109.

at about $90 million.[8] However, in the case of the Production Credit System this may well represent an overestimate of the interest savings to the System since the average rate paid on the intermediate credit bank debentures was substantially less than 2 percent throughout the period of the highest governmental investment. Of course, the rate paid was favorably influenced by the existence of the interest-free government capital. A rough estimate indicated a total interest savings through June 30, 1960 of about $60 million. The estimates of the subsidy and savings do not take into account the $13.5 million of franchise taxes paid by the FICB's. As of June 30, 1960, the total of the surplus of the Federal and Intermediate Credit Banks and the accumulated earnings of the Production Credit Associations equaled $193 million. These surplus accounts represent almost all of the earnings of the Production Credit System since dividends paid on stock owned by members totaled less than $9 million from 1933 through mid-1960.[9]

I have not included in the estimates $277 million of interest rate reductions on Federal Land Bank mortgages for the period from July 11, 1933 through June 30, 1944, and $57 million on Land Bank commissioner loans for a somewhat shorter period of time which was authorized by Congress and paid directly from the Treasury.[10] These interest rate subsidies were probably not necessary for the continued existence of the Federal Land Bank System, though the subsidy placed downward pressure on the interest rates that could be charged by other lenders and thus had the effect of increasing the share of total farm mortgages held by the Federal Land banks.

The comparisons between the interest subsidy or interest savings made possible by the provision of governmental capital to the Federal Land Bank System and the Intermediate Credit System, and the reserve and surplus accounts of these two systems, indicate that the net returns exceeded the interest cost or savings. However, in terms of the competitive relationships of these institutions or systems to other lenders, the fact that the net earnings were in excess of the interest costs or savings is not necessarily the

---

[8]From the time of organization through June 30, 1954, Saulnier, Halcrow and Jacoby estimate that the interest-free capital provided to the Production Credit corporations was 1.9 billion dollar-years and to the FICB's, 1.8 billion dollar-years. (Saulnier, et al., op. cit., p. 191.) Between June 30, 1954 and June 30, 1960, 537 million dollar-years of interest-free capital was provided to the System.

[9]27th Annual Report of the Farm Credit Administration, 1959-60, p. 37. In addition, PCA's have paid $4.6 million in patronage refunds.

[10]Saulnier, et al., op. cit., p. 95.

relevant consideration. Two other factors need to be taken into account. The first is the importance of the interest savings or costs relative to the volume of loans outstanding during the period under consideration, and the second is the extent to which these systems have accumulated assets and retained them as a result of the interest-free capital after the government capital has been retained. The first of these is relatively easy to ascertain. In the case of the Federal Land Bank System, the estimated interest subsidy ranged from $67 to $161 million. If the dollar-years of mortgages outstanding is calculated for the period from 1932 through 1947, when most of the interest subsidy occurred, there were 26 billion dollar-years of mortgages outstanding.[11] Thus the interest subsidy, when converted to an annual basis, was somewhere between 0.25 percent and 0.62 percent. In other words, the interest charged to borrowers could have been reduced by approximately these amounts. To illustrate, an agency that did not receive such a subsidy might have to charge an interest rate of 5 percent. Because of the interest rate subsidy, the Federal Land Bank System could have offered an interest rate ranging from 4.38 percent to 4.75 percent. In the case of the Intermediate Credit System for the period from 1934 through June 30, 1960, there were 16.2 billion dollar-years of credit provided and the cost or value of the interest subsidy ranged from $60 to $90 million.[12] This amounted to 0.37 to 0.55 percent of the credit provided. When compared to an interest rate of 6 percent, the competitive advantage provided was reasonably substantial.

Whether the present or prospective competitive position of the two credit systems has been improved by the provision of interest-free governmental capital depends primarily upon the extent that the savings provided by such capital was passed on to borrowers during the period that the savings were available. If all savings had been passed on to borrowers, then the System retained little or no competitive advantage from the provision of the interest-free capital. On June 30, 1947, by which time the Land Bank System had retired all of its governmental capital, the net worth minus the capital stock of the entire System was approximately $215 million. This was equal to approximately 22 percent of the total mortgages outstanding on that date. Thirteen years later the net worth minus

---

[11]Estimated by the simple summation of the amount of farm mortgages held by the Federal Land banks at the end of each year, 1932 through 1947. See 27th Annual Report of the Farm Credit Administration, 1959-60, p. 63.

[12]Estimate of dollar-years of credit is the sum of loans and discounts outstanding on June 30 for the years 1934-60, inclusive for the Federal Intermediate Credit banks. See 27th Annual Report of the Farm Credit Administration, 1959-60, p. 91.

the value of the capital stock was $366 million. This amounted to approximately 15 percent of the mortgages outstanding at that time. Two inferences may be drawn from these data. First, it is quite possible that little or none of the interest subsidy was in fact passed on to borrowers prior to 1947. It is possible that this failure to pass on the savings was accidental and grew out of the very favorable loss experience during the 1940's and the very low and unanticipated interest cost on Federal Land Bank bonds. Second, it does not appear that the Land Bank System has used its favorable net worth position as of June 30, 1947 to pass on savings to borrowers since that time.[13] The addition to net worth other than the increased value of the capital stock has been very substantial in the thirteen years since 1947. The ratio of net worth minus capital stock to loans outstanding continued to increase through 1953 and did not return to the 1947 level until 1955.[14] The decline in the ratio since 1956 has been due to the rather significant expansion in the volume of new loans made and which by June 30, 1960, had not made much contribution to the surplus accounts. The Federal Land Bank System now has a very sound and favorable capital structure; earnings on its surplus accounts could contribute substantially to lower interest rates on future mortgages. However, there is no indication from the recent behavior of the System that there is any intention to halt the growth in the reserve and surplus accounts.

The Federal Intermediate Credit System had net worth in addition to farmer- and government-owned capital stock of $193 million on June 30, 1960. The average amount of loans and discounts outstanding for the Intermediate Credit Banks during 1959-60 was approximately $1.3 billion. Thus the surpluses and accumulated earnings of the System equaled 15 percent of loans. The loss experience of the PCA's has averaged less than a third of a percent of the average amount of loans outstanding. Thus the ratio of net worth, excluding the value of all stock, to loans outstanding of 15 percent is many times larger than any amount that might be needed to cover losses and is also more than double in absolute amount the government stock now in the Intermediate Credit System. It seems reasonable to assume that much of the interest saving has been added to the surplus and earned income accounts, and has not

---

[13]Between June 30, 1947 and June 30, 1959 the (compound) growth rate of the surplus accounts for the Land Banks and Associations was about 4.2 percent. During the same period the average dividend return to borrowers on capital stock was 4.6 percent. Since June 30, 1952 the dividend rate has averaged 3.9 percent.

[14]The ratios of net worth minus capital stock to mortgages outstanding were as follows as of June 30: (in percent)

1952 — 26	1954 — 25	1956 — 20	1958 — 18	1960 — 15
1953 — 27	1955 — 23	1957 — 18	1959 — 16	

yet been passed on to borrowers. In other words, I do not think anyone would be alarmed if the surplus and earned income accounts of the System were now $100 to $140 million instead of $193 million.

C. Specialization by Lenders.

As noted earlier, a large number of institutions and individuals loan to farmers. During the past 40 years, and especially since 1932, the federally owned or supervised agencies have become significant factors in the provision of credit to farmers, even though private sources of credit are still approximately four times as important as the public or cooperative sources. The data in Table IV-14 indicate that the growth of the federally owned or sponsored credit agencies has not resulted in any significant transfer of business from the two major institutional lenders to farmers, namely banks and insurance companies. The growth of the federal agencies has been at the expense of the miscellaneous group of lenders, in which individuals, merchants and dealers probably predominate. One implication of this series of developments might be that the Federal Land banks, the PCA's, and the Farmers Home Administration have not effectively competed with the banks and insurance companies for the farm credit business. The trends noted, of course, are not conclusive evidence of any lack of competition, since in the absence of the federal agencies the banks and insurance companies might have expanded their agricultural loan business substantially, also at the expense of the other or miscellaneous group.

Some evidence on the degree of competition between the federally owned or sponsored credit agencies and the other major institutional lenders may be ascertained by determining the degree of specialization by each of the important institutional lenders. There are three aspects of specialization which will be considered, for mortgages and non-real estate credit separately. The first is concerned with the characteristics of the borrower, such as his location, tenure, and net worth. The second is the purposes for which the loan funds were borrowed and the extent to which different institutions lend for varying purposes. The third aspect of specialization is concerned with the size and term of loan provided by the lending agency and the relationship between value of security and the loan. The picture which emerges is that while there is a considerable overlap among the various agencies with respect to each of the categories of specialization, each institution seems to have one or more areas in which it has a relatively unique role, and on the whole there has been a rather high degree of stability in these patterns.

1. Mortgage Credit.

a. Region. Prior to the establishment of the Federal Land Bank System there were two types of farm mortgage lenders that gave agriculture access to national sources of credit. These were the insurance companies and the mortgage companies. Both of these institutional lenders displayed a high degree of regional specialization with concentration in the North Central states and the Southern Plains. The first decade of operation of the Land Banks and the joint stock Land Banks did not reduce the degree of penetration of the insurance companies in the North Central states; the insurance companies' share of outstanding farm mortgages increased from 18 percent in 1917 to 30 percent in 1928, and the North Central states provided the same share of the total mortgages held by the insurance companies in both years, namely 78 percent. The insurance companies wrote very few mortgages in the whole of the northeast or the southeastern part of the United States, and even by the late twenties held relatively few mortgages in the Mountain or Pacific states. Thus a significant share of American agriculture did not have reasonably good access to national credit markets for obtaining farm mortgage loans. With only minor exceptions the Federal Land banks by the late twenties tended to hold relatively large proportions of the total farm mortgage debt in those regions where the insurance companies were relatively unimportant and tended to hold relatively small proportions of the debt in those regions where the insurance companies were very important.

Since the late twenties the degree of regional specialization has declined somewhat but it is still true that about half of all the farm mortgages held by the insurance companies are on farm property in the North Central states, and the insurance companies' share of the total mortgages outstanding in these same states is currently almost as large as in 1928 and significantly larger than in 1917. The decline in the importance of the North Central states as a source of loans of the insurance companies is thus not due to the incursions by the Federal Land banks into that area but due to the fact that the region's share of all farm mortgage debt has declined from 65 percent in 1917 to slightly more than 40 percent currently. The insurance companies, in expanding their relative and absolute importance outside the North Central states, have continued to specialize to a very considerable degree from the standpoint of location.

b. Purposes of Farm Mortgage Loans. One of the major objectives of Federal Land Bank legislation in 1916 was to increase owner-operatorship of farm real estate. Such an objective might imply that a rather large fraction of the farm mortgage loans made by the Federal Land banks would be for the purchase of real estate. In fact, quite the opposite situation prevails. Throughout most of their history the Land Bank mortgages have been used primarily for refinancing other indebtedness. The situation which prevailed in mid-1956 seems to be fairly typical. The purposes for mortgage loans made in the previous few months indicated that only 15 percent of the total value of mortgages written was for the purchase of real estate. During the same period of time, 31 percent of the funds committed for farm real estate mortgages by life insurance companies were used for the purchase of real estate.[15]

It is reasonably clear that no one of the institutional lenders is, or all of the institutional lenders taken as a group are, the major factor in the transfer of real estate from one owner to another. For a period ending March 1, 1959, it was estimated that 67 percent of all farm purchases involved the use of credit. The distribution of the credit-financed purchases was estimated as follows: sellers, 43 percent; commercial banks, 18 percent; insurance companies, 14 percent; Federal Land Banks, 10 percent; and other sources, 15 percent.[16] Thus it will be seen that the number of purchases financed by sellers was greater than that of the three major institutional lenders combined, and furthermore that commercial banks were more important than either the insurance companies or the Federal Land banks, when importance is measured in terms of the number of transfers involved. It is probably true, in terms of the amount of funds committed, that insurance companies committed more than any of the other institutional lenders, since the average size of insurance company mortgages was twice that of the Federal Land banks and three times that of commercial banks.[17]

A considerable amount of detail is available on the purposes of mortgage loans made by insurance companies and the Federal Land banks. Since there has been little change in the use of the proceeds

---

[15]Data for insurance companies and Land Banks from Betty A. Case, Farm Mortgage Loans Held by Life Insurance Companies, ARS 43-58 (October 1957), p. 6. Comparable data are not available for commercial banks. However, on June 30, 1956, 56 percent of outstanding real estate mortgages (as measured by amount outstanding) had had the purchase of farm land as the original purpose. Since real estate mortgages originally used to purchase land probably had longer maturities than real estate mortgages for other purposes, an analysis comparable to that for the insurance companies and Land Banks (based on loans recently made) would indicate a lower percentage of mortgage funds used to purchase real estate than 56 percent. See Federal Reserve Bulletin (February 1957), p. 134.

[16]The Farm Real Estate Market, ARS 43-110 (October 1959), p. 22. See Table IV-15 for additional data.

[17]See Paul L. Holm, "Financing Farm Land Transfers," Agricultural Finance Review, Vol. 21 (July 1959), p. 22; and Betty A. Case, Farm Mortgage Loans Held by Life Insurance Companies, ARS 43-58 (October 1957), p. 17.

over time, the data given in Table IV-15 for 1956 can be considered rather typical of the period between 1950 and 1959.

It is of interest to note the previous holders of loans refinanced by the Federal Land banks. Data are available for two periods for the last 100 loans made by each Land Bank prior to June 15, 1956 and June 15, 1957 (see Table IV-16).[18] The results are not especially surprising. Most of the refinancing of real estate mortgages is of loans held by lenders that grant relatively short-term loans — the commercial banks and others. These data are consistent with the view that sellers of farm land and some commercial banks are willing to make loans that would not be made by the Land Banks. After the ratio of the debt to the value of the pledged property decreases, the Land Banks become able and willing to take over the mortgage. This pattern of making and refinancing loans is probably a significant factor in explaining some of the differences in interest rates that one may observe.

D. Size and Term of Mortgage Loans.

1. Size.

The larger average size of farm mortgages recorded by life insurance companies than by Federal Land banks is probably a function of differences in appraisal policies and differences in interest rate policy.[19] Apparently the Federal Land banks follow a

---

[18] The data for the period ending June 15, 1956 given in Table IV-16 are not consistent with the similar data for the same period for the Federal Land banks given in Table IV-15. In Table IV-15, it is indicated that 48 percent of the amount loaned by the Federal Reserve banks was for refinancing indebtedness: in Table IV-16, 43 percent is given. Other differences may be noted. The reason for these differences is that in Table IV-15 loans are classified by major purpose, while in Table IV-16 the distribution of the actual use of borrowed funds has been estimated from the available data.

[19] The average sizes of farm mortgages recorded by the principal lenders have been as follows:

	1940	1950	1959
Federal Land banks	3,820	4,740	11,620
Insurance companies	5,760	9,760	21,960
Banks	2,000	3,740	6,600
Individuals	1,670	4,250	10,860
Misc.	2,830	4,390	8,390
All lenders	2,370	4,700	10,000

Sources: 1940 and 1950: Betty A. Case, Farm Mortgage Loans Held by Life Insurance Companies, U.S.D.A., ARS 43-58 (October 1957) p. 17. 1959: V.E. Eitel, "Characteristics of Farm Mortgages Recorded, January 1 to March 31, 1959: A Preliminary Report," U.S.D.A., ARS (August 1960), p. 7.

TABLE IV-15

Percentage Distribution of Farm Mortgage Loans Made by the Federal Land Banks and Life Insurance Companies, by Major Purpose of Loan, United States, 1956

Purpose of loan	Percentage of total funds			
	January 1 to June 30		July 1 to December 31	
	Federal Land banks[a]	Life insurance companies[b]	Federal Land banks[c]	Life insurance companies[d]
	Percent	Percent	Percent	Percent
Purchase of real estate	15	31	14	40
Refinancing of farm real estate mortgages	48	36	51	28
Refinancing of other indebtedness	10	15	12	13
Improvements to land and buildings	11	8	10	10
Other	16	10	13	9
Total	100	100	100	100

[a]Analysis of last 100 loans closed by each Land Bank prior to June 15, 1956.

[b]Percentage of amount committed January 1 to June 30, 1956. Data reported by 12 life insurance companies, which held 48 percent of the total amount of farm-mortgage loans held by all life insurance companies on January 1, 1957.

[c]Analysis of last 100 loans closed by each Land Bank prior to December 15, 1956.

[d]Percentage of amount committed July 1 to December 31, 1956. Data reported by 12 life insurance companies, which held 48 percent of the total amount of farm-mortgage loans held by all life insurance companies on January 1, 1957.

Source: Agricultural Finance Review, Vol. 20 (April 1958), p. 7.

TABLE IV-16

Purposes for Which Land Bank Loans Were Used Based on a Sample of the Last 100 Loans Made by Each Land Bank Prior to June 15, 1956, and June 15, 1957

Purpose	Percent the amount of new money advanced for each purpose is of the total amount advanced	
	June 15, 1956	June 15, 1957
1. To refinance a real estate mortgage held by:		
A. Insurance companies	6.2	2.2
B. Commercial banks	8.3	9.9
C. Production Credit associations	.7	.7
D. Others	13.8	14.0
Subtotal	29.0	26.8
2. To refinance chattel mortgages, notes and accounts held by:		
A. Commercial banks	7.5	5.6
B. Production Credit associations	2.6	2.2
C. Others	3.6	3.3
Subtotal	13.7	11.1
3. To buy real estate	20.1	24.6
4. Repairs and improvements:		
A. Buildings	14.7	14.1
B. Land	2.8	3.8
Subtotal	17.5	17.9
5. Other purposes:		
A. To purchase farm machinery	3.0	1.4
B. To purchase livestock	1.3	1.8
C. For general farm operations	7.7	6.0
D. For all other purposes	7.7	10.4
Total	100.0	100.0

Source: Annual Report of the Farm Credit Administration 1956-57, p. 16.

more rigid approach to appraisal of farm land than do the insurance companies, and until recently the Land Banks have been limited by law to a loan equal to 65 percent of the appraised value of the property and from this loan the borrower had to purchase the 5 percent stock in the local loan association. As a result of legislation in 1959 the loan can be 65 percent of the appraised value plus the amount required to purchase the stock. With respect to interest rates charged, each Land Bank follows the policy of uniform interest rates, regardless of the absolute size of the mortgage or the relationship between equity and debt.[20] Insurance companies can adapt the interest rate to the particular circumstances and in this way very effectively compete with the Land Banks even though most of the time the average interest rate charged by the insurance companies is higher than that charged by the Land Banks.

2. Term.

The Federal Land banks pioneered the long-term amortized loan in agriculture, and this innovation has come to play a major role in credit in the nonfarm sector of the economy, especially in the housing field. Apparently only the insurance companies among the major agricultural lenders have found it either necessary or desirable to follow the Federal Land banks in this practice. Both banks and individuals currently write mortgages for five-year terms or less.[21] It was not until after the mid-thirties that the insurance companies substantially lengthened the average terms of their mortgages. The very short term of the large volume of loans held by banks and individuals indicates a considerable degree of specialization by lenders in providing mortgage credit to farmers. Either a large proportion of farmers are not able to obtain long-term mortgages from the Federal Land banks or the insurance companies, or they find it simpler and more convenient to obtain a mortgage for a relatively short-term purpose from banks or individuals.

3. Value of Security and Debt.

The major institutional lenders are more conservative than other lenders with respect to the percentage of the purchase price

---

[20]Interest rates do vary from one Federal Land Bank to another, however.

[21]For data on terms of mortgages see Betty A. Case, op. cit., pp. 7 and 23, and V. E. Eitel, op. cit., p. 2. In 1917-21, the average terms of mortgages were: insurance companies, 7.5 years; banks, 2.7 years; and individuals, 3.7. In 1959 the average terms were: insurance companies, 19.1; banks, 4.5; and individuals, 6.6. The Federal Land banks had an average term of 30.9 years in the earlier period and 25.7 years in 1959.

of farm land that they are willing to finance. Somewhat surprising, at least to me, is the fact that of the three major institutional lenders, commercial banks have given a higher ratio of credit to purchase price of farm lands transferring ownership than either insurance companies or the Federal Land banks in all years since 1955, except 1961 when insurance companies had a higher ratio. Table IV-17 presents data on the distribution of credit-financed farm purchases by the source of credit and the percentage of credit of purchase price for each source of credit for several recent years. In every year, the lenders other than the major institutional lenders loaned a higher fraction of the purchase price.

4. Summary.

There appears to be a considerable degree of specialization by the various lenders in the farm mortgage field. The Land Banks appear to be primarily a refinancing agency; to a lesser degree the life insurance companies play a similar role. The major factor in the original financing of farm real estate transfers is the sellers of the land, and commercial banks are involved in the financing of a larger proportion of transfers than any other institutional lender. A presumption of limited competition is evidenced by the distribution of mortgages of various sizes among the lending agencies. Most large farm mortgages are written by insurance companies and the Land Banks tend to emphasize mortgages of moderate size while the majority of mortgages written by commercial banks are relatively small. With respect to term or maturity of mortgages, almost all of the mortgages with terms of 30 years or more are written by the Land Banks and the Farmers Home Administration. The introduction of the long-term amortized mortgage by the Land Banks has had little effect on the term of loans written by banks or individuals, though life insurance companies have apparently responded by more than doubling the term of their farm mortgages over the past four decades.

While the degree of regional concentration by the various lenders has declined somewhat in the last four decades, the insurance companies have maintained a high degree of specialization in the farm areas where the average real estate value per farm is above the national average and farm income per farm is relatively high. The Land Banks and commercial banks have tended to be more important in the remaining areas of the nation.

The individual who needs or desires to purchase real estate with a down payment of less than 35 percent will, in general, be able to obtain it only from sellers and other noninstitutional lenders or the Farmers Home Administration.

(horizo

TABLE IV-17

Credit-Financed Farm Purchases: Percentage Financed by Specified Lenders, and Amount of Credit Extended as Percentage of Purchase Price, United States Years Ending March 1, 1955-61[a]

Source of credit	Percentage of credit-financed purchases				Credit as percentage of purchase price[b]			
	1955	1957	1959	1961	1955	1957	1959	1961
	Pct.	Pct.	Pct.	Pct.	Pct.	Pct.	Pct.	Pct.
Sellers (individuals)	34	41	43	42	68	71	71	73
Commercial banks	20	18	18	14	52	54	59	57
Insurance companies	19	16	14	15	49	52	54	60
Federal land banks	9	10	10	11	51	51	55	56
Individuals other than sellers	9	5	6	9	60	61	61	65
Two or more lenders	2	4	2	2	63	74	63	67
Other sources	7	6	7	7	70	71	73	67
Total or average	100	100	100	100	59	63	64	67

[a]Most of the sales probably occurred in the preceding six months.

[b]Many purchasers of farm real estate offer land that they already own as additional security for the land being purchased. Thus the amount of debt as a percentage of the purchase price for purchases reported here is considerably higher than it would be if loans were secured by only the land purchased, and is also considerably higher than the ratio of this debt to the value of the farm real estate security.

Source: The Farm Real Estate Market, ARS 43-110 (CD-53) (October 1959), p. 22.

E. Non-Real Estate Credit.

On the basis of the available data it is not possible to consider the degree of specialization of various non-real estate lenders in the same degree of detail as was possible for mortgage credit. Very little is known about the sources of supply of perhaps 40 percent of all non-real estate credit and reasonably detailed information is available for other lenders, during the last decade, only for a single date, June 30, 1956.[22] At the time of the loan survey on June 30, 1956, approximately two million farmers had loans outstanding with commercial banks for purposes other than the purchase of real estate, 250 thousand farmers had loans from the Production Credit Associations, and 175 thousand farmers had loans with the Farmers Home Administration, 136 thousand of whom had operating loans. In terms of non-real estate debt outstanding on that date, the banks had almost 4 1/2 times as much as the PCA's and slightly more than seven times as much as the Farmers Home Administration.

The available comparative data permit some general conclusions with respect to the extent of specialization by the three major institutional lenders noted above. Unless otherwise indicated, the comparisons made are for operating loans with the Farmers Home Administration and all loans at insured commercial banks, except for farm real estate loans. Thus the data for the commercial banks include some farm mortgages, though most of the debt is evidenced by notes. The commercial banks have a substantially smaller average size of loan outstanding than do the other two institutions. The Production Credit Associations averaged \$3,420 per borrower, the Farmers Home Administration, \$3,210 and the insured commercial banks, \$1,920.[23] As would be expected, the commercial banks make far more small loans than do the other institutions. In the case of the commercial banks, 38 percent of their borrowers had less than \$500 in debt outstanding, while 19 percent of the Production Credit Association borrowers had less than \$500 outstanding and only 10 percent of the Farmers Home Administration borrowers had debts less than \$500.[24] Apparently borrowers feel that commercial banks have a very considerable advantage in making relatively small loans.

While the age distributions of borrowers from Production Credit Associations and commercial banks are almost identical, the Farmers Home Administration is clearly serving a group of farmers

---

[22]Sources for this section are based on R. W. Bierman and Betty A. Case, "The Farmers Home Administration and Its Borrowers," Agricultural Finance Review, Vol. 21 (July 1959), pp. 40-67 and sources indicated in that article, footnote 2, p. 41.

[23]Bierman and Case, op. cit., pp. 48-49.

[24]Ibid., p. 63.

that it was originally intended to serve. The Farmers Home Administration is more likely to have a tenant as a borrower than the commercial banks which, in turn, are more likely to have a tenant as a borrower than the Production Credit Associations. With respect to all loans outstanding, the Farmers Home Administration has approximately a fifth of their borrowers with a net worth of less than $3,000. The commercial banks have 13 percent, and the Production Credit Associations only 7 percent. Borrowers with net worths in excess of $25,000 constitute 32 percent of all borrowers from the Production Credit Association and only 19 and 6 percent of the borrowers from insured commercial banks and Farmers Home Administration, respectively.

The 1956 survey indicates that the Production Credit Associations relative to the commercial banks tend to lend to farmers who are relatively well established as measured by the assets that they own. The commercial banks seem to serve a very wide spectrum of the farm operator population and tend to have a very large proportion of the small loans. The Farmers Home Administration, in addition to providing operating loans for relatively young and tenant farmers, also provides loans for the acquisition of real estate for the same groups to a much greater extent than is true of other lending institutions.

In my Research Study, "The Credit Programs Supervised by the Farm Credit Administration," I attempted to evaluate the effect of the establishment of the Intermediate Credit System, including the Production Credit Associations, upon the terms and types of credit made available to farmers. One of the major objectives of that system was to provide farmers with loans of intermediate term, say from six months to 3 to 5 years in duration. The evidence brought together there indicated, first, that banks were providing credit of terms of a year or more in substantial amount; second, that until 1955 the Production Credit Associations did not make loans of a maturity in excess of a year; and third, it was pointed out that the 1956 survey showed that almost half of the non-real estate credit provided by banks was for intermediate-term purposes and that of the intermediate-term loans more than half had original maturities of a year or more and about a seventh had original maturities of three years or more. Furthermore, the evidence indicated that a large fraction of the intermediate-term loans had been renewed during 1956 and that of all the renewals about three-quarters had been planned. On the whole, the evidence indicated that the commercial banks were fulfilling an important role in the intermediate-term credit field and that their terms were at least as favorable as the PCA's. It is possible that the PCA's have not had too much of a competitive impact upon the banks with respect to the terms on which credit is offered to farmers.

The Production Credit Associations have tended to concentrate on relatively large loans compared to the size of loans made by commercial banks. On the whole, the Production Credit Associations have tended to serve a relatively large fraction of farmers who have net worths considerably above the national average for all farmers. Most of the farmers served by the Production Credit Associations would certainly have been provided credit by commercial banks if the Production Credit Associations were not in existence. The Production Credit Associations make loans to only about an eighth as many farmers as do commercial banks. The Farmers Home Administration has tended to serve a clientele that either because of low net worth or the size of loan required could not have obtained the credit, at least in the same amount, from other institutional lenders.

F. Interest Rate Competition.

A major political factor in the establishment of the Federal Land Bank System and the Federal Intermediate Credit banks was the complaint of the high cost of borrowing funds for farmers. Mr. R. B. Tootell, Governor of the Farm Credit Administration, testified before a congressional committee in 1956 that it was his belief that the credit agencies supervised by the Farm Credit Administration had not had any significant effect on interest rates paid by farmers, but that the major impact of the cooperative farm system had been upon the conditions on which credit was available and the availability of credit.[25] On the basis of the work that I have done I have found no evidence that contradicts Mr. Tootell's conclusion to any significant degree.

In my Research Study, "The Credit Programs Supervised by the Farm Credit Administration," I estimated that the Federal Land banks may have reduced the cost of mortgage credit to farmers by approximately two-tenths of 1 percent, and that this reduction occurred not because the interest rates charged by other lenders were lower than they would have been in the absence of the Land Bank System, but because the Land Banks wrote a significant volume of mortgages at a rate lower than that charged by other lenders. In other words, the Land Banks do charge a lower rate of interest than do the rest of the lenders, and when borrowers are either able or willing to meet the loan conditions of the Land Banks, they are able to obtain credit at a lower money rate of interest than they can obtain it from others. In order to obtain the lower rate of interest they

---

[25] Farm Credit Act of 1956, Hearings Before a Subcommittee of the Committee on Agriculture and Forestry, United States Senate, 84th Congress, 2nd Session, April 23 and 24, 1956, p. 39.

must purchase stock equal to 5 percent of the amount borrowed and unless they receive a dividend on that stock equal to the interest paid on the mortgage, part of the interest rate differential between the Land Banks and other institutional lenders may disappear. However, since 1947, it should be noted, the ratio of dividends to capital stock outstanding has averaged approximately 4.6 percent, which is roughly equal to the interest rate on Land Bank mortgages. This means that most or all of the difference between the interest rate charged by the Federal Land banks and other lenders has constituted a net saving.

In the study referred to, the conclusion that the Federal Land banks have not had an impact on the interest rate charged by other lenders was based on two types of evidence. First, there did not appear to be any narrowing of the differential between the interest rates charged by the various lenders and returns on high grade bonds for the period from 1910 to date. Second, insurance companies, whose primary objective is to maximize the return on their investment portfolio, have increased their share of the holdings of total farm mortgage debt which they certainly would not have done had the profitability of such investments declined to any important degree.

It has been pointed out that the reduction in the cost of farm mortgages has been greater than the possible saving in interest rates for those farmers who borrowed from the Federal Land banks because of the virtual elimination of the commission on mortgages that was so prevalent prior to 1917. Data collected in 1914 and 1915 indicated that the collection of commissions on new and extended mortgages amounted, on an annual basis, to about 0.5 percent of the outstanding mortgage debt.[26] By 1930 it was estimated that the cost of commissions each year was about 0.2 percent of the debt outstanding.[27] And at present, commissions are relatively uncommon. There is no way of knowing if the virtual elimination of the commission was due to the competitive influence of the Land Banks, which have never charged commissions. The trend toward the elimination of the commission may well have been similar to the trend toward equalization of regional rates of interest, which was well underway before 1917.

Commissions were important mainly in areas that had to import the credit for farm mortgages. Commissions were negligible in the

---

[26]C. W. Thompson, Costs and Sources of Farm-Mortgage Loans in the United States, U.S.D.A., Bul. No. 384 (July 31, 1916), pp. 2 and 9-10.

[27]Secretary of Agriculture, The Farm Debt Problem, House Doc. No. 9, 73rd Congress, 1st Session (March 27, 1933), p. 17.

New England states in 1914-15. They amounted to 0.3 percent in Iowa, but were 1 percent or more in several plains and western states. In general local credit institutions did not charge commissions and it seems likely that as these institutions developed with the growth of the state, commissions would have declined in any case. However, the Federal Land banks did provide a mechanism for attracting capital from national markets without requiring commissions and thus made it possible to eliminate commissions on the share of the mortgages held by those institutions.

Efforts to determine the effect of the Intermediate Credit System on interest rates on short-term loans have not given particularly illuminating results. It first needs to be noted that information on the cost of short-term credit for years prior to 1930 is rather meager. Reasonably reliable estimates for commercial banks probably exist for 1921 and 1930.[28] On the basis of these and other data it appears that for the period from 1920 through 1929 short-term farm loans from commercial banks probably carried an interest rate of 7.5 to 8.0 percent. For 1950 through 1959 the average rate for banks and Production Credit Associations was about 6.3 percent.

Probably the most sensitive indicator of changes in the cost of short-term business credit is the rate on prime commercial paper of 4- to 6- months maturity. During the 1920's the average annual rate on prime commercial paper was 5.1 percent; during the 1950's the rate was 2.6 percent. Thus the margin between the rate on short-term farm loans over prime commercial paper increased from approximately 2.5 or 3.0 percent during the twenties to about 3.8 percent during the fifties. Comparisons with other short-term interest rates, such as bank loans to business or rates on Federal Intermediate Credit Bank debentures, gave similar results.

The widening of the margin certainly does not imply that the Intermediate Credit System has resulted in an increase in the cost of short-term farm credit. Many other factors could be responsible for the increased margin — changes in the type and maturity of loans, increased operating costs, increased services.

A simple comparison of interest rates charged by various lenders is not adequate, of course, to reflect all of the considerations involved in competition among lenders. Two lenders may charge the same rate, but other conditions of the loan agreement or of the loans made may vary substantially. Differences in the size of the loan, the maturity of the loan, the ratio of the loan to the security,

---

[28]American Institute of Banking, Farm Credit Administration, 1934, pp. 90-92.

or the degree of risk accepted by the lender can mean that similarity of interest rates charged has little meaning. However, for the two main sets of comparisons that have been made — between the Federal Land banks and the insurance companies and between the Production Credit Associations and the banks — most of these differences seem to be rather unimportant. No one of the groups of lenders has specialized in high risk loans; in fact, quite the contrary seems to have been the case. The Land Banks have written mortgage loans with longer terms than insurance companies, but have also followed more stringent appraisal policies. The Production Credit Associations have probably loaned funds under conditions that were less risky than have been accepted by commercial banks, on the average. Only the Farmers Home Administration has attempted to make loans that involved an amount of risk substantially greater than that generally acceptable to the major private lending institutions.

G. Summary of Part II.

In Part I of this monograph it was shown that despite the great importance of capital when measured as the ratio of capital to output, or capital per worker, or as an expense, the supply of capital to agriculture has come primarily from internal sources. It was estimated that farm operators and landlords together provided about 90 percent of all the capital used in agriculture. In the early pages of Part II it was shown that the credit utilized by agriculture was derived from a wide variety of sources. Of the major institutional sources of credit, banks were the most important, supplying in excess of a quarter of agricultural credit in recent years. Next most important were the insurance companies which have supplied from 10 to 13 percent of total credit since 1940. All of the federally owned or supervised credit agencies are currently supplying about a fifth of farm credit. Individuals, merchants, dealers, and other miscellaneous groups of creditors are more important than any one of the institutional lenders and now provide approximately 40 percent of the farm credit outstanding.

The federally owned or supervised credit agencies either have had or still do have an element of government subsidy. In the case of the Land Bank System and the Intermediate Credit System, the subsidy was derived from the provision of interest-free capital, though other elements of subsidy still exist. All of the governmental capital in the Land Bank System was retired by June 30, 1947, and approximately three-fourths of the government capital invested in the Intermediate Credit System has now been retired. It is uncertain how much of a competitive advantage has been derived as a result of these subsidies. There is no way of determining how much of the subsidy was passed on to borrowers and how much was retained in net worth accounts. I lean to the view that a large part of the subsidy, or alternatively the saving in interest, was added to net worth accounts, especially after 1940. Both systems appear to have relatively high ratios of net worth to credit outstanding, even after one deducts the value of capital stock. Moreover, both systems seem to be adding to surplus accounts a very large share of their earnings and it is not at all clear that any significant advantage is currently being passed on to present borrowers. Unless the systems run into a very adverse period or expand at a rapid rate, it is reasonable to assume that at some time in the future net interest rates to borrower members will reflect the advantage derived from adding a part, perhaps a large part, of the interest subsidy or savings to the net worth accounts of the two systems.

The extent of specialization by different lenders was discussed in some detail, especially in the farm mortgage credit field. It is clear that there is a considerable degree of specialization, with each major type of lender tending to emphasize a rather specific type of mortgage. Differences were found with respect to the size of the mortgage, the term of the mortgage, the location of the borrower, the ratio of debt to the value of the asset pledged and the purposes for which the mortgages were made. It was found for example that the Land Banks were primarily refinancing institutions, that most loans for the transfer of farm real estate were made by sellers, and that of the institutional lenders, commercial banks and insurance companies were more important in this activity than were the Land Banks.

In the non-real estate credit field the differences were somewhat less sharp. It is rather well established that the Farmers Home Administration serves a clientele many of whom would have difficulty obtaining funds from other lenders. It was also fairly clear that the Production Credit Associations tend to serve farmers with relatively high net worths and who need a substantial amount of credit, but who could obtain credit from commercial banks.

The discussion of the degree of specialization by lenders may imply that there is a lack of competition in the farm credit field. I do not believe that this conclusion is warranted. Our discussion has emphasized the differences among the major institutional lenders and in a general way between the institutional lenders and individuals. But two points must be borne in mind. First, the institutional lenders all do some business that is competitive with another type of lender. It is at the extremes, large versus small loans, low equity versus high equity, short versus long term, where there is little direct competition between the major types of institutional lenders. In the middle, so to speak, the insurance companies and the Land Banks do compete for farm mortgages and the commercial banks and the Production Credit Associations serve similar borrowers. Second, there is a considerable degree of competition among any one of the groups of private institutional lenders and to a degree between certain of the federally owned or supervised credit agencies. Our discussion of the insurance companies, for example, has perhaps left the impression that we were here dealing with a single monolithic agency. In fact, quite the opposite is the case since in the areas where insurance companies do a significant part of the farm mortgage business, several insurance companies are seeking to gain the available business. In most agricultural areas a farmer has the choice of several banks with which to do business and while there is undoubtedly a considerable continuity of relationship between an individual farmer and an individual bank, the available data indicate that there is a considerable uniformity of interest rates among banks in a given area. Uniformity of rates can, of course, imply concerted action as well as competition. However, the fact that commercial bank loan rates to farmers are at approximately the same level as the rates found necessary by the Production Credit Associations implies that the bank rates are probably at or near the competitive level. It may also be noted that the Federal Land banks make loans for purposes similar to the purposes of some of the loans made by the Production Credit Associations. The existence of competition within various institutional groups and the degree of overlap among the major lending groups appear to provide a considerable degree of competition in the loans made to farmers.

III. AGRICULTURAL CREDIT POLICY

The present juncture in the development of American agriculture is a particularly difficult moment to define an adequate and desirable agricultural credit policy, but this is also a time when it is important that appropriate decisions be made. American agriculture is today faced with many difficult adjustment problems. Agricultural credit policy may be able to play some small role in facilitating those adjustments. It is equally important that we remember that inappropriate decisions with respect to agricultural credit may only increase the adjustment difficulties and place greater downward pressure on the returns to agricultural resources, especially labor. The present situation is one in which any change from current credit policies and institutions must be evaluated with great care. It would be far better to make no change in the farm credit situation than to adopt measures that might increase farm adjustment problems.

Changes in credit policy alone can make relatively little contribution to the solution of problems confronting farmers today. It may well be true that many individual farmers would find it profitable to use more credit and acquire new capital resources.

Unless other measures are taken to reduce the total quantity of resources used in agriculture, the final effect will be either to lower the level of net agricultural income or to increase the cost to the government of maintaining net agricultural income at any given level. The first of these effects would be considered to be desirable by no one and the second seems to make little economic or political sense.

No change should be made in credit policy that will lead to an increase in agricultural output unless there are other substantial benefits to be derived from the change. This statement may appear to be trite and unnecessary. After all, who would want to modify credit policy primarily to increase agricultural output? Two comments seem appropriate. First, there is a belief, how widespread I do not know, that a reduction in interest costs would result in an improvement of farm income. It seems obvious to many that any reduction in farmers' cost must necessarily benefit farmers. As is so often the case, what seems obvious from an unsophisticated economic analysis is fallacious, and the true effect is the opposite. Second, despite the fact that it is almost universally recognized that American agriculture is confronted with a surplus problem, many federal government agricultural programs have the obvious and direct consequence of increasing agricultural output. The agricultural conservation payments which subsidize investments that increase land productivity, the program for importation of foreign nationals for agricultural work, the Department of Agriculture's watershed program, and federal investment in irrigation and reclamation, are examples of programs that increase agricultural output, reduce the demand for labor in agriculture and contribute to the adjustment problems confronting farmers. It would be wholly inappropriate to modify agricultural credit policy in such a way that it also worked at cross purposes with the objective of increasing the return to farm families and unnecessarily required a more rapid rate of out-migration from agriculture.

The above comments are not meant to imply that any change in credit policy or any governmental program that has the effect of increasing agricultural output is to be condemned. Our national objectives as they relate to agriculture imply more than a satisfactory or reasonable level of income for farm people. These objectives also imply that agricultural products be produced efficiently and that the existing inequality of income distribution in agriculture should not be enlarged. American agriculture, through rapid advances in efficiency and productivity, has contributed substantially to the economic growth of our nation and it can continue to do so in the future, even though agriculture is now a relatively small segment of the national economy. Programs or activities that have an impact on net output with a value equal to or greater than all costs incurred should be inaugurated or maintained unless they have negative consequences for other important national objectives.[1]

If there were monopolistic elements in the supply of agricultural credit and the degree of monopoly could be reduced or eliminated by credit policy, the criterion of efficiency would commend such a change in credit policy, or if there were a gap in the provision of credit to agriculture due either to lack of knowledge or particular institutional arrangements such as property rights or legal restraints upon lending institutions, favorable considerations should be given to measures that would eliminate this gap. The present imbalance between output and demand at prevailing farm prices should not be used as an excuse to immobilize credit policy, though this imbalance must be recognized before undertaking any modification of agricultural credit policy, and the gain from changing the policy should be a clear and definite one.

A. Major Agricultural Credit Problems.

The earlier parts of this study and the other Research Studies dealing with farm credit programs have identified three major actual or potential farm credit problems. These problems will now be described briefly.

1. A large fraction of the short- and intermediate-term credit available to agriculture depends upon commercial banks whose source of loanable funds largely depends upon the bank deposits made locally. As a result, it is possible that a decline in income in a community may result in a restriction on loanable funds for farm operators at a time when the demand for such funds has increased. The possibility also exists that a general recession or depression might result in a sufficient reduction of bank deposits to force banks not to renew many outstanding loans or to prevent them from making new loans when such loans would alleviate economic distress among farmers. It cannot be said that either facet of this particular problem would never arise in actuality (though I think the probability of either one arising is very low indeed), despite the existence of the

[1]The comparison of the value of the net output and of the cost should be a marginal comparison and both private and social returns and costs should be included. Furthermore, the marginal gain and the marginal cost should be evaluated in terms of the prices that prevail after the program or activity has been undertaken. If the evaluation is made on the basis of prices that prevail prior to the program or activity, the scale will be too large in terms of the criterion of efficiency.

unit banking system in virtually all of the major agricultural regions.[2] Certainly the post-World War II recessions have not been of sufficient severity to have had a significant influence on the supply of loanable funds to farmers by commercial banks, nor have commercial banks restricted the amount of credit made available to farmers during the period of declining net farm operator income since 1951. It may be that in agricultural areas that have been adversely affected by weather conditions, lending institutions may not have been able to meet their increased credit needs from local sources. There was a substantial expansion in the volume of emergency loans of the Farmers Home Administration between January 1, 1956 and July 1, 1958. Whether this expansion was due to the inability or unwillingness of local banks to supply the loans or to the relatively favorable terms on which emergency credit is made available, the writer does not know. Undoubtedly both elements were involved. It may be noted that in the areas of heaviest concentration of emergency loans, the volume of loans at commercial banks increased during the same period of time.

2. The credit facilities for the transfer of farm real estate from one owner to another, especially into the hands of farm operators, may be inadequate to the task of achieving an orderly and reasonably rapid expansion in the size of farm operating units. As was noted in Part II, about two-thirds of all farm transfers involve the use of credit and of those farm transfers involving credit, the major institutional lenders financed less than one-half. Institutional lenders, either for legal or other reasons, generally cannot provide a loan in excess of 65 percent of the appraised value of the property involved. Given the fact that the total capital involved in a family-size unit of sufficient scale to provide a reasonable income for the farm family ranges from $50 to $100 thousand or more in many agricultural areas, few farm operators can acquire the necessary capital to become owner-operators when the down payment requirements are of this magnitude. The old saw that in order to become an owner-operator one either has to inherit or marry the land may be more true year by year, though it does need to be remembered that the fraction of land held by owner-operators has not declined in recent years and as a nation we apparently have too many rather than too few farm operators.

I do not think that we have sufficient knowledge to say with a high degree of certainty that the present arrangements for the transfer of land from one owner to another inhibit the expansion of

---

[2]Correspondent relations among unit banks, especially between country banks and city banks, undoubtedly help rural banks to meet local credit demands that may exceed the local credit supply.

farm size. Two opposite forces seem to be at work. First, the relatively large down payments required probably do limit for most farmers the size of the operating unit that they can purchase. Many farm operators have adjusted to this particular circumstance by renting additional land as a means of increasing the size of their operating unit. This is clearly indicated by the increase in numbers and average size of part-owner farms. Second, the large size of the down payment required to purchase land improves the relative position of existing owner-operators in acquiring land that becomes available for sale in their own community. In 1949 for example, 23 percent of all land purchases made were for the purpose of farm enlargement. Ten years later, 42 percent of the purchases made were for that purpose.[3] Farm enlargement, of course, is favored by other considerations and it is impossible to know how much of the increased importance of farm enlargement as the objective of land purchase has been due to the credit situation.

3. The credit requirements of farmers who require a very large ratio of debt to assets to achieve an economic size unit may not be adequately met by existing credit institutions. At the present time the Farmers Home Administration is the only credit agency that appears to be in a position to provide credit for those farmers who have potential managerial ability but need to borrow 80 to 90 percent of the total value of assets, capital as well as land, required to establish an economic size farm unit, and the limits that have been placed upon the Farmers Home Administration as to the size of the operating unit that can be established may mean that there exists a group of farmers, either actual or potential, who cannot become established on adequate sized units. The reason for considering this situation to be a problem rests more upon grounds of equity than upon grounds of economic efficiency. The inequity that exists in the present situation is presumably that most adequate sized farm units that are likely to exist in the future will be acquired either by inheritance or gift and cannot be acquired by individuals with limited financial resources. However, there is grave danger in moving too rapidly to eliminate such an inquity. The danger is that the farm operator who has such a high ratio of debt to the value of total assets is placed in considerable jeopardy of losing his net assets if adversity strikes him. It may well be for most persons with demonstrated managerial ability but limited financial assets that renting the land required for an adequate sized farm unit represents the superior alternative. This may be particularly true at the present juncture because of the relatively low net returns on farm land.

On the basis of the material presented in Parts I and II of this monograph and the other studies dealing with the farm credit

---

[3] The Farm Real Estate Market (October 1959), p. 15.

agencies, there are three aspects of the farm credit picture that I do not consider to present problems of major significance. These are aspects of farm credit that at one time or another in the development and consideration of credit policy have been raised as important issues. Whether they were issues at one time is largely irrelevant. The first is the cost of farm credit. The cost of short-term and production credit obtained from the major institutional lenders and the cost of farm mortgage credit from all sources appear to be at reasonable levels. The Production Credit Associations and the Federal Intermediate Credit banks, which appear to be efficiently operated organizations and can be considered to provide a competitive benchmark, do not appear to be able to provide farmers with credit at significantly lower rates of interest than provided by commercial banks. While the Federal Land banks provide mortgage credit at interest rates lower than that offered by any other category of lenders, this lower cost seems to be available primarily for a rather standardized type of mortgage which fails to meet the requirements of the vast majority of borrowers. Given the higher elements of risk that are involved in the mortgages made by many other lenders, the interest rate differentials do not appear to be unduly large.

The second is the maturity or term of agricultural credit. Farmers appear to have available to them credit on a wide variety of maturities ranging from very short-term notes to mortgages of 33 to 40 years. There may be some basis for the view that too little credit is available on terms of 3 to 7 years to cover capital investments on tenant-operated farms or on owner-operated farms with an existing mortgage. There have been some fairly significant changes in the number and importance of intermediate-term loans in recent years, and it appears likely that if there is sufficient demand for loans of the maturities noted that the supply will become available.

The third is the coordination of agricultural credit to monetary and fiscal policy. If consideration is restricted to loans made directly to farmers, I do not believe that there is any important problem involved in coordinating agricultural credit and monetary and fiscal policy, with the possible exception of those loanable funds that are made available by congressional appropriation and the difficulties that arise out of limitations on interest rates that can be either charged or paid. Agricultural credit should be subject to the same elements of restraint, discipline, or encouragement that is implied by the general efforts to constrict or expand the available money and credit supply. If interest rates rise as a result of an effort to reduce the rate of expansion of credit, agriculture should and does face the impact of the higher interest rates. Restrictions on bank credit through open-market operations or changing reserve ratios has an impact on the supply of commercial bank credit to agriculture just as it affects the supply of credit provided by banks in general.

There is a special and important, at least potentially, agricultural credit problem that has not been covered in the earlier parts of this study or in other studies referred to. It perhaps should not be posed as a problem, but more as a question that needs to be considered in conjunction with the evaluation of present agricultural credit policy or in connection with any suggested change in that policy. The question may be put as follows: Is there a significant danger of a large increase in foreclosures or other forms of distress transfer of farms if there were to be a decline in the value of farm land? Such a decline in the value of farm land might or might not be accompanied by a reduction in net farm operator income from recent levels. A decline in land prices could occur simply as a result of a re-evaluation of attitudes toward the price of farm land. Such a re-evaluation might be a consequence of a change in the rate at which future returns are discounted, either because of a general rise in interest rates or due to certain subjective elements. It could also be due to a substantial recombination of agricultural resources which had the effect of lowering the marginal product of land.

As has been indicated earlier, the ratio of total debt, including non-real estate debt as well as mortgage debt, to the total value of farm assets, has been lower in recent years than at any time since 1910 except for the years immediately following World War II. Compared to the early part of the 1920's the recent ratio certainly appears to be quite favorable. However, the ratio of all debt or of mortgage debt to the value of assets does not adequately depict the circumstances of farms that are mortgaged. Only a minority of farms are now mortgaged or have been since 1890 when data first became available. Thus the ratio of mortgage debt to value of farm real estate on the farms actually mortgaged is substantially higher than the ratio for all farms. Data are available for several decades only for full-owner farms, but their circumstances do not seem to be very different from that of all farms. In 1920 it was estimated that the ratio of mortgage debt to the value of mortgaged full-owner farms was 29 percent. In 1956 the ratio was 27 percent. Following 1920, the decline in land values and a transfer of non-real estate credit to mortgage credit increased the ratio to 42 percent in 1925 and it was still 40 percent in 1930.[4] The percentage of full-owner-operated farms with mortgages was 33.1 percent in 1956, which was somewhat less than in 1920 when 37.2 percent were

---

[4]Data from Statistical Abstract of the United States, 1959, p. 628 and The Farm Debt Problem, House Doc. No. 9, 73d Congress, 1st Session (March 27, 1933), pp. 8 and 15.

mortgaged. These comparisons with 1920, which indicate a rough equivalence for the years 1920 and 1956, are not meant to imply that foreclosures and distress transfers in the future are going to approximate the seriousness of the situation that prevailed from 1920 through 1935. It may be noted that a larger fraction of full-owner farms were mortgaged in 1940, namely 41 percent, than in either 1920 or 1956; that the ratio of debt to the value of these mortgaged farms was 42 percent; and that distress transfers, which averaged about 1.5 percent of all farms annually in 1940-41, gradually declined and have since stabilized at a level of approximately two-tenths of 1 percent. But the economic conditions that followed 1940, which included a rising land market and increasing levels of farm income, both in dollar and real terms, may be no more typical of the future than what happened after 1920.

Estimates of the distribution of the ratio of debt to value on mortgaged full-owner farms are available for 1925, 1928, 1932 and 1956. I have arbitrarily selected the part of the distribution representing ratios of 80 percent or more for these four years. The following percentage of mortgaged farms had debt value ratios of 80 percent or more: 1925, 7.7 percent; 1928, 9.8 percent; 1932, 13.1 percent; and 1956, 4.6 percent.[5] Between 1925 and 1928 farm land prices declined by about 5 percent and between 1925 and 1932 by about a third.[6] The inability of farmers to service their debts in the period from 1925 into the thirties was due, of course, to the very sharp decline in net farm income. But had the decline in land values been due primarily to a fall in land prices independent of current farm income, there would have been a considerable number of distress transfers of real estate during the period.

The present circumstances of farmers with a high ratio of debt to the value of their real estate perhaps does not call for more than a note of caution. It is most unlikely, given the present political climate, that net farm operator income will be permitted to decline significantly in the years immediately ahead. But a policy that would result in a significant increase in the number of farms operating with a high ratio of mortgage debt to value of land must recognize the possibility of a sharp increase in distress transfers and must weigh this negative aspect against the gains that might be achieved by such a policy.

---

[5] 1954 Census of Agriculture, Vol. III, Pt. 5, pp. 72-73; The Farm Debt Problem, p. 16; and David L. Wickens, Farm Mortgage Credit, U.S.D.A., Technical Bulletin No. 288 (1932), p. 57.

[6] Agricultural Finance Review, Vol. 21 (July 1959), p. 148.

B. Policy Recommendations for Agricultural Credit Policy.

Any significant change in agricultural credit policy must recognize that a major dilemma exists. This dilemma grows out of the fact that the average size of farm operating units must increase substantially over the next few years if the average return to farm families is to more closely approximate the returns realized by families owning comparable resources in the rest of the economy. The increase in the average size of operating units is required because of the impact of economic growth upon the structure of agriculture and because of the desirability of narrowing the gap between the returns to comparable human resources in the farm and nonfarm sectors.[7] Agricultural credit policy can be only one of a number of policies required to achieve the necessary adjustments. Other programs and measures must in fact play a much larger role than credit policy.

Stated briefly, the major purpose of agricultural credit policy should be to facilitate the recombinations of agricultural resources and to supply the credit needed for any new capital required or desirable as a result of the increased size of farm operating units and the reduction in labor input. In achieving this objective the major function of agricultural credit is to make possible the orderly transfer of existing capital and land resources in agriculture from the present farm operating units to a smaller number of larger and more efficient operating units. Credit policies should not be used to encourage the acquisition of new capital resources in agriculture, though the only reasonable restraint upon the acquisition of new resources is that credit not be subsidized and the borrowers should be required to pay the full cost of the credit utilized. Limited amounts of subsidized credit, as provided by the Farmers Home Administration in its operating emergency and farm ownership programs, may be justified in terms of other goals achieved, but it needs to be recognized that other goals are realized only at the expense of some aggravation of the already substantial adjustment problems of agriculture.

It is conceivable that credit should aid in the transfer of resources, especially labor out of agriculture, and thus make a contribution to agriculture's external adjustment problem. The few comments that I make here should not be considered as recommendations but are intended to be merely suggestive of the possible role that some type of credit might play in speeding up the transfer of resources out of agriculture. Other measures, such as the continuous

---

[7] An increase in the size of farm operating units must be accompanied by a decline in the absolute employment of labor in all categories if average farm family incomes, including the incomes of hired workers, are to increase.

maintenance of high levels of nonfarm employment; positive educational, informational, and employment services designed to ease the transition; and assistance in locating housing in nonfarm communities, are likely to contribute much more than anything that can be done through credit.

Credit programs that may merit some consideration as a means of improving the mobility of farm residents and easing the adjustment process might include the following: (a) a federal loan program for rural schools which would provide credit at low or zero interest rates for the construction of school buildings and purchase of transportation equipment; (b) a nonrecourse loan for farmers who are leaving agriculture made on the basis of the appraised value of all physical assets used in agriculture and perhaps also including household equipment; such loans would assure farmers of a minimum return on their assets and would make funds available to them to arrange for a change in residence;[8] (c) long-term, low interest rate loans to be made available by the federal government to attract nonfarm employment to rural communities; such loans might be combined with managerial assistance and should be made only in those circumstances where there is a reasonable chance that the business could be profitable after a period of years; (d) long-term and low interest rate loans for farm families that move from farm to nonfarm communities to cover the costs of movement, cost of maintenance for the family during the first few months and the amount of down payment on a house.

These suggestions may appear to be somewhat unorthodox. If credit programs are to have any role in easing and speeding up the adjustment process, traditional types of credit are likely to prove inadequate and different forms of credit involving in all likelihood some element of subsidy must be made available. Direct grants could be used as a substitute for credit in the four roles noted above. However, direct grants may be less achievable from the political standpoint and might, in fact, be less appealing to the recipients than would specialized loans of the kind described.

The remainder of the monograph is devoted to a presentation of a series of general recommendations with respect to farm credit policy. The recommendations deal exclusively with loans available to farmers for the acquisition of real estate and capital items and for operating and consumption purposes. The loan activities of the

---

[8] Such loans would be made a few months in advance of the actual sale of the assets involved. It would be necessary to use some such technique as a public auction if actual sales value were less than the appraised value.

Commodity Credit Corporation, the Rural Electrification Administration, or the banks for cooperatives are excluded from consideration.

1. The legal, institutional and economic framework should encourage a variety and diversity of credit sources for farmers. This condition is now reasonably well met by agricultural credit policy in the United States. Most farmers do have a variety of credit sources available to them and such variety is necessary if their credit needs are to be effectively met. Credit institutions organized for profit such as commercial banks, institutions organized cooperatively, such as Land Banks and the Production Credit Associations, and governmentally owned and operated credit agencies such as the Farmers Home Administration tend both to compete with each other and to complement each other. This recommendation is certainly consistent with maintaining and encouraging the Land Banks and the Production Credit Associations and the Intermediate Credit Banks. The recommendation is inconsistent, however, with any measures that would aid the federally sponsored agencies in becoming the dominant element in the supply of agricultural credit. One may conclude, both from their structure and their past history, that the federally sponsored agencies do not have sufficient flexibility to provide all or even most of the credit used by farmers. Both the Land Banks and the Production Credit System have found it necessary or desirable to standardize their operations to a very substantial degree, but the credit needs of farmers are very diverse and cannot be met by a limited number of forms of credit. The extent of standardization has probably resulted primarily from two influences. First is the practice of having a single rate of interest on all mortgages written by each Land Bank and on all loans made by each Production Credit Association. The characteristics of these institutions make it extremely difficult for them to charge varying rates dependent upon the size of the loan, the degree of risk involved, or the term of the loan. The second element leading to standardization is a result of one of the great strengths of these two institutions, namely their ability to obtain funds from national credit markets. Relatively low risk farm loans may well be required to sell bonds or debentures at attractive rates.

These comments about certain characteristics of the federally sponsored credit agencies are neither meant to degrade those agencies nor to imply that they do not play an important or necessary role in agricultural credit. Each of the other agencies has significant limitations, and no one of them could serve all or most of the credit needs of agriculture. Commercial banks have legal and ideological limitations that would prevent them from becoming an important element in the supply of long-term credit to agriculture. The fact that individuals play such an important role in the provision of credit for real estate transfers indicates that there is an important sector of the mortgage credit market not now being filled by the institutional lenders as a group.

The purpose of the remarks about the federally sponsored agencies is to underscore another point, namely that subsidies should not be used to allow or encourage the cooperative agencies to expand their share of the farm loan business. The past history of these organizations, especially since 1940, does not imply that either one of them has any intention of expanding its role by the use of governmental subsidies. The Federal Land Banks have already repaid all of the governmental capital invested in them, and the Production Credit System is making rapid strides in the same direction. Certain elements of subsidy or special treatment still prevail, only the Production Credit Associations are subject to all state and federal income taxes and all other state and local taxes applicable to any business. The franchise taxes paid by the Intermediate Credit Banks are probably less than a private business firm would pay on the same earnings and, in any case, the franchise taxes are perhaps more appropriately considered as a flexible payment of interest on governmental capital than as a tax.[9] The Federal Land banks pay very few taxes. The Land Banks and Land Bank Associations are not subject to the federal income tax, nor to state and local income taxes; and Federal Land Bank bonds are still exempt from state and local income taxation, though subject to all federal income taxes. Since other financial institutions such as insurance companies do receive special federal income tax treatment, it is not at all certain what would constitute fair and equitable taxation of the Land Banks and of the Intermediate Credit Banks. Yet the implicit subsidy involved here is probably important enough to warrant removing whatever competitive advantage may be derived from the current special treatment.

2. The amount of subsidized credit made available for farmers should be limited and provided only to carefully defined groups of farmers or in carefully defined circumstances. Farmers as a whole can obtain no long-run gain in income from low subsidized interest rates. Existing owners of land can realize a capital gain from a lowering of the interest rate, but individuals who purchase land subsequent to the lowering of the rate would gain nothing from the

---

[9]The franchise tax paid by the Intermediate Credit Banks is equal to 25 percent of its earnings remaining after it has allocated 25 percent of those earnings to a reserve account. Moreover, the maximum amount of the franchise tax is equal to the amount of government capital invested in the Banks multiplied by the average rate on all U.S. Government obligations issued to the public during the preceding fiscal year.

existence of a low and subsidized farm mortgage rate.[10] Any monetary gain that farmers might realize as a result of reduced interest rates would be rather promptly offset by a reduction in the return on the capital resources that they themselves owned. This would come about as a result of increased agricultural output and reduction in the prices of farm products. In addition, a subsidized interest rate would lower the demand for labor and result either in a reduction in farm employment or a lowering of the return to existing workers in agriculture. Only if credit were rationed so that the amount used at the lower interest rate were not greater than before would farmers gain an amount equal to the reduction in the interest cost. Such rationing would not only present insuperable administrative difficulties, but would also introduce significant inequities within agriculture and result in economic inefficiency.

3. The Federal Intermediate Credit banks and commercial banks should be urged to reappraise the role of the Intermediate Credit Banks in rediscounting agricultural paper or in making loans to commercial banks using agricultural papers as security. One of the original objectives of the Intermediate Credit Bank System was to provide a source of funds for commercial banks and other credit or financing institutions serving agriculture. For a variety of reasons the Intermediate Credit Banks were never used to any considerable extent in this way by the commercial banks. One of the reasons for the small use of the Intermediate Credit Bank service was the small margin permitted between the bank and the Intermediate Credit Banks discount rate and the rate charged the farmer.

Since there is no legal limitation on the total charges made by Production Credit Associations for the provision of credit to farmers because most such associations charge fees in addition to the specified interest rate, the Intermediate Credit Banks should not have to impose a requirement that the interest cost to the borrower be equal to the Intermediate Credit Banks discount rate plus a specified margin. If commercial banks rediscounted with or borrowed from the Intermediate Credit Banks, the credit that commercial banks could provide would be less dependent upon variations in the amount of their deposits. While many, if not most, country commercial banks have relationships with correspondent banks that provide them access to funds, there are undoubtedly many situations in which a cordial relationship between the Intermediate Credit Banks and commercial banks in rural areas could serve to stabilize the supply of credit available to a community. Because of the limited number of Production Credit Associations — there are

---

[10] In fact, a farmer with limited capital may find it more difficult to purchase land when interest rates are low because of the increase in the absolute amount of equity required.

now less than 500 — many farmers can borrow from Production Credit Associations only at the cost of some inconvenience. There would seem to be some benefits to be derived by making the facilities of the Intermediate Credit Banks available to borrowers through a much larger number of credit institutions.

4. Federal insurance programs for two types of agricultural credit should be established. One should be for long-term real estate mortgage credit and the other for intermediate-terms from three to ten years. The objective of these two insurance programs should be primarily that of aiding in the establishment of adequate sized farm production units. As has been indicated earlier the amount of capital required to establish an efficient farm operating unit has grown substantially in recent decades and will continue to grow in the future. The difficulty of obtaining adequate capital may be increasing and may become even greater in the future. The insurance program for mortgage credit should differentiate between two general categories of situations. First, an insurance program should be made available to all lenders for the more or less standard institutional mortgage loan involving a ratio of debt to value of the real estate of 65 percent or less. Any mortgage that met certain standards such as the reasonableness of the appraised value, the character of the borrower, and a suitable relationship between estimated earnings and required payments on the mortgage would be acceptable for such insurance. There should be no actual or implied control over the interest rates charged, since such controls generally mean that the program would be operative only part of the time. Second, an insurance program should be developed for real estate mortgages which provide low equity, long maturities, and perhaps partial amortization. Such mortgages should be available only under rather stringent conditions; (a) the farm unit to be established should be of adequate size to provide a satisfactory level of income under reasonably good management; (b) the insurance should be made available only on the basis of farm plans developed and followed by the borrowers. Professional service for developing the plans should be provided and a degree of management assistance supplied during at least a specified number of years or until the amount of the mortgage has been reduced to a level assumed reasonable for a standard mortgage insurance contract.

The other type of insurance program should be made available for intermediate-term credit. The value of the non-real estate physical assets required for an efficient operating unit is often measured in tens of thousands of dollars. In the past and at present most of the funds required for this investment have been supplied by farm operators. But if the process of adjustment in farm sizes is to be speeded up, a special program may be required to supply credit for these needs. An insurance program for intermediate-term credit of this kind should be operated in much the same way as the insurance program for the long-term low equity mortgage financing and could be administered by the same agency.

If agricultural credit is to play more than a passive role in the recombinations of resources that appear both desirable and, to a degree, inevitable, some rather drastic changes in the types of credit available must be made. However, the dangers and difficulties in these undertakings should not be underestimated. An insurance program for the more or less standard farm mortgage loan would probably not add significantly to the supply of mortgage credit, but would protect credit institutions under unforeseen adverse economic circumstances.

There are two main difficulties that should be evaluated in connection with the other insurance programs. First, these programs may add substantially to the supply of farm credit, particularly in the mortgage field, and thus result in a further increase in the price of land. I know of no way of measuring the possible impact of such a program on the price of land. Reasonably reliable statistical estimates can be made of the impact of a reduction in the interest rate on land prices, but I have not been able to devise a test for the effect of greater availability of credit. But it appears reasonably certain, at least to me, that these programs would result in an increase in the demand for land. As a result of the program there would be more potential land buyers who could meet the equity requirements than would be the case if the programs did not exist. Given the low average level returns on land at present, the net effect might not be very large. But I do not know how we can be certain even of that. Second, there is a considerable danger, given the present prices of land, that farm operators who participated in such low equity financing would be subjected to a loss of their own limited capital. Even if the real estate mortgages were only partially amortized, the fixed payments required annually would still be of a very considerable magnitude on efficient operating units in many parts of American agriculture. Thus the potential gains in economic efficiency that might result from such insurance programs need to be weighed against the costs that would be involved if any considerable fraction of farmers participating in the program were forced to liquidate their enterprises.

5. <u>The various interest rate ceilings or limitations that effect agricultural credit, whether imposed by federal or state governments, should be removed.</u> Currently the Federal Land banks cannot charge more than 6 percent on their farm mortgage loans and until quite recently they could not pay more than 5 percent on bonds

issued.[11] Many states have limits on the interest rate charged on agricultural loans. If such limits are effective and enforced on the major institutional lenders, the net consequence to the farmer is that of increasing his cost of borrowing. When it becomes unprofitable for the institutional lenders to loan at these rates, farmers who require credit are then forced to turn to other types of institutions and pay higher interest rates. Admittedly in many instances the legal rates are not enforced or various subterfuges are used to avoid them. The Production Credit Associations, for example, in several states with interest rate limitations, are able to function only by charging various kinds of fees. Banks can and have avoided such interest rate ceilings by requiring that the borrower keep a minimum proportion of his loan on deposit with the bank. If there had been an excuse for such ceilings and limitations, the credit markets serving agriculture today seem to be sufficiently competitive to make the effects of these ceilings and limitations both capricious and undesirable. Certainly when it is seen that a cooperative farm credit group such as the Production Credit Associations, with excellent access to national credit markets, with some element of government subsidy, and operating exclusively for the interest of the farmer borrowers, finds it necessary to in fact violate the interest rate ceilings in many states, it should seem obvious that these ceilings are not serving a reasonable function.

---

[11]It has been noted earlier that interest rates charged by a given Federal Land Bank or a Production Credit Association are uniform at any given time, though rates vary from bank to bank or association to association. This description of interest rate policy does not indicate that the level of rates charged fails to reflect changes in interest rates over time. In fact, the rates charged by the two sets of institutions are quite responsive to general changes in interest rates as reflected by the costs of borrowing through the issuance of Land Bank bonds or Intermediate Credit Bank debentures.

Research Study Five

FEDERAL CREDIT PROGRAMS IN THE HOUSING SECTOR OF THE ECONOMY: AN AGGREGATIVE ANALYSIS

James Gillies
University of California
Los Angeles

"I suggest that our Federal Housing Programs are in urgent need of reappraisal which, if not agonizing, ought to be at least bold, imaginative and searching. Instead of continuing and expanding activities which were developed to deal with the problems of yesteryear, we must re-examine their place in a high level economy and in the light of the federal government's commitments under the Employment Act."

Leo Grebler
Proceedings of the American Economic Association, May 1960, pp. 330-331.

PREFACE

This report, Federal Credit Programs in the Housing Sector of the Economy: An Aggregative Analysis, was prepared for the Commission on Money and Credit during the summer of 1960. Its major purpose is to highlight the impact of various federal housing credit programs on prices, resource allocation, economic stability and economic growth.

The study is not a research study of the normal type, since the analysis is based almost entirely upon facts presented in the various related reports presented to the Commission. I have not, therefore, documented the material on which the conclusions in this report are based; the sources of all facts mentioned in this study are the Research Studies listed in the Appendix. I do not wish to imply, however, that the authors of the other reports would necessarily have drawn the same conclusions from the facts that they present, as I have.

In addition to the heavy borrowing from the Studies presented to the Commission, I have had the good fortune of having had almost daily discussions of the subject matter of this study with my colleagues – Leo Grebler, Fred Case, Lee Burns, David Huff and Frank Mittelbach – of the Real Estate Research Program of the Graduate School of Business Administration at UCLA. They do not necessarily agree with all or any of my conclusions – and in certain instances strongly disagree.

I am also indebted to Bertrand Fox, Eli Shapiro and George Brinnegar for their astute observations and penetrating suggestions.

James Gillies

Los Angeles

January 1962

SUMMARY AND RECOMMENDATIONS[1]

1. There are three major government programs in the housing sector of the economy: underwriting activities, secondary market operations, and community development programs.

2. In general the government credit programs for housing in the decade of the fifties have:

- been noncompetitive with traditional, institutional lenders;
- operated over the period to increase prices and costs;
- increased the flow of funds into residential constructions by approximately $18 billion—an amount equivalent to 12 percent of all expenditure on residential construction during the period;
- increased the total housing stock by an additional 1.5 million units beyond what would have been built without the programs;
- operated to reinforce general stabilization programs;
- had no appreciable influence on the federal budget;
- not materially improved the housing status of the very low-income groups in society.

The costs of the federal government programs in the 1950's have been indirect costs—the loss of alternative types of production, and the inflationary impact.

3. Specifically, the underwriting programs have:

- substantially increased the proportion of residential mortgage debt held by lending institutions;
- influenced the flow of building resources towards single family home construction;
- eased the terms and conditions under which mortgage money could be borrowed;
- increased mortgage lending competition in local market areas;
- markedly increased the amount of mortgage lending activity by commercial banks;
- enabled mutual savings banks to expand their holdings of residential mortgages;
- increased the proportion of residential mortgage loans in life insurance companies' portfolios;
- had little impact on savings and loan associations;
- assisted mortgage bankers in increasing their level of activities;
- improved the flow of mortgage funds among markets within the nation;

---

[1]The summary points are stated in terms of broad generalizations and, as with all generalizations, have qualifications.

- increased the flow of investment capital into the housing sector;
- increased house construction from 7 to 15 percent in the decade of the fifties above the level which would have been attained without the programs;
- diverted resources into housing from other long-term types of investment opportunities;
- contributed to the general rise in prices during the decade;
- been no charge against the federal budget for insuring operations, and only a very modest charge for direct lending operations;
- contributed to short-run stabilization policies;
- contributed to the rising interest rates on government securities.

4. There are two major secondary market facilities—the Federal Home Loan Bank System and the Federal National Mortgage Association.

Specifically, the Federal Home Loan Bank System has:

- contributed to the rate of growth of savings and loan associations in the residential mortgage market;
- increased the volume of house construction 2 to 3 percent above the level that would have been attained without the FHLBS;
- exerted some pressure on short-term money rates;
- operated without charge to the federal budget;
- operated, on occasion, counter to short-run stabilization policy;
- little likelihood of being an effective fiscal policy weapon during a serious depression.

The Federal National Mortgage Association has:

- increased the flow of resources into the residential mortgage market;
- increased residential construction 4 to 6 percent above the level that would have been attained if the FNMA had not operated;
- increased prices and costs in the housing sector;
- increased the proportion of VA-guaranteed loan financing in the nation;
- been a direct charge against the federal budget;
- operated in the short-run in an anti-stabilization fashion;
- influenced short-term money rates;
- possibilities for operation as an effective compensatory fiscal device in periods of serious depression.

5. Direct participation programs in the housing sector are of three types–community facilities operations, public housing and urban renewal.

The Community Facilities Program has:

- not influenced aggregate levels of prices, employment or growth;
- not influenced national monetary, debt and fiscal policy;
- been only a minor charge against the federal budget;
- had very little fiscal flexibility.

The Public Housing Program has:

- had no impact on aggregate levels of prices, employment and growth in the 1950's;
- not influenced national monetary, debt, or fiscal policy;
- been only a minor charge against the federal budget;
- had very little fiscal flexibility.

The Urban Renewal Program has:

- had no impact on general levels of prices, employment, or growth;
- not influenced general monetary, debt, or fiscal policies;
- no fiscal flexibility;
- been only a minor charge against the federal budget.

I. INTRODUCTION

The environment within which federal credit programs in the housing sector operated in the 1950's was exceedingly different from the environment which gave birth to the programs in the early 1930's. When the Federal Home Loan Bank System was organized, financial institutions involved in residential mortgage financing were faced with a major liquidity crisis; when the Federal Housing Administration insured loan program was introduced, housing construction in the nation was less than 100,000 units annually; when the Home Owners Loan Corporation was established, borrowers were losing their homes and some municipalities were insolvent; when the Public Housing Administration was conceived, elimination of unemployment was of more direct concern than elimination of slums. In short, the programs were developed in a period of serious depression as much to help solve the problems generated by the depression as to meet specific housing needs. Indeed, they were designed to bring order out of chaos in the mortgage market, to support financial institutions, to stimulate employment, and to finance municipal government.

In the post-World War II period, the situation has been completely different. The economy has operated at or close to full employment, lending institutions have grown substantially, and funds are flowing into the residential mortgage market at unprecedented rates. In only one year during the decade of the fifties were there less than one million nonfarm housing units constructed in the nation, and in the decade over $163 billion was spent on residential construction. Residential mortgage debt outstanding increased from $53.6 billion in 1950 to $145.3 billion at the end of 1959, and in 1959 the net increase in mortgage debt outstanding was approximately $19 billion. In fact, in 1955, 1956, and 1959 nearly 50 percent of all funds invested in mortgages, corporate securities and federal and municipal long-term bonds were placed in mortgages.

There can be no doubt that federal credit programs played an important part in housing and mortgage markets in the past decade. Housing starts financed with FHA-insured or VA-guaranteed loans ranged from a high of 51 percent of all private housing starts in 1950 and 1955 to a low of approximately 24 percent in 1958. In no year during the 1950's was government-under-written residential mortgage debt less than 40 percent of total residential mortgage debt outstanding and at the end of 1959 government-under-written residential mortgage debt amounted to $54 billion—a sum greater than the total outstanding debt of all state and local governments combined.

The impact of the government programs, however, extends beyond the underwriting operations of the FHA and the VA. The Federal

Home Loan Bank System has played an important role in the growth of savings and loan associations in the past decade. Similarly, the FNMA with its various programs has influenced patterns of mortgage activity. Finally, direct lending programs under the aegis of various government agencies have been in operation in the housing sector.

Given this large volume of activity, during periods of relatively full employment, by federal credit programs designed primarily to meet the problems of depression, it is indeed pertinent, if not imperative, to ascertain what the actual impacts of the programs have been on other sectors of the economy. Have the programs led to major reallocation of resources in favor of housing or have they acted primarily to raise prices? Have they improved operations of lending institutions in the mortgage market or have they created privileged positions? Have they contributed to improved housing in the nation or have they merely changed the pattern of house construction? Have they led to instability in the economy as a whole at the price of stability in the housing sector? Have they worked with or against general monetary policy to maintain full employment? Have they contributed to the problems of managing the public debt? Have they been a major expense to the Treasury? Have they contributed to fiscal flexibility? Have they contributed to economic growth? Only by answering these and related questions is it possible to evaluate the appropriateness of current housing programs for a near full-employment economy; similarly, it is impossible to recommend changes in existing programs or adoption of new ones without a clear understanding of the impact of current programs on the economy.

Evaluation of the operation of various government housing programs automatically implies the existence or establishment of criteria against which to measure activities. In this study, programs are evaluated in terms of the programs themselves—their objectives and the degree to which these objectives have been achieved. Secondly, programs are examined in relation to their impact outside of the sector in which they are designed to operate, particularly in terms of national goals for the economy and society. Finally, they are assessed in terms of the general structure of the society in which they operate; for example, programs in the United States are normally considered to be most desirable when they strengthen the framework of a free-enterprise economy.

While all three types of evaluations are used in assessing programs, the expanding pattern of activity of federal credit programs in the housing sector makes particularly pressing an understanding of (1) the relationship of the programs to other financial segments of the economy and (2) the relationship of housing programs to monetary, fiscal, and debt management policy. The housing programs are so large and so pervasive that they cannot be considered in terms of housing goals alone; they are integrally linked with over-all programs designed to maintain full employment, price stability, and economic growth. Consequently, these relationships are given special attention throughout the report.

Implicit in a choice of criteria for evaluation of federal housing programs is acceptance of the basic premise that there is a need for housing programs in the United States. However, the questions may well be raised—should there be underwriting of mortgage loans? Should efforts be made to remove inadequate housing? Should veterans be accorded special advantages in the residential mortgage markets, etc.? The answers to these and associated queries depend to some extent on the opportunity cost to society of having such programs, but unquestionably they depend much more upon society's evaluation—through Congress—of social priorities. Certainly, from the pragmatic view of assessing policy it is more meaningful to assume that the programs are an integral part of the social and economic structure of the nation and to determine how they can operate effectively, in terms of efficient resource allocation and over-all national economic policy, than to debate the question of whether or not they should exist. Consequently, in this study the programs are assumed to be a fact of the political, social, and economic life of the nation.

In analyzing national objectives, it is essential to deal with aggregates. And yet, in studying housing and mortgage activities this can be particularly misleading, since housing and mortgage operation are oriented toward local markets. The initiation of housing demand depends on conditions in local areas and the granting of a mortgage loan is made by an officer of a local lending institution or an individual in a local area. The wide range of differences among local areas and even among lending institutions within local areas make aggregative judgments about housing and mortgage markets difficult. This is not to argue that national policies do not affect local markets, but rather to suggest that activities in local areas can determine the efficiency of national programs. It is for this reason that the role of individual lending institutions is implicitly given great emphasis in this study.

Direct lending programs of the federal government in the housing sector are also reviewed. During the 1950's these programs, in relation to total activity in the economy as a whole and the housing sector in particular, have been small. However, the programs have important implications for monetary, debt, and fiscal policy, especially when there is a general change in levels of economic activity, and therefore they are examined in some detail.

The analysis is divided among five sections: a description of the programs; the impact of the programs on financial institutions; the effect of the programs on resource allocation, price levels and economic growth; the influence of the activities on monetary, debt, and fiscal policy; and a final section of recommendations for changes in the programs and suggestion for additions to the federal credit programs in the housing sector. The Home Owners' Loan Corporation is not discussed in the report and the thorny questions raised by the Shaw-Gurley hypothesis are not examined in detail.

II. THE MAJOR PROBLEMS

Since the early 1930's, when the federal government first took an active role in housing markets, four basic types of housing programs have evolved: underwriting programs, secondary facility operations, community development activities and emergency aids. With the exception of the first two types of operations, about the only thing in common among the programs is that they deal with housing; and, currently, with the exception of the VA-guarantee program, and the Federal Home Loan Bank System, they are all administered by the Housing and Home Finance Agency. In philosophy, as well as economic impact, they differ greatly.

Underwriting Programs[1]

The two major underwriting programs in the housing area are the Veterans Administration home loan guarantee program established by the Servicemen's Readjustment Act of 1944 as amended (58 Stat. 284) and the home and project mortgage insurance programs of the Federal Housing Administration (FHA) authorized by Sections 203 (b) and 207 of Title II of the National Housing Act of 1934 as amended (48 Stat. 1246). In addition, there are the FHA property improvement program; the VA direct home loan program established in 1950 to provide loans in areas of the nation where VA loans were unavailable; and finally, a large number of specialized FHA-insured loan programs for senior citizen housing, victims of natural disasters, urban renewal and redevelopment programs, military and defense housing, mobile home parks and cooperative housing projects.

The FHA program, originally established to generate demand for housing, thereby stimulating employment and bringing order out of the then existing chaos in the mortgage market, has long

---

[1]This material is drawn largely from George F. Break, "Federal Loan Insurance Programs for Housing," Research Study One in Federal Credit Agencies, prepared for the Commission on Money and Credit (Englewood Cliffs, N.J.: Prentice-Hall, Inc., 1963).

outlived its original functions. Indeed, currently, the objectives of the program are to promote sound financing of real property, stabilization in the mortgage market and improved housing standards. Similarly, the VA program, inaugurated to enable servicemen to acquire housing standards that they presumably would have had if they had not entered the services, has been replaced, if not explicitly at least implicitly, by the goal of providing servicemen with mortgage credit at terms more favorable than those generally available in the market.

The genius of the FHA program (and the VA-guarantee operations) at its inauguration was that it operated on both the supply and demand side of the mortgage market at the same time. In essence, it created a new environment within which mortgage lending took place. By enabling borrowers to acquire loans for longer periods of time, at higher ratio to lending value and at lower interest rates than were available under conventional financing, the program stimulated housing demand. At the same time by underwriting some of the risk of mortgage lending it encouraged borrowers to make such loans. It is important to note, however, that the lower interest rate was probably not the most significant change for borrowers under the program—the important factors were the longer terms and higher ratio loans.

It is of course fundamental to the successful operation of the FHA-insured and VA-guaranteed programs that lending institutions be willing to make loans. The initiation of the program, with the exception of the direct lending operations under the VA, lies with private lenders. Consequently, FHA and VA operations must be and are closely allied to lending policies and philosophies—which vary greatly from market to market—of private lenders. Since lenders have alternative investment opportunities the FHA and VA programs cannot retain their effectiveness when they are out of line with general investment market conditions.

There can be no doubt about the success of the FHA and VA operations. In fiscal 1958, new FHA and VA commitments to insure exceeded $10 billion and amounted to over 58 percent of all commitments acquired by all federal credit programs. Indeed, in the decade 1949-59, FHA and VA credit commitments were $27 billion greater than those of all other programs of the federal government. Translated in terms of the market for housing this volume of commitments meant that in seven of the years between 1946 and 1958 FHA and VA mortgage recordings exceeded 30 percent of all nonfarm mortgage recordings of $20,000 or less, and from the end of 1945 to the end of 1956 about 50 percent of all nonfarm institutional residential mortgage lending was insured or guaranteed. At the end of 1957, FHA and VA commitments underwrote about 44 percent of all residential mortgage debt outstanding in the United States.

In terms of the volume of new construction the pattern is somewhat less clear. In three of the post-World War II years—1947, 1950 and 1955—FHA-insured and VA-guaranteed loans were utilized to finance 50 percent or more of all private nonfarm housing starts. In other years, for example 1957-58, the programs were involved in financing less than 30 to 35 percent of the total.

Neither the FHA nor VA program has required extensive Treasury support. Indeed, the FHA program has consistently taken in more funds from insurance operations, fees and default proceedings than it has expended for administration and to meet obligations. On the average during the last decade receipts have exceeded disbursements by $44 million per year.

The VA program, on the other hand, levies no guarantee fee equivalent to the FHA insurance premium and pays its obligations in cash, and therefore it has always required funds from the federal budget. These have been modest, amounting to only $315 million by mid-1959, an amount only slightly higher than the programs existing assets—$295 million. The VA direct lending program is financed by funds borrowed from the Treasury through a revolving fund operation. As of the end of 1959 annual net budget expenditures amounted to $85 million.

In essence, therefore, the FHA and VA programs have been essentially self-supporting during a period of great activity. Whether this will continue to be the case depends on whether or not the nation experiences a major economic collapse with an extremely high level of mortgage default. Barring this situation, the FHA will continue to be self-supporting. If the VA direct lending program were stopped, as recommended by President Eisenhower in the 1960 Budget Message, and the operations of the VA transferred to the FHA, the charge to the budget would be even less.

Secondary Market Facilities

There are two programs with which the federal government is associated that provide facilities for the purchase and sale of mortgages—the Federal Home Loan Bank System and the Federal National Mortgage Association.

The Federal Home Loan Bank System.[2] The Federal Home Loan Bank System was established by Congress in 1932 as a central

---

[2]For a complete analysis of the operations of the Federal Home Loan Bank System see Ernest Bloch, "The Federal Home Loan Bank System," Research Study Three in Federal Credit Agencies, prepared for the Commission on Money and Credit (Englewood Cliffs, N.J.: Prentice-Hall, Inc., 1963).

reserve system for institutions engaged in residential financing. While it was organized to serve all types of lending institutions, through the years the FHLB System has been used primarily by savings and loan associations.

The system consists of three parts: the Board, the 11 district banks, and the member institutions. All the outstanding stock of the banks is owned by member institutions so in one sense it is now a private organization, but the Board, which consists of three members appointed by the President, has considerable authority and sufficient responsibilities to make the System an integral part of the credit structure of the nation. The Board plays an important role in the selection of the officers and directors of member banks and all debentures of the banks are issued on a consolidated basis by the Board. Moreover, the Board administers the Federal Savings and Loan Insurance Corporation, which insures the savings in all federal savings and loan associations and in those state chartered institutions which apply and qualify for insurance. The Board also charters savings and loan associations and in the early 1930's was associated with the operation of the Home Owners Loan Corporation.

The original function of the System was, and remains, to assist member institutions in their operations by supplying a secondary credit accommodation for members. The need for such an institution is essential, given the general nature of savings and loan associations operations. Associations receive the funds which they invest from individuals who in turn are given shares (in mutual associations) or investment certificates (in stock associations). The majority of shareholders consider the association much like a bank in that they expect to be able to withdraw their funds on demand. While there is a time stipulation with respect to removal of funds in associations, by any meaningful definition the liabilities of associations are highly liquid.

At the same time, associations invest the bulk of their funds—again as a legal requirement—on the security of residential real property. The majority of their assets are in the form of long-term mortgages—traditionally highly illiquid assets. Consequently, they are financial institutions which operate with liquid liabilities backed up by almost completely illiquid assets. Under such circumstances, the need for a source of liquidity is apparent, and since liquidity must come from selling or pledging mortgages, it follows that such liquidity involves a secondary market for mortgages.

Through the years the importance of the FHLB as a liquidity source to meet major withdrawals has declined—or at least moved into the background. In the post World War II period and particularly during the 1950's the FHLB has functioned more as a lender of first resort for member institutions than as a liquidity source. In other words, member associations have utilized the services of the banks to obtain funds to meet short-run situations. This use has developed since the balance between savings growth and the demand for funds in the postwar period has not always been equal—in the periods of rapid recovery after recession in 1950, 1955 and 1959 the demand for mortgage advances increased more rapidly than savings in associations, and in those years advances outstanding from the FHLB increased $380, $550 and $840 million, respectively. In addition, advances were highest in areas of greatest growth—the Far West, Southwest and Middle West. Consequently, the FHLB System has added to its original function of providing a source of liquidity in case of emergency the additional function of providing funds to meet short-run needs, and it has thereby increased the volume of funds that associations can effectively invest in residential real property. Because of both operations—short- and long-run—it is fair to conclude that the FHLB has transferred some liquidity problems from the associations to the System.

The impact of the FHLB System on association growth has unquestionably been substantial. During the postwar period, share capital in savings and loan associations throughout the nation increased from about $11 billion in 1948 to $48 billion in 1958. In fact, approximately 32 percent of all the savings growth in lending institutions that lend on the security of residential real property occurred in savings and loan associations. On a regional basis the pattern of growth is even more remarkable; for example, in California assets of savings and loan associations increased by 300 percent between 1948 and 1958.

Clearly, one of the most significant factors in the growth has been the insurance of shareholder's accounts and investment certificates by the FSLIC. Without this insurance, the savings public, mindful of the problems of many commercial institutions in the 1930's, would probably not have been as willing to place their funds in associations—even with the opportunity of earning higher rates of return than in other comparable institutions.

Moreover, the liquidity provided by the FHLB's to member institutions has had an important bearing on the lending patterns and policies of associations. They have been able to advance more funds to finance residential real estate transactions because of this facility than otherwise would have been the case.

The Federal Home Loan Bank Board is not supported by the Treasury. Its income from operations more than offsets expenses, and therefore it is not a net charge against the federal budget.

The Federal National Mortgage Association.[3] The need for a national market for residential mortgages was recognized in the first housing legislation enacted by the federal government dealing directly with mortgage lending. Provisions were made in the National Housing Act of 1934 for the private chartering of a facility to purchase and sell mortgages, but private funds to inaugurate such an institution were not forthcoming. Consequently, in 1938 Congress created the Federal National Mortgage Association with the broad purpose of providing a secondary market for FHA-insured mortgages, plus some related activities. During the next decade the FNMA's operations, in terms of volume, were relatively insignificant but in 1948 it was given authority to purchase VA-guaranteed loans and since that time it has been of varying degrees of importance in the mortgage market.

Since 1954, when the Association was reorganized under the Housing Act of that year, the FNMA has had three basic activities: (1) a secondary market function, (2) a special assistance function, and (3) a management and liquidation function. Each activity is operated as a special section of the Association.

The secondary market function relates to the original purposes for which the FNMA was established. Under the program the FNMA buys and sells FHA and VA loans ostensibly at market prices. It is expected that the program will eventually operate without expense to the government and that it will at some future date be transferred to private ownership. Funds for operation come from sale of securities to the public; and although it was intended that the program be limited in scope, purchases in 1957, for example, were almost $1 billion—close to a record amount for any one year.

The second segment of FNMA's operations—the Special Assistance Function—is financed entirely by the Treasury and is essentially directed at purchasing mortgages written for special housing programs. Under this aspect of FNMA operations it was never contemplated that mortgages would be purchases at par—although there is still some debate as to how prices actually should be determined. Until 1958 when Congress authorized a special $1 billion anti-recession housing program purchases were quite modest.

---

[3]For a brilliant, albeit controversial, analysis of the operations of the FNMA see Jack Guttentag, "The Federal National Mortgage Association," Research Study Two in Federal Credit Agencies, prepared for the Commission on Money and Credit (Englewood Cliffs, N.J.: Prentice-Hall, Inc., 1963).

The third function of the FNMA—the management and liquidation of the existing portfolio—was organized to liquidate the holdings acquired by the Association during its earlier years (1938-54) of operations. As of the middle of 1960 little progress had been made in this program; in fact, because of additional purchases the total portfolio of FNMA holdings increased from the $2.5 billion level of 1954 to $5.5 billion by the end of 1959—an amount equivalent to 9.0 percent of all underwritten mortgage debt.

In analyzing the financing of FNMA's operations, it is important to distinguish between the periods prior and since 1954. In the early period (1938-54) FNMA purchased $4.6 billion of mortgages, paid and accrued dividends of $100 million, and increased assets by $200 million. It acquired the funds to support the program from mortgage sales of $1.5 billion, repayments of $500 million, foreclosure gains of $100 million, net income of $200 million (retained earnings), and $2.6 billion net investment by the United States Government. In the period since 1954, an additional $4.7 billion has been spent—$4.6 billion of which has been for mortgage purchases. The money to finance the acquisitions has come primarily from a net investment of the public in notes and debentures issued by the FNMA in the amount of $2.4 billion and common stock sales of $100 million; mortgage sales and repayments of $1.4 billion; and other miscellaneous operations.

Between 1954 and 1959, the Treasury's investment in FNMA increased by only $0.3 billion, while the net total increase in the mortgage portfolio was $3.0 billion. In the previous period (1938-54) the Treasury's investment was $2.6 billion when purchases were $4.6. It is clear, therefore, that since 1954 there has been a substitution of private for public monies in the operation of FNMA, although it has not been as extensive as contemplated since it has been impossible to substitute private funds for public in the liquidation of the existing portfolio. The Treasury's investment in 1959 was still over $2.6 billion.

In terms of the total volume of residential mortgage debt in the nation the size of activity of FNMA is not large. At no time during the period of 50-59 did it hold more than 3.7 percent of all residential mortgage debt or 8.5 percent of FHA-insured mortgage loans. Its holdings of VA-guaranteed loans were higher, amounting to as much as 13 percent of all loans outstanding in 1953. On the other hand, when flows rather than holdings are considered, the significance of FNMA operation appears greater. In 1949, 1957, and 1959 it accounted for about one-tenth of the net flow of funds into residential mortgages and in 1957 as much as one-quarter of the net flow into government-underwritten programs.

Federal Credit Programs for Community Development[4]

The federal credit programs for community development differ in scope and form the underwriting and secondary market programs. Whereas the latter are designed to improve operations of a market served primarily by private funds, the former involve direct government expenditures in areas where private funds have seldom been utilized. The one type of program is designed to provide an environment within which private institutions can operate more effectively; the other is involved in performing functions where private funds do not operate at all.

The major programs for community development are operated as constituent agencies of the HHFA—the Urban Renewal Administration, the Public Housing Administration, and the Community Facilities Administration.

The Urban Renewal Administration. The Urban Renewal Administration administers Title I of the Housing Act of 1949 as amended, which created a variety of community renewal and redevelopment programs designed to assist communities in improving the use of land. As originally contemplated, the program was based on the economic proposition that as cities age, improvements on land grow old and lose their value. If the market automatically assured that all land would be placed in its highest and best use there would be no problem, but for a variety of reasons real property markets do not operate so perfectly. Consequently, through time much land is utilized in something less than its most optimum manner. Because of the difficulties in assembling land, and the expense of clearing it, private developers are reluctant to attempt programs in older sections of communities, even though in terms of location land may be extremely appropriate for new development.

Under Title I of the Housing Act of 1949 the federal government cooperates with local communities through local Community Redevelopment Agencies in placing land back in its raw state. Once an area is approved for redevelopment the Community Redevelopment Agency acquires the land, clears it, and offers it for sale to the highest private bidder willing to develop it in harmony with the over-all plans for the use of land within the city. However, the price paid by a developer is normally less than the cost of acquiring and clearing—consequently, there is a loss in the transaction. The

---

[4]Much of the material on which this discussion is based, came from an unpublished Research Study prepared for the Commission on Money and Credit by Professors Robert C. Turner and Joseph Ewers of Indiana University, entitled, "Federal Credit Programs for Community Development."

URA pays two-thirds of the difference between the cost of acquiring and clearing the land and the price received for it in the market place; the local community pays the rest. If the community absorbs all the expenses of planning the project, and the land, when cleared, is used for a public purpose, the URA will advance three-quarters of the difference between the cost and revenue. The community's share may be in the form of noncash contributions such as general improvements made in the area within the preceding three years.

In addition to this major function, the URA provides planning grants, demonstration grants and loans to assist local communities. Planning advances assist communities in financing the long and expensive process of preparing a renewal program and must be repaid, with interest at the current cost of government borrowing, when the program is completed. Demonstration grants are available up to two-thirds of the total cost when a community conducts an operation which will prove valuable to other localities in their operations. Similar grants are available on a fifty-fifty basis to state planning agencies to assist communities with populations of less than 50,000 in their planning and to other agencies for regional and metropolitan planning. The URA also supplies technical aid to local agencies.

Once a program is approved, URA will lend money to local community redevelopment agencies on both a short- and a long-term basis. Short-term, or temporary loans, provide working capital for the local organization to finance acquisition and clearance of land. If land is not sold, the temporary loan may be converted into a long-term loan with a 40-year maturity. In addition, the URA loan contract may be pledged as collateral for a private loan.

The local community must have a "workable program" for urban renewal before it is eligible for assistance. In essence, the workable program calls for a local effort to prevent slum and blight through codes and ordinances, a program of relocation for people displaced by a project, and administrative and fiscal responsibility for carrying out the project. As of the end of 1959, the URA granted relocation allowances up to \$200 per person and \$3,000 per business concern to assist the resettlement of displaced people and firms. Any local obligations issued to finance projects are exempt from federal income tax.

As of June 30, 1959, 385 cities had 647 projects in some state of operation—355 in actual execution. At the end of October 1959, planning advances netted \$16 million and total net disbursement for project loans, \$66 million. Commitments are much larger—they were approximately \$1.75 billion at the end of 1958. The Treasury has authority to borrow \$1 billion for direct loans by the URA but administrative and capital grants are made from special appropriations. As of the end of 1958 total public outlay for all projects for all purposes was $381 million in cash and noncash expenditures.

The Public Housing Administration. Public housing programs were included in legislation of the early 1930's, but it was not until the Housing Act of 1937 that public housing was given formal recognition. Basically, the program calls for financing of construction to homes for low-income groups and annual subsidies to maintain the low-rental character of the projects. The program's fundamental nature has changed little since 1937.

The Public Housing Administration operates in conjunction with local housing authorities which serve as the local administrative agencies for communities within which public housing is constructed. The PHA provides two types of credit aids to local housing authorities—temporary loans to finance land acquisition and construction and long-term loans for permanent financing.

In actual practice, however, the PHA advances little money. Rather the local housing authority obtains funds from private lenders using the PHA to support the tax-exempt obligations of local agencies. Such bonds are serial obligations with a maximum life of 40 years, with level payment amortization. They are guaranteed by the PHA since the PHA on an annual basis agrees to subsidize projects to the extent that costs of debt service, maintenance, and repair exceed revenues.

Projects are administered by local housing authorities, which are responsible for renting, management, and maintenance. In addition, the community must grant complete real and personal property tax exemption to the project although the local authority must make payments to the community up to a maximum of 10 percent of rent receipts in lieu of taxes.

The program is essentially slum clearance to the extent that for every unit of public housing constructed with federal assistance one unit of unsafe, unsanitary housing must be removed. In addition, limits are placed on the costs of construction per room and standards for occupancy eligibility have been established.

As pointed out above, funds to finance construction have come primarily from the sale of securities by local housing authorities rather than from the Treasury. The obligation of the government is essentially one of guaranteeing the bonds through assuring the annual subsidy. The annual subsidy in 1958 amounted to $98.8 million, although the maximum which might have been called for was $121.2 million. The government's payments have been increasing because costs are rising much faster than rent revenues, and if current trends continue payments will continue to increase since new projects are receiving considerably more annual subsidy than old.

There has been a sharp decline in direct lending under the PHA program, and at the end of 1959 total loans amounted to less than \$100 million and were financed from PHA receipts. In years when construction of public housing is high the Treasury is called upon to advance funds. For example, at the close of 1952 PHA loans totaled \$900 million.

At the local level, payments in lieu of taxes have generally exceeded the tax revenue from the area before public housing was constructed. On the other hand, if the land had been used by private developers it is probable that local tax revenues would have been greater. It has been estimated that this loss to the community is about \$200 per unit per year.

At the end of 1957 there were 450,000 public housing units owned or managed by local housing authorities. Obviously, the program has long since outlived its original function of providing employment during the depression and is maintained to provide housing for low-income groups.

The Community Facilities Administration. The Community Facilities Administration operates a number of programs designed to assist small communities—less than 10,000 population—in improving public facilities (sewage disposal and water supply) and for public works planning. In addition, it has responsibilities for lending to institutions of higher education for student and faculty housing, lending to hospitals for housing nurses and interns, supervising the school construction program under the U.S. Office of Education loan program, and liquidating expired activities such as the RFC public agency loan programs, Alaska housing loans, war public works loans under the Lanham Act and the prefabricated housing loan program.

The program of CFA to small communities is in the traditional pattern—both construction and permanent financing loans are made. All projects must be economically sound and are financed only if other sources of credit are unavailable at reasonable terms. Interest rates approximate the cost of federal borrowing.

Advances for public works planning were authorized under the Housing Act of 1954. Such advances are made on an interest-free basis to encourage communities to maintain a reserve of public works projects which could be activated in case of a major recession and to improve the general quality of public works design and building. Advances are repayable when the project is actually started. As of the end of 1960 these two programs were not large—less than \$52 million.

III. THE DIRECT IMPACT OF FEDERAL CREDIT AGENCIES ON INSTITUTIONAL RESIDENTIAL MORTGAGE LENDING

The impact of federal credit agencies on private sources of funds in the housing sector varies immensely among programs and among types of suppliers. The major institutional source of funds for financing residential housing are savings and loan associations, commercial banks, life insurance companies and mutual savings banks. The insurance and guarantee programs and secondary market operations have had an immense effect on these institutions, but the community facilities programs have been almost irrelevant to the action of such lenders. On the other hand, the community facilities operations along with portions of the other programs have had some impact on the bond market—both short- and long-term. However, since the community facilities programs have had minor impact, they will be considered only briefly.

Community Development Programs

Community Facilities Administration. Advances to communities for planning of public facilities and to small communities to finance public works programs totaled approximately $50 million by the end of 1960. Loans under these programs are of the type that other lenders would not make, and indeed loans are only made when funds are unavailable from other sources. It follows, therefore, that the programs have had no direct impact in terms of replacing private funds with public. In addition, the total of operations is so small that it is doubtful that it has had any impact on the general level of interest rates at which the federal government has been able to borrow funds.

Public Housing.[1] Financing for public housing is acquired through the issuance of long-term tax-exempt housing authority bonds and short-term temporary notes. When the bonds or notes are purchased by the traditional lending institutions they are considered as part of the bond portfolio and therefore are not in direct competition for funds that are used to finance residential housing, but rather with other demands for short-term financing.

There is no doubt that temporary public housing notes which comprise almost 50 percent of the short-term tax-exempt security market effect the market. Moreover, they probably have an impact on the market for all short-term securities although this is difficult to identify and quantify. Lending institutions, particularly commercial banks, have therefore been affected by this operation, but in

[1]For a complete analysis of the public housing programs see Robert M. Fisher, Twenty Years of Public Housing (New York: Harper and Brothers, 1959).

their bond portfolio, not their mortgage lending. The same is true of long-term tax-exempt housing authority bonds, and although the amount of the impact is difficult to measure, it is probable that they compete more directly for funds that might otherwise be invested in long-term mortgages than do the short-term offerings.

It is generally believed that in order to have a major impact on the market the volume of long-term issues must approach $500 million. Since recent issues have been in the neighborhood of $100 million it is doubtful that they are having any immediate impact on rates. More significantly, it is unlikely that they are siphoning any significant amount of funds from the residential mortgage market.

Urban Renewal. The direct impact of urban renewal on private lenders has as yet been insignificant. While projects may have led to private financing of redevelopment, little or no direct financing from traditional lenders has been involved. As the program develops this situation may, however, change.

In summary, it is correct to state that the impact of the community facilities programs on the traditional sources of private funds has been relatively slight. In fact, it is limited to the changes in yields on tax-exempt short-term paper and long-term bonds and their effect on the general bond market. Although this is not insignificant it is minor in relation to over-all fiscal and monetary operations in the economy. Moreover, there is little competition between private and public lenders in this area of operation—public monies are utilized primarily in areas where private lenders are unwilling to invest.

Underwriting Programs

There are two basic factors that underscore any analysis of the relationship of private financial institutions to FHA-insured or VA-guaranteed loan programs. First, all funds advanced through these programs, with the minor exception of the direct loan program of the VA, come from financial institutions. Indeed, the very operation of the programs depends upon the willingness of private institutions to make insured and/or guaranteed loans—the initiation function rests with the private lenders. Second, while the initiation function does rest with private lenders the position of the FHA and VA is not completely passive because through their policies they are able to create an environment conducive to mortgage lending, and thereby induce lenders to make residential mortgage loans. Consequently, the actions of the FHA and VA strongly influence the operations of private mortgage lenders, and to some degree the reverse is also true. In a word, the underwriting programs and private financial institutions are closely allied—they have an impact on each other.

The relationship of underwriting programs to different types of institutions varies, but there are certain general results of the programs which have affected all lenders. The underwriting of default risk, the development of some homogeneity in the security behind mortgage loans (through establishing appraisal and construction standards), the insistance on amortization and the experience record on loans with high ratio of loan to lending value have effected the policies of all types of lenders regardless of whether or not they make FHA or VA loans.

Commercial Banks. The underwriting programs of the federal government have probably had more influence on commercial bank residential mortgage lending than on any other type of private financial institution. Prior to the 1930's commercial banks, both because of law and tradition, made very few residential mortgage loans. Indeed, for many years nationally chartered banks were restricted from making any residential real estate loans and it was not until 1916 that they were permitted to make urban mortgage loans of not more than one-year maturity. In 1927 restrictions were eased to the extent that five-year first mortgage loans of not more than 50 percent of the value of the property were permitted. State laws have been somewhat less restrictive so state banks made a much larger volume of mortgage loans than those with national charters, but together in 1930, all commercial banks held only 11.1 percent of the total mortgage debt outstanding on one- to four-family nonfarm homes.

Even if the laws had been more permissive there is some doubt that commercial banks would have taken a more active part in the residential mortgage market. Traditionally, commercial bank managers have viewed their function as financing commerce, primarily through short-term loans. Given the nature of their deposit liabilities most banks' officers felt that it was inappropriate to make long-term, highly illiquid mortgage loans on the security of residential real property, and stayed out of such lending.

The National Housing Act of 1934, creating the Federal Housing Administration, established a new period in residential mortgage lending for commercial banks. The insurance program of the FHA reduced the risk of lending and greatly increased the liquidity of first mortgage loans. Moreover, when loans were insured, federal restrictions on the terms and conditions of mortgages originated by national banks were relaxed. Consequently, banks were able to enter the market on a competitive basis with other lenders.

The success of the FHA insured program unquestionably was instrumental in the progressive liberalization of the laws governing conventional mortgage lending by banks to the point that currently national banks may make fully amortized loans up to 75 percent of the property's value, for 20 years. The total portfolio of mortgage loans, (excluding FHA-insured and VA-guaranteed loans), may not exceed a bank's unimpaired capital and surplus or 60 percent of its time and savings deposits, whichever is greater.

The commercial banks rapidly capitalized on the lending opportunities provided by the FHA program. The proportion of all nonfarm residential mortgage debt held by commercial banks increased to 18.5 percent in 1946. Since then it rose briefly to over 20 percent in 1947 and 1948 but subsequently declined to a level of 13.8 percent in 1959. However, as a proportion of total bank assets mortgage loans have increased continuously from 3.4 percent in 1946 to 8.4 percent in 1959; and as a proportion of total bank time deposits, from 15 percent to 31.1 percent in the same period. The decline in the proportion of all residential nonfarm mortgage debt held by banks is a result, therefore, not of a smaller participation of banks in the mortgage market, but a more rapid increase on the part of other lenders.

Commercial banks have been very active in the FHA and VA lending field. In 1946, 36.5 percent of all FHA-VA mortgage debt in the United States was held by commercial banks; by 1959 the proportion had declined to 15.7 percent but FHA-VA loans still made up 45.6 percent of commerical banks' residential mortgage loan portfolios, and the dollar volume of loans held increased from $2.3 billion in 1946 to $9.3 billion in 1959. This increase, does not change the fact that the position of commerical banks in residential mortgage lending relative to other lenders has declined steadily through the postwar period and that banks in the 1950's shifted their portfolios from FHA-VA loans to conventional.

An analysis of net changes in banks' holdings of nonfarm residential mortgage loans on a yearly basis indicates the reasons for these shifts. In the period 1947-59, the dollar volume of lending fell below $1 billion in 1949, 1951-53 and 1957. Not only did the volume drop but the proportion of total lending also declined sharply, and most significantly, bank conventional mortgage lending changed almost as sharply as FHA and VA lending. In other words, in spite of interest rate ceilings and rigid yield patterns on underwritten loans in years of tight money all types of bank residential mortgage lending declined.

Examination of changes in commercial bank mortgage lending patterns in relation to other types of bank investment indicates that the fluctuation in mortgage lending activity is no greater than in other types of bank operations. When there is a restrictive credit policy, bank investments contract regardless of whether they are FHA-insured, conventional mortgages, or commercial loans.

Generalizations with respect to bank mortgage lending must be made with care. There are considerable regional differences in the approach to lending reflecting differing local conditions, and even within areas there are sharp variations in management philosophy with respect to mortgage lending. Within a local mortgage market it is not unusual to find banks that eagerly seek mortgage loans, banks that will take loans if they seem particularly good, and banks that will not make any mortgage loans except as a customer accommodation.

The impact of the underwriting programs on commercial banks therefore may be summarized as follows:

(1) The proportion of commercial banks' assets placed in residential mortgage loans has increased substantially as a result of the FHA and VA programs. In fact, in the postwar period alone it increased from 3.4 percent to 8.4 percent.

(2) The experience with FHA and VA programs has led to a liberalization of conventional lending regulations and a substantial expansion of conventional loans. In fact, in 1959, 54.4 percent of all loans held by commercial banks (approximately $5.1 billion) were conventional—an amount equivalent to 12.5 percent of all conventional residential mortgage debt outstanding in the nation.

(3) Banks' mortgage lending policies are much more influenced by changes in national monetary policy than by changes in FHA and VA programs. Mortgage lending is an accepted part of bank activity—and a relatively stable part—but mortgage lending by banks is not a stable part of over-all mortgage lending in the nation. This lack of general stability is a result of general monetary policies, not specific changes in the underwriting programs.

(4) The volume of residential mortgage lending varies markedly among banks and among local market areas.

Savings and Loan Associations. The underwriting programs, *per se*, have probably affected the operations of savings and loan associations less than any other type of lending institutions.

Throughout the entire span of the history of organized financial institutions in the United States, savings and loan associations have played a dominant part in the financing of real property. Indeed, the raison d'être of savings and loan associations is to gather together funds for lending on the security of real property. Laws regulating their operations are designed primarily to prevent them from lending beyond a certain amount on other types of securities rather than to restrict the amount and type of mortgage loans that they can make.

The development of the FHA-insured program in 1934 with its emphasis on higher ratio of loan to lending values, longer terms, and amortization was not particularly important for the savings and loan business. Associations had been able to make, and actually had made, amortized loans for years with extended maturities, and while the insurance provision against default was important, the real need of associations in the 1930's was a program to provide liquidity for portfolios. Total liquidity, not individual mortgage liquidity, was the requirement. Consequently, savings and loan associations have made relatively few FHA-insured loans.

In the period following World War II, savings and loan associations rapidly increased their position in the residential real estate market. In 1946 associations made 32.9 percent of all nonfarm mortgage recordings of $20,000 or less; by 1950 the share had fallen to 31.3 percent, but in 1958 it was up to 38.4. Between 1950 and 1959 the dollar volume of advances increased from $5,060 million to $10,516 million—more than 100 percent. During the same period the total dollar volume of funds advanced by life insurance companies declined while advances by commercial banks and mutual savings banks increased about 60 percent. The total amount of mortgage loans held by savings and loan associations increased from $11.2 billion in 1950 to $42.9 billion in 1958, and commercial bank holdings increased from $11.1 billion to $18.3 billion.

The significant fact associated with the great increase in holdings of mortgages by savings and loan associations is that the increase came about primarily through an expansion of conventional lending. In 1950 savings and loan associations throughout the nation had $734 million in FHA-insured loans. By 1958 this had increased to $2.1 billion; whereas in 1950 savings and loan associations held 6.6 percent of all FHA-insured loans in the nation, in 1958 holdings were only 5.0 percent of the total. In 1950 approximately 6.2 percent of savings and loan association loans were FHA-insured, but in 1958 the proportion was approximately 5.0 percent.

Participation by savings and loan associations in the VA-guaranteed loan program has been considerably greater than in the FHA-insured. In 1950, 22.4 percent of all VA loans were held by savings and loan associations, but the proportion dropped to 15.6 percent in 1958. In terms of absolute amounts, savings and loan associations

TABLE V-1

Nonfarm Mortgage Recordings of $20,000 or less, by Type of Lender, 1940-58

(Dollar amounts in millions)

Year	Savings and Loan Associations	Insurance Companies	Commercial Banks	Mutual Savings Banks	Individuals and Others	Total Number	Total Volume
1940	$1,284	$ 334	$ 1,006	$ 170	$1,238	1,456,000	$ 4,031
1941	1,490	404	1,166	218	1,454	1,628,000	4,732
1942	1,171	362	886	166	1,359	1,351,000	3,943
1943	1,238	280	753	152	1,440	1,274,000	3,861
1944	1,560	257	878	165	1,746	1,446,000	4,606
1945	2,017	250	1,097	217	2,068	1,639,000	5,650
1946	3,483	503	2,712	548	3,344	2,497,000	10,589
1947	3,650	847	3,004	596	3,631	2,567,000	11,729
1948	3,629	1,016	2,664	745	3,828	2,535,000	11,882
1949	3,646	1,046	2,446	750	3,941	2,488,000	11,828
1950	5,060	1,618	3,365	1,064	5,073	3,032,000	16,179
1951	5,295	1,615	3,370	1,013	5,111	2,878,000	16,405
1952	6,452	1,420	3,600	1,137	5,409	3,028,000	18,018
1953	7,365	1,480	3,680	1,327	5,896	3,164,000	19,747
1954	8,312	1,768	4,239	1,501	7,154	3,458,000	22,974
1955	10,452	1,932	5,617	1,858	8,627	3,913,000	28,484
1956	9,532	1,799	5,458	1,824	8,475	3,602,000	27,088
1957	9,217	1,472	4,264	1,430	7,861	3,246,000	24,244
1958	10,516	1,460	5,204	1,640	8,568	3,441,000	27,388

Source: Housing and Home Finance Agency, Housing Statistics — Annual Data, Washington, D.C. (March 1961), p. 52.

TABLE V-2

Percentage Distribution of Nonfarm Mortgage Recordings of $20,000 or less, by Type of Lender, 1940-58

(Based on dollar volume)

Year	Savings and Loan Associations	Insurance Companies	Commercial Banks	Mutal Savings Banks	Individuals and Others	Total
1940	31.9%	8.3%	25.0%	4.2%	30.7%	100.0%
1941	31.6	8.5	24.6	4.6	30.7	100.0
1942	29.7	9.2	22.5	4.2	34.5	100.0
1943	32.1	7.3	19.5	3.9	37.3	100.0
1944	33.9	5.6	19.1	3.6	37.8	100.0
1945	35.8	4.4	19.4	3.8	36.6	100.0
1946	32.9	4.8	25.6	5.2	31.6	100.0
1947	31.1	7.2	25.6	5.1	31.0	100.0
1948	30.5	8.6	22.4	6.3	32.2	100.0
1949	30.9	8.8	20.7	6.3	33.3	100.0
1950	31.3	10.0	20.8	6.6	31.4	100.0
1951	32.3	9.8	20.5	6.2	31.2	100.0
1952	35.8	7.9	20.0	6.3	30.0	100.0
1953	37.4	7.5	18.6	6.7	29.9	100.0
1954	36.2	7.7	18.5	6.5	31.1	100.0
1955	36.7	6.8	19.7	6.5	30.3	100.0
1956	35.2	6.6	20.2	6.7	31.3	100.0
1957	38.0	6.1	17.6	5.9	32.4	100.0
1958	38.4	5.3	19.0	6.0	31.3	100.0

Source: See Table V-1.

TABLE V-3

Percentage Holdings of Total Residential Mortgage Debt Outstanding, By Type Of Lender, 1950-60

	1950	1960
Savings and Loan Associations	25.0	36.7
Life Insurance Companies	20.7	18.0
Mutual Savings Banks	13.2	15.2
Commercial Banks	19.3	12.8
Individuals and Others	21.8	17.3
Total	100.0	100.0

Source: Housing and Home Finance Agency, Housing Statistics–Annual Data, Washington, D.C., (March 1961), pp. 58-59.

TABLE V-4

Nonfarm Mortgage Recordings of $20,000 or Less By Type of Lender and Type of Loan, 1958
(In millions of dollars)

	Conventional	FHA	VA	Total
Savings and Loan Associations	$ 9,557	$ 514	$ 445	$10,516
Commercial Banks	3,758	1,279	167	5,204
Insurance Companies	989	437	34	1,460
Mutual Savings Banks	841	500	299	1,640
Mortgage Companies	2,497	1,743	893	5,133
Others	3,330	78	27	3,435
ALL LENDERS	$20,972	$4,551	$1,865	$27,388

Sources: Federal Housing Administration; Veterans Administration; U.S. Savings and Loan League.

TABLE V-5

Percentage Distribution of Nonfarm Mortgage Recordings of $20,000 or less, By Type of Lender and Type of Loan, 1958
(Based on dollar volume)

	Conventional	FHA	VA	Total
Savings and Loan Associations	90.9%	4.9%	4.2%	100.0%
Commercial Banks	72.2	24.6	3.2	100.0
Insurance Companies	67.7	29.9	2.4	100.0
Mutual Savings Banks	51.3	30.5	18.2	100.0
Mortgage Companies	48.6	34.0	17.4	100.0
Others	96.9	2.3	0.8	100.0
ALL LENDERS	76.6%	16.6%	6.8%	100.0%

Sources: Federal Housing Administration; Veterans Administration; United States Savings and Loan League.

TABLE V-6

Residential Mortgage Debt
Outstanding, 1946-59

Year	Billions of Dollars
1946	28.1
1947	33.8
1948	39.6
1949	44.9
1950	53.6
1951	61.4
1952	68.9
1953	77.1
1954	87.2
1955	100.6
1956	112.1
1957	121.3
1958	133.0
1959	148.2

Source: See Table V-3.

TABLE V-7

Outstanding Mortgage Debt, One- to Four-Family Nonfarm Residences, by Percentage of Holdings, by Type of Lenders, and by Type of Loan, 1958

	Percent of Total				Percent of Holdings			
Type of Holder	FHA	VA	Conventional	Total	FHA	VA	Conventional	Total
Private Financial Institution	83.3	86.2	81.3	82.8	18.7	23.8	57.5	100.0
Savings & Loan	8.9	23.2	45.5	33.6	4.9	15.8	79.2	100.0
Life Insurance	30.1	24.5	14.2	19.5	28.7	28.7	42.6	100.0
Commercial Banks	22.1	11.0	12.6	14.0	29.5	17.9	52.6	100.0
Mutual Savings Banks	22.2	27.5	9.1	15.7	26.3	39.9	33.8	100.0
FNMA	6.0	7.9	0.0	2.9	38.0	62.0	0.0	100.0
Other Federal Agencies	0.0	0.0	1.7	1.0	0.0	0.0	100.0	100.0
Individuals and Others	10.7	5.8	17.0	13.3	15.0	10.1	74.9	100.0
Total	100.0	100.0	100.0	100.0	18.6	22.9	58.5	100.0

Source: Developed from Housing and Home Finance Agency, Housing Statistics, (March 1961), p. 59.

increased their holdings of VA-guaranteed loans from \$2.5 billion in 1950 to \$6.6 billion in 1958. In spite of this relatively high level of holdings it is important to note that only 4.2 percent of all VA-guaranteed loans made in the nation in 1958 were by savings and loan associations, although associations made 38.4 percent of all residential nonfarm mortgage loans of \$20,000 or less in that year. Obviously, the great bulk of savings and loan mortgage lending is in conventional loans. Indeed, in 1958, 90.9 percent of all loans made by savings and loan associations were conventional, 4.9 percent were FHA-insured and 4.2 percent were VA-guaranteed; at the same time only 77 percent of all recordings in the nation were conventional, 17 percent FHA-insured and 6 percent VA-guaranteed. (See Table V-5).

In terms of total lending, it is apparent that savings and loan associations do not need the insured or guaranteed programs to increase the volume of their operations. Moreover, they do not need to hold a high volume of such loans in their portfolios for liquidity purposes—they depend on other sources. Indeed, the extent to which they are holding such loans is creating some portfolio management problems since the yields on FHA and VA mortgages have not risen as rapidly as the price which savings and loan associations are paying for savings.

Life Insurance Companies. Life insurance companies differ from other institutional mortgage lenders in two important respects—first, they are for the most part nonlocal with reference to any particular local market—their funds are not derived from the savings of any one area and basic lending decisions are usually made outside the area; and second, they differ from other institutional lenders in that they are not faced with the possibility of unforeseeable demand for funds within relatively short periods of time.

Life insurance companies are admirably qualified for a role in the long-term mortgage market. Their liabilities at any one time are small relative to total policy commitments and are actuarially calculable. They can therefore invest in the long-term mortgage market with equanimity. Like commercial banks, they can participate in various investment markets and therefore constantly search for means and methods of maximizing their returns consistent with safety.

Insurance companies have always made mortgage loans a substantial portion of their portfolios, although the amount has varied over time. In the 1920's mortgage loans accounted for as much as 40 percent of all investments, but during the depression holdings were reduced; and in 1946 mortgages were a historic low of 14.8 percent of insurance companies' assets.

The FHA-insured and VA-guaranteed loan programs originally had a particular attraction for life insurance companies because they could be bought and sold. Consequently, in the postwar period, life insurance companies made a large volume of such loans. In 1949, 23 percent of all FHA-insured mortgage loans in the United States were made by life insurance companies and 48.5 percent of all life insurance mortgage lending was devoted to such loans. VA-guaranteed loans also played an important part in life insurance mortgage lending activity, as holdings increased from $844 million in 1947 to over $7.3 billion in 1956. In 1958, life insurance companies recorded 5.3 percent of all nonfarm mortgage loans of $20,000 or less; 67.7 percent of the loans were conventional, 24.6 percent FHA-insured and 2.4 percent VA-guaranteed. In that same year, life insurance companies held 31 percent of all FHA-insured loans in the nation and 25 percent of all VA-guaranteed loans, and 27 percent of their holdings were in FHA's and 34 percent in VA's.

In essence, the impact of the FHA-insured and VA-guaranteed programs on life insurance company operations has been to enable companies to buy and sell mortgages more easily; in fact, to permit their access in and out of the mortgage market. Prior to the FHA and VA programs this was difficult to do; consequently, the FHA and VA programs have given insurance companies more flexibility in managing their total portfolios. In addition, the programs probably encouraged lending in certain areas where life insurance company managers were not confident of the soundness of the mortgage market. In this way, the programs have helped the movement of funds throughout the nation. In addition, while the proportion of assets invested in mortgages by life insurance companies is slightly less than it was in the 1920's, probably a larger proportion of life insurance mortgage loans are in residential real property than would be the case if the FHA and VA programs had not been inaugurated.

Mutual Savings Banks. Mutual savings banks once dominated the institutional residential mortgage lending picture. However, since 1912 the share of the mortgage debt held by mutual banks has tended to decline. In 1958 mutual banks made about 6.0 percent of all nonfarm mortgage recordings of $20,000 or less and they distributed their loans as follows: 51.3 percent conventional, 30.5 percent FHA-insured and 18.2 percent VA-guaranteed. In terms of the absolute amounts of funds advanced they were the smallest institutional lender in 1958.

The FHA-insured and VA-guaranteed loan programs have been of considerable importance to the mutual savings banks. As of December 31, 1958, mutual savings banks held 22 percent of all outstanding FHA-insured mortgage debt on one- to four-family nonfarm residences, and 28 percent of all VA-guaranteed debt.

Much more important, however, is the fact that 27 percent of the holdings of mutual savings banks were in FHA-insured loans and 55 percent in VA-guaranteed loans. Only 18 percent of the aggregate portfolios of such institutions was in conventionals.

Mutual banks, unlike savings and loan associations, were not originally chartered to make mortgage loans and therefore they have a range of investment opportunities. Restricted in operations to the eastern states, mutual savings banks originally were able to acquire only a limited number of mortgage loans. However, after the development of FHA and VA programs, the savings banks' role increased substantially. Clearly the programs have been instrumental in mutual savings banks' expanded operations in the mortgage market in the postwar period, and therefore, have led to the channeling of more funds into the mortgage market.

Mortgage Companies. While mortgage companies differ from other types of institutional lenders, they play an important role in mortgage markets and have had considerable impact on the lending programs of the traditional institutional lenders.

Mortgage companies primarily are engaged in originating mortgage loans for, or for the purpose of selling to, institutional investors, arranging construction financing between the time of commencement of construction and the issuance of permanent mortgage money, and servicing loans. Companies vary tremendously in their operations, and since they are subject to only limited state or federal regulation there is a broad range of activities within which they can engage.

In the post-World War II period mortgage companies have been most active in the FHA-insured and VA-guaranteed markets. On the basis of advance commitments from lenders, and sometimes without such commitments, they arrange the financing of home building. Early in 1960, it was estimated that mortgage companies were servicing close to $30 billion of mortgages or almost one-quarter of the total mortgage debt in the nation.

Mortgage companies are able to operate because lenders are willing to buy FHA-insured and VA-guaranteed loans on properties they have never appraised, held by individuals that they have never checked for credit. They are buying, in essence, the insurance and the guarantee. The result is that funds are transferred from areas of capital surplus to areas of capital shortage. The growth of the mutual savings banks in the mortgage market would have been impossible without the mortgage bankers, and it is doubtful if insurance company participation would have been so great without the benefit of these organizations.

In essence, the mortgage companies developed to meet a need that was created when FHA and VA operations were successful in creating (at least partially) a national market for mortgages. Moreover, the collateral functions of mortgage banks in arranging interim financing, normally through commercial bank short-term credit, and "warehousing" loans has been an important factor in the postwar residential market.

Summary. The underwriting programs of the federal government have changed the nature of residential mortgage markets and lending institutions have reacted in different ways to these changes.

The FHA and VA programs have increased the volume of institutional mortgage lending in the nation. Prior to 1935 less than 60 percent of the nonfarm residential mortgage debt was held by institutional lenders; by 1950 the proportion was 80 percent and at the end of 1958 it was approximately 81 percent. As a result, in 1958 every type of lending institution had a larger proportion of its assets in residential nonfarm mortgages than in 1920. Clearly, the FHA and VA programs have not acted to replace private credit by public credit–indeed, the reverse is true, the programs have expanded the amount of private credit in the mortgage market.

Among private lenders, the FHA and VA programs have increased competition for mortgage loans over the long term. Commercial banks have become more competitive in the mortgage market because of the changes in law developed through the National Housing Act, and mutual savings banks and life insurance companies have expanded their operations because of the ability to buy and sell FHA and VA loans in the market primarily through mortgage companies. Savings and loan associations are the only lenders which did not experience a change of important magnitude in the nature of their operations because of the FHA and VA programs.

The degree to which various institutions have participated in FHA and VA programs have varied over time, according to changes in returns to be earned on such loans in relation to other returns in the investment market. This has been particularly true of commercial and mutual savings banks and insurance companies; less so for savings and loan associations. Associations are not as keenly affected by changes in rates as other types of lending institutions because they hold only a small proportion of their mortgage portfolios in insured and guaranteed loans.

The variation in the proportion of FHA and VA loans made by institutions is closely linked to the fact that FHA and VA have consistently operated with fixed interest rates. As a result, market forces do not set the return, and when it is out of line with other earnings lenders shift out of such lending. While in actual practice discounting can make up some of the difference between fixed and actual yields, there is little doubt that the fixed rate has caused some disorder in the mortgage market in the postwar period.

Secondary Market Facilities

The two organizations providing secondary market facilities have different impacts on different types of lenders and therefore are considered separately.

The Federal Home Loan Bank System.[2] To all practical purposes, the impact of the Federal Home Loan Bank System has fallen entirely on savings and loan associations, and the impact has been very important. While it is impossible to separate the importance of differing economic and institutional forces, it is probably true that savings and loan associations could not have grown to the extent they have in the past two decades without the services of the Federal Home Loan Bank System. Given the experience of investors and shareholders in savings and loan associations in the early years of the depression, it is unlikely that the public would have been willing to place their funds in associations again in such volume if such accounts were not insured by the Federal Savings and Loan Insurance Corporation. Some dimensions of the importance of the FSLIC is demonstrated by the fact that in 1960, 64 percent of all associations in the nation holding 94 percent of the total assets of the business had insurance of accounts.

Less dramatic in its appeal to the public, but equally if not more significant in the operations of the savings and loan association business, has been the impact of the Federal Home Loan Bank System. Prior to the development of the System, savings and loan associations had to depend upon commercial banks as a source of liquidity and often associations were unable to arrange liquidity at the time they needed it most.

The FHLB System through the 11 district banks serves as a reservoir of credit for all member institutions. A savings and loan association in a district may become a member by buying stock in the district bank, and currently, member institutions own all the stock in such banks. Individual associations must buy stock equivalent to a minimum of 2 percent of home loans to qualify for membership. A member institution can obtain two types of advances from its bank: short-term and long-term.

---

[2]This discussion is based largely on Ernest Bloch's "The Federal Home Loan Bank System," Research Study Three in Federal Credit Agencies, prepared for the Commission on Money and Credit (Englewood Cliffs, N.J.: Prentice-Hall, Inc., 1963).

The amount of advances available to any member depends upon the Federal Home Loan Bank Act and the regulations and policies of district banks. The policy of the Board in 1960 was to limit advances to 12.5 percent of members' savings accounts plus 2.5 percent for emergencies, and 5 percent of separate advances with a maturity of not less than five years. At no time could advances exceed 12 times the capital stock owned by the member institution. Moreover, the regulations of the Board provide that the Board of Directors and Executive Committee of each district bank can establish a line of credit not in excess of a member's borrowing capacity. These lines are reviewed every 15 months and revised as necessary, and they set forth the types and amounts of advances that a member institution may obtain.

Short-term advances are normally made for less than a year and are used primarily to meet short-run changes in the needs of a member association. Whenever there is a discrepancy between commitments to loan and the inflow of current savings, an association may borrow on a short-term basis to meet its commitments. Such advances are unsecured, except for the capital stock held by a member in a district bank, and they are repayable without penalty anytime within the maturity date.

Long-term advances, on the other hand, clearly increase the volume of money available for lending on the security of real property. Such advances are secured by the capital stock of the borrower, collateral of first mortgages on one- to four-family homes where the unpaid principal and balance does not exceed $35,000 and obligations of the United States or obligations fully guaranteed by the United States. Each district bank may use its own judgment in determining the collateral value of mortgages. All long-term advances are amortized although they may be repaid without penalty and terms of repayment may be renegotiated. Flexibility is the keynote in such operations.

The interest rate charged on advances changes over time and differs among banks. The rate depends on the nature, terms, and length of the advance but is kept within certain limits by law. Legally rates cannot exceed 6 percent—in 1960 they approached 5.75 percent, while during World War II they were as low as 1.5 percent. The differential among rates often means that associations in certain districts are more inclined to use the facilities of their bank than others. Since the funds loaned by a district bank are obtained by the sale of debentures in the national market this activity operates to move money from a surplus to a deficit area.

Loans must be repaid in full plus interest and any expenses accrued because of the transaction. The district banks have never lost any money on the advance operations.

In 1958 a special type of advance, limited to 5 percent of the withdrawable share capital or investment certificates of a member association, was arranged because of the particularly favorable time for floating FHLB debentures. The Board was able to obtain money relatively cheaply and therefore took advantage of the situation to increase the volume of funds available for lending by member associations.

There is no question that the ability to obtain both short- and long-term advances, plus the security of a source of liquidity in case of emergency, plays an important role in the operation of individual savings and loan associations. Consequently, changes in the practices of the FHLB must be made with care and with sufficient prior announcement to permit individual associations to adjust their operations in light of proposed changes. Since the FHLB is the liquidity source for associations, given the nature of most of their assets, any drastic changes in operational policy—such as occurred in 1955 when secondary credit was drastically reduced—can create major problems for individual institutions.

On balance the effect of the FHLB on savings and loan associations has been to facilitate their growth and to increase the proportion of assets which they can invest on the security of real property by providing them with (1) a source of short-term liquidity with flexible repayment schedules, (2) a source of long-term funds, (3) a source of final liquidity, and (4) insurance of accounts.

The Federal National Mortgage Association.[3] To all intents and purposes since 1954 the Federal National Mortgage Association has been a quite different operation than it was prior to that time. Consequently, analysis of its impact on lending institutions is restricted to operations since the Charter Act of that year.

Basically, the Federal National Mortgage Association was designed to operate as a true secondary market for mortgages of all types, and when it does it will unquestionably be of major importance for all lenders. At present, it has little immediate impact on savings and loan associations or commercial banks and only indirectly on life insurance companies and mutual savings banks. The fact that holdings of mortgages by FNMA have consistently increased since the Charter Act indicates to most lenders that it is operating essentially as a direct source of funds for mortgages and therefore is in competition with traditional lenders.

---

[3]For details of these operations see Jack Guttentag, "The Federal National Mortgage Association," Research Study Two in Federal Credit Agencies, prepared for the Commission on Money and Credit (Englewood Cliffs, N.J.: Prentice-Hall, Inc., 1963).

The small amount of use made of FNMA by lenders is indicated by the fact that in the period 1954-59, bank and trust companies accounted for only 10 percent of the purchases of FNMA; savings and loan associations, 5 percent; and insurance companies, 1 percent. The rest of FNMA's purchases were from mortgage companies—some 84 percent.

In a very real sense, FNMA in the past five years has been a purchaser of last resort for mortgage companies, and indeed has contributed greatly to the successful operation of mortgage companies, to the extent that companies always had a place to dispose of their mortgages. It is, of course, important to note that mortgage bankers do not primarily originate loans for sale to FNMA—rather they prefer to sell to institutional lenders, not only because of the advantages of working out permanent relationships, but because it normally enables them to maintain the servicing of the loan. If mortgages that are sold to the FNMA are subsequently resold, the mortgage company can easily lose the servicing contract.

The need by mortgage companies of a purchaser of last resort arises from two reasons: (1) Mortgage companies often warehouse loans and occasionally are caught between a rising rate of interest on commercial loans and the yield on their mortgages. Under such circumstances they can dispose of their inventory to FNMA; and (2), when lending institutions are unwilling to make FHA-insured or VA-guaranteed loans in the mortgage market, mortgage companies have sold mortgages to the FNMA, using the FNMA in essence as a direct source of funds. In this manner, mortgage bankers are able to stay active in the market and the FNMA has been responsible for a greater amount of FHA and VA lending than might otherwise have occurred.

In the final analysis, the FNMA has had little direct affect on institutional mortgage lending in the past five years. However, to the extent that it has made it more possible for mortgage companies to operate successfully and, in turn, to the extent that mortgage companies have been able to assist in the movement of funds throughout the nation—particularly to life insurance companies and mutual savings banks—the operation has been indirectly influential. Moreover, the "special assistance functions" have been very important for VA lending at certain periods.

Summary

An analysis of the impact of various federal credit agencies on lending institutions clearly indicates that as yet the community facilities programs have had little direct impact and that the FNMA as now operating is not sharply influencing major institutional lenders' activities. On the other hand, the Federal Home Loan

Bank System with its constituent elements has been, and continues to be, a major factor in increasing the growth and improving the operations of savings and loan associations.

The FHA-insured and VA-guaranteed programs have had a major impact on lending institution operations. The FHA has influenced the operation of commercial banks, and, in the mortgage market, that of the life insurance companies and mutual savings banks, and thereby increased competition within the market. The VA program has had the same result.

The important impact of FHA and VA on institutional residential lending cannot be understood in a purely aggregative analysis. Mortgage lending originates in local areas in local markets. The FHA and VA have made it possible for the transfer of funds from surplus areas to scarcity regions through the auspices of insurance company and mutual bank decisions and mortgage bank operations. Only by assessing what this interflow of funds has meant to local markets is it truly possible to understand the impact of FHA and VA programs on institutions in mortgage markets. The difference in the use of the programs among markets is immense; moreover, the extent to which the programs are used in many ways depends upon the nature and structure of institutions in local markets. It is a major error to evaluate the impact of these programs on a national basis alone; and the solution to many problems associated with mortgage lending may well be found in changing the pattern of lending institutions in local markets, rather than in attempting to change the somewhat ephemeral national mortgage market.

IV. THE INDIRECT IMPACT ON THE ECONOMY OF FEDERAL CREDIT AGENCIES IN HOUSING

While most government housing programs inaugurated in the past two decades had as their basic purpose the solution of particular problems in housing or mortgage market operations, they have also had significant side effects. The most important of these have been the impacts on prices, both in the housing and other sectors of the economy, and the distribution of resources; the implications of the programs for over-all economic stability; and the significance of the programs to total growth in the economy. Since the programs are diverse, they are analyzed separately.

Community Development Programs

Community Facilities Administration. To date the public facility programs and advances for public works planning have been so small that they have had no appreciable affect on the use of resources, price levels, or economic stability in any aggregative sense. They may have had some local impacts, depending upon the nature of the labor and material markets, in a particular area, but on balance the influence has been small.

Advance planning grants in 1958 supported local expenditures of \$820.6 million, and in the period 1954-58 the approved advances of \$28 million supported projects costing an estimated \$1.4 billion. Given the fact that aggregate gross national produce for the period 1954-58 was approximately \$2 trillion, the improbability of the programs' having any significant impact on resource allocation or economic growth is apparent. If the program continues at its present dimensions its future impact will be equally slight.

Urban Renewal. It is estimated that the total public outlay in cash and noncash expenditures for urban renewal through 1958 has been \$381 million, and this expenditure has triggered private construction expenditures of \$2.0 billion—\$894 million for private housing, \$207 million for industrial development and \$869 million for public and semipublic facilities. Since during the period of 1949-58 total construction expenditures were \$410 billion, it is apparent that in an aggregative sense the program has had little or no impact on the flow of resources into the construction industry. Again, in certain local areas the impact may have been significant.

The decade of the 1950's, is unsatisfactory for estimating the potential influence of urban renewal on the distribution of resources and the rate of economic growth in the nation. The fifties have been a period of experimentation and development for urban renewal. They have been a period when the problems of initiating a completely new concept of land clearance have been worked out, tested in the courts and sold to the public. It will be in the 1960's that urban renewal will begin to be a positive factor of some proportions in the economy.

It seems apparent that urban renewal will become an accepted activity in almost every large city and many smaller cities throughout the nation, and if the 1960 relationship between urban renewal and gross national product remains constant and current trends in gross national product continue, by 1975 approximately \$3.7 billion annually will be spent in the United States on this program. A carefully considered analysis places annual expenditures at \$3 billion by 1970, of which about \$600 million will be federal government contributions. When the program reaches such proportions it will begin to have an impact beyond local areas.

If the 1960's is a period of full employment, urban renewal programs will have to be completed at the cost of foregoing some other type of activity. It appears that the impetus for urban renewal is such that not only will it continue, but it will grow in the next decade despite the opportunity costs. To this extent, the program is countercyclical in impact. On the other hand, there is little possibility that urban renewal in its present form, with such a large local government contribution, could expand in depression periods, and therefore, if renewal (as it is now known) is to be done, it must be done in periods of growth and expansion. In its present form, it is not an effective anti-depression weapon.

Public Housing. In the post-World War II period the total volume of public housing, averaging 2 to 5 percent of all housing starts annually, has not been of significant volume to have a major impact on the flow of resources, prices, or economic growth in the nation. Inasmuch as for every unit of public housing constructed, one unit of substandard housing is removed it is reasonable to conclude that the quality of the housing stock throughout the nation has been modestly improved. However, the rapid deterioration of public housing units requires that even such a limited statement be made with qualifications.

As in the case of urban renewal, the impact in some local areas may have been significant on prices and employment, particularly in 1951 and 1952 when the program was at its postwar peak.

Obviously, to the extent that public housing is constructed in periods of full employment it contributes to pressure on prices. The fact that such pressures have been small in the past few years is merely because the total volume of public housing construction has been small.

Underwriting Programs

Unlike the community facilities programs, the federal underwriting programs have had important impacts on the economy in general and the housing sector in particular; but there is much debate and uncertainty as to the exact nature of such impacts.

It is probably true that the FHA-insured and VA-guaranteed programs have resulted through the years in increasing the use of credit for the purchase of housing, and therefore have increased the flow of resources into the housing sector. In 1929 total outstanding nonfarm mortgage debt on one- to four-family properties was 21.5 percent ($18.9 billion) of total private outstanding long-term debt and in 1957 it was 43.4 percent ($126.9 billion). Since the FHA and VA programs did not involve direct lending, the increase in the proportion of private long-term outstanding debt is a response to changing portfolio operations of lending institutions. In 1929 savings and loan associations had 99.1 percent of their savings in mortgages; life insurance companies had 12.6 percent of policy reserves in one- to four-family nonfarm residential mortgages; mutual banks had 24.9 percent and commercial banks 11.8 percent of time deposits so invested. In 1958 savings and loan associations had 90.8 percent of savings, life insurance companies 26.1 percent of policy reserves, mutual savings banks 45.9 percent, and commercial banks 29.7 percent of time deposits in one- to four-family nonfarm residential mortgages.

Savings and loan associations have probably been less influenced by the FHA and VA programs than any other type of institutional lender and have had a smaller change in the proportion of savings invested in one- to four-family nonfarm residential mortgages than any of the other three lenders. There is little doubt that the increase in the proportion of commercial bank time deposits, the proportion of life insurance reserves and the increase in mutual savings bank holdings are partially a result of the FHA and VA programs. In other words, the organizations that are not specifically and primarily mortgage lenders increased the proportion of their assets which they were willing to invest in residential mortgages because of the underwriting programs.

The importance of the FHA and VA programs cannot be underestimated. Between 1954 and 1957 FHA and VA operations equalled about 30 percent of the amount of all home mortgage loans recorded of $20,000 or less. At the end of 1957 underwritten mortgage debt amounted to $51.6 billion—42.6 percent of all such debt. Its net increase of more than $22 billion in the period 1953-57 accounted for more than 40 percent of the increase in total residential debt. Almost $4.5 billion a year moved into FHA and VA loans in the period 1953-57.

What has been the effect of the increased flow of mortgage money into the residential housing market—has it meant higher prices or more construction, or both? What has it meant to the terms and conditions under which mortgage funds could be borrowed? What has it meant to the rate of economic growth in the nation and the stability of economic activity?

To the extent that an increased flow of money into the mortgage market occurred at a time of full employment of resources the effect must have been an increase in prices—not only of houses, but of all factors of production in the economy. In the immediate post-World War II when demand for all goods and services was very strong the FHA and VA programs which encouraged borrowing and induced lenders to advance funds on the security of real property resulted in substantial price rises in the housing sector. This conclusion is supported by the fact that in the period 1946-50 there was a greater relative increase in mortgage debt than in housing output. The impact of the programs was felt primarily in higher construction costs and housing prices.

In the period since 1950, when there has been more unemployed resources, programs have had considerable affect on the real volume of output. A systematic quantitative analysis suggests that in the period 1948-56 as a whole the FHA and VA mortgage programs stimulated construction from at least $1 billion to as much as $4 billion annually (in 1957-58 dollars) or from 8 to 30 percent.

That these conclusions must be utilized with care is demonstrated by an examination of the relation between changes in the volume of real output and increases in mortgage debt. For example, while the amount of money invested in mortgages between 1955 and 1959 increased 50 percent, the amount of housing constructed increased only 20 percent. Or in other words, for every 100 houses financed under the terms, conditions and prices in 1959, 164 could have been financed if terms, conditions, and prices had not changed since 1950. While no one would argue that all price rises in the economy were due to the FHA and VA underwriting programs, at the same time it is important to note that price effects of the programs were significant.

There can be more certainty about the point that the FHA-insured and VA-guaranteed programs have altered the flow of resources within the residential housing market. During the 1920's single-family houses accounted for about 62 percent of all private nonfarm dwelling units constructed, but in the decade 1949-58 slightly over 87 percent of all units were single houses. Again, of course, the impact of other factors must not be neglected. The general increase in the use of the automobile in the post-World War II period, compared to the 1920's, made it possible for people to live beyond areas served by mass rapid transit systems—the suburbs—and suburban living was conducive to single-family home construction.

Finally, it appears that the FHA-insured and VA-guaranteed loan programs had the greatest direct benefit to middle-income groups. Neither high- nor low-income earners utilized the programs extensively. To the extent that the FHA increased the capacity of people to borrow for homeownership by encouraging the increased use of amortized loans, longer maturities, and lower down payments it clearly enabled a greater proportion of the population to obtain their own homes.

If, as it appears, the FHA and VA programs have been influential in increasing the flow of resources into housing, what effect has this had on the economic growth of the nation? The answer depends upon how the resources that were utilized for housing would have been used if housing had not been constructed, and the answer is no one knows for certain. Since the financing of resources used in housing came from financial institutions (particularly commercial banks, life insurance companies, and mutual savings banks in the

FHA and VA part of the market), and assuming that the volume of savings in the nation would have been the same regardless of whether or not housing was constructed, then it is reasonable to assert that there would have been expansion in those areas which these institutions were willing to finance if the FHA and VA programs were inoperative. Commerical banks might have expanded consumer credit and therefore encouraged more consumer goods buying; or they might have advanced additional funds to industrial firms for plant and equipment expansion. Mutual savings banks and life insurance companies would probably have increased their holdings of government obligations which would have meant either a lower interest rate on such securities or more construction of public facilities. Given the present state of economic techniques of analysis, it is impossible to analytically measure what the alternative use of resources in the economy would have been in order to give a complete answer to the question of how the FHA and VA programs have influenced economic growth.

The impact of the programs on economic stability are better understood, particularly in the short run. It is generally recognized that in short-run periods the demand for housing is closely associated with the terms and conditions under which credit is available to finance acquisition. In turn, the cost of borrowing funds is closely allied to general monetary conditions, and the FHA and VA have been particularly influential in the mortgage market because they have operated essentially with fixed rates.

When economic activity is relatively high, and rising, the demand for investment capital is strong and interest rates rise. During such periods, because their rates are fixed, the relative position of the FHA-insured loan and VA-guaranteed loan in the market deteriorates. Consequently, lenders transfer their resources into other types of investments. While it is true that discounting procedures operate to equalize the rate of return on FHA's and VA's with other types of investments, such action is possible only to the extent that builders are able to pass the discount on to purchasers—but this cannot always be done, since it is resisted by many types of builders and some lenders. The net result is that in periods of rising interest rates FHA and VA lending declines.

The reverse situation is, of course, also true. When the demand for capital declines the relative attractiveness of FHA and VA loans increases, and purchasers (many of whom postponed action when FHA and VA funds were unavailable) come into the market and demand loans. As a result, the volume of FHA and VA lending increases, precisely at a time when the economy is moving out of a period of high level activity. In this very positive sense, therefore, the FHA and VA programs have been countercyclical—they have expanded when other activities declined.

Do the facts of the housing market in the period since 1950 fit the above analysis? In 1950 51 percent of all housing starts in the United States were financed with loans underwritten by an agency of the federal government, but by 1953 the proportion was 38 percent. While there were restrictions placed on construction by the Korean War during the early part of this period, there is little doubt that the basic underlying factors stimulating housing demand were present in the economy; but mortgage funds were difficult to obtain. Total housing starts dropped from 1.352 million in 1950 to 1.068 million in 1953 during a period of very high economic activity in the nation. By the end of 1953 and early in 1954 when the economy was less buoyant, total housing starts increased almost 200,000—20 percent—and the share of starts financed by the FHA and VA increased from 38 percent in 1953 to 49 percent in 1954. Through 1955, housing starts and the proportion underwritten by federal programs continued to increase, although not as rapidly, until in 1956 when the economy was operating at high levels, housing starts dropped 30 percent and the share of insured and guaranteed loans from 51 to 42 percent of all starts.

The pattern is clear. In the short run, housing starts in the decade of the 1950's increased most during periods of general economic decline because in those periods terms and conditions under which funds could be borrowed were most attractive (FHA and VA) to purchasers. Concurrently, in periods of declining return on other types of investment, and only in such periods, were FHA and VA loans attractive to investors.

Further confirmation of this pattern of activity is apparent in the fact that FHA and VA programs in the 1950's were utilized most by those lenders who could shift funds among various types of investment outlets—life insurance companies, commercial banks and mutual savings banks. The savings and loan associations were relatively unaffected, since the bulk of their funds were invested in conventional loans, and they continued to make such loans on sound property, regardless of the situation in the FHA and VA markets. Since the conventional market increased substantially in size, they were able to increase their share of all residential mortgage lending to about 40 percent of the market.

The countercyclical position of the FHA and VA programs in the housing market and the economy as a whole depends entirely on the proposition that economic conditions do not deteriorate to the extent that the basic underlying demand conditions for housing declines, i.e., population growth slows down, mobility drops, incomes decline, etc. During a period of prolonged unemployment it is very doubtful that changes in the terms and conditions of mortgage credit of the magnitude envisaged in FHA and VA operations could have much countercyclical effect.

Within the context of changes in housing construction during periods of relatively full employment of resources the FHA and VA also serve as effective countercyclical weapons to the extent that by Administrative order—selective credit controls—changes in terms and conditions can be made to bring about changes in construction. It has been strongly stated that selective controls on down payments, etc., are the most effective way of achieving countercyclical aims, and therefore interest rate ceilings should be removed.[1] In support of this position it would appear that if interest rate ceilings were removed from FHA-insured and VA-guaranteed loans such mortgages would still be somewhat lower priced to the borrower than conventional loans, assuming lenders are willing to accept lower returns in exchange for some insurance of risk. At the same time the rate would be competitive with other rates and therefore fluctuations in the total volume of housing starts would be less. There would be more stability in the housing sector. It would be a mistake to think that starts would be completely stable, for the amount of funds advanced by lenders would still vary with alternative rates of return on other investments and particular portfolio situations.

While removing the interest rate ceilings would possibly remove some of the countercyclical activity of housing, it is important to remember that the maximum interest rate ceiling on government-insured or guaranteed loans was never intended for such a purpose in the first place. If it is desirable to limit the total amount of FHA-insured and VA-lending such a goal can be achieved more efficiently through selective credit controls. A case can be made that housing should not be expected to bear the brunt of adjustments which should be controlled through over-all fiscal and monetary policy. On balance the evidence suggests that the freeing of interest rates on FHA and VA loans would serve both the housing sector and the rest of the economy well.

It is apparent that the FHA and VA programs have had major impacts throughout the entire economy in terms of allocation of resources, prices, economic stability and probably economic growth. The programs have led to a greater flow of funds into the mortgage market and therefore an increase in the use of resources for residential construction; they have contributed to the rising price of housing, and they have had a very important stabilization impact in the short run in the post-World War II period. They have unquestionably led to a greater amount of single-family home construction than otherwise would have taken place, and they may well have led to better construction and land planning. They have changed the

---

[1]Leo Grebler, Housing Issues in Economic Stabilization Policy (New York: National Bureau of Economic Research, 1960).

pattern of mortgage lending to the completely amortized long-term loan, and they have probably led to a general increase in the loan-to-value ratio on housing. It is doubtful that they have in the past decade influenced conventional mortgage rates. The demand for funds has been so great that lenders have been able to place their loans without difficulty—and instead of conventional rates being lowered to compete with FHA and VA's, the problem has been one of increasing FHA and VA rates to compete with other returns in the conventional mortgage and general money market.

Secondary Market Facilities

The Federal Home Loan Bank System. Unlike the underwriting programs, the effects of the Federal Home Loan Bank System's operations on economic activity in the economy are less direct. The entire influence of the System has been exerted through its influence on savings and loan associations and the change it has brought in their operation.

There can be no doubt that the FHLB and its related activities have been an important factor in the growth of savings associations. It is very doubtful that associations would have been able to attract as large a share of the savings in the nation as they have without the FHLB. In 1947, savings and loan associations held 8.7 percent of all individual savings in the United States but by 1959 they had 26.8 percent of such savings. This tremendous increase—from $9.8 billion to $54.5 billion—was invested primarily in mortgages and therefore increased the amount of money available to finance housing transfers and construction. Moreover, the great bulk of it was invested in conventional loans.

To the extent that savings and loan associations were able to increase the supply of mortgage funds available to finance conventional loans in the post-World War II period, they contributed to a greater amount of real resources flowing into the housing market. It is estimated that this increased total output from 2 to 3 percent during the 1950's. The Federal Home Loan Bank Board through its advances also enabled savings and loan associations to expand their activities. While it is difficult to estimate the exact amount of net long-term advances during the decade, at the end of 1957 they amounted to $518 million, and short-term advances were $746 million, for a total of $1.2 billion. There is no doubt that with the growth of savings and loan associations these activities are of increased importance. In 1950, for example, advances by the FHLB to member associations equalled 27 percent of the increase in loans made by savings and loan associations in that year, in 1955 they equalled more than 20 percent of the increase in loans. The FHLB has become an important element in controlling the total volume of mortgage credit placed in the market by associations.

In July 1955, during the upswing in economic activity the Chairman of the FHLB encouraged member banks to limit their commitments for advances, and in September the Board started a program of formal restraints to force associations to relate their lending to their cash flows. In October, the restraints were relaxed because of the inability of associations to make rapid adjustments. In spite of these actions, however, advances from the FHLB rose from $688 million in February 1955 to $1,061 million in July and $1,275 million in September, as builders turned more and more to savings and loan associations for funds during a period of tight money.

Advances do not lead to a net increase in mortgage lending of savings and loan associations over a long period of time since they must be repaid, but they do permit savings and loan associations to place more money in the market than otherwise would be the case because they even out the flow of funds through offices.

On balance, the FHLB has increased the amount of resources flowing into the conventional mortgage market, has probably reduced fluctuations of a short-run nature in the amount of conventional funds advanced and has contributed to stability in conventional lending. The impact on total levels of prices has probably not been important, although in 1959 savings and loan associations made 40 percent of all residential mortgage recordings of $20,000 or less. The impact on economic growth has been limited to the extent that savings and loan associations have increased the volume of construction in the nation. While not nearly as important in direct terms as the underwriting programs the influence should not be ignored in analyzing and determining general economic policies.

The Federal National Mortgage Association.[2] The impact of the FNMA has probably been more important in terms of economic stability and stability of activity within the housing sector than it has on the general level of prices, the total volume of construction output or economic growth. Analysis of the impact of operations are complicated by the fact that activities of the FNMA have changed often, and sometimes rapidly, through the years.

There seems to be little doubt that operations of the FNMA were significant in the increase in housing in the 1953-54 period. At that time FNMA was operating under the one-for-one program whereby it agreed to buy from the buyers of its mortgages an equal

---

[2] For a fuller discussion of these points see Jack Guttentag, "The Federal National Mortgage Association," Research Study Two in Federal Credit Agencies, prepared for the Commission on Money and Credit (Englewood Cliffs, N.J.: Prentice-Hall, Inc., 1963), and his "The Short Cycle in Residential Construction," American Economic Review (June 1961), pp. 275-298.

TABLE V-8

Percentage Distribution of Savings of Individuals in Selected Media, 1947-59

Year	Savings & Loan Assns.	Mutual Savings Banks	Com'l Banks	Credit Unions	U.S. Savings Bonds	Postal Savings	Total
1947	8.7	15.7	30.9	0.4	41.2	3.1	100.0
1948	9.5	15.9	30.1	0.5	41.1	2.9	100.0
1949	10.4	16.1	29.2	0.6	41.0	2.7	100.0
1950	11.4	16.3	28.7	0.7	40.4	2.5	100.0
1951	12.7	16.5	28.9	0.9	38.8	2.2	100.0
1952	14.3	16.8	29.2	1.1	36.6	2.0	100.0
1953	16.0	17.0	29.4	1.2	34.6	1.8	100.0
1954	17.9	17.2	29.3	1.3	32.8	1.5	100.0
1955	20.0	17.4	28.7	1.5	31.1	1.3	100.0
1956	21.8	17.6	28.5	1.7	29.4	1.0	100.0
1957	23.2	17.6	29.8	1.9	26.7	0.8	100.0
1958	24.6	17.5	30.8	2.0	24.5	0.6	100.0
1959	26.8	17.~~2~~1	30.8	2.2	22.5	0.5	100.0

Source: Housing and Home Finance Agency, Housing Statistics — Annual Data, Washington, D.C. (March 1961), p. 75.

amount of loans within one year. Since private lenders were unwilling at this time to give commitments, primarily because of the attractive earnings on investments of other types, the willingness of the FNMA to make commitments permitted builders to acquire construction financing which they otherwise might not have been able to obtain. As a result, residential construction was stimulated.

At the start of the housing expansion in 1953, the FNMA was a net seller of loans but as the building boom continued it became a net buyer. In other words, it placed additional funds in the market at a time when the building industry was operating at high levels. Between mid-1954 and mid-1955 it was a net purchaser of $409 million of loans.

Although this was a procyclical action on the part of the FNMA and was important in starting building activity, from the point of view of the total volume of building, once the boom was started the activities of the FNMA were unimportant. It was only a minor factor in speeding up and maintaining the expansion.

In July 1955, the FNMA reduced the price at which it offered to sell its FHA and VA loans from its "management and liquidation" portfolio but sales were few and during the year the Association continued to be a net supplier of funds to the mortgage market.

In 1956, as housing construction declined action was taken through the FNMA to increase the supply of funds in the market. Under provisions of the Housing Act of 1956 the amount of stock which sellers of mortgages to FNMA had to acquire was reduced from 3 to 2 percent of the loans sold. The provision for stock acquisition which was included in the Charter Act was intended to discourage sales to the FNMA and to transfer ownership of the Association to private lenders. The provision was very much disliked by lenders, and therefore when there was a temporary need of funds in the housing market the occasion was used to reduce the stock purchase requirement.

By the Charter Act the FNMA was also permitted to issue forward commitments for secondary market purchases. As a result, sales of underwritten mortgages to the FNMA rose sharply in the fall of 1956—in fact, sales were so great that FNMA would have exhausted its funds if it had not administratively ruled that it would not buy any mortgages originated less than four months before the time of sale. Altogether in 1956 and 1957 the FNMA purchased $1.6 billion of loans, of which $1.4 were VA-guaranteed. In fact, purchases in 1957 were greater than in any other year in the Association's history, and amounted to 18 percent of all FHA and VA loans made that year. There is no question that this activity was an important element in the insured and guaranteed home loan mortgage market, and in the latter part of 1957 FHA housing starts recovered substantially—up 30 percent in the last quarter over the preceding year.

On the other hand, the total volume of activity of the FNMA was not sufficient to stop a decline in underwriting operations. In 1957 FHA and VA loans combined were 35.5 percent less than in 1956; but clearly, they would have been even smaller if the FNMA program had been inoperative. In 1959 FNMA was again very active in the market, when purchases approached $2 billion and sales were practically negligible.

The FNMA financed its activities in the 1950's through sale of securities and short-term borrowing. In 1957 it sold $2.3 billion of securities to the public of which all but $200 million had maturities of less than 10 months, and in 1959 it sold $1.3 billion of securities, all but $200 million of which had maturities of less than 10 months. Given the general compartmentalization of security markets it is doubtful if this financing diverted many funds from the mortgage market. On balance, the activities of the FNMA were essentially all a net gain for the mortgage market.

In general, it would appear that the impact of FNMA on construction was usually below 6 percent a year, although there were variations. Given the general high levels of activity in the economy, the possibilities of the FNMA actually extending the output of housing in the economy without raising prices or limiting other types of operations were quite small. In the 1950's the transfer of resources among various types of construction activity was so great that the operations of the FNMA on the residential sector was primarily to generate inflationary forces.

The special assistance programs had different implications. When it operated to assure the availability to borrowers of VA-guaranteed loans at rates below the mortgage market, it involved massive purchases of loans and a tremendous amount of direct government financing. Under such circumstances, lenders who sold their loans made windfall profits—and indeed, the lack of logic of the program is apparent when it is recognized that many of the VA loans were made at a discount to the veteran and then sold at par to the FNMA. In such circumstances it was not the veteran who received the supposed benefit.

In essence, if the FNMA is to support the FHA and VA markets it must "make a market" for these securities; in the 1950's it did not do so Through the years the FNMA simply bought—and seldom sold. Many of its activities have been hedged by requirements of eligibility and restrictions. It could not act as an agency through which buyers and sellers could get together. Consequently, one of the fundamental purposes of the FNMA, as originally designed, was not achieved. Similarly it is doubtful that the FNMA had any major impact on eliminating yield differentials on mortgages in various areas, although to the extent that it operated in any submarket of the mortgage market it had some effect.

In summary, therefore, an analysis of FNMA's operations indicate (although generalizations are difficult because operations have varied so extensively,) that:

(a) The FNMA did not have extensive influence in directing resources into construction. In no year did it influence more than 6 percent of total construction and usually less than 4 percent.

(b) Operations of the FNMA during the 1950's were probably inflationary in the economy as a whole and the housing sector in particular.

(c) The FNMA operated in a procyclical fashion inasmuch as it increased the supply of mortgage funds in the market during periods when building activity was increasing; and it reduced declines in the housing sector when mortgage money markets were tightened.

(d) It was a very important factor at specific periods in keeping the FHA and VA programs in operation. Without the FNMA the volume of such financing would have been less.

(e) It did not make a market for insured and guaranteed loans and, except for mortgage companies, it did not operate as a lender of last resort.

Summary

During the 1950's the community facilities programs had little or no impact on levels of economic activity, price changes, and resource allocation in an aggregative sense, although they were significant in local markets. The underwriting programs led to an increase in the flow of resources into the housing market, a change in the types of housing constructed, a modification of terms and conditions under which mortgage funds were advanced, an increase in institutional competition for mortgage funds, and an increase in the price of housing and probably all prices in general. The programs acted as unstabilizing factors in the housing sector but have been significant stabilizing forces in the economy as a whole.

On balance, the Federal Home Loan Bank Board operated to encourage cyclical activity in housing and in the economy, although in the future this may not be true. The FNMA was important in supporting the volume of FHA and VA lending and acted in a procyclical fashion in the economy as a whole and in a countercyclical fashion in the housing market. It did not operate as an effective secondary mortgage market, and it was in general an inflationary force in the economy.

V. THE IMPACT OF FEDERAL CREDIT PROGRAMS IN HOUSING ON MONETARY, FISCAL, AND DEBT POLICY

The major programs in housing in the United States were inaugurated in the 1930's when the problems of the economy were unemployment and a general breakdown in the financial sector. Since the end of World War II the economy has been operating at relatively high levels of activity. Therefore, the environment within which the housing programs operated in the past decade has been quite different from the one for which they were designed. Consequently, the impacts of the programs on the economy have changed, and for determining policy it is essential to determine as precisely as possible what the impacts have been in relation to new conditions and new problems.

In this section the impact of housing programs on monetary, fiscal, and debt policy are examined in relation to the general goals for the economy of stable prices, high levels of employment, efficient allocation of resources and an optimum rate of economic growth.

Community Development Programs

Community Facilities Administration. Activity under the loans to communities for both public facilities and public works planning has been so small that it has had no impact on monetary, fiscal, or debt policy. Funds advanced for planning have amounted to only \$12.6 million since the program was inaugurated, and the public facilities loans of \$40.7 million pay interest equivalent to what it costs the Treasury to obtain the money. There has, therefore, been practically no drain on the budget to finance these programs.

By any measure, it would appear that the programs have as yet had little effect on the economy and its operations.

Urban Renewal. As of the end of 1959, the urban renewal program had little impact on the federal budget. Total payments for planning advances amounted to only \$16 million and net loans were \$66 million. Total public outlay for all purposes for all projects was about \$400 million compared to total federal cash outlays during the same period of \$700 billion—obviously, a small proportion.

An impact on the budget, however, is being created because of the increased commitments issued by the urban renewal administration and the growing speed at which urban renewal projects are developing. It is estimated that by 1970 government contributions to urban renewal will amount to about $600 million annually. The extent to which this affects national fiscal and debt policies will depend on the size of the economy and the federal budget at that time.

In general, regardless of the size of operations, the urban renewal program is not well established for fiscal flexibility. The time lags between the initiation of projects and their completion—some have been in one stage or another of development for ten years—clearly suggests that expenditures cannot be rapidly changed to meet national objectives. In addition, as long as local communities must make a major contribution to the financing of such programs it is unlikely that they can be speeded up in periods of unemployment. The only time that a local municipality will undertake additional costs is in periods of general high level activity. If urban redevelopment is to be incorporated into an over-all program of fiscal policy, then the nature of local responsibility for the program will have to be changed.

It is also possible that federal contracts to guarantee privately secured loans might also lead to fiscal difficulties. When private loan funds are scarce the demand for direct federal loans will rise, and this could occur at a time when general fiscal policy would call for restraint. However, by the nature of the commitment such loans would have to be honored.

As the program expands, the demand for funds to finance projects will increase. While some of the necessary money may come from taxes, the major portion will have to be raised by borrowing. The impact of such borrowing on money markets could well influence rates and therefore be a significant factor in the determination of monetary policy.

These observations all pertain to the future and are hinged on the proposition that the nature of the program will not be effectively changed in the next decade. So far, during the period of its operation, from 1949-60, the program has had very little, if any, impact on the money market or the federal budget. Certainly, it has not influenced national monetary and fiscal policies.

Public Housing. The demands for funds from the Treasury to support public housing operations have been relatively small compared to the total expenditures of the Treasury during the period 1946-59. Expenditures that have been made suggest that the program has been countercyclical, i.e., expenditures have been highest during periods of rising employment. If the number of people who needed low-income housing declined during prosperity, theoretically, the program could be made countercyclical. Unfortunately, there is little evidence to suggest that needs for such housing do in acutality decline as economic conditions improve. On the other hand, the unfilled need for such housing is extensive, and it is not without possibility that a backlog of such projects could be prepared for development in case of a decline in economic conditions. It should be noted that the program is not appropriate to assist in short-run economic adjustments because of the time lag between conception and actual construction. Moreover, as in the case of urban renewal, the initiation for such projects must come from local governments, and it is unlikely that they would be as willing to provide their share of the costs of such operations in depressed periods as they are in periods of relative prosperity.

Since 1950, net federal outlays for all parts of public housing programs have been largest in 1951 and 1952, 1957 and 1958. In 1953, expenditures were lowest and in 1954 and 1955 there was a negative outlay. Consequently, in those years during the 1950's when the economy was most active, expenditures on public housing by the federal government were greatest and vice-versa. The federal public housing program as currently constituted did not operate in a countercyclical fashion during the 1950's.

Although direct federal expenditures on public housing have had virtually no impact on the federal budget—cash payments have never exceeded more than .01 percent of total federal cash payments to the public in any one year, there is a potential effect because the government guarantees the bonds sold by public housing authorities to the public. There are two types of such securities; both are sold to private bidders and both are tax-exempt and guaranteed by the Public Housing Administration. The short-term notes are used primarily for working capital although they have also been used for other purposes in recent years. There is no question that they are important in the money market, for in the ten-year period, 1950-60, they accounted for about half of all short-term tax-exempt securities brought to the market by all borrowers. The long-term bonds are serial obligations with a maximum life of 40 years with maturity dates designed so that debt service is level over the life of the loan. While these borrowings have no direct impact on the federal budget they do create a contingent liability inasmuch as the guarantee behind the obligations is the annual contribution of the government to the projects. Under this financial arrangement the guarantee cannot be less than the yearly debt service of all outstanding obligations of local housing authorities; the discounted value of all known future commitments as of July 1, 1957 was estimated at $3.4 billion. As the volume of public housing operations increases, the size of this liability will also increase.

There is no doubt that public housing authority securities have influenced the money market. During 1951, 1952, and 1953 when the Treasury expanded its lending to PHA the interest rate on both short- and long-term government securities increased. While unquestionably the dominant factors in the market were the change in the Federal Reserve policy following the Accord in 1951 and the need for funds arising out of the Korean conflict, it is probable that short-term requirements for PHA had some impact on rates at that time.

Temporary PHA notes make up about half of the market for short-term tax-exempt securities so they clearly have an impact on such financing. Since their maturities have been designed to attract corporate funds held to meet quarterly tax payments, the market is broadened to some extent, but their influence on the costs of short-term credit cannot be ignored. Inasmuch as they are advertised two weeks in advance and are sold on the day after the regular Monday offering of Treasury bills, they come into direct competition with the bill market.

Tax-exempt long-term housing authority bonds have about 10 percent of the long-term exempt market. They compete with other government issues, private and public offerings, as well as mortgages for long-term funds, so it is doubtful that they have much impact on the market.

Finally, with respect to the relationship of public housing to the federal budget, it is estimated that the tax-exempt status of PHA bonds costs the Treasury about $50.00 per unit, an amount equivalent to $22.3 million in 1958.

In terms of over-all monetary policy public housing financial operations are not of a sufficient magnitude, except in the short-term tax-exempt market, to be an effective weapon for monetary control. In the 1950's the program may have exercised some upward pressure on rates, but there is no evidence that it had any impact on general monetary policies.

On balance, it is fair to conclude that in the 1950's the Public Housing Administration operations had little if any impact on the budget or monetary policy and had slight cyclical tendencies. It is also proper to conclude that it is an impractical program for assuring effective operation of fiscal policies in the short run, although with some basic revisions it might be developed into an effective countercyclical program for major depression situations.

Underwriting Programs

The direct impacts of the underwriting programs on debt, fiscal, and monetary policy are not as large as might seem likely, given the size of the programs. Through all their years of operations the budgetary costs of the programs—even when direct lending is considered—have been very small. The $315 million of budget expenditures for the VA program has been more than matched by the $398 million of excess of receipts over expenditures under the FHA operations. Total direct loans of the VA by mid-1959 were approximately $751 million.

The indirect impacts have been large. Certainly, the use of the FHA and the VA programs by institutions has substantially increased the proportion of total residential mortgage debt held by institutions and has drawn the mortgage market in general closer to monetary influence. Moreover, the underwriting of risk, which in many respects has made mortgages more homogeneous debt instruments, has led to freer substitution of mortgages for other types of investments, and vice versa, than was true prior to the early 1930's. The programs have brought mortgage lending to a situation where not only can it affect monetary, debt, and fiscal policy, but in turn monetary, debt, and fiscal policy have a good chance of influencing mortgage lending.

Although exact measures are impossible, it is probable that the underwriting of mortgages by agencies of the federal government has forced interest rates on government securities up. The fact that mortgages have become substitutes for Government bonds in the portfolios of many institutions clearly makes it necessary for the Treasury to offer more competitive rates when borrowing. The extent of the substitution is not known, but immediately following World War II many lenders, particularly savings and loan associations and life insurance companies, made massive transfers of assets from Government bonds to insured or guaranteed mortgage loans, and such action continued in varying degrees throughout the 1950's.

Given the fact that total insurance and guarantees in force in 1957 amounted to $51.6 billion or 42.6 percent of the total residential mortgage debt of $121.2 billion, it is unquestionable that underwriting and guarantees had some effect on the structure of general interest rates. It is important to note that they probably had more <u>direct</u> affect on general interest rates than on conventional mortgage rates, since during the 1950's FHA and VA loans <u>were not</u> substitutes for conventional loans but for "Governments."

The insurance provision of the FHA has implications for interest rates and debt management in the future.[1] Under provisions of the

---

[1] For a complete analysis of the economic significance of the mortgage insurance fund see Ernest M. Fisher and Chester Rapkin, <u>The Mutual Mortgage Insurance Fund</u> (New York: Columbia University Press, 1956).

Housing Act of 1934, as amended, the Commissioner of the FHA was "authorized upon application by the mortgagee to insure.....any mortgage offered to him within one year from the date of its execution which is eligible for insurance...." In order to provide such insurance the Commissioner is empowered "to issue to mortgagees, upon receipt of title of defaulted properties, debentures of the Mutual Mortgage Insurance Fund such debentures to be due and payable three years after the first day of July following the maturity date of the mortgage in exchange for which the debenture is issued." The interest rate on debentures is determined by the Commission and all debentures are fully guaranteed as to principal and interest by the United States.

During the first 20 years of its operations the Fund insured over $18 billion of mortgages and operated with considerable profit. In fact, it paid off all advances for capital and expenses from the Treasury and credited the balance to surplus. At the end of 1955 the Mutual Mortgage Insurance Fund was insuring about $15 billion of property at current market price.

The liabilities of the Fund, however, are less than the outstanding balances because the property is always taken over in exchange for debentures. If a property can be held until market conditions improve (assuming that it was foreclosed because of a general depression), experience indicates that general recovery of all economic activity will increase the value of foreclosed properties, and indeed, the Fund may not experience any loss. The fact of possibility of recovery does not, however, remove the obligation of the Treasury to guarantee several billion dollars of debentures of the Mutual Insurance Fund. Issuing such debentures would increase the availability of funds in the market and, presuming they come out during a depression, could well operate in an important countercyclical manner.

To date the demands for debentures have been so small (approximately $30 million in 20 years against receipts of more than $400 million in fees and premiums) that they have had no effect on money rates, fiscal or debt policy.

The very nature of FHA and VA financing has important implications for monetary policy. The fact that since the introduction of the FHA and VA programs most mortgages are completely amortized on the level payment principle means that it is possible for the credit demands for mortgage financing to vary substantially on both sides of zero. During a period of decline in house building it is possible for repayments to be larger than the demand for funds for new financing. Consequently, the housing sector could be a new supplier of funds to the economy at a time when economic activity is declining. If repayments are immediately reinvested by lending institutions in some other type of operation the effect would be countercyclical. If housing activity were at an extremely low ebb, it is more probable, however, that institutions would buy bonds or securities of the federal government, thus transferring to the government sector the task of improving general economic conditions.

In addition, the fixed payment feature of amortized loans leads to a sharp variation in the proportion of income spent by consumers on housing when income varies. If a sharp depression occurred with a substantial drop in money income payments, a higher proportion of income would have to go to mortgage payments and the volume of uncommited funds for other uses would decline. Therefore, countercyclical policies geared at expanding consumer expenditures would be difficult to implement because a large proportion of consumers' income is committed to mortgage payments. In a sense, the fixed amortized loan payments is a built-in destabilizer in the economy.

Finally, there is much concern about the general objectives of FHA and VA operations and general monetary policy directed toward stabilizing levels of economic activity. It is generally true that in periods of serious economic inactivity alteration of the terms and conditions under which mortgage credit is available has relatively little effect on the volume of real estate activity. However, in the short run changes in the terms and conditions of credit available to finance housing have an important and immediate impact on demand; while a tightening of terms will not necessarily destroy demand, it will certainly lead to its postponement.

As a result any monetary policy designed to restrict credit causes a rise in rates and yields, and the volume of FHA-insured and VA-guaranteed lending drops. Since presumably the reason for a policy of tight money is to limit an overexpansion in the economy, the action of the FHA and VA programs is clearly countercyclical, but at the cost of reducing residential construction.

In fact, in the post-World War II period, largely because of the FHA and VA programs, residential housing activity has operated in a countercyclical manner. It has reinforced monetary policy. But have fixed interest rates been a necessary condition for this result? The answer is uncertain, but it is possible that selective controls could obtain the same result, and indeed, they may have been more important than fixed rates in keeping residential housing operating in a countercyclical fashion in the postwar period. If such is the case, rates should be released and allowed to seek their natural level, which would be below the conventional rate because of the insurance provision and the marketability of such loans. Selective controls could then be utilized to direct resources in and out of the housing market as necessary.

While there are sound arguments on both sides of this question, it is probable that a freeing of the interest rates would not lead to substantially less compensating activity on the part of housing in the economy, and there would be some advantages—the most important being that (1) funds would flow into the mortgage market in a more even manner, (2) the practice of discounting would be discontinued, and (3) the management of mortgage portfolios by lenders—who in the last analysis must advance the funds—would be eased. When lenders feel that the general tendency for rates is to rise, they are reluctant to tie up large portions of their funds in insured and guaranteed loans, even when the possibilities for their sale is present. Indeed, savings and loan associations, which in some areas are paying 4.5 percent plus for savings, find that they must carry the share of their portfolios invested in VA loans at a loss. They therefore attempt to sell them, and this lowers the price of such loans and leads to a loss in operations for the lender. Given this past experience it is unlikely that a lender will be eager to advance as large a portion of his funds in such securities in the future, unless rates move with the market.

While using discretionary powers substitutes the "rule of men" for "rule by law" and implicitly suggests that sufficient data and wisdom are available to permit such discretionary powers to perform effectively, the advantages of free rates for the over-all economy and the housing market outweigh the advantages of fixed rates for short-run economic stabilization.

In summary, the underwriting programs have:

(a) Had little impact on the budget; indeed, they have operated at a net profit to the Treasury.

(b) Raised some questions of debt management, particularly in relation to the issuance of debentures from the Mutual Mortgage Insurance Fund in case of a massive decline in economic activity.

(c) Been highly sensitive to monetary policy because of the immediate response in housing demand to changes in terms and conditions under which mortgage funds are advanced and because mortgage rates are sensitive to general money rates.

(d) Influenced fiscal policy only indirectly to the extent that the programs have altered levels of employment and expenditures in the housing industry.

Secondary Market Facilities

The Federal Home Loan Bank System.[2] The FHLB System had considerable influence on monetary, fiscal, and debt policy during the 1950's. While the System and its member institutions have operated primarily with private funds have not been a charge against the U.S. Treasury, the manner in which the System has operated has had important implications for general policy.

The Federal Home Loan Bank System is tied to the Treasury in two manners: (1) All bonds, notes, debentures, and other obligations sold by the FHLBS must have the approval of the Treasury with respect to maturities, interest rates, terms, conditions, and prices and must be sold only at a period of time approved by the Treasury; and (2) the Secretary of the Treasury is authorized to purchase up to $1 billion of the System's obligations. A careful analysis indicates that at no time has the Treasury limited the Board in its actions, and indeed, has acted primarily as a source of technical information concerning how an issue should be placed. Moreover, the Treasury has not bought the securities of the System, although it does have the right and obligation to do so in case of an emergency. In no manner has the System drawn on the funds of the Treasury for operation.

The impact of the FHLBS operations on fiscal and monetary policy is perhaps more indirect. The FHLBS has stimulated the construction of residential properties by assisting the growth of savings and loan associations and providing associations with a source of credit. To this extent it encouraged expenditures during the past decade.

The impact has in fact actually been more direct to the extent that the FHLB made advances to member institutions. The Banks were a source of funds of both a short- and long-term nature, and at the end of 1957 advances amounted to $1.3 billion or 3.0 percent of members' savings capital. Short-term advances assisted associations in meeting commitments that fell due when savings were not available, and long-term advances fed funds to associations to meet increased demands for loans.

The manner in which such advances are made has an impact on general fiscal and credit policy. To the extent that banks expand advances during periods of general inflation in the economy they

---

[2]For a more detailed analysis see Ernest Bloch, "The Federal Home Loan Bank System," Research Study Three in Federal Credit Agencies, prepared for the Commission on Money and Credit (Englewood Cliffs, N.J.: Prentice-Hall, Inc., 1963).

tend to be procyclical, and vice-versa. If the FHLB increases advances when monetary policy calls for restraint, the System acts against the general policy in the economy—and through the postwar period there are indications that this has happened. In 1955, for example, during a period when a general policy of restraint was being exercised, advances to member associations increased from $688 million in February to $1.2 billion in September.

The pressure on the System to provide advances is strongest during general periods of restraint because it is at such times that borrowers turn to savings and loan associations for funds. High rates of return on alternative forms of investment lead commercial banks and life insurance companies to enter other markets, and therefore builders seek funds from associations which in turn seek advances from the FHLB. The net result is that the FHLBS may operate in a manner counter to that desired from a national point of view.

The FHLBS raises money for advances from sale of debentures in the capital market. The calibre of its obligations is such that the System has had no trouble in raising all the funds it wanted from the capital market in the 1950's, although of course the rate paid has been increased to maintain competition with other forms of obligations. The issuance of consolidated bonds of the System has been limited by administrative action of the FHLBB to 12 times the total capital and statutory reserves of the banks, but at no time since 1937 has this ratio been approached. In fact, the highest ratio of obligations to total capital of the banks was 2.4 to 1 in 1950. In 1957 it was 1.2 to 1. This is considerably less than the 1957 ratio of 12 to 1 in Federal Land banks and 7 to 1 in the Federal National Mortgage Association.

Through the years the obligations of the FHLB have been purchased by commercial banks but there has been a steady increase in the proportion of such obligations held by the public. While there are few data available concerning nonbank buyers, on balance it would appear that such purchasers are less inflationary than those of banks. The issuing of such a volume of debentures has probably contributed to the general rise in money rates in the decade of the fifties.

It is interesting to note that over the long run the System has placed more money into the market than it has taken out. The Home Loan Banks purchase government securities as counterparts to members' payment for stock or deposits of surplus funds, and, of course, associations themselves hold Governments to meet reserve requirements. Between 1948 and 1959 the System as a whole provided $2 billion more funds, i.e., purchased Governments, than it withdrew, i.e., sold FHLB consolidated debentures. The System has been a new borrower only in 1950 ($400 million), 1955 ($250 million) and in 1959 ($320 million)—years in which it was relatively easy to float issues. On balance, the System has not placed a heavy burden on postwar capital markets.

In summary:

(a) The FHLB System makes no demands from the U.S. Treasury for funds to support its operations and therefore has no direct effect on the size of the federal debt.

(b) The large volume of FHLB debentures issued in the market has probably exerted some, although not a great deal of, pressure on the upward movement of interest rates at certain periods in the past decade. However, on balance the System as a whole has purchased more "Governments" than it has sold "obligations."

(c) The timing and amount of advances by banks to member associations can have important procyclical and anti-monetary policy results. Timing of advances has been much more coordinated with association needs than with general needs of the economy.

The Federal National Mortgage Association.[3] The FNMA has had varying effects on monetary, debt, and fiscal policy throughout its history. Prior to the Charter Act of 1954 the FNMA was financed largely by the Treasury. Since then, with the exception of the special assistance program and the sale of stock to the Treasury, FNMA has been operating through the sale of debentures to the public.

In 1959 the Treasury owned about $90 million of preferred stock in the Association, and the Association paid a dividend on such stock equivalent to the average interest rate paid by the government on the total national debt. Common stock is issued to the organizations from whom FNMA purchases mortgages; at the end of 1958 the value of stock outstanding was approximately $37 million.

In order to finance its operations the Association issued debt obligations equivalent to ten times the capital and surplus account, and as of the end of 1958 such outstanding obligations amounted to $1.1 billion. The debenture bonds were not guaranteed by the government and they are not tax exempt. Practically all the issues have

---

[3]Much of this analysis is based on Jack Guttentag, "The Federal National Mortgage Association," Research Study Two in Federal Credit Agencies, prepared for the Commission on Money and Credit (Englewood Cliffs, N.J.: Prentice-Hall, Inc., 1963).

been short term and, while the amount is not large in relation to total short-term issues in the capital market, they have had some impact on raising short-term rates. With the government entering into more and more short-term financing the FNMA's operations have added pressure to the market.

At the mid-point of 1959, approximately 20 percent of the debentures of FNMA were owned by commercial banks, 9 percent by mutual savings banks, 4 percent by insurance companies and 67 percent by all others—savings and loan associations, nonfinancial corporations, state and local governments, corporate pension trust funds, foreign accounts, dealers and brokers, and those banks and insurance companies not reported in any surveys of holdings. From the point of view of operations in secondary markets as conceived after the Act of 1954 it is apparent that the operations of the FNMA are not a heavy drain, indeed only a very modest charge, against the federal budget.

In two other parts of the FNMA operations the Treasury has played an important part. Practically the entire portfolio of loans held by the FNMA in its "liquidation and management" operations was originally financed by the Treasury. While this operation has ceased, and the sale of mortgages has reduced the obligations of the Treasury, the existence of the portfolio is a clear indication of the extent to which the government can be involved in the mortgage market through the FNMA. In addition, under the special assistance portion of the FNMA's operations, in September 1958, $1 billion was appropriated to the FNMA to purchase Veterans Administration guaranteed loans. The need for special assistance of this type is directly related to the fact that the VA-guaranteed loan rate was pegged substantially below conventional and FHA-insured rates. In order to assure the availability of such loans, therefore, the FNMA had to purchase them from lenders and had to pay "above the market rate." Between 1954 and 1959 all appropriations to FNMA—approximately $2.5 billion—were authorized under the special assistance function.

It is clear to the extent that Congress authorizes FNMA to extend and continue its special assistance operations there will be a drain on the U.S. Treasury. It is also clear, from the past experiences of the FNMA, that it is not easy to transfer these costs to the private market. Special assistance programs become a direct lending operation of the federal government.

During the 1950's, in what many consider its major function of "making a market" for federally underwritten mortgages, the FNMA was not particularly successful, primarily because of restrictions on the type of mortgages it could buy and unrealistic price policies. In actual fact, instead of operating as a market, the FNMA was a net purchaser of mortgages which lenders wished to unload. In its efforts to be a self-supporting operation, the Association tried to sell its holdings at prices equal to what it paid for them and since it frequently paid over market prices, it was unsuccessful in doing so.

Finally, to the extent that the FNMA supported the FHA and VA markets, the program operated to stabilize construction but to destabilize the economy as a whole. The sale of FHA and VA loans to the FNMA occurred in periods of rising economic activity which led to additional funds in the mortgage market at the very time other agencies of the government were trying to reduce inflationary pressures.

In summary, since the Charter Act of 1954, the FNMA has:

(a) Utilized the funds of the Treasury for special assistance programs which on balance have exerted an upward pressure on prices.

(b) Operated primarily in a procyclical fashion — Associations' holdings have risen more rapidly during periods of rising construction and least rapidly during periods of falling construction.

(c) Had relatively little impact on monetary policy.

VI. CONCLUSIONS AND RECOMMENDATIONS

Analysis of the operations of the federal credit programs in the housing sector clearly indicates that the programs, in varying degrees, have influenced the allocation of resources, price levels, and the rate of growth in the economy. It is also apparent that the programs have led to important institutional changes in the financial structure of the economy and that they have worked both with and against general monetary, fiscal, and debt policies.

If it is assumed that the general goal of the economic system is to operate with stable prices and sufficient growth to maintain reasonably full employment and that these goals are to be achieved through judicious fiscal, monetary, and debt management, it is evident that certain changes must be made in housing programs if they are to make their contribution to these objectives. At the same time housing programs have certain goals in themselves, and any changes recommended in order to assure general economic goals must be assessed against their impact on the goals of the programs. In the last analysis, when there is a fundamental conflict between the two ends the solution must be chosen in relation to a general evaluation of which is more important—general economic goals or housing goals. Recommendations are given in two parts: First, recommendations for changes in programs as they currently exist are made in relation to their impact on monetary, debt, and fiscal policy. Second, in the latter part of this chapter new programs are considered in relation to total housing goals, and these too are analyzed in relation to monetary, debt, and fiscal policy.[1]

Community Development Programs

Community Facilities Administration. To date the community facilities programs, both in terms of advances for planning and direct loans for construction of public works, have had little impact on resource allocation, price levels or economic growth in an aggregative sense. The volume has simply been too small to influence general economic activity.

In terms of general criteria for the operation of such programs both parts measure up well. Lending for public works construction is done at the cost of borrowing money by the Treasury, and therefore the charge against the budget is small. Moreover, loans are only made when a community cannot obtain funds from a traditional private source. Advance planning grants are, of course, a direct charge against the budget, but the amount involved is extremely small.

In terms of its objective of creating a shelf of public works in communities throughout the nation, the planning program has been ineffective for the simple reason that communities are inclined to build projects once they are planned plus the fact that the general growth of urban areas has led to a great need for additional facilities. If such a shelf of public works projects is an important countercyclical weapon, it is essential that the Community Facilities Administration have the right to designate the time at which projects planned under planning grants advanced from the Administration are put into execution.

The potentialities of the programs for stabilizing the economy in case of a major depression are somewhat limited. Local authorities, given the restraints of current methods of municipal finance, will not build public works projects during a major decline in economic activity. Therefore, even though they can obtain funds inexpensively from the CFA they will not initiate projects. In order for CFA to be an effective weapon for fiscal policy during a depression the Administration must stand ready to make direct grants for public works operations.

---

[1]For another evaluation of housing programs see Ernest M. Fisher, A Study of Housing Programs and Policies (Washington: Housing and Home Finance Agency, 1960).

In terms of developing stand-by policies to meet the needs of a depression, it is necessary for the CFA to explore the problems involved in developing such a program, particularly in terms of timing and administration. In periods of serious depression public facilities construction in local areas may well prove to be an effective method of rapidly increasing government expenditures.

Public Housing. During the last half of the decade of the fifties the public housing program had little impact on resource allocation, price levels or the rate of economic growth, in the nation as a whole. However, certain aspects of the operation have had some influence on monetary policy. Public housing operations are not in competition with private institutional lenders and have had little or no effect on the operations of these institutions.

The impact of public housing on monetary policy is indirect and arises out of the sale of short-term public housing notes. In certain periods in the past decade these notes have amounted to as much as one-half of all tax-exempt government-guaranteed bills in the market. They have competed for funds against other offerings and have forced rates up.

While it is recognized that such financing has been relatively inexpensive for the Public Housing Administration in a direct sense, it may well be that in the long run the pressure on prices created by the offerings may have made the gain more illusory than real. Moreover, since the Public Housing Administration is involved in essentially long-term operations—the building and financing of housing—it would be wise to take the PHA out of the short-term market. This could be done through developing a revolving fund—originally supported by the Treasury—to provide the short-term needs of the Authority.

Public Housing operations in the post-World War II period have not operated in a countercyclical manner, although the total impact has been very slight. In those years when the economy was most active public housing expenditures were highest. The lag between planning and execution of such projects is such that public housing is not an effective short-run stabilization weapon.

There is some doubt as to whether or not public housing, as presently constituted, can be an effective fiscal policy weapon in periods of serious depression. All public housing must be initiated at the local level and the financial impecunity of local municipalities during depressions makes it somewhat uncertain as to whether or not such projects would be initiated at the time when they were most needed. If public housing is to be adopted as a method of implementing increased government expenditures in the face of a serious depression, study should be undertaken as to how such programs can be implemented without cost to local municipalities but with local municipal support.

In terms of the total over-all objective of public housing of providing satisfactory accommodations for low-income members of society there is no question that this objective has not been fulfilled. Moreover, there is considerable concern as to whether or not public housing as constituted will ever be an effective answer to the need. The experience with existing operations indicates that the construction of massive centers of such housing with specified admission requirements does little more than create new areas of inadequate housing. It is clear that the entire public housing approach needs rigorous examination and indeed experimentation with new approaches. As presently constituted, the public housing program is neither effectively achieving its major purposes nor making a contribution to general programs promoting full employment, stable prices, and economic growth.

Urban Renewal. During its first decade of operations, 1949-59, the urban renewal program had little aggregative impact on employment, prices, and the rates of economic growth. Similarly, primarily because of its size, the program had little influence on monetary, fiscal, or debt policy.

As the program grows, and the existence of current commitments and a backlog of a decade of experience indicates that it will, it will have an increasingly larger impact on the economy, and on monetary, debt, and fiscal policy.

The basic pressure of an increased program will fall on the Treasury, since it will consist of a substantial expansion of direct grants to finance the cost of "writing down" the acquisition price of property. The effect of this increased Treasury obligation will depend to a considerable extent on how the funds are acquired and levels of general economic activity in the economy. If funds are obtained by Treasury borrowing of newly created money from banks, there will be a substantial expansionary impact on the economy at the time of acquisition. On the other hand, if funds are obtained by tapping the private money income stream, expenditures on urban renewal will merely offset expenditures on private investment. To the extent that new funds are placed in the economy through operation of urban redevelopment and there are unemployed resources the impact will be chiefly on output; at full employment the impact will be primarily on prices.

The urban renewal program does not in its present form lend itself to effective fiscal policy. The time between the start of a project and its completion is extremely long and there is little or no flexibility in its operation. As in the case of public housing and community facilities programs the initiative for the projects must come from local areas and it is unlikely that communities would be willing to support such projects during periods of serious economic depression.

The lack of fiscal compensatory operations is intensified by the fact that the major contribution of the federal government to the program—the capital grant—is made when the project is completed, regardless of the nature of conditions in the economy at the time. Since the capital grant is a necessary condition for the success of the entire project it would be better to carry it as a capital outlay for bringing property into new use rather than as an expense. It could thereby be advanced over the life of the project. In this manner some flexibility could be introduced into the financing of the programs.

Possibly many of the problems associated with financing urban renewal could be alleviated by the creation of an urban renewal bank. The function of the bank would be to loan funds to finance redevelopment projects that are economically sound. It would be operated on the basis that only those projects which can pay for themselves through increased real property tax returns would be undertaken. Under such circumstances a bank could provide low cost, long-term capital to absorb a current deficit, with the assurance that the ultimate increase in local tax revenues would generate the funds to retire the loans. The bank would operate as a bank making intelligent investment decisions, and the redevelopment program would be removed from the complications of direct Treasury financing.

Urban redevelopment as originally conceived was a plan for placing land into its highest and best use. Through the years, for many good reasons, this basic premise has been almost lost as various social problems have been related to urban renewal operations. With the increasing size of urban renewal and the prospective impact of the program on fiscal policy and monetary policy the program should be restudied to clearly differentiate the social and economic impacts.

<u>Summary</u>. Direct federal government programs in the housing sector should be related to over-all policies for economic activity in the nation primarily through their impact on fiscal policy. None of the current programs, as they are now instituted, contributes to the operation of compensatory fiscal policy, nor is there any manner under their present structure by which they can be tied into fiscal policy. From the point of view of short-run stabilization the lag between commencement and completion of projects is so long that the programs cannot be utilized for fiscal policy purposes, and in the long run the fact that the initiation of projects lies with local municipalities, which must participate financially to a certain extent

in projects, indicates that such programs will not be started in the depth of a serious economic depression.

The impact of the programs on monetary policy comes primarily through the volume of short-term Public Housing Administration issues in the market, which has exerted an upward pressure on interest rates.

In order to relate the programs to national goals of economic policy it is recommended:

(1) That programs planned under planning advances for public works made by the Community Facilities Administration be commenced only under authority of the Community Facilities Administration and that the Community Facilities Administration give permission for the execution of such projects in light of general fiscal policy.

(2) That the Public Housing Administration finance its short-run operations out of a revolving fund and that it cease to issue short-term obligations.

(3) That the Public Housing Administration explore new means and methods of meeting the housing needs of low-income groups without direct government construction.

(4) That capital grants under the Urban Redevelopment Program be advanced through the economic life of the improvement placed on the redeveloped land and that costs of construction and development be financed through long-term issues of obligations.

(5) That study be given the possibilities of converting the Urban Renewal Administration lending operations into an Urban Renewal Bank operation designed to finance urban renewal on a sound economic basis.

(6) That all direct participating programs develop plans whereby the federal government can absorb the local communities' portion of the cost of any program when in the light of general fiscal policy it appears in the public interest to stimulate expenditure in the nation.

Underwriting Programs

The underwriting programs have had important implication for resource allocation, prices, and economic growth in the nation since their inception and they have also been influenced by, and in turn have influenced general monetary, fiscal, and debt policy. What changes are necessary in these programs to help them better achieve over-all national economic and housing objectives?

The underwriting programs in housing measure up well to many of the standards set for federal credit programs. In essence they have been self supporting and they have operated through existing financial institutions, although they have had some influence in changing the importance of different types of institutions in the market. In addition, they have led to a great institutionalization of mortgage debt which has brought mortgage lending more directly under the influence of monetary, fiscal, and debt management programs.

Given this operating record there is little reason to recommend a major change in the method by which the programs are organized. It is unreasonable, however, to maintain part of the underwriting operation outside of the central housing agency of the federal government. Therefore, it is recommended that the VA-guaranteed loan program be transferred for administrative operations to the FHA and that the VA program be terminated as soon as feasible, inasmuch as it is reasonable to believe that the basic purpose for which it was established has been accomplished. The direct lending program of the VA should be operated in conjunction with the Voluntary Home Mortgage credit program and the FHA Certified Agency program. Direct lending should not take place in areas where FHA-insured loans are available.

Perhaps the most controversial portion of the FHA and VA operations is the fixed interest rate policy. It is argued that such fixed rates serve as "built-in" stabilizers in the economy.

As has been pointed out, when the economy prospers and interest rates rise, FHA and VA lending drops and house construction slows down, and vice versa. In a very real sense, therefore, the fixed rates while dampening total housing operations have operated in a general countercyclical fashion to reinforce over-all monetary policy. These same objectives can be obtained by selective controls, and the freeing of rates would lead to a more orderly operation of the mortgage market. Lenders would be able to arrange portfolio operations more easily and borrowers would still receive the advantage of acquiring loans at below conventional rates because of the insurance. Moreover, the practice of discounting, with its inflationary impact on housing prices, would be eliminated.

The importance of selective controls in housing as adjuncts to over-all monetary policies cannot be overestimated. Selective controls involve decision making which can be effective only if based on sound evidence. It is therefore recommended that the FHA inaugurate a substantial program of research on local market operations to assure a proper flow of information for basic decision-making purposes.

Through the years the FHA has devoted considerable attention to increasing single-family home construction. With the increased urbanization of the nation efforts should be made to encourage rental building by insuring high ratio of loan to lending value loans on rental housing and attempts should be made to permit special slow rate of amortization over the full life of the property. In this manner, persons owning housing units that are rented would be provided an offset to the advantage accruing to homeowners through current income tax policies.

It is unrealistic for the FHA to have to go to Congress each year to obtain additional authority to insure loans. The limit should be raised to guarantee effective operation of the program in a growing economy and to remove the current minor harassment involved in getting it increased annually.

Finally, through the years the insurance provisions of the FHA have become exceedingly complex. Efforts should be made to simplify the insurance procedures, possibly by establishing one formula for one- to four-family housing, one for rental housing and one for cooperative housing.

In order to assure the coordination of the federal underwriting programs in the housing sector of the economy with national objectives of full employment, stable prices, and economic growth it is recommended that:

(1) The VA-guaranteed loan program administration be incorporated within the FHA-insured loan operations.

(2) Interest ceiling on FHA and VA loans be removed.

(3) HHFA sponsor research on housing and mortgage markets at both the local and national level.

(4) FHA insurance procedures be simplified.

Secondary Market Facilities

The Federal Home Loan Bank System. The Federal Home Loan Bank System has increased the flow of funds into the mortgage market through stimulating the growth of savings and loan associations by its policy of advancing funds to associations to meet both short- and long-term needs. The System is operated without charge to the federal government and has no direct impact on the budget. However, the System's operations have important implications for monetary and fiscal policy and the general housing objectives of the nation.

The FHLBS cannot directly assist in the operation of fiscal policy—either in the short or the long run. The only way in which the System can influence the pattern of expenditure in the nation is to increase or decrease advances. In the short run savings and loan associations' patterns of operations are too inflexible to respond to rapid changes in advances; and since the System's prime purpose is to operate as a liquidity source for associations it cannot abandon this function to meet the needs of national fiscal policy. Moreover, in the long run the System cannot be expected to make a major contribution to fiscal policy since in the depths of a depression it could only increase advances to member associations—it could not operate to generate housing demand.

The System raises its funds for advances to members through sale of securities. In the past it has offered many of these funds in the short-term market and it is probable that these offerings have placed pressure on short-term rates. Inasmuch as the funds are utilized to facilitate long-run mortgage lending it is recommended that the Board develop a means and methods of financing in the "more than one year" market, and thereby relieve pressure on the short-term market.

Since a fundamental purpose of the System is to provide a secondary credit accommodation for member associations, it is absolutely essential that associations be able to count on the System's performing such a function. Therefore, it is recommended that the System should not make any major change in its operations without notifying member associations well in advance—possibly 9 to 12 months. Unless this is done associations cannot honor their commitments.

The System should not expand its "long-term" advance operations beyond the level of the late 1950's—roughly 1.2 times its capital. The result of such operations is primarily to take funds out of the capital market and redirect them into mortgage lending through savings and loan associations. The fundamental function of the System is to provide liquidity for its members, and a sharp rise in its long-term advances to members makes it more difficult to perform such a function. For example, when a program of long-term advances redirects resources of the nation into housing and thereby causes an upward shift in prices, the requirement of price stability might force the System to attempt to adjust the flow of resources into housing by restricting advances. With an even larger portion of associations' operations dependent on borrowed funds this becomes more difficult to do.

The thesis has been strongly advanced that nonbank financial intermediaries play a significant and much underrated role in the creation of credit—that they are much more than brokers of loanable funds. If such is the case, i.e., that commercial banks and savings and loan associations are indistinguishable in their capacity to create credit, it can be argued that central banking operations in the 1950's were too narrow in scope. It would appear, however, that orderly activity in the housing and mortgage markets can be assured by continued operations of the Federal Home Loan Bank System and that it is not feasible at this time for savings and loan associations to be brought more directly under the control of the Federal Reserve System. It is recommended that:

(1) The Federal Home Loan Bank System transfer its financing operations to the long-term market.

(2) All changes in policy with respect to the availability of commitments be made at least 9 to 12 months in advance.

(3) Borrowing be limited to the amounts necessary to facilitate orderly operation of the System as a source of liquidity for member associations.

The Federal National Mortgage Association. Since the Charter Act of 1954, the FNMA has had two major areas of operations—special assistance and secondary market. In neither respect has it operated in an optimum manner.

Special assistance programs should not, by and large, be operated through the FNMA. If the ceiling on FHA-insured and VA-guaranteed loans were removed, one of the pressure areas for such operations would automatically be eliminated; but even if this does happen, the FNMA should not be utilized to support the VA market. Constituted as it is, when it is used for such a purpose, the net result is that the advantages of the support go to lending institutions and not the veteran and that at best it can operate only on a random basis, creating windfall profits for certain institutions. FNMA support for special housing programs is much more deceptive than direct lending programs and probably less effective. On balance it would appear that the major function properly remaining for the special assistance portion of the FNMA program is to operate as a lender of last resort. This is a program that can easily be abused and it might be well to consider reinstatement of the one-for-one program if such a function is to be continued.

If the FNMA is to act as a secondary market, efforts should be made to eliminate operating in a procyclical fashion. The removal of fixed rates on FHA and VA loans would be a first step in such a direction, but it is also important for the FNMA to adopt a price policy whereby it leads the market instead of following it. The most important need is the establishment of a true secondary market ~~for~~ for mortgages. It is recommended that consideration be given to means and methods of transferring the FNMA from a mortgage support program to a true market operation.

Supplementary Needs in the Housing Sector

Mortgage Markets. Analysis of the financial system indicates that during the past 50 years it has responded well to the needs for channeling funds into the residential mortgage market. The proportion of all funds invested in housing has increased rapidly, the cost of borrowing over the long term has been reduced, the amortized loan has made residential mortgage lending more sound, and there has been some improvement in the flow of funds among markets. The Federal Home Loan Bank System has provided liquidity for the major institutional mortgage lender and has tapped the general financial market for funds for residential mortgage lending, and the FNMA has improved the marketability of mortgages. The proportion of home-ownership in the nation has increased and the total housing stock has been expanded.

In spite of the fine record, future long-term growth in the housing sector could be restrained if the prospective increase in demand for capital through the coming years is not met by increased savings, or if there are unnecessary restraints on the movement of funds into the mortgage market. Efficient as past operations have been, there is still need for some change if the challenge of housing the prospective population increase is to be met.

Lending Institutions. In the final analysis the funds to finance housing must come from savings and more and more of these savings are being channeled into the mortgage market through institutional lenders. The demand for funds is generated by and large in local markets and lenders operate to a considerable degree in response to local market situations. It is important that all lenders be permitted to compete effectively in such markets not only to assure a substantial flow of funds into mortgage lending but to guarantee a competitive local market situation. It is therefore recommended that laws and regulations limiting the mortgage lending activities of commercial banks and life insurance companies be changed. Specifically, these institutions should be permitted to make mortgage loans under the same terms and conditions as savings and loan associations. The basic change would be an equalization in the permissible ratio of loan to lending value.

The regulations limiting the proportion of savings and time deposits which commercial banks can lend on the security of real property should be raised from the current level of 60 percent, and efforts should be made to create uniform state laws governing real estate lending operations of life insurance companies. A division should be established within the Federal Reserve System equivalent to the Federal Home Loan Bank to act as a liquidity source for residential mortgage. Such a division should not be utilized for short-run liquidity needs, as in the case with the FHLB, but should operate as a lender of last resort in times of general liquidity crisis. It is recommended that mutual savings banks be federally chartered and that the rules and regulations governing their operations be completely re-examined, particularly with reference to the acquisition of mortgages.

The advantages of increasing participation of lending institutions in the mortgage market are fundamentally (1) that competition in local markets would increase with salutory effects, and (2) that additional funds would flow into the mortgage market as demand conditions warranted.

The importance of operating at the local market level cannot be overemphasized. It is at this point that mortgage lending takes place, and it is in the local market where the basic impact of lending policies is felt. It is fundamental therefore that efforts be made to remove state and local restrictions limiting lending on the security of real property.

<u>The Intermarket Movement of Mortgage Funds</u>. In spite of the loan participation program of savings and loan associations, the Voluntary Home Mortgage Credit Program, and the operations of the FHLB and FNMA, the difference in effective mortgage rates among regions and local areas is much greater than seems justified by origination and service costs, given equal risks. Efforts must be made to improve the flow of money among areas.

One major institutional residential mortgage lender, the life insurance company, is in an admirable position to operate as a marginal supplier of funds in markets. Restrictions and regulations have often prohibited life insurance companies from fulfilling such a function. This problem should be solved by establishing uniform laws governing lending operations in all states.

The free flow of funds among local markets will never take place until there is a national market for mortgages. The difference among the securities behind conventional loans makes it almost impossible for such loans to be treated as homogeneous and therefore susceptible to purchase and sale in a national market. On the other hand, experience has demonstrated that FHA-insured and VA-guaranteed loans can be and are bought and sold. The FNMA was originally established to provide a market for such loans, and it is essential that it perform this important function. Care should be taken in establishing the working rules of such an institution that it does not act to support the mortgage market, or a section of it, in opposition to general economic trends and policies.

TABLE V-9

An Estimate of New Housing Starts in the Decade of the Sixties

Increase in non-farm households	10,100,000
Add: Housing units lost through destruction, conversion to other use, merger, etc.	3,500,000
Increase in vacancies	400,000
Seasonal and other "second home" requirements	750,000
Gross need for new housing units	14,750,000
Less: Units supplied by conversion, trailers, public housing, etc.	1,250,000
New private non-farm housing starts	13,500,000
Annual average	1,350,000

Source: The Next Decade, United States Savings and Loan League, 1959, p. 18.

TABLE V-10

Estimated Residential Construction Expenditures and Increase in Residential Mortgage Debt, 1960-1970
(1958 prices)
(In billions of dollars)

Year	Residential Construction Expenditures*	Increase in Residential Mortgage Debt
1960	19.1	11.9
1961	20.0	12.2
1962	21.0	13.0
1963	22.0	13.6
1964	22.9	14.2
1965	24.0	14.9
1966	25.0	15.5
1967	26.2	16.2
1968	27.4	17.0
1969	28.6	17.7
1970	29.9	18.5

*Includes additions and alterations, but excludes repair and maintenance.

Source: The Next Decade, United States Savings and Loan League, 1959, p. 20.

Central Mortgage Bank. For many years there have been recommendations that a Central Mortgage Bank be established to supplement existing institutions in the mortgage market. A bank is recommended (1) to operate in alleviating the impact of "tight money" policies on the mortgage market by standing ready to purchase mortgages at such times, (2) to assist in attracting more funds into the mortgage market by selling securities to pension funds, etc., on the grounds that a debt instrument of the bank would be much more acceptable to many investors than mortgages, both for legal and preference reasons.

A Central Mortgage Bank will create important problems for economic stabilization if it is organized as has sometimes been proposed. Given the general needs for economic stabilization it would seem more appropriate to organize a facility, without a market support program, to issue mortgage bonds to investors who will hold bonds but not mortgages. To some extent the FHLBS and the FNMA have operated in this manner by issuing debentures. However, if the need for mortgage funds in the next decade is as large as has been predicated, it will be important to tap new sources of funds, and this should be done through a Central Mortgage Bank limited to issuing bonds against the security of mortgages but not designed to support the mortgage market at all times and under all conditions.

Steps to improve existing organizations and the flow of funds into the market by removing restrictions on existing institutional lenders are much more important at this time than the immediate organization of a central bank and indeed may be necessary first steps before an effective bank can be established.[2]

Direct Lending Programs. The direct lending programs have been almost entirely involved in improving the housing stock in local municipalities. In order to improve the administrative effectiveness of these programs it is recommended that study be given means and methods of simplifying the operations of these programs at both the local and federal level. Since local housing in the last analysis is a local responsibility, it is further recommended that federal agencies rigorously insist on an active local "workable program" for elimination of blight and slums before direct federal aid of any type is advanced.

Administration. By any definition the United States is now an urban nation. Over 66 percent of the population lives in metropolitan

---

[2]See Oliver Jones and Leo Grebler, The Secondary Mortgage Market (Los Angeles: Graduate School of Business Administration, University of California, 1961).

areas and a large percentage of the population increase in the decade of the fifties was in urban regions. In addition, government programs in the housing sector are among the largest in the economy. It follows that there should be a Secretary of Housing and Metropolitan Affairs in the federal cabinet and that the HHFA and related activities should be co-ordinated in a Department of Housing and Urban Affairs.

This change should be accompanied by the appointment of a senior officer in the Department of Housing and Urban Affairs with the prime responsibility of co-ordinating housing programs with national monetary, debt, and fiscal policies.

APPENDIX

Given the nature and purpose of this study, I have made no attempt to specifically document each fact on which the analysis in the report is based. However, the interested reader will find sources for all the facts in various published and unpublished reports of the Commission on Money and Credit. I have drawn most heavily from George F. Break, "Federal Loan Insurance for Housing"; Ernest Bloch, "The Federal Home Loan Bank System"; and Jack Guttentag, "The Federal National Mortgage Association." All of these Research Studies appear in Federal Credit Agencies (Englewood Cliffs, N.J.: Prentice-Hall, Inc., 1963).

I have also used the monographs submitted to the Commission by the financial trade associations: The Savings and Loan Business: Its Purposes, Functions, and Economic Justification, prepared by Leon T. Kendall for the United States Savings and Loan League; The Commercial Banking Industry, prepared by The American Bankers Association; and Mortgage Companies: Their Place in the Financial Structure, prepared by Miles L. Colean for the Mortgage Bankers Association of America. These monographs are available from Prentice-Hall, Inc.

Finally, I have drawn from unpublished documents prepared at various times and for various purposes for the Commission. The most important of these are Robert C. Turner and Joseph Ewers, "Federal Credit Programs for Community Development" and Leo Grebler, "The Influence of Credit Policies on Housing."

Research Study Six

SOURCES OF FUNDS AVAILABLE TO FEDERAL LENDING AGENCIES

Robert C. Turner
Ross M. Robertson
Indiana University

THE PURPOSE AND PLAN OF THE RESEARCH STUDY

The problem of ascertaining the sources of funds available to federal lending agencies is at once disarmingly simple and annoyingly complex. Analytically, it is simple in the sense that funds of the lending agencies can come from only tow sources—from tax monies (appropriations) or from the proceeds of securities sold to private investors. Complexities emerge as we try, agency by agency, to add up for a span of years the precise amounts obtained for ultimate lending. Moreover, there is the problem of deciding what we mean by a federal lending agency. Some units of the federal government clearly extend credit on much the same basis as a private lender; in exchange for a promissory note or other evidence of debt they disburse funds that are to be repaid on an agreed maturity date. But at least two governmental agencies, the Commodity Credit Corporation and the Federal National Mortgage Association, are engaged in price support operations, and the question arises whether an extension of credit in the accepted sense of the word actually takes place. Finally, certain agencies guarantee or insure loans, and the analyst must ask himself in what way these agencies extend credit, for it is obvious that private institutions do the lending while the government simply absorbs most of the risk.

In order to keep this paper of manageable length and to present an analysis that is both comprehensive and helpful, we have arbitrarily and somewhat ruthlessly simplified some of the conceptual problems. For example, because the Commodity Credit Corporation largely performs its function by making nonrecourse loans to farmers, conventional practice classifies the CCC as a lending agency. For this reason we have included CCC loans in some of the summary tables. Yet it is clear that the Commodity Credit Corporation is in no meaningful or usual sense an extender of credit. Making loans on the basis of agricultural commodities offered as collateral, the Corporation is repaid only if prices of the products rise above the support prices so that "borrowing" farmers can gain by repaying their loans. In the event that prices of supported products fall below support levels before the maturity dates of notes, the Corporation simply takes title to the "collateral" and has no recourse against borrowing farmers to recoup losses. It is inaccurate to speak of such a heads-you-win-tails-we-lose agreement as a true extension of credit, and in our final summation of fund sources borrowings from the Treasury for crop price supports are neglected. It may be argued, of course, that the Federal National Mortgage Association, which has as a major objective the support of prices of federally underwritten mortgages, performs a function not unlike that of the CCC. Yet, as we shall see, FNMA does stand to gain as well as lose from its transactions, as do the private operators who deal with the agency. For this reason, we have included FNMA among federal lending agencies for purposes of analysis.

We have followed a similar procedure in dealing with the guaranteeing and insuring agencies, chiefly the Veterans Administration and the Federal Housing Administration. It may be of passing interest to be reminded of the magnitudes involved; the fact remains that the actual loans are made by private parties, and, while in the case of the VA guarantee of loans there is an element of subsidy, credit extension does not take place as it does when the Veterans Administration makes a direct loan to a veteran.

The ultimate purpose of this monograph is to examine the economic effects of federal lending as agencies obtain funds from the Treasury or as a result of entering into the money and capital markets. Preceding the discussion of these presumably different effects will be a summary presentation of the programs and magnitudes involved. The paper is therefore divided into two parts. In Part I we first set forth the amounts of outstanding loans, guarantees, and insurance for major federal programs. Since the Bureau of the Budget, in making its estimates, omits outstanding loans for certain "quasi-public" credit programs, it is necessary to make a separate reckoning for certain activities of the Farm Credit Administration, the Federal Home Loan Bank Board, and the Federal National Mortgage Association. We then go on to list the sources and amounts of funds available to the federal lending agencies. The most important categories are borrowings in the private capital market and borrowings from the U.S. Treasury, but stock purchases by private parties and by the Treasury constitute a modest source of funds. Only a small amount of funds are obtained nowadays from direct Treasury appropriations, but it will be necessary to note the magnitude of this source as well as the amounts added to sources through repayment of previous loans, earnings from fees and interest, and sales of assets.

The data having been presented, it will then be possible in Part II to see what effect the different ways of obtaining funds may have both on the economy and on the acceptability of the several programs to the voting public. In this section the authors make no attempt to assess the merits of the lending programs. It is simply our purpose to indicate, on the assumption that the voters through their congressional representatives have demanded certain programs, how financing may be selected that will achieve stated objectives and at the same time remain consistent with stabilization policy. In this connection it will be necessary to describe how certain agencies, the "quasi-public" ones in Bureau of the Budget terminology, obtain funds in the money and capital markets by selling the so-called "agency issues."

I. AMOUNTS AND SOURCES OF FUNDS, BY LENDING AGENCY

Perhaps the most useful introduction to our subject may be obtained from a glance at Table VI-1. This table shows actual and estimated totals of both direct loans and guarantees and insurance for major federal credit programs outstanding at the end of fiscal years 1959, 1960, and 1961. Because we are concerned only with domestic lending programs, foreign loans are not included in the table.[1]

---

[1] The magnitudes of foreign loans are substantial. Four categories — Treasury Department: Loan to United Kingdom; Export-Import Bank; Department of State: International Cooperation Administration; and Development Loan Fund — accounted for an estimated $11,584 million of direct loans and investments outstanding at the end of fiscal 1961, so that the total of direct loans estimated for fiscal 1961 would be $24,690 million if the foreign figures were included. On the other hand, guarantees and insurance of foreign loans are negligible, the Development Loan Fund accounting for only $20 million. If foreign agencies were included, the grand total of Table VI-1 would be $97,872 million. (See Special Analysis of Federal Credit Programs in the 1961 Budget, page 6.)

TABLE VI-1

Outstanding Loans, Guarantees and Insurance for Major Federal Credit Programs Classified by Agency or Program
(in millions)

Agency or program	1959 actual		1960 estimate		1961 estimate	
	Direct loans and investments	Guarantees and insurance	Direct loans and investments	Guarantees and insurance	Direct loans and investments	Guarantees and insurance
Housing and Home Finance Agency:						
Federal National Mortgage Association	$3,440		$3,541		$3,679	
Urban Renewal Administration	71	$273	126	$426	144	$645
Community Facilities Administration	585		792		965	
Federal Housing Administration	318	28,414	345	32,872	368	37,332
Public Housing Administration	89	3,335	93	3,527	94	3,819
Veterans Administration	1,053	30,300	1,380	30,207	1,465	29,850
Department of Agriculture:						
Rural Electrification Administration	2,974		3,188		3,415	
Farmers Home Administration	914	169	939	161	918	144
Commodity Credit Corporation	2,251	230	1,245	414	1,037	271
Department of Commerce: Maritime Administration	207	191	190	303	175	503
Civil Aeronautics Board		17		28		34
Interstate Commerce Commission		3		64		158
Expansion of defense production	204	335	193	357	178	304
Small Business Administration	339	64	438	85	548	102
Department of Health, Education, and Welfare	31		69		120	
Total by type of assistance	12,476	63,331	12,539	68,444	13,106	73,162
Grand total	75,807		80,983		86,268	

Source: Special Analysis of Federal Credit Programs in the 1961 Budget, p. 6, (adjusted to exclude foreign loans).

The figures largely speak for themselves. It may be worth pointing out that the increase of $9.8 billion in the grand total of guarantees and insurance since the end of 1959 primarily reflected increased insurance of mortgage loans by the Federal Housing Administration. Programs of the FHA and the VA account for more than 90 percent of the total of guarantees and insurance, most of the remainder being long-term obligations of the Public Housing Administration. Both the guaranteed and the unguaranteed portions of outstanding loans are included in the total of guarantees and insurance, so that these gross figures are not a proper measure of the contingent liability of the federal government. The major program for which the contingent liability differs materially from the principal amount of the loans is the Veterans Administration guaranty program; by the end of 1961, the U.S. liability was estimated at about $13.3 billion lower than the amount of nearly $30 billion shown.

Perhaps more meaningful as an indicator of the size of federal credit programs was the actual volume of new commitments to these programs. Table VI-2 shows, as nearly as it is possible to do in so brief a space, the approximate magnitude of lending and guaranteeing and insuring activity in recent years. According to the Bureau of the Budget, commitments are defined simply as approval by federal agencies of direct loans and of insurance or guarantees of private loans, but some commitments do not result in an actual credit extension. Again, both the unguaranteed or uninsured positions of loans are included in the totals found in the guarantee and insurance columns. The estimated $3.15 billion of new commitments for 1961 was a surprisingly small quantity in view of the general impression that the government is extremely active as a lender.

It is important to observe that there are excluded from these amounts what a good many people would consider the most important credit activity of the federal government — that of the quasi-public agencies.[2] Of the quasi-public agencies three, Banks for Cooperatives, Federal Intermediate Credit banks, and Federal Land banks are supervised by the Farm Credit Administration. Another agency, the Federal Home Loan banks, is under the supervision of

---

[2]However, total commitments overstate, perhaps by as much as $2 billion, the net amount of credit assistance extended by the federal government, the reason being that two or more types of assistance may sometimes be provided for the same borrower or the same property at different stages in the financing process. Thus a loan insured by the FHA or guaranteed by the VA may later appear as a mortgage purchase by FNMA.

the Federal Home Loan Bank Board. Finally, with respect to its secondary market operations only, the Bureau of the Budget classifies the Federal National Mortgage Association, supervised by the House and Home Finance Agency, as a quasi-public agency.[3] Table VI-3 shows the outstanding loans for these institutions at the end of fiscal 1958 and fiscal 1959.

Following, by major categories, are the federal lending agencies (engaged in domestic credit programs) contained in the authors' check list. The grouping under the headings of Agriculture, Business, Housing, and Miscellaneous conforms to the classification used in other Commission studies.

Agencies Administering Federal Credit Programs

Agriculture

- Farm Credit Administration
  - Federal Land banks
  - Production Credit Associations
  - Federal Intermediate Credit banks
  - Banks for Cooperatives
- Farmers Home Administration
- Rural Electrification Administration
- Commodity Credit Corporation
- Veterans Administration (farm loans)

Business

- Small Business Administration
- Veterans Administration (business loans)
- Interstate Commerce Commission (railroad loans)
- Maritime Administration
- Civil Aeronautics Board
- Defense Loans
  - Federal Reserve banks (guarantees)
  - Treasury Department (direct loans)

---

[3]The Bureau of the Budget includes the 12 Federal Reserve banks in the category of quasi-public credit institutions. If the Federal Reserve banks were still making direct loans to American business, a case could be made for including them as lending agencies. However, Federal Reserve banks typically lend only to the member banks of the System as a part of their ordinary central bank functions. Such an extension of Federal Reserve credit is more properly considered a part of the money-creating process than part of a federal credit program as such programs are defined in the present context.

TABLE VI-2

New Commitments for Major Federal Credit Programs
Classified by Type of Assistance, Major Agency, or Program

(in millions)

Agency or program	1959 actual		1960 estimate		1961 estimate	
	Direct loans and invest- ments	Guar- antees and insur- ance	Direct loans and invest- ments	Guar- antees and insur- ance	Direct loans and invest- ments	Guar- antees and insur- ance
Housing and Home Finance Agency:						
Federal National Mortgage Asso- ciation	$1,184		$1,459		$1,306	
Urban Renewal Administration	110	$313	115	$301	123	$340
Community Facilities Adminis- tration	227		234		155	
Federal Housing Administration	23	8,753	37	13,583	33	12,005
Public Housing Administration	296	110	268	126	342	157
Veterans Administration	205	2,633	357	2,567	6	2,296
Department of Agriculture:						
Rural Electrification Administra- tion	276		350		301	
Farmers Home Administration	322	40	278	13	232	13
Commodity Credit Corporation	543	3,003	242	1,825	279	1,561
Department of Commerce: Maritime Administration	2	48		259		201
Civil Aeronautics Board		15		10		10
Interstate Commerce Commission		4		100		80
Expansion of defense production		128		96		79
Small Business Administration	233	48	256	46	323	58
Department of Health, Education, and Welfare	32		43		46	
Total by type of assistance	3,453	15,095	3,639	18,926	3,146	16,800
Grand total	$18,548		$22,565		$19,946	

Source: Special Analysis of Federal Credit Programs in the 1961 Budget, p. 4, (adjusted to exclude foreign loans).

Housing

Housing and Home Finance Agency
- Federal Housing Administration
- Public Housing Administration
- Federal National Mortgage Association
- Community Facilities Administration
- Urban Renewal Administration

Veterans Administration (home loans)
Federal Home Loan banks

TABLE VI-3

Outstanding Loans for Major Quasi-Public Credit Programs
Classified by Agency and Program

(in millions)

Agency	June 30, 1958	June 30, 1959
Farm Credit Administration:		
Banks for Cooperatives	$408	$526
Federal Intermediate Credit banks	1,227	1,547
Federal Land banks	1,989	2,262
Federal Home Loan Bank Board: Federal Home Loan banks	929	1,537
Housing and Home Finance Agency: Federal National Mortgage Association (secondary market operations)	1,394	1,574
Total	5,947	7,446

Source: Special Analysis of Federal Credit Programs in the 1961 Budget, p. 9.

Miscellaneous

Office of Education (college loans)
Bureau of Indian Affairs
Veterans Administration (life insurance loans)
Other minor loans

We come now to the task of adding up the funds available to the federal lending agencies. Three problems in arithmetic complicate the task. First, although data were requested in accordance with a standard form, the several agencies varied this form to suit their own institutional peculiarities. Second, some agencies furnished data on a June 30 rather than on a December 31 basis, making it impossible to obtain strickly comparable totals. Finally, a few agencies did not furnish data on a standard form, largely because the source of funds to them was clearly governmental appropriations. The amount of funds in these cases thus has to be inferred from the magnitudes of their loans.

As remarked above sources of funds to the lending agencies are basically two. An agency may obtain its funds from the Treasury, thus using money raised by federal taxation or by the sale of U.S. Treasury obligations. Alternatively, an agency may go to the capital market, obtaining money by the sale of its securities there. It is possible to subdivide these two sources of funds into further categories, and this we have done in order to show as much detail as possible even though the increased detail is not particularly helpful for analytical purposes. The six categories into which sources of funds were divided for purposes of interrogation are as follows:

A. Bonds, debentures, or notes sold and outstanding in the private market, not government secured.

B. Bonds, debentures, or notes sold and outstanding in the private market, government secured.

C. Bonds, debentures, or notes issued in connection with borrowings from the government to obtain loanable funds.

D. Capital stock held by the government.

E. Capital stock held by private parties.

F. Funds obtained from government appropriations, repayments on principal, sales of mortgages, and earnings.

In the interest of assisting the reader to make his way through these data as readily as possible, the agencies will be discussed in the order they are set down in the checklist. Approximate totals of fund sources, by categories, will be found in Appendix B.[4]

Agricultural Agencies

Farm Credit Administration. The three agencies under the supervision of the Farm Credit Administration are the Federal Land banks, the Federal Intermediate Credit banks, and the Banks for Cooperatives.

As will be seen from Appendix Tables VI-A1 and VI-A2, the preponderance of funds available to the Federal Land banks comes from the sale of securities in the private capital market.[5] Issues of the Federal Land banks are denominated "bonds," though many of them are in the note and certificate range in U.S. Treasury terminology. The variance in the range of maturities of these issues (a matter to be discussed briefly in Part II) is apparent from Table VI-A3, which shows the issues of this agency as of December 31, 1959.

The mechanics of Federal Land Bank lending suggest the methods used by all of the Farm Credit Administration agencies. When a

---

[4]The six categories of information contained in the tables are not exclusive, a few minor unclassified sources of funds having come to light as the work proceeded. For example, the Federal Home Loan banks obtain some funds from deposits of their members, and no category of tables was provided for this single case.

[5]Tables designated VI-A1, VI-A2, etc. are found in Appendix A.

farmer wishes to have access to the long-term credit provided by the Federal Land banks, he goes to his local Federal Land Bank Association (known, until 1959, as a National Farm Loan Association) to obtain the loan and is required to purchase stock in the association equal to 5 percent of the amount borrowed. The association, in turn, makes an equivalent investment in stock of the Federal Land Bank. The loan is then made by the Federal Land Bank and endorsed by the local association, risks in most cases being shared equally by the local association, of which there are now about 800, and the Land Bank of the district in which it is located. Although the Land Banks were originally capitalized by the federal government, government capital stock has been retired. As Table VI-A2 shows, the capital stock held by the local associations has increased during the past five years at a rate averaging more than $10 million per annum.

A comparison of the sources of funds available to the Federal Land banks from the sale of their agency issues (Table VI-A1) with the magnitudes of loans made by the agency in recent years shows that sources consistently lag behind loan figures by an amount fluctuating around $200 million. The discrepancy is accounted for by the fact that loans can be made from certain items in the Land Banks' now substantial net worth of around $400 million.

The Federal Intermediate Credit banks, although organized on somewhat the same principle as the Federal Land banks, present a few complexities, partly because of slightly different structure and partly because of recent changes in legislation. Until January 1, 1957, the Production Credit System consisted of (1) local Production Credit Associations from which farmers could obtain short-term production loans, (2) Federal Intermediate Credit banks, which furnished to the local associations the funds lent to farmers, and (3) Production Credit Corporations, one for each district, through which the federal government provided equity funds to the local associations. As of January 1, 1957, pursuant to the Farm Credit Act of 1956, the Production Credit Corporations become part of the Federal Intermediate Credit banks in the several districts.

As in the case of the Federal Land banks, farmers wishing to borrow from a Production Credit Association must purchase capital stock in the association amounting to 5 percent of the amount borrowed. But the Production Credit Associations do not in turn buy stock in the Federal Intermediate Credit banks, though in accordance with the Farm Credit Act of 1956 class B stock may be issued by the Federal Intermediate Credit banks as patronage refunds to the Production Credit Associations.

Tables VI-A4 to VI-A10 should assist the reader to a comprehension of this agency's recently shifting structure. Tables VI-A4 to VI-A7 show the sources of funds to the Federal Intermediate Credit banks proper. Table VI-A8 shows the capital stock contribution of the federal government to the now superseded Production Credit Corporations, footnote 2 of that table providing the essential details of changes resulting from the Federal Credit Act of 1956. Table VI-A9 indicates the capital stock contribution of the federal government to the Production Credit Associations, and Table VI-A10 shows the capital stock contribution of members of the Production Credit Association. As Table VI-A3 did for the Federal Land Bank bonds, Table VI-A11 describes some of the characteristics of the Federal Intermediate Credit Bank debentures as of the end of 1959. Again, the name of the issues may be somewhat misleading, for they have short maturities, generally lying in the range of a long Treasury bill or a certificate of indebtedness.

The third major agency under the Farm Credit Administration is the Federal Banks for Cooperatives. Procedures followed in making the agency's three types of loans (long-term facility loans, short-term working-capital loans, and commodity loans) are approximately the same. For the first two types of loans borrowers must purchase stock in the lending bank, or make a guaranty-fund payment, equal to 5 percent of the loan amount. For commodity loans, made ordinarily to mature at the end of the current marketing year, a stock purchase or quaranty-fund payment of only 1 percent of the loan is required.

Tables VI-A12 to VI-A15 furnish the detail of the origination of loanable funds during the 1950's. The most important source of funds, as indicated in Table VI-A12 is the private market in which debentures bearing rather short maturities are sold. The Banks for Cooperatives benefit from the largest capital stock contribution made by the federal government to a Farm Credit Administration agency (see Table VI-A13), but this source of funds has been declining in recent years as the capital stock held by borrowing cooperatives has risen substantially in amount (Table VI-A14). As Table VI-A15 indicates, net earnings on government capital stock outstanding furnish a minor source of funds.

Table VI-A16 gives detailed characteristics of the issues of this agency as of December 31, 1959. Of the five agency issues, this one, totaling $363 million at the end of 1959, is the smallest in total amount and the least complex.

Farmers Home Administration. Administrative expenses of the Farmers Home Administration are largely met by direct annual appropriations from Congress, which in the past three fiscal years have amounted to about $31 million annually. A small amount of administrative expenses, amounting in fiscal 1959 to about $1 million, comes from the Farm-Tenant Mortgage Insurance Fund.

The funds for the current direct loan programs of the Farmers Home Administration come almost exclusively from two sources. These are borrowings from the Treasury and a Revolving Loan Fund of approximately $145 million, the latter available only for disaster (emergency) loans. At the end of fiscal 1959, the Farmers Home Administration had gross loans of $829.5 million. Of the total amount of loans outstanding, approximately $293 million was being provided at the end of fiscal 1959 by borrowings from the Treasury. The greater part of these funds was obtained from the Treasury in exchange for promissory notes of varying maturities, usually in the neighborhood of five years (see Table VI-A17). At the same time an additional amount of some $29 million was obtained from the Treasury for the Farm-Tenant Mortgage Insurance Fund. The Disaster Loan Revolving Fund of approximately $145 million (see Table VI-A18) provided loans of approximately $74 million at the end of fiscal 1959, and any payments made on these loans from the Revolving Fund can be used for relending to farmers. The balance of the direct loans to farmers obviously comes from funds made available by previous appropriations, amounting to approximately $508 million. Insured farm loans at the end of fiscal 1959 standing at approximately $161 million, were, of course, made by private lenders and are therefore not included in these estimates.

Not included in any of the amounts above was about $32.1 million in loans held by the Farm Tenant-Mortgage Fund on June 30, 1959. About $30.1 million of this amount represents insured loans once held by private lenders and later sold to the government under the secondary market repurchase agreement contained in each insured loan agreement. The balance of about $2 million represents loans made from funds of the Farm-Tenant Mortgage Insurance Fund for sale in blocks to private lenders.

Rural Electrification Administration. The REA, operative since 1935, has made its loans for the most part to cooperatives. The REA has financed generating plants and transmission and distribution lines for construction in rural areas and in some cases has provided funds for telephone facilities.

Loans, repayments, and net changes in outstandings resulting from REA activity are shown in Table VI-A19. During the 1950's, total borrowings of $2,485,237,000 less repayments of $577,104,000 left a net change of approximately $1.9 billion in outstanding notes given to the Treasury in exchange for funds.

Commodity Credit Corporation. It was noted previously that the Commodity Credit Corporation is in no real sense a lending agency. For the sake of completeness, however, some data are provided.

A literal reading of the figures suggests that during the decade of the 1950's the CCC lent more than $22 billion and received back almost half as much. Actually, however, more than $13 billion of "loans repaid or charged off" are accounted for as "collateral acquired in settlement." In other words, in repayment of their obligations farmers from 1950 through 1958 relinquished ownership of stored crop to which they had previously held title. The CCC, of course, sold some of this "collateral" in domestic and foreign markets, but a great deal of it remained in storage and some of it had to be destroyed. Such operations certainly did require financing, as Table VI-A20 shows. During the years 1950-59, the Corporation borrowed from the government more than $9.5 billion. A minor source of funds, as indicated in Table VI-A21, were borrowings in the early 1950's from banks acting as agents under price support programs for peanuts and wool. Throughout the decade the government's "capital stock" contribution remained constant at $100 million.

Veterans Administration. Strictly speaking, the Veterans Administration makes no direct farm loans, though it has guaranteed farm loans in ever-decreasing amounts during the 1950's. However, the direct loan program for purchasing homes includes residences on farms, and about 5 percent of the direct loans made to veterans are for the purchase of a farm.

Business Agencies

Small Business Administration. The Small Business Administration makes business loans, either with or without bank participation. Since the start of its Financial Assistance Program in September 1953, the Small Business Administration has approved 18,271 business loans totaling $856.3 million. Of this amount, $115.7 million were loans that were for one reason or another cancelled, leaving net approvals of $740.6 million. Actual disbursements of government funds by the Small Business Administration have amounted to only $476 million, with funds disbursed by participating banks totaling $193.2 million. Out of this total of $669.2 million there have been repayments and other credits of $240.6 million. Business loans outstanding on December 31, 1959, thus approximated $428.6 million.[6]

---

[6]See Thirteenth Semiannual Report of the Small Business Administration, six months ending December 31, 1959, p. 52.

Through December 31, 1959, net commitments on disaster loans, after cancellations of loans, totaled $82.9 million, of which the Small Business Administration share was $79.7 million and the share of loans disbursed was $76.8 million. Charge-offs and delinquencies through December 31, 1959, indicated that of this amount approximately $1.8 million constituted actual and estimated losses.[7]

Table VI-A22 shows the loanable funds obtained from government appropriations and from earnings made available to the Revolving Fund of the Small Business Administration. A total of $540 million has been made available through appropriations, and income from interest and fees totaled an additional $35 million. The sum of these sources is thus more than sufficient to account for SBA loans outstanding at the end of 1959.

Veterans Administration (business loans). Guaranteed and insured business loans of the Veterans Administration have amounted to $294 million in the years 1950-58, but repayments have amounted to $417 million. The outstanding amount of guaranteed and insured business loans of the Veterans Administration has been steadily reduced since 1953. Since there are no direct business loans of this agency, there is no problem of ascertaining sources of funds.

Interstate Commerce Commission (railroad loans). The Interstate Commerce Commission is authorized to guarantee private lenders against loss on loans to railroads for the purpose of financing the acquisition, construction, or maintenance of capital equipment. In 1959, $60.8 million of such loans were made, and none was repaid or charged off. Since no direct loans are made by this agency, there is no problem of sources of funds.

Maritime Administration. The Maritime Administration has made no new commitments for direct loans since 1956. During the 1950's direct loans, totaling $135.6 million were made in the calendar years 1955, 1956, and 1957. Sources of funds for these loans were government appropriations.

Insured loans of the Maritime Administration, all made in the years 1954-59, have totaled $365 million, and insured loans repaid or charged off in the 1950's have totaled $113 million.

Civil Aeronautics Board. In the two years in which is has had authority to guarantee loans to airlines (1958 and 1959), the Civil Aeronautics Board guaranteed slightly more than $25 million of such loans. Repayments of $1.2 million left $23.9 million of loans outstanding as of December 31, 1959. CAB makes no direct loans, and there is no sources-of-funds problem.

---

[7] Ibid., p. 56.

Defense Loans. Under Section 301 of the Defense Production Act of 1950 certain departments of the government are authorized to guarantee loans by private or public agencies to defense contractors and subcontractors. Under Section 302 of the Defense Production Act the President is authorized to make direct loans or to participate in private loans for certain defense purposes; under Section 303 of the same Act the General Services Administration may make advances on purchase commitments for strategic materials and equipment.

Although the volume of Section 301 guaranteed loans and repayments was large during the 1950's, amounting to $13.3 billion of loans and $13 billion of repayments, only $340 million of such loans was outstanding at the end of 1959. More important for purposes of this paper are the Section 302 loans, which may be either direct or participation loans, and the Section 303 loans which are direct advances. All told, Section 302 and Section 303 loans came to just under $608 million for the years 1950-59; of this amount $186.4 million was outstanding at the end of 1959.

Direct loans under Section 302 totaled $280.2 million for the years 1951-59, no such loans being made in the calendar year 1959. In the same period the General Services Administration rendered advances of $234.3 million, of which only $8.7 million was outstanding at the end of 1959. Purchases by the Department of Defense of principal balances of loans guaranteed by the Army and Navy amounted during the 1950's to just under $50 million. Thus, the government's direct advances, financed by appropriations, amounted to approximately $464 million. Of this total something more than $180 million was outstanding at the end of 1959.

Housing Agencies

Federal Housing Administration. As remarked at the beginning of this monograph, the Federal Housing Administration presents no source-of-funds problem because it makes no direct loans. Nevertheless, FHA-insured loans have been such an important part of the government's housing program in the postwar period that a word about the agency's budget expenditures is in order.

As Professor George Break has shown in his study, Federal Loan Insurance for Housing,[8] by mid-1959 the amount of home and project mortgages insured by FHA had passed $45 billion; with property improvement loans of nearly $12 billion, the total of FHA-

---

[8]George F. Break, "Federal Loan Insurance for Housing," Research Study One in Federal Credit Agencies, prepared for the Commission on Money and Credit (Englewood Cliffs, N.J.: Prentice-Hall, Inc., 1963).

insured credit amounted to $57 billion. While carrying out this massive program through the postwar period, FHA receipts from insurance premiums and from sale of assets acquired in default proceedings have each year exceeded the agency's administrative expenses and payments on defaulted mortgages. Consequently, as Professor Break has pointed out, FHA budget expenditures have been negative each year of the 1950's, averaging -$44 million a year from 1950 to 1959.

Public Housing Administration. The Public Housing Administration obtains its funds, except for a nominal $1 million obtained from capital stock sold to the government, through borrowing from the Treasury and through the use of its own corporate assets (acquired from earnings) available for lending. Table VI-A23 reveals the substantially decreased volume of credit extended by the Public Housing Administration since 1953, this reduction reflecting both a modest drop in activity and a change in PHA financing policy that depends more on guarantee of private loans than upon direct lending.

Loan commitments by PHA to local authorities under annual contribution contracts are disbursed either as direct federal loans or as guarantees of private temporary loans. After a direct PHA loan is initially made, it may be repaid upon arrangement of short-term financing (12 months or less) with a commercial bank or refunded with guaranteed financing, such financing taking the form of 40-year serial bonds sold to private investors. An annual federal contribution covers the debt service on these bonds. These contributions are met out of appropriations, which have increased in recent years to substantial amounts—$115 million in fiscal 1959, $131 million in fiscal 1960, and a projected $146 million in fiscal 1961.

As Table VI-A23 shows, except in 1957 outstanding PHA indebtedness to the Treasury has decreased in each of the last six years. In 1959, borrowings from the Treasury fell to a nine-year low of $75 million and repayments to the Treasury to $83 million, leaving an outstanding indebtedness to the Treasury of only $27 million. Besides this modest amount owing the Treasury, PHA has about $65 million of corporate assets available for lending on a revolving basis.

Federal National Mortgage Association. No federal lending agency surpasses the Federal National Mortgage Association in its various and imaginative tapping of fund sources. As Jack Guttentag has remarked in his monograph, The Federal National

Mortgage Association,[9] in examining FNMA's sources of funds it is useful to distinguish between the periods before and after the effective date of its Charter Act. Sources of FNMA funds from 1938 to the end of 1954 were primarily U.S. Treasury contributions and secondarily sales of previously purchased mortgages. At the end of 1954, FNMA's mortgage portfolio of $2.5 billion was just about equal to the net investment of the U.S. Government out of appropriations.

FNMA's Charter Act of 1954 authorized the substantial substitution of private for federal funds in both the secondary market operations and the management and liquidation functions. The law originally provided for both secondary market debentures and management and liquidation notes and debentures, the maximum aggregate amount of such debentures not to exceed FNMA's holdings of cash, mortgages, and Treasury obligations or $3,350 million, whichever was smaller. As indicated in Table VI-A24, something more than $2.4 billion of FNMA debentures was outstanding as of December 31, 1959. About $.8 billion of these obligations was used to retire Treasury investment in the management and liquidation portfolio, which stood at approximately $2 billion at the end of 1959. The remaining $1.6 billion was used to increase mortgage holdings through the secondary market operations. Thus, from the beginning of 1955 through 1959, the Treasury's investment was limited to relatively small amounts of preferred stock and short-term FNMA borrowings from the Treasury between debenture issues.

As shown in Table VI-A25, at the end of 1959 borrowings from the Treasury amounted to almost $2.7 billion, approximately $2.6 billion of this amount being in the form of notes to Treasury on account of special assistance functions and managements and liquidations functions. An additional amount of $139 million was owed Treasury in short-term notes issued to finance secondary market operations, and, as Table VI-A26 indicates, $143 million of preferred stock was owned by Treasury.[10]

---

[9]Jack Guttentag, "The Federal National Mortgage Association," Research Study Two in Federal Credit Agencies, prepared for the Commission on Money and Credit (Englewood Cliffs, N. J. Prentice-Hall, Inc., 1963).

[10]Since the end of 1959 these figures have changed, more perhaps in 1960 than usual, and so, for that matter, have those presented in Table VI-A28. For example, in August 1960, $797 million of Fanny May debentures were retired by borrowing that sum from Treasury. Moreover, since April 1960, Fanny May has been selling a new issue, the "short-term discount note," to be discussed later.

Table VI-A27 shows the amounts of common stock held by private parties. Purchase of this stock by private mortgage lenders is prerequisite both to obtaining a commitment from FNMA and to selling mortgages to FNMA. As the amount of a little over $53 million outstanding at the end of 1959 suggests, purchase of capital stock is an unimportant source of funds. It is nevertheless an important symbol—a sign that activities carried on by the Association have an intimate relationship with the private market.

Tables VI-A24 to VI-A27 indicate the basic sources of funds available to FNMA on an annual basis. More than most agencies, FNMA depends upon its operations for replenishment of its funds obtained from public and private sources. In this agency the most important "revolving-fund" items are mortgage sales, repayments on principal, proceeds of foreclosures and interest payments on mortgages (see Table VI-A29).

Community Facilities Administration. CFA makes loans for college housing, for public facilities, and for public works planning. At the end of 1959 there were net approvals of $459 million in loans to private colleges and universities and $461 million to public colleges and universities for a total of $920.2.[11] Loans totaling $15.7 million had been approved to assist hospitals in the development of housing for student nurses and interns. Upon approval of a college housing loan the Administration enters into a loan agreement with the borrowing institution by which the government proposes to buy bonds to be issued for the project, at a specified rate of interest, with the provision that no other equally favorable or more favorable bids are submitted when the bonds are offered for public sale. Through the end of 1959, HHFA was committed to purchase 767 bond issues with an aggregate volume of $730 million. As Table VI-A30 shows, however, less than $600 million had actually been disbursed from funds obtained by borrowing from the Treasury.

The Public Facility Loan Program, enacted in 1955, authorized the Housing Administrator to purchase, through the CFA, the securities and obligations of, or make loans to, states and their political subdivisions and other instrumentalities designated under state law. A fund of $100 million, operated on a revolving basis, has been provided for the program. In order to finance specific public projects priority is to be given the construction proposed by smaller municipalities—i.e., towns or other political subdivisions with under 10,000 inhabitants. As in all the housing programs, there is a considerable lag between original authorization and final payment for construction. A very small amount of municipal bonds

---

[11] Thirteenth Annual Report, 1959, Housing and Home Finance Agency, p. 256.

was purchased in 1957. In 1958 loans amounted to about $11 million and in 1959 to about $24 million. As indicated in Table VI-A31, funds for Public Facility Loans have been obtained from the Treasury in amounts slightly greater than required to make these purchases in 1958 and 1959.

The CFA also supervises a Program of Advances for Public Works Planning, initiated by the Housing Act of 1954. A revolving fund of $48 million in undisbursed balances and advances outstanding, of which $30 million has been appropriated to date, is available for loans to states, municipalities, and other public agencies for the purpose of planning public works that can readily be placed under construction. Advances become due and repayable without interest when the public works planned are finally placed under construction. As of December 31, 1959, something more than $29.4 million of advances had been approved net of cancellations, and a little more than $5 million of advances had been repaid into the revolving fund. Up to the end of 1959 government appropriations in the amount of $24 million had been obtained for this purpose.

Urban Renewal Administration. This agency makes loans in three categories. Relatively small in volume are the so-called planning advances made for the purpose of financing necessary surveys and plans in preparation of an urban renewal project before the execution of a loan and grant contract. These funds may be lent to local public agencies for a specific project or for a general renewal program, or they may be advanced for area surveys to determine whether urban renewal projects are feasible. Advances of this sort are repaid from any funds available to a local agency for financing the planned project.

Expenditures incurred by local public agencies for expenses past the planning stage may be financed by loans from URA, which bear interest at not less than the going federal rate. These fall into two categories — temporary and definitive. "A contract for a temporary loan generally will be made for such period of time as may reasonably be required to complete the project. A definitive, or long-term, loan will be made available only to finance the capital value of that portion of a project area which is leased for redevelopment rather than sold, and its duration may not exceed 40 years."[12]

The Housing Act of 1959 increased the agency's authority to enter into loan contracts. There is now no limit to such contracts. Authority to borrow from the Treasury in order to make such loans is still limited to $1 billion, but the President has discretionary

[12] Ibid., p. 269.

power to permit borrowing from the Treasury beyond the statutory limit. The reason for the change to unlimited authority for loan contracts is that most of the funds contracted to be lent are not actually disbursed. Instead, the contract may be used by a local public agency as security to borrow private funds at more favorable rates of interest. The contracts thus serve as guarantees rather than direct loans.

Table VI-A32 shows the annual borrowings from the Treasury for the purposes of obtaining loanable funds. Outstanding at the end of 1959 was $98 million of such borrowings. This amount may seem large compared to URA outstanding loans, for at the end of 1959 only a little more than $2 million were outstanding as planning advances and about $7.2 million were outstanding as direct federal loans. However, as 1959 borrowings and repayments suggest (Table VI-A32), the agency has a substantial loan turnover. More than $8 million of planning advances were made in 1959 and more than $6 million repaid; more than $96 million of other loans were made and about $89 million either repaid or refunded. At the end of 1959 URA had guaranteed more than $165 million of urban renewal loans.

Veterans Administration (housing loans). The Direct Loan Program of the Veterans Administration was established to make direct loans in rural areas and in small cities and towns ("housing credit shortage areas") where VA-guaranteed loans by private lenders are not available. The maximum loan available to a veteran is $13,500. The residence purchased may be on a farm, but the basic objective is the purchase of the home and not the farm. Actually, about 95 percent of the direct loans made have been for the purpose of obtaining housing in a city or town.

Table VI-A33 shows for the years 1950-59 the amounts of funds obtained from Treasury borrowing, and Table VI-A34 shows for the same period sums available from principal repayments, sales of loans, and earnings used to operate the direct loan program only. At the end of 1959, approximately $1.4 billion was available for lending on a revolving-fund basis. Of this amount, close to $1.2 billion was outstanding in the form of direct loans to veterans.[13]

Federal Home Loan Bank System. The System through its 11 regional Federal Home Loan banks provides the means whereby member institutions may obtain advances to meet unusual or heavy withdrawal demand by savers and for meeting fluctuating demands,

---

[13]These magnitudes are larger than those shown in the Annual Report of the Administration of Veterans Affairs for 1959 because they are for December 31 instead of June 30. Compare pp. 81-82 of the 1959 Annual Report.

mainly seasonal, for mortgage loans. Member institutions may include mutual savings banks and insurance companies as well as savings and loan associations but members at the end of 1959 comprised 4,599 savings and loan associations out of a total of 4,624.

The Federal Home Loan Bank System is, of course, not a central bank but another type of financial intermediary — an intermediary that provides a central source of pre-existing funds for member institutions. The sources of funds are chiefly FHLB capital stock, deposits of members with the Banks, and consolidated FHLB obligations sold on the open market. Retained earnings also provide a small source of funds.

When the FHLB system was established in 1932, the U.S. Treasury subscribed for capital in the amount of $125 million. In 1951 the last of this government-owned stock was retired, and since then the stock owned by member institutions has more than trebled, amounting at the end of 1959 to $866 million (see Table VI-A35). Because members are required by statute to own stock equivalent to 2 percent of the total unpaid principal of mortgages on one- to four-family dwellings, capital contributions of member associations are a continuing and important source of funds. At the end of 1959, 27 percent of the aggregate funds of the Banks were represented by the capital stock subscriptions of member institutions.

A somewhat variable source of funds for the Federal Home Loan Bank System is deposits of members. At the end of 1959 these deposits amounted to $590 million or 18 percent off aggregate funds. At the previous year end, however, deposits amounted to $819 million, and by the end of June 1960, they were back up to $734 million, about one-fifth of which were demand deposits and the remainder time deposits.

By all odds the most important source of FHLB funds in recent years has been the consolidated obligations of the System. As Table VI-A36 shows, nearly $1.8 billion of these obligations was outstanding at the end of 1959. At that time these sources of funds comprised 55 percent of total major Bank funds. As indicated in Table VI-A37, nine issues of the agency were outstanding at the end of 1959, all save one to mature within eight months. Typically the Federal Home Loan banks offer issues maturing in less than a year, a clear exception being a 5-year issue of 1958 that will not mature until April 3, 1963.

A final and minor source of funds is retained earnings of $72 million, which are available for making advances to member institutions. Table VI-A38 indicates the growth of these earnings during the decade of the 1950's.

Miscellaneous Agencies

Office of Education. By the end of June 1959, the Office of Education had obligated almost $31 million to 1,197 institutions of higher learning for student loans.[14] By the end of fiscal 1959 more than $1 million was obligated for loans to private schools to finance the purchase of special equipment for use in teaching science, mathematics, and foreign languages. For these two main purposes nearly $71 million has been made available from government appropriations.

Bureau of Indian Affairs. Table VI-A39 summarizes the small and relatively unimportant sources of funds available to the Bureau of Indian Affairs during the 1950's. Footnotes marked with a single and double asterisk indicate the major fund transactions of recent years.

Veterans Administration. From 1950 to 1958 holders of VA insurance policies borrowed net about $218 million. (Borrowings in previous years account for the rest of the $358 million of these loans outstanding at the end of 1958.) Sources of these funds were, of course, the cash values built up by policyholders through premium payments.

Other. Treasury Department loans to the District of Columbia for the construction of public works amounted net to almost $11 million in the years 1953-58. In the same years civil defense loans of the Treasury Department totaled net just over $5 million. Combined loans of the Post Office Department and the General Services Administration under the lease-purchase program for public buildings amounted to just over $42 million in the years 1956-58.

II. FEDERAL LENDING AGENCIES AND THEIR FINANCING ALTERNATIVES

We have come a long and tortuous way through data that must now be summarized. The reader is cautioned again that the data with which we have had to work were obtained from many sources and from agency officers of varying degrees of authority and that within the limits of the time available it was impossible to obtain from the agencies a reconciliation of every minor inconsistency. Nevertheless, we are now in a position to indicate to a degree of accuracy sufficient for practical purposes the ways in which lending agencies have in the 1950's obtained their funds. The question then arises, what difference does it make? Can the economist say that one source of funds is preferable to another?

---

[14]Annual Report of the U.S. Department of Health, Education, and Welfare, 1959, p. 148.

Summary of Sources of Funds Available to Lending Agencies

The tables of Appendix A for the most part present sources-of-funds data furnished directly by the lending agencies. These tables are in each relevant instance designated as falling in one of six categories — A, B, C, D, E, or F — corresponding with the six categories listed on p. 515 above. Addition of the data in the tables and other data in the text gives the results found in Tables VI-B1 to VI-B7 which are found in Appendix B.[1] It will be observed that two separate additions were made for the Category C tables, one including and the other excluding borrowings from the Treasury by the Commodity Credit Corporation. As remarked above, the authors feel that the Commodity Credit Corporation is not a lending agency and that the inclusion of these large sums in the sources of funds unduly inflates the totals; nevertheless, the CCC data may be useful for some comparative purposes.

Some of the fund sources that escaped inclusion in the tables can be roughly identified. Thus, the Federal Land banks regularly make credit use of some $200 million of a net worth of twice that amount. The Farmers Home Administration has in effect lent $32 million from funds of the Farm-Tenant Mortgage Fund that were not included in the agency's tables.[2] Public Housing Administration funds in the amount of $65 million were available from earnings. Maritime Administration loans in the amount of $132 million and Defense loans in the amount of $180 million net were financed by appropriations. Thus, a total of $265 million can be included in Category F from earnings and about $312 million should be included in this category from direct appropriations.

One large fund source remains to be considered. As observed earlier, a variable but important source of funds for the Federal Home Loan banks is deposits of members of the FHLB System.

---

[1] An effort was made to put data on a calendar rather than on a fiscal year basis, but at the time of interrogation some agencies simply could not provide end-of-year figures. However, with the exception of the Rural Electrification Administration the magnitudes are not large, and for the purposes of present approximation it seemed better to make additions as of the date reported rather than to interpolate end-of-year data.

[2] Farmers Home Administration loans from 1950 on are approximately accounted for by the two sources of funds indicated in Tables VI-A17 and VI-A18. As indicated in the text, gross loans of the Administration presently outstanding amount to nearly $830 million, a sum that is possible because more than $500 million is available to the Administration from appropriations made before 1950.

These deposits amounted at the end of 1959 to $590 million. The average end-of-year deposits of members for the five years 1955-59 was $689 million; for the ten years 1950-59 the average was $571 million.

The most useful generalization emerging from these data is the approximate division of funds into private sources on the one hand and into government (Treasury) sources on the other. The most important private source (almost $8 billion) is the sale of debt instruments not secured by the government in the capital market (Category A). The sale of government-secured issues in the private market (Category B) has now ceased and was unimportant in the 1950's. Capital stock in lending agencies held by private parties (Category E) amounted at the end of 1959 to almost $1.3 billion. Deposits of System members with the Federal Home Loan banks brought the private sources of funds to about $9.8 billion at the end of 1959.

At the end of 1959 total agency borrowings from the government (Category C) amounted to approximately $7.8 billion. If we add to this figure about $ .5 billion of government-owned capital stock (Category D) and the total of $5.1 billion of loanable funds obtained from government appropriations, principal repayments, sales of loans, and earnings during the years 1950-59 (Category F), we obtain a total of $13.3 billion available from government sources.

These data are summarized in column 2 of Table VI-4. It is perhaps worth noting that if from Category F we subtract some $3.1 billion of funds originating in Fanny May sales of mortgages and repayments on mortgages, there is a remarkably even division between private and government sources of funds.

Because some of the more than $23 billion of funds from these several sources was available to the agencies at the beginning of the decade, we may obtain a total of sources of funds available during the 1950's by adding the net change in outstandings for Categories A through E to the total of Category F. The net change in outstandings for Categories A, B, and E, the private sources of funds, is about $9.5 billion. The net change in outstandings for Categories C and D plus the total of Category F comes to something more than $11.4 billion. When we add to the private sources the net addition during the decade of more than $ .3 billion of deposits of the FHLB System members with Federal Home Loan banks, private funds available to the agencies add to about $7.8 billion. Something over $19 billion of funds thus became available to the federal lending agencies from one source or another during the decade of the 1950's.

TABLE VI-4

Sources of Funds Available to Federal Lending Agencies
1950 – 1959

(in thousands)

	January 1, 1950	December 31, 1959	Net Change
Public			
Category C - Bonds, debentures, or notes issued in connection with borrowings from government, excluding CCC	$1,352,193	$7,762,068	$6,409,875
Category D - Capital stock held by the government	523,850	463,873	- 59,977
Category F - Funds obtained from appropriations, repayments, etc.	--	4,463,406	4,463,406
Subtotal	$1,876,043	$12,689,347	$10,813,304
Category F not included in tables	--	600,000	600,000
Total, Public	$1,876,043	$13,289,347	$11,413,304
Private			
Category A - Bonds, debentures, or notes sold in private market, not government secured	$1,412,132	$ 7,916,624	$ 6,504,492
Category B - Bonds, debentures, or notes sold in private market, government secured	10,453	--	- 10,453
Category E - Capital stock held by private parties	274,524	1,275,571	1,001,047
Subtotal	$1,697,109	$9,192,195	$7,495,086
Deposits of System Members with FHLB	267,000	589,000	322,000
Total, Private	$1,964,109	$9,781,195	$7,817,086
Grand Total	$3,840,152	$23,070,542	$19,230,390

Private Versus Public Sources of Funds

We come now to the question whether private sources of funds or public sources of funds are preferable for use by the lending agencies. It seems clear at the outset that activities of the lending agencies are not likely to exert a net downward pressure on the economy, a restrictive influence being conceivable only in the unlikely event that the agencies as a whole should one day receive in repayments per accounting period more than they issue in loans. On the contrary, it seems clear that the influence of the lending agencies will almost always be on the expansionary side, for we would not have them at all if it were felt that private lenders could and would meet all the demands that Congress wants met. We then have first to inquire whether government or private funds will have the more stimulating effect on the economy.

In analyzing this question, it should be recalled that in either event (assuming no net expansion of the money supply by the banking system) the effect of the entire transaction is to siphon funds out of the private economy and then to inject them back into the economy via the lending activity of a government agency. Agency lending, viewed alone, tends to have a stimulating effect on the economy in that it adds to the total supply of funds available for spending. Moreover, the lent funds will presumably all be spent; otherwise the borrowers would not have borrowed them. What remains to be determined, however, is the extent to which the raising of funds exerts an offsetting contractionary effect on the spending stream.

If the funds are obtained from the Treasury, the Treasury can in turn obtain funds either by borrowing or by taxing. If the funds were obtained by a corresponding increase in taxes, it is probable that there would indeed be a contractionary effect to offset the stimulating effect of the lending, resulting in little <u>net</u> effect on the total spending stream. This is true because taxpayers' marginal propensity to consume is assumed to be high. Increased taxes would therefore cause an almost equivalent decrease in spending, though a small portion of the monies taxed away would have been saved. If, however, the funds were raised by either Treasury borrowing or the sale of agency issues, the funds would come primarily out of the saving stream. If economic conditions at the time were such that at current rates the supply of saved funds was tending to exceed the demand for loanable funds, as would probably be the case during periods of recession, the borrowing operation would exert little or no contractionary influence on the spending stream. If, on the other hand, the borrowing took place at a time when investment spending was tending to outrun, and was in fact limited by, the available supply of loanable funds, then the borrowing operation would exert a contractionary influence sufficient, conceivably, to offset the expansionary influence of the agency lending.

We know of no way to measure the extent to which the financing of such lending by the Treasury has been reflected, or in the future might be reflected, in increased tax rates. It seems probable that public attitudes toward the size of the debt are such that any increase in Treasury financing because of agency lending activity would be reflected to some extent in higher tax rates than would otherwise be enacted. If this presumption is correct, we may conclude that raising funds from Treasury sources would tend to have a somewhat less stimulating effect than raising them from agency issues.

In the above analysis, we assumed that there was no expansion in the money supply by the banking system so that funds obtained for agency lending purposes had to be siphoned out of the income stream. It is always possible for the central bank to inject reserves into the banking system and thus permit an expansion in the money supply as needed to provide the funds for agency lending, whether the banks buy the securities themselves, buy other existing issues and thus release funds for the purchase of Treasury or agency issues, or make new loans and thus meet a demand for funds that might otherwise have been obtained from the supply of funds available for purchase of Treasury or agency issues. It there is such an expansion of the money supply, it would make no difference whether the funds were obtained by agency issues or by Treasury issues except to the limited extent that the Treasury would probably find it easier than would the several agencies to tailor issues in such a way as to finance borrowing through the commercial banking system.

To summarize and reduce this abstract discussion to more understandable terms, we may conclude that agency lending financed by the Treasury would tend to be somewhat less stimulating than lending that is financed by the sale of agency issues in times of boom, when a restrictive monetary policy is likely to be in effect and when public pressure to run a surplus in the federal budget is strong. In times of recession, when approximately the opposite conditions might prevail, it would make little, if any, difference which method of financing were chosen. Finally, over the entire cycle the effect of revolving-fund lending activity, such as that typically carried on by Fanny May in its selling and buying of mortgages, is probably nil.

Moreover, even in times of high and rising business activity, the economic impact of agency lending is not likely to be great. In 1959, a boom year for the agencies, when they extended several times as much credit as in the immediately preceding year, total lending and purchases of mortgages in the amount of about $6 billion was little more than 1 percent of gross national product. When we reflect that some portion of this credit, though certainly not all of it, would have been offered by private lenders in some form or other, it is hard to conclude that federal lending activity is likely to interfere seriously with broad objectives of stabilization policy.

We have left out of account the obvious destabilizing effects of FHA-insured and VA-guaranteed mortgages on the urban residential mortgage market of the 1950's, partly because the subject has been treated in other papers and partly because these agencies are not primarily direct lenders. It is as well demonstrated as almost any fact of recent American economic history that the federally underwritten mortgage, largely an urban credit instrument, was the chief cause of swings in housing starts from 1952 to 1959 that ran counter to cyclical changes in output generally. This countercyclical result–housing starts rising with falling general activity and falling with rising general activity–was clearly the result of maintaining rigid coupons on FHA and VA loans. It is nevertheless worth observing that none of the direct lending agencies discussed in this monograph had as drastic an effect on private markets as did the Federal Housing Administration and the Veterans Administration, which, except for the relatively small volume of VA direct loans, simply insured or guaranteed loans made by private lenders.

If there are no compelling reasons of stabilization objectives for preferring private to government sources of funds, can a case be made <u>on other grounds</u> for requiring the lending agencies to choose one financing alternative rather than another? In favor of financing via the Treasury the argument can be advanced that interest costs to the agencies are lower than for the federal government and that the lending agencies can pass on the savings to borrowers, preferred for one reason or another by Congress, in the form of lower rates.[3] On the side of requiring the lending agencies to go to the private capital markets is the contention that agency officers are thereby made aware of the economic facts of life, that they are forced to price their own loans realistically, and that a roadblock is thus placed in the way of uninhibited lending by agencies not adequately restricted by the general language of congressional directives. In order to assess the weight of these arguments it is necessary to examine briefly the issues by which lending agencies tap the private market for funds.

The "federal agency securities," or more simply the "agency issues," have unquestionably increased in volume and in market importance during the past decade (see Table VI-5 and Chart VI-1).

---

[3]The authors wish to underscore the essential point of this argument, that, if the people in the democracy determine that a subsidy, for one reason or another, ought to be accorded a sector or group in society, then there is no reason for stopping short of implementing that subsidy in the most effective and efficient manner possible. We are not here concerned with the "cost" of funds to the people as taxpayers, since interest payments are in any case a transfer payment, and no net pressure is exerted on the economy in the aggregate through either type of borrowing.

TABLE VI-5

Interest-Bearing Securities Issued by Federal Agencies But Not Guaranteed by the United States Government, 1953 – 1960

(millions of dollars)

Quarters Ending	FICB	FLB	B for C	S. Total	FNMA	FHLB	S. total	Total
1953								
Mar.31	717	863	110	1,690	-	306	306	1,996
June30	781	868	110	1,759	-	251	251	2,010
Sept.30	793	875	110	1,778	-	349	349	2,127
Dec.30	634	941	110	1,685	-	414	414	2,099
1954								
M	617	940	110	1,667	-	204	204	1,871
J	725	1,007	120	1,852	-	115	115	1,967
S	776	1,017	120	1,913	-	179	179	2,092
D	641	1,030	120	1,791	-	273	273	2,064
1955								
M	699	1,085	120	1,904	570	141	711	2,615
J	793	1,117	110	2,020	570	341	911	2,931
S	824	1,133	110	2,067	570	535	1,105	3,172
D	657	1,263	110	2,030	570	975	1,545	3,575
1956								
M	702	1,321	110	2,133	670	878	1,548	3,681
J	834	1,322	133	2,289	670	929	1,599	3,388
S	861	1,437	143	2,441	770	918	1,688	4,129
D	705	1,437	143	2,285	770	963	1,733	4,018
1957								
M	767	1,519	185	2,471	1,220	724	1,944	4,415
J	924	1,552	182	2,658	1,620	738	2,358	5,016
S	948	1,600	207	2,755	1,685	765	2,450	5,205
D	886	1,599	222	2,707	2,687	826	3,513	6,220
1958								
M	971	1,625	191	2,787	3,064	476	3,540	6,327
J	1,159	1,646	199	3,004	1,962	456	2,418	5,422
S	1,205	1,687	232	3,124	1,897	616	2,513	5,637
D	1,116	1,743	252	3,111	1,897	714	2,611	5,722
1959								
M	1,206	1,792	258	3,256	1,947	699	2,646	5,902
J	1,456	1,888	284	3,628	2,087	992	3,079	6,707
S	1,524	1,986	320	3,830	2,287	1,402	3,689	7,519
D	1,356	1,986	364	3,706	2,437	1,774	4,211	7,917
1960								
M	1,416	2,047	360	3,823	2,637	1,293	3,930	7,753
J	1,600	2,137	330	4,067	3,081	1,259	4,340	8,407

Source: Treasury Bulletin.

CHART VI-1

INTEREST-BEARING SECURITIES ISSUED BY FEDERAL AGENCIES BUT NOT GUARANTEED BY THE UNITED STATES GOVERNMENT, 1953-1960, BY QUARTERS*

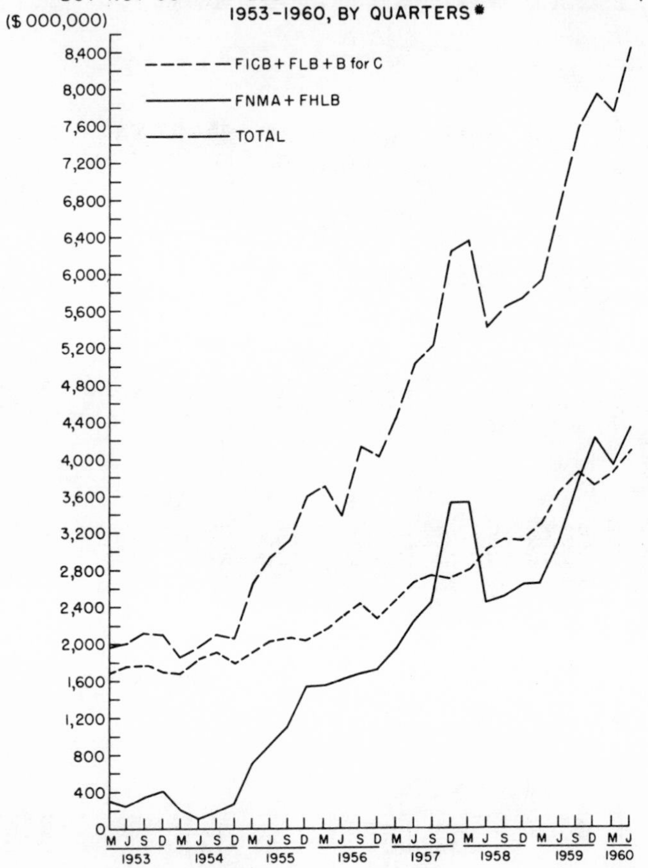

*End of quarter figures
SOURCE: TREASURY BULLETIN

Moreover, they are becoming progressively better known, as both small and institutional investors gain experience with them. Nevertheless, these issues are not accepted by the market as being equal in quality to the regular Treasury list. Against the admitted advantages of higher yields for given maturities, investors weigh the somewhat more limited marketability and thinner market of the agency issues.

A word or two about the structure of the market for agency issues and a few generalizations about their price behavior relative to the Treasury list may assist the reader. To date, no adequate formal study of the agency issues has been done, and most of the information concerning them must be obtained from traders in the market. Detailed statistical studies really should be made to support the comments that follow, but these remarks represent a consensus of knowledgeable dealers.

As indicated previously, there are presently five agency issues—Federal Land Bank bonds, Federal Intermediate Credit Bank debentures, Banks for Cooperative debentures, Federal National Mortgage Association notes and debentures, and Federal Home Loan Bank notes. In the spring of 1960 Fanny May began to issue short-term discount notes, comparable in maturity to commercial paper, and an announcement has recently been made of a forthcoming issue of revenue bonds by the Tennessee Valley Authority. These new issues of Fanny May and the TVA may portend new experimentation in the direction of having government agencies tap the private capital markets.

The pricing and sale of agency issues follows procedures not unlike those of the Treasury list, except that they are a little less formal and somewhat more complex. When an agency is required to raise new funds it will, of course, anticipate its needs by several weeks. After internal discussions of the need for funds, their probable cost, and appropriate maturities, advice is simultaneously sought from Treasury officials, officials of the Federal Reserve Bank of New York, and prospective takers of the issue. The Treasury is primarily concerned with suggesting changes in timing to avoid conflict with upcoming Treasury financing. The Treasury may likewise suggest maturities consistent with its own current financing, though Treasury officials will not ordinarily impose on the agencies a decision inconsistent with dealer advice. While the procedure is not required, agency officers in New York invariably check with the trading desk of the Federal Reserve Bank of New York before making final decisions.

The New York agency officer and his Washington counterpart are crucial figures in the marketing of agency issues. John Knox in New York and Robert Ferguson, his Federal Credit Administration counterpart in Washington, perform a large part of the pricing and marketing function for the Federal Land banks, the Federal Intermediate Credit banks, and the Banks for Cooperatives; John Claiborne in New York and Arthur Hemstreet in the Federal National Mortgage Association office in Washington handle the Fanny May issues. Finally, Everett Smith in New York and Worth Folger and Robert Day in Washington handle the Federal Home Loan Bank issues.

Once internal discussion and preliminary talks with the Treasury have been completed, these agency representatives telephone their most important buyers to inquire what terms will be required to make an issue go. After a consensus has been obtained, discussions are carried on between New York and Washington offices, with prices and maturities being finally determined. The New York representatives then call their dealers and clients to solicit subscriptions at the determined price. Each buyer will, of course, have a good idea of where large portions of the issue can be placed, but the dealers themselves take positions in the issues.

In general, new offerings are priced to yield 40 to 50 basis points (1/2 percent or somewhat less) more than Treasury issues of comparable maturity. However, in a strong bond market — i.e., when yields are falling rather steadily—the spread between agency issues and the comparable Treasuries narrows to perhaps 25 to 30 basis points. In a sour market — i.e., in a market characterized by rapidly rising yields (though not necessarily by "disorderly" conditions in Federal Reserve terminology) — the spread may widen to as much as 70 to 75 basis points.

The agreement among dealers on the approximate extent of differentials between Treasury and agency yields is so marked that there seems little reason to question the existence of the differences just cited. A spot check by the authors of market differentials during the period 1957-60 bears out market conclusions about prices of new issues.[4] The Federal Reserve Bank of Chicago, remarking that the relationship between yields on agency securities and Treasury securities has remained roughly the same over the past decade, notes that agency securities have customarily carried an interest rate of around one-third to two-thirds of 1 percent above the rate on Treasury securities.[5]

---

[4]Differentials on old issues were less predictable though substantially the same, but differences tend to disappear as comparable securities approach maturity.

[5]"Federal Agency Securities," Business Condition, Federal Reserve Bank of Chicago (August 1960), p. 14. For a study of yield relationships between these categories of securities see also Report of the Special Committee to Study the Federal Home Loan Bank System, U.S. Savings and Loan League, 1956, pp. 28-32.

Generalization about the ownership of the agency issues is less satisfactory. The Treasury makes a regular survey of ownership of these issues; within the last year savings and loan associations and corporations have been added to the categories of surveyed institutions, improving the detail (see Table VI-6). Yet the amount of securities in the "all other investors" category, which includes banks and insurance companies not included in the survey, is so large that anything like a definite assignment of percentages of totals owned is impossible. However, data from Federal Reserve flow-of-funds accounts suggests that the proportion of the non-guaranteed debt owned by commercial banks has dropped from about 80 percent to about 25 percent between 1950 and 1958. Meanwhile, consumers and nonprofit organizations increased their holdings from approximately 10 percent to between 25 and 30 percent of the total, nonbank savings institutions increased their holdings from practically nothing to about 15 percent, and, state and local governments increased their ownership from nothing to between 5 and 10 percent. Insurance company holdings, varying over the decade, have apparently never amounted to more than 5 percent of the total.[6]

Comparison of the ownership of Treasury issues with that of agency issues suggests no great difference in the relative importance of the several classes of holders. However, commercial banks as a group hold about 30 percent of the marketable Treasury issues as compared with a maximum of 25 percent holding of the agency issues.

As noted above, two government agencies have recently experimented with issues calculated to test new money market potentials. With its Short-Term Discount Notes, Fanny May has raised more than $400 million since April 1960, and more than $300 million of these securities were outstanding in October 1960. As might have been expected, these notes yield more than Treasury bills of comparable maturities; having most of the advantages of commercial paper, they unquestionably tap a market not previously reached by other agencies. Similarly, TVA, now authorized to sell $750 million of bonds to finance future power production, has seized on the idea of selling power revenue bonds with a first claim on net power proceeds from the operation of all existing and future TVA power facilities.[7] Again, a new segment of the bond market will be attracted, and the total job of public financing (including debt management) may thereby be facilitated.

---

[6] Ibid., p. 14.
[7] Basic Data on TVA and Its Revenue Bond Financing, brochure of the Tennessee Valley Authority, 1960

TABLE VI-6

Summary of Treasury Survey of Ownership of Agency Issues

Interest Bearing Securities Issued by Federal Agencies But Not Guaranteed by the United States Government
(Par values – in millions of dollars)
June 30, 1960

	Tot. Amt. Outstand'g.	Commercial Banks	Mtl. Savings Banks	Insurance Companies Life	Insurance Companies Fire, Casualty and Marines	Savings & Loan Associations	Corporations	U.S. Government Investment Accounts and Federal Reserve Banks	Held by All Other Investors	Memorandum: Held by Corporate Pensions Trust Funds
Banks for Cooperatives	330	39	19	1	4	2	79	-	186	4
Federal Home Loan Banks	1,259	187	60	13	15	162	252	4	566	16
Fed. Intermed. Credit Banks	1,600	202	88	15	22	5	275	3	990	26
Federal Land Banks	2,137	337	135	32	45	9	72	-	1,507	154
Fed. Nat'l. Mort. Assoc.	3,081	477	202	33	72	194	382	9	1,712	110
Totals	8,407	1,242	504	94	158	372	1,060	16	4,961	310

Source: Treasury Bulletin, September, 1960, p. 54.

The fact remains that no clear-cut advantages over orthodox Treasury financing emerge from an examination of the methods used in floating the agency issues. Moreover, it is apparent that in recent years the lending agencies, particularly Fanny May and the Federal Home Loan banks, have entered the market for funds just when the Treasury was having trouble with its own financing, this despite careful checking with the Treasury in anticipation of a new issue. It is possible that the lending agencies succeed in getting no better financing than they would through the Treasury but at somewhat higher cost to ultimate borrowers.

To some financial analysts and not a few bond dealers the question of cost of financing misses the point. They would argue that forcing agencies into the market for funds makes them examine realistically the terms of their own lending and other credit-extending activities. Fanny May, they say, is made to realize that mortgages cannot be bought at 100 when the market for them is 94 and that borrowing short to lend long is usually a poor proposition. Or the Federal Home Loan banks will not be tempted to lend to members at less than going rates of interest and thus encourage undue extension of credit by the savings and loan associations.

On its face, the "roadblock" argument — that a market check on a program may be effective in reducing its scope and making it amenable to the demands of the private sector — makes sense. Yet we must ask ourselves if such a check can really be expected to be, or should be, a deterrent to objectives set by Congress.

A consideration of recent episodes indicates how little we may expect in the way of a roadblock effect, once Congress has approved certain objectives. We may take a random example. While the total volume of farm mortgage loans rose from $1.7 billion in 1950 to $2.8 billion in 1958, the proportion of the loans made by Federal Land banks rose from 12 percent to 22 percent. As interest rates increased, the gap between Federal Land Bank rates and the rates charged by their immediate competitors, commercial banks and insurance companies, widened. But could anyone really have expected the Federal Land banks to keep their rates in lock step with those of their competitors and thus have repelled a rising proportion of the total business?

Let us take another example. The most casual inspection of Table VI-5 and Chart VI-1 reveals a tendency observers have frequently remarked — that increases in debt of the Federal Home Loan banks increased sharply in 1955 and 1959, following upsurges in home building in 1954 and 1958. Similarly, Fanny May increased its activity as the Federal Reserve tightened interest rates in 1956-57 and again in late 1958 and 1959. Does anyone honestly believe that the requirement that these agencies go to the market for funds affected the course of their lending activity?

We probably get the clearest view of our problem when we reflect that the federal lending agencies are government institutions. No amount of reference to their functions as "business-type" activities can change the fact that these agencies were created to intervene in the private economy. And the mere fact that the capital stock of certain of the agencies is owned by private parties should not disguise the fact that they are government agencies pure and simple. The Federal Home Loan banks may be owned by member institutions — but they still have a put on the Treasury for $1 billion should the going ever get rough. Fanny May may sell all the "stock" it can to private mortgage companies, but the fact remains that the agency still goes to the private market for funds to help Treasury stay under the debt ceiling — and comes back to Treasury when the heat is off.

Like the Federal Reserve System, the lending agencies were created by the people for public purposes. In presenting ways of tapping fund sources, we must be guided by the ultimate objectives of these public agencies — as determined by the national legislature — and not by some vain hope that we can make them more like private institutions or less effective than they can be. The criteria of ultimate objectives still may leave open the alternative of private funds; but until more compelling reasons for using the agency issues as substitutes for Treasury issues are forthcoming, it seems less expensive and less cumbersome to furnish funds through the Treasury. The people are not likely to achieve better public institutions by disguising the fact that they are public.

APPENDIX A

TABLE VI-A1

Federal Land Banks

Category A. Consolidated Federal Farm loan bonds sold and outstanding in the private market, nongovernment secured, as source of loanable funds, 1950-59.

(in thousands)

Year[a]	Outstanding at end of Year	Issued	Retired	Net change in outstandings
1949	$ 715,707			
1950	714,842	none	865	-$ 865
1951	784,479	$71,450	$ 1,813	+ 69,637
1952	816,082	229,900	198,297	+ 31,603
1953	935,938	307,100	187,244	+119,856
1954	1,029,962	379,609	285,586	+ 94,024
1955	1,190,962	236,500	75,500	+161,000
1956	1,437,099	605,300	359,163	+246,137
1957	1,599,389	813 000	650,711	+162,290
1958	1,742,961	800,000	656,428	+143,572
1959	1,985,920	738,000	495,041	+242,960

[a]Year ended December 31.

Source: Farm Credit Administration.

TABLE VI-A2

Federal Land Banks

Category E. Capital stock held by Federal Land Bank Associations[1]
1950-59
(in thousands)

Year a/	Outstanding at end of year	Sold	Retired	Net change in outstandings
1950	$60,197			+$2,311
1951	62,902			+ 2,705
1952	67,204			+ 4,302
1953	72,628			+ 5,424
1954	78,135			+ 5,507
		(No Information)		
1955	88,896			+10,761
1956	102,016			+13,120
1957	112,608			+10,592
1958	123,210			+10,602
1959	138,888			+15,678

[a]Year ended December 31.

[1]Name changed from National Farm Loan Associations to Federal Land Bank Associations, effective December 31, 1959, by Farm Credit Act of 1959.

Source: Farm Credit Administration.

TABLE VI-A3

Federal Land Bank Bonds

(Outstanding as of the close of business December 31, 1959)

Millions of Dollars	Issue Dated	Rate	Maturity	Bid	Asked	Yield to Maturity
$124	8/2/54	2 1/4	2/1/60	99 22/32	99 26/32	4.81
89	2/2/59	3 3/4	2/1/60	99 26/32	99 30/32	4.55
201	5/1/59	3 7/8	4/20/60	99 18/32	99 22/32	4.92
107	2/1/55	2 1/2	6/1/60	98 24/32	99	5.04
118	1/5/60	5 3/8	10/20/60	100	100 2/32	5.29
83	2/14/58	3 3/8	4/3/61	97 12/32	97 20/32	5.36
120	11/3/58	4	9/20/61	97 8/32	97 24/32	5.39
125	5/1/57	4	5/1/62	96 28/32	97 12/32	5.21
98	8/25/59	4 7/8	8/20/62	99 4/32	99 12/32	5.13
122	5/1/58	2 3/4	5/1/63	91 28/32	92 8/32	5.31
108	5/1/58	3 1/4	5/2/66	89 8/32	89 24/32	5.17
72	2/15/57	4 1/8	2/15/72-67	92	93	4.90
75	10/1/57	4 1/2	10/1/70-67	96	97	4.86
86	4/1/59	4 1/4	3/20/68	94 16/32	95 16/32	4.92
100	2/2/59	4 3/8	3/20/69	95	96	4.92
60	7/15/57	4 5/8	7/15/69	97 16/32	98 16/32	4.82
83	2/14/58	3 1/2	4/1/70	88	89	4.88
85	1/5/60	5 1/8	7/20/70	100 28/32	101 4/32	4.99
60	5/1/56	3 1/2	5/1/71	87	88	4.89
109	9/14/56	3 7/8	9/15/72	89	90	4.94

Source: C. J. Devine and Company, quotation sheet dated January 4, 1960.

TABLE VI-A4

Federal Intermediate Credit Banks

Category A. Consolidated debentures sold and outstanding in the private market, nongovernment secured, as source of loanable funds, 1950-59.
(in thousands)

Year a/	Outstanding at end of year	Issued	Retired	Net change in outstandings
1950	$ 507,470	$ 741,760	$ 724,215	+$17,545
1951	669,605	1,098,510	936,375	+162,135
1952	703,730	1,116,555	1,082,430	+ 34,125
1953	618,720	1,048,595	1,133,605	- 85,010
1954	634,930	996,495	980,285	+ 16,210
1955	656,945	1,055,330	1,033,315	+ 22,015
1956	704,700	1,133,550	1,085,795	+ 47,755
1957	886,350	1,354,100	1,172,450	+181,650
1958	1,115,500	1,560,300	1,331,150	+229,150
1959	1,356,200	1,958,500	1,717,800	+240,700

[a] Year ended December 31.

Source: Farm Credit Administration.

TABLE VI-A5

Federal Intermediate Credit Banks

Category D. Capital stock held by the government, 1950-59.
(in thousands)

Year a/		Outstanding at end of year	Sold to Government	Repaid to Government	Net change in outstandings
1950	1/	$60,000	-	-	-
	2/	-	-	-	-
1951	1/	60,000	-	-	-
	2/	2,650	$2,650	-	+$ 2,650
1952	1/	60,000	-	-	-
	2/	6,850	4,725	$ 525	+4,200
1953	1/	60,000	-	-	-
	2/	2,800	100	4,150	-4,050
1954	1/	60,000	-	-	-
	2/	1,400	-	1,400	-1,400
1955	1/	60,000	-	-	-
	2/	2,400	1,000	-	+1,000
1956	1/	60,000	-	-	-
	2/	-	1,250	3,650	-2,400
1957	1/	82,904	27,405 b/	4,501	+22,904
	2/	-	-	-	-
1958	1/	79,909	1,700	4,695	-2,995
	2/	-	-	-	-
1959	1/	90,139	14,600	4,370	+10,230
	2/	-	-	-	-

[a]Year ended December 31.
[b]Exchange of PCC stock for FICB class A.

[1]Capital stock.
[2]Paid-in surplus.

Source: Farm Credit Administration.

TABLE VI-A6

Federal Intermediate Credit Banks

Category E. Capital stock held by Production Credit Associations[1]
1950-59
(in thousands)

Year a/	Outstanding at end of year	Issued	Retired	Net change in outstandings
1950				
1951				
1952				
1953				
1954				
1955				
1956				
1957	$ 8,959	$ 8,959	$	$+8,959
1958	15,524	6,565		+6,565
1959	20,504	4,980		+4,980

[a]Year ended December 31.

[1]The Farm Credit Act of 1956 authorized patronage refunds from credit bank earnings in class B stock which may be issued to and held only by Production Credit Associations. Participation certificates in payment of patronage refunds are issued to other financing institutions borrowing from or rediscounting with the Credit Banks.

Source: Farm Credit Administration.

TABLE VI-A7

Federal Intermediate Credit Banks

Category F. Funds obtained by warnings from Government-owned Capital Stock, 1950-59 [b].
(in thousands)

Year a/	Earnings	Deductions from Earnings	Net Earnings
1950	$12,139	$ 9,045	$ 3,094
1951	17,077	15,490	1,587
1952	23,567	20,044	3,523
1953	22,244	20,561	1,683
1954	18,957	15,199	3,758
1955	17,461	16,241	1,220
1956	27,511	27,215	296
1957	40,765	38,978	1,787
1958	46,234	36,963	9,271
1959	62,441	56,677	5,764

[a]Year ended December 31.
[b]Agency reported earnings from capital stock rather than from appropriations.

Source: Farm Credit Administration.

TABLE VI-A8

Production Credit Corporations [1]

Category D. Capital stock held by the government, 1950-59.
(in thousands)

Year a/	Outstanding at end of year	Sold to government	Repaid to government	Net change in outstandings
1950	$ 42,235	-	$ 4,000	-$4,000
1951	39,235	-	3,000	- 3,000
1952	36,235	-	3,000	- 3,000
1953	35,860	-	375	- 375
1954	31,735	-	4,125	- 4,125
1955	31,350	-	385	- 385
1956	29,235	-	2,115	- 2,115
2/ 1957	0	-	(1,830 b/ (27,405	(-1,830 (-27,405
1958	-	-	-	-
1959	-	-	-	-

[a]Year ended December 31.

[b]$1,830,000 - amount of PCA stock outstanding 12/31/56; transferred to Governor equal amount of PCC stock canceled.

$27,405,000 - exchanged for FICB class A stock.

[1]Effective January 1, 1957, pursuant to the Farm Credit Act of 1956, the Production Credit Corporations were merged in the Federal Intermediate Credit banks in their respective Farm Credit districts.

[2]Under the Farm Credit Act of 1956, $27,405,000 of Production Credit Corporation capital was transferred to the Federal Intermediate Credit banks and $2,595,000 of the revolving fund was paid into the U.S. Treasury as miscellaneous receipts leaving a revolving fund of $60 million at January 1, 1957, available to the Governor of PCA for capitalising Production Credit Associations.

Source: Farm Credit Administration.

TABLE VI-A9

Production Credit Associations

Category D. Capital stock provided from Government funds [1]
1950-59.
(in thousands)

Year a/	Outstanding at end of year	Sold to PCCs	Repaid	Net change in outstandings
1950	$15,728	$ 965	$7,533	-$6,568
1951	11,371	1,015	5,372	- 4,357
1952	7,596	100	3,875	- 3,775
1953	4,946	640	3,290	- 2,650
1954	3,165	160	1,941	- 1,781
1955	2,160	-	1,005	- 1,005
1956	1,830	250	580	- 330
1957	1,870	1,830 b/	10	+ 1,870
1958	4,450	2,860	280	+ 2,580
1959	3,575	245	1,120	- 875

[a] Year ended December 31.
[b] PCA stock outstanding 12/31/56 transferred to Governor; equal amount of PCC stock canceled.

[1] Prior to January 1, 1957, the 12 Production Credit Corporations, wholly Government owned, subscribed to class A capital stock of PCAs. Since January 1, 1957, a U.S. Treasury revolving fund of $60 million has been available to the Governor of the Farm Credit Administration for capitalizing Production Credit Associations.

Source: Farm Credit Administration.

TABLE VI-A10

Production Credit Associations

Category E. Capital stock held by members of the associations, 1950-59.

(in thousands)

Year a/	Outstanding at end of year	Sold	Retired	Net change in outstandings
1950	$ 71,145			+$ 6,277
1951	82,911			+ 11,766
1952	90,442			+ 7,531
1953	93,014			+ 2,572
1954	94,610			+ 1,596
		(No Information)		
1955	98,362			+ 3,752
1956	102,685			+ 4,323
1957	111,758			+ 9,073
1958	131,981			+ 20,223
1959	157,161			+ 25,180

[a]Year ended December 31.

Source: Farm Credit Administration.

TABLE VI-A11

Federal Intermediate Credit Bank Debentures

(Outstanding as of the close of business December 31, 1959)

Millions of dollars	Issue dated	Rate	Maturity	Bid	Asked	Yield to maturity
$181	5/4/59	4 1/8	2/1/60	99 28/32	99 31/32	4.44
171	6/1/59	4 1/2	3/1/60	99 28/32	99 31/32	4.58
150	7/1/59	4.45	4/4/60	99 25/32	99 28/32	4.85
152	8/3/59	4 7/8	5/2/60	99 26/32	99 30/32	4.97
118	9/1/59	4.65	6/1/60	99 23/32	99 26/32	5.04
133	10/1/59	5 1/4	7/5/60	99 30/32	100 1/32	5.12
128	11/2/59	5.20	8/1/60	99 30/32	100	5.15
131	12/1/59	5 1/4	9/1/60	99 30/32	100	5.22
171	1/4/60	5 3/8	10/3/60	100	100 2/32	5.29

Source: C. J. Devine and Company, quotation sheet dated January 4, 1960.

TABLE VI-A12

Banks for Cooperatives

Category A. Debentures sold and outstanding in the private market, nongovernment secured, as source of loanable funds, 1950-59.

(in thousands)

Year a/	Outstanding at end of year	Issued	Retired	Net change in outstandings
1950	$ 30,000	b/$ 30,000	-	+$ 30,000
1951	70,000	b/ 40,000	-	+ 40,000
1952	110,000	b/ 40,000	-	+ 40,000
1953	110,000	b/ 70,000	$ 70,000	-
1954	120,000	b/ 120,000	110,000	+ 10,000
1955	170,000	c/ 70,000	80,000	- 10,000
1956	142,800	c/ 145,000	112,200	+ 32,800
1957	221,800	c/ 366,800	287,800	+ 79,000
1958	252,000	c/ 329,500	299,300	+ 30,200
1959	363,500	c/ 648,000	536,500	+ 111,500

[a]Year ended December 31.

[b]Obligations of the Central Bank for Cooperatives.

[c]Consolidated obligations of the 13 Banks for Cooperatives.

Source: Farm Credit Administration.

TABLE VI-A13

Banks for Cooperatives

Category D. Capital stock held by the Government, 1950-59 (in thousands)

Year a/	Outstanding at end of year	Sold to government	Repaid to government	Net change in outstandings
1950	$178,500	-	-	-
1951	178,500	-	-	-
1952	178,500	-	-	-
1953	178,500	-	-	-
1954	150,000	-	$28,500	-$28,500
1955	150,000	-	-	-
1956	147,314	-	2,687	- 2,687
1957	141,588	-	5,726	- 5,726
1958	134,799	-	6,789	- 6,789
1959	126,339	-	8,459	- 8,459

[a]Year ended December 31.

Source: Farm Credit Administration.

TABLE VI-A14

Banks for Cooperatives

Category E. Capital stock held by farmers' marketing, purchasing and general service cooperatives, 1950-59.
(in thousands)

Year a/	Outstanding at end of year	Sold	Retired	Net change in outstandings
1950	$16,647			$+1,116
1951	20,346			+3,699
1952	20,483			+ 137
1953	19,806			+ 677
1954	19,904			+ 98
		(No Information)		
1955	20,618			+ 714
1956	21,098			+ 480
1957	26,355			+5,257
1958	32,088			+5,733
1959	40,136			+8,048

[a]Year ended December 31.

Source: Farm Credit Administration

TABLE VI-A15

Banks for Cooperatives

Category F. Funds obtained from earnings, 1950-59 [b].
(in thousands)

Year a/	Earnings	Deductions from earnings	Net earnings
1950	$ 9,820	$ 3,647	$ 6,173
1951	12,245	5,491	6,754
1952	13,618	6,386	7,232
1953	13,374	5,890	7,484
1954	13,582	6,909	6,673
1955	13,721	5,888	7,833
1956	15,261	8,198	7,063
1957	18,922	12,006	6,916
1958	20,389	11,230	9,159
1959	25,723	17,578	8,145

[a] Year ended December 31.
[b] Excluding administrative appropriations and expenses, except that administrative expenses are included if they are paid out of earnings rather than from special government appropriation.

Source: Farm Credit Administration.

TABLE VI-A16

Banks for Cooperatives' Debentures

(Outstanding as of the close of business December 31, 1959)

Millions of dollars	Issue dated	Rate	Maturity	Bid	Asked	Yield to maturity
$113	8/3/59	4 7/8	2/1/60	99 30/32	100 1/32	4.35
112	10/1/59	5 3/8	4/4/60	100 1/32	100 4/32	4.78
138	12/1/59	5 1/4	9/1/60	99 29/32	100	5.22

Source: C. J. Devine and Company, quotations sheet dated January 4, 1960.

TABLE VI-A17

Farmers Home Administration

Category C. Bonds, debentures, or notes issued in connection with borrowings from the government for loanable funds, 1950-59

(in thousands)

Year [a]	Outstanding at end of year	Borrowings	Repaid	Net change in outstandings
1950	$ 30,810	$128,000	$ 97,190	$+30,810
1951	57,836	147,500	120,474	+27,026
1952	78,369	153,000	132,467	+20,533
1953	116,795	164,000	125,574	+38,426
1954	172,377	182,000	126,418	+55,582
1955	159,853	145,400	157,924	-12,524
1956	150,798	163,000	172,055	- 9,055
1957	256,907	285,500	179,391	+106,109
1958	253,862	209,500	212,545	- 3,045
1959	293,552	281,500	241,810	+39,690

[a]Year ended June 30.

Source: Farmers Home Administration.

TABLE VI-A18

Farmers Home Administration

Category F. Loanable funds obtained from government appropriations and earnings, 1950-59[b].
(in thousands)

Year[a]	Government appropriations	Earnings: Income from interest, fees, etc.	Earnings: Expenses for dividends, interest, etc.	Earnings: Net	Total
Carried Forward	$45,400				
1950	1,350				
1951	30,000[c]				
1952					
1953					
1954	68,500[c]				
1955					
1956					
1957					
1958					
1959					

[a]Year ended June 30.

[b]Excluding administrative appropriations and expenses, except that administrative expenses are included if they are paid out of earnings rather than from special government appropriation.

[c]The amounts shown in 1951 and 1954 were appropriated to the Disaster Loan Revolving Fund to augment that Fund.

Source: Farmers Home Administration.

TABLE VI-A19

Rural Electrification Administration

Category C. Notes issued in connection with borrowings from the Secretary of the Treasury for loanable funds, 1950-59.

Fiscal Year a/	Outstanding at end of year	Borrowings	Repaid	Net change in outstandings
1950	$1,281,136	$285,000	$19,057	$+265,943
1951	1,526,715	280,000	34,420	+245,580
1952	1,731,326	240,000	35,389	+204,611
1953	1,932,722	235,000	33,604	+201,396
1954	2,091,132	205,000	46,589	+158,411
1955	2,206,524	180,000	64,608	+115,392
1956	2,343,228	210,000	73,296	+136,704
1957	2,518,951	255,000	79,277	+175,723
1958	2,727,752	300,237	91,436	+208,801
1959	2,923,326	295,000	99,428	+195,572

[a]Year ended June 30.

Source: Rural Electrification Administration

TABLE VI-A20

Commodity Credit Corporation

Category C. Bonds, debentures, or notes issued in connection with borrowings from the government for loanable funds 1950-59.

(in thousands)

Year a/	Outstanding at end of year	Borrowings	Repaid	Net change in outstandings
1950	$ 2,736,000	$1,445,000	$1,275,000	$+ 170 000
1951	2,025,000	667,000	1,378,000	- 711 000
1952	2,169,000	878,000	734,000	+ 144 000
1953	3,948,000	3,554,000	1,775,000	+1,779,000
1954	5,532,000	4,008,000	2,424,000	+1,584,000
1955	9,875,000	4,727,000	384,000	+4,343,000
1956	11,640,000	3,327,000	1,562,000	+1,765,000
1957	12,786,000	4,007,000	2,861,000	+1,146,000
1958	12,153,000	4,390,000	5,023,000	- 633,000
1959	12,074,000	4,321,000	4,400,000	- 79,000

[a] Year ended December 31.

Source: Commodity Credit Corporation.

TABLE VI-A21

Commodity Credit Corporation

Category B. Bonds, debentures, or notes issued in connection with borrowings from banks.
(in thousands)

Year[a]	Outstanding at end of year	Sales	Repaid	Net change in outstandings
1950	$ 791	$47,480	$57,142	$-9,662
1951	3,624	96,834	94,001	+2,833
1952	505	9,875	12,994	-3,119
1953	-	100	605	- 505
1954	-	-	-	-
1955	-	-	-	-
1956	-	-	-	-
1957	-	-	-	-
1958	-	-	-	-
1959	-	-	-	-

[a] Year ended December 31.

Note: Borrowings from banks acting as agents under Price Support Programs for Peanuts and Wool.

Source: Commodity Credit Corporation.

TABLE VI-A22

Small Business Administration

Category F. Loanable funds obtained from government appropriations and earnings to Revolving Fund, 1950-59[b].
(in thousands)

Year[a]	Government appropriations	Earnings			Total
		Income from interest, fees, etc.	Expenses for interest, etc.[c]	Net	
1950					
1951					
1952					
1953					
1954 (11 mos)	$ 55,000	$ 32	$ 1,591	-$1,559	$ 53,441
1955	25,000	853	3,604	- 2,751	22,249
1956	45,000	2,450	7,295	- 4,845	40,155
1957	95,000	5,620	10,670	- 5,050	89,950
1958	120,000	10,196	17,025	- 6,829	113,171
1959	200,000	15,552	20,751	- 5,199	194,801

[a]Year ended June 30.
[b]Excluding administrative appropriations and expenses, except that administrative expenses are included if they are paid out of earnings rather than from special government appropriations.
[c]Includes administrative expenses of business and disaster loans authorized for payment from Revolving Fund, and allowance for losses.

Source: Small Business Administration.

TABLE VI-A23

Public Housing Administration

Category C. Bonds, debentures or notes issued in connection with borrowings from the government for loanable funds 1950-1959.

(in thousands)

Year [a]	Outstanding at end of year	Borrowings	Repaid	Credit by Treasury for loss	Net Change in outstandings[1]
1950	$349,000	$ 12,000	-		$+ 12,000
1951	489,000	140,000	-		+140,000
1952	655,000	431,000	$265,000		+166,000
1953	655,000	550,000	550,000		-
1954	215,000	439,000	879,000		-440,000
1955	61,000	145,000	299,000		-154,000
1956	38,000	195,817	213,000	$5,817	-23,000
1957	41,000	196,000	192,996	3	+3,000
1958	35,000	135,000	141,000		-6,000
1959	27,000	75,000	83,000		-8,000

[a] Year ended June 30.

[1] Credit by U.S. Treasury for Loss sustained by PHA on loan to LHA.

Source: Public Housing Administration.

TABLE VI-A24

Federal National Mortgage Association

Category A. Bonds, debentures, or notes sold and outstanding in the private market, government secured, as sources of loanable funds, 1950-59.
(in thousands)

Year a/	Outstanding at end of year	Sales	Repaid	Net change in Outstandings
1950				
1951				
1952				
1953				
1954				
1955	$ 570,374	$ 570,374		+ $570,374
1956	770,374	300,000	$ 100,000	+ 200,000
1957	2,687,435	2,317,061	400,000	+1,917,061
1958	1,897,344	1,897,344	2,687,435	- 790,091
1959	2,437,344	1,340,000	800,000	+ 540,000

[a]Year ended December 31.

Source: Federal National Mortgage Association.

TABLE VI-A25

Federal National Mortgage Association

Category C. Bonds, debentures, or notes issued in connection with borrowings from the government for loanable funds, 1950-59.

(in thousands)

Year [a]	Outstanding at end of year	Borrowings	Repaid	Net change in outstandings
1950	$ 1,310,322	$ 1,310,381	$ 59	+ $1,310,322
1951	1,813,221	513,838	10,939	+ 502,899
1952	2,199,508	1,498,845	1,112,558	+ 386,287
1953	2,375,000	304,043	128,551	+ 175,492
1954	2,448,518	2,780,548 [b]	2,707,030 [b]	+ 73,518
1955	2,001,781	2,368,222 [c]	2,814,959 [c]	- 446,737
1956	2,162,734	659,433	498,480	+ 160,953
1957	958,680	964,532	2,168,586	- 1,204,054
1958	1,703,576	1,775,521	1,030,625	+ 744,896
1959	2,698,428	2,110,576	1,115,724	+ 994,852

[a] Year ended December 31.
[b] Includes $2,375,000 exchange of notes
[c] Includes $2,114,925 exchange of notes

Source: Federal National Mortgage Association.

TABLE VI-A26

Federal National Mortgage Association

Category F. Capital stock held by the government, 1950-59
(in thousands)

Year a/	Outstanding at end of year	Sold to government	Retired	Net change in outstanding
1950	$ 20,000			
1951	20,000			
1952	20,000			
1953	20,000			
1954	92,820	$92,820	$20,000	$+72,820
1955	92,820			
1956	92,820			
1957	142,820	50,000		+50,000
1958	142,820			
1959	142,820			

[a] Year ended December 31, 1959.

Source: Federal National Mortgage Association.

TABLE VI-A27

Federal National Mortgage Association

Category E. Common stock held by private parties, 1950-59
(in thousands)

Year a/	Outstanding at end of year	Issued	Retired	Net change in outstandings
1950				
1951				
1952				
1953				
1954	$ 1	$ 1	-	$+ 1
1955	2,582	2,581	-	+ 2,581
1956	14,683	14,683	-	+12,101
1957	33,023	33,023	-	+18,340
1958	38,287	38,287	-	+ 5,264
1959	53,373	53,373	-	+15,086

[a]Year ended December 31, 1959.

Source: Federal National Mortgage Association.

TABLE VI-A28

Federal National Mortgage Association
Notes and Debentures[1]

(Outstanding as of the close of business December 31, 1959)

Millions of dollars	Issue dated	Rate	Maturity	Bid	Asked	Yield to maturity
150	6/10/59	4 1/2	3/10/60	99 28/32	99 31/32	4.56
100	10/13/59	5.30	4/11/60	100 1/32	100 4/32	4.77
200	11/10/59	5 1/8	5/10/60	99 31/32	100 1/32	4.99
100	2/10/59	4	6/10/60	99 10/32	99 18/32	5.04
797	1/20/58	3 5/8	8/23/60	99 1/32	99 4/32	5.05
200	12/10/59	5.35	9/12/60	100	100 2/32	5.23
150	9/23/59	5 1/8	9/11/61	99 16/32	99 24/32	5.27
200	2/10/58	3 1/2	2/13/62	95 24/32	96 8/32	5.40
150	3/10/58	3 1/4	3/11/63	93 12/32	93 28/32	5.36
100	11/10/58	4 1/8	11/12/63	95 12/32	95 28/32	5.34
100	12/10/57	4 3/8	6/10/65	95 24/32	96 8/32	5.17
100	3/10/58	3 5/8	3/10/68	89 24/32	90 8/32	5.10
90	4/10/59	4 3/8	4/10/69	94 16/32	95 16/32	4.99

[1]The short-term discount notes, issued exclusively through A. G. Becker and Company, Incorporated, did not appear until April 1960.

Source: C. J. Devine and Company, daily quotation sheet dated January 4, 1960.

TABLE VI-A 29

Federal National Mortgage Association

Combined Operations

Loanable funds obtained from principal repayments; sales of mortgages and earnings, 1950-59 (in thousands)

Calendar Year	Principal repayments and sales of mtgs. a/	Earnings: Income from interest, fees, etc. b/	Earnings: Expenses for dividends interest, etc. c/ d/	Earnings: Net	Total
1950	$ 513,662	$ 52,253	$ 40,887	$ 11,366	$ 525,028
1951	166,587	67,221	70,389	(3,168)	163,419
1952	134,812	84,066	85,204	(1,138)	133,674
1953	314,840	102,830	72,733	30,097	344,937
1954	625,496	102,973	144,271	(41,298)	584,198
1955	188,527	109,390	74,716	34,674	223,201
1956	129,420	121,554	83,596	37,958	167,378
1957	147,539	169,660	133,299	36,361	183,900
1958	666,186	192,758	158,535	34,223	700,409
1959	234,873	234,050	194,280	39,770	274,643
Totals	3,121,942	1,236,755	1,057,910	178,845	3,300,787

[a] Includes $8,006 repayments on RFC mortgages and DHC Purchase Money Notes acquired in 1954.
[b] Includes surplus adjustments: $256 in 1951, $44 in 1952 and $689 in 1958.
[c] Includes surplus adjustments: ($102) in 1951, $29 in 1953 and $689 in 1958.
[d] Includes administrative expense which is all paid from earnings.

Note: The Association is a self-supporting corporation – it receives no appropriation of funds for the payment of its administration or other expenses. The principal source of funds for the purchase of mortgages is borrowings from the public and from the United States Treasury.

TABLE VI-A30

Community Facilities Administration

(College Housing Loans)

Category C. Bonds, debentures, or notes issued in connection with borrowings from the government for loanable funds, 1950-59.

(in thousands)

Year a/	Outstanding at end of year	Borrowings	Repaid	Net change in outstandings
1950				
1951				
1952	$ 2,000	$ 2,000	-	$ +2,000
1953	20,000	18,000	-	+18,000
1954	51,500	31,500	-	+31,500
1955	81,500	30,000	-	+30,000
1956	116,112	55,000	20,388	+34,612
1957	227,857	111,745	-	+111,745
1958	388,857	161,000	-	+161,000
1959	594,418	211,955	6,394	+205,561

[a] Year ended June 30.

Source: Community Facilities Administration.

TABLE VI-A31

Community Facilities Administration

(Public Facility Loans)

Category C. Bonds, debentures, or notes issued in connection with borrowings from the government for loanable funds, 1950-59.

(in thousands)

Year a/	Outstanding at end of year	Borrowings	Repaid	Net change in outstandings
1950				
1951				
1952				
1953				
1954				
1955				
1956				
1957	$ 1,400	$ 1,400	-	$ +1,400
1958	13,700	12,300	-	+12,300
1959	37,951	24,251	-	+24,251

[a]Year ended June 30.

Source: Community Facilities Administration.

TABLE VI-A32

Urban Renewal Administration

Category C. Notes issued in connection with borrowings from the Treasury for loanable funds, 1950-59.
(in thousands)

Year a/	Outstanding at end of year	Borrowings	Repaid	Net change in outstandings
1950	$ 500	$ 500	--	$ +500
1951	3,000	2,500	--	+2,500
1952	10,000	9,000	$ 2,000	+7,000
1953	28,000	23,000	5,000	+18,000
1954	38,000	10,000	--	+10,000
1955	48,000	10,000	--	+10,000
1956	48,000	--	--	--
1957	53,000	12,000	7,000	+5,000
1958	73,000	20,000	--	+20,000
1959	98,000	118,000	93,000	+25,000

[a]Year ended June 30.

Source: Urban Renewal Administration

TABLE VI-A33

Veterans Administration

Category C. Bonds, debentures, or notes issued in connection with borrowings from the government for loanable funds, 1950-59.

(in thousands)

Year a/	Outstanding at end of year	Borrowings	Repaid	Net change in outstandings
1951	$ 150,000	$ 150,000	-	+ 150,000
1952	219,962	69,962	-	+ 69,962
1953	316,213	96,251	-	+ 96,251
1954	429,210	112,997	-	+ 112,997
1955	533,745	104,535	-	+ 104,535
1956	630,900	97,155	-	+ 97,155
1957	730,507	99,607	-	+ 99,607
1958	877,844	147,337	-	+ 147,337
1959	1,089,383	211,539	-	+ 211,539

[a] Year ended December 31.

Source: Veterans Administration.

TABLE VI-A34

Veterans Administration

Category F. Loanable funds obtained from government appropriations and earnings, Direct Loan Progam, operated on a revolving fund basis, 1950-59.[b]

(in thousands)

Year[a]	Government appropriations plus principal repayments and sales of loans to private investors	Earnings			Total
		Income from interest, fees, etc.	Expenses for dividends, interest, etc.	Net held as reserve for losses	
1951)[c]	$ 4,039	$ 3,000	$ 2,000	$ 1,000	$ 5,039
1952)[c]	14,913	5,000	3,000	2,000	16,913
1953)[c]	14,966	17,444	14,302	3,142	18,108
1954	37,851	11,884	6,992	4,892	42,743
1955	34,478	15,310	8,270	7,040	41,518
1956	29,745	18,364	10,891	7,473	37,218
1957	31,126	22,480	14,348	8,132	39,258
1958	43,008	30,062	19,252	10,810	53,818
1959	49,247	35,882	21,874	14,008	63,255

[a]Year ended December 31.
[b]Excluding administrative appropriations and expenses, except that administrative expenses are included if they are paid out of earnings rather than from special government appropriation.
[c]Earnings partly estimated.

Source: Veterans Administration.

TABLE VI-A35

Federal Home Loan Banks

Category E. Capital stock held by private parties (member institutions), 1950-59.

(in thousands)

Year[a]	Outstanding at end of year	Sold	Retired	Net change in outstandings
1950	$182,546	n.a.	n.a.	$+46,307
1951	270,652	n.a.	n.a.	+88,106
1952	315,488	n.a.		+44,836
1953	368,524	n.a.		+53,036
1954	437,904	n.a.		+69,380
1955	515,517	$78,002	$ 389	+77,613
1956	607,120	92,734	1,131	+91,603
1957	685,383	79,848	1,585	+78,263
1958	768,627	83,546	302	+83,244
1959	865,509	97,894	1,012	+96,882

[a]Year ended December 31.

Source: Federal Home Loan Bank Board.

TABLE VI-A36

Federal Home Loan Banks

Category A. Bonds or notes sold and outstanding in the private market, nongovernment secured, as source of loanable funds, 1950-59.
(in thousands)

Year [a]	Outstanding at end of year	Sales	Repaid	Net change in outstandings
1950	$ 561,000	$ 737,000	$ 382,500	$ 354,500
1951	529,500	843,500	875,000	-31,500
1952	448,550	548,550	629,500	-80,950
1953	413,500	453,500	488,550	-35,050
1954	273,000	328,000	468,500	-140,500
1955	975,000	1,236,000	534,000	702,000
1956	963,000	1,378,000	1,390,000	-12,000
1957	826,000	1,276,000	1,413,000	-137,000
1958	714,235	808,000	919,765	-111,765
1959	1,773,660	1,833,000	773,575	1,059,425

[a] Year ended December 31.

Source: Federal Home Loan Bank Board.

TABLE VI-A37

Federal Home Loan Bank Notes

(Outstanding as of the close of business December 31, 1959)

Millions of dollars	Issue dated	Rate	Maturity	Bid=	Asked	Yield to maturity
80	4/15/59	3.80	1/15/60	99 30/32	100	3.70
199	5/21/59	4 3/8	2/15/60	99 28/32	99 31/32	4.53
310	7/23/59	4 7/8	2/15/60	99 30/32	100 1/32	4.50
124	6/15/59	4 1/2	3/15/60	99 29/32	99 31/32	4.70
247	8/17/59	4.65	4/15/60	99 26/32	99 29/32	4.90
240	11/16/59	5 1/8	5/16/60	99 31/32	100 1/32	5.00
181	9/15/59	5	6/15/60	99 27/32	99 30/32	5.07
134	10/15/59	5.40	7/15/60	100	100 3/32	5.16
275	4/15/58	3 1/8	4/15/63	93 20/32	94 4/32	5.09

Source: C. J. Devine and Co., quotation sheet dated January 4, 1960.

TABLE VI-A38

Federal Home Loan Banks

Category F. Loanable funds obtained from earnings, 1950-59[b]

(in thousands)

Year[a]	Earnings: Income from interest, fees, etc.	Earnings: Expenses for dividends, interest, etc.	Total
1950	$ 16,479	$ 14,171	2,308
1951	22,075	21,398	677
1952	24,381	23,142	1,239
1953	29,833	28,704	1,129
1954	31,958	30,790	1,168
1955	41,381	39,176	2,205
1956	64,904	63,127	1,777
1957	70,278	68,536	1,742
1958	64,024	62,523	1,501
1959	90,555	88,363	2,192

[a] Year ended December 31.

[b] Excluding administrative appropriations and expenses, except that administrative expenses are included if they are paid out of earnings rather than from special government appropriations.

Note: Included in Expenses are allocations to Statutory Reserve. Net earnings represent the annual increments to undivided profits, which could be considered loanable funds.

Source: Federal Home Loan Bank Board.

TABLE VI-A39

Bureau of Indian Affairs

Category F. Loanable funds obtained from government appropriations and earnings, Revolving Credit Program, 1950-59.[b]

(in thousands)

Year a/	Government Appropriations	Earnings				Total
		Income from interest fees, etc.		Expenses for dividends, interest, etc.	Net	
1950	$ 3,000		$ 43		$ 43	$ 3,043
1951	2,400	$ 232*	67		299	2,699
1952	800	320*	115		435	1,235
1953	1,000	364*	161		525	1,525
1954	-	425*	172		597	597
1955	-	350*	126		476	476
1956	-	354*	172	187**	339	339
1957	-	430*	182	314**	298	298
1958	-	206*	135	472**	-131	-131
1959	-	51*	217	540**	-272	-272

[a]Year ended June 30.

[b]Excluding administrative appropriations and expenses, except that administrative expenses are included if they are paid out of earnings rather than from special government appropriation.

*These amounts represent cash settlements for loans of livestock which originally were to be repaid "in kind." The Act of May 24, 1950 (25 U.S.C. 443) authorized acceptance of cash in lieu of livestock and the deposit of such settlements in the revolving fund for loans.

**The credit program administered by the Bureau of Indian Affairs involves several different facets: (1) Financing for Indians from the same lending institutions that serve other citizens, (2) loans from the revolving credit fund and tribal moneys, and (3) liquidation of inactive "reimbursable loans" and "repayment cattle" programs. The same staff administers all credit activities. From 1950 through 1955, administrative expenses were paid from appropriated gratuity funds. In 1956, the Interior Department Appropriation Act provided for a portion of the credit administrative expenses to be paid from the revolving loan fund. Since that time, expenses for administering the credit activities of the Bureau have been paid partly from gratuity funds and partly from the revolving fund for loans,

Source: Bureau of Indian Affairs.

APPENDIX B

TABLE VI-B1

Sources of Funds Available to Federal Lending Agencies

Bonds, debentures, or notes sold and outstanding in the private market, nongovernment secured as sources of loanable funds, 1950-59. (Summary of Category A) (in thousands)

Year	Outstanding at end of year	Sales	Repaid	Net change in outstandings
1950	$1,813,312	$1,508,760	$1,107,580	+ 401,180
1951	2,053,584	2,053,460	1,813,188	+ 240,272
1952	2,078,362	1,935,005	1,910,227	+ 24,778
1953	2,078,158	1,879,195	1,879,399	- 204
1954	2,057,892	1,825,104	1,844,371	- 20,266
1955	3,503,281	3,168,204	1,722,815	+1,445,389
1956	4,017,973	3,561,850	3,047,158	+ 514,692
1957	6,220,974	6,126,961	3,923,961	+2,203,001
1958	5,722,040	5,395,144	5,894,078	- 498,934
1959	7,916,624	6,517,500	4,322,916	+2,194,585

TABLE VI-B2

Sources of Funds Available to Federal Lending Agencies

Bonds, debentures, or notes sold and outstanding
in the private market, government secured,
as sources of loanable funds, 1950-59,
(Summary of Category B)
(in thousands)

Year	Outstanding at end of year	Sales	Repaid	Net change in outstandings
1950	$ 791	$47,480	$57,142	$-9,662
1951	3,624	96,834	94,001	+2,833
1952	505	9,875	12,994	-3,119
1953	--	100	605	- 505
1954	--	--	--	--
1955	--	--	--	--
1956	--	--	--	--
1957	--	--	--	--
1958	--	--	--	--
1959	--	--	--	--

TABLE VI-B3

Sources of Funds Available to Federal Lending Agencies

Bonds, debentures, or notes issued in connection with borrowings from the government for loanable funds, 1950-59.
(Summary of Category C including CCC borrowings)
(in thousands)

Year [a]	Outstanding at end of year	Borrowings	Repaid	Net change in outstandings
1950	$ 5,707,768	$3,180,881	$1,391,306	$+1,789,575
1951	6,064,773	1,900,838	1,543,833	+ 357,005
1952	7,065,176	3,281,807	2,281,404	+1,000,403
1953	9,391,741	4,944,29	2,617,729	+2,326,565
1954	10,977,749	7,769,045	6,183,037	+1,586,008
1955	14,967,415	7,710,157	3,720,491	+3,989,666
1956	17,129,784	4,707,406	2,545,037	+2,162,369
1957	17,574,314	5,932,784	5,488,254	+ 444,530
1958	18,226,603	7,150,895	6,498,606	+ 652,289
1959	19,836,068	7,648,821	6,039,356	+1,609,465

[a]For the most part year ended December 31, but a few agencies reported as of June 30.

TABLE VI-B4

Sources of Funds Available to Federal Lending Agencies

Bonds, debentures, or notes issued in connection with borrowings from the government for loanable funds, 1950-59.
(Summary of Category C not including CCC borrowings)

Year	Outstanding at end of year	Borrowings	Repaid	Net change in outstandings
1950	$2,971,768	$1,735,881	$ 116,306	$+1,619,575
1951	4,039,773	1,233,838	165,833	+1,068,005
1952	4,896,176	2,403,807	1,547,404	+ 856,403
1953	5,443,741	1,390,294	842,729	+ 547,565
1954	5,445,749	3,761,045	3,759,037	+ 2,008
1955	5,092,415	2,983,157	3,336,491	- 353,334
1956	5,489,784	1,380,406	983,037	+ 397,369
1957	4,788,314	1,925,784	2,627,254	- 701,470
1958	6,073,603	2,760,895	1,475,606	+1,285,289
1959	7,762,068	3,327,821	1,639,356	+1,688,465

[a]For the most part year ended December 31, but a few agencies reported as of June 30.

TABLE VI-B5

Sources of Funds Available to Federal Lending Agencies

Capital stock held by the government, 1950-59.
(Summary of Category D)
(in thousands)

Year [a]	Outstanding at end of year	Sold to government	Returned	Net change in outstandings
1950	$473,485	$ 965	$51,330	$-50,365
1951	412,756	3,665	64,394	-60,729
1952	410,181	4,825	7,400	- 2,575
1953	403,106	740	7,815	- 7,075
1954	440,120	92,980	55,966	+37,014
1955	439,730	1,000	11,390	- 390
1956	432,249	1,550	9,032	- 7,482
1957	470,182	77,405	39,472	+37,933
1958	462,978	4,560	11,764	- 7,204
1959	463,873	14,845	13,949	+ 896

[a]For the most part year ended December 31, but a few agencies reported minor amounts as of June 30.

TABLE VI-B6

Sources of Funds Available to Federal Lending Agencies

Capital stock held by private parties, 1950-59.
(Summary of Category E)
(in thousands)

Year	Outstanding at end of year	Sold[a]	Retired[a]	Net change in outstandings
1950	$ 330,535			+$ 56,011
1951	436,811			+ 106,276
1952	493,617			+ 56,806
1953	553,972			+ 60,355
1954	630,554			+ 76,582
1955	725,975			+ 95,421
1956	847,602			+ 121,627
1957	978,086			+ 130,484
1958	1,109,717			+ 131,631
1959	1,275,571			+ 165,854

[a]Detailed breakdown of amounts sold and retired not available for certain agencies.

TABLE VI-B7

Sources of Funds Available to Federal Lending Agencies

Loanable funds obtained from government appropriations, principal repayments, sales of loans, and earnings, 1950-59.[b]
(Summary of Category F)
(in thousands)

Year[a]	Government appropriations, principal repayments, sales of loans, etc.	Earnings			Total
		Income from interest, fees, etc.	Expenses for dividends interest, etc.	Net	
1950	$563,412	$ 90,734	$ 67,750	$22,984	$586,396
1951	203,026	121,917	114,768	7,149	210,175
1952	150,525	151,067	137,776	13,291	163,816
1953	330,806	176,250	132,190	44,060	374,866
1954	786,847	179,983	205,752	-25,769	761,078
1955	249,505	198,592	147,895	50,697	300,202
1956	207,165	250,570	200,509	50,061	257,226
1957	281,165	328,337	278,051	50,286	331,451
1958	834,194	364,004	306,000	58,004	892,198
1959	521,590	464,471	400,063	64,408	585,998
Totals	$4,128,235	$2,325,925	$1,990,754	$335,171	$4,463,406

[a]For the most part year ended December 31, but a few agencies reported minor amounts as of June 30.

[b]Excluding administrative appropriations and expenses, except that administrative expenses are included if they are paid out of earnings rather than from special government appropriations.

Research Study Seven

ANALYSIS OF THE TECHNICAL COMPONENTS OF THE FEDERAL CREDIT PROGRAMS

J. Fred Weston*
University of California
Los Angeles

INTRODUCTION

Federal credit programs now aggregate outstandings of some $100 billion. This magnitude suggests a substantial potential influence on the economy. Among the many issues suggested by the programs, this study deals with an analysis of the behavior of the technical components of the federal credit programs. Its central focus is: Given the basis for and the objectives of the programs, how can their implementation be made most effective?

The federal credit programs may be grouped into four major types, listed in order of the degree of government participation:

1. Government-sponsored credit institutions

2. Government insurance programs

---

*Dr. David A. Snell, Dr. Y.S. Cho, and Mr. Youngil Lim assisted in gathering data upon which the analysis is based. The Division of Research of the Graduate School of Business Administration UCLA, provided research assistance in the final stages of the study. Among those who helped with comments were my colleagues, Neil H. Jacoby and Leo Grebler, but neither agrees with all the views expressed.

3. Government guarantee programs

4. Direct lending by government

Government-sponsored credit institutions are federally chartered. Although they usually receive an initial contribution of government capital, they are intended to be self-supporting to the extent that government sponsorship enables them to raise funds by selling their obligations in the open capital markets at favorable rates. They lend to other financial intermediaries which in turn lend to private borrowers. For example, Federal Land banks sell their own bonds, using mortgages of individual farms as security. Loans to farmers are made through Federal Land Bank Associations.

Government insurance programs are no different in principle from other kinds of insurance, except that a government agency is the underwriter. For example, the Federal Housing Administration insures residential mortgage loans made by private lenders. Premiums paid by borrowers are expected to cover losses and other expenses of the insurance system.

In a credit guarantee program, a government agency promises to bear losses incurred. The borrower may be, but usually is not, charged a fee. The Veterans Administration, for example, guarantees residential mortgage loans made by private lenders to veterans who are not charged a fee for the guarantee provided.

Government agencies may also lend directly to private borrowers. Examples are the loans to business firms made directly by the Small Business Administration and the Export-Import Bank.

THE NATURE OF THE TECHNICAL COMPONENTS OF CREDIT

There are three major technical components of a credit program: price, credit standards, and credit terms.

Price

Price may refer to interest rates or to the size of the fee charged for licensing, insuring, or guaranteeing. The direct loans of the Small Business Administration might carry interest fees above or below the market. The Federal Housing Administration could charge an insurance rate equal to, smaller than, or larger than actuarial requirements. The government as insurer may specify permissible levels of interest rates charged on loans. The rates may be fixed or flexible, at or below the market.

Credit Standards

Credit standards are non-price allocating criteria. They are used in the credit field because the risk of non-repayment of obligations by some applicants may be so high as to require interest charges beyond conventionally acceptable rates. Given customary ranges for the price of funds, credit standards permit rationing of available funds among potential users.

Credit standards usually are related to the three "C's" of credit: character, capacity, and capital. Character refers to the evidence of moral dependability of the borrower. Capacity refers to his ability as a businessman or an agriculturist and to his earning power generally. Capital refers to the financial position of the prospective borrower. Here the central criteria are his liquidity position and his wealth (or equity) position in relation to obligations already outstanding.

The selection of credit standards is particularly crucial to the operation of government credit programs. For example, should the FHA residential mortgage insurance program use credit evaluation to avoid high-risk borrowers, or should it deliberately seek to make funds available to borrowers who would otherwise be unable to obtain financing from private sources? Should the Small Business Administration emphasize capital or capacity in its credit appraisals?

Because credit standards relate to a number of factors, a complex mix of requirements may be employed. The potential richness of the combinations of standards that may be employed enlarges the dimensions of the credit "commodity." As a consequence, the credit standards employed will determine the group to receive financing. Government credit programs may substantially widen the availability of funds or may channel funds to limited groups determined by the nature of credit standards employed.

Credit Terms

Credit terms define the nature of the credit commodity or product. Clear examples are the size of the down payment or the ratio of down payment to total value, the maturity of the contract, and repayment provisions. Whether or not qualified potential borrowers become active demanders for funds is influenced more by the nature of the credit as established by credit terms than by the "price." Indeed, the maturity of the loan, which establishes the required monthly outlays by the borrower, may be more influential than the interest rate charged in determining his ability to meet an obligation.

These factors are related to other forms of institutional gaps. Lenders may be unfamiliar with the general lending area, such as financing exports to foreign countries. Or the lending area may be regarded as one of high risk, as in the small business lending field where business mortality rates are high. Natural catastrophes, such as fires, floods, and earthquakes, and economic catastrophes, such as major business recessions, may call for direct-lending programs to meet needs that private lenders could not be expected to fill.

Another group of bases for federal credit programs is subsumed under the heading, "greater social returns." There are numerous possible social reasons for the existence of federal credit programs. For example, a public insurance scheme can reduce risks through combinations; as a result, social returns are increased. Moreover, as a consequence of the reduction in risks, greater resources may flow into the area. As government insurance schemes may be applied in a number of areas, the selection of the best possible area for a particular scheme is likely to be based on the identification of a social priority.

In insurance programs, the government is better able to bear catastrophic risks than either private insurance carriers or individual lenders. In areas of high risk, such as loans to exporters, which are subject to catastrophes like balance-of-payment restrictions by foreign countries or political revolution, the risk is more appropriately borne by the government than by private groups.

High social returns may also be realized from projects that aid particular groups. An illustration is an electrification program which might, if carried out on a fragmentary basis by private lenders, prove to be unduly risky, but would lead to greater productivity in agriculture as a whole. Or, funds may be allocated to a group of veterans in recognition of their contributions to the defense of the nation. A related field is maritime, railroad, or airline financing, on grounds both of potential contributions to national defense and of increasing the general productivity of the economy through improved methods of distribution.

There is a problem in determining the social priority of a group, for it is often difficult to distinguish between social priority and political strength. When political strength is the basis for the program, the economic costs may be substantial and the true social gains minimal.

The next two bases for programs are the sensitivity and the effectiveness of areas for achieving certain economic goals such as stability and/or growth. If these areas could be identified effectively, they would represent potentially a sound basis for federal credit programs.

The justification for federal credit programs in the export field has been the assertion that foreign governments have been performing services for their own business firms in these areas. This is in turn related to certain political goals of governments which might be furthered by credit programs.

Relation between Basis and Form of Programs

Table VII-1 also summarizes the relationship between the basis for a federal credit activity and the related form that the federal credit program takes. Different causes sometimes call for the same appropriate form of activity, and sometimes for a different form of activity. An important distinction will subsequently be noted, however, between similar types of federal credit programs and the actual employment of the programs.

Lack of competition among lending sources might justifiably call for antitrust activity. Characteristically, however, the situation is likely to be one of oligopoly rather than of overt monopoly practices. As a consequence, in the financial area, as in others, it may be difficult for antitrust action to provide a really effective remedy. Therefore, multiplying the sources of financial supply through direct government lending or government-sponsored lending associations may be the more appropriate action. However, before federal programs can be justified, more action in the direction of chartering additional lending facilities would be salutory.

Similarly, a second cause of an inadequate flow of funds to a particular area may be institutional patterns in the flow of savings. These may represent legal rules setting out restrictions on the percentage of assets that insurance companies may invest in common stocks, legal lists for investment of trusts, etc. The legal rules and the institutional framework should be carefully examined for possible change before a government program is instituted. A first step should be to foster increased competition between different types of lending institutions by broadening the permissible range of lending authority now relatively specialized due to legal rules.

When the chronic credit gap is, in fact, caused by high risk, either direct lending or a government-sponsored lending program may be appropriate. The lending program may be either direct lending or substitution of government credit for private credit by financing a privately organized institution. Through insurance, a federal program may reduce risks by the principle of combination of risks. A federally sponsored program may pool private capital so that it is better able to bear risks, as in the Small Business Administration program. The government may find it necessary to make direct loans, as in the same program, because neither pooling through insurance nor pooling of private capital through government-sponsored lending institutions seems effective.

The existence of a credit gap because of secular decline in the industry represents a special form of high-risk barrier. A credit program may properly be called for, but its nature may be substantially modified in order to meet a changed objective. A federal credit agency that finances in an area where a gap has occurred because of such a secular decline will result in misallocation of resources if the lending activity operates so as to keep resources in the area. The proper use of a credit program in this situation, however, is to assist in an orderly transition or migration of resources out of the area.

When a credit gap exists because private lenders are unfamiliar with the area, direct lending by the government may have the effect of providing a demonstration. The government experience in the unfamiliar area may establish that profitable lending can be undertaken by private lenders.

It is clear that when the gap results from catastrophes of the kind referred to earlier, the only form of credit program that is likely to be effective is a direct-lending program by the government itself.

There is an interrelationship between credit gaps and social priorities in that it is not likely that a federal credit program would be organized to fill a credit gap unless some aspect of social priority were involved. Hence, the second group of bases for programs referred to as social priorities differs only in degree of emphasis, rather than in kind. Three distinctive areas are identified under social priorities: high social returns, economic goals, and political goals.

A distinction should be made between two forms of high social returns. One form is the existence of social gains that may be achieved through an insurance program. Such a program could be justified on grounds that total national product is increased. However, although the total is increased, the allocation of resources is redirected, as, for example, to housing in the FHA program.

In addition, under the category of high social returns a social priority emphasis may exist in which particular groups are likely to employ direct lending or guarantee schemes, because the impact sought is a relatively direct one.

Multiple forms of federal credit programs might be employed to achieve economic goals, such as operating in cyclically sensitive areas or growth-responsive areas. Although these programs may overlap, some aimed to achieve other objectives. Federal credit programs for economic goals are likely to place stronger emphasis on economic stability and growth than on income redistribution.

When the objective is to compete with the lending or credit insurance programs of foreign governments, or to achieve certain political goals, almost any form of credit program that meets these specifications is appropriate. In practice, when the emphasis is on political goals, direct lending is likely to be relied upon heavily.

Although different forms of federal credit programs, based on differing objectives, may seem to overlap, several important generalizations may be made. For example, when insurance schemes are employed, the objective is likely to be general social gains. In using such schemes, care must be exercised to examine the social priorities implied in the social gains. When the objective or basis is primarily income redistribution, a direct-lending program may be the most effective. When the basis for programs is high risk and unfamiliarity, federal sponsorship of direct-lending agencies may be the best way to develop familiarity and experience in the area.

But what must be emphasized is that, although the same general forms of federal credit programs may be employed to reach different objectives, there will be substantial variation in the way in which a particular program will be used in different agencies. The second major thesis of this study is that the combined bases and form of a federal credit program will strongly influence the preferred behavior of the technical components of that program. To illustrate this proposition, it is necessary to review specific federal credit programs. The discussion is organized under the four major forms of federal credit programs.

FEDERALLY SPONSORED CREDIT ACTIVITIES

Federally sponsored credit agencies operate most significantly in the agricultural credit field. The Federal Land banks, operating through Federal Land Bank Associations, advance long-term mortgage funds to agriculture. The Federal Intermediate Bank System provides for three- to five-year working capital loans to agriculture. The Federal Land banks illustrate the use of the technical components of credit in a federally sponsored credit agency.

The bases for the long-term mortgage lending program in agriculture through a federal credit agency are manifold. Clearly long-term credits to agriculture represent a high-risk area. The high risk results from the price fluctuations and the economic instability that were experienced particularly in the pre-World War II period. This general instability, coupled with a low elasticity of demand for agricultural products and with other hazards, such as crop failures, clearly establishes agriculture as a high-risk area. Furthermore, the evident lack of familiarity with many aspects of agriculture also heightened the risk prospects as viewed by private lenders.

Because of the relative isolation and the limited mobility of farm borrowers, particularly before World War II, it has been argued that there was lack of effective competition among private lenders in providing long-term credits to agriculture. The secular decline in agriculture aggravated the risk elements. Finally, a number of social priorities were recognized for increasing the flow of long-term funds to agriculture. On grounds of social stability, it is desirable that farm tenancy be reduced in favor of ownership. Also, family ownership is preferred to wide holding of agricultural land by large corporations.

The Federal Land banks were created by Congress in 1916, capitalized by a federal contribution of $9 million, and supervised by the Federal Farm Loan Board.[1] Until the serious depression of the 1930's, the participation of the Federal Land Bank System in the farm mortgage market was relatively modest. By 1928 its share of the market was about 12 percent.[2] During the period between 1916 and 1928, life insurance companies increased their share of the market from some 15 percent to 22 percent. The participation of commercial banks declined somewhat, to about 11 percent, whereas individuals and other accounted for some 50 percent. The main inroads of the Federal Land banks into the farm mortgage market were clearly made at the expense of individuals, who formerly dominated the market.

The share of the market attained by the Federal Land banks before the serious depression of the 1930's seems to have resulted from their more favorable terms and standards of lending. In general, the interest rate charged on mortgage loans by these banks was 1 percent above their cost of borrowing. As their costs of borrowing benefited in part from their tax-exempt status and from the recognition of contingent support by the Treasury, their

---

1R.J.Saulnier, H.G. Halcrow, and N.H. Jacoby, Federal Lending and Loan Insurance, National Bureau of Economic Research (Princeton: Princeton University Press, 1958), pp. 15-154.

2The data in this section are based on material in D. Gale Johnson, "Agricultural Credit, Capital and Credit Policy in the United States," Research Study Four of this volume.

interest rates were from .5 to 1.5 percent below the rates charged by private lenders. It is clear also that borrowers who could not qualify for loans from private lenders were able to obtain loans through the Federal Land Bank System. The Federal Land Bank System was also an innovator in providing longer maturities and a higher ratio of loan to value in its early years.

With the widespread defaults during the 1930's, the Federal Land banks played an emergency role. A total of $314 million was supplied by Congress in 1932 and 1933. By 1939 the share of the farm mortgage market held by the Federal Land banks had risen to almost 31 percent.

The foregoing brief review of the development of the Federal Land banks has been necessary in order to place their present activity in proper perspective. By 1958 their share of the farm mortgage market had declined to about 18 percent. Life insurance companies had increased their share of the market to about 25 percent, while banks and trust companies had enlarged theirs from about 7 percent in 1939 to almost 14 percent in 1958.

The Federal Land banks still charge interest rates .5 to 1.5 percent lower than the rates charged by private lenders. Why, then, has their share of the market declined? For one thing, private lenders have matched the Federal Land banks in providing longer maturities and relatively higher ratios of loan to value. In fact, there is evidence that private lenders grant better credit terms as measured by the ratio of loan to value. Private lenders have moved up to advancing loans equal to 65 percent of appraised values. The appraisal method of the Federal Land banks, however, has been based on estimates of future earning power. These estimates have been relatively conservative, so that the loans obtainable from Federal Land banks have been smaller than those obtainable from private lenders. Moreover, the Federal Land banks seem to have required increasingly higher credit ratings from farm mortgage applicants.

In the light of the behavior of the Federal Land banks, how may their performance with regard to the technical components of credit be evaluated? From one standpoint, the operations of the Federal Land banks have been almost ideal. They performed an important role in limiting the destabilizing effects of the agricultural recession of the 1930's. Currently, in a relatively high income-level economy, they compete with private lenders on the basis of price alone. In order to qualify, however, for the lower interest rate obtainable on Federal Land Bank loans, the borrower must present a reasonably high credit rating and must be able to accept a lower ratio of loan to value. This suggests that the lower interest rate is related to the higher credit standing of borrowers.

Thus, the Federal Land banks have accomplished their objectives of demonstrating that mortgages with long maturities providing for systematic amortization can be made successfully in the farm mortgage field. The Federal Land banks continue as a test operation against which to measure the performance of private lenders.

However, a gap still seems to exist. Increasingly, for technological reasons, farm operations have moved to larger size units. This decreases the ability of individual farmers to finance the purchase of farm units. The result would be an increase in farm tenancy and the concentration of the ownership of farm land in the hands of corporate enterprise.

This trend poses a dilemma. If credit is more available for agriculture, the flow of resources into agriculture may be stimulated, and the surplus problem will become more serious. On the other hand, not to fill this gap is to acquiesce in trends with undesirable social and political consequences. Hence, a strong case can be made for a mortgage credit program enabling an experienced and reasonably able agriculturist to obtain the necessary funds to finance the purchase of a farm unit.

Under such a program, down-payment requirements would be much lower, and maturities would be extended far beyond those presently available. The program would have to be administered by a farm credit agency with the ability to be selective with regard to the background, the experience, and the capabilities of the individual applying for a loan. In addition, it would have to be able to evaluate the program, which the applicant presents as the basis for obtaining a loan under so favorable conditions. The selling of such property to corporate buyers would have to be restricted so as to prevent loans obtained for the purpose of benefiting from the rise in capital value that would be realized by holding title for a limited time. The program can be defended on grounds of preserving the possibility of freedom of entry for the individual farm operator in the face of trends that make such entry increasingly difficult.

If soundly conceived, such a program would have to operate on an insurance basis, rather than with federal subsidy. Federally sponsored credit agencies in agriculture presently operate without any subsidy except their ability to raise funds at lower rates than could a private organization. The implied contingent responsibility of the Treasury permits these agencies to raise funds at lower cost than could private agencies. On the other hand, because they have sought to be self-sufficient and free of direct federal subsidy, the federal agencies have operated as private lenders. As this seems to be the nature of federally sponsored organizations, the program would call for a federal agency to provide insurance and, hence, for a pooling of risks in this form of agricultural lending.

As the objectives involve primarily social goals, it is recommended that the technical components of credit be responsive to general market movements in interest rates but operate below the markets in terms of the interest rates charged for the degree of risk taken. In addition, credit standards and credit terms would not vary with the cycle as those of private lenders tend to do, but would operate below the market on a fixed and relatively inflexible basis. Another contribution of the federal insurance program would be the provision for a moratorium on amortization payments when declines in agricultural income are due to economic or crop conditions beyond the control of individual farm operators.

This review of the operation of a federal credit program based primarily on federal sponsorship suggests a number of interim conclusions. When the basis for the program is high risk or lack of familiarity, federal sponsorship of an organization that groups risks and thereby reduces them, provides valuable leadership to private lenders who find that they can develop various institutional arrangements to approximate the risk reduction achieved by the federal agency. After the innovations of the federal agency have been matched, it then operates in approximately the same manner as private lenders. It may, in fact, impose somewhat higher credit terms and credit standards in order to ration its lower-cost credit to the best-qualified potential users.

On the other hand, when the program is designed primarily to achieve a social goal, such as the desired form of farm ownership, either an insurance, a guarantee, or a direct-lending program is called for. The credit standards in such a program should operate consistently below those demanded by the private market in view of the level of risk. Furthermore, instead of using conventional and traditional standards as a basis for rationing credit, the emphasis is shifted from potential security that might be offered by the applicant to his character and ability. There would be an increased exposure to risk, requiring a greater contingent support from the financing powers of the federal government.

The same analysis and principles set forth in connection with long-term mortgage credit for agriculture are equally applicable to the provision of intermediate-term credit of three to ten years to meet the working capital needs of agricultural units.

FEDERAL CREDIT INSURANCE PROGRAMS

The insured mortgage program of the Federal Housing Administration is the clearest example of credit insurance administration by a federal agency. The initial purpose of the FHA program was to generate demand for housing in order to offset the severe depression in housing activity and to reform the mortgage market. Current objectives of the program have been stated primarily in terms of promoting sound financing of real property, of stabilizing the mortgage markets, and of improving housing standards. At this point, however, the insurance program as such must fundamentally be justified on grounds of social priorities.

The development of a residential mortgage insurance program has effects that are not immediately apparent. The use of an insurance program in the housing field is an ideal application of insurance principles because mortgage insurance on homes represents the combining of a large number of independent risks. The act of combining these risks reduces the over-all risk, for the risk of high loss ratios to the insurer is lower than for individual lenders. Thus, whether or not the FHA program had any special objectives, the insurance scheme is an effective risk-reducing device with social gains.

The complete justification for such an insurance program, however, would be the social priority of the group for which the program had been developed. Otherwise, there are a wide variety of possible areas to which the insurance scheme could be applied. The question might therefore be raised whether or not the FHA type of housing insurance program could be equally well carried out on a completely private basis. The difficulty is that, whereas individual risks satisfy the condition of nonconnexity, fluctuations in over-all business conditions exert an overwhelming influence. The covariant of the probability of losses on individual houses owing to changes in general economic conditions is very great. Thus a private insurer would be subject to the catastrophic hazard that general economic conditions could deteriorate. With a government insurance agency, it is understood that the federal government carries a contingent responsibility to come to the rescue of the insurance organization if a general economic decline of serious magnitude should develop. If the risks of the fluctuations in general business could be avoided, a private housing insurance agency would be entirely feasible.

Turning to an analysis of the technical components of the Federal Housing Administration Mortgage Insurance Program, it should be recognized that the FHA brought about what may truly be termed a revolution in home mortgage credit practices. Down payments were reduced, maturities were extended, and provision was made for systematic amortization of principal. The practices first developed by the HOLC and applied by the FHA on a continuing basis were subsequently followed by private lenders. As a consequence, the total amount of housing credit was probably increased because of the successful demonstration of liberalized credit terms for residential mortgage loans.

Interest rates have characteristically been lower than rates charged on conventional loans. In addition, the insured housing loan interest rates have been inflexible after a ceiling level is reached. The lower level of interest rates represents a subsidy to home buyers if interest rates are not at a ceiling. If the lower rate is operative, thus providing a subsidy, this represents a social gain in a broad sense. On the other hand, if interest rates rise so that the interest rate ceiling becomes effective, funds are diverted by private lenders from the insured mortgage field to more profitable alternatives.

The justification for an interest rate ceiling is twofold: it is presumed to prevent lenders from benefiting from the insurance feature by limiting the amount of interest they may charge. But if it results in diversion of funds to other places, the program becomes inoperative so that the first possible objective of the interest rate ceiling is not achieved.

A second justification given for the use of the interest rate ceiling is that it becomes effective in a period of a strong business upswing. By diverting funds from housing to other investment, the ceiling is said to reduce the amount of activity in the housing field during the business upswing, with a countercyclical effect. The diverted funds, however, are more likely to flow into the business lending area where interest rates will rise relatively during the business upswing. But business borrowing during the business upswing is less sensitive to interest rate rises. Hence, the effect of the countercyclical dampening of lending in the housing field is to stimulate lending in the business loan area, with a net effect of contributing to economic instability. If the funds had stayed in the housing area at higher rates of interest, it is unlikely that they would have been utilized to the same degree, because the demand for housing loans is likely to be more sensitive to interest rate variations than are business loans.

If it is argued in rebuttal that lending institutions are likely to lend the same aggregate amount during a business upswing, the claim that less diversion of funds would take place with removal of interest rate ceilings is questionable. But, at worst, the effect of the interest rate ceiling is to dampen activity in the housing field and perhaps to stimulate it in the business loan area. My own judgment is that interest rate ceilings reduce instability of housing activity, contribute to increased instability in the business investment sector, and produce other economic distortions as a form of price rigidity.

With regard to the utilization of credit standards, the operations of the FHA leave something to be desired. The outstanding fact about the FHA Insured Underwriting Program is that the bulk of the lending has been to middle-income borrowers for medium-priced homes.[3] The FHA program has excluded the highest-income groups and the lowest-income groups. The thin coverage of the lower-income groups by the FHA insured mortgage program represents a serious equity problem, for the group that most needs the benefits of the program does not participate proportionately. A high percentage of the lower-income groups is forced into forms of lending which involve higher interest rates and more restrictive mortgage terms.

This illustrates the problem referred to previously. In a government credit insurance program in which the actual lending activity is conducted by private lenders, they will employ credit standards that give them the maximum amount of protection in a loan program. It follows, therefore, that the credit standards employed by private lenders will militate against those whose credit standards are the lowest. Thus, if the basis for the FHA insurance program is the social gains that can be achieved by a grouping of independent risks through a government program, the past record of the FHA in the home mortgage field, aside from the interest rate ceiling, has been an outstanding one. On the other hand, if the primary basis for the program is the social stability gained by broadening homeownership, a parallel program is required in which the possibilities of home-ownership are extended to lower-income groups. It is to be noted that a public housing program does not meet this goal, because it is a rental program rather than an ownership program. But the experience with the FHA insurance program indicates that, if the objective of aiding homeownership of lower-income groups is to be attained, a supplementary FHA direct-lending program is required.

The nature of the parallel FHA direct-lending program in the housing field may be briefly sketched. In the new program, credit standards would be employed in a directly opposite way from the present FHA program. Both price and credit terms would be varied inversely to the credit standards presented by prospective borrowers.

A schedule of relationships would be drawn up and, if the income of the borrower were below a specified level, the price of the home to be financed would be at a related maximum figure. For this maximum figure, the loan could be made fully by the FHA. As the size of the mortgage, the price of the house, and the income of the borrower rose, the FHA loan would be limited, but a private lender could be a co-lender to an increasing degree.

---

[3] J.E. Morton, Urban Mortgage Lending (Princeton: Princeton University Press, 1956), pp. 6, 27-29.

Two other elements in the program are recommended: In the event of default, the FHA should attempt to work out terms, particularly in the area of the lengthening of maturity, to enable the borrower successfully to resume payments on the mortgage. This would carry out the spirit and the tradition of the Home Owners Loan Corporation established in the depression to refinance existing home mortgages held by private lenders.

The great risk of any credit program is the risk of an over-all economic downturn. Thus, a strong argument could be presented that when disposable personal income drops by a given percentage –for example, 5 percent–within a three- to five-quarter period of time, abatement of mortgage payments would be provided for. If maximum economic stability is the dominating goal, the provision could appropriately be for abatement of mortgage payments in both the insured and direct-lending programs for a specified period of time. Thus there would be an automatic moratorium on all home mortgage payments under FHA programs.

If, on the other hand, need and ability to pay are the main criteria, the abatement of the mortgage payments would be extended only to the supplementary FHA direct-lending subsidy program established for low-income groups. Economic stability would represent a secondary objective rather than a primary objective.

A strong case can also be made for applying the principle of a moratorium on government-sponsored mortgage programs to industries or geographic areas that are temporarily depressed. This would represent applying the principle of abatement on the basis of lack of ability to pay where the cause is associated, not with the individual borrower, but rather with broader economic circumstances.

In review, the FHA Insured Mortgage Program may have acted more as a subsidy to lenders than to borrowers. Lenders have utilized the insured programs when interest rates associated with the FHA programs have been competitive with rates that could be obtained on conventional loans. While lower down payments and longer maturities represented more favorable terms, the insurance feature of the FHA loans may have justified a larger rate differential than actually existed. On the other hand, participation by lower-income groups in the FHA insurance program has not been adequate. Alterations in the technical components of the FHA Insured Mortgage Program have been proposed which would further extend its availability to lower-income groups.

FEDERAL GUARANTEE PROGRAMS

A wide variety of federal guarantee programs have been employed. They have functioned in the following areas: Guarantees of loans under Section 301 of the Defense Production Act of 1950 have been made by the Atomic Energy Commission and the various branches of the armed services, as well as by the Department of Commerce and the General Services Administration. The Commodity Credit Corporation provides a guarantee of loans for the marketing of agricultural commodities. The Public Housing Administration has guaranteed short-term notes and long-term obligations sold to private investors by local housing authorities to finance construction and operating costs of PHA-approved low-rent housing projects. The Veterans Administration has guaranteed loans to veterans for the purchase or improvement of farm properties or homes and for the establishment or expansion of businesses. The International Cooperation Administration guaranteed private investment in selected countries. In the field of transportation, the U.S. Maritime Commission (now the Maritime Administration) guaranteed loans to war contractors under Regulation V during World War II. At present, guarantees are provided for loans to railroads for equipment and property loans. Also, there are guarantees of loans for small feeder airline companies.

Many of these guarantee programs are now inoperative. Of those remaining, some, in fact, represent a form of price-support subsidy, such as the Commodity Credit Corporation's guarantee of loans for the marketing of agricultural commodities. At the other extreme, the Defense Production guaranteed loans are virtually inoperative. The most active of the guarantee programs are the aircraft loans, the railroad transportation loans, and the Veterans Administration guaranteed loans in the housing field.

Public Law 85-307, enacted September 7, 1957, authorizes the Civil Aeronautics Board to guarantee any lender against loss of interest and of 90 percent of principal on approved loans for aircraft purchases up to a total of $5 million for each borrower. Maturities are limited to 10 years; interest rates run relatively high, with a guarantee fee standardized at .375 percent. The program is too new and too small for adequate evaluation.

The Transportation Act of 1958 authorized the Interstate Commerce Commission to guarantee lenders against loss of principal and interest on loans made to railroads for financing or refinancing of equipment or property. Maturities are limited to 15 years. The railroads did not take the initiative in the enactment of such a program, nor have they used the program to any great extent.

The Veterans Administration guarantees in the housing field constitute a more active and significant program. The credit terms provided by the VA program are more liberal than those of the FHA Insured Mortgage Program. The kind of guarantee provided by the Veterans Administration virtually absolves the private lender from risk. Lenders are given complete protection so long as the value of the property is 40 percent of the outstanding loan principle at the time of default.

The pattern of value of homes and annual income of home buyers has been about the same for the VA-guaranteed loans as for the FHA-insured loans. The VA program has aided primarily the middle-income groups of veterans. But the program has not afforded aid to the lowest-income groups corresponding to their proportion in the total veteran population, because VA policy specifically excluded low-income applicants.

It appears somewhat anomalous that a program that seeks to reward veterans for their contributions to the nation should, in effect, discriminate against those veterans who happen to be in low-income groups. It would seem that veterans in low-income groups should receive special consideration in the kind of supplementary FHA program described in the previous section.

Review of the guarantee programs suggests that they usually involve a subsidy or a social priority. The guarantee program for loans to railroads could be justified on the basis of avoiding too rapid decline in the flow of resources to an industry that is clearly in a secular decline. On the other hand, loans to the small feeder airlines were intended to stimulate the growth of an industry in its early stages in an area where the operation of the market system might not develop a supplementary airline transportation system as early as deemed desirable in the national interest.

But both loans to protect against too rapid secular decline and loans to promote rapid secular growth involve relatively high risks. It is doubtful, on the basis of principles already set forth in the discussion of federal credit insurance programs, that programs involving high risks and social priorities are likely to be effectively operated through private lenders. If there is justification for such programs at all, their goals are likely to be met more effectively if a direct-lending program is used instead of a guarantee program. Also, because a guarantee program to be really effective usually involves a subsidy or a social priority, credit prices, terms, and standards should be operated relatively inflexibly below the market. This would achieve the social priority objectives, but would perhaps have undesirable effects on the cyclical pattern of business activity. The social priority objective may properly dominate so long as the programs are not so large as to interfere with federal programs designed to increase economic stability and growth.

DIRECT LENDING BY GOVERNMENT AGENCIES

A wide variety of government agencies engage in direct lending. To illustrate the principles associated with direct government lending activities, this discussion is limited to two illustrations drawn from the business and international finance fields, as the previous examples were drawn primarily from agriculture and housing. The two agencies here examined are the Small Business Administration and the Export-Import Bank of Washington, D.C.

The Small Business Administration is a successor to the Reconstruction Finance Corporation, which was in existence from 1931 through 1955. The Small Business Administration operates to fill certain institutional credit gaps. At least two credit gaps are represented in lending to small business: high risk and unfamiliarity. Such lending is inherently risky because of the high mortality rate among small businesses; the lack of management depth, resulting in undue dependence upon a single individual; the lack of a full range of management competences; and the thinness of financial reserves to meet a temporary reversal. There is much evidence that considerable opportunity for profitable lending to small business exists. Small businesses often arise in new growth areas. The rewards for successful penetration into new growth areas can be very substantial.

The second gap involved in lending to small business is lack of familiarity. The success of the Veterans Administration Guaranteed Business Loan Program immediately after World War II demonstrates that private lenders had overlooked numerous opportunities in making term loans to small business. The relative success of the VA-guaranteed loan program stimulated private lenders to follow its example. The innovators among private lenders who went into the small business term-loan field found the rewards relatively high.[4]

The existence of two types of gaps calls for distinct policies. When the gap is caused by high risk, technical components below the market may properly be employed. When, however, the gap is unfamiliarity with this kind of lending, federal and governmental agencies should simply seek to demonstrate that by following credit policies reflecting market conditions, a successful lending program can be established.

The activities of the Small Business Administration may be exampled in the light of the principles set forth. The SBA has followed a policy of relatively inflexible interest rates–approxi-

---

[4]Saulnier, Halcrow, and Jacoby, op. cit., p. 285.

mately 5.5 percent—without recognizing differential risks among borrowers or changing money market conditions. The inflexibility of interest rate policies suggests the application of high credit standards.

The fundamental weaknesses of the SBA direct-lending program are revealed by the principles that led to the establishment of the Small Business Investment Company program. The fundamental contradiction is this: with the higher-than-average probability of losses among small business firms, a lender must be compensated for the extra risks he assumes. In a straight loan program, either interest rates must be relatively high to compensate for higher-than-average loss ratios, or some participation in successful performance must be permitted, or the agency must plan to operate at a target level of loss.

The continuation both of an invigorated SBA program and of the SBIC program is recommended. The SBIC program will first be discussed to indicate what would remain for a reinvigorated SBA direct-lending program.

The SBIC program provides for a subsidy, mainly in the form of a special tax treatment or of long-term low-interest credits from the government, to financial intermediaries for loans to small business. The SBIC's, with a minimum of private investment, have access to a substantial volume of government funds. If losses occur in their lending programs, they can be passed through to the private investors and charged against ordinary income. On the other hand, if the lending operations of the SBIC's are successful, the fact that loans are in the form of convertibles or debts with warrants attached permits participation in the high profitability or increased market values of the equities of the firms in which investments are made. Clearly the odds are shifted in favor of the SBIC's by the twin provisions of tax concessions on the one hand, and participation in the rewards of successful investments on the other. The prospects for the SBIC's have been so favorable that they have perhaps given rise to speculative excesses in the market prices of their securities.

With the spectacular development of the SBIC's, the question may be raised whether or not the role of direct lending remains for the SBA. Experience to date suggests that the SBIC's have focussed primarily on companies in growth and romantic industries, such as electronics, plastics, chemicals, etc. On the other hand, the vast majority of small businesses are in the wholesale and retail trade areas where similar opportunities for spectacular growth generally do not exist. It is in this area particularly that the Small Business Administration can still perform an important role. A deliberately flexible interest rate policy should be followed in order to gear the level of interest rates to the amount of risk involved. Furthermore, experimentation should be developed in aiming at a given volume of lending activity by the SBA related to given levels of interest rates.

If the SBA is to perform its role of providing familiarity with a relatively high-risk and uncertain area, a deliberate policy of experimentation should be followed with target amounts of loss recognized in the early years of a reinvigorated program. This would illustrate the policy of altering technical components of credit to adjust to differences in the credit standards presented by potential borrowers, as well as to general money market conditions. It would use the direct-lending program to discover whether or not the small business lending gap is a reality or a myth. Only by the actual experiment of a relatively large-scale risk-accepting program would it be possible to ascertain the actual magnitude of the small business financing need. Certainly the many opportunities for dynamic and vigorous experimentation and innovation in the small business financing area have not yet been fully exploited, especially in comparison with the successful innovations of federal credit agencies in the agriculture and housing credit fields.

A second example of direct lending is the Export-Import Bank, first established in 1934 and modified by subsequent legislation. It was finally established on a permanent basis by an act of August 9, 1954, with its lending authority increased to $7 billion in 1958. The activities of the Export-Import Bank include direct lending, participation loans, and credit insurance, principally on political risks, but more recently on commercial risks as well. This discussion will focus on the direct-lending activities of the Export-Import Bank.

The Export-Import Bank primarily provides credit insurance in connection with short-term loans, but direct financing and participation financing on medium-term loans are also provided. On medium-term loans, the exporter may obtain direct financing of 68 percent of the export value. The interest rate depends upon the credit position of the buyer who is being financed, credit conditions in the United States, and the credit position of the exporter himself. The Export-Import Bank also lends directly on project loans to private business (either United States or foreign companies) or directly to foreign governments on long-term loans.

It will be noted that the direct lending of the Export-Import Bank is limited to medium- and long-term credit. It is presumed that credit for periods of less than one year is obtainable on satisfactory terms from private sources. The bank also encourages proposals for the purchase, by private investors or by commercial banks, of all or part of its portfolio of individual credits. This policy encourages private lenders to participate after the loan has been seasoned to a certain extent.

Over the period 1934-59, the Export-Import Bank disbursed some $10 billion in credits. Ninety-nine percent of the Export-Import Bank loans have exceeded $250,000; virtually all the loans of the Export-Import Bank have been large loans.[5]

With regard to interest rates, Congress permitted the Export-Import Bank management to establish its own scale of charges. Among federal credit agencies, the Export-Import Bank seems to have been almost unique in adopting a flexible interest rate policy. Most loans to foreign governments carried rates of about 2 1/2 to 3 1/2 percent per annum. Loans to foreign or domestic business enterprises have been in the range of 4 to 5 percent, and the special exporter-importer credits have been extended at 6 to 7 percent rates of interest.[6]

The rates of interest charged have reflected the general level of interest rates at the time the Export-Import Bank was raising its own funds. Thus they have also reflected borrowing costs to the Export-Import Bank when it had to go into the market for funds, rather than current money-market conditions at the time it made the loan.

The rates of interest charged by the Export-Import Bank have been below market rates, that is, below the rates the borrower would have had to pay if he had tried to borrow the money directly. Against this must be counterbalanced the consideration that these are "tied" loans. As the borrower must spend the money on American-manufactured goods, the loan represents a subsidy to American manufacturers in the sense that they do not have to compete in world markets in order to make the sale.

Turning to credit standards and credit terms, a number of generalizations may be made. On the whole, the loans of the Export-Import Bank have been "sound business loans." By amount, 99 percent were made to large and generally strong borrowers. The bank has suffered only one default in the entire history of its operation. The losses written off between the time of its establishment in 1934 and the end of 1959 equalled .028 percent of total loans authorized.[7] There is no question that such lending represents the application of highly conservative credit standards.

On the other hand, the policies of the Export-Import Bank have been defended in the following terms: Given its limited resources in relationship to the potential demands upon it, the U.S. Export-

---

[5] Export-Import Bank of Washington, D.C., Annual Reports.
[6] Ibid.
[7] Ibid.

Import Bank has chosen to concentrate on very large loans of high quality to large, well-established borrowers. As the loans are "tied" loans, the goods must be purchased in the United States. Hence, the large volume of goods purchased in the United States through Export-Import Bank lending gives indirect aid to a far larger number of exporters than the number who receive direct-lending aid from the Export-Import Bank.

Recognition of the preceding arguments points up a fundamental dilemma for the SBA and the Export-Import Bank lending policies, and for the operation of federal credit agencies generally. Federal credit programs are set up in support of a principle. The recognized existence of an institutional lending gap or the furtherance of a social goal leads to the establishment of the program. On the other hand, the funding of the program falls short of the potential claims that would justifiably be made upon it on the basis of the fundamental principles of the loan program involved. As a consequence, the lending agency must resort to some device for rationing its limited funds among a large number of potential competing users. Because it would be politically inexpedient to attempt the rationing process through high interest rate charges, the rationing is characteristically performed in the same manner as private lenders ration funds when interest rates are set below the market rates that would be required, given the level of risks involved.

The application of relatively stringent credit standards accomplishes a number of objectives for the government lending agency. First, it does ration limited funds among a large number of potential competing users. Second, it enables the lending agency to demonstrate a low loss ratio, thus establishing a record of high respectability in the conduct of its lending function. This in turn may be a basis for increasing the size of the commitment made to the agency in subsequent congressional enactments.

However, the limited size of appropriations in the face of the potential applications of the principle upon which the federal credit program was established in the first place is likely to have a perverse effect. The limited resources are actually allocated to borrowers who, among the potential users, least need the aid.

CONCLUSIONS

Federal credit programs may be grouped to provide a framework for evaluating the appropriate behavior of their technical components. The three major groupings are: (1) imperfections in the market mechanism for evaluating private product, (2) divergence of private and social product, and (3) distributive goals.

Imperfections in the Market Mechanism

Imperfections in the market mechanism are primarily gaps in the credit market. These include an institutional framework which interferes with the flow of funds, unfamiliarity and high-risk areas, and areas that seem to be either in secular decline or inadequately developed to support lending at that stage.

Private lenders seem to overestimate the risks involved in making loans in such credit markets. The charges and the terms required for providing financing would be so high as to discourage the development of such areas. Consistent with general national economic goals, federal credit programs could properly be instituted.

The preferred behavior of the technical components follows from the nature of the need giving rise to the programs. The technical components of the federal credit program should seek to operate flexibly at the market. The market is determined, however, by the improvements in the market mechanism attained by federal participation in the area, rather than by what private lenders would charge if they could somehow be induced to operate in the area. Thus, the market conditions as experienced by the federal credit agency are likely to enable price, credit terms, and credit standards to be lower than those that would have to be exercised by private lenders. The price policy of the federal credit agency should be to stimulate what the market mechanism would produce if it were operating more efficiently and if the imperfections and frictions that prevent private sellers from operating in the area had been removed.

Depending upon the area, the proper form of the government program could be sponsorship, insurance, guarantee, or direct lending. Where sponsorship stimulates the accumulation of pools of credit capital, as in the farm credit field, it may be effective. An insurance or guarantee program is likely to be most appropriate where there is nonconnexity of risks, as in housing or farm mortgage lending programs. Direct-lending programs will probably be most appropriate where extreme unfamiliarity with the area or extremely high risks may inhibit the pooling of private capital under sponsorship, or lack of nonconnexity of risks may make an insurance or guarantee program inappropriate.

Divergence of Private and Social Product

Another major set of circumstances which would call for a federal credit program concern the divergence of private and social product. Thus, the rural electrification program could be justified initially by the need to increase productivity in agriculture by increasing the availability of more efficient sources of power. The social value of increasing social stability by broadening home-ownership might justify the housing program. In addition, the economic goals of increasing cyclical stability and increasing the growth rate of the economy as a whole represent social values to which a private credit price policy would not fully contribute. This could be the basis for FHA insurance of housing, a cyclically sensitive area; both the Small Business Administration program as well as the Export-Import Bank stimulation of United States exports may be justified by their potential contribution to growth. In addition, the political goals of increased world economic stability, as well as political stability, which contributes to the enhancement of national security in the world as a whole, represent social products of great value.

The appropriate behavior of the technical components of such programs should be based on the principle that the programs should be carried forward to the point where the cost of an incremental program activity would not be exceeded by the marginal social-value product thereby engendered. Translated into practical policy considerations, this would call for behavior of the technical components at prices below the market operative if reliance had to be placed upon private institutions for carrying out the programs. But these prices for the government agency will represent "market" prices in the sense of equating marginal social costs with marginal social-value product. Furthermore, the technical components should behave flexibly, related to variations in the costs of conducting credit programs by the government agency.

The rural electrification program at its present stage of maturity may no longer meet a social-value product test. A similar conclusion might be reached with regard to the FHA housing insurance program, or that perhaps it could now be operated by a private institution.

When economic stability was the goal, federal credit agencies may have been too timid in the use of the technical components of credit. One possible weapon of great power which might appropriately have been used is the partial or complete, temporary or prolonged, moratorium on payments under various government programs when a general economic decline makes payments by borrowers difficult. The principle of a moratorium on payments in government credit programs during a period of general economic decline would provide another important and powerful built-in stabilizer.

With regard to stimulation of growth, government programs have been too timid in financing small and new businesses in new growth areas. Also, in comparison with other countries, the U.S.

Government has lagged in the development of export credit insurance programs. In addition, the very powerful use of export subsidies by other countries might be followed. Thus, export subsidies might well be provided in industries of decreasing internal costs or industries promising substantial external economies.

Distributive Goals

Finally, a third basis for credit programs exists where there are distributive goals, where the government seeks to enhance the income or welfare position of particular groups on the basis of specified social priorities. The identification of areas for which government programs are appropriate must necessarily represent a judgment reflecting the value system of the decision-maker. No objective norms are possible. But distributive goals are related to programs for farming, housing, small business, and certainly for catastrophe situations. On some, such as the catastrophic area, there is little argument as to the appropriateness of the government program. On others, considerable disagreement may be expressed.

An important principle to recognize is that, when the government's goal is redistribution of income or wealth, the most appropriate form of the program is likely to involve direct activity on the part of the government, as contrasted to a program involving sponsorship, insurance, or guarantee.

Where political consensus has established a government credit program in which distribution goals are the aim of the program, technical components may appropriately be below those that would have been employed by private lenders upon the particular area of government credit activity. Technical components in this connection should not only be below the market, but probably should also be relatively inflexible. The degree to which they should be flexible will depend upon the relative emphasis placed upon distributive goals and the goals of economic growth or stability when a program combines both elements. So long as the magnitude of such programs is small, the distributive goals may take precedence over other goals. When the magnitude of such programs becomes large, the distributive goals have to be balanced against broader economic effects.

The applications of these criteria suggest that both more and less are needed in government credit programs. Upon the principle that federal programs that seek to improve upon the market mechanism should seek to approximate market prices, the FHA ceiling on interest rates is clearly inappropriate. Among the government credit programs based on divergence of private and social product, the programs in rural electrification and some of the housing and farm programs should be curtailed or their directions should be altered.

In this connection, programs to further economic growth and stability have probably been timid and inadequate. More flexibility in repayment provisions might properly be exercised. More imaginative programs in support of industries with a relative advantage in the export business might appropriately be followed. In addition, more imaginative use of experimentation with flexibility and variety in prices, credit terms, and credit standards, in lending in the business and international fields might appropriately be employed.[8] Further, more flexible use of credit terms and credit standards could well be employed to aim at distributive goals as well as social stability goals in both agriculture and housing.

---

[8]The stimulating power for the economy as a whole and the beneficial effects on private lenders themselves of earlier programs are described in N.H. Jacoby, "Government Loan Agencies and Commercial Banking," American Economic Review, 32 (March 1942), pp. 250-260.